About Pearson

Pearson is the world's learning company, with presence across 70 countries worldwide. Our unique insights and world-class expertise comes from a long history of working closely with renowned teachers, authors and thought leaders, as a result of which, we have emerged as the preferred choice for millions of teachers and learners across the world.

We believe learning opens up opportunities, creates fulfilling careers and hence better lives. We hence collaborate with the best of minds to deliver you class-leading products, spread across the Higher Education and K12 spectrum.

Superior learning experience and improved outcomes are at the heart of everything we do. This product is the result of one such effort.

Your feedback plays a critical role in the evolution of our products and you can reachus@pearson.com. We look forward to it.

About Pearson

Pearson is the world's learning company with presence across 70 countries worldwide. Our unique insights and world-class expertise comes from a long history of working closely with renowned teachers, authors and thought leaders, as a result of which, we have emerged as the preferred choice for millions of teachers and learners across the world.

We believe learning opens up opportunities, creates fulfilling careers and hence better lives. We hence collaborate with the best of minds to deliver you class-leading products, spread across the Higher Education and K12 spectrum.

Superior learning experience and improved outcomes are at the heart of everything we do. This product is the result of one such effort.

Your feedback plays a critical role in the evolution of our products and you can contact us at reachus@pearson.com. We look forward to it.

Leadership in Organizations

Eighth Edition

Gary Yukl

Nishant Uppal

Pearson

First Impression, 2017
Second Impression, 2018

This edition is manufactured in India and is authorized for sale only in India, Bangladesh, Bhutan, Pakistan, Nepal, Sri Lanka and the Maldives. Circulation of this edition outside of these territories is UNAUTHORIZED.

Published by Pearson India Education Services Pvt. Ltd, CIN: U72200TN2005PTC057128.

Head Office: 15th Floor, Tower-B, World Trade Tower, Plot No. 1, Block-C, Sector 16, Noida 201 301, Uttar Pradesh, India.

Registered Office: 4th Floor, Software Block, Elnet Software City, TS 140, Block 2 & 9, Rajiv Gandhi Salai, Taramani, Chennai 600 113, Tamil Nadu, India.
Fax: 080-30461003, Phone: 080-30461060
Website: www.in.pearson.com, Email: companysecretary.india@pearson.com

Printed in India by: Tara Art Printers Pvt. Ltd.

Table of Contents

Preface to the Indian Edition

It gives me immense pleasure to introduce the eighth edition of *Leadership in Organizations* to our readers. This edition aspires to deepen the understanding of leadership in global business, both in knowledge and practice, by drawing perspectives from the latest advancements in international business. The chapters and cases included in this edition focus upon the theoretical, empirical, and policy and practitioner aspects of a wide range of topics including subordinate management, motivation, and job satisfaction among others. The geographical spread of topics and cases presented in the present edition provide a truly global flavor.

The leaders in an organization can be an asset that could be leveraged upon to improve business performance. Since the early 1980s, leadership has remained a topic of academic exploration given the dynamic relationship between organizations, workers, and workplace and the extremely volatile and uncertain business environment. *Leadership in Organizations, 8e,* attempts to spread this virtue and presents the complex person-job-organization-environment relationship.

The eighth edition is organized in the following way:

- The first three chapters focus on individual as leader and attempts to simplify otherwise complex nature of leadership.
- Chapter 4 then presents the role of feedback in terms of usefulness of views from varied sources in decision making.
- Managing and leadership change have become the primary function of leaders in VUCA times. Chapter 5 explains the role and responsibility of leaders in such situations.
- Chapters 6 to 10 explain and critically analyze another critical role of the leader, more specifically in perpetually transforming and evolving business environment, and dealing with people.
- Chapter 10 also links behaviors and dispositions of a leader with the vision and mission of organizations. Leaders are not only responsible for crafting socially relevant business goals, but also for embarking upon them while taking the organization with them.
- While leaders are responsible for designing socially relevant organizations, they must be attentive to the definition of society for their organizations. Organizations engage into boundary spanning and finding places in each corner of society. This makes leaders responsible for ensuring high ethical and moral standards so that their organizations can make decisions that are least ambiguous and most benefitting for the larger segment of the society. This is the main theme of chapters 13 and 14.
- Finally, in order to meet the objectives and functions of leaders in organization, the book also outlines various methods through which leaders can develop themselves. Leadership skills are dynamic and contextual and hence deserve continuous attention. The last chapter deals with this leadership issue and presents some scientific ways in which leaders are currently being trained and nurtured.

I believe that this edition will respond well to the needs of the global business diaspora including academics, policy makers, and organizations. I hope that it will provide stimulus for research and propel further development in international business.

Lastly, I would like to acknowledge the peers and the editors who have reviewed and worked tirelessly towards evaluating the current edition. I am also grateful to Dr Ajit Prasad, Director, Indian Institute of Management Lucknow, whose continuous encouragement to link theory with practice motivated me to take up the current project. I would also like to acknowledge the immense support offered by my beloved wife, Deepti. Without their contribution this project would not have been possible.

About the Adapter

Nishant Uppal is faculty of Organization Behavior in the Human Resources Management Group, Indian Institute of Management Lucknow. He earned his PhD in Organizational Behavior and Human Resource Management from the Indian Institute of Management, Indore.

He has published a number of papers in world-renowned journals such as *Personality and Individual Differences*, *Studies in Higher Education*, *International Journal for Selection and Assessment*, *Personnel Review*, *Journal for International Business and Entrepreneurship Development*, and *Journal for Global Business Advancement*. He specializes in the fields of leadership, change management, knowledge management, organizational adaptation, job design, organizational structure, and personality.

Introduction: The Nature of Leadership

Learning Objectives

After studying this chapter, you should be able to:

- Understand the different ways leadership has been defined.
- Understand the controversy about differences between leadership and management.
- Understand why it is so difficult to assess leadership effectiveness.
- Understand the different indicators used to assess leadership effectiveness.
- Understand what aspects of leadership have been studied the most during the past 50 years.

Leadership is a subject that has long excited interest among people. The term connotes images of powerful and dynamic individuals who command victorious armies, direct corporate empires, or lead political parties or even nations. The exploits of brave and clever leaders are the essence of many legends and myths. Much of our description of history is the story of military, political, religious, and social leaders who are credited or blamed for important historical events, even though we do not understand very well how the events were caused or how much influence the leader really had. For example, historians and scientists still wonder what caused the initial successes and subsequent failures of political leaders, such as Napoleon in France, Saddam Hussein in Iraq, or Indira Gandhi in India.

The widespread fascination with leadership may be because it is such a mysterious process, as well as one that touches everyone's life. Why did certain leaders (e.g., Gandhi, Mohammed, Mao Tse-tung) inspire such intense fervor and dedication? How did certain leaders (e.g., Julius Caesar, Alexander the Great, Ashoka, or Akbar) build great empires? Why did some rather undistinguished people (e.g., Adolf Hitler, Claudius Caesar, or Chandragupta Maurya) rise to positions of great power? Why do some leaders have loyal followers who are willing to sacrifice their lives for them (e.g., Subhash Chandra Bose and Nelson Mandela), while other leaders are so despised that subordinates conspire to murder them (like emperor Shah Jahan of the Mughal dynasty in India and Louis XVI of France).

From Chapter 1 of *Leadership in Organizations*, Eighth Edition. Gary Yukl. Copyright © 2013 by Pearson Education, Inc. Publishing as Prentice Hall. All rights reserved.

Questions about leadership have long been a subject of speculation, but scientific research on leadership did not begin until the twentieth century. The focus of much of the research has been on the determinants of leadership effectiveness. Social scientists have attempted to discover what traits, abilities, behaviors, sources of power, or aspects of the situation determine how well a leader is able to influence followers and accomplish task objectives. There is also a growing interest in understanding leadership as a shared process in a team or organization and the reasons why this process is effective or ineffective. Other important questions include the reason why some people emerge as leaders, the determinants of a leader's actions, and whether a leader is born as one. However, the predominant concern has been the effectiveness of leadership.

Some progress has been made in probing the mysteries surrounding leadership, but many questions remain unanswered. In this text, major theories and research findings on leadership effectiveness will be reviewed, with particular emphasis on managerial leadership in formal organizations such as business corporations, government agencies, hospitals, and universities. This chapter introduces the subject by considering different conceptions of leadership, different ways of evaluating its effectiveness, and different approaches for studying leadership.

Definitions of Leadership

Once upon a time, six blind men lived in a village. One day, the other villagers told them, "Hey, there is an elephant in the village today."

They had no idea what an elephant was. They decided, "Even though we will not be able to see it, let us go and feel it anyway." All of them went to the elephant and each one of them touched it.

"Hey, the elephant is a pillar," said the first man, who touched the elephant's leg.

"Oh, no! It is like a rope," said the second man, who touched the tail.

"No, no! It is like a thick branch of a tree," said the third man, who touched the trunk of the elephant.

"It is like a big hand fan," said the fourth man, who touched the ear.

"It is like a huge wall!" exclaimed the fifth man, who touched the belly of the elephant.

"It is like a solid pipe," said the sixth man, who touched the tusk of the elephant.

They began to argue about the elephant and each one of them insisted that he was right. It seemed as if they were getting agitated. A wise man was passing by and saw this. He stopped and asked them, "What is the matter?" They said, "We cannot agree on what the elephant is like." Each one of them described what he thought about the elephant. The wise man calmly explained, "All of you are right. The reason each one of you is describing it differently is because each one of you touched a different part of the elephant. So, actually, the elephant has all those features that all of you said."

"Oh!" everyone exclaimed. There were no more fights, and they were happy that they were all right.

No wonder, the elephant in our context is *leadership*.

The term *leadership* is a word taken from the common vocabulary and incorporated into the technical vocabulary of a scientific discipline without being precisely redefined. As a consequence, it carries extraneous connotations that create ambiguity of meaning (Janda, 1960). Additional confusion is caused by the use of other imprecise terms such as *power*, *authority*, *management*, *administration*, *control*, and *supervision* to describe similar phenomena. An observation by Bennis (1959, p. 259) is as true today as when he made it many years ago:

> Always, it seems, the concept of leadership eludes us or turns up in another form to taunt us again with its slipperiness and complexity. So we have invented an endless proliferation of terms to deal with it . . . and still the concept is not sufficiently defined.

Researchers usually define leadership according to their individual perspectives and the aspects of the phenomenon which is of most interest to them. In 2016, a search in scholarly databases (e.g., EBSCO, J-STOR, Springer, PsycINFO) of published articles using the term "leadership" returned over 40,000 articles. You might wonder if researchers, scholars, consultants, or leaders were the cause of this problem. After a comprehensive review of the leadership literature, Northouse (2006) concluded, "There are almost as many definitions of leadership as there are persons who have attempted to define the concept." The stream of new definitions has continued unabated since Northouse made his observation. Leadership has been defined in terms of traits, behaviors, influence, interaction patterns, role relationships, and occupation of an administrative position. Table 1 shows some representative definitions presented over the past 50 years.

Most definitions of leadership reflect the assumption that it involves a process whereby intentional influence is exerted over other people to guide, structure, change, and facilitate activities and relationships in a group or organization. The numerous definitions of leadership appear to have little else in common. For example, they differ in whether their unit of analysis and focus of observation is a leader or a follower. Traditionally, researchers focusing on the behavior and outcome of leaders observe and analyze questions such as who exerts influence, the intended purpose of the influence, the manner in which influence is exerted, and the outcome of an influence attempt. More recently, researchers such as Uhl-Bien et al. have also started to question the behavior and outcome of followers and view leadership as a consequence of social interactions between leaders and followers.

These differences are not just a case of scholarly nitpicking; they reflect deep disagreement about the identification of leaders and leadership processes. Researchers who differ in their conception of leadership select different phenomena to investigate, and interpret the results in different ways. Researchers who have a very narrow definition of leadership are less likely to discover things that are unrelated to or inconsistent with their initial assumptions about effective leadership.

Because leadership has so many different meanings to people, some theorists question whether it is even useful as a scientific construct (e.g., Alvesson & Sveningsson, 2003; Miner, 1975). Nevertheless, most behavioral scientists and practitioners seem to believe leadership is a real phenomenon that is important for the effectiveness of organizations. Interest in the subject continues to increase, and the deluge of articles and books about leadership shows no sign of abating.

Specialized Role or Shared Influence Process?

A major controversy involves the issue of whether leadership should be viewed as a specialized role or as a *shared influence process*. One view is that all groups have role specialization, and the leadership role has responsibilities and functions that cannot be shared too widely without jeopardizing the effectiveness of the group. The person with primary responsibility to perform the *specialized leadership role* is designated as the "leader." Other members are called "followers" even though some of them may assist the primary leader in

TABLE 1	Definitions of Leadership

- Leadership is "the behavior of an individual . . . directing the activities of a group toward a shared goal" (Hemphill & Coons, 1957, p. 7).
- Leadership is "the influential increment over and above mechanical compliance with the routine directives of the organization" (Katz & Kahn, 1978, p. 528).
- Leadership is "the process of influencing the activities of an organized group toward goal achievement" (Rauch & Behling, 1984, p. 46).
- "Leadership is about articulating visions, embodying values, and creating the environment within which things can be accomplished" (Richards & Engle, 1986, p. 206).
- "Leadership is a process of giving purpose (meaningful direction) to collective effort, and causing willing effort to be expended to achieve purpose" (Jacobs & Jaques, 1990, p. 281).
- Leadership "is the ability to step outside the culture . . . to start evolutionary change processes that are more adaptive" (Schein, 1992, p. 2).
- "Leadership is the process of making sense of what people are doing together so that people will understand and be committed" (Drath & Palus, 1994, p. 4).
- Leadership is "the ability of an individual to influence, motivate, and enable others to contribute toward the effectiveness and success of the organization . . ." (House et al., 1999, p. 184).
- "Leadership is thoughtful innovation and motivated communication" (Mumford, 2000, p.27).
- "Three elements of leadership are wisdom, intelligence, and creativity" (Sternberg & Vroom, 2002, p. 302).
- "Leadership is the capacity to make strategic choices in complex and ambiguous situations" (Waldman et al., 2004, p. 356).
- "Leadership is an outcome of close interaction between genetic, social, and personality factors" (Arvey, et al., 2006, p. 2).
- "Leadership is mastery, creating congruence between form and content, and defining purpose" (Ladkin, 2008, p. 32).
- "Leadership is defining outcomes such as direction, alignment, and commitment" (Drath et al., 2008, pp. 635-653).
- "Leadership is a dynamic, interactive influence process to achieve an objective" (O'Reilly et al., 2010, p. 104).
- "Leadership is co-created in systems of interconnected relationships and richly interactive contexts" (Fairhurst & Uhl-Bien, 2012, p. 1043).
- "Leadership is to exert disproportionate non-coercive influence on followers, and finding such followers who would allow themselves to be influenced" (Uhl-Bien et al., 2014, p. 84).
- "Leadership is changing" (Chrobot-Mason, et al., 2016, p. 298).

carrying out leadership functions. The distinction between leader and follower roles does not mean that a person cannot perform both roles at the same time. For example, a department manager who is the leader of department employees is also a follower of higher-level managers in the organization. Researchers who view leadership as a specialized role are likely to pay more attention to the attributes that determine selection of designated leaders, the typical behavior of designated leaders, and the effects of this behavior on other members of the group or organization.

Another way to view leadership is in terms of an influence process that occurs naturally within a social system and is diffused among the members. Writers with this perspective believe it is more useful to study "leadership" as a social process or pattern of relationships rather than as a specialized role. According to this view, various leadership functions may be carried out by different people who influence what the group does, how it is done, and the way people in the group relate to each other. Leadership may be exhibited both by formally selected leaders and by informal leaders. Important decisions about what to do and how to do it are made through the use of an interactive process involving many different people who influence each other. Researchers who view leadership as a shared, diffuse process, are likely to pay more attention to the complex influence processes that occur among members, the context and conditions that determine when and how they occur, the processes involved in the emergence of informal leaders, and the consequences for the group or organization.

Type of Influence Process

Controversy about the definition of leadership involves not only who exercises influence, but also what type of influence is exercised and the outcome. Some theorists would limit the definition of leadership to the exercise of influence resulting in enthusiastic commitment by followers, as opposed to indifferent compliance or reluctant obedience. These theorists argue that the use of control over rewards and punishments to manipulate or coerce followers is not really "leading" and may involve the unethical use of power.

An opposing view is that this definition is too restrictive because it excludes some influence processes that are important for understanding why a leader is effective or ineffective in a given situation. How leadership is defined should not predetermine the answer to the research question of what makes a leader effective. The same outcome can be accomplished with different influence methods, and the same type of influence attempt can result in different outcomes, depending on the nature of the situation. Even people who are forced or manipulated into doing something may become committed to it if they subsequently discover that it really is the best option for them and the organization. The ethical use of power is a legitimate concern for leadership scholars, but it should not limit the definition of leadership or the type of influence processes that are studied.

Purpose of Influence Attempts

Another controversy about which influence attempts are part of leadership involves their purpose and outcome. One viewpoint is that leadership occurs only when people are influenced to do what is ethical and beneficial for the organization and themselves. This definition of leadership does not include influence attempts that are irrelevant or detrimental to followers, such as a leader's attempts to gain personal benefits at the follower's expense.

An opposing view would include all attempts to influence the attitudes and behavior of followers in an organizational context, regardless of the intended purpose or actual beneficiary. Acts of leadership often have multiple motives, and it is seldom possible to determine the extent to which they are selfless rather than selfish. The outcomes of leader actions usually include a mix of costs and benefits, some of which are unintended, making it difficult to infer purpose. Despite good intentions, the actions of a leader are sometimes more detrimental than beneficial for followers. Conversely, actions motivated solely by a leader's personal needs sometimes result in unintended benefits for followers and the organization. Thus, the domain of leadership processes to study should not be limited by the leader's intended purpose.

Influence Based on Reason or Emotions

Most of the leadership definitions listed earlier emphasize rational, cognitive processes. For many years, it was common to view leadership as a process wherein leaders influence followers to believe it is in their best interest to cooperate in achieving a shared task objective. Until the 1980s, few conceptions of leadership recognized the importance of emotions as a basis for influence.

In contrast, some recent conceptions of leadership emphasize the emotional aspects of influence much more than reason. According to this view, only the emotional, value-based aspects of leadership influence can account for the exceptional achievements of groups and organizations. Leaders inspire followers to willingly sacrifice their selfish interests for a higher cause. For example, leaders can motivate soldiers to risk their lives for an important mission or to protect their comrades. The relative importance of rational and emotional processes and how they interact are issues to be resolved by empirical research, and the conceptualization of leadership should not exclude either type of process.

Influence or Persuasion

From the leadership perspective, it is necessary to differentiate between the most commonly interchanged processes—influence and persuasion. Where persuasion is to spur someone to action or to make a decision without actually earning his or her sincere consensus, influencing requires convincing and attempting to earn mindshare as a prerequisite to action or decision. Consequently, persuasion is reasoning with someone so that he or she would believe or do something, while influence, on the other hand, is the ability to affect the manner of thinking of another. For example, Mahatma Gandhi had influence over people, so no persuasion was required to make people follow him during the Dandi March.[1]

Direct and Indirect Leadership

Most theories about effective leadership focus on behaviors used to directly influence immediate subordinates, but a leader can also influence other people inside the organization, including peers, bosses, and people at lower levels who do not report to the leader. Some theorists make a distinction between direct and indirect forms of leadership to help explain how a leader can influence people when there is no direct interaction with them (Hunt, 1991; Lord & Maher, 1991; Yammarino, 1994).

A chief executive officer (CEO) has many ways to influence people at lower levels in the organization. Direct forms of leadership involve attempts to influence followers when interacting with them or using communication media to send messages to them. Examples include sending memos or reports to employees, sending e-mail messages, presenting speeches on television, holding meetings with small groups of employees, and participating in activities involving employees (e.g., attending orientation or training sessions, company picnics). Most of these forms of influence can be classified as direct leadership.

Indirect leadership has been used to describe how a chief executive can influence people at lower levels in the organization who do not interact directly with the leader (Bass, Waldman, Avolio, & Bebb, 1987; Waldman & Yammarino, 1999; Yammarino, 1994). One form of indirect leadership by a CEO is called "cascading." It occurs when the direct influence of the CEO is transmitted down the authority hierarchy of an organization from the CEO to middle managers, to lowerlevel managers, to regular employees. The influence can

---

[1]The Dandi March was an act of nonviolent civil disobedience in colonial India initiated by Mahatma Gandhi to produce salt from seawater, as was the practice of the local populace until British officials introduced taxation on salt production, deemed their sea-salt reclamation activities illegal, and then repeatedly used force to stop it. The 24-day march began on 12 March 1930 as a direct action campaign of tax resistance and nonviolent protest against the British salt monopoly. It gained worldwide attention, which gave impetus to the Indian Independence Movement and started the nationwide Civil Disobedience Movement.

involve changes in employee attitudes, beliefs, values, or behaviors. For example, a CEO who sets a good example of ethical and supportive behavior may influence similar behavior by employees at lower levels in the organization.

Another form of indirect leadership involves influence over formal programs, management systems, and structural forms (Hunt, 1991; Lord & Maher, 1991; Yukl & Lepsinger, 2004). Many large organizations have programs or management systems intended to influence the attitudes, skills, behavior, and performance of employees. Examples include programs for recruitment, selection, and promotion of employees. Structural forms and various types of programs can be used to increase control, coordination, efficiency, and innovation. Examples include formal rules and procedures, specialized subunits, decentralized product divisions, standardized facilities, and self-managed teams. In most organizations only top executives have sufficient authority to implement new programs or change the structural forms.

A third form of indirect leadership involves leader influence over the organization culture, which is defined as the shared beliefs and values of members (Schein, 1992; Trice & Beyer, 1991). Leaders may attempt either to strengthen existing cultural beliefs and values or to change them. There are many ways for leaders to influence an organization's culture. Some ways involve direct influence (e.g., communicating a compelling vision or leading by example), and some involve forms of indirect influence, such as changing the organizational structure, reward systems, and management programs. For example, a CEO can implement programs to recruit, select, and promote people who share the same values (Giberson, Resick, & Dickson, 2005).

Administrative theorists describe the essential roles and tasks of managers as planning, organizing, leading, and controlling. As a result, managers make many decisions and get involved in the nitty-gritty of day-to-day operations. However, according to Peter Drucker, effective leaders do not make many decisions. They focus on important ones that have an impact on the larger aspects of the organization. They try to think through what is generic and strategic, rather than solve daily problems or put out fires. While a manager is responsible for crafting and implementing policies in an organization, a leader continuously analyzes, creates, and challenges the existing practices and policies. Finally, managers' concerns are limited to maintaining the existing structures and processes of the organization for producing the desired results while leaders shape and craft vision and associate people around the vision.

The interest in indirect leadership is useful to remind scholars that leadership influence is not limited to the types of observable behavior emphasized in many leadership theories. However, it is important to remember that a simple dichotomy does not capture the complexity involved in these influence processes. Some forms of influence are not easily classified as either direct or indirect leadership. Moreover, direct and indirect forms of influence are not mutually exclusive, and when used together in a consistent way, it is possible to magnify their effects.

Leadership or Management

There is a continuing controversy about the difference between leadership and management. It is obvious that a person can be a leader without being a manager (e.g., an informal leader), and a person can be a manager without leading. Indeed, some people with the job title "manager" do not have any subordinates (e.g., a manager of financial accounts). Nobody has proposed that managing and leading are equivalent, but the degree of overlap is a point of sharp disagreement.

Some writers contend that leadership and management are qualitatively different and mutually exclusive (e.g., Bennis & Nanus, 1985; Zaleznik, 1977). The most extreme distinction assumes that management and leadership cannot occur in the same person. For these writers, leaders and managers differ with regard to their values and personalities. Managers value stability, order, and efficiency, and they are impersonal, risk-averse, and focused on short-term results. Leaders value flexibility, innovation, and adaptation; they care about people as well as economic outcomes, and they have a longer-term perspective with regard to objectives and strategies. Managers are concerned about how things get done, and they try to get people to perform better. Leaders are concerned with what things mean to people, and they try to get people to agree about the most important things to be done. Bennis and Nanus (1985, p. 21) proposed that "managers are people who do things right, and leaders are people who do the right thing." However, the empirical research does not support the assumption that people can be sorted neatly into these two extreme stereotypes. Moreover, the stereotypes imply that managers are generally ineffective. The term *manager* is an occupational title for a large number of people, and it is insensitive to denigrate them with a negative stereotype.

Other scholars view leading and managing as distinct processes or roles, but they do not assume that leaders and managers are different types of people (Bass, 1990; Hickman, 1990; Kotter, 1988; Mintzberg, 1973; Rost, 1991). How the two processes are defined varies somewhat, depending on the scholar. For example, Mintzberg (1973) described leadership as one of the 10 managerial roles. Leadership includes motivating subordinates and creating favorable conditions for doing the work. The other nine roles (e.g., resource allocator, negotiator) involve distinct managing responsibilities, but leadership is viewed as an essential managerial role that pervades the other roles.

Kotter (1990) proposed that managing seeks to produce predictability and order, whereas leading seeks to produce organizational change. Both roles are necessary, but problems can occur if an appropriate balance is not maintained. Too much emphasis on the managing role can discourage risk taking and create a bureaucracy without a clear purpose. Too much emphasis on the leadership role can disrupt order and create change that is impractical. According to Kotter, the importance of leading and managing depends in part on the situation. As an organization becomes larger and more complex, managing becomes more important. As the external environment becomes more dynamic and uncertain, leadership becomes more important. Both roles are important for executives in large organizations with a dynamic environment. When Kotter surveyed major large companies in a dynamic environment, he found very few had executives who were able to carry out both roles effectively.

Rost (1991) defined management as an authority relationship that exists between a manager and subordinates to produce and sell goods and services. He defined leadership as a multidirectional influence relationship between a leader and followers with the mutual purpose of accomplishing real change. Leaders and followers influence each other as they interact in noncoercive ways to decide what changes they want to make. Managers may be leaders, but only if they have this type of influence relationship. Rost proposed that leading was not necessary for a manager to be effective in producing and selling goods and services. However, leading is essential when major changes must be implemented in an organization, because authority is seldom a sufficient basis for gaining commitment from subordinates or for influencing other people whose cooperation is necessary, such as peers and outsiders.

Defining managing and leading as distinct roles, processes, or relationships may obscure more than it reveals if it encourages simplistic theories about effective leadership. Most scholars seem to agree that success as a manager or administrator in modern organizations also involves leading. How to integrate the two processes has emerged as a complex and important issue in organizational literature (Yukl & Lepsinger, 2005). The answer will not come from debates about ideal definitions. Questions about what to include in the domain of essential leadership processes should be explored with empirical research, not predetermined by subjective judgments.

A Working Definition of Key Terms

It is neither feasible nor desirable at this point in the development of the discipline to attempt to resolve the controversies over the appropriate definition of leadership. Like all constructs in social science, the definition of leadership is arbitrary and subjective. Some definitions are more useful than others, but there is no single "correct" definition that captures the essence of leadership. For the time being, it is better to use the various conceptions of leadership as a source of different perspectives on a complex, multifaceted phenomenon.

In research, the operational definition of leadership depends to a great extent on the purpose of the researcher (Campbell, 1977). The purpose may be to identify leaders, to determine how they are selected, to discover what they do, to discover why they are effective, or to determine whether they are necessary. As Karmel (1978, p. 476) notes, "It is consequently very difficult to settle on a single definition of leadership that is general enough to accommodate these many meanings and specific enough to serve as an operationalization of the variable." Whenever feasible, leadership research should be designed to provide information relevant to a wide range of definitions, so that over time it will be possible to compare the utility of different conceptions and arrive at some consensus on the matter.

We define leadership broadly in a way that takes into account several things that determine the success of a collective effort by members of a group or organization to accomplish meaningful tasks. The following definition is used:

> Leadership is the process of influencing others to understand and agree about what needs to be done and how to do it, and the process of facilitating individual and collective efforts to accomplish shared objectives.

The definition includes efforts not only to influence and facilitate the current work of the group or organization, but also to ensure that it is prepared to meet future challenges. Both direct and indirect forms of influence are included. The influence process may involve only a single leader or it may involve many leaders. Table 2 shows the wide variety of ways leaders can influence the effectiveness of a group or organization.

In this text, leadership is treated as both a specialized role and a social influence process. More than one individual can perform the role (i.e., leadership can be shared or distributed), but some role differentiation is assumed to occur in any group or organization. Both rational and emotional processes are viewed as essential aspects of leadership. No assumptions are made about the actual outcome of the influence processes, because the evaluation of outcomes is difficult and subjective. Thus, the definition of leadership is *not* limited to

TABLE 2	What Leaders Can Influence

- The choice of objectives and strategies to pursue.
- The motivation of members to achieve the objectives.
- The mutual trust and cooperation of members.
- The organization and coordination of work activities.
- The allocation of resources to activities and objectives.
- The development of member skills and confidence.
- The learning and sharing of new knowledge by members.
- The enlistment of support and cooperation from outsiders.
- The design of formal structure, programs, and systems.
- The shared beliefs and values of members.

processes that necessarily result in "successful" outcomes. How leadership processes affect outcomes is a central research question that should not be biased by the definition of leadership. The focus is clearly on the process, not the person, and they are not assumed to be equivalent. Thus, the terms *leader*, *manager*, and *boss* are used interchangeably in this text to indicate people who occupy positions in which they are expected to perform the leadership role, but without any assumptions about their actual behavior or success.

The terms *subordinate* and *direct report* are used interchangeably to denote someone whose primary work activities are directed and evaluated by the focal leader. Some writers use the term *staff* as a substitute for subordinate, but this practice creates unnecessary confusion. The term connotes a special type of advisory position, and most subordinates are not staff advisors. Moreover, the term *staff* is used both as a singular and plural noun, which creates a lot of unnecessary confusion. The term *associate* has become popular in business organizations as another substitute for subordinate, because it conveys a relationship in which employees are valued and supposedly empowered. However, this vague term fails to differentiate between a direct authority relationship and other types of formal relationships (e.g., peers, partners). To clarify communication, this text continues to use the term *subordinate* to denote the existence of a formal authority relationship.

The term *follower* is used to describe a person who acknowledges the focal leader as the primary source of guidance about the work, regardless of how much formal authority the leader actually has over the person. Unlike the term *subordinate*, the term *follower* does not preclude leadership processes that can occur even in the absence of a formal authority relationship. Followers may include people who are not direct reports (e.g., coworkers, team members, partners, outsiders). However, the term *follower* is not used to describe members of an organization who completely reject the formal leader and seek to remove the person from office; such people are more appropriately called "rebels" or "insurgents."

Indicators of Leadership Effectiveness

Like definitions of leadership, conceptions of leader effectiveness differ from one writer to another. The criteria selected to evaluate leadership effectiveness reflect a researcher's explicit or implicit conception of leadership. Most researchers evaluate leadership effectiveness in terms of the consequences of influence on a single individual, a team or group, or an organization.

One very relevant indicator of leadership effectiveness is the extent to which the performance of the team or organization is enhanced and the attainment of goals is facilitated (Bass, 2008; Kaiser, Hogan & Craig, 2008). Examples of objective measures of performance include sales, net profits, profit margin, market share, return on investment, return on assets, productivity, cost per unit of output, costs in relation to budgeted expenditures, and change in the value of corporate stock. Subjective measures of effectiveness include ratings obtained from the leader's superiors, peers, or subordinates.

Follower attitudes and perceptions of the leader are another common indicator of leader effectiveness, and they are usually measured with questionnaires or interviews. How well does the leader satisfy the needs and expectations of followers? Do they like, respect, and admire the leader? Do they trust the leader and perceive him or her to have high integrity? Are they strongly committed to carrying out the leader's requests, or will they resist, ignore, or subvert them? Does the leader improve the quality of work life, build the self-confidence of followers, increase their skills, and contribute to their psychological growth and development? Follower attitudes, perceptions, and beliefs also provide an indirect indicator of dissatisfaction and hostility toward the leader. Examples of such indicators include absenteeism, voluntary turnover, grievances, complaints to higher management, requests for transfer, work slowdowns, and deliberate sabotage of equipment and facilities.

Leader effectiveness is occasionally measured in terms of the leader's contribution to the quality of group processes, as perceived by followers or by outside observers. Does the leader enhance group cohesiveness, member cooperation, member commitment, and member confidence that the group can achieve its objectives? Does the leader enhance problem solving and decision making by the group, and help to resolve disagreements and conflicts in a constructive way? Does the leader contribute to the efficiency of role specialization, the organization of activities, the accumulation of resources, and the readiness of the group to deal with change and crises?

A final type of criterion for leadership effectiveness is the extent to which a person has a successful career as a leader. Is the person promoted rapidly to positions of higher authority? Does the person serve a full term in a leadership position, or is he or she removed or forced to resign? For elected positions in organizations, is a leader who seeks reelection successful?

It is difficult to evaluate the effectiveness of a leader when there are so many alternative measures of effectiveness, and it is not clear which measure is most relevant. Some researchers attempt to combine several measures into a single, composite criterion, but this approach requires subjective judgments about how to assign a weight to each measure. Multiple criteria are especially troublesome when they are negatively correlated. A negative correlation means that trade-offs occur among criteria, such that as one increases, others decrease. For example, increasing sales and market share (e.g., by reducing price and increasing advertising) may result in lower profits. Likewise, an increase in production output (e.g., by inducing people to work faster) may reduce product quality or employee satisfaction.

Immediate and Delayed Outcomes

Some outcomes are more immediate than others. For example, the immediate result of an influence attempt is whether followers are willing to do what the leader asks, but a delayed effect is how well followers actually perform the assignment. The effects of a leader can be viewed as a causal chain of variables, with each *"mediating variable"* explaining the effects of the preceding one on the next one. An example is provided in Figure 1. The farther along in the causal chain, the longer it takes for the effect to occur. For criteria at the end of the causal chain, there is a considerable delay (months or years) before the effects of the leader's actions are evident. Moreover, these end-result criteria are more likely to be influenced by extraneous events (e.g., the economy, market conditions). When the delay is long and there is considerable "contamination" of end-result criteria by extraneous events, then these criteria may be less useful for assessing leadership effectiveness than more immediate outcomes.

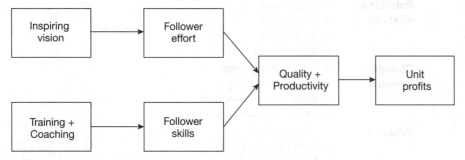

FIGURE 1 Causal Chain of Effects from Two Types of Leader Behavior

In many cases, a leader has both immediate and *delayed effects* on the same criterion. The two types of effects may be consistent or inconsistent. When they are inconsistent, the immediate outcome may be very different from the delayed outcomes. For example, profits may be increased in the short run by eliminating costly activities that have a delayed effect on profits, such as equipment maintenance, research and development, investments in new technology, and employee skill training. In the long run, the net effect of cutting these essential activities is likely to be lower profits because the negative consequences slowly increase and eventually outweigh any benefits. The converse is also true: increased investment in these activities is likely to reduce immediate profits but increase long-term profits.

What Criteria to Use?

There is no simple answer to the question of how to evaluate leadership effectiveness. The selection of appropriate criteria depends on the objectives and values of the person making the evaluation, and people have different values. For example, the top management may prefer different criteria than other employees, customers, or shareholders. To cope with the problems of incompatible criteria, delayed effects, and the preferences of different stakeholders, it is usually best to include a variety of criteria in research on leadership effectiveness and to examine the impact of the leader on each criterion over an extended period of time. Although multiple conceptions of effectiveness, similar to multiple conceptions of leadership, serve to broaden our perspective and enlarge the scope of inquiry, this significantly adds to the complexities of evaluating leadership effectiveness. In fact, thousands of studies on leader behavior and its effects have been conducted over the past half century, but the bewildering variety of behavior constructs used for this research makes it difficult to compare and integrate the findings. As a possible solution to this complexity, Yulk (2012, p. 68) recently presented a hierarchical taxonomy of leadership behavior against which leadership effectiveness can be measured. Table 3 reproduces the various facets of the taxonomy.

Yulk (2012, p. 68) has given the following description of the various mega-categories listed in the first column of Table 3:

> For task-oriented behavior, the primary objective is to accomplish work in an efficient and reliable way. For relations-oriented behavior, the primary objective is to increase the

TABLE 3	Hierarchical Taxonomy of Leadership Behaviors
Task-oriented	• Clarifying • Planning • Monitoring operations • Problem solving
Relations-oriented	• Supporting • Developing • Recognizing • Empowering
Change-oriented	• Advocating change • Envisioning change • Encouraging innovation • Facilitating collective learning
External	• Networking • External monitoring • Representing

quality of human resources and relations, which is sometimes called "human capital." For change-oriented behavior, the primary objectives are to increase innovation, collective learning, and adaptation to the external environment. For external leadership behavior, the primary objectives are to acquire necessary information and resources and to promote and defend the interests of the team or organization. In addition to these differences in primary objectives, each meta-category includes unique specific behaviors for achieving the objectives. The relevance of each component behavior depends on aspects of the situation, and the effect is not always positive for the primary objective or for other outcomes.

This description is further elaborated in Chapter 3. However, to conclude, it can be said that it is important to recognize that observable leadership behaviors differ from skills, values, personality traits, or roles. These other constructs are informative; however, they differ in important ways from observable leadership behaviors and leadership effectiveness.

Major Perspectives in Leadership Theory and Research

The attraction of leadership as a subject of research and the many different conceptions of leadership have created a vast and bewildering literature. Attempts to organize the literature according to major approaches or perspectives show only partial success. One of the more useful ways to classify leadership theory and research is according to the type of

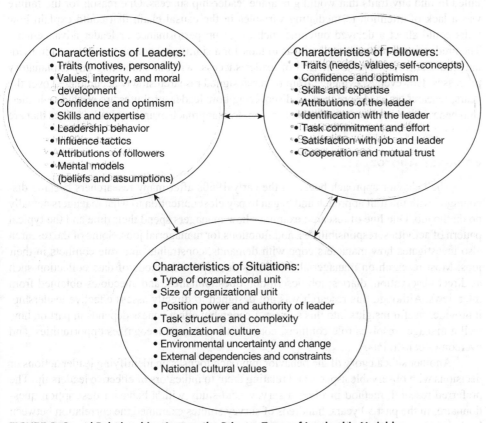

Characteristics of Leaders:
• Traits (motives, personality)
• Values, integrity, and moral development
• Confidence and optimism
• Skills and expertise
• Leadership behavior
• Influence tactics
• Attributions of followers
• Mental models (beliefs and assumptions)

Characteristics of Followers:
• Traits (needs, values, self-concepts)
• Confidence and optimism
• Skills and expertise
• Attributions of the leader
• Identification with the leader
• Task commitment and effort
• Satisfaction with job and leader
• Cooperation and mutual trust

Characteristics of Situations:
• Type of organizational unit
• Size of organizational unit
• Position power and authority of leader
• Task structure and complexity
• Organizational culture
• Environmental uncertainty and change
• External dependencies and constraints
• National cultural values

FIGURE 2 Causal Relationships Among the Primary Types of Leadership Variables

variable that is emphasized the most. Three types of variables that are relevant for understanding leadership effectiveness include: (1) characteristics of leaders; (2) characteristics of followers; and (3) characteristics of the situation. All those variables relate with each other in a very complex manner. Figure 2 shows examples of key variables and the likely causal relationships among them within each category.

Most leadership theories emphasize one category more than the others as the primary basis for explaining effective leadership, and leader characteristics have been emphasized most often over the past half-century. Another common practice is to limit the focus to one type of leader characteristic, namely traits, behavior, or power. To be consistent with most of the leadership literature, the theories and empirical research reviewed in this text are classified into the following five approaches: (1) *trait approach*, (2) *behavior approach*, (3) *power-influence approach*, (4) *situational approach*, and (5) *integrative approach*. Each approach is described briefly in the following sections.

Trait Approach

One of the earliest approaches for studying leadership was the trait approach. This approach emphasizes attributes of leaders such as personality, motives, values, and skills. Underlying this approach was the assumption that some people are natural leaders, endowed with certain traits not possessed by other people. Early leadership theories attributed managerial success to extraordinary abilities such as tireless energy, penetrating intuition, uncanny foresight, and irresistible persuasive powers. Hundreds of trait studies conducted during the 1930s and 1940s sought to discover these elusive qualities, but this massive research effort failed to find any traits that would guarantee leadership success. One reason for the failure was a lack of attention to mediating variables in the causal chain that could explain how traits could affect a delayed outcome such as group performance or leader advancement. The predominant research method was to look for a significant correlation between individual leader attributes and a criterion of leader success, without examining any explanatory processes. However, as evidence from better designed research slowly accumulated over the years, researchers made progress in discovering how leader attributes are related to leadership behavior and effectiveness. A more recent trait approach examines leader values that are relevant for explaining ethical leadership.

Behavior Approach

The behavior approach began in the early 1950s after many researchers became discouraged with the trait approach and began to pay closer attention to what managers actually do on the job. One line of research examines how managers spend their time and the typical pattern of activities, responsibilities, and functions for managerial jobs. Some of the research also investigates how managers cope with demands, constraints, and role conflicts in their jobs. Most research on managerial work uses descriptive methods of data collection such as direct observation, diaries, job description questionnaires, and anecdotes obtained from interviews. Although this research was not designed to directly assess effective leadership, it provides useful insights into this subject. Leadership effectiveness depends in part on how well a manager resolves role conflicts, copes with demands, recognizes opportunities, and overcomes constraints.

Another subcategory of the behavior approach focuses on identifying leader actions or decisions with observable aspects and relating them to indicators of effective leadership. The preferred research method involves a survey field study with a behavior description questionnaire. In the past 50 years, hundreds of survey studies examined the correlation between leadership behavior and various indicators of leadership effectiveness. A much smaller number of studies used laboratory experiments, field experiments, or critical incidents to determine how effective leaders differ in behavior from ineffective leaders.

Power-Influence Approach

Power-influence research examines influence processes between leaders and other people. Like most research on traits and behavior, some of the power-influence research takes a leader-centered perspective with an implicit assumption that causality is unidirectional (leaders act and followers react). This research seeks to explain leadership effectiveness in terms of the amount and type of power possessed by a leader and how power is exercised. Power is viewed as important not only for influencing subordinates, but also for influencing peers, superiors, and people outside the organization, such as clients and suppliers. The favorite methodology has been the use of survey questionnaires to relate leader power to various measures of leadership effectiveness.

Other power-influence research used questionnaires and descriptive incidents to determine how leaders influence the attitudes and behavior of followers. The study of influence tactics can be viewed as a bridge linking the power-influence approach and the behavior approach. The use of different influence tactics is compared in terms of their relative effectiveness for getting people to do what the leader wants.

Participative leadership is concerned with power sharing and empowerment of followers, but it is firmly rooted in the tradition of behavior research as well. Many studies used questionnaires to correlate subordinate perceptions of participative leadership with the *criteria of leadership effectiveness* such as subordinate satisfaction, effort, and performance. Laboratory and field experiments compared autocratic and participative leadership styles. Finally, descriptive case studies of effective managers examined how they use consultation and delegation to give people a sense of ownership for decisions.

Situational Approach

The situational approach emphasizes the importance of contextual factors that influence leadership processes. Major situational variables include the characteristics of followers, the nature of the work performed by the leader's unit, the type of organization, and the nature of the external environment. This approach has two major subcategories. One line of research is an attempt to discover the extent to which leadership processes are the same or unique across different types of organizations, levels of management, and cultures. The primary research method is a comparative study of two or more situations. The dependent variables may be managerial perceptions and attitudes, managerial activities and behavior patterns, or influence processes.

The other subcategory of situational research attempts to identify aspects of the situation that "moderate" the relationship of leader attributes (e.g., traits, skills, behavior) to leadership effectiveness. The assumption is that different attributes will be effective in different situations, and that the same attribute is not optimal in all situations. Theories describing this relationship are sometimes called *contingency theories* of leadership. A more extreme form of situational theory ("leadership substitutes") identifies the conditions that can make hierarchical leadership redundant and unnecessary.

Integrative Approach

An integrative approach involves more than one type of leadership variable. In recent years, it has become more common for researchers to include two or more types of leadership variables in the same study, but it is still rare to find a theory that includes all of them (i.e., traits, behavior, influence processes, situational variables, and outcomes). An example of the integrative approach is the self-concept theory of charismatic leadership, which attempts to explain why the followers of some leaders are willing to exert exceptional effort and make personal sacrifices to accomplish the group objective or mission.

Level of Conceptualization for Leadership Theories

Another way to classify leadership theories is in terms of the *level of conceptualization* or type of constructs used to describe leaders and their influence on others. Leadership can be described as (1) an intra-individual process, (2) a dyadic process, (3) a group process, or (4) an organizational process. The levels can be viewed as a hierarchy, as depicted in Figure 3. What level is emphasized will depend on the primary research question, the type of criterion variables used to evaluate leadership effectiveness, and the type of mediating processes used to explain leadership influence. Typical research questions for each level are listed in Table 4. The four levels of conceptualization, and their relative advantages and disadvantages, are described next.

Intra-Individual Processes

Because most definitions of leadership involve influence processes between individuals, leadership theories that describe only leader attributes are rare. Nevertheless, a number of researchers used psychological theories of personality traits, values, skills, motivation, and cognition to explain the decisions and behavior of an individual leader. Roles, behaviors, or decision styles are also used for describing and comparing leaders. Examples can be found in theories about the nature of managerial work and the requirements for different types of leadership positions. Individual traits and skills are also used to explain a person's motivation to seek power and positions of authority, and individual values are used to explain ethical leadership and the altruistic use of power.

Knowledge of intra-individual processes and taxonomies of leadership roles, behaviors, and traits provide insights that are helpful for developing better theories of effective leadership. However, the potential contribution of the intra-individual approach to leadership is limited, because it does not explicitly include what most theorists consider to be the essential process of leadership, namely influencing others such as subordinates, peers, bosses, and outsiders.

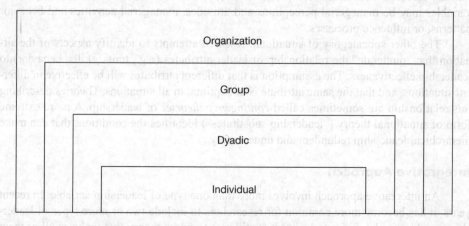

FIGURE 3 Levels of Conceptualization for Leadership Processes

TABLE 4	Research Questions at Different Levels of Conceptualization

Intra-Individual Theories

- How leader traits and values influence leadership behavior
- How leader skills are related to leader behavior
- How leaders make decisions
- How leaders manage their time
- How leaders are influenced by role expectations and constraints
- How leaders react to feedback and learn from experience
- How leaders can use self-development techniques

Dyadic Theories

- How a leader influences subordinate motivation and task commitment
- How a leader facilitates the work of a subordinate
- How a leader interprets information about a subordinate
- How a leader develops a subordinate's skills and confidence
- How a leader influences subordinate loyalty and trust
- How a leader uses influence tactics with a subordinate, peer, or boss
- How a leader and a subordinate influence each other
- How a leader develops a cooperative exchange relationship with a subordinate

Group-Level Theories

- How different leader-member relations affect each other and team performance
- How leadership is shared in the group or team
- How leaders organize and coordinate the activities of team members
- How leaders influence cooperation and resolve disagreements in the team or unit
- How leaders influence collective efficacy and optimism for the team or unit
- How leaders influence collective learning and innovation in the team or unit
- How leaders influence collective identification of members with the team or unit
- How unit leaders obtain resources and support from the organization and other units

Organizational-Level Theories

- How top executives influence members at other levels
- How leaders are selected at each level (and implications of the process for the firm)
- How leaders influence organizational culture
- How leaders influence the efficiency and the cost of internal operations
- How leaders influence human relations and human capital in the organization
- How leaders make decisions about competitive strategy and external initiatives
- How conflicts among leaders are resolved in an organization
- How leaders influence innovation and major change in an organization

Dyadic Processes

The dyadic approach focuses on the relationship between a leader and another individual who is usually a subordinate or another type of follower. The need to influence direct reports is shared by leaders at all levels of authority from chief executives to department managers and work crew supervisors. The explanation of leader influence is usually in terms of how the leader causes the subordinate to be more motivated and more capable of accomplishing task assignments. These theories usually focus on leadership behavior as the source of influence, and on changes in the attitudes, motivation, and behavior of an individual subordinate as the influence process. Reciprocal influence between the leader and follower may be included in the theory, but it is usually less important than the explanation of leader influence over the follower.

An example of a dyadic leadership theory is the leader-member exchange (LMX) theory, which describes how dyadic relationships evolve over time and take different forms, ranging from a casual exchange to a cooperative alliance with shared objectives and mutual trust. Although the LMX theory recognizes that the leader has multiple dyadic relationships, the focus is clearly on what happens within a single relationship. Much of the research on power and influence tactics is also conceptualized in terms of *dyadic processes*. Most theories of transformational and charismatic leadership were initially conceptualized primarily at the dyadic level.

Since real leaders seldom have only a single subordinate, some assumptions are necessary to make dyadic explanations relevant for explaining a leader's influence on the performance of a group or work unit. One assumption is that subordinates have work roles that are similar and independent. Subordinates may not be homogeneous with regard to skills and motives, but they have similar jobs. There is little potential for subordinates to affect each other's job performance, and group performance is the sum of the performances by individuals. An example of minimum interdependence is a district sales unit in which sales representatives work separately and independently of each other and sell the same product in different locations or to different customers. However, when there is high interdependence among group members, a high need for collective learning, and strong external dependencies, a group-level theory is needed to explain how leadership can influence group performance.

The dyadic theories do not include some leadership behaviors that are necessary to facilitate collective performance by a team or organization. Moreover, some of the dyadic behaviors that are effective in terms of dyadic influence will be ineffective with regard to team performance or organizational performance. For example, attempts to develop a closer relationship with one subordinate (e.g., by providing more benefits) may be dysfunctional if they create perceptions of inequity by other subordinates. Efforts to empower individual subordinates may create problems when it is necessary to have a high degree of coordination among all of the subordinates. The extra time needed by a leader to maximize performance by an individual subordinate (e.g., providing intensive coaching) may be more effectively used to deal with problems that involve the team or work group (e.g., obtaining necessary resources, facilitating cooperation and coordination).

Another limitation of most dyadic theories is inadequate attention to the context. In most dyadic theories of effective leadership, aspects of the situation are likely to be treated as moderator variables that constrain or enhance leader influence on individual subordinates. The dyadic theories underestimate the importance of the context for determining what type of leadership is necessary to enhance collective performance by multiple subordinates.

Group Processes

When effective leadership is viewed from a group-level perspective, the focus is on the influence of leaders on collective processes that determine team performance. The explanatory influence processes include determinants of group effectiveness that can be influenced by leaders, and they usually involve all members of a group or team, not only a single subordinate. Examples of these collective explanatory processes include how well the work is organized to utilize personnel and resources, how committed members are to perform their work roles effectively, how confident members are that the task can be accomplished successfully ("potency"), and the extent to which members trust each other and cooperate in accomplishing task objectives. The leadership behaviors identified in dyadic theories are still relevant for leadership in teams, but other behaviors are also important.

As compared to the dyadic theories, most group-level theories provide a much better explanation of effective leadership in teams with interactive members, but these theories also have limitations. The need to describe leader influence on member motivation is usually recognized, but the theory may not include psychological processes that are useful for explaining this influence. The need to influence people and processes outside of the team is usually recognized, but external relationships are usually viewed from the perspective of the team. The focus is on the efforts of leaders to improve team performance (e.g., by getting more resources), but the implications of leader actions for other subunits or the larger organization are seldom explicitly considered. Shared leadership is more likely to be included in a group-level theory than in a dyadic theory, but distributed leadership by multiple formal leaders is seldom explicitly included, even though it is common in some types of teams (e.g., military combat units with a commander and an executive officer).

Organizational Processes

The group approach provides a better understanding of leadership effectiveness than dyadic or intra-individual approaches, but it has some important limitations. A group usually exists in a larger social system, and its effectiveness cannot be understood if the focus of the research is limited to the group's internal processes. The organizational level of analysis describes leadership as a process that occurs in a larger "open system" in which groups are subsystems (Fleishman et al., 1991; Katz & Kahn, 1978; Mumford, 1986).

The survival and prosperity of an organization depends on adaptation to the environment and the acquisition of necessary resources. A business organization must be able to market its products and services successfully. Adaptation is improved by anticipating consumer needs and desires, assessing the actions and plans of competitors, evaluating likely constraints and threats (e.g., government regulation, input scarcity, hostile actions by enemies), and identifying marketable products and services that the organization has unique capabilities to provide. Some examples of activities relevant for adaptation include gathering and interpreting information about the environment, identifying threats and opportunities, developing an effective strategy for adapting to the environment, negotiating agreements that are favorable to the organization, influencing outsiders to have a favorable impression of the organization and its products, and gaining cooperation and support from outsiders upon whom the organization is dependent. These activities are aspects of "strategic leadership."

Survival and prosperity also depend on the efficiency of the transformation process used by the organization to produce its products and services. Efficiency is increased by finding more rational ways to organize and perform the work, and by deciding how to make the best use of available technology, resources, and personnel. Some examples of leadership responsibilities include designing an appropriate organizational structure, determining authority relationships, and coordinating operations across specialized subunits of the organization.

As compared to dyadic or group-level theories of leadership, organization-level theories usually provide a better explanation of financial performance. Distributed leadership is less likely to be ignored in an organization-level theory, because it is obvious that an organization has many designated leaders whose actions must be coordinated. Management practices and systems (e.g., human resource management, operations management, strategic management) are also ignored or downplayed in dyadic and team leadership theories, but in theories of organizational leadership the need to integrate leading and managing is more obvious (Yukl & Lepsinger, 2004). More attention is likely for subjects such as organizational structure and culture, organizational change, executive succession, and influence processes between the CEO and the top management team or board of directors. A limitation of most theories of organizational leadership is that they do not explain influence processes for individual leaders (except sometimes for the chief executive), or influence processes within teams (except in some cases the top-management team).

Multi-level Theories

Multi-level theories include constructs from more than one level of explanation (Klein, Dansereau, & Hall, 1994; Rousseau, 1985). For example, the independent and dependent variables are at the same level of conceptualization, but moderator variables are at a different level. An even more complex type of multi-level theory may include leader influence on explanatory processes at more than one level and reciprocal causality among some of the variables. Multi-level theories of effective leadership provide a way to overcome the limitations of single-level theories, but it is very difficult to develop a multi-level theory that is parsimonious and easy to apply. The level of conceptualization has implications for the measures and methods of analysis used to test a theory, and multi-level theories are usually more difficult to test than single-level theories (Yammarino, Dionne, Chun, & Dansereau, 2005). Despite the difficulties, there is growing interest in developing and testing multi-level theories of leadership.

Other Bases for Comparing Leadership Theories

Key variables and level of conceptualization are not the only ways to compare leadership theories. This section briefly describes three other types of distinctions commonly used in the leadership literature: (1) *leader-centered* versus *follower-centered theory*, (2) universal versus contingency theory, and (3) *descriptive* versus *prescriptive theory*. Each type of distinction is better viewed as a continuum along which a theory can be located, rather than as a sharp dichotomy. For example, it is possible for a theory to have some descriptive elements as well as some prescriptive elements, some universal elements as well as some contingency elements, and an equal focus on leaders and followers.

Leader-Centered or Follower-Centered Theory

The extent to which a theory is focused on either the leader or followers is another useful way to classify leadership theories. Most leadership theories emphasize the characteristics and actions of the leader without much concern for follower characteristics. The leader-focus is strongest in theory and research that identifies traits, skills, or behaviors that contribute to leader effectiveness. Most of the contingency theories also emphasize leader characteristics more than follower characteristics.

Only a small amount of research and theory emphasizes characteristics of the followers. Empowerment theory describes how followers view their ability to influence important events. Attribution theory describes how followers view a leader's influence on events and outcomes. The leader substitutes theory describes aspects of the situation and follower attributes that make a hierarchical leader less important. The emotional contagion theory of charisma describes how followers influence each other. Finally, theories of self-managed groups emphasize sharing of leadership functions among the members of a group; in this approach, the followers are also the leaders.

Theories that focus almost exclusively on either the leader or the follower are less useful than theories that offer a more balanced explanation. Most theories of leader power emphasize that influence over followers depends on follower perceptions of the leader as well as on objective conditions and the leader's influence behavior.

Descriptive or Prescriptive Theory

Another important distinction among leadership theories is the extent to which they are descriptive or prescriptive. Descriptive theories explain leadership processes, describe the typical activities of leaders, and explain why certain behaviors occur in particular situations. Prescriptive theories specify what leaders must do to become effective, and they identify any necessary conditions for using a particular type of behavior effectively.

The two perspectives are not mutually exclusive, and a theory can have both types of elements. For example, a theory that explains why a particular pattern of behavior is typical for leaders (descriptive) may also explain which aspects of behavior are most effective (prescriptive). However, the two perspectives are not always consistent. For example, the typical pattern of behavior for leaders is not always the optimal one. A prescriptive theory is especially useful when a wide discrepancy exists between what leaders typically do and what they should do to be most effective.

Universal or Contingency Theory

A universal theory describes some aspect of leadership that applies to all types of situations, and the theory can be either descriptive or prescriptive. A descriptive universal theory may describe typical functions performed to some extent by all types of leaders, whereas a prescriptive universal theory may specify functions all leaders must perform to be effective.

A contingency theory describes some aspect of leadership that applies to some situations but not to others, and these theories can also be either descriptive or prescriptive. A descriptive contingency theory may explain how leader behavior varies from one situation to another, whereas a prescriptive contingency theory describes effective behavior in a specific situation.

The distinction between universal and contingency theories is a matter of degree, not a sharp dichotomy. Some theories include both universal and situational aspects. For example, a prescriptive theory may specify that a particular type of leadership is always effective but is more effective in some situations than in others. Even when a leadership theory is initially proposed as a universal theory, limiting and facilitating conditions are usually found in later research on the theory.

Summary

Leadership has been defined in many different ways, but most definitions share the assumption that it involves an influence process for facilitating the performance of a collective task. Otherwise, the definitions differ in many respects, such as who exerts the influence, the intended beneficiary of the influence, the manner in which the influence is exerted, and the outcome of the influence attempt. Some theorists advocate treating leading and managing as separate roles or processes, but the proposed definitions do not resolve important questions about the scope of each process and how they are interrelated. No single, "correct" definition of leadership covers all situations. What matters most is how useful the definition is for increasing our understanding of effective leadership.

Most researchers evaluate leadership effectiveness in terms of the consequences for followers and other organization stakeholders, but the choice of outcome variables has differed considerably from researcher to researcher. Criteria differ in many important respects, including how immediate they are, and whether they have subjective or objective measures. When evaluating leadership effectiveness, multiple criteria should be considered to deal with these complexities and the different preferences of various stakeholders.

Leadership has been studied in different ways, depending on the researcher's methodological preferences and definition of leadership. Most researchers deal only with a narrow aspect of leadership, and most empirical studies fall into distinct lines of research such as the trait, behavior, power, and situational approaches. In recent years, there has been an increased effort to cut across and integrate these approaches.

Level of analysis is another basis for classifying leadership theory and research. The levels include intra-individual, dyadic, group, and organizational. Each level provides some unique insights, but more research is needed on group and organizational processes, and more integration across levels is needed.

Another basis for differentiating theories is the relative focus on leader or follower. For many years, the research focused on leader characteristics and followers were studied only as the object of leader influence. A more balanced approach is needed, and some progress is being made in that direction.

Leadership theories can be classified as prescriptive versus descriptive, according to the emphasis on "what should be" rather than on "what occurs now." A final basis for differentiation (universal versus contingency) is the extent to which a theory describes leadership processes and relationships that are similar in all situations or that vary in specified ways across situations.

Review and Discussion Questions

1. What are some similarities and differences in the way leadership has been defined?
2. What are the arguments for and against making a distinction between leaders and managers?
3. Why is it so difficult to measure leadership effectiveness?
4. What criteria have been used to evaluate leadership effectiveness, and are some criteria more useful than others?
5. What are the trait, behavior, and power-influence approaches, and what unique insights does each approach provide about effective leadership?
6. Is leadership described as an intra-individual, dyadic, group, or organizational process in most leader-ship theories and research?
7. Compare descriptive and prescriptive theories of leadership, and explain why both types of theory are useful.
8. Compare universal and contingency theories. Is it possible to have a theory with both universal and contingent aspects?

Key Terms

behavior approach	dyadic processes	power-influence approach
contingency theories	follower-centered theory	prescriptive theory
criteria of leadership	integrative approach	shared influence process
effectiveness	leader-centered theory	situational approach
delayed effects	level of conceptualization	specialized leadership role
descriptive theory	mediating variable	trait approach

Nature of Managerial Work

Learning Objectives

After studying this chapter, you should be able to:

- Understand the different roles and activities commonly required for managers.
- Understand how managerial roles and activities are affected by aspects of the situation.
- Understand how managers cope with demands, constraints, and choices confronting them.
- Understand the importance of external activities and networking for managers.
- Understand how managers solve problems and make decisions.
- Understand how managers can make effective use of their time.

Leadership is an important role requirement for managers and a major reason why managerial jobs exist. This chapter examines findings from research on the nature of managerial work. The research involves analysis of data from a variety of sources, including observation of managers, diaries in which managers describe their own activities, interviews with managers who explain what they do and why they do it, and job description questionnaires in which managers rate the importance of different types of *managerial activities*. One major purpose of this research has been to identify patterns of activity that are common to all types of managers. Another major purpose has been to compare activity patterns for different types of managers, or managers in different situations. These "comparative" studies examine the extent to which the behavior of a manager is influenced by the unique role requirements of the situation.

Most descriptive research on managerial activities was not designed to determine how activities are related to effective leadership, but the research provides some insights about the subject. One important skill is time management. The final section of the chapter describes guidelines to help managers use their time wisely, cope with *demands*, and handle *role conflicts*.

Activity Patterns for Managers

To discover what managers do and how they spend their time, researchers used descriptive methods such as direct observation, diaries, and interviews. The researcher attempted to find answers to questions such as how much time managers spend alone or interfagers use different forms of interaction (e.g., telephone, scheduled meetings, unscheduled meetings, written messages), where the interactions occur, how long they last, and who initiated them. Reviews of this research find some consistent activity patterns for most types of managerial positions (Hales, 1986; McCall, Morrison, & Hannan, 1978; Mintzberg, 1973). This section of the chapter reviews major findings about the nature of managerial work.

Pace of Work Is Hectic and Unrelenting

The typical manager works long hours, and many managers take work home. In part, this workload can be traced to the preferences of people in managerial positions. Having trained their minds to search for and analyze new information continually, most managers do this type of searching automatically and find it difficult to forget about their jobs when at home or on vacation. The typical manager's day seldom includes a break in the workload. Managers receive almost continuous requests for information, assistance, direction, and authorization from a large number of people, such as subordinates, peers, superiors, and people outside the organization. The research on managerial activities contradicts the popular conception of managers as people who carefully plan and orchestrate events, and then sit in their office waiting for the occasional exception to normal operations that may require their attention.

Content of Work Is Varied and Fragmented

Managers typically engage in a variety of activities each day, and many of them are brief in duration. Mintzberg's (1973, p. 33) observations of executives found that "half of the activities were completed in less than 9 minutes, and only one-tenth took more than an hour." The activities of managers tend to be fragmented as well as varied. Interruptions occur frequently, conversations are disjointed, and important activities are interspersed with trivial ones, requiring rapid shifts of mood. A manager may go from a budget meeting to decide millions of dollars in spending to a discussion about how to fix a broken water fountain (Sayles, 1979).

Many Activities are Reactive

The fragmented nature of managerial activity reflects the fact that many interactions are initiated by others, and much of a manager's behavior is reactive rather than proactive in nature. A common stereotype of managers is that they spend a considerable part of their time in careful analysis of business problems and development of elaborate plans to deal with them. However, the descriptive studies find that most managers devote little time to reflective planning. The fragmented activities and continual heavy demands characteristic of managerial work make it difficult for managers to find the long periods of unallocated time necessary for this type of activity. Reflective planning and other activities that require large blocks of time, such as team building and training subordinates in complex skills, are usually preempted by "fire fighting" activities involving immediate operational problems. What little time managers spend alone in the office is typically used to read correspondence, check and send e-mail messages, handle administrative paperwork, write reports or memos, and scan journals or technical publications. Most managers gravitate toward the active aspects of their jobs, and they tend to focus on specific, immediate problems rather than general issues or long-term strategies.

Problems occur in a mostly random order, and managers choose to react to some problems as they become aware of them, while others are ignored or postponed. There are more problems than a manager can handle at any given time, and only a few of them will get immediate attention. The importance of a problem is a major determinant of whether it will be recognized and handled, but it is often unclear how important a problem really is.

A manager is more likely to respond to a problem when there is pressure for immediate action due to a crisis, deadline, or expectations of progress by someone important, such as the manager's boss or an external client (McCall & Kaplan, 1985). In the absence of such pressure, a problem is more likely to get action when it is perceived to be similar to other problems that a manager has solved successfully in the past, when the problem is perceived to be clearly within the manager's domain of responsibility, and when the manager perceives that the actions and resources necessary to solve the problem are available. Managers are likely to ignore a problem or postpone dealing with a problem when there is no external pressure for action, it is fuzzy and difficult to diagnose, it is the primary responsibility of other managers or subunits, or it cannot be solved without additional resources and support that would be difficult or impossible to obtain.

Interactions Often Involve Peers and Outsiders

Although much of the leadership literature focuses on the relationship between leader and subordinates, the descriptive research has found that managers typically spend considerable time with persons other than direct subordinates or the manager's boss. These contacts may involve subordinates of subordinates, superiors of the boss, lateral peers, subordinates of lateral peers, and superiors of lateral peers. In addition, many managers spend considerable time with people outside the organization, such as customers, clients, suppliers, subcontractors, people in government agencies, important people in the community, and managers from other organizations. Kotter (1982) found that the network of relationships for general managers often consisted of hundreds of people inside and outside of their organization (see Figure 1).

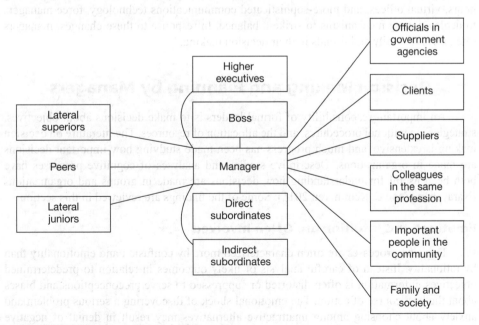

FIGURE 1 A Manager's Network of Contacts

The high incidence of lateral and external interactions can be explained in terms of a manager's need for information about complex and uncertain events that influence the operations of his or her organizational subunit, and the manager's *dependence* on the cooperation and assistance of numerous people outside the immediate chain of command (Kotter, 1982). A large network of contacts provides information about current events within or outside of the organization that may affect the manager's job performance and career. In addition, *networks* can be used to obtain assistance for solving problems or making changes. The ability to assemble a coalition of internal and external supporters is especially important to make innovative changes and ensure that they will be implemented successfully (Kanter, 1983). Managers use different parts of their network for different purposes and extend the network as needed to accomplish a particular objective (Ibarra & Hunter, 2007; Kaplan, 1988).

Networks are developed in a variety of ways, such as (1) talking with people before, during, and after meetings, ceremonies, and social events in the organization; (2) serving on special committees, interest groups, and task forces; (3) joining civic groups, advisory boards, and social clubs; and (4) attending workshops, trade shows, and meetings of professional associations. Cooperative relationships are established and maintained by showing respect and positive regard, offering unconditional favors (e.g., passing on useful information, offering to help with a problem), keeping in touch, and showing appreciation for favors received, especially those requiring a significant effort on the part of the person doing it. The process of networking is a perpetual activity for managers. Old relationships need to be maintained and new ones established as people in key positions change, the organization changes, and the external environment changes. Good network relationships in the organization are associated with greater influence over subordinates (e.g., Bono & Anderson, 2005).

A significant, yet often ignored, aspect of a manager's interactional network is family, friends, and other societal relations. These factors of the network pose great demands on the manager's work and personal life. The competing demands of work and society have assumed increased relevance for managers in recent years, and the divide between personal and professional life has become increasingly narrower. Various socio-cultural changes, such as rising numbers of women in the work force, an ageing population, unrelenting working hours, virtual offices, and more-sophisticated communications technology, force managers to deploy coping mechanisms to strike a balance. In response to these changes, managers often involve family and friends in their decision making.

Decision Making and Planning by Managers

An important responsibility of formal leaders is to make decisions about objectives, strategies, operational procedures, and the allocation of resources. The literature on decision making is extensive, and much progress has been made studying how important decisions are made in organizations. Descriptive studies and analyses of cognitive processes have both been useful for understanding how decisions are made in groups and organizations (Narayanan, Zane & Kemmerer, 2011). Some of the findings are reviewed in this section.

Emotions and Intuition are Often Involved

Decision processes are often characterized more by confusion and emotionality than by rationality. Instead of careful analysis of likely outcomes in relation to predetermined objectives, information is often distorted or suppressed to serve preconceptions and biases about the best course of action. The emotional shock of discovering a serious problem and anxiety about choosing among unattractive alternatives may result in denial of negative evidence, wishful thinking, procrastination, vacillation between choices, and panic reactions by individual managers or by decision groups (Janis & Mann, 1977). The greater the job demands and stress for a manager, the less likely it is that a prolonged search or careful analysis of potential costs and benefits will be made (Hambrick, Finkelstein, & Mooney, 2005). Instead, a highly stressed executive is more likely to respond to serious threats and problems by relying on solutions used in the past or by imitating the practices of similar companies. Individuals with strong negative affect (fear, anger, depression) are more likely to use dysfunctional methods for decision making than individuals with positive affect (Ganster, 2005).

Decisions often reflect the influence of intuition rather than conscious rational analysis of available alternatives and their likely outcomes (Dane & Pratt, 2007; Salas, Rosen & DiazGranados, 2010; Simon, 1987). Experienced managers try to determine if a problem is familiar or novel, and for familiar ones they can apply past experience and learned procedures to determine the best course of action. However, failure to classify a problem accurately is likely to result in a poor decision on how to resolve it. When managers become attached to mental models that are no longer adequate, it is more difficult for them to recognize novel problems or innovative solutions (Narayanan et al., 2011). Involving other people can improve the quality of problem diagnosis and decision choice, but only if appropriate processes are used by the group.

Important Decisions are Disorderly and Political

Much of the management literature describes decisions as discrete events made by a single manager or group in an orderly, rational manner. This picture is sharply contradicted by the descriptive research on managerial work and related research on managerial decision making (Cohen & March, 1974; McCall & Kaplan, 1985; Schweiger, Anderson, & Locke, 1985; Simon, 1987). Managers are seldom observed to make major decisions at a single point in time, and they are seldom able to recall when a decision was finally reached. Some major decisions are the result of many small actions or incremental choices taken without regard to larger strategic issues.

Important decisions in organizations typically require the support and authorization of many different people at different levels of management and in different subunits of the organization. It is common practice for a manager to consult with subordinates, peers, or superiors about important decisions when an immediate response is not required. The person who initiates the decision process may not be the person who makes the final choice among action alternatives. For example, a section supervisor with a problem may point out the need for a decision to his or her boss, the department manager. The department manager may consult with the plant manager or with managers in other departments who would be affected by the decision. Even when not consulted in advance, the plant manager may review the department manager's decision and approve, reject, or modify it.

The different people involved in making a decision often disagree about the true nature of a problem and the likely outcomes of various solutions, due to the different perspectives, assumptions, and values typical of managers from different functional specialties and backgrounds. When managers have different mental models for explaining the cause of a problem, it is more difficult to reach agreement about a good solution (Mumford, Friedrich, Caughron, & Byrne, 2007).

A prolonged, highly political decision process is likely when decisions involve important and complex problems for which no ready-made, good solutions are available, when many affected parties have conflicting interests, and when a diffusion of power exists among the parties. The decision process may drag on for months or years due to delays and interruptions as a proposal is sidetracked by opponents, preempted by immediate crises, or recycled back to its initiators for revisions necessary to make it suitable to managers whose support is needed (Mintzberg, Raisinghani, & Theoret, 1976). For decisions involving major changes in organizational strategies or policies, the outcome will depend to a great extent on the influence skills and persistence of the individual managers who desire to initiate change and on the relative power of the various coalitions involved in making or authorizing these decisions (Kanter, 1983; Kotter, 1982, 1985).

Routine Decisions are Different

Not all decisions involve major changes or prolonged political processes. Managers make many less momentous decisions in the process of solving operational problems, setting shortterm goals, assigning work to subordinates, setting up work schedules, authorizing the expenditure of funds for supplies or equipment, and approving pay increases. These decisions often involve problems for which ready-made and low-risk solutions are available, the manager has the authority to make a decision, few important people will be affected by the decision, little conflict exists about objectives or solutions, and pressure is felt for a quick decision due to a deadline or a crisis. Managers usually make this type of decision either alone or after briefly consulting with a few people, and only a short period of problem analysis and search for solutions is likely to occur (McCall & Kaplan, 1985). Although these decisions are less important, they require appropriate technical knowledge by the manager and the capacity to find a good balance between lengthy, systematic analysis and quick, decisive action. A hasty decision based in limited information may fail to solve the problem, but the problem may get worse and be more difficult to resolve if the manager delays a decision to get more information.

Most Planning Is Informal and Adaptive

An important type of decision for managers is planning how to achieve objectives, implement changes, and conduct important activities. Planning is often described in the managerial literature as primarily a formal process of written objectives, strategies, policies, and budgets, cascading from top management down the hierarchy, with even more detailed versions at each lower level of management. The descriptive studies find that planning by managers is often informal and implicit. Kotter (1982) found that general managers develop agendas consisting of goals and plans related to their job responsibilities and involving a variety of short-term and long-term issues. The short-term (1–30 days) objectives and plans are usually quite specific and detailed, but the longer-term (5–20 years) agenda items are usually vague, incomplete, and only loosely connected. A new manager begins the process of developing this agenda immediately, but initially it is likely to be rough and incomplete. Over time, as managers gather more information about their organization or subunit (e.g., operations, people, politics, markets, competitors, problems, and concerns), the agendas are refined and expanded (Gabarro, 1985; Kotter, 1982).

Kotter also found that the implementation of agenda items is also a gradual, continuous process. Managers use a variety of influence techniques during their daily interactions with other people to mobilize support and shape events. The agenda guides the manager in making efficient use of random encounters and brief interactions with relevant people in the manager's network of contacts.

In his study of top executives, Quinn (1980) found that most of the important strategic decisions were made outside the formal planning process, and strategies were formulated in an incremental, flexible, and intuitive manner. In response to major unforeseen events, the executives developed tentative, broad strategies that allowed them to keep their options open until they had more opportunity to learn from experience about the nature of the environment and the feasibility of their initial actions. Strategies were refined and implemented simultaneously in a cautious, incremental manner that reflected the need to develop a political coalition in support of a strategy as well as to avoid the risks of an initial, irreversible commitment to a particular course of action. Instead of a top-down, formal process, overall objectives and strategies for the firms were more likely to be the result of a "bottom-up" political process in which the objectives and strategies of powerful individuals and organizational subunits are reconciled and integrated. The formal, annual plans were merely a confirmation of strategic decisions already reached through the informal political process.

Managerial Roles

The early descriptive research on managerial work was concerned primarily with providing a description of activity patterns. Then, the focus of descriptive research shifted to classifying the content of managerial activity in terms of its purpose. A major difficulty in this research has been to determine what behavior categories are meaningful, distinct, and relevant for classifying observed activities of managers. In attempting to resolve this question, different researchers have developed taxonomies of *managerial roles* or functions.

Mintzberg's Taxonomy of Roles

Mintzberg (1973) developed a taxonomy of 10 managerial roles to use for coding the content of activities observed in a study of executives (see Table 1). These roles account for all of a manager's activities, and each activity can be explained in terms of at least one role, although many activities involve more than one role. The managerial roles apply to any manager, but their relative importance may vary from one kind of manager to another. The roles are largely predetermined by the nature of the managerial position, but each manager has some flexibility in how to interpret and enact each role. Three roles deal with the interpersonal behavior of managers (leader, liaison, figurehead), three roles deal with information-processing behavior (monitor, disseminator, spokesperson), and four roles deal with decision-making behavior (entrepreneur, disturbance handler, resource allocator, negotiator). Each type of role will be described in more detail.

TABLE 1	Mintzberg's Managerial Roles

Information Processing Roles

- Disseminator
- Monitor
- Spokesperson

Decision-Making Roles

- Entrepreneur
- Disturbance handler
- Resource allocator
- Negotiator

Interpersonal Roles

- Liaison
- Figurehead
- Leader

Leader Role.   Managers are responsible for making their organizational subunit function as an integrated whole in the pursuit of its basic purpose. Consequently, the manager must provide guidance to subordinates, ensure that they are motivated, and create favorable conditions for doing the work. A number of managerial activities are expressly concerned with the leader role, including hiring, training, directing, praising, criticizing, promoting, and dismissing. However, the leader role pervades all managerial activities, even those with some other basic purpose.

Liaison Role.   The liaison role includes behavior intended to establish and maintain a web of relationships with individuals and groups outside of a manager's organizational unit. These relationships are vital as a source of information and favors. The essence of the liaison role is making new contacts, keeping in touch, and doing favors that will allow the manager to ask for favors in return.

Figurehead Role.   As a consequence of their formal authority as the head of an organization or one of its subunits, managers are obliged to perform certain symbolic duties of a legal and social nature. These duties include signing documents (e.g., contracts, expense authorizations), presiding at certain meetings and ceremonial events (e.g., retirement dinner for a subordinate), participating in other rituals or ceremonies, and receiving official visitors. The manager must participate in these activities even though they are usually of marginal relevance to the job of managing.

Monitor Role.   Managers continually seek information from a variety of sources, such as reading reports and memos, attending meetings and briefings, and conducting observational tours. Some of the information is passed on to subordinates (disseminator role) or to outsiders (spokesperson role). Most of the information is analyzed to discover problems and opportunities, and to develop an understanding of outside events and internal processes within the manager's organizational subunit.

Disseminator Role.   Managers have special access to sources of information not available to subordinates. Some of this information is factual, and some of it concerns the stated preferences of individuals desiring to influence the manager, including people at high levels of authority. Some of the information must be passed on to subordinates, either in its original form or after interpretation and editing by the manager.

Spokesperson Role.   Managers are also obliged to transmit information and express value statements to people outside their organizational subunit. Middle managers and lower-level managers must report to their superiors; a chief executive must report to the board of directors or owners. Each of these managers is also expected to serve as a lobbyist and public relations representative for the organizational subunit when dealing with superiors and outsiders. As Mintzberg (1973, p. 76) points out, "To speak effectively for his organization and to gain the respect of outsiders, the manager must demonstrate an up-to-the-minute knowledge of his organization and its environment."

Entrepreneur Role.   The manager of an organization or one of its subunits acts as an initiator and designer of controlled change to exploit opportunities for improving the existing situation. Planned change takes place in the form of improvement projects such as development of a new product, purchase of new equipment, or reorganization of formal structure. Some of the improvement projects are supervised directly by the manager, and some are delegated to subordinates. Mintzberg (1973, p. 81) offers the following description of the way a manager deals with improvement projects:

The manager as a supervisor of improvement projects may be likened to a juggler. At any one point in time he has a number of balls in the air. Periodically, one comes down, receives a short burst of energy, and goes up again. Meanwhile, new balls wait on the sidelines and, at random intervals, old balls are discarded and new ones added.

Disturbance Handler Role.   In the disturbance handler role, a manager deals with sudden crises that cannot be ignored, as distinguished from problems that are voluntarily solved by the manager to exploit opportunities (entrepreneur role). The crises are caused by unforeseen events, such as conflict among subordinates, the loss of a key subordinate, a fire or accident, a strike, and so on. A manager typically gives this role priority over all of the others.

Resource Allocator Role.   Managers exercise their authority to allocate resources such as money, personnel, material, equipment, facilities, and services. Resource allocation is involved in managerial decisions about what is to be done, in the manager's authorization of subordinates' decisions, in the preparation of budgets, and in the scheduling of the manager's own time. By retaining the power to allocate resources, the manager maintains control over strategy formation and acts to coordinate and integrate subordinate actions in support of strategic objectives.

Negotiator Role.   Any negotiations requiring a substantial commitment of resources will be facilitated by the presence of a manager having the authority to make this commitment. Managers may participate in several different types of negotiations, including negotiations with unions involving labor-management contracts or grievances; contract negotiations with important customers, suppliers, or consultants; employment negotiations with key personnel; and other nonroutine negotiations (e.g., acquisition of another firm, application for a large loan).

Role Conflicts

The discussion of characteristic managerial roles emphasizes the types of activities commonly expected of managers, regardless of the type of position. However, many different people ("role senders") in an organization exert pressure on the manager to conform with their beliefs about the proper way to behave ("*role expectations*"). At times, different people make incompatible demands on the manager, creating "role conflicts" (Kahn, Wolfe, Quinn, & Snoek, 1964; Pfeffer & Salancik, 1975). For example, managers often find themselves beset by conflicting demands from superiors and subordinates. The conflict may involve a disagreement about the relative priority of two different roles, or about the manner in which a particular role should be carried out. In trying to reconcile conflicting role expectations, a manager is likely to be more responsive to the expectations of superiors, because they wield more power over a manager than do subordinates (Kahn et al., 1964). However, the manner in which a role conflict is resolved also depends in part on how important the issue is to each role sender (Salancik et al., 1975). A manager who is able to reconcile successfully the divergent concerns of superiors and subordinates is more likely to be effective (Mann & Dent, 1954; Mann & Hoffman, 1960; Tsui, 1984; Tsui, Ashford, St. Clair, & Xin, 1995).

In addition to role expectations from other people, a leader's perception of role requirements will depend on the nature of the task. Role expectations from subordinates or superiors are sometimes inconsistent with objective task requirements, especially when the nature of the task or the external environment changes while norms and beliefs about proper leadership behavior remain the same. Here again, the leader has a role conflict: conform to expectations from role senders and be less effective in facilitating group performance, or do what is necessary to accomplish the task and take a chance on being initially rejected by role senders.

Demands, Constraints, and Choices

Mintzberg's (1973) managerial roles describe the type of required activities that are common to most managerial and administrative positions. However, descriptive research indicates that managers also have unique role requirements that are specific to a particular type of managerial position in a particular type of organization. Stewart (1967, 1976, 1982) formulated a model for describing different types of managerial jobs and understanding how managers do them. The model was based on extensive research using observation, interviews, and diaries, and it has three core components.

Core Components

Demands, *constraints*, and choices define the job of a manager and strongly influence the behavior of anyone who occupies the position. Demands and constraints are situational influences on the leader and affect the scope of the leader's choice of actions.

Demands.   Demands are the required duties, activities, and responsibilities for someone who occupies a managerial position. Demands include standards, objectives, and deadlines for work that must be met, and bureaucratic procedures that cannot be ignored or delegated, such as preparing budgets and reports, attending certain meetings, authorizing expenditures, signing documents, and conducting performance appraisals. Other demands depend on particular individuals, such as the requirement by the boss that the manager knows operational details, or an important customer's insistence on dealing with the manager instead of a subordinate.

Constraints.   Constraints are characteristics of the organization and external environment limiting what a manager can do. They include bureaucratic rules, policies, and regulations that must be observed, and legal constraints such as labor laws, environmental regulations, securities regulations, and safety regulations. Another type of constraint involves the availability of resources, such as facilities, equipment, budgetary funding, supplies, personnel, and support services. The technology used to do the work constrains the options for how the work will be done. The physical location of facilities and distribution of personnel among work sites limits the opportunities for face-to-face interaction. Market considerations such as the preferences of clients and customers are constraints on the type of products and services that may be provided by the manager's organizational unit.

Choices.   Choices are the activities that a manager may do but is not required to do. Choices include the opportunities available to someone in a particular type of managerial position to determine what to do and how to do it. Demands and constraints limit choices in the short run, but over a longer time period, a manager has some opportunities to modify demands and remove or circumvent constraints, thereby expanding choices. Examples of major choices include the objectives for the manager's unit, the priorities attached to different objectives, the strategies selected to pursue objectives, the aspects of the work in which the manager gets personally involved, how and with whom the manager spends time, what responsibility is delegated to whom, and how the manager attempts to influence different people. In a sense, these choices can be described in terms of Kotter's (1982) concepts as what agendas to set, what contacts to make to build a network, and how to influence people to implement the agendas.

Managerial jobs differ greatly in the amount and type of demands and constraints the job holder faces. However, even within the same job, the demands and constraints will vary depending on the perception of the job holder. They are not entirely determined by objective conditions but result instead from the dynamic interaction between manager and role senders. By their choices, managers influence demands. For example, agreeing to serve on a committee adds to a manager's demands. Moreover, people differ in the way they interpret role expectations, and one person will perceive a demand where another may not. For example, one operations manager believes that a bureaucratic regulation must be observed exactly, whereas another operations manager in the same company perceives more flexibility in what can be done.

Situational Determinants

There are differences in the pattern of demands, constraints, and choices for different types of managerial jobs, depending on aspects of the situation such as the type of organization and the nature of the work. Based on Stewart's research, three factors were found to be important for comparing managerial jobs with respect to behavioral requirements.

Pattern of Relationships.   The demands made on a manager by superiors, subordinates, peers, and persons outside the organization influence how the manager's time is spent and how much skill is needed to fulfill role requirements. More time is needed to deal with subordinates when they have interlocking jobs requiring coordination; new assignments must be made frequently; it is important but difficult to monitor subordinate performance, and automatic compliance with orders and requests is not assured. More time is needed to deal with superiors when the manager is highly dependent on them for resources or assignments, and they make unpredictable demands. More time is needed to deal with peers when the manager is dependent on them for services, supplies, cooperation, or approval of work outputs. More time is needed for outsiders (e.g., clients, customers, suppliers, subcontractors) when the manager is highly dependent on them and must negotiate agreements, carry out public relations activities, create a good impression, and act discreet. Having to establish relationships with many people for short periods of time, as opposed to dealing with the same people repeatedly, further complicates the manager's job, especially when it is necessary to impress and influence people quickly. The extent to which subordinates, peers, and superiors make incompatible demands on a manager determines how much role conflict the manager will experience.

Work Pattern.   Stewart found that the pattern of role requirements and demands affected managerial behavior, and somewhat different patterns of behavior were associated with different types of managerial jobs. The following factors were useful for classifying managerial jobs: (1) the extent to which managerial activities are either self-generating or a response to the requests, instructions, and problems of other people; (2) the extent to which the work is recurrent and repetitive rather than variable and unique; (3) the amount of uncertainty in the work; (4) the extent of managerial activities requiring sustained attention for long periods of time; and (5) the amount of pressure to meet deadlines. For example, more initiative and planning of activities are required in a predominantly self-generating job (e.g., product manager, research manager, training director) than for a predominantly responding job with unpredictable problems and workload variations that are beyond the manager's control (e.g., production manager, service manager). Stewart suggested that the work pattern associated with some kinds of managerial jobs tends to be habit forming. A person who spends a long time in one position may grow accustomed to acting in a particular way and will find it difficult to adjust to another managerial position with different behavioral requirements.

Exposure.   Another aspect of a managerial job that determines what behavior and skills are required is the amount of responsibility for making decisions with potentially serious consequences, and the amount of time before a mistake or poor decision can be discovered. There is more "*exposure*" when decisions and actions have important, highly visible consequences for the organization, and mistakes or poor judgment can result in loss of resources, disruption of operations, and risk to human health and life. There is less exposure when decisions do not have immediate consequences, or when decisions are made by a group that has shared accountability for them. Examples of high-exposure jobs include product managers who must recommend expensive marketing programs and product changes that may quickly prove to be a disaster, project managers who may fail to complete projects on schedule and within budget, and managers of profit centers who are held accountable for their unit's costs and profits.

How Much Discretion Do Managers Have?

A managerial position makes various demands on the person who occupies it, and the actions of the occupant are constrained by laws, policies, regulations, traditions, and scope of formal authority. Despite these demands and constraints, some choice of behavior remains, particularly with respect to what aspects of the job are emphasized, how much time is devoted to various activities, and how much time is spent with different people. The research showed that even for managers with similar jobs, there was considerable variability of behavior (James & White, 1983; Kotter, 1982; Stewart, 1976, 1982). For example, Stewart found that some bank managers emphasized staff supervision, whereas some others delegated much of the internal management to the assistant manager and concentrated on actively seeking out new business.

In part, variability of behavior within the same job occurs because of its multiple performance dimensions. Within the boundaries imposed by the priorities of higher management, a person may choose to devote more effort to some objectives than to others. For example, activities involving development of new products may get more attention than cost reduction, quality improvements, development of new export markets, or improvement of safety practices. Development of subordinates to groom them for promotion may get more attention than team building or training in skills necessary to improve performance in the present job.

The trade-offs inherent among performance dimensions and lack of time to do everything well make it inevitable that different people will define the same job in different ways. How this job definition is done will reflect a manager's interests, skills, and values, as well as the changing role expectations of the individuals whose destinies are intertwined with the managers.

Variability in the same job is also due to the way in which a manager deals with role conflicts. Role expectations for a leader are seldom absolute or comprehensive, and a leader usually has considerable discretion to shape his or her role over time. Given enough time, a skillful leader may be able to reconcile role requirements that were initially incompatible. Leaders with a record of successful decisions and demonstrated loyalty to the organization are given more freedom to redefine their role and initiate innovations. However, flexibility is greater for role expectations that do not involve central values of symbolic importance to organization members (Biggart & Hamilton, 1984).

Other Determinants of Managerial Work

Stewart's broad perspective on the demands and constraints is not typical of most research on the situational determinants of leader behavior. Most studies investigate only one or two aspects of the situation at a time, and different aspects of the situation are examined from one study to the next. This narrow approach makes it difficult to detect the influence of unmeasured situational variables or to compare results across studies. Despite these limitations, the research indicates that managerial activities are influenced by several situational variables, including level of management, subunit size, *lateral interdependence*, crisis conditions, and stage in the organizational life cycle.

Level of Management

Job responsibilities and the skills necessary to carry them out vary somewhat for managers at different authority levels in the organization (Jacobs & Jaques, 1987; Katz & Kahn, 1978; Lucas & Markessini, 1993). Higher-level managers are usually more concerned with exercise of broad authority in making long-range plans, formulating policy, modifying the organization structure, and initiating new ways of doing things. Decisions at this level usually have a long time perspective, because it is appropriate for top executives to be thinking about what will happen 10 to 20 years in the future. Middle managers are primarily concerned with interpreting and implementing policies and programs, and they usually have a moderately long-time perspective (two to five years). Low-level managers are primarily concerned with structuring, coordinating, and facilitating work activities. Objectives are more specific, issues are less complex and more focused, and managers typically have a shorter time perspective (a few weeks to two years).

A manager at a high level in the authority hierarchy of an organization typically has more responsibility for making important decisions, including determination of organizational objectives, planning of strategies to obtain objectives, determination of general policies, design of the organizational structure, and allocation of resources. As one goes down through the authority hierarchy, managers have less discretion and freedom of action. Lower-level managers must operate within the constraints imposed by formalized rules and policy decisions made at higher levels. Blankenship and Miles (1968) found that lower-level managers had less discretion, were required more often to consult with superiors before taking action on decisions, and made the final choice in a decision less often.

Consistent with this difference in job requirements and discretion across levels is the relative importance and amount of time devoted to different managerial activities and roles (Allan, 1981; Luthans, Rosenkrantz, & Hennessey, 1985; McCall & Segrist, 1980; Mintzberg, 1973; Paolillo, 1981). The *job description research* found that planning, strategic decision making, and public relations are more important activities for top managers than for lower-level managers (Hemphill, 1959; Katzell, Barrett, Vann, & Hogan, 1968; Mahoney, Jerdee, & Carroll, 1965; Page & Tornow, 1987; Tornow & Pinto, 1976). The research on managerial roles found that the resource allocator, spokesperson, and figurehead roles are more important for top-level managers than for lower-level managers. High-level managers are usually more dependent on people outside the organization, and research on managerial activities and networking shows that they spend more time interacting with outsiders than do most managers at lower levels (Luthans, Rosenkrantz, & Hennessey, 1985; McCall, Morrison, & Hannan, 1978; Michael & Yukl, 1993). Research on social networks finds that external ties with important people are a valuable resource to top executives, but spending too much time in external relations can distract from their internal management responsibilities and undermine their effectiveness (Balkundi & Kilduff, 2005). Lower-level managers tend to be more concerned with technical matters, staffing (personnel selection and training), scheduling work, and monitoring subordinate performance. The number of activities carried out each day is greater for lower-level managers, and the time spent on each activity tends to be less (Kurke & Aldrich, 1983; Mintzberg, 1973; Thomason, 1967; Walker, Guest & Turner, 1956).

Size of Organizational Unit

The implications of work unit size or "span of control" for leader behavior have been investigated in several types of research, ranging from studies with small groups to studies on chief executives. Kotter studied general managers and concluded that managers of the larger organizational subunits had more demanding jobs in comparison to managers of smaller units. Decisions are more difficult due to the sheer volume of issues and activities and the lack of detailed knowledge a manager is likely to have. Because larger units are likely to have a more bureaucratic structure, managers must cope with more constraints (e.g., rules, standard procedures, and required authorizations). Consistent with this analysis, Kotter (1982) found that general managers in larger organizational units had larger networks and attended more scheduled meetings.

When a manager has a large number of subordinates, it is more difficult to get all of them together for meetings, or to consult individually with each subordinate. Thus, leaders tend to use less participative leadership or to limit it to an "executive committee" or to a few trusted "lieutenants." Heller and Yukl (1969) found that as span of control increased, upper-level managers made more autocratic decisions, but they also used more delegation. Both decision styles allow a manager who is overloaded with responsibilities to reduce the amount of time needed to make decisions. Lower-level managers in this study also made more autocratic decisions as span of control increased, but they did not use more delegation, perhaps because delegation was less feasible for them. Blankenship and Miles (1968) found that as span of control increased, managers relied more on subordinates to initiate action on decisions, and this trend was much more pronounced for upper-level managers than for lower-level managers.

As the size of a work unit increases, so does the administrative workload. Managers spend more time on planning, coordinating, staffing, and budgeting activities (Cohen & March, 1974; Hemphill, 1950; Katzell et al., 1968). The increase in coordination requirements is magnified when the subordinates have highly uncertain and interdependent tasks. Sometimes part of the increased administrative burden can be delegated to a second in command, to a coordinating committee composed of subordinates, or to new coordinating specialists who serve as staff assistants. In many cases, however, the leader is expected to assume the responsibility for providing direction and integration of group activities.

Managers of large work units have less opportunity for interacting with individual subordinates and maintaining effective interpersonal relationships with them (Ford, 1981). Less time is available to provide support, encouragement, and recognition to individual subordinates (Goodstadt & Kipnis, 1970). Problems with subordinates are likely to be handled in a more formalized, impersonal manner, and managers are more likely to use warnings and punishment (Kipnis & Cosentino, 1969; Kipnis & Lane, 1962). When a subordinate has a performance problem, the manager is less likely to provide individualized instruction and coaching.

As a group or work unit grows larger, separate subgroups, cliques, or factions are likely to emerge. The subgroups often compete for power and resources, creating conflicts and posing a threat to group cohesiveness and teamwork. Thus, the leader of a large group or work unit needs to devote more time to building group identification, promoting cooperation, and managing conflict. The pressure to carry out more administrative activities may cause the leader to neglect group maintenance activities until serious problems arise.

External Dependencies

The extent to which a leader's subunit is dependent on other subunits in the same organization ("lateral interdependence") or on external groups will affect leader behavior to a considerable extent. As interdependence increases with other subunits, coordination with them becomes more important and there is more need for mutual adjustments in plans, schedules, and activities (Galbraith, 1973; Mintzberg, 1979). Lateral interdependence represents a threat to the subunit because routine activities must be modified more frequently to accommodate the needs of other subunits, with a resulting loss in autonomy and stability (Hunt & Osborn, 1982; Sayles, 1979). Research on activity patterns of managers finds results consistent with this picture. As lateral interdependence increases, the external activities of a leader become more important, managers spend more time in lateral interactions, and they build larger networks with contacts in other parts of the organization (Hammer & Turk, 1987; Kaplan, 1984; Kotter, 1982; Michael & Yukl, 1993; Stewart, 1976; Walker, Guest, & Turner, 1956; Yanouzas, 1964).

The leader's role in lateral relations includes functions such as gathering information from other subunits, obtaining assistance and cooperation from them, negotiating agreements, reaching joint decisions to coordinate unit activities, defending the unit's interests, promoting a favorable image for the unit, and serving as a spokesperson for subordinates. The extent to which a leader emphasizes each of these activities depends on the nature of the lateral relationship. For example, when a unit provides services on demand to other units, acting as a buffer for subordinates against these external demands is a primary concern of the leader (Sayles, 1979).

Just as the leader tries to reconcile demands from above and below, so also is it necessary to make compromises in seeking to reach agreements with other units. Subordinates expect the leader to represent their interests, but it will not be possible to maintain an effective working relationship with other units unless the leader is also responsive to their needs. Salancik et al. (1975) conducted a study of managers in an insurance company to investigate this kind of role conflict. They found that to maintain a cooperative effort, managers with interdependent work activities tended to become more responsive to each other's needs. The greater the number of peers a manager had to interact with on a regular basis, the less responsive the manager was to the desires of subordinates.

External dependencies are also increased by reliance on outside suppliers, consultants, and contractors that provide supplies, materials, or services when needed on a just-in-time basis. Many companies now use a "virtual" or "networked" form of organization and outsource most activities to other organizations. Some of the leaders in these organizations are expected to function more like entrepreneurs than traditional managers, which requires more knowledge about information technology and more skills in project management (Horner-Long & Schoenberg, 2002). The managers must identify strategic opportunities, negotiate joint ventures with people in other organizations, build strategic alliances, and coordinate interdependent activities in dozens of locations spread around the globe.

Crisis Situations

When there is an immediate crisis or disruption of normal operations, the role expectations for the leader are likely to change. Unusual challenges for leaders can be created by a variety of different events such as a terrorist attack, a serious accident or shooting incident with many fatalities, a natural disaster (flood, tornados, earthquake), a cyber attack, a financial crisis or hostile takeover attempt, or a health emergency with widespread illness or deaths. Leaders of organizations affected by such crises will be expected to be more assertive, directive, and decisive (Mulder & Stemerding, 1963).

Let us look at a real-life incident to understand this further. Mallika Jagad, a 24-year-old banquet manager, was serving at an event at the Taj Mahal Palace Hotel, Mumbai, on November 26, 2008, along with 35 other employees. At around 9:30 p.m., the first gunshots from terrorists storming the Taj were heard. Jagad quickly took charge of the situation, made everyone lie down and switch off their mobile phones, and separated husbands and wives to reduce the risk to families, while maintaining calm among other employees. There were no casualties in this part of the hotel where Jagad was in charge.

When Kadam Singh Kang, who was the General Manager of the hotel, heard about the terrorist attack, he immediately left a conference at another property to attend to the crisis. He took charge as he arrived at the hotel, supervising evacuation and coordinating other rescue efforts. He said, "If the hotel comes down, I will be the last person to leave" (Deshpande & Raina, 2011).

Peterson and Van Fleet (2008) found that respondents from nonprofit organizations preferred leaders to use more problem-solving and directive behavior and less supportive behavior in crisis situations than in noncrisis situations. A study conducted aboard warships found that in crisis situations navy officers were more directive, autocratic, and goal-oriented (Mulder, Ritsema van Eck, & de Jong, 1970). Officers who showed initiative and exercised power in a confident and decisive manner were usually more effective. A study of bank managers found that effective managers were more flexible in their behavior when a crisis disrupted normal operations (Mulder, de Jong, Koppelaar & Verhage, 1986).

As yet, there is only a limited amount of research on leadership in extreme contexts involving a serious crisis or disruption (DeChurch, Burke, Shuffler, Lyons, Doty & Salas, 2011; Hannah, Uhl-Bien, Avolio, Cavarretta, 2009; Stewart, 1967, 1976). Nevertheless, it is already evident from the descriptive research that effective leaders show initiative in defining the problem, identifying a solution, directing the response to the crisis, and keeping people informed about events. Given the increasing frequency of such events for many types of organizations, much more research is needed.

Stage in the Organizational Life Cycle

Organizations move along a life cycle similar to biological organisms. There is a birth stage, a growth stage, a maturity stage, and a decline or revitalization stage (Quinn & Cameron, 1983). By examining important processes during each stage, it is possible to identify changing demands, constraints, and choices (Baliga & Hunt, 1988; Hunt, Baliga, & Peterson, 1988).

In the initial stage of the organization's evolution, a primary management responsibility is to communicate a vision of the proposed organization to potential external stakeholders (e.g., banks, investors, suppliers) who can provide necessary resources to establish the organization. Once the organization is founded, other key responsibilities include identifying and acquiring the technology needed to perform the work, recruiting the key personnel needed to staff the organization, inspiring commitment by the new members, and designing appropriate management systems (e.g., information systems, control systems, reward systems).

As the organization grows rapidly, the management responsibilities concerned with internal demands (e.g., staffing, motivation, organization of work, resource allocation, coordination) become as important as those related to external demands. In the maturity phase, when the organization's key products or services become fully developed and the market stabilizes, a primary management responsibility is to structure the work and develop procedures to increase the efficiency of operations, and to maintain member morale and motivation in a time of increasing controls and declining opportunity for advancement.

Eventually, the organization will encounter severe environmental threats (e.g., new competitors, declining demand for its products and services). In this crisis phase, the primary responsibility of management is to determine how to adapt and survive. New strategies must be identified, members of the organization must be influenced to support them, resources must be found to finance the changes, credibility must be reestablished with external stakeholders, and the structure of the organization must be changed to be consistent with the new strategy. The success of this effort will determine whether the organization declines or is revitalized.

Social Changes Affecting Managerial Work

Managerial work is being affected by sweeping changes in economics, politics, communications technology, and cultural values (Dess & Picken, 2000). The trend toward globalization continues to accelerate as foreign competition intensifies, foreign markets become more important, and more companies become multinational or participate in cross-national joint ventures. Managerial responsibilities increasingly involve international issues, and managers must be able to understand, communicate with, and influence people from different cultures. Cultural diversity of the workforce within organizations is increasing as well. To build cooperative relationships requires considerable empathy, respect for diversity, and understanding of the values, beliefs, and attitudes of people from different cultures.

New computer and telecommunications technology is changing the nature of work and making it possible to provide more detailed, timely information to anyone who needs it. However, increased information about the organization's operations and environment can be both a blessing and a curse. It takes a clear sense of objectives and priorities and strong cognitive skills to deal with the deluge of information and make sense out of it. Moreover, as electronic communication becomes more important, leaders will need to adjust their behavior to fit the new technologies.

Changes in the structure of organizations present yet another challenge. Many organizations are being decentralized into smaller, semiautonomous units, flattened by eliminating layers of middle management, or restructured around product teams that cut across functional or geographical lines. Team-based organizations have more shared leadership, and team leaders are expected to be more of a coach and facilitator and less of a director and controller.

Another trend is increased reliance on outside suppliers, consultants, and contractors that provide supplies, materials, or services when needed on a just-in-time basis. In contrast to a vertically integrated firm, many new companies with internet and e-commerce activities use a "virtual" or "networked" form of organization and outsource most activities to other organizations. Leadership scholars have begun to investigate possible differences in managerial skills and role requirements for these virtual companies. Despite many similarities in roles, the leaders are expected to function more like entrepreneurs than traditional managers, which requires more knowledge about information technology and more skills in project management (Horner-Long & Schoenberg, 2002). The managers must identify strategic opportunities, negotiate joint ventures with people in other organizations, build strategic alliances, and coordinate interdependent activities in dozens of locations spread around the globe.

Limitations of the Descriptive Research

Most of the research on managerial activity patterns and roles was conducted decades ago, and as noted earlier, there have been major changes in the context for managerial work and the technology used for information processing and communication. Only a few studies have been conducted in the past decade (e.g., Dierdorff, Rubin & Morgeson, 2009; Tengblad, 2006). The limited findings suggest that much remains the same, but it is also obvious that some things have changed. More research is needed on managerial roles and activities that may be affected by the new technology, by globalization, and by new forms of organization (e.g., virtual teams, teambased organizations, joint ventures).

Most of the observational research on the nature of managerial work was designed to describe the typical pattern and content of managerial activities, not to answer directly the question of what activity patterns or behavior patterns are necessary and effective. Discovering that many managers carry out a particular activity does not tell us whether it is essential for managerial effectiveness. Even the results from the situational research may be misleading. The most prevalent behavior pattern in a particular type of managerial job or situation is not necessarily the most effective one.

Job description studies measure the perceived importance of various activities and responsibilities for the job. This research reveals similarities and differences in skill requirements across various types of managerial positions. The primary purpose of the research is to facilitate development of compensation systems, selection procedures, and performance appraisal procedures, not to determine how managerial behavior is related to managerial effectiveness. The importance ratings made by many managers may be biased by shared stereotypes or implicit theories about effective leaders. As yet, there is little evidence to demonstrate that the managerial activities and behaviors rated most important are also the ones related most strongly to criteria of managerial effectiveness.

Other descriptive studies have analyzed data from interviews with managers predetermined to be effective (Kanter, 1982; Kotter, 1982; Kotter & Lawrence, 1974), or with managers from organizations designated as effective (Peters & Austin, 1985; Peters and Waterman, 1982). These researchers attempted to find common themes that might explain why the managers were effective. However, the studies did not compare effective managers to ineffective managers. More reliable insights would be gained if researchers compared behavior patterns for effective managers and ineffective managers of the same type and explicitly examined the relation of managerial behavior patterns to the requirements of the managerial job situation.

Guidelines for Managers

The chaotic and demanding nature of managerial work makes time management one of the most important administrative skills for leaders. This section presents guidelines (see summary in Table 2) for managing time wisely, coping with demands, and handling role conflicts. The guidelines are based on research, practical experience, and recommendations by consultants.

TABLE 2	Guidelines for Managers

- Understand the reasons for demands and constraints.
- Expand the range of choices.
- Determine what you want to accomplish.
- Analyze how you use your time.
- Plan daily and weekly activities.
- Avoid unnecessary activities.
- Conquer procrastination.
- Take advantage of reactive activities.
- Make time for reflective planning.
- Identify important problems that can be solved.
- Look for connections among problems.
- Experiment with innovative solutions.

- **Understand the reasons for demands and constraints.**

It is essential to learn how others perceive the manager's role and what they expect. Perception of demands and constraints inevitably involves subjective judgments, but many managers fail to take the time necessary to gather sufficient information on which to base these judgments. Do not assume that everyone agrees with your vision, priorities, or ideas about effective management. Before one can satisfy people or modify their expectations, it is necessary to understand what they really desire. Understanding role expectations requires frequent face-toface interaction, asking questions, listening to others rather than constantly preaching, being sensitive to negative reactions (including nonverbal cues), and trying to discover the values and needs underlying a person's opinions and preferences.

- **Expand the range of choices.**

Too many managers focus on the demands and constraints and fail to give adequate consideration to opportunities to define the job in different ways. It is essential to step back from the job and see it in a broader strategic perspective. It is usually possible to be proactive with superiors about defining the job in a way that allows more discretion, especially when role ambiguity is already present due to poorly-defined responsibilities. Choices may be expanded by finding ways to avoid demands and reduce constraints. A manager's planning and agenda development should include a conscious analysis of the demands and constraints limiting current effectiveness, and how they can be reduced, eliminated, or circumvented.

- **Determine what you want to accomplish.**

Time is a scarce resource that must be used well if the manager is to be effective. The key to effective time management is knowing what you want to accomplish. A person with a clear set of objectives and priorities can identify important activities and plan the best way to use time; without clear objectives, no amount of planning will improve time management. The objectives and priorities may be informal, as with Kotter's (1982) mental agendas, but they need to be identified by a deliberate, conscious process.

- **Analyze how you use your time.**

It is difficult to improve time management without knowing how time is actually spent. Most managers are unable to estimate very accurately how much time they spend on different activities. Most time management systems recommend keeping a daily log of activities for one or two weeks. The log should list each activity in 15-minute blocks of time. It is helpful to indicate the source of control over each activity (e.g., self, boss, subordinates, others, organizational requirements) and whether the activity was planned in advance or is an immediate reaction to requests and problems. Typical time wasters should be noted on the log (e.g., unnecessary interruptions, meetings that run too long, searching for misplaced items). The time log should be analyzed to identify how important and necessary each activity is. Consider whether the activity can be eliminated, combined with others, or given less time. Identify whether too many activities are initiated by others, and whether adequate time is allowed for activities that are important but not urgent.

- **Plan daily and weekly activities.**

The extensive practitioner-oriented literature on time management shows considerable agreement about the importance of planning daily and weekly activities in advance (e.g., Webber, 1980). When planning daily activities, the first step is to make a to-do list for the day and assign priorities to each activity. This type of prioritized activity list may be used with a calendar showing required meetings and scheduled appointments to plan the next day's activities. Most of the discretionary time should be allocated to high-priority activities. If insufficient time is available to do important activities with immediate deadlines, reschedule or delegate some activities that are less important. The task of juggling the various activities and deciding which to do is a difficult but essential component of managerial work. Remember that it is more efficient to do a series of similar tasks than to keep switching from one type of task to another. Sometimes it is possible to schedule similar activities (e.g., several telephone calls, several letters) at the same time during the day. In addition, it is wise to take into account natural energy cycles and biorhythms. Peak alertness and efficiency occur at different times of the day for different people, and peak periods should be used for difficult tasks that require creativity.

- **Avoid unnecessary activities.**

Managers who become overloaded with unnecessary tasks are likely to neglect activities that are important for attaining key objectives. Managers may accept unnecessary tasks because they are afraid of offending subordinates, peers, or the boss, and they lack the self-confidence and assertiveness to turn down requests. One way to avoid unnecessary tasks is to prepare and use tactful ways to say no (e.g., say that you could only do the task if the person does some of your work for you; suggest other people who could do the task faster or better; point out that an important task will be delayed or jeopardized if you do what the person requests). Some unnecessary but required tasks can be eliminated by showing how resources will be saved or other benefits attained. Unessential tasks that cannot be eliminated or delegated can be put off until slack times. Sometimes when a task is put off long enough, the person who requested it will discover that it is not needed after all.

- **Conquer procrastination.**

Even when it is obvious that an activity is important, some people delay doing it in favor of a less important activity. One reason for procrastination is the fear of failure. People find excuses for delaying a task because they lack self-confidence. One remedy for a long, complex task is to divide it into smaller parts, each of which is easier and less intimidating. Deadlines are also helpful for overcoming procrastination. When setting deadlines for completion of difficult tasks, it is better to allow some slack and set a deadline that is earlier than the date when the task absolutely must be completed. However, having some slack should not become an excuse for not starting the task. Schedule a definite time early in the day to begin working on unpleasant tasks that tend to be procrastinated. Such tasks are more likely to get done if tackled first before the daily stream of demands provides excuses to avoid them.

- **Take advantage of reactive activities.**

Although some degree of control over the use of one's time is desirable, it is not feasible for a manager to plan in advance exactly how each minute of the day will be spent. The unpredictable nature of the environment makes it essential to view chance encounters, interruptions, and unscheduled meetings initiated by others not just as intrusions on scheduled activities, but rather as opportunities to gain important information, discover problems, influence others, and move forward on implementation of plans and informal agendas. Obligations that might otherwise be time wasters, such as required attendance at some meetings and ceremonial occasions, can be turned to one's advantage (Kotter, 1982; Mintzberg, 1973).

- **Make time for reflective planning.**

Managers face relentless pressures for dealing with immediate problems and responding to requests for assistance, direction, or authorization. Some of these problems require immediate attention, but if managers become too preoccupied with reacting to day-to-day problems, they have no time left for the reflective planning that would help them to avoid many of the problems, or for the contingency planning that would help them cope better with unavoidable problems. Therefore, it is desirable to set aside some time on a regular basis for reflective analysis and planning. Listen to Antonia Bryson, a deputy commissioner in New York City's Department of Environmental Protection (Haas, 1994, p. 60):

> What happens in government is that you always tend to get caught up in crises. . . But it's helpful to sit back at the end of every week and ask, is this part of my long-term plan of what I want to accomplish while I am in this job?. . . The higher up you go, the more you have to constantly examine how you are setting your own priorities. Are you going to the right meetings? Are you going to too many meetings? Are you using your staff members effectively to make sure you yourself are spending time on the right things and accomplishing what you want to get accomplished?

Making time for reflective planning requires careful time management. One approach is to set aside a block of private time (at least one to two hours) each week for individual planning. Another approach is to schedule periodic strategy sessions with subordinates to encourage discussion of strategic issues. Still another approach is to initiate a major improvement project, delegate primary responsibility to a subordinate or task force, and schedule regular meetings with the individual or group to review plans and progress.

- **Identify important problems that can be solved.**

A manager always faces more problems than can be resolved. Therefore, it is desirable for the manager to evaluate (1) whether a problem can be solved within a reasonable time period with available resources and (2) whether it is worthwhile to invest the time, effort, and resources on this problem rather than on others (Isenberg, 1984; McCall & Kaplan, 1985). Descriptive research on effective managers suggests that they give priority to important problems that can be solved, rather than ignoring these problems or trying to avoid responsibility for them by passing the problem to someone else or involving more people than necessary to diffuse responsibility for decisions (Peters & Austin, 1985; Peters & Waterman, 1982). Managers should attempt to avoid or postpone action on problems that are either trivial or intractable. Of course, some problems are so important that they should not be postponed even when the initial probability of a successful solution is low.

- **Look for connections among problems.**

In the process of trying to make sense out of the streams of problems, issues, and opportunities encountered by a manager, it is important to look for relationships among them rather than assuming that they are distinct and independent (Isenberg, 1984). A broader view of problems provides better insights for understanding them. By relating problems to each other and to informal strategic objectives, a manager is more likely to recognize opportunities to take actions that contribute to the solution of several related problems at the same time. Finding these connections is more likely if the manager is able to remain flexible and open-minded about the definition of a problem and actively considers multiple definitions for each problem.

• **Experiment with innovative solutions.**

Effective managers are more willing to experiment actively with innovative approaches for solving problems, rather than spending an excessive amount of time studying them. Whenever possible, experiments are conducted initially on a small scale to minimize the risk, and ways are found to obtain the information necessary to evaluate results. In some cases, an action is taken not because the manager believes it is the best way to solve a problem, but rather because taking limited action is the only way to develop an adequate understanding of the problem (Isenberg, 1984; Quinn, 1980). Peters and Waterman (1982, p. 13) found that managers in effective companies had a bias for action characterized as "do it, fix it, try it." One manager described the following approach for quickly introducing innovative products: "Instead of allowing 250 engineers and marketers to work on a new product in isolation for 15 months, they form bands of 5 to 25 and test ideas out on a customer, often with inexpensive prototypes, within a matter of weeks" (Peters & Waterman, 1982, p. 14).

Summary

The descriptive research found that managerial work is inherently hectic, varied, fragmented, reactive, disorderly, and political. Brief oral interactions predominate, and many of these involve people outside the manager's immediate work unit and chain of command. Decision processes are highly political, and most planning is informal and adaptive. This activity pattern occurs, in part, because managers face several dilemmas. To carry out their responsibilities, managers need to obtain recent, relevant information that exists only in the heads of people who are widely scattered within and outside the organization; they need to make decisions based on information that is both overwhelming and incomplete; and they need to get cooperation from people over whom they have no formal authority.

Identifying meaningful and widely applicable categories to describe the content of managerial work has been a problem for a long time. One approach is the taxonomy of managerial roles proposed by Mintzberg. Another approach is represented by job description research that asks managers to rate the importance of different activities and responsibilities for their jobs.

Some of the descriptive research has examined differences in behavior related to aspects of the managerial situation. Stewart identified several situational influences on leader behavior. The pattern of interactions with subordinates, peers, superiors, and outsiders is affected by a manager's dependency on these people, by the demands they make on a manager, and by the type of work for which the manager is responsible.

Comparative research on managers in different situations reveals several other aspects of the situation that affect managerial behavior, including level of management, size of the organizational unit, lateral interdependence, crisis conditions, and stage in the organizational life cycle. Managerial work is being altered by sweeping societal trends such as globalization, workforce diversity, the pace of technological change, and the emergence of new forms of organizations.

Despite all the demands and constraints a manager faces, some choice of behavior remains. Even managers in similar positions define their roles differently. There are choices in what aspects of the job to emphasize, how to allocate one's time, and with whom to spend it. Managers will be more effective if they understand the demands and constraints in their job situation, and work to expand their choices.

Finally, effective managers are more proactive in their behavior. Even when reacting to unforeseen events, their behavior more closely reflects their objectives and priorities.

Effective leaders devote time to identifying current problems for which a solution can be found, and they prepare how to respond to unavoidable but predictable problems and disruptions. When a problem occurs, they quickly identify the cause and take decisive action to direct the work unit's response. Effective leaders also keep people informed about progress in efforts to deal with a serious crisis.

Review and Discussion Questions

1. Briefly describe typical activity patterns in managerial work.
2. What does descriptive research tell us about managerial decision making, planning, and problem solving?
3. Briefly describe Mintzberg's 10 managerial roles. Are some roles more important than others?
4. Briefly describe how managerial behavior is influenced by the nature of the job situation, according to Stewart.
5. How are managerial activities and behavior affected by level of management, unit size, external dependencies, and crises?
6. How much latitude do managers have in what they do and how they do it? Which term ("captains of their destiny" or "prisoners of their fate") best describes managers?
7. Why do managers have so much difficulty managing their time?
8. What are some guidelines for time management?

Key Terms

constraints	job description research	role conflicts
demands	lateral interdependence	role expectations
dependence	managerial activities	time management
exposure	managerial roles networks	

CASE 1

Acme Manufacturing Company

Steve Arnold is a production manager at Acme Manufacturing Company in New Jersey. When he drove into the parking lot at the plant on Tuesday morning at 8:35, Steve was already 35 minutes late for work. He had overslept that morning because the previous night he had stayed up late to finish the monthly production report for his department. He parked his car and entered the rear of the plant building. Passing through the shipping area, Steve spotted his friend George Summers and stopped to ask how work was progressing on the new addition to George's house.

Entering the office at 8:55, Steve greeted his secretary, Ruth Sweeney, and asked whether anything urgent needed his immediate attention. Ruth reminded him of the staff meeting at 9:30 with Steve's boss—Frank Jones, the vice president for Production—and the other production managers. Steve thanked Ruth for reminding him (he had forgotten about the meeting) and continued on to his adjoining inner office to look for the memo announcing the meeting. He vaguely remembered getting the memo in an email one or two weeks earlier, but did not take the time to read it or look at the attached materials.

His phone rang, and it was Sue Bradley, the sales vice president, who was inquiring about the status of a rush order for one of the company's important clients. Steve promised to look into the matter and get back to her later in the day with an answer. Steve had delegated the rush order last week to Lucy Adams, one of his production supervisors, and he had not thought about it since then. Stepping back into the outer office, Steve asked Ruth if she had seen Lucy today. Ruth reminded him that Lucy was at a training workshop in California. She would be difficult to reach until the session ended late in the afternoon, because the workshop facilitators regard cell phone calls and text messages as an unnecessary distraction.

Going back into his office, Steve emailed a message to Lucy asking her to call him as soon as possible. Then, he resumed his search for the memo about the meeting with his boss and the other production managers. He finally found it in his large collection of unprocessed emails. The purpose of the meeting was to discuss a proposed change in quality control procedures. By now it was 9:25, and there was no time to read the proposal. He hurried out to get to the meeting on time. During the meeting, the other production managers participated in the discussion and made helpful comments or suggestions. Steve was not prepared for the meeting and did not contribute much except to say that he did not anticipate any problems with the proposed changes.

The meeting ended at 10:30, and Steve returned to his office, where he found Paul Chen, one of his production supervisors, waiting for him. Paul wanted to discuss a problem caused in the production schedules by a major equipment breakdown. Steve called Glenda Brown, his assistant manager, and asked her to join them to help rearrange the production schedules for the next few days. Glenda came in shortly and the three of them worked on the production schedules. At 11:25, Ruth came in to announce that Mr. Ferris was waiting and he claimed to have an appointment with Steve at 11:30. Steve looked at his calendar but could not find any entry for the appointment. Steve asked Ruth to tell Mr. Ferris that he would be ready shortly.

The schedules were completed around 11:40. Since it was nearly noon, Steve invited Mr. Ferris to join him for lunch at a nearby restaurant. During lunch Steve learned that Mr. Ferris was from one of the firms that provided materials used in the production process at Acme, and the purpose of the meeting was to inquire about some changes in material specifications the company had requested. As Mr. Ferris talked, Steve realized that he would not be able to answer some of the technical questions. When they returned to the plant at 1:15, Steve introduced Mr. Ferris to an engineer who could answer his questions.

Soon after Steve walked back to his office, his boss (Frank Jones) stopped in to ask about the quality report for last week. Steve explained that he had given top priority to finishing the monthly production report and would do the quality report next. Frank was irritated, because he needed the quality data to finalize his proposal for new procedures, and he thought Steve understood this task was more urgent than the production report. He told Steve to get the quality data to him as soon as possible and left. Steve immediately called Glenda Brown and asked her to bring the quality data to his office. The task of reviewing the data and preparing a short summary was not difficult, but it took longer than he anticipated. It was 2:40 by the time Steve completed the report and attached it to an e-mail to his boss.

Looking at his calendar, Steve noticed that he was already late for a 2:30 meeting of the plant safety committee. The committee meets weekly to review safety problems, and each department sends a representative. Steve rushed out to the meeting, which was held in another part of the plant. The meeting was dull this week, without any important issues or problems to discuss.

The meeting ended at 3:30, and as Steve walked back through his section of the plant, he stopped to talk to his assistant manager. Glenda wanted some advice on how to resolve a problem in the production assignments for the next day. They discussed the problem for about a halfhour. When Steve returned to his office at 4:05, his secretary was just leaving. She reported that Lucy had called before leaving to fly home from the conference.

Steve was feeling tired and decided it was time for him to go home also. As he drove out of the parking lot, Steve reflected that he was getting further behind in his work. He wondered what he could do to get better control over his job.

CASE 2
Training or Sales

On the eve of his annual appraisal meeting with his supervisors, Anil and Vikas, where his promotion is to be decided, Nishant was in a dilemma.

As the Regional Training Head (Northern Region) of a leading financial sector firm dealing in life and general insurance, mutual funds, and other non-banking financial products in India, Nishant is responsible for conducting training need analysis, developing content, and ensuring quality training. The training programs are designed to fulfill the development requirements of employees of the firm as well as those of various channel partners. Channel partners include some leading banks, broking houses, and direct agents.

He has a team of eight direct-reporting Area Training Managers (ATMs) who are based in various locations in North India such as New Delhi (3); Lucknow, Uttar Pradesh (1); Jaipur, Rajasthan (1); Ludhiana, Punjab (1); and Chandigarh (2). Each ATM has two to three Training Managers under them. In all, Nishant has a team of 28 training professionals.

There are four Regional Training Heads (RTHs) across India. This position has dual reporting. All RTHs report to the National Training Head, Anil, and the respective Regional Sales Heads (RSHs). RSHs have teams across the regions, called Area Offices, each office having one ATM. Figure 2 shows the organizational chart.

While dual reporting at RTH level is a natural structural necessity of the firm, this adds great ambiguity and complexity. For example, sometimes, ATMs are required to travel across their areas to conduct training. They are eligible to travel by cars provided to them by an official vendor. Often, sales employees also travel by the same car. Though it appears to be a nominal issue, it has led to significant conflict in area offices. Sales Managers (SMs)

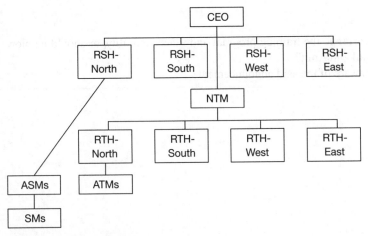

FIGURE 2 Organizational Chart

who are eligible to travel only by local transport and not official cars started to fix training dates according to their travel plan to a particular city. This led to a marked increase in the travel cost of ATMs.

Another common issue is the scheduling of training programs. Often, SMs try to schedule training programs for channel partners toward the beginning of the month, mostly during the first week. This is because at the end of the month, they have sales target pressures and training occupies the time that they wish to spend on sales. In addition, in case there is a new product launch, which is a regular feature, they want their channel partners to be equipped with the expertise and sales aid materials, such as brochures, towards the beginning of the month. In one of the area offices, because of an extremely competitive environment, two SMs who were due for their promotions wanted to schedule the training program for different channel partners at the same time. Sunita, the ATM, was in a fix and did not know which SM to support. Both SMs had persuaded and even threatened her to select to conduct programs for their channel partner at the same time.

Nishant had to regularly intervene and have joint meetings with RSHs, Area Heads, and ATMs to devise strategies to resolve such conflicts. There have been several such instances and he has been successful and greatly appreciated for his acumen and timely action. However, this time, it is different.

Vikas, an RSH, was very successful at meeting targets, considered an aggressive go-getter, and known across the firm as "the bull." This made him the favorite RSH of the National Head and the company CEO, Amit. In fact, Amit used to consult Vikas in almost all the major decisions of the firm. All the employees knew about the close bond between the two. As a result, Vikas used to get things done by everyone else and no one could refuse him.

Vikas' brother was getting married in a nearby town. He was very happy and excited about the event. In a sales meeting with his SMs the day before Nishant's appraisal, while distributing sweets, he made a surprising announcement — he had arranged travel for all his team members to attend the wedding ceremony.

Later that morning, he summoned Nishant and asked him to arrange an outbound training program for his SMs and other team members, in the town where the wedding ceremony is to take place. Such outbound training programs are a regular feature, and the cost is borne by the training department. Outbound training programs require cost approvals and diligent preparations. However, it was evident to Nishant that this time, it was not about the training.

Nishant, on the verge of his promotion, was greatly conflicted.

Questions

1. Should Nishant arrange the training program and ignore morality, or should he blow the whistle to Anil and Amit?
2. Is Amit already aware of the said announcement?

Effective Leadership Behavior

From Chapter 3 of *Leadership in Organizations*, Eighth Edition. Gary Yukl. Copyright © 2013 by Pearson Education, Inc. Publishing as Prentice Hall. All rights reserved.

Effective Leadership Behavior

Learning Objectives

After studying this chapter, you should be able to:

- Understand why so many different behavior categories have been proposed.
- Understand what research methods have been used to study leadership behavior.
- Understand how leader behavior can be described with either broad or specific categories.
- Understand why task and relations behaviors are important for leadership effectiveness.
- Understand why change-oriented behaviors are important for effective leadership.
- Understand how specific types of task and relations behavior can be used effectively.

This chapter will review research on the types of leadership behavior most likely to influence subordinate satisfaction and performance. The chapter begins by describing different approaches used for classifying leadership behaviors that are relevant for effective leadership. Next is a description of several broad behavior categories that have influenced much of the research over the past half century. Methods for studying the effects of leader behavior are described next, and the results found in research on task-oriented and *relations-oriented behavior* are reviewed and evaluated. The final part of the chapter describes some specific types of task and relations behaviors that are important for effective leadership.

Ways for Describing Leadership Behavior

A major problem in research on the content of leadership behavior has been the identification of behavior categories that are relevant and meaningful for all leaders. In research on managerial activities studies have produced a somewhat different set of behavior categories, making it difficult to compare and integrate the results across studies. A similar condition exists for the behavior research described in this chapter. As a consequence, the past half century of research has produced a bewildering variety of behavior concepts pertaining to managers and leaders (see Bass, 1990; Fleishman et al., 1991). Sometimes different terms are used to refer to the same type of behavior. At other times, the same term is defined differently by various theorists. What is treated as a general behavior category by one theorist is viewed as two or three distinct categories by another theorist. What is a key concept in one taxonomy is absent from another. With so many divergent taxonomies, it is difficult to translate from one set of behaviors to another.

There are several reasons why taxonomies developed to describe leadership behavior are so diverse (Fleishman et al., 1991; Yukl, 1989). Behavior categories are abstractions rather than tangible attributes of the real world. The categories are derived from observed behavior in order to organize perceptions of the world and make them meaningful, but they do not exist in any objective sense. No absolute set of "correct" behavior categories can be established. Thus, taxonomies that differ in purpose can be expected to have somewhat different constructs. For example, taxonomies designed to facilitate research and theory on managerial effectiveness differ from taxonomies designed to describe observations of managerial activities, or taxonomies designed to catalog position responsibilities of managers and administrators.

Another source of diversity among taxonomies, even for those with the same purpose, is the possibility that behavior constructs can be formulated at different levels of abstraction or generality. Some taxonomies contain a small number of broadly defined behavior categories, whereas other taxonomies contain a larger number of narrowly focused behavior categories. For example, *task-oriented behavior* is a broad meta-category, clarifying work roles is a midrange category, and setting clear performance goals is a specific, narrow category. They are all abstract behavior categories, but goal setting is a part of *clarifying*, which is a part of task behavior (see Table 1). In the same way, relations-oriented behavior is a broad meta-category, *developing* is a midrange relations behavior, and providing career advice is a very specific type of developing. The optimal level of abstraction for the behavior categories in a taxonomy depends upon the purpose of the taxonomy. For research on effective leadership, the broad *meta-categories* are less useful than more specific behavior categories.

A third source of diversity among behavior taxonomies is the method used to develop them. Some taxonomies are developed by examining the pattern of covariance among behavior items on a behavior description questionnaire describing actual managers (factor analysis method); some taxonomies are developed by having judges group behavior examples according to perceived similarity in content or purpose (judgmental classification); and some taxonomies are developed by deduction from theory (theoretical-deductive approach). Each method has its own associated biases, and the use of different methods results in somewhat different taxonomies, even when the purpose is the same.

TABLE 1	Examples of Behaviors at Different Levels of Abstraction	
Broad, Abstract Categories	**Task-oriented Behavior**	
Middle-range Categories	Clarifying	Monitoring
Specific Categories	Assigning work	Observing how the work is done
	Setting task goals	Reading weekly sales reports
	Explaining policies	Holding progress review meetings
Observed Incident	The manager set a goal to increase sales by 10%	The manager checked the new display to see if it was done right

When a combination of methods has been used, one method is usually more important than others for selecting the behavior categories.

Another possible and significant source of diversity among leadership taxonomies is the hierarchical position of the leader. Mintzberg (1983) has proposed a particular taxonomy for this situation. According to him, any organization will typically have five components in its hierarchical structure: strategic apex (top-level managers who are charged with overall responsibility for the organization); technostructure (analysts who have responsibility for erecting specific forms of standardization in the organization); support staff (people who fill in the staff units and who provide indirect services for the organization); middle line (managers who connect the operating core to the strategic apex); and operating core (employees who perform the basic work related to the production of products and services). Each component has competing leadership responsibilities and, as a result, the components often come into conflict with one another. Authors of various taxonomies chose one component of an organization to describe the leadership behavior.

When different taxonomies are compared, it is obvious that there are substantial differences in the number of behaviors, the range of behaviors, and the level of abstraction of the behavior concepts. Some taxonomies have only a few broad categories, some have many specific behaviors, and some have a few broad categories with specific component behaviors. Some taxonomies are intended to cover the full range of leader behaviors, whereas others only include the behaviors identified in a leadership theory (e.g., theories of charismatic or *transformational leadership*).

Major Types of Leadership Behavior

Most theories and research on effective leadership behavior involve one or two broadly defined behaviors (sometimes called *meta-categories*). This section of the chapter briefly describes several meta-categories that are relevant for effective leadership, and they are explained in more detail later in this chapter.

Task and Relations Behaviors

Much of the early theory and research on effective leadership behavior was strongly influenced by work at Ohio State University during the 1950s. The initial task of the researchers was to identify categories of relevant leadership behavior and develop questionnaires to measure how often a leader used these behaviors. A preliminary questionnaire was used by samples of military and civilian personnel to describe the behavior of their supervisors (Fleishman, 1953; Halpin & Winer, 1957; Hemphill & Coons, 1957). Analysis of the questionnaire responses indicated that subordinates perceived their supervisor's behavior primarily in terms of two broadly defined meta-categories.

One set of behaviors involves concern for relationships and was labeled *consideration*. This behavior category included doing personal favors for subordinates, finding time to listen to a subordinate with a problem, backing up or defending a subordinate, consulting with subordinates on important matters, being willing to accept suggestions from subordinates, and treating a subordinate as an equal.

The other set of behaviors was involved concern for task objectives and was labeled *initiating structure*. This behavior category included assigning tasks to subordinates, maintaining definite standards of performance, asking subordinates to follow standard procedures, emphasizing the importance of meeting deadlines, criticizing poor work, and coordinating the activities of different subordinates.

TABLE 2	Similar Behavior Constructs in Early Leadership Research	
Task-oriented	**Relations-oriented**	**Source**
Initiating Structure	Consideration	Fleishman (1953); Halpin & Winer (1957)
Instrumental Leadership	Supportive Leadership	House (1971)
Goal Emphasis; Work Facilitation	Supportive Leadership; Interaction Facilitation	Bowers & Seashore (1966); Taylor & Bowers (1972)
Performance Behavior	Maintenance Behavior	Misumi & Peterson (1985)

Other researchers also developed questionnaires with scales for task and relations behaviors, although the labels and component behaviors varied somewhat from version to version (see Table 2). It was widely accepted that leaders must use some task and relations behaviors to be effective, and these two meta-categories influenced most of the early leadership theories.

Change-oriented Behavior

The early leadership theory and research paid little attention to behaviors directly concerned with encouraging and facilitating change. In the 1980s, some change-oriented behaviors were included in theories of charismatic and transformational leadership, but leading change was still not explicitly recognized as a separate dimension or meta-category. Evidence for the construct validity of change-oriented meta-category was later found by researchers in Sweden and the United States (Ekvall & Arvonen, 1991; Yukl, 1997, 1999a; Yukl, Gordon, & Taber, 2002).

Verification that change-oriented behavior is a distinct and meaningful meta-category extended the earlier research and provided important insights about effective leadership. Each of the three meta-categories has a different primary purpose, and they are all relevant for effective leadership. Task-oriented behavior is primarily concerned with accomplishing the task in an efficient and reliable way. Relations-oriented behavior is primarily concerned with increasing mutual trust, cooperation, job satisfaction, and identification with the team or organization. Change-oriented behavior is primarily concerned with understanding the environment, finding innovative ways to adapt to it, and implementing major changes in strategies, products, or processes. Examples of each type of behavior are shown in Table 3.

Some specific types of leader behavior in a meta-category affect only one objective, but other types of behavior affect more than one objective. For example, when a leader consults with team members about the action plan for a project, the result may be more commitment to the project (human relations), better use of available personnel and resources (task efficiency), and discovery of more innovative ways to satisfy the client (adaptation). When a leader provides coaching for an employee, the result may be improved productivity (task efficiency), an increase in employee skills relevant for career advancement (human relations), and better implementation of an innovative new program (adaptive change).

More recently, researchers (e.g., Chatterjee & Hambrick, 2007; Gerstner, Konig, Enders, & Hambrick, 2013; Wales, Patel, & Lumpkin, 2013) have started to pay attention to the change-oriented behavior of leaders. Some leaders in organizations provide the requisite force for overcoming inertia. They strategically propel dynamic actions in path-divergent domains such as higher number and size of acquisitions or the adaptation of discontinuous technologies. As a result, they lead to a high degree of variation in organizational performance—big wins or big losses.

| TABLE 3 | Examples of Task, Relations, and Change-oriented Behaviors |

Task-oriented Behaviors

- Organize work activities to improve efficiency.
- Plan short-term operations.
- Assign work to groups or individuals.
- Clarify what results are expected for a task.
- Explain priorities for different task objectives.
- Set specific goals and standards for task performance.
- Explain rules, policies, and standard operating procedures.
- Direct and coordinate work activities.
- Monitor operations and performance.
- Resolve immediate problems that would disrupt the work.

Relations-oriented Behaviors

- Provide support and encouragement to someone with a difficult task.
- Express confidence that a person or group can perform a difficult task.
- Socialize with people to build relationships.
- Recognize contributions and accomplishments.
- Provide coaching and mentoring when appropriate.
- Consult with people on decisions affecting them.
- Empower people to determine the best way to do a task.
- Keep people informed about actions affecting them.
- Help resolve conflicts in a constructive way.
- Use symbols, ceremonies, rituals, and stories to build team identity.
- Encourage mutual trust and cooperation among members of the work unit.
- Recruit competent new members for the team or organization.

Change-oriented Behaviors

- Monitor the external environment to detect threats and opportunities.
- Interpret events to explain the need for change.
- Study competitors and outsiders to get ideas for improvements.
- Envision exciting new possibilities for the organization.
- Encourage people to view problems or opportunities in a different way.
- Develop innovative new strategies linked to core competencies.
- Encourage and facilitate innovation and entrepreneurship in the organization.
- Encourage and facilitate collective learning in the team or organization.
- Experiment with new approaches for achieving objectives.
- Make symbolic changes that are consistent with a new vision or strategy.
- Encourage and facilitate efforts to implement major change.
- Announce and celebrate progress in implementing change.

Participative Leadership

Another behavior category identified in the early leadership research is *participative leadership*, which is also called *empowering leadership* and *democratic leadership*. It involves a leader's use of decision procedures that allow other people such as subordinates to have some influence over decisions that will affect them (Coch & French, 1948; Heller & Yukl, 1969; Likert, 1961, 1967; Vroom & Yetton, 1973). The use of empowering decision procedures reflects a strong concern for relations objectives such as subordinate commitment and development, but it can also involve a concern for task objectives such as decision quality. The content of leader decisions may involve task objectives (plan work procedures), relations objectives (determine how to improve employee benefits), change objectives (identify innovative new initiatives), or some combination of the three types of objectives. Participative decision procedures such as consultation or a joint decision can be used with peers and outsiders (e.g., suppliers, clients) as well as with subordinates.

Transformational Leadership

Another behavior meta-category that was identified in the 1980s is usually called *transformational leadership* (Bass, 1985), but other terms for it include *visionary leadership* and *inspirational leadership*. The component behaviors vary for different theories and measures of transformational leadership, but they usually include a few relations-oriented behaviors such as supporting and developing, a few change-oriented behaviors such as articulating an appealing vision and encouraging innovative thinking, and a few behaviors that are difficult to classify into a single meta-category (e.g., leading by example, talking about personal values, making self-sacrifices for the team or organization). Some of the same behaviors are also described in theories of *charismatic leadership*.

External Leadership Behaviors

Theories and research on dyadic leadership seldom include boundary-spanning behaviors, in part because information about a leader's behavior is typically obtained only by surveying subordinates who have little opportunity to observe how their leader interacts with people outside the work unit or organization. However, just as the research on managerial work identified important boundary-spanning roles and activities, the research on leadership of groups and organizations has identified relevant boundary-spanning behaviors. Three distinct and broadly defined categories of external behavior are *networking*, environmental scanning, and representing (Luthans & Lockwood, 1984; Stogdill, Goode, & Day, 1962; Yukl et al., 2002; Yukl & Van Fleet, 1982; Yukl, Wall, & Lepsinger, 1990).

Networking involves building and maintaining favorable relationships with peers, superiors, and outsiders who can provide desired information, resources, and political support. The behavior category includes attending professional conferences and ceremonies, joining social networks, socializing informally, doing favors, and using impression management tactics such as ingratiation.

Environmental scanning (also called *external monitoring*) includes collecting information about relevant events and changes in the external environment, identifying threats and opportunities for the leader's group or organization, and identifying best practices that can be imitated or adapted. The scanning may be carried out by using a leader's network of contacts, by studying relevant publications and industry reports, by conducting market research, and by studying the decisions and actions of competitors and opponents.

Representing includes lobbying for resources and assistance from superiors, promoting and defending the reputation of the leader's group or organization, negotiating agreements with peers and outsiders such as clients and suppliers, and using political tactics to influence decisions made by superiors or governmental agencies. Proactive influence tactics are commonly used for lobbying and negotiating.

Methods for Studying the Effects of Leader Behavior

Several types of research methods have been used to study the effects of leader behavior. By far, the most common method is the use of survey research with behavior description questionnaires filled out by subordinates. Each subordinate indicates how often the leader has been using the behaviors, and then the behavior scales are correlated with measures of criterion variables such as subordinate satisfaction, turnover, task commitment, and performance.

Another type of study uses descriptions of leader behavior obtained from observation, diaries, *critical incidents*, or interviews with leaders and subordinates. The behavior descriptions are coded into categories and related to measures of leader effectiveness. Case studies and biographies of famous leaders can also be content analyzed to identify behaviors used by effective (or ineffective) leaders.

A small number of studies have involved an experiment in which leader behavior is manipulated by the researchers to determine how it affects the attitudes or performance of subordinates. Some laboratory experiments used student groups with leaders who were instructed to use a designated pattern of behavior. Other lab experiments asked people to read scenarios or view a video with leaders who use different patterns of behavior, then indicate how they would likely respond to each type of leader. A few field experiments involved leaders in actual organizations who were trained to use particular types of behavior.

Historiography is another method of studying leadership behavior. Although it has been criticized for author biases and, consequently, the associated controversies, this has proven to be a very informative source for deducing leadership behaviors. For example, in a historiometric study of the U.S. presidents, Deluga (1997) suggested that some of the most and least successful presidents were highly narcissistic, while others of the same type were not. This study also found that presidential narcissism predicted charisma, creativity, war avoidance, great decisions, mean levels of overall greatness, and consensus of greatness.

Each type of method has advantages and limitations, and the most appropriate method depends in part on the research question. The use of multiple methods is highly recommended to minimize the limitations of a single method. Unfortunately, multimethod studies are very rare. It is more common for researchers to select a method that is familiar, well accepted, and easy to use rather than determining the most appropriate method for their research question.

Example of a Critical Incident Study

Yukl and Van Fleet (1982) conducted a study using critical incidents and survey questionnaires for different samples of military leaders. In critical incidents describing Air Force officers in the Korean War, the task-oriented behaviors found most often in effective incidents included clarifying roles and objectives, planning operations, emphasizing performance, and solving immediate problems. The relations-oriented and transformational behaviors found most often in effective incidents included coaching and developing, inspiring confidence and optimism, and leading by example. The results from the incidents were compared to survey results for a sample of platoon leaders in a simulated combat field exercise conducted at Fort Bragg in North Carolina. After the combat exercise, subordinates used a questionnaire to describe their platoon leader's behavior, and squad performance was evaluated by independent judges. The specific leader behaviors that correlated significantly with performance were the same ones found to be important in the earlier analysis of critical incidents.

Example of Diary Incident Study

An example of research based on analysis of incident diaries is provided by Amabile, Schatzel, Moneta, and Kramer (2004). Leader behavior in 26 project teams was described in diary incidents recorded by members for several weeks. Researchers coded the leader behaviors into specific categories of behavior identified in previous research. The analysis of results showed that effective leaders used more relations-oriented behaviors such as providing psychological support, consulting with team members, and providing recognition, but they also used more task behaviors such as clarifying roles and objectives, monitoring progress, and dealing with work-related problems. How and when a behavior was used were as important as what type of behavior was used. The effects of negative behavior (inappropriate or inept actions or failure to take appropriate action when it was needed) were usually stronger than the effects of positive behavior. Ineffective behaviors sometimes initiated a negative spiral of actions and reactions between the leader and subordinates with unfavorable consequences for the project team.

Examples of Field Experiments

Field experiments are difficult to conduct in real organizations, and only a small number of them have been used to investigate the effects of leadership behavior. Hand and Slocum (1972) trained managers in a steel plant to use more consideration behavior, and 18 months after the training was completed, these managers were rated more effective than managers in the control group (Hand & Slocum, 1972). The results for managers trained to use more task-oriented behavior were inconclusive.

In another field experiment, Wexley and Nemeroff (1975) found that training hospital supervisors to use more consideration behavior resulted in higher subordinate satisfaction and attendance measured two months after the training. Latham and Saari (1979) found that training first-line production supervisors to use more relationship-oriented behaviors (e.g., active listening, use of praise) resulted in higher performance ratings for these supervisors one year after training. Porras and Anderson (1981) found that human relations training designed to increase the use of some relationship-oriented behaviors (e.g., active listening, praise, consultation) resulted in a significant 17 percent increase in worker productivity six months after training was completed. Finally, in a study of production supervisors in a furniture factory, productivity improved (six months to two years after training) in three of the four departments in which supervisors were trained to use more praise with subordinates (Wikoff, Anderson, & Crowell, 1983).

In summary, the experiments in field settings found that relations-oriented behavior usually resulted in higher subordinate satisfaction and productivity. Task-oriented leadership was seldom manipulated in the leadership experiments, but some field experiments on goal setting (a specific type of task-oriented behavior) found that setting clear, specific, and challenging performance goals for subordinates improved their performance (Locke & Latham, 1990).

Interpreting Causality in Leader Behavior Research

Unless leader behavior is manipulated in an experimental study, it is very difficult to determine causality. For other research methods such as survey studies, there is more than one plausible interpretation of causality. When a positive correlation is found, the researchers usually assume the leader's behavior influenced the criterion variable (see Figure 2A). For example, a significant correlation between consideration and subordinate performance is usually interpreted as showing that considerate leaders cause subordinates to be more motivated and productive. However, it is also possible that causality is in the opposite direction, and leader behavior is influenced by the criterion variable (see Figure 2B). For example, leaders are more supportive to subordinates with high performance than to subordinates with low performance. Several experiments conducted in a laboratory setting with university students demonstrated that causality can operate in both directions (Day, 1971; Day & Hamblin, 1964; Farris & Lim, 1969; Herold, 1977; Lowin & Craig, 1968; Misumi & Shirakashi, 1966; Sims & Manz, 1984).

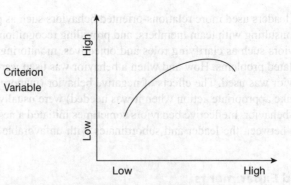

FIGURE 1 Leader Behavior vs Criterion Variable

Source: Pierce, J. R., & Aguinis, H., "The too-much-of-a-good-thing effect in management," *Journal of Management* (2013), Vol. 39(2), pp. 313-338.

Another possibility is that both leader behavior and the criterion variable are affected in the same way by a third variable (see Figure 2C). In many studies, the measures of leader behavior and the criterion variable are obtained from the same respondents. The correlation will be inflated if both measures are biased in the same way. For example, well-liked leaders are rated high on both consideration and effectiveness by subordinates, whereas disliked leaders are rated low on both variables. This type of bias is unlikely when the criterion variable is measured independently of leader behavior, but rater attribution biases can still occur (see Figure 2D). For example, raters who know the leader's group has high performance may assume that the leader uses relevant behaviors more than is really true.

An important, yet often ignored, plausible causal relationship between leadership behaviors and related outcomes is that there can be a "too much of a good thing" (TMGT) effect. TMGT (Grant & Schwartz, 2011; Pierce & Aguinis, 2013) refers to an apparent paradox in organizations, where an antecedent remains beneficial to some extent, but becomes harmful when taken too far. Recently, researchers (e.g., Harris & Russell, 2013) observed that although some leadership types, such as servant leadership and contingent reward leadership, are useful for the performance of subordinates, they become counterproductive beyond a threshold level. This suggests that there can also be a nonlinear (e.g., inverted U-shaped, as shown in Figure 1) relationship between leadership behavior and criterion variable.

Effects of Task and Relations Behaviors

In the early days of research on effects of leadership behavior, hundreds of studies were conducted to determine the influence of task-oriented and relations-oriented behavior on indicators of leadership effectiveness such as subordinate satisfaction, subordinate performance, and ratings of leader effectiveness by superiors. Scholars have used meta-analyses to examine the overall results (e.g., Fisher & Edwards, 1988; Judge, Piccolo, & Illies, 2004). However, the results are difficult to interpret when several different behavior measures, types of criteria, and research methods are included in the same analysis. Findings in the behavior research are described separately for survey studies and other types of research.

General Findings

The only consistent finding in the survey research was a positive relationship between consideration and subordinate satisfaction. Subordinates are usually more satisfied with a leader who is considerate, although the relationship was weaker when the measures of

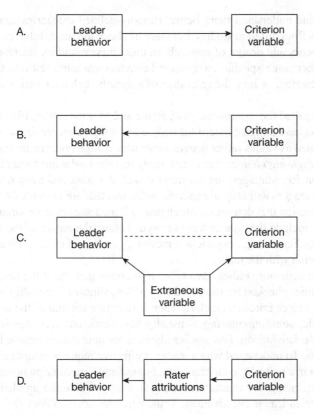

FIGURE 2 Possible Causes of a Correlation Between Leader Behavior and Criterion

behavior and satisfaction were not from the same source. Task-oriented behavior was not consistently related to subordinate satisfaction. In some studies, subordinates were more satisfied with a structuring leader, but other studies found the opposite relationship or no significant relationship. This pattern of results suggests the possibility of a curvilinear relationship such that satisfaction is highest for a leader who uses a moderate amount of task-oriented behavior.

In the survey studies, measures of leadership effectiveness had a weak positive correlation with task-oriented behavior and relations-oriented behavior, but once again the results were not consistent across studies. The weakest results were found in studies with an independent, objective measure of effectiveness such as group performance.

The results from experiments and studies with critical incidents, diaries, and interviews are more consistent, and they generally support the proposition that effective leaders guide and facilitate the work to accomplish task objectives, while at the same time maintaining cooperative relationships and teamwork. It is likely that all leaders need to use some task-oriented and relations-oriented behaviors.

Evaluation of the Behavior Research

Much of the behavior research suffers from the tendency to look for simple answers to complex questions, and it is not surprising that meta-analyses of survey studies find only weak positive relationships between effective leadership and meta-categories such as task and relations behavior. Behavior taxonomies are descriptive aids that can help us to analyze complex events and understand them better. Broadly-defined categories can be useful for comparing results from different studies, but there has been too much reliance on them in the formulation of theory and design of research. In most survey studies, the researchers failed to consider whether some specific component behaviors are more relevant than others for the leadership situation, or how the relevance of a specific behavior varies across different situations.

In a theory called the *managerial grid*, Blake and Mouton (1964, 1982) proposed that effective managers have a high concern for people and a high concern for production. These concerns are defined as values rather than as behaviors. A high concern for both people, and production (the "*high-high leader*") does not imply that the leader must use all forms of task and relations behavior. Managers are overloaded with demands and must ration their time. Thus, effective managers will only use specific behaviors that are relevant for their situation. Aspects of the situation that determine which task-oriented and relations-oriented behaviors are most relevant include the type of team or organization, the nature of the task, and characteristics of subordinates (e.g., experience, motives, gender and cultural diversity, trust and loyalty, identification with the team).

Most of the behavior studies have other limitations that make the results difficult to interpret. Few studies checked for the possibility of a nonlinear relationship between behavior and the performance criterion (such as when a moderate amount of the behavior is optimal). For example, some *monitoring* is usually beneficial, but an excessive amount can reduce subordinate satisfaction. Few studies checked for interactions among behaviors with interrelated effects. To understand why a leader is effective requires examination of how the behaviors interact in a mutually consistent way. For example, monitoring operations is useful for discovering problems, but unless something is done to solve the problems, monitoring will not contribute to leader effectiveness. Thus, when necessary, effective leaders will use other behaviors (e.g., problem solving, coaching) in combination with monitoring.

The descriptive studies of managerial work and research using case studies and biographies suggest that complementary behaviors are woven together into a complex tapestry such that the whole is greater than the sum of the parts (Kaplan, 1988). A leader's skill in selecting and enacting appropriate behaviors is related to the success of the outcome, and unless a behavior is used in a skillful way it may not be effective. The overall pattern of leadership behavior is more important than how often a particular type of behavior is used, and different patterns of behavior may be used to accomplish the same outcome.

The behavior research provides some useful insights about effective leadership, but more research is needed to understand how effective leaders adapt their behavior to the situation and are able to be flexible as the situation changes. Most of the behavior research has examined how leaders act toward subordinates, and more research is needed on boundary-spanning behaviors, which can be as important for effective leadership.

In the remainder of this chapter, specific types of task and relations behavior are explained and guidelines provided for using the behaviors effectively in most situations where they are relevant. The guidelines are based on applied research in leadership, on suggestions by practitioners, and on relevant theory and research in the management literature (e.g., project management, operations management, performance management, and human resources management).

Planning Work Activities

Short-term planning of work activities means deciding what to do, how to do it, who will do it, and when it will be done. The purpose of *planning* is to ensure efficient organization

TABLE 4	Guidelines for Action Planning

- Identify necessary action steps.
- Identify the optimal sequence of action steps.
- Estimate the time needed to carry out each action step.
- Determine starting times and deadlines for each action step.
- Estimate the cost of each action step.
- Determine who will be accountable for each action step.
- Develop procedures for monitoring progress.

of the work unit, coordination of activities, and effective utilization of resources. *Planning* is a broadly defined behavior that includes making decisions about objectives, priorities, strategies, organization of the work, assignment of responsibilities, scheduling of activities, and allocation of resources among different activities according to their relative importance. Special names are sometimes used for subvarieties of planning. For example, *operational planning* is the scheduling of routine work and determination of task assignments for the next day or week. *Action planning* is the development of detailed action steps and schedules for implementing a new policy or carrying out a project. *Contingency planning* is the development of procedures for avoiding or coping with potential problems or disasters. Finally, planning also includes determining how to allocate time to different responsibilities and activities ("time management").

Planning is mostly a cognitive activity involving processing of information, analyzing, and deciding. Planning seldom occurs in a single behavior episode; instead it tends to be a prolonged process that occurs over a period of weeks or months. Most planning involves formulation of informal and implicit agendas, rather than formal, written documents and agreements. Because planning is a cognitive activity that seldom occurs as a single discrete episode, it is difficult to observe (Snyder & Glueck, 1980). Nevertheless, some observable aspects include writing plans, preparing written budgets, developing written schedules, and meeting with others to formulate objectives and strategies. Planning is most observable when a manager takes action to implement plans by communicating them to others and making specific task assignments.

The importance of planning and organizing has long been recognized in the management literature (Carroll & Gillen, 1987; Drucker, 1974; Fayol, 1949; Quinn, 1980; Urwick, 1952). Evidence of a relationship between planning and managerial effectiveness is provided by a variety of different types of studies (e.g., Boyatzis, 1982; Carroll & Gillen, 1987; Kim & Yukl, 1995; Kotter, 1982; Morse & Wagner, 1978; Shipper & Wilson, 1992; Yukl, Wall, & Lepsinger, 1990). Recommended steps for action planning are shown in Table 4).

Clarifying Roles and Objectives

Clarifying is the communication of plans, policies, and role expectations. Major subcategories of clarifying include (1) defining job responsibilities and requirements, (2) setting performance goals, and (3) assigning specific tasks. The purpose of clarifying behavior is to guide and coordinate work activity and make sure people know what to do and how to do it. It is essential for each subordinate to understand what duties, functions, and activities are required in the job and what results are expected. Even a subordinate who is highly competent and motivated may fail to achieve a high level of performance if confused about responsibilities and priorities. Such confusion results in misdirected effort and neglect of important responsibilities in favor of less important ones. The more complex and multifaceted the job, the more difficult it is to determine what needs to be done.

Clarifying behavior is likely to be more important when there is substantial role ambiguity or role conflict for members of the work unit. Less clarifying is necessary if the organization has elaborate rules and regulations dictating how the work should be done and subordinates understand them, or if subordinates are highly trained professionals who have the expertise to do their jobs without much direction from superiors.

A number of different types of studies have found a positive relationship between clarifying and managerial effectiveness (Alexander, 1985; Bauer & Green, 1998; Kim & Yukl, 1995; Van Fleet & Yukl, 1986b; Wilson et al., 1990; Yukl, Wall, & Lepsinger, 1990). Evidence from many studies (including some field experiments) indicates that setting specific, challenging goals usually improves performance (see Locke & Latham, 1990).

Guidelines for Clarifying

The following guidelines indicate how leaders can effectively assign tasks to subordinates and clarify subordinate roles and responsibilities (see Table 5 for summary).

- **Clearly explain an assignment.**

When assigning tasks, use clear language that is easy to understand. If more than one task is involved, explain one task at a time to avoid confusion. Describe what needs to be done, say when it should be done, and describe the expected results. Explain any organization rules or standard procedures that must be followed by anyone who does that type of task.

- **Explain the reason for the assignment.**

Unless it is obvious already or there is no time for it, explain why the task is necessary and important, and why you have selected the person to be responsible for it. Understanding the purpose of an assignment can increase task commitment and facilitate subordinate initiative in overcoming obstacles.

- **Check for understanding of the assignment.**

Be alert for indications that the person does not understand your instructions or is reluctant to do what is asked (e.g., a puzzled expression or hesitant response). For a complex task that the person has not done previously, it is useful to probe for understanding. For example, ask how the person expects to carry out the task.

- **Provide any necessary instruction in how to do the task.**

If the person needs instruction in how to do a task, demonstrate and explain the procedures one step at a time using simple, clear language. Point out both correct and incorrect

TABLE 5	Guidelines for Clarifying Roles and Objectives

- Clearly explain an assignment.
- Explain the reason for the assignment.
- Check for understanding of the assignment.
- Provide any necessary instruction in how to do the task.
- Explain priorities for different objectives or responsibilities.
- Set specific goals and deadlines for important tasks.

procedures, and explain the cues that indicate whether a procedure has been done correctly. If the task involves an observable procedure that only takes a short time to complete, and the person lacks experience doing it, demonstrate the procedure, then have the person practice it while you observe and provide feedback and coaching.

- **Explain priorities for different objectives or responsibilities.**

Tasks often involve more than one type of objective, and there may be trade-offs among the objectives. For example, the objectives may involve both quantity and quality of the work, and when too much time is devoted to one objective the other may suffer. There is no simple way to determine priorities, but they should reflect the importance of the task for the manager's unit and the organization. It is essential to explain the relative priorities of different objectives and provide guidance on how to achieve an effective balance among them.

- **Set specific goals and deadlines for important tasks.**

Clear, specific performance goals are often useful to guide efforts and increase task motivation. The goals may involve the performance of individual subordinates or the overall performance of a team or work unit. The goals should be challenging but realistic given the difficulty of the task, subordinate skills, and available resources needed for the work. For a task that needs to be completed by a definite time and date, it is useful to set a specific deadline for the overall task, and sometimes for each important step.

Monitoring Operations and Performance

Monitoring involves gathering information about the operations of the manager's organizational unit, including the progress of the work, the performance of individual subordinates, the quality of products or services, and the success of projects or programs. Monitoring can take many forms, including observation of work operations, reading written reports, watching computer screen displays of performance data, inspecting the quality of samples of the work, and holding progress review meetings with an individual or group. Many organizations use video cameras to observe operations and increase security, and monitoring of telephone calls and internet correspondence is commonly used to check on quality for customer service representatives. To assess performance for retail facilities and service centers, it is sometimes useful to have somebody disguised as a customer visit them to observe how well the employees provide customer service. The appropriate type of monitoring depends on the nature of the task and other aspects of the situation.

Monitoring provides much of the information needed for planning and problem solving, which is why it is so important for managerial effectiveness (Meredith & Mantel, 1985). Information gathered from monitoring is used to identify problems and opportunities, as well as to formulate and modify objectives, strategies, plans, policies, and procedures. Monitoring provides the information needed to evaluate subordinate performance, recognize achievements, identify performance deficiencies, assess training needs, provide coaching and assistance, and allocate rewards such as a pay increase or promotion. When monitoring is insufficient, a manager will be unable to detect problems before they become serious (problems such as declining quality, low productivity, cost overruns, behind-schedule projects, employee dissatisfaction, and conflicts among employees).

The appropriate degree of monitoring will depend on the competence of the subordinate and the nature of the work. More frequent monitoring is desirable when subordinates are inexperienced and insecure, when mistakes have serious consequences, when the tasks of subordinates are highly interdependent and require close coordination, and when disruptions in the workflow are likely from equipment breakdowns, accidents, materials shortages, personnel shortages, and so forth. Monitoring of performance is most difficult when the work involves unstructured, unique tasks for which results can be determined only after a long time interval. For example, it is more difficult to evaluate the performance of a research scientist or human resource manager than the performance of a sales representative or production manager. Monitoring too closely or in ways that communicate distrust can undermine subordinate self-confidence and reduce intrinsic motivation.

As noted previously, monitoring indirectly affects a manager's performance by facilitating the effective use of other behaviors. The amount of research on the effects of monitoring by leaders is still limited, but evidence that monitoring is related to managerial effectiveness is provided by several studies using a variety of research methods (e.g., Amabile et al., 2004; Jenster, 1987; Kim & Yukl, 1995; Komaki, 1986; Komaki, Desselles, & Bowman, 1989; Komaki & Minnich, 2002; Yukl, Wall, & Lepsinger, 1990).

Guidelines for Monitoring

The following guidelines describe effective ways to monitor operations and the performance of subordinates (see summary in Table 6).

- **Identify and measure key indicators of performance.**

Accurate, timely information about the operations and performance of the work unit is essential for effective leadership by the work unit manager. When performance involves multiple criteria, they should all be measured and used for evaluation performance. It is a common mistake to focus on one or two indicators that are easy to measure, even though they do not provide a complete and accurate picture of unit performance.

- **Monitor key processes as well as outcomes.**

Processes that determine outcomes should be measured in addition to the outcomes themselves to gain a better understanding of causal relationships and to detect problems earlier. For example, quality problems can be resolved more effectively by identifying the critical steps in the production process or service activity where they occur and measuring them continuously to detect and resolve them quickly.

- **Measure progress against plans and budgets.**

Interpretation of information about operations is aided by relating it to plans, forecasts, and budgets. For example, at appropriate times (e.g., monthly or quarterly) compare actual

TABLE 6	Guidelines for Monitoring Operations

- Identify and measure key performance indicators.
- Monitor key process variables as well as outcomes.
- Measure progress against plans and budgets.
- Develop independent sources of information.
- Conduct progress review meetings at appropriate times.
- Observe operations directly when it is feasible.
- Ask specific questions about the work.
- Encourage reporting of problems and mistakes.
- Use information from monitoring to guide other behaviors.

expenditures to budgeted amounts to identify any discrepancies. If expenditures exceed budgeted amounts, investigate to determine the reason for the discrepancy and determine if there is a problem that requires corrective action.

- **Develop independent sources of information.**

Instead of relying on a single source for information, it is better to compare information from multiple sources. Using multiple sources makes it less likely that important information will be lost or discounted. Multiple sources can be found by enlisting the aid of other people who have relevant information, such as peers, customer and clients, or members of the organization below the level of immediate subordinates. For example, a top executive in one company made it known that he would have breakfast in the company cafeteria at a particular time on certain days, and invited any employees who were interested to join him for an informal discussion of company operations.

- **Conduct progress review meetings at appropriate times.**

Progress review meetings provide an opportunity to review and discuss a subordinate's progress in a project or assignment. The optimal frequency and timing for progress review meetings varies, depending on the nature of the task and the competence of the subordinate. More frequent meetings are appropriate for a subordinate who is learning a new job or who is unreliable. The timing of meetings depends partly on when performance data will be available and when key action steps are scheduled for completion.

- **Observe operations directly.**

Information about operations can be obtained from reports and progress review meetings, but there is no substitute for direct observation. Walking around to observe operations and talk to employees is especially useful for middle managers and top executives who tend to become isolated from day-to-day operations. Visiting work sites and different facilities of the company are also ways to see for yourself how things are going and check on the accuracy of reports about operations. The success of a visit to a work site depends partly on how the visit is arranged and conducted. Most visits should be unannounced and made by the manager alone. If advance notice is provided, people will probably try to make a favorable impression, making it difficult to assess how things are normally done. If the manager brings along several staff assistants, employees are likely to be more inhibited about what they say.

- **Ask specific questions.**

When conducting progress review meetings or observing operations, managers should use their knowledge about the work processes and their subordinates to ask specific questions and obtain vital information about the work. A probing but nonjudgmental style of questioning is better than a critical tone. Questions usually elicit better information if worded in an openended way rather than asking for a simple yes or no answer. Since questions reflect a manager's concerns, it is an effective way to communicate those concerns to people even while getting information from them.

- **Encourage reporting of problems and mistakes.**

The success of monitoring depends on getting accurate information from people who may be reluctant to provide it. Subordinates are often afraid to inform their boss about problems, mistakes, and delays. Even a subordinate who is not responsible for a problem may be reluctant to report it if likely to be the target of an angry outburst (the "kill the messenger" syndrome). Thus, it is essential to react to information about problems in a constructive, nonpunitive way. Show appreciation for accurate information, even if it is not favorable, and help subordinates learn from mistakes rather than punishing them.

- **Use information from monitoring to guide other behaviors.**

When monitoring reveals that a subordinate has been highly effective, it is an opportunity to provide praise. If performance is below targeted levels or a project is behind schedule, the leader should acknowledge the problem rather than ignoring it and initiate actions to deal with it. It may be necessary to revise the action plan and schedule if it is unrealistic, to provide more resources for the task, or to provide coaching if the subordinate lacks adequate skills.

Supportive Leadership

Supportive leadership (or "supporting") includes a wide variety of behaviors that show consideration, acceptance, and concern for the needs and feelings of other people. Supportive leadership helps to build and maintain effective interpersonal relationships. A manager who is considerate and friendly toward people is more likely to win their friendship and loyalty. The emotional ties that are formed make it easier to gain cooperation and support from people on whom the manager must rely to get the work done. It is more satisfying to work with someone who is friendly, cooperative, and supportive than with someone who is cold and impersonal, or worse, hostile, and uncooperative. Improvements in job satisfaction are likely to result in less absenteeism, less turnover, less alcoholism, and less drug abuse (Brief, Schuler, & Van Sell, 1981; Ganster, Fusilier, & Mayes, 1986; Kessler, Price, & Wortman, 1985). Supportive leadership may increase a subordinate's acceptance of the leader, trust of the leader, and willingness to do extra things for the leader.

Some forms of supporting behavior increase subordinate self-confidence and reduce the amount of stress in the job. Stress is reduced by showing appreciation, listening to problems and complaints, providing assistance when necessary, expressing confidence in the person, doing things to make the work environment more enjoyable, and buffering the person from unnecessary demands by outsiders. Stress is increased by making unreasonable demands, pressuring the person to work faster, being overly critical, and insisting on compliance with unnecessary bureaucratic requirements. Although results in research on the effects of considerate, supportive leadership are not consistent, it is likely this type of behavior will improve subordinate satisfaction and performance in many situations.

Guidelines for Supporting

The following guidelines indicate ways that managers can use supporting effectively with subordinates and others (see Table 7 for summary).

- **Show acceptance and positive regard.**

Due to the considerable position power of most managers, subordinates are especially sensitive to indications of acceptance and approval (or rejection and criticism). Outbursts of anger, harsh criticism, and personal insults are stressful regardless of the source, but especially when the source is someone who has considerable position power. There are many ways to show acceptance and concern for people in your day-to-day behavior. Supportive leadership means being polite and considerate. Maintain a pleasant, cheerful disposition. Spend some time with subordinates to get to know them better and find out about their

TABLE 7	Guidelines for Supporting

- Show acceptance and positive regard.
- Provide sympathy and support when the person is anxious or upset.
- Bolster the person's self-esteem and confidence.
- Be willing to help with personal problems.

interests, recreational activities, family, and hobbies. Remember prior conversations with the person, including details about the person's family and activities. If necessary, keep a notebook with this type of information about each subordinate. Be discreet about things that are told to you in confidence (don't spread gossip about the personal lives of subordinates or team members).

- **Provide sympathy and support when the person is anxious or upset.**

Show understanding and sympathy for someone who is upset by stress and difficulties in the work. Take time to listen to the person's concerns. Try to understand why the person is anxious or frustrated, and when appropriate, offer coaching, advice, and personal assistance. For example, pitching in to help subordinates do their work when the workload is unusually high is an effective way to demonstrate support. Job stress for subordinates can be reduced by buffering them from frivolous complaints and unrealistic demands made by outsiders or higher management.

- **Bolster the person's self-esteem and confidence.**

Indicate that the person is a valued member of the organization. Express confidence in the person when assigning a difficult task. When someone is discouraged due to job problems and setbacks in a difficult task, supportive managers will say things to help boost a person's self-confidence. When mistakes or performance problems occur, supportive managers deal with them in a constructive manner instead of "blowing up" and criticizing the person harshly. It is important to indicate a sincere desire to help someone learn from mistakes and overcome performance problems.

- **Be willing to help with personal problems.**

Effective managers are willing to help an employee deal with personal problems (e.g., family problems, financial problems, substance abuse) when assistance is requested or it is clearly needed because the person's performance is being adversely affected. Examples of things that a manager can do include helping the person identify and express concerns and feelings, helping the person understand the reasons for a personal problem, providing factual information that will help the person, referring the person to professionals who can provide assistance, helping the person identify alternatives, and offering advice (Burke, Wier, & Duncan, 1976; Kaplan & Cowen, 1981).

Developing Subordinate Skills

Developing includes several managerial practices that are used to increase a subordinate's skills and facilitate job adjustment and career advancement. Key component behaviors include mentoring, coaching, and providing developmental opportunities. Developing is usually done with a subordinate, but it may also be done with a peer, a colleague, or even with a new, inexperienced boss. Responsibility for developing subordinates can be shared with other members of the work unit who are competent and experienced. For example, some leaders assign an experienced subordinate to serve as a mentor and coach for a new employee.

The descriptive research suggests that most effective managers take an active role in developing the skills and confidence of subordinates (Bradford & Cohen, 1984; McCauley, 1986). Developing is usually regarded as primarily a relations-oriented behavior, but it can also contribute to the attainment of task-related objectives, such as improved quantity and quality of employee performance. Developing offers a variety of potential benefits for the manager, the subordinate, and the organization. One benefit is to foster mutually cooperative relationships. Potential benefits for subordinates include better job adjustment, more skill learning, greater self-confidence, and faster career advancement. The leader can gain a sense of satisfaction from helping others grow and develop. Potential benefits for the organization include higher employee commitment, higher performance, and better preparation of people to fill positions of greater responsibility in the organization as openings occur.

Guidelines for Developing

Guidelines for developing subordinate skills and confidence are described in this section and summarized in Table 8.

• **Show concern for each person's development.**

The most basic principle of mentoring is to have a genuine concern about the personal development and career progress of subordinates. A manager should encourage each subordinate to set ambitious career goals that are realistic in terms of the person's ability and consistent with the person's interests. Encourage the person to set specific goals for self-development. Respond enthusiastically to requests for advice or assistance. Provide social–emotional support as well as career-related support.

• **Help the person identify ways to improve performance.**

Before trying to improve task performance, it is essential to discover what is being done correctly and incorrectly. One diagnostic approach is to jointly review step by step how the person carries out the task to determine whether any essential steps are omitted, unnecessary steps are included, or key steps are performed incorrectly. When discussing ways to improve performance, it is usually better to begin by inviting the person to do a self-assessment rather than by making your own diagnosis of the person's performance. The person may already be aware of weaknesses and will be less defensiveness if asked to identify them rather than being told by you. However, in some cases, the person does not understand why his or her performance is not better. Even a highly motivated person may be unable to improve beyond

TABLE 8	Guidelines for Developing

- Show concern for each person's development.
- Help the person identify ways to improve performance.
- Be patient and helpful when providing coaching.
- Provide helpful career advice.
- Help the person prepare for a job change.
- Encourage attendance at relevant training activities.
- Provide opportunities to learn from experience.
- Encourage coaching by peers when appropriate.
- Promote the person's reputation.

the current level of performance without assistance. When appropriate, suggest additional things the person should consider to improve performance.

- **Be patient and helpful when providing coaching.**

An essential quality for effective coaching is patience. Don't expect people to learn everything immediately or do everything right the first time. It takes time to learn complex skills, and learning is inhibited when someone is anxious and frustrated. A person who is experiencing difficulty in doing a task will become even more anxious and upset if you are critical and impatient. Be helpful and supportive when a person is frustrated and discouraged by slow progress or repeated mistakes. For example, tell the person how you experienced the same frustrations in mastering a particularly difficult aspect of the task. If the person lacks self-confidence, say you are confident that he or she will be able to learn a new procedure or skill.

- **Provide helpful career advice.**

Provide career guidance and advice about how to deal with career problems, such as lack of advancement, interpersonal conflicts, burnout, and mid-career crisis. Many subordinates need help in developing specific strategies for achieving their career objectives. It may be useful to identify career paths and promotion opportunities in the organization and explain the advantages and pitfalls of various assignments or potential job changes. Share insights learned from experience with problems or choices similar to those now faced by a subordinate. If appropriate, introduce the person to other people in the organization who can be trusted to provide good career advice. To avoid being overbearing about career advice, ask a subordinate to indicate ways you can be helpful in the career planning process.

- **Encourage attendance at relevant training activities.**

Another way to facilitate skill development by subordinates is to encourage them to attend relevant workshops and courses. Inform subordinates about developmental opportunities and explain why they are relevant to a subordinate's needs, interests, and career ambitions. Encourage subordinates to take advantage of opportunities to attend assessment centers or multisource feedback workshops that provide useful feedback about strengths and weaknesses. Make it easier for subordinates to attend developmental activities by planning work schedules to allow time for them. If feasible, provide financial compensation to pay for outside courses. Bring in outside experts to conduct special training sessions for subordinates.

- **Provide opportunities to learn from experience.**

Provide special projects and assignments that require the subordinate to assume new responsibilities and apply new skills. Some of these assignments may involve delegation of responsibilities previously carried out by the manager (e.g., prepare a budget, conduct a meeting, present a proposal to top management). Sometimes the best approach for developing skills is to assign a challenging task without giving detailed instructions, and allow the person to discover how to carry out the task and to deal with problems encountered along the way. In a developmental assignment, provide coaching when needed to help the person learn from successes and failures.

- **Encourage coaching by peers when appropriate.**

The responsibility to develop subordinates may be shared with other members of the work unit who are competent and experienced. Peers are a valuable source of advice and support in organizations. Although coaching and mentoring by peers occurs informally, it can be encouraged and facilitated by the manager. One example is the practice of assigning a competent subordinate to serve as a mentor and coach for a new employee. It is also useful to have a subordinate with special knowledge coach other employees who are less experienced.

- **Promote the person's reputation.**

A manager can promote the reputation of a subordinate by telling superiors and peers about the person's achievements and expertise. It is also helpful to introduce the person to important people in the organization. A subordinate's visibility and contacts can be enhanced by selecting the person to serve on committees or projects that provide an opportunity to interact with important people in the organization. High visibility assignments provide an opportunity for a subordinate to demonstrate competence in carrying out important responsibilities.

Providing Praise and Recognition

Recognizing involves giving praise and showing appreciation to others for effective performance, significant achievements, and important contributions to the organization. Although it is most common to think of recognition as being given by a manager to subordinates, this managerial practice can also be used with peers, superiors, and people outside the work unit. The primary purpose of recognizing, especially when used with subordinates, is to strengthen desirable behavior and task commitment. Recognizing is primarily a relations behavior, but like developing, it can contribute to the attainment of task objectives as well.

Three major forms of recognizing are praise, awards, and recognition ceremonies. Praise consists of oral comments, expressions, or gestures that acknowledge a person's accomplishments and contributions. It is the easiest form of recognition, but it is underutilized by many managers. Most praise is given privately, but it can be used in a public ritual or ceremony as well. Leaders usually have less discretion in the use of awards or recognition ceremonies, because organizations often have programs and policies specifying the criteria and procedures for this type of recognition. Nevertheless, even low-level leaders have options to be very creative about informal awards.

Awards include things such as a certificate of achievement, a letter of commendation, a plaque, a trophy, a medal, or a ribbon. Awards can be announced in many different ways, including an article in the company newsletter, a notice posted on the bulletin board, a picture of the person (e.g., "employee of the month") hung in a prominent place, over a public address system, in regular meetings, and at special ceremonies or rituals. Giving formal awards is a symbolic act that communicates a manager's values and priorities to people in the organization. Thus, it is important for awards to be based on meaningful criteria rather than favoritism or arbitrary judgments. An award that is highly visible allows others to share in the process of commending the recipient and showing appreciation for his or her contributions to the success of the organization. The basis for making the award is more important than the form of the award. Some managers are creative about using awards, and they look for new and unusual awards to use with "planned spontaneity." Examples include home-baked bread, flowers, a bottle of wine, and a picture of the employee with the CEO.

A recognition ceremony ensures that an individual's achievements are acknowledged not only by the manager but also by other members of the organization. Recognition ceremonies can be used to celebrate the achievements of a team or work unit as well as those of an individual. Special rituals or ceremonies to honor particular employees or teams can have strong symbolic value when attended by top management, because they demonstrate concern for the aspects of behavior or performance being recognized. Milliken & Company (Peters & Austin, 1985) use a unique version of a recognition ceremony.

> Once each quarter a "Corporate Sharing Rally" is held to allow work teams to brag about their achievements and contributions. Each of the "fabulous bragging sessions" has a particular theme such as improved productivity, better product quality, or reduced costs. Attendance is voluntary, but hundreds of employees show up to hear teams make short five-minute presentations describing how they have made improvements relevant to the theme. Every participant receives a framed certificate, and the best presentations (determined by peer evaluation) get special awards. In addition to celebrating accomplishments and emphasizing key values (represented by the themes), these ceremonies increase the diffusion of innovative ideas within the company.

Most studies that measure contingent reward behavior with leader behavior questionnaires find a positive correlation with subordinate satisfaction, but results for subordinate performance are inconsistent (Podsakoff, Skoder & Tov, 1982; Podsakoff & Todor, 1985). Praise is often given along with tangible rewards, and in much of the research it is difficult to separate their effects. Another source of ambiguity is the limited influence of most managers on the distribution of tangible rewards (e.g., bonus, pay increase, promotion). Formal policies, incentive programs, and union contracts for determining employee compensation and benefits usually provide very limited reward power to managers at the lower and middle levels in large organizations. It is difficult to interpret the results from surveys that fail to take into account constraints on leader reward behavior and the effects of company policies and programs (Podsakoff, Todor, Grover, & Huber, 1984).

The results are easier to interpret in a survey study or incident study when respondents describe how their leader uses praise. Survey research on the effects of praise and recognition suggest that this type of behavior can be beneficial when used in a skillful way under favorable conditions (e.g., Kim & Yukl, 1995; Yukl et al., 1990). Descriptive studies in organizations suggest that effective leaders provide more recognition to subordinates for their achievements and contributions (Kouzes & Posner, 1987; Peters & Austin, 1985). In a rare field experiment on the effects of praise, Wikoff, Anderson, and Crowell (1983) found that increasing the use of praise by supervisors resulted in improved performance by their employees.

Guidelines for Recognizing

The following guidelines for recognizing are based on the research literature on positive reinforcement and the descriptive literature on practices of managers in effective organizations. The guidelines are concerned with the following questions: what to recognize, when to give recognition, who to recognize, and what form of recognition to use (see summary in Table 9).

- **Recognize a variety of contributions and achievements.**

Managers tend to think of recognition as appropriate only for major achievements, thereby limiting their opportunity to gain the benefits from this potent managerial practice. Recognition should be provided for a variety of other things, including demonstration of initiative and extra effort in carrying out an assignment or task; achievement of challenging

TABLE 9	Guidelines for Recognizing

- Recognize a variety of contributions and achievements.
- Actively search for contributions to recognize.
- Recognize improvements in performance.
- Recognize commendable efforts that failed.
- Do not limit recognition to high-visibility jobs.
- Do not limit recognition to a few best performers.
- Provide specific recognition.
- Provide timely recognition.
- Use an appropriate form of recognition.

performance goals and standards; personal sacrifices made to accomplish a task or objective; helpful suggestions and innovative ideas for improving efficiency, productivity, or the quality of the work unit's products or services; special efforts to help someone else (e.g., coworker, customer) deal with a problem; and significant contributions made to the success of other individuals or teams.

- **Actively search for contributions to recognize.**

Before recognition can be given for contributions and accomplishments, it is necessary to determine what things are important for the success of the work unit and consistent with the values and ideals of the organization. It is helpful to spend some time each day looking for examples of effective behavior to recognize. Many managers tend to notice and criticize ineffective behavior by subordinates or peers but fail to notice and praise effective behavior. It is also helpful to establish periodic awards, such as the "employee of the week," that require a manager to spend some time on a regular basis looking for examples of effective performance among subordinates. Kouzes and Posner (1987) recommend setting a personal goal to find and praise at least one subordinate each day for some exemplary behavior or significant contribution.

- **Recognize improvements in performance.**

Some managers believe that it is inappropriate to recognize performance improvements if an individual's level of performance is still only average or substandard. However, some form of recognition for improvements is important to encourage and strengthen efforts toward additional improvement. Improvements can be recognized in a way that also communicates an expectation of continuing progress toward excellence. Recognition of improvement is especially relevant for new employees who are just learning a new task and for employees who do not have much self-confidence.

- **Recognize commendable efforts that failed.**

Another fallacy is that recognition must be limited to successful efforts. Sometimes recognition is necessary for unsuccessful efforts to perform an important activity with a low probability of success. For example, Ore-Ida fires off a cannon to celebrate the "perfect failure" when research scientists terminate a project that is failing rather than prolong it at great cost to the company (Peters & Waterman, 1982). In another example, when someone suggests an improvement but it does not appear to be feasible, the manager should thank the person and explain why the idea could not be implemented in order to encourage further suggestions in the future.

- **Do not limit recognition to high-visibility jobs.**

Everyone has a desire for recognition and appreciation, and even people who are a little embarrassed by recognition still desire and value it. It is a common tendency to provide recognition to individuals whose performance and achievements are highly visible, while largely ignoring people whose contributions are less visible and whose performance is harder to measure. It is better to recognize contributions and achievements by employees in all jobs, regardless of their status or visibility. Recognition should be given to people in support functions as well as to people in line functions with easily quantifiable performance, such as production and sales. With a little effort, it is possible to find examples of effective behavior and indicators of successful performance for any type of job.

- **Do not limit recognition to a few best performers.**

The question of who to recognize also relates closely to the basis for giving recognition and the amount of recognition. Some managers believe that recognition should be limited to a few best performers in each type of job, thereby creating strong competition among people. However, Peters and Austin (1985) found that effective organizations recognize many winners rather than only a few. For example, it is better to provide awards for the top 75 percent of sales representatives than only for the top 10 percent. It is better to give an award to everyone who exceeds a challenging performance standard rather than to recognize only the person with the best performance. Extreme forms of competition create undesirable side effects, such as unwillingness to help competitors and resentment by people who perform exceptionally well but receive little or no recognition merely because someone else does a little better, often due to a lucky break. It is feasible to recognize many "heroes" or "winners" and still have different amounts of recognition for different levels of performance. Unless the people with the best performance receive a greater amount of recognition, their accomplishments will be unnecessarily diminished and the desired benefits from recognition may not be realized.

- **Provide specific recognition.**

Praise is more likely to be successful if it is specific. Instead of a general comment commending someone for doing an assignment well, it is better to explain why you think the person did the assignment well. Indicate the basis for your judgment, point out examples of special effort or effective behavior, and explain why the person's accomplishments are important to you and to the organization. In the case of praise for good suggestions, explain how the person's ideas were used and how they benefited the organization or contributed to the success of a project. Specific praise is more believable than general praise, because it shows that you actually know what the person has done and have a sound basis for a positive evaluation. In addition, citing specific examples of effective behavior communicates what behaviors you value and guides the person toward repeating these behaviors in the future.

- **Provide timely recognition.**

Research on positive reinforcement suggests that it is more effective when given reasonably soon after the behavior to be reinforced. Thus, managers should try to identify effective behavior and provide recognition for it promptly. As Peters and Waterman (1982) point out, one of the benefits of "management by walking around" is to help find examples of good behavior and provide immediate praise for it. However, recognition for any particular type of achievement or contribution by a person can be overdone. It is not necessary or effective to praise someone every day for the same thing.

- **Use an appropriate form of recognition.**

There is no simple, mechanical formula for determining what type of recognition to use. The appropriate form of recognition will depend on the type and importance of the achievement to be recognized, the norms and culture of the organization, and the characteristics of the manager and recipient. Whatever form of recognition is used, it must be sincere. Most people are able to detect efforts to manipulate them with praise or awards. Managers should avoid overusing a particular form of recognition, because its effect can be diminished if it becomes too commonplace.

Summary

The early research on leader behavior was dominated by a focus on broadly defined metacategories of task-oriented behavior and relations-oriented behavior. Over a period of more than three decades, hundreds of studies were conducted to see how the two types of behavior were correlated with criteria of leadership effectiveness, such as subordinate satisfaction and performance. Many studies were also conducted to test contingency theories that attempt to explain how leaders can adapt their task-oriented and relations-oriented behaviors to changing situations.

Results from the survey research are weak and inconsistent, but when combined with results from other methods such as critical incidents and experiments, a clearer picture emerges. The overall pattern of results suggests that effective leaders have a high concern for task objectives and interpersonal relationships, and they use specific types of behavior that are relevant for their leadership situation. Examples of specific task-oriented behaviors include planning, clarifying, and monitoring. Examples of specific relations-oriented behaviors include supporting, developing, and recognizing.

Another broadly-defined behavior category identified in the early leadership research is participative leadership. It involves several types of decision procedures used by leaders to improve the quality of decisions and commitment to implement them.

Change-oriented leadership behavior is used to influence innovation, collective learning, and the successful implementation of major changes in an organization. Transformational leadership includes a mix of relations and change behaviors plus some additional aspects of behavior not easily classified into other categories.

Boundary-spanning behaviors for leaders are another broad category that includes behaviors used by leaders in interactions with peers, superiors, and outsiders. Examples include networking, environmental scanning, and representing.

Review and Discussion Questions

1. Why are behavior taxonomies important for research and theory on effective leadership?
2. What are the limitations of using only broad meta-categories in theory and research?
3. How can a leader's behavior reflect a high concern for both task and relations?
4. How are task-oriented and relations-oriented behaviors related to effective leadership?
5. How are planning, clarifying, and monitoring related to subordinate satisfaction and performance?
6. What are some guidelines for planning, clarifying, and monitoring?
7. How are supporting, developing, and recognizing related to subordinate satisfaction and performance?
8. What are some guidelines for supporting, developing, and recognizing?

Key Terms

change-oriented behavior	initiating structure	relations-oriented behavior
clarifying	meta-categories	supportive leadership
consideration	monitoring	task-oriented behavior
critical incidents	networking	transformational
developing	participative leadership	leadership
high-high leader	planning recognizing	

CASE 1

Consolidated Products

Consolidated Products is a medium-sized manufacturer of consumer products with nonunionized production workers. Ben Samuels was a plant manager for Consolidated Products for 10 years, and he was well liked by the employees. They were grateful for the fitness center he built for employees, and they enjoyed the social activities sponsored by the plant several times a year, including company picnics and holiday parties. He knew most of the workers by name, and he spent part of each day walking around the plant to visit with them and ask about their families or hobbies.

Ben believed that it was important to treat employees properly so they would have a sense of loyalty to the company. He tried to avoid any layoffs when production demand was slack, figuring that the company could not afford to lose skilled workers who are so difficult to replace. The workers knew that if they had a special problem, Ben would try to help them. For example, when someone was injured but wanted to continue working, Ben found another job in the plant that the person could do despite having a disability. Ben believed that if you treat people right, they will do a good job for you without close supervision or prodding. Ben applied the same principle to his supervisors, and he mostly left them alone to run their departments as they saw fit. He did not set objectives and standards for the plant, and he never asked the supervisors to develop plans for improving productivity and product quality.

Under Ben, the plant had the lowest turnover among the company's five plants, but the second worst record for costs and production levels. When the company was acquired by another firm, Ben was asked to take early retirement, and Phil Jones was brought in to replace him.

Phil had a growing reputation as a manager who could get things done, and he quickly began making changes. Costs were cut by trimming a number of activities such as the fitness center at the plant, company picnics and parties, and the human relations training programs for supervisors. Phil believed that training supervisors to be supportive was a waste of time. His motto was: "If employees don't want to do the work, get rid of them and find somebody else who does."

Supervisors were instructed to establish high-performance standards for their departments and insist that people achieve them. A computer monitoring system was introduced so that the output of each worker could be checked closely against the standards. Phil told his supervisors to give any worker who had substandard performance one warning, then if performance did not improve within two weeks, to fire the person. Phil believed that workers don't respect a supervisor who is weak and passive. When Phil observed a worker wasting time or making a mistake, he would reprimand the person right on the spot to set an example.

Phil also checked closely on the performance of his supervisors. Demanding objectives were set for each department, and weekly meetings were held with each supervisor to review department performance. Finally, Phil insisted that supervisors check with him first before taking any significant actions that deviated from established plans and policies.

As another cost-cutting move, Phil reduced the frequency of equipment maintenance, which required machines to be idled when they could be productive. Because the machines had a good record of reliable operation, Phil believed that the current maintenance schedule was excessive and was cutting into production. Finally, when business was slow for one of the product lines, Phil laid off workers rather than finding something else for them to do.

By the end of Phil's first year as plant manager, production costs were reduced by 20 percent and production output was up by 10 percent. However, three of his seven supervisors left to take other jobs, and turnover was also high among the machine operators. Some of the turnover was due to workers who were fired, but competent machine operators were also quitting, and it was becoming increasingly difficult to find any replacements for them. Finally, talk of unionizing was increasing among the workers.

Questions

1. Describe and compare the managerial behavior of Ben and Phil. To what extent does each manager display specific relations behaviors (supporting, developing, recognizing) and specific task behaviors (clarifying, planning, monitoring)? To what extent does each manager use participative or inspirational leadership?
2. Compare Ben and Phil in terms of their influence on employee attitudes, short-term performance, and long-term plant performance, and explain the reasons for the differences.
3. If you were selected to be the manager of this plant, what would you do to achieve both high employee satisfaction and performance?

CASE 2

Air Force Supply Squadron

Colonel Pete Novak was assigned to command an air force squadron that airlifted supplies to combat units during the Korean War. The squadron had more than 200 men and several cargo planes. When he assumed command, the situation was bleak. They were short of supplies, personnel, and replacements. Organization and coordination were poor, and there was little cooperation and teamwork among different sections. Morale was low due to the unrelenting workload, the constant bickering and disagreements, and the stress of flying into combat zones.

Colonel Novak held a meeting of the squadron to introduce himself and talk about how important their mission was to the success of the war effort. He talked about how the men in the front lines were counting on the squadron to bring them the supplies and ammunition they needed to keep the enemy from overrunning the country. He reminded them that every man had a vital function in the operation of the squadron.

Then Colonel Novak set out to learn about more about the men in his unit, beginning with the officers. He held frequent staff meetings with the section heads and some key noncommissioned officers (NCOs) to discuss the methods used to carry out the mission of the squadron. He visited the enlisted men at work and off duty, talking to them and showing a personal interest in them. He listened to their complaints, and whenever possible tried to deal with their concerns about the poor living conditions at the base. He flew along with the airplane crews on some of the supply missions. On one occasion, when supplies were desperately needed at the front lines and the squadron was shorthanded, he pitched in and worked beside the men all during the night to load the planes.

It was not long before Colonel Novak had learned each person's name, what his job was, and something about his background. As he found out more about the capabilities of the men, he reorganized the squadron to place people where the best use could be made of their skills and experience. In staff meetings, disagreements were discussed and worked out, and responsibilities were assigned when all concerned were present. Authority was clearly delegated to reduce confusion and duplication of orders. The NCOs were held responsible for the actions of their men and, within limits, their decisions were enforced without question.

Within two months, the effects of the changes were evident. The officers and enlisted men learned what was expected of them and began to see themselves as an essential part of a well-run organization. They began to take pride in their ability to accomplish their mission despite the hardships. Morale and teamwork improved. Before long the squadron became one of the most efficient in Korea.

Copyright © 1985 by Gary Yukl

Questions

1. What effective leadership behaviors were exhibited by Colonel Novak?
2. What does this case illustrate about effective leadership?
3. Compare the leadership behavior in this case with the behavior in the preceding case.

CASE 3

Attitude and Performance

Nishant is in a fix (refer to Case 2 in Chapter 2). Two of his team members, Area Training Managers (ATMs), Vishal Sharma and Harmeet Singh, have applied for a promotion. Recently, the Regional Training Head (RTH) of the Western region had left to join a life insurance firm. The Corporate HR team released an internal job posting (IJP[1]) to fill this vacancy. On the very morning of the IJP announcement, during a conference call, Anil, the National Training Head (NTH), had informed the RTHs and advised them to send one ATM from each region for the upcoming interviews. He had clearly announced that the RTHs should decide in time and effectively, as none of them can send more than one nomination.

As such, both Vishal and Harmeet have been performing team members, and are often appreciated by the internal sales team as well as by channel partners. All ASMs were aware of this IJP and the respective ASMs for Vishal and Harmeet were pursuing their promotion with Nishant. Ideally, both of them should have been offered the opportunity to apply; however, Anil's mandate was very clear.

---

[1]Internal Job Posting (IJP) is released on an organization's intranet and a common e-mail is sent to all employees. It is a very transparent process, where information is symmetrical across the organization. This is to promote the internal recruitment culture in the organization.

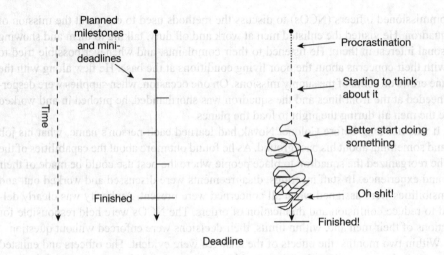

FIGURE 3 Task-Oriented Attitude vs Relationship-Oriented Attitude

Although Vishal and Harmeet are almost identical in their performance and are known for timely completion of assigned tasks, they differ in many aspects. For example, their ways of approaching goals are entirely different (see Figure 3). On the one hand, Vishal judiciously plans all tasks and executes them accordingly, while on the other, Harmeet goes by the wind, leaving him with leeway to adjust for contingencies. Although Harmeet sometimes struggles with deadlines, strict adherence to plans always helps Vishal in effectively conducting training programs. Often, Harmeet comes up with the excuse that he does not wish to trouble stakeholders by pressuring them and because everyone works in an uncertain and dynamic work environment, there must always be some buffer for exigencies. This behavior of Harmeet makes his contemporary managers think of him as friendly and adjusting.

Vishal, on the contrary, often ignores and rejects demands from internal sales personnel and channel partners for rescheduling training programs. According to him, demands are always endless and, consequently, when you start to accommodate such demands, no training program will ever reach a logical conclusion. He always quoted the example that if movie theatres started accounting for the convenience of all viewers, there will be no Fridays. His contemporary managers are sometimes frustrated with such a task-oriented attitude; however, their supervisors remain extremely happy with Vishal, as this means completion of tasks in a timely and effective manner.

In all, apart from different ways to approach a task, Vishal and Harmeet both remain performers.

Nishant is now confused about which name to propose for the IJP. He has no logical reason for rejecting either of them. And he is sure that across the country, these two are the most eligible and likely contenders for the RTH position.

Questions

1. Between Vishal and Harmeet, who should be Nishant's choice for the training department? Why?
2. Between task and relationship orientation, what should be the job profile of an RTM for the training department in a life insurance firm?

Participative Leadership and Empowerment

Learning Objectives

After studying this chapter, you should be able to:

- Understand different forms of participative leadership and empowerment.
- Understand the major findings in research on consequences of participative leadership.
- Understand the situations in which participative leadership is most likely to be effective.
- Understand when and how to use consultation.
- Understand the potential benefits and risks of delegation.
- Understand when and how to use delegation.

Making decisions is one of the most important functions performed by leaders. Many of the activities of managers and administrators involve making and implementing decisions. Participative leadership involves efforts by a leader to enlist the aid of others in making important decisions. Democratic societies uphold the right of people to influence decisions that will affect them in important ways. Involving others in making decisions is often a necessary part of the political process for getting decisions approved and implemented in organizations. Delegation is a distinct type of power-sharing process that occurs when subordinates are given responsibility and authority for making some types of decisions formerly made by a manager. Empowerment involves the perception by members of an organization that they have the opportunity to determine their work roles, accomplish meaningful work, and influence important events.

Participative leadership, *delegation,* and empowerment are subjects that bridge the power and behavior approaches to leadership. The research on participative leadership and delegation emphasizes the leader's perspective on power sharing. The research on empowerment emphasizes the follower's perspective. Taken together, the two different perspectives provide a better understanding of effective leadership in organizations. This chapter describes the theory and research findings on participative leadership and empowerment.

Nature of Participative Leadership

Participative leadership involves the use of various *decision procedures* that allow other people some influence over the leader's decisions. Other terms commonly used to refer to aspects of participative leadership include *consultation, joint decision making, power sharing, decentralization, empowerment,* and *democratic management.* Participative leadership can take many forms and includes several specific decision procedures. Although primarily a relationsoriented behavior, participative leadership also has implications for achieving task objectives and implementing change.

Varieties of Participation

A variety of different decision procedures may be used by a manager, and they involve different amounts of influence over a decision by subordinates or group members. Scholars have proposed several different taxonomies of decision procedures, and there is no agreement about the optimal number of decision procedures or the best way to define them. However, most leadership scholars would recognize the following four decision procedures as distinct and meaningful:

Autocratic Decision.   The manager makes a decision alone without asking for the opinions or suggestions of other people, and these people have no direct influence on the decision; there is no participation.

Consultation.   The manager asks other people for their opinions and ideas and then makes the decision alone after seriously considering their suggestions and concerns.

Joint Decision.   The manager meets with others to discuss the decision problem and make a decision together; the manager has no more influence over the final decision than any other participant.

Delegation.   The manager gives an individual or group the authority and responsibility for making a decision; the manager usually specifies limits within which the final choice must fall, and prior approval may or may not be required before the decision can be implemented.

The four decision procedures can be ordered along a continuum ranging from no influence by other people to high influence (see Figure 1). Some researchers differentiate between subvarieties of these basic four procedures. For example, Tannenbaum and Schmidt (1958) distinguished two varieties of autocratic decision: one in which the leader merely announces an autocratic decision ("tell" style) and the other in which the leader makes the decision alone but uses influence tactics such as rational persuasion ("sell" style) to gain support for it. The same writers also distinguished between a leader who announces a decision and is willing to modify it only if there are strong objections, and a leader who presents a tentative

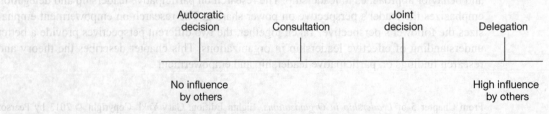

FIGURE 1 Continuum of Decision Procedures

proposal and actively encourages people to suggest ways to improve it (but retains the right to make the final choice). Vroom and Yetton (1973) distinguished between consulting with individuals and consulting with a group. A joint decision may involve only a single subordinate or several people, and for group decisions, a number of different decision procedures can be used. Varieties of delegation are described later in the chapter.

Decision procedures are abstract descriptions of pure or ideal types; the actual behavior of managers seldom occurs in ways that neatly fit these descriptions. Consultation often occurs informally during the course of repeated interactions with other people rather than at a single point of time in a formal meeting. Consultation may occur during brief contacts in the hall, after a meeting or social event, at lunch, or on the golf course. Actual behavior may involve a mix of elements from different decision procedures, such as consulting about problem diagnosis but not about final choice among solutions, or consulting about final choice among a limited set of predetermined solutions. Participative leadership has a dynamic quality and may change over time. For example, what was initially consultation may become a joint decision as it becomes evident that there is consensus about the best alternative. What was initially a group decision may become consultation when it becomes obvious that the group is deadlocked and the leader must make the final decision.

It is also important to distinguish between overt procedures and actual influence. Sometimes what appears to be *participation* is only pretense. For example, a manager may solicit ideas and suggestions from others but ignore them when making the decision. Likewise, the manager may ask subordinates to make a decision, but do it in such a way that the subordinates are afraid to show initiative or deviate from the choices they know their boss prefers.

Potential Benefits of Participative Leadership

Participative leadership offers a variety of potential benefits, but whether the benefits are achieved depends on who the participants are, how much influence they have, and other aspects of the decision situation (see Figure 2). Four potential benefits include higher decision quality, higher decision acceptance by participants, more satisfaction with the decision process, and more development of decision-making skills. Several explanations have been proposed for the positive effects of participation (Anthony, 1978; Cooper & Wood, 1974; Likert, 1967; Maier, 1963; Mitchell, 1973; Strauss, 1963; Vroom & Yetton, 1973).

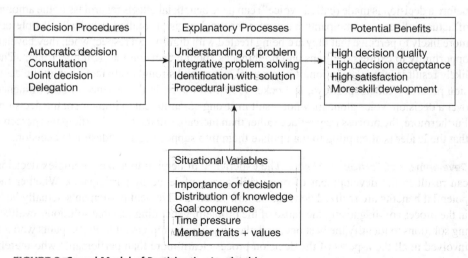

FIGURE 2   Causal Model of Participative Leadership

Situational variables that enhance or limit the effects of participation are discussed later in the chapter as part of the theories developed to explain why this form of leadership is not effective in all situations.

Decision Quality.   Involving other people in making a decision is likely to increase the quality of a decision when participants have information and knowledge lacked by the leader and are willing to cooperate in finding a good solution to a decision problem. Cooperation and sharing of knowledge will depend on the extent to which participants *trust* the leader and view the process as legitimate and beneficial. If participants and the leader have incompatible goals, cooperation is unlikely to occur. In the absence of cooperation, participation may reduce rather than increase decision quality. Even high cooperation does not guarantee that participation will result in a better decision. The decision process used by the group will determine whether members are able to reach agreement, and it will determine the extent to which any decision incorporates the members' expertise and knowledge. When members have different perceptions of the problem or different priorities for the various outcomes, it is difficult to discover a high-quality decision. The group may fail to reach agreement or settle for a poor compromise. Finally, other aspects of the decision situation such as time pressures, the number of participants, and formal policies may make some forms of participation impractical.

Decision Acceptance.   People who have considerable influence in making a decision tend to identify with it and perceive it to be their decision. This feeling of ownership increases their motivation to implement it successfully. Participation also provides a better understanding of the nature of the decision problem and the reasons why a particular alternative was accepted and others rejected. Participants gain a better understanding of how they will be affected by a decision, which is likely to reduce any unwarranted fears and anxieties about it. When adverse consequences are likely, participation allows people an opportunity to express their concerns and help to find a solution that deals with these concerns. Finally, when a decision is made by a participative process considered legitimate by most members, then the group is likely to apply social pressure on any reluctant members to do their part in implementing the decision.

Satisfaction with the Decision Process.   Research on procedural justice (e.g., Earley & Lind, 1987; Lind & Tyler, 1988) found that the opportunity to express opinions and preferences before a decision is made (called "voice") can have beneficial effects regardless of the amount of actual influence participants have over the final decision (called "choice"). People are more likely to perceive that they are being treated with dignity and respect when they have an opportunity to express opinions and preferences about a decision that will affect them. The likely result is more perception of procedural justice and stronger satisfaction with the decision process (Roberson, Moye, & Locke, 1999). However, in the absence of real influence over a decision, voice alone may not result in strong commitment to implement the decision. Furthermore, the process may reduce rather than increase satisfaction if participants perceive that the leader is attempting to manipulate them into supporting an undesirable decision.

Development of Participant Skills.   The experience of helping to make a complex decision can result in the development of more skill and confidence by participants. Whether the potential benefits are realized depends on how much involvement participants actually have in the process of diagnosing the cause of the problem, generating feasible solutions, evaluating solutions to identify the best one, and planning how to implement it. Participants who are involved in all the aspects of the decision process learn more than participants who merely contribute to one aspect. For participants with little experience in making complex decisions, learning also depends on the extent to which participants receive coaching and encouragement from the leader during difficult stages of the decision process.

Objectives for Different Participants

The potential benefits of participation are not identical for all types of participants. The leader's objectives for using participation may differ depending on whether participants are subordinates, peers, superiors, or outsiders.

Downward consultation may be used to increase the quality of decisions by drawing on the knowledge and problem-solving expertise of subordinates. Another objective is to increase subordinate acceptance of decisions by providing a sense of ownership. A third objective may be to develop the decision-making skills of subordinates by giving them experience in helping to analyze decision problems and evaluate solutions. A fourth objective is to facilitate conflict resolution and team building.

Lateral consultation with people in different subunits may be used to increase decision quality when peers have relevant knowledge about the cause of a problem and likely solutions. When cooperation from other managers is necessary to implement a decision, consultation is a way to increase their understanding and commitment. Lateral consultation facilitates coordination and cooperation among managers of different organizational subunits with interdependent tasks. However, consultation should be limited to decisions for which it is appropriate, so that time is not wasted in unnecessary meetings.

Upward consultation allows a manager to draw on the expertise of the boss, which may be greater than the manager's expertise. In addition, upward consultation allows a manager to find out how the boss feels about a problem and is likely to react to various proposals. On the other hand, excessive consultation with a boss suggests a lack of self-confidence and initiative for the subordinate. A manager with authority to make decisions is wise to avoid becoming too dependent on the boss when making these decisions.

Consulting with outsiders such as clients and suppliers helps ensure that decisions affecting them are understood and accepted. It is also a way to learn more about their needs and preferences, strengthen external networks, improve coordination, and solve mutual problems.

Research on Effects of Participative Leadership

Since the pioneering studies by Lewin, Lippitt, and White (1939) and Coch and French (1948), social scientists have been interested in studying the consequences of participative leadership. The research has continued for more than a half century using a variety of methods. Field experiments compared leaders who used participative procedures to leaders who made autocratic decisions (e.g., Coch & French, 1948; Fleishman, 1965; French, Israel, & As, 1960; Latham & Yukl, 1975, 1976; Lawrence & Smith, 1955; Morse & Reimer, 1956). Survey field studies asked subordinates to indicate how much involvement they had in decisions, or to rate the leader's general use of participative decision procedures, and the effects of participation were assessed by relating it to subordinate satisfaction with the leader, subordinate task commitment, subordinate performance, or ratings of leader effectiveness by higher management (e.g., Kim & Yukl, 1995; Likert, 1967; Yukl & Van Fleet, 1982).

Example of an Experimental Field Study

Bragg and Andrews (1973) conducted a quasi-experimental study in a hospital laundry department. The foreman of the laundry department typically made decisions in an autocratic manner, and he was persuaded by the chief administrator to try a participative approach. The 32 workers in the laundry department were told that the purpose of the group meetings was to make their jobs more interesting, not to increase productivity, which was already high. The workers and union were told that the participation program would be discontinued if they found it unsatisfactory. Over the next 18 months, meetings were held whenever the workers wanted to discuss specific proposals about hours of work, working procedures, working conditions, minor equipment modifications, and safety matters. In addition to these group meetings, the foreman consulted regularly with individuals and smaller groups of workers to discuss problems and new ideas.

Worker attitudes were measured at two-month intervals for 14 months with a questionnaire. The attitude data showed some initial doubts about the participation program, after which workers became increasingly more favorable toward it. Productivity during the first 18 months of the program increased 42 percent over that for the department during the prior year, whereas for similar departments in two other hospitals (the comparison groups), productivity declined slightly during the same period of time. Attendance in the department, which was high initially, became even better after the participation program was introduced, whereas for other nonmedical departments in the same hospital (the comparison groups), it became worse. The results were statistically significant and showed that the participation program was highly successful.

After the program had been in effect for three years, neither the workers nor the supervisor had any desire to return to the old autocratic style of management. The success of the program encouraged the introduction of participation in the medical records section, where it resulted in the elimination of grievances and a sharp reduction in turnover. However, an attempt to introduce a participation program in the nursing group was much less successful, due primarily to lack of support by the head nurse and resistance by administrative medical personnel.

Findings in Participation Research

Findings in the quantitative research on the effects of participative leadership are summarized in several literature reviews and meta-analyses (Cotton et al., 1988; Leana, Locke, & Schweiger, 1990; Miller & Monge, 1986; Sagie & Koslowsky, 2000; Spector, 1986; Wagner & Gooding, 1987). All the reviewers noted the lack of consistent strong results in the research.

Survey studies with all data from the same respondents (the subordinates) usually found positive effects of participation, whereas survey studies with independent measures of outcomes had weaker and less consistent results. No effort was made in most survey studies to identify the particular mix of decision procedures that were used or to determine whether these procedures were appropriate for the types of decisions being made. In effect, the studies tested only the general hypothesis that more is better when it comes to participation.

Results from the laboratory experiments did not support the effectiveness of participative leadership. In contrast, most field experiments and quasi-experimental studies showed positive results, although the results are sometimes difficult to interpret. Most of the studies involved a participation program introduced by the organization rather than participative behavior by an individual manager, and participation was usually combined with other types of interventions, such as more supportive behavior by the leader, better training of subordinates, use of goal setting, or better procedures for planning and problem solving, making it difficult to determine which consequences were due to participation.

Most descriptive case studies support the benefits of participative leadership (Bradford & Cohen, 1984; Kanter, 1983; Kouzes & Posner, 1987; Peters & Austin, 1985; Peters

& Waterman, 1982). This research found that effective managers used a substantial amount of consultation and delegation to empower subordinates and give them a sense of ownership for activities and decisions.

Overall, the results from research on the effects of participative are not sufficiently strong and consistent to draw any firm conclusions. Participative leadership sometimes results in higher satisfaction, effort, and performance, and at other times it does not. The lack of consistent results about the effectiveness of participative leadership probably reflects the fact that each type of participative decision procedure is effective in some situations but not in others. Few studies incorporated situational variables in a systematic manner or investigated whether different procedures are more effective for different types of decisions. This question is the subject of a contingency theory developed by Vroom and Yetton (1973).

Normative Decision Model

The importance of using decision procedures that are appropriate for the situation has been recognized for some time. Building on earlier approaches, Vroom and Yetton (1973) proposed a model to identify the situations that determine whether a specific type of decision procedure will be effective. This contingency theory was called the *normative decision model*.

Vroom and Yetton identified five decision procedures for decisions involving multiple subordinates, including two varieties of autocratic decision (A-I and A-II), two varieties of consultation (C-I and C-II), and one variety of joint decision making by the leader and subordinates as a group (G-II). The procedures are defined in Table 1. The decision procedure used

TABLE 1	Decision Procedures in Normative Decision Model
A-I	You solve the problem or make the decision yourself, using information available to you at the time.
A-II	You obtain the necessary information from your subordinates and then decide the solution to the problem yourself. You may or may not tell your subordinates what the problem is in getting the information from them. The role played by your subordinates in making the decision is clearly one of providing necessary information to you, rather than generating or evaluating alternative solutions.
C-I	You share the problem with the relevant subordinates individually, getting their ideas and suggestions, without bringing them together as a group. Then you make the decision, which may or may not reflect your subordinates' influence.
C-II	You share the problem with your subordinates as a group, obtaining their collective ideas and suggestions. Then you make the decision, which may or may not reflect your subordinates' influence.
G-II	You share the problem with your subordinates as a group. Together you generate and evaluate alternatives and attempt to reach agreement (consensus) on a solution. Your role is much like that of chairperson. You do not try to influence the group to adopt your preferred solution, and you are willing to accept and implement any solution that has the support of the entire group.

Based on Vroom and Yetton (1973, p. 13).

by a leader affects the quality of a decision and decision acceptance by the people who are responsible for implementing the decision. These two mediating variables jointly determine how the decision will affect the performance of the leader's team or work unit.

Decision Acceptance and Quality

Decision acceptance is the degree of commitment to implement a decision effectively. Acceptance is important whenever a decision must be implemented by subordinates or has implications for their work motivation. In some cases, subordinates are highly motivated to implement a decision made by the leader because it is clearly beneficial to them or because the leader uses influence tactics to gain their commitment to the decision. However, subordinates may not accept an autocratic decision for other reasons. For example, subordinates may resent not being consulted, they may not understand the reasons for the decision, and they may see it as detrimental to their interests. A basic assumption of the model is that participation increases decision acceptance if it is not already high, and the more influence subordinates have in making a decision, the more they will be motivated to implement it successfully. Thus, decision acceptance is likely to be greater for joint decision making than for consultation, and for consultation than for an autocratic decision.

Decision quality refers to the objective aspects of the decision that affect group performance aside from any effects mediated by decision acceptance. The quality of a decision is high when the best alternative is selected. For example, an efficient work procedure is selected instead of less efficient alternatives, or a challenging performance goal is set instead of an easy goal. Decision quality is important when there is a great deal of variability among alternatives and the decision has important consequences for group performance. If the available alternatives are approximately equal in consequences, or if the decision has no important consequences for group performance, then decision quality is not important. Examples of task decisions that are usually important include determination of goals and priorities, assignment of tasks to subordinates who differ in skills, determination of work procedures for complex tasks, and determination of ways to solve technical problems.

Situational Variables

The effect of the decision procedures on decision quality and acceptance depends on various aspects of the situation, and a procedure that is effective in some situations may be ineffective in other situations. The effectiveness of a decision procedure depends on several aspects of the decision situation, including the importance and complexity of the decision, the distribution of relevant information, subordinate attitudes regarding the decision, and leader dependence on subordinates to implement the decision. The causal relationships among the variables are shown in Figure 3.

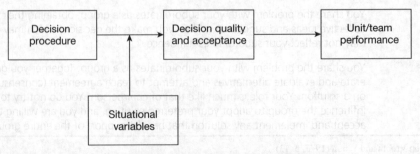

FIGURE 3 Causal Relationships in the Normative Decision Model

The effect of participation on decision quality depends on the distribution of relevant information and problem-solving expertise between leader and subordinates. The model assumes that participation will result in better decisions if subordinates possess relevant information and are willing to cooperate with the leader in making a good decision. Cooperation depends on the extent to which subordinates share the leader's task objectives and have a relationship of mutual trust with the leader. The model assumes that consultation and joint decision making are equally likely to facilitate decision quality when subordinates share the leader's objectives. However, when subordinates have incompatible objectives, consultation usually results in higher-quality decisions than joint decision making, because the leader retains control over the final choice.

Decision Rules

The model provides a set of rules for identifying any decision procedure that is not appropriate in a given situation because decision quality and/or acceptance would be jeopardized by using that procedure (see Table 2). The rules are based on the assumptions discussed earlier about the consequences of different decision procedures under different conditions. For some decision situations, the model prescribes more than one feasible decision procedure. Any decision procedure not excluded in a decision rule can be used for that situation.

TABLE 2	Decision Rules in the Normative Decision Model

1. When the decision is important and subordinates possess relevant information lacked by the leader, an autocratic decision (A-I, A-II) is not appropriate because an important decision would be made without all of the relevant, available information.

2. When decision quality is important and subordinates do not share the leader's concern for task goals, a group decision (G-II) is not appropriate because these procedures would give too much influence over an important decision to uncooperative or even hostile people.

3. When decision quality is important, the decision problem is unstructured, and the leader does not possess the necessary information and expertise to make a good decision, the decision should be made by interaction among the people who have the relevant information (C-II, G-II).

4. When decision acceptance is important and subordinates are unlikely to accept an autocratic decision, an autocratic decision (A-I, A-II) is not appropriate because the decision may not be implemented effectively.

5. When decision acceptance is important and subordinates are likely to disagree among themselves about the best solution to an important problem, autocratic procedures (A-I, A-II) and individual consultation (C-I) are not appropriate because they do not provide the opportunity to resolve differences through discussion and negotiation among subordinates and between the subordinates and the leader.

6. When decision quality is not important but acceptance is important and unlikely to result from an autocratic decision, the only appropriate procedure is a group decision (G-II), because acceptance is maximized without risking quality.

7. When decision acceptance is important and not likely to result from an autocratic decision, and subordinates share the leader's task objectives, subordinates should be given equal partnership in the decision process (G-II), because acceptance is maximized without risking quality.

Based on Vroom and Yetton (1973).

Vroom and Yetton (1973) developed decision process flowcharts to simplify the application of the rules and assist managers in identifying the feasible set of decision procedures for each situation. When more than one decision procedure remains in the "feasible set," then other criteria can be used to determine which decision procedure to use. Both time pressure and subordinate development are included in the extended model by Vroom and Jago (1978).

One limitation of the normative decision model is its complexity, and the extended model is even more complex than the original one. A simplified model that is easier for managers to use was proposed by Yukl (1990), and it is shown in Table 3. This simplified model indicates which of three decision procedures (autocratic, consultation, and joint decision) is optimal when the priorities are (1) protect decision quality, (2) gain decision acceptance, and (3) save time.

Summary

The normative decision model is probably the best supported of the contingency theories of effective leadership. It focuses on specific aspects of behavior, it includes meaningful intervening variables, and it identifies important aspects of the situation moderating the relationship between behavior and outcomes. However, the model deals with only a small part of leadership, and the complexity of the model makes it difficult for leaders to apply.

Guidelines for Participative Leadership

Building on the participation research and the normative decision model, some tentative guidelines are proposed for using participative leadership. Guidelines for

TABLE 3	Simplified Version of the Normative Decision Model	
	Subordinate Acceptance of Decision	
Decision Quality	Not Important or Assured with Autocratic Decision	Important and Not Assured with Autocratic Decision
Not important	AUTOCRATIC	GROUP
Important, but the leader has sufficient information; members share the leader's goals	AUTOCRATIC	GROUP
Important, but the leader has sufficient information; members do not share the leader's goals	AUTOCRATIC	CONSULTATION
Important and the leader lacks essential information; members share the leader's goals	CONSULTATION	GROUP
Important and the leader lacks essential information; members don't share the leader's goals	CONSULTATION	CONSULTATION

Based on Yukl (1990).

diagnosing the situation are presented first, followed by some guidelines for encouraging participation (see Table 4).

Diagnosing Decision Situations

The following sequence is a relatively easy way to determine whether a participative procedure is feasible and appropriate for a particular decision situation.

- **Evaluate how important the decision is.**

Decision quality is likely to be important if the decision has important consequences for the manager's work unit or the overall organization and if some of the alternatives are much better than others. Decision quality is also more important when the manager's position has high exposure (i.e., mistakes are very visible and will reflect poorly on the manager).

- **Identify people with relevant knowledge or expertise.**

Participative decision procedures are appropriate when a manager lacks relevant information possessed by others such as subordinates, peers, or outsiders. This situation is likely when the decision problem is complex and the best way to resolve the problem is not evident from the data or from the manager's prior experience with similar problems. A decision is more complex when it involves many possible alternatives, the outcomes of each alternative are difficult to predict, and the alternatives involve trade-offs among several important criteria. For complex decisions, it is essential to identify people who have relevant knowledge and expertise, and a good network of contacts is invaluable for identifying such people.

- **Evaluate likely cooperation by participants.**

Participation is unlikely to be successful unless the prospective participants are willing to cooperate in finding a good solution to the decision problem. Cooperation is more likely when the decision is important to followers and they perceive that they will actually have some influence over the final decision. If people perceive that a leader is trying to manipulate them, then consultation is unlikely to increase either decision quality or decision acceptance.

TABLE 4	Guidelines for Participative Leadership

How to Diagnose Decision Situations:

- Evaluate how important the decision is.
- Identify people with relevant knowledge or expertise
- Evaluate likely cooperation by participants.
- Evaluate likely acceptance without participation.
- Evaluate whether it is feasible to hold a meeting.

How to Encourage Participation:

- Encourage people to express their concerns.
- Describe a proposal as tentative.
- Record ideas and suggestions.
- Look for ways to build on ideas and suggestions.
- Be tactful in expressing concerns about a suggestion
- Listen to dissenting views without getting defensive.
- Try to utilize suggestions and deal with concerns.
- Show appreciation for suggestions.

Cooperation is also unlikely if potential participants have task objectives that are incompatible with those of the manager. When there is doubt about the motives of potential participants, it is advisable to consult with a few of them individually to determine whether a group meeting would be productive. It is unwise to hold a meeting with a hostile group of people who want to make decisions that are contrary to the interests of the manager. When people with relevant information have different objectives, then some consultation may be useful to diagnose the cause of a problem and identify promising alternatives, but the final choice of an alternative must remain with the manager.

Another reason for lack of cooperation is that the potential participants simply do not want to become involved in making decisions they view as the manager's responsibility. The opportunity to participate may be rejected by the followers who are already overloaded with work, especially when the decisions do not affect them in any important way. Just as many people decline to vote in local elections, not everyone will be enthusiastic about the opportunity to participate in making organizational decisions.

- **Evaluate likely acceptance without participation.**

A time-consuming participative procedure is not necessary if the manager has the knowledge to make a good decision and it is likely to be accepted by subordinates or others who must implement it or who will be affected by it. An autocratic decision is more likely to be accepted if the manager has considerable position and personal power over group members or has the persuasive skills to "sell" the decision successfully. Acceptance of an autocratic decision is also likely if the decision is to do something people already want to do, or the decision appears to be a reasonable response to a crisis situation. Finally, acceptance of autocratic decisions is more likely when people have cultural values that emphasize obedience to authority figures.

- **Evaluate whether it is feasible to hold a meeting.**

Consulting with people separately or holding a group meeting usually requires more time than making an autocratic decision and telling people to implement it. It is especially difficult to hold a meeting if the number of people who need to be involved is large and they are widely dispersed. In many crisis situations, time is not available either for extensive consultation with individuals or for a lengthy group meeting to decide how to react to the crisis. In this situation, a leader who knows what to do and takes charge in a decisive way is likely to be more effective than one who is very participative (e.g., Yun, Samer, & Sims, 2005). Nevertheless, even in a crisis situation, a leader should remain responsive to suggestions made by knowledgeable subordinates. Under the stress of a crisis, a leader is unlikely to notice all of the problems that require attention or to think of all the actions that need to be taken.

Encouraging Participation

Consultation will not be effective unless people are actively involved in generating ideas, making suggestions, stating their preferences, and expressing their concerns. Some guidelines for encouraging more participation include the following.

- **Encourage people to express their concerns.**

Before making changes that will affect people in significant ways, it is useful and considerate to consult with them. This guideline applies to peers and outsiders as well as subordinates. One form of consultation that is often appropriate is to hold special meetings with people who will be affected by a change to identify their concerns and deal with them.

- **Describe a proposal as tentative.**

More participation is likely if you present a proposal as tentative and encourage people to improve it, rather than asking people to react to a plan that appears complete. In the latter case, people will be more inhibited about expressing concerns that appear to be criticism of the plan.

- **Record ideas and suggestions.**

When someone makes a suggestion, it is helpful to acknowledge the idea and show that it is not being ignored. One approach is to list ideas on a flipchart, blackboard, or computer display when they are expressed. In an informal meeting, if there is no easy way to display ideas, make notes to avoid forgetting a person's ideas and suggestions.

- **Look for ways to build on ideas and suggestions.**

Most people quickly focus on the weaknesses of an idea or suggestion made by someone else without giving enough consideration to its strengths. It is helpful to make a conscious effort to find positive aspects of a suggestion and mention them before mentioning negative aspects. Many times an initial idea is incomplete, but it can be turned into a much better idea with a little conscious effort. Thus, rather than automatically rejecting a suggestion with obvious weaknesses, it is useful to discuss how the weaknesses could be overcome and to consider other ideas that build on the initial one.

- **Be tactful in expressing concerns about a suggestion.**

If you have concerns about a suggestion, express them tactfully to avoid threatening the self-esteem of the person who made the suggestion and discouraging future suggestions. Some negative examples include the following:

> You aren't serious about that?
> That has been tried before and it doesn't work.

Concerns should be expressed in a way that indicates qualified interest rather than outright rejection. It is usually possible to express concerns in the form of a question using the terms *we* and *us* to emphasize a shared effort, as shown in the following example:

> Your suggestion is a promising one, but I am concerned about the cost. Is there any way
> we could do it without exceeding our budget?

- **Listen to dissenting views without getting defensive.**

In order to encourage people to express concerns and criticisms of your plans and proposals, it is essential to listen carefully without getting defensive or angry. Use restatement of a person's concerns in your own words to verify that you understand them and to show you are paying attention. Avoid making excuses, and instead try to consider objectively whether revisions are needed.

- **Try to utilize suggestions and deal with concerns.**

People will stop making suggestions if you dismiss them without serious consideration or simply ignore them in making a final decision. It is important to make a serious effort to utilize suggestions and deal with concerns expressed by people with whom you have consulted. The potential benefits from participation will not occur if people perceive that a request for suggestions was done just to manipulate them.

- **Show appreciation for suggestions.**

People will be more likely to cooperate in making decisions and solving problems if they receive appropriate credit for their helpful suggestions and ideas. Compliment someone for good ideas and insights. It is important to thank people and show appreciation for helpful suggestions. Explain how an idea or suggestion was used in the final decision or plan. Explain how the proposal or plan was modified to incorporate a person's suggestion or respond to his or her concerns. If a suggestion is not used, thank the contributor and explain why it was not feasible to use the suggestion.

Limitations of Participative Decision-Making

> *"Let us go to the swimming pool," Rajesh, the group representative of an MBA class of 45 students, announced to the entire batch.*
>
> *Their class had an exhaustively long day. After four long lectures, two quizzes, and one presentation, they were left with no energy. But they had another long day tomorrow, which again consisted of several stressful events. Hence, they needed an energizer and refreshments. "Oh, fantastic!" exclaimed Sunita. "Indeed, it is great weather for swimming. Let's also grab some snacks on the way. What shall we get?"*
>
> *Ramit suggested, "We can grab some chips, cold drinks, and some sandwiches." What do you say?"*
>
> *"Great, but should we have chips and cold drinks? Should we not protect our throats from infection before tomorrow's presentations? I hope you noticed that microphones did not function properly today and we practically had to shout during today's presentation," said Sunita.*
>
> *Arjun said, "In fact, instead of snacks, we can go out for dinner. I hear this new restaurant by the river is serving amazing dishes."*
>
> *Sunita agreed, "That's great. We will anyway need to go to the market to buy stationary for tomorrow's presentation."*
>
> *"Dinner sounds good, but why not pizza?" asked Prakash. "I have some discount coupons. This way, we will save money and time. But we don't have the stationary; perhaps Rajesh can go to the market to buy it."*
>
> *Rajesh agreed to do so. However, on his way to buy the stationary, he wondered what had happened to their plans to refresh and energize. Weren't they supposed to go swimming?*

Undoubtedly, participative decision-making (PDM) has several advantages; however, it sometimes poses unique challenges for leaders. For example, Lam, Chen, and Schaubroeck, (2002); and Sagie and Aycan (2003) found that the relationship between PDM and group performance is contingent upon the culture of the group. Here are some disadvantages or limitations of PDM:

- **Time Consuming and Stressful:** This may be one of the most significant limitations of PDM. With an increase in team size and diversity, arriving at a conclusion and decision is often stressful and time consuming. Inputs and ideas start pouring in from all the members, sometimes with great variations. Collating, combining, and articulating all inputs might be extremely exhaustive.

- **Security Issues:** For some issues that require privacy and confidentiality, involving multiple members in decision-making might lead to compromises.

- **Volunteer Silence:** Some members might choose not to participate. Compelling them may lead to suboptimal decisions.

- **Group Thinking:** Groupthink is a psychological phenomenon. This behavior is observed in groups where the participants' desire for harmony or conformity in the group often results in an irrational or dysfunctional decision-making outcome. Group members often try to minimize conflict and reach a consensus decision. They actively suppress any dissenting viewpoints and isolate themselves from outside influences, thus surpassing critical evaluation alternative viewpoints.

- **Manipulation:** Managers sometimes use participative decision-making as a politically correct way to implement their own decisions. For example, managers may form a committee of subordinates who are either sycophants or those who have already accepted the decision informally.

- **Complexity of Technology and Organizations:** Organizations and technology are so complicated these days that specialized employees are required for each job. Employees cannot extend beyond a particular limit in participation. Those who can participate in decisions relating to marketing may be less useful when decisions related to finance are to be taken.

Delegation

As noted earlier, delegation involves the assignment of new responsibilities to subordinates and additional authority to carry them out. Although delegation is usually regarded as a variety of participative leadership, it is different in some important ways from the other forms of participative leadership such as consulting and joint decision making. A manager may consult with subordinates, peers, or superiors, but in most cases delegation is appropriate only with subordinates. Delegation has somewhat different situational determinants than consultation (Leana, 1987). For example, a manager who is overloaded with work is likely to use more delegating but less consulting. Delegation often involves the shifting of primary responsibility for a particular type of decision to an individual or group, whereas the other participative procedures do not involve a similar redefinition of roles. With all these differences, it is not surprising that a factor analysis of leader behavior questionnaires usually yields a distinct factor for delegating (Yukl & Fu, 1999).

Varieties of Delegation

The term *delegation* is commonly used to describe a variety of different forms and degrees of power sharing with individual subordinates. Major aspects of delegation include the variety and magnitude of responsibilities, the amount of discretion or range of choice allowed in deciding how to carry out responsibilities, the authority to take action and implement decisions without prior approval, the frequency and nature of reporting requirements, and the flow of performance information (Sherman, 1966; Webber, 1981).

In its most common form, delegation involves assignment of new and different tasks or responsibilities to a subordinate. For example, a person who is responsible for manufacturing something is also given responsibility for inspecting the product and correcting any defects that are found. When new tasks are assigned, the additional authority necessary to accomplish the tasks is usually delegated also. For example, a production worker who is given new responsibility for ordering materials is given the authority (within specified constraints) to sign contracts with suppliers.

Sometimes delegation involves only the specification of additional authority and discretion for the same tasks and assignments already performed by the subordinate. For example, a sales representative is allowed to negotiate sales within a specified range of prices, quantities, and delivery dates, but cannot exceed these limits without prior approval from the sales manager. Delegation is increased by giving the sales representative more latitude in setting prices and delivery dates.

The extent to which a subordinate must check with the boss before taking action is another aspect of delegation. There is little or no delegation for someone who must ask the boss what to do whenever there is a problem or something unusual occurs. There is moderate delegation when the subordinate is allowed to determine what to do but must get approval before implementing decisions. There is substantial delegation when the subordinate is allowed to make important decisions and implement them without getting prior approval. For example, a sales representative who was not allowed to make adjustments for damaged goods and late deliveries without checking first is given permission to resolve these matters in the future without getting prior approval.

Reporting requirements are another aspect of delegation that is subject to considerable variation. The amount of subordinate autonomy is greater when reports are required only infrequently. For example, a department manager must report department performance on a weekly basis rather than on a daily basis. Autonomy is also greater when reports describe only results rather than describing both the results and the procedures used to accomplish them. For example, a training director must report to the vice president for human resources the number of employees who were trained in each subject area and the overall training expenses for the month, but not the types of training methods used, the number of trainers, or the training expenses in different categories.

The flow of performance information involved in monitoring a subordinate's activities is also subject to variation. Subordinate autonomy is greater when detailed information goes directly to the subordinate, who is then allowed to correct any problems. A subordinate is likely to have less autonomy when detailed performance information goes first to the boss and is subsequently passed on to the subordinate. There is an intermediate amount of subordinate autonomy when detailed performance information goes to both parties simultaneously.

Klein et al. (2006) explained the concept of dynamic delegation. Dynamic delegation refers to a shift in active leadership that occurs "when a senior leader takes over strategic direction of the team, assuming a more active and influential role in the team, or, conversely, when a senior leader cedes strategic direction, assuming a more passive role and implicitly or explicitly delegating the active leadership role to a more junior leader." Klein et al. (2006) observed dynamic delegation in medical teams in an emergency trauma center during the treatment of a victim of a car accident. The patient arrived by helicopter and was immediately surrounded by the trauma team. The attending surgeon strolled into the trauma center a few minutes after the patient's arrival. He glanced at the team and the patient, said nothing, grabbed a chair and slouched there, approximately eight feet from the foot of the patient's bed, drinking a soda and making notes in a chart. A few minutes later, when the patient moaned a few times in pain, the attending surgeon put down his soda and notes, got up, strode to the patient's bedside, stood right next to the surgical fellow, queried the fellow for a moment, directed the team to perform specific tests and procedures, and then returned to his chair, soda, and notes, apparently confident of the team's ability to treat the patient's injuries without his further involvement. In this incident, which was typical of many of the patient-care episodes, researchers have observed active leadership getting shifted, in a matter of minutes, from the fellow (when the attending surgeon was initially slouched in his chair, drinking a soda) to the attending surgeon (when he stood at the bedside, directing the team), and back to the fellow (when the attending surgeon returned to the chair).

Potential Benefits from Delegation

There are many different reasons for delegating (Leana, 1986; Newman & Warren, 1977; Preston & Zimmerer, 1978; Yukl & Fu, 1999). Table 5 shows the results found in a study that asked managers in several organizations about the importance of various reasons for delegation to a subordinate. Delegation offers a number of potential advantages if carried out in an appropriate manner by a manager. One potential advantage is the improvement of decision quality. Delegation is likely to improve decision quality if a subordinate has more expertise in how to do the task than the manager. Delegation is also likely to improve decision quality when the subordinate's job requires quick responses to a changing situation and the lines of communication do not permit the manager to monitor the situation closely and make rapid adjustments. A subordinate who is closer to the problem than the manager and has more relevant information can make quicker and better decisions about how to resolve the problem. The result may be better customer service and reduced administrative costs. However, delegation is not likely to improve decision quality if the subordinate lacks the skills to make good decisions, fails to understand what is expected, or has goals incompatible with those of the manager.

Another potential advantage of delegation is greater subordinate commitment to implement decisions effectively. The commitment results from identification with the decision and a desire to make it successful. However, commitment is unlikely to improve if a subordinate views delegation as a manipulative tactic by the manager, considers the task impossible to do, or believes the newly delegated responsibilities are an unfair increase in workload.

Delegation of additional responsibilities and authority can make a subordinate's job more interesting, challenging, and meaningful. Enriched jobs are sometimes necessary to attract and retain competent employees, especially when the organization has limited opportunities for advancement to higher-level positions. Giving junior managers more responsibility and authority, with a commensurate increase in salary, reduces the likelihood that they will be lured away to other companies in times of stiff competition for managerial talent. However, delegation will only increase the satisfaction of a subordinate who desires more responsibility, has the skills necessary to handle new responsibilities, and is able to experience some success in accomplishing a challenging task. Delegation will decrease job

TABLE 5	Percent of Managers Who Rated a Reason for Delegating As Moderately or Very Important
Develop subordinate skills and confidence	97%
Enable subordinates to deal with problems quickly	91%
Improve decisions by moving them close to the action	89%
Increase subordinate commitment to a task	89%
Make the job more interesting for subordinates	78%
Reduce your workload to manage time better	68%
Satisfy superiors who want you to delegate more	24%
Get rid of tedious tasks you don't want to do	23%

Adapted from Yukl and Fu (1999).

satisfaction if the subordinate is constantly frustrated due to a lack of sufficient authority and resources to carry out new responsibilities, or to a lack of ability to do the work.

Delegation is an important form of time management for a manager who is overloaded with responsibilities. By delegating less important duties and functions to subordinates, a manager frees additional time for more important responsibilities. Even when a manager could do the delegated tasks better than subordinates, it is a more efficient use of the manager's time to concentrate on those functions that will have the greatest influence on the performance of the manager's organizational unit. Without delegation, a manager is not likely to have sufficient discretionary time to do some complex tasks that are important but not urgent.

Delegation can be an effective method of management development. Organizations need to develop managerial talent to fill vacant positions at higher levels of authority. Delegation is a way to facilitate development of the skills necessary to perform key responsibilities in a higher position. When delegation is used for developmental purposes, however, it is usually necessary for the manager to do more monitoring and coaching. Thus, when used for this purpose, delegation may not reduce a manager's workload.

Reasons for Lack of Delegation

With all of these potential advantages from delegation, it would seem as if it should occur whenever appropriate. However, there are several reasons some managers fail to delegate as much as they should (Leana, 1986; Newman & Warren, 1977; Preston & Zimmerer, 1978; Yukl & Fu, 1999). Results from a study that asked managers in several companies about the importance of different reasons for not delegating are shown in Table 6.

Some aspects of a manager's personality are associated with failure to delegate, including a strong need for power, insecurity, a high need for achievement, and difficulty in forming relationships. Some managers enjoy the exercise of power over subordinates and the feeling of being in charge. Delegation would require sharing power with subordinates and reducing their dependence.

Delegation is never absolute, because a manager continues to be responsible for the work activities of subordinates. To avoid the risk of mistakes, a manager who is insecure may

TABLE 6	Percentage of Managers Who Rated a Reason for Not Delegating As Moderately or Very Important	
Keep decisions involving confidential information		87%
Keep tasks and decisions that are very important		76%
Keep tasks and decisions central to your role		73%
Keep tasks for which mistakes are highly visible		58%
Keep tasks you can do better than subordinates		51%
Keep tasks that are difficult to explain to subordinates		43%
Keep tasks that are difficult to monitor		39%
Keep tasks that are interesting and enjoyable		24%

Adapted from Yukl and Fu (1999).

delegate sensitive tasks only to a few trusted subordinates, or not at all. Furthermore, allowing a subordinate to demonstrate competence in performing managerial responsibilities may create a competitor for the manager's job.

Managers with a high need for achievement often prefer to retain important, challenging tasks rather than delegating them to subordinates (Miller & Toulouse, 1986). Managers who take pride in solving important problems may be reluctant to relinquish that activity or admit others could do it as effectively. Reluctance to delegate may be supported by biases in perception of one's own performance. One experiment found that managers rated quality of performance higher when they were directly involved in supervising a task, even though actual quality was the same as for a delegated task (Pfeffer, Cialdini, Hanna, & Knopoff, 1998).

Failure to delegate is also related to characteristics of the subordinates, such as task expertise and shared objectives. Managers are reluctant to delegate significant responsibilities to subordinates who lack the necessary expertise (Ashour & England, 1972; Leana, 1986; Yukl & Fu, 1999). Even if a subordinate has the expertise, delegation of significant responsibility is unlikely if the person seems indifferent about task objectives (McGregor, 1960). This perception may be inaccurate initially, but distrust by the manager may eventually make it a self-fulfilling prophecy (Argyris, 1964). Sometimes distrust of subordinates is determined more by personality problems in the manager than by the actual characteristics of the subordinates (Johnston, 2000).

The reader should not assume that only insecure, power hungry managers are reluctant to delegate. Even managers who become successful at empowering people often say it was personally difficult, as the following example shows (O'Toole, 1995).

> Ben Cohen, the cofounder of Ben and Jerry's (Ice Cream), who believes strongly in empowerment. When describing how difficult it was, he explained how it was not natural to ask questions of employees when he already knew the answer, to listen patiently when they said something that wasn't right, or to ask them for ideas when he was eager to express ideas of his own.

The potential for delegation also depends on the nature of the work and the amount of authority possessed by the leader. A lack of leader authority to make decisions or change how the work is done limits the potential for delegation. Another constraint is when subordinates have highly interdependent jobs. Even if people have shared objectives, they may disagree about priorities and the best way to accomplish the objectives. In this situation empowering individuals to act on their own increases the danger they will be working at cross-purposes. To achieve coordination and avoid destructive conflicts, it will be necessary to devote more time to meetings to plan joint activities and solve operational problems. In this type of situation, it is more feasible to use consultation or to delegate authority for a task to a team rather than to individual subordinates.

Research on Consequences of Delegation

Much less empirical research is available on leader delegation than on leader consultation with individuals or a group. Studies on the amount of delegation used by supervisors find that it is correlated with subordinate performance (e.g., Bauer & Green, 1996; Leana, 1986; Schriesheim, Neider, & Scandura, 1998). However, the direction of causality is difficult to determine in survey research. It is not clear whether delegation improves performance, if improved performance results in more delegation, or if both effects are occurring simultaneously. Moreover, descriptive studies of leaders make it evident that delegation can harm performance if used when it is not appropriate for the situation. More longitudinal, experimental research is needed to investigate direction of causality and the facilitating conditions (e.g., mutual trust, shared objectives, leader's self-confidence, and the subordinate's desire for more responsibility).

In a study of five Turkish companies, Pellegrini and Scandura (2006) found that the effectiveness of delegation is subject to national cultures. According to them, subordinates in high power distance cultures may expect the leader to take charge and give orders, rather than delegate decision-making authority to the subordinates. Employees in high uncertainty avoidance national cultures may prefer to be told exactly what to do instead of the ambiguity of being delegated a challenging task. Similarly, Chin and Aryee (2007) in a study of employees in a Chinese manufacturing setup, found that the positive influence of delegation is contingent upon the individual cultural value orientation of traditionality (commitment to, respect for, and acceptance of the customs and norms of a traditional society). Delegation positively enhanced self-concept for individuals who were low in traditionality but did not enhance self-concept for high traditionality individuals. Their finding suggests that employees do not uniformly interpret the signal that delegation conveys and pick up cues depending upon their cultural values.

Guidelines for Delegating

This section of the chapter provides some tentative guidelines for effective use of delegation by managers. Although research on delegation is still very limited, there is considerable agreement in the practitioner literature about when and how to use delegation effectively. Guidelines for what to delegate are presented here first, followed by guidelines on how to delegate.

What to Delegate

The selection of tasks to delegate depends in part on the purpose of the delegation. Some guidelines on what to delegate are the following (see Table 7).

- **Delegate tasks that can be done better by a subordinate.**

Some responsibilities can be done better by a subordinate than by a manager. Better performance by a subordinate is likely when the person has more expertise, when the person is closer to the problem and can obtain more timely information about it, or because the manager simply does not have the time necessary to do the task properly. Such responsibilities are usually good candidates for delegation, regardless of the purpose.

- **Delegate tasks that are urgent but not high priority.**

When the purpose is to reduce excessive workload, the best tasks for delegation are ones that are urgent but not high priority. These tasks must get done quickly, but the manager does not have time to do all of them. Some of the tasks may be things that a subordinate

TABLE 7	Guidelines for What to Delegate

- Tasks that can be done better by a subordinate.
- Tasks that are urgent but not high priority.
- Tasks relevant to a subordinate's career.
- Tasks of appropriate difficulty.
- Both pleasant and unpleasant tasks.
- Tasks not central to the manager's role.

cannot do as well as the manager, but it is better for them to be done by a subordinate than not at all. Delegation of these tasks frees more time for a manager to do higher priority tasks.

- **Delegate tasks relevant to a subordinate's career.**

If the purpose of delegation is to develop subordinate skills, the responsibilities must be ones relevant to the subordinate's career objectives. Developmental delegation is likely to include special projects that allow a subordinate the opportunity to struggle with a challenging task and exercise initiative and problem solving. Preparation of a subordinate to take over the manager's job or to advance to a similar job in another unit requires delegating some important managerial responsibilities, including the ones that the subordinate initially may not do as well as the manager. Some of these delegated tasks may be irrelevant to the subordinate's current job and, in fact, may take time away from the subordinate's regular work.

- **Delegate tasks of appropriate difficulty.**

Delegated tasks should be challenging for a subordinate, but not so difficult as to offer little hope of doing them successfully. The tasks should be difficult enough so that some mistakes are likely to occur, because mistakes are an integral part of the learning experience. However, the task should not be so difficult and important that mistakes will undermine the subordinate's self-confidence and ruin his or her reputation. Delegation for developmental purposes should be carried out gradually. As the subordinate learns how to handle the initial responsibilities, additional responsibilities can be delegated.

- **Delegate both pleasant and unpleasant tasks.**

Some managers keep all of the pleasant tasks for themselves and delegate only tedious, boring tasks to subordinates. Such tasks will not enrich subordinate jobs and are likely to reduce rather than increase subordinate job satisfaction. On the other hand, some managers with a martyr complex delegate only pleasant tasks and retain for themselves all of the disagreeable ones. This approach leaves a gap in the development of subordinates and is likely to make the manager's job more stressful than it should be. Delegation should include both pleasant and unpleasant tasks. The unpleasant tasks should be shared by subordinates or rotated among them to avoid perceptions of favoritism and inequity in work assignments.

- **Delegate tasks not central to the manager's role.**

Tasks that are symbolically important and central to a manager's role should not be delegated. These responsibilities include such things as setting objectives and priorities for the work unit, allocating resources among subordinates, evaluating the performance of subordinates, making personnel decisions about pay increases and promotions for subordinates, directing the group's response to a crisis, and various figurehead activities for which an appearance by the manager is expected (Mintzberg, 1973). When it is necessary to develop subordinate skills related to these responsibilities, another form of participation such as consultation and group decisions can be used rather than delegation. For example, strategic planning may be carried out in planning meetings in which subordinates provide ideas and suggestions, but the responsibility for strategic decisions is not delegated to individual subordinates.

How to Delegate

The success of delegation depends as much on how it is carried out as on what is delegated. The following guidelines are designed to minimize problems and avoid common pitfalls related to assignment of tasks and delegation of authority (see Table 8). The first

TABLE 8	Guidelines for How to Delegate

- Specify responsibilities clearly.
- Provide adequate authority and specify limits of discretion.
- Specify reporting requirements.
- Ensure subordinate acceptance of responsibilities.
- Inform others who need to know.
- Monitor progress in appropriate ways.
- Arrange for the subordinate to receive necessary information
- Provide support and assistance, but avoid reverse delegation.
- Make mistakes a learning experience.

four guidelines are for the initial meeting held to delegate responsibilities to a subordinate, and the last five guidelines describe steps the manager should take afterward to ensure that delegation will be successful.

- **Specify responsibilities clearly.**

When delegating, it is essential to make sure the subordinate understands the new responsibilities. Explain the results expected for a delegated task or assignment, clarify objectives and priorities, and inform the person about any deadlines that must be met. Check for comprehension by asking the subordinate to restate your expectations, or by questioning the subordinate about important aspects of the task. In the case of an inexperienced subordinate, you may want to ask the person to prepare action plans for you to review before the plans are implemented.

- **Provide adequate authority and specify limits of discretion.**

Unless adequate resources are provided, the subordinate is unlikely to be successful in carrying out a delegated task. When assigning new responsibilities, determine the appropriate amount of authority needed by the subordinate to carry them out. Specify clearly the subordinate's scope of authority and limits of discretion. Authority includes funds that can be committed, resources that can be used, decisions that can be made without prior approval, and agreements that can be negotiated directly with outsiders or other units in the organization.

- **Specify reporting requirements.**

It is important for a subordinate to understand the types of information that must be reported, how often reports are expected, and the manner in which progress will be monitored (e.g., written reports, progress review meetings, presentations in department meetings, and formal performance evaluations). The frequency and timing of progress reviews will depend on the nature of the task and the competence of the subordinate. More frequent checking is appropriate for critical tasks with high exposure and high cost of mistakes and for subordinates who lack experience and confidence. As a subordinate demonstrates the ability to perform delegated tasks, the frequency of reporting can be reduced. Progress reports should emphasize results, but the means for accomplishing delegated tasks should not be ignored entirely. It is important to ensure use of procedures that are legal, ethical, and consistent with organizational policy.

- **Ensure subordinate acceptance of responsibilities.**

If delegation is to be successful, the subordinate must accept the new assignments and be committed to carrying them out. In some cases, acceptance is not a problem, because the assignments are interesting and important for the subordinate's career advancement. However, a subordinate may be reluctant to admit doubts and concerns about new assignments. It is useful to allow the subordinate to participate in determining what tasks will be assigned and how much authority will be delegated. With developmental delegation, it is useful to discuss how the delegated tasks are relevant to the person's career advancement. If the subordinate lacks self-confidence, it is helpful to express confidence in the person's ability to do a good job.

- **Inform others who need to know.**

People who are affected by the delegation and people whose cooperation and assistance are necessary for the subordinate to do the delegated tasks should be informed about the subordinate's new responsibilities and authority. Unless informed about the delegation by you, these people may doubt the subordinate's authority and ignore his or her requests and directions. The people who need to be informed may include other subordinates, subordinates of your subordinate, peers in other units, your boss, and outsiders such as clients and suppliers.

- **Monitor progress in appropriate ways.**

With delegated tasks, as with all tasks, it is important to monitor progress and provide feedback to the subordinate. It is difficult to achieve an optimal balance between control and delegation, and progress review meetings enable a manager to monitor subordinate progress without having to supervise too closely on a day-to-day basis. The subordinate is given considerable latitude to deal with problems without interference, yet is free to ask for advice and assistance whenever it is needed. When authority is delegated, a manager and subordinate should decide on the type of performance measures and progress indicators to collect.

- **Arrange for the subordinate to receive necessary information.**

It is usually best to have all detailed information about the subordinate's performance flow directly to the subordinate, with less detailed summary information coming to the manager at less frequent intervals. However, in the case of developmental delegation with an inexperienced subordinate, detailed information may be collected more frequently to check closely on the progress of the subordinate. In addition to performance information, the subordinate will need various types of technical and general information to carry out the delegated tasks effectively. Keep the subordinate informed about changes that affect his or her plans and schedules. If possible, arrange for relevant technical information to flow directly to the subordinate and help the subordinate establish his or her own sources of essential information.

- **Provide support and assistance, but avoid reverse delegation.**

A manager should provide psychological support to a subordinate who is discouraged or frustrated, and encourage the person to keep going. For newly delegated tasks, it may be necessary to provide more advice and coaching about procedures for doing some aspect of the work. However, it is important to avoid reverse delegation, in which control is reasserted over a task that was previously delegated. When a subordinate asks for help with problems, he or she should be asked to recommend a solution. The manager can help the person evaluate whether the solution is feasible and appropriate.

- **Make mistakes a learning experience.**

It is important to recognize that mistakes are inevitable for delegated tasks. Mistakes and failures should be treated seriously, but the response should not be one of criticism and blame. Instead, the episode should become a learning experience for both parties as they discuss the reason for the mistake and identify ways to avoid similar mistakes in the future. If it becomes obvious that the subordinate does not know how to do some essential aspect of the work, the manager should provide additional instruction and coaching.

Perceived Empowerment

The theory and research reviewed earlier in this chapter examines power sharing and participation from the perspective of leader behavior and decision procedures. The emphasis has been on what is done to allow more influence over work-related decisions and to create conditions that foster initiative and self-determination. Additional insights can be gained by examining follower perceptions, needs, and values.

Nature of Psychological Empowerment

The term *psychological empowerment* describes how the intrinsic motivation and selfefficacy of people are influenced by leadership behavior, job characteristics, organization structure, and their own needs and values. Theories of psychological empowerment attempt to explain when and why efforts to empower people are likely to be successful. Participative practices and *employee involvement programs* do not necessarily reduce feelings of powerlessness or leave people feeling that their work is meaningful and worthwhile (Conger & Kanungo, 1988). For example, allowing people to determine how to do a trivial and demeaning task is unlikely to increase their feelings of self-worth and self-fulfillment. Delegating responsibility for a more significant task will not be empowering if people lack the skills and knowledge required to perform the task successfully and are worried about failure. The opportunity to elect a leader may do little to reduce feelings of powerlessness if the choice is between candidates who are equally unsatisfactory.

The defining elements of psychological empowerment have been suggested by various scholars, but as yet there has been only limited research on this question (e.g., Bowen & Lawler, 1992; Conger & Kanungo, 1988; Kanter, 1983; Spreitzer, 2008; Thomas & Velthouse, 1990). A study by Spreitzer (1995) found support for the proposition that psychological empowerment includes four defining elements: (1) meaning, (2) *self-determination,* (3) *self-efficacy,* and (4) impact. More empowerment will be felt when the content and consequences of the work are consistent with a person's values, the person has the capability to determine how and when the work is done, the person has high confidence about being able to do it effectively, and the person believes it is possible to influence important events and outcomes. The emphasis on these four elements links psychological empowerment to earlier theory and research on work motivation (e.g., Bandura, 1986; Shamir, 1991), job design (e.g., Fried & Ferris, 1987; Hackman & Oldham, 1980), participative leadership (e.g., Sagie & Koslowsky, 2000; Vroom & Jago, 1978), and organizational programs for employee involvement (e.g., Cotton, 1993; Lawler, 1986).

How Leaders Can Increase Empowerment

The theory and research on psychological empowerment makes it evident that participative leadership and delegation are not the only types of leadership behavior that can make people feel empowered. Other types of leadership behavior can directly affect psychological empowerment, and these behaviors may also enhance the effects of participative leadership and delegation (Ahearne, Mathieu & Rapp, 2005; Forrester, 2000; Howard, 1998; Konczak

TABLE 9	Guidelines for Empowering

- Involve people in making decisions that affect them.
- Delegate responsibility and authority for important activities.
- Provide access to relevant information.
- Provide resources needed to carry out responsibilities.
- Change management systems to be consistent with empowerment.
- Remove bureaucratic constraints and unnecessary controls.
- Express confidence and trust in people.
- Provide coaching and advice when requested.
- Encourage and support initiative and problem solving.
- Recognize important contributions and achievements.
- Ensure that rewards are commensurate with responsibilities and contributions.
- Ensure accountability for the ethical use of power.

et al., 2000; Vecchio, Justin & Pearce, 2010; Zhang & Barthol, 2010). For example, the leader can encourage a subordinate to view problems as opportunities, encourage innovative thinking, act supportive when the subordinate is discouraged, provide resources needed to deal with problems in the work, and remove unnecessary bureaucratic restraints. A leader who wants subordinates to be more empowered must also avoid being defensive when subordinates question the leader's proposals and decisions. Ways to empower subordinates are summarized in Table 9.

Empowerment Programs

Efforts to increase employee empowerment often involve organizational programs rather than just an individual leader's actions with direct subordinates. A variety of different empowerment programs have been used, including self-managed teams, democratic structures and processes, and employee ownership of the company (Heller, 2000; Lawler, Mohrman, & Benson, 2001; Yukl & Becker, 2007; Yukl & Lepsinger, 2004). Some of these empowerment programs for organizations are described briefly.

Leader Selection and Assessment

More empowerment is likely when members elect their leaders for limited terms, which is a common practice in voluntary organizations, professional associations, and democratic political units (e.g., city councils, school boards, state legislatures). Most private business organizations have leaders who are appointed rather than elected, but some companies use a hybrid form of selection. The leaders are selected by a council of representatives who were elected by the members (c.f., de Jong & van Witteloostuijn, 2004). For example, in some employee-owned companies, the employees select top management and can vote to replace them if their performance is not satisfactory (Heller, 2000). Regardless of how a leader is selected, the influence of members is greater when they participate actively in assessing leader performance, especially if they are able to remove a leader with unsatisfactory performance.

Democratic Decision Procedures

Empowerment is also increased when the formal procedures for making important decisions give members significant influence over these decisions. In some organizations, the charter specifies that a meeting or referendum must be held to allow members to decide important matters by a majority vote. In large organizations where direct participation is not feasible, an alternate form of empowerment that is sometimes used is to have elected representatives from each major subunit on the governing council, or to allow lower-level members to elect one or more representatives to serve on the board of directors. In many public sector organizations, members also have the right to attend open meetings of the board or council to express opinions about important issues before a decision is made. The election of leaders and the use of policy-making councils or boards with elected members are common in public sector organizations and professional associations, but they are rare in private sector business organizations in the United States.

In some European countries, the board of directors for a company is required by law to include members representing employees, and some organizations have an employee council with elected representatives from different subunits (Heller, 2000). In Germany, for example, the labor union members of the board can vote on important decisions and have a voice in the selection of the CEO. The European Union has adopted guidelines for increasing empowerment with works councils and other structural arrangements and processes.

Shared Leadership Responsibilities

Empowerment is also increased when leadership responsibilities are shared by members of a small organization or team rather than invested in a single leader. One example is the growing use of self-managed teams in business organizations. The most extreme form of shared leadership occurs when all important decisions are made collectively, and leadership responsibilities for daily operations are distributed among the members and rotated frequently. This form of empowerment is most likely to be found in small employee-owned businesses, cooperatives, and voluntary organizations. An example of a "bossless organization" is provided by Vanderslice (1988) in her case study of the Moosewood Restaurant.

> Moosewood is a small, collectively owned organization that has been financially sound for the 15 years it has existed. The restaurant has 18 members, and all of them are involved in making important decisions such as policy changes, selection and dismissal of members, financial issues, wages and benefits, and selection of suppliers. In addition, there are usually 4 to 6 temporary workers who are not involved in decision making but who may be accepted as regular members after a year of apprenticeship. Areas of responsibility are rotated among the members. The time an individual remains responsible for a particular job depends on the logical cycle of the task and the individual's interest in doing it. All jobs are open to any member who wants to learn to do them, and members are encouraged to take a turn at every job. Job rotation spreads expertise and responsibility among collective members rather than lodging it in one or two managers. All jobs pay the same hourly rate, and income from the 15% service charge is shared by all members. Some power differences exist, but they are based on demonstrated expertise and commitment to the organization. Accountability is regulated through internalized values and group pressure. However, confronting a member about inappropriate behavior is still an unresolved problem.

Information Sharing

It is difficult for employees to influence decisions or assess the effectiveness of top executives unless they have access to accurate information about business performance, plans, goals and strategies, and many companies are reluctant to share this information with employees (Lawler, Mohrman, & Ledford, 1998). Open book programs are one way to empower employees through communication and learning. As the name suggests, top management "opens the books" to employees to give them a clear understanding of financial information, such as revenues, profits, and costs. To be successful, this type of program should also provide training that will enable employees to understand the information and use it to improve company performance.

Consequences of Empowerment Programs

Potential benefits from empowerment have been identified by scholars (e.g., Block, 1987; Howard, 1998; Thomas & Velthouse, 1990). The benefits include (1) stronger task commitment, (2) greater initiative in carrying out role responsibilities, (3) greater persistence in the face of obstacles and temporary setbacks, (4) more innovation and learning, and stronger optimism about the eventual success of the work, (5) higher job satisfaction, (6) stronger organizational commitment, and (7) less turnover.

Some potential costs and risks have also been identified (e.g., Baloff & Doherty, 1989; Bowen & Lawler, 1992; Eccles, 1993). Examples include (1) higher costs for selection and training, (2) higher labor costs for skilled employees, (3) inconsistent service quality, (4) inappropriate decisions by some employees, (5) customer feelings of inequity about unequal treatment, (6) opposition by middle managers who feel threatened, and (7) conflicts from raising employee expectations beyond what top management is willing to concede.

As yet only a few studies have examined the consequences of psychological empowerment (e.g., Howard & Wellins, 1994; Koberg, Boss, Senjem, & Goodman, 1999; Konczak

TABLE 10	Conditions Facilitating Psychological Empowerment	
Condition	Unfavorable	Favorable
Organization structure	High centralization and formalization	Very decentralized, low formalization
Competitive strategy	Low cost, standard product or service	Customized, highly differentiated product/service
Task design and technology	Simple, repetitive task and reliable technology	Complex, non-routine task, unreliable technology
Duration of relation with customers/clients	Brief transactions during a short-time interval	Repeated interaction in a continuing relationship
Dominant cultural values in the organization	Reliable, efficient operations without any mistakes	Flexibility, learning, and participation
Employee traits	Low achievement motivation, external locus of control, and emotional stability	High need for achievement, internal locus of control, and emotional stability
Employee ability	Unskilled, inexperienced	Highly skilled professional
Employee tenure	Temporary employee	Regular, continuing employee
Employee ownership and rewards for success	None or very little	Employees are shareholders or co-owners
Employee involvement programs	None	Extensive programs strongly supported by top management
Mutual trust	Low	High

et al. 2000; Spreitzer, 1995; Spreitzer, Kizilos, & Nason, 1997). One example of this research is a survey of 406 manufacturing companies in the United Kingdom (Waterson, Clegg, Bolden, Pepper, Warr, & Wall, 1999); 22% of the companies reported little or no improvement in overall performance, 32% claimed moderate gains, and 46% reported substantial performance gains. In general, the results in research on effects of empowerment programs have been mixed and inconclusive.

It is too early to reach any firm conclusions about the consequences of empowerment programs, but the combined evidence from these studies and related lines of research suggest that the potential benefits are unlikely to occur unless conditions are favorable. The conditions that can strengthen or weaken feelings of empowerment have been suggested by a number of writers (e.g., Argyris, 1998; Forrester, 2000; Gratton, 2004; Randolph, 1995; Spreitzer, 1996; Yukl & Becker, 2006), and they include characteristics of the organization, the members, and the national culture (see Table 10).

Summary

Participative leadership involves efforts by a manager to encourage and facilitate participation by others in making decisions that would otherwise be made by the manager alone. Participation can take many forms, ranging from revising a tentative decision after receiving protests, to asking for suggestions before making a decision, to asking an individual or group to jointly make a decision, to allowing others to make a decision subject to the manager's final authorization. Involving others in making decisions is often necessary for getting decisions approved and implemented in organizations. Even when it is not necessary to consult with others before making a decision, a manager may still prefer to do so in order to obtain the potential benefits, which include better decision quality and greater acceptance of decisions.

Many studies have been conducted on the outcomes of using participation, but the research evidence is not sufficiently strong and consistent to draw any firm conclusions. Lack of consistent results about the effectiveness of participative leadership probably means that various forms of participation are effective in some situations but not in others. Participation is unlikely to be effective if potential participants do not share the leader's objectives, if they do not want to take responsibility for helping to make decisions, if they distrust the leader, or if time pressures and the dispersion of participants make it impractical to consult with individuals or hold group meetings. Group forms of participation are unlikely to be effective unless the manager has sufficient skills in managing conflict, facilitating constructive problem solving, and dealing with common process problems that occur in groups.

Vroom and Yetton developed a model of participative leadership to help managers identify the appropriate decision procedures in different situations. The situational variables are characteristics of the decision situation that determine whether a particular decision procedure will increase or decrease decision quality and acceptance. The model was extended by Vroom and Jago to include other criteria and aspects of the situation. Research on these models is limited, but it provides moderate support for them. The findings suggest that managers are likely to be more effective if they use decision procedures that are appropriate for the situation.

Delegation involves the assignment of new responsibilities and additional authority to individual subordinates or to a team. The potential benefits of delegation include better decisions, increased subordinate motivation, more satisfying jobs for subordinates, development of subordinate skills, and reduction of work overload for a manager. Lack of confidence in subordinates and desire to consolidate power prevent some managers from delegating as much as they should. Research on the consequences of using delegation is still limited, but the findings suggest it can be effective when used for appropriate decisions and carried out in a competent manner.

Psychological empowerment involves a combination of meaningful work, high self-efficacy, self-determination, and ability to influence relevant events. Leaders can affect the psychological empowerment of followers in many ways, and participative leadership and delegation are only two of the relevant behaviors. Organizations can implement empowerment programs that will increase the influence of employees on important decisions and the selection and assessment of leaders. Whether an employee feels powerful or powerless also depends on aspects of the job, the organization, and the employees.

Review and Discussion Questions

1. What has been learned from the research on participative leadership?
2. What determines the success of a participative decision?
3. Briefly explain the Vroom-Yetton normative model of leadership.
4. What are some guidelines on how to encourage participation?
5. What are the potential benefits of delegation, and when is it most likely to be successful?
6. What are some guidelines on what to delegate?
7. Why do some managers find it so difficult to delegate or share power?
8. What are essential elements of psychological empowerment?

Key Terms

autocratic decision	delegation	participation
consultation	employee involvement	psychological empowerment
decision acceptance	programs	self-efficacy
decision procedure	goal congruence	self-determination
decision quality	normative decision model	trust

CASE 1

Echo Electronics

Paul Sanchez is the production manager for Echo Electronics, a small company that makes and distributes communications equipment. Paul's direct subordinates are the supervisors of the four production departments in the company's manufacturing plant. Six months ago, the engineering manager at Echo Electronics proposed a plan to install new computerized workstations to increase productivity in the plant. It seemed to be a good idea to Paul, and he welcomed the change. The CEO also approved the plan, and the new equipment was installed immediately.

Three months later, Paul was surprised and disappointed to find that the expected increase in productivity did not occur. In fact, productivity and quality actually decreased. The marketing manager told Paul that several of their best customers complained about receiving

Echo equipment that was defective. Paul does not believe that the problem lies with the new workstations. Technicians from the firm that built the workstations recently checked them and found that they were operating properly. Paul talked to someone at another company that uses the workstations, and his contact reported that they were having great success with them.

When Paul discussed the problem with his four production supervisors, he found that they shared his concern but did not agree among themselves about the cause of the problem. Reasons given for the decline in performance included poor design of the workstations, inadequate training of the production workers who operate them, and lack of financial incentives for increasing productivity. The supervisors also told Paul that the production workers have strong feelings about the workstations. Morale declined, and two employees quit because they were upset about the changes made in the way the work is done.

This morning, Paul received a phone call from the CEO who just received the production figures for last month and was calling to express concern about them. The CEO indicated that the problem was Paul's to solve, but he must take immediate steps to deal with it. The CEO wants to know by next week what steps Paul will take to reverse the decline in productivity and product quality.

SOURCE: Adapted from a case by Timothy R. Hinkin and used with his permission.

Questions

1. What actions could Paul have taken to prevent the problem?
2. What steps should Paul take now to deal with the problem?

CASE 2

Alvis Corporation

Kathy McCarthy was the manager of a production department in Alvis Corporation, a firm that manufactures office equipment. The workers are not unionized. After reading an article that stressed the benefits of participative management, Kathy believed that these benefits could be realized in her department if the workers were allowed to participate in making some decisions that affect them. Kathy selected two decisions for an experiment in participative management.

The first decision involved vacation schedules. Each summer the workers are given two weeks vacation, but no more than two workers can go on vacation at the same time. In prior years, Kathy made this decision herself. She would first ask the workers to indicate their preferred dates, then she considered how the work would be affected if different people were out at the same time. It was important to plan a vacation schedule that would ensure adequate staffing for all of the essential operations performed by the department. When more than two workers wanted the same time period, and they had similar skills, she usually gave preference to the workers with the highest productivity.

The second decision involved production standards. Sales had been increasing steadily over the past few years, and the company recently installed some new equipment to increase productivity. The new equipment would make it possible to produce more with the same number of workers. The company had a pay incentive system in which workers received a piece rate for each unit produced above a standard amount. Separate standards existed for each type of product, based on an industrial engineering study conducted a few years earlier. Top management wanted to readjust the production standards to reflect the fact that the new equipment made it possible for the workers to earn more without working any harder. The savings from higher productivity were needed to help pay for the new equipment.

Kathy called a meeting of her 15 workers an hour before the end of the work day and explained that she wanted them to discuss the two issues and make recommendations. Kathy figured that the workers might be inhibited about participating in the discussion if she were present, so she left them alone to discuss the issues. Besides, Kathy had an appointment to meet with the quality control manager. Quality problems had increased after the new equipment was installed, and the industrial engineers were studying the problem in an attempt to determine why quality had gotten worse rather than better.

When Kathy returned to her department just at quitting time, she was surprised to learn that the workers recommended keeping the standards the same. She had assumed they knew the pay incentives were no longer fair and would set a higher standard. The worker speaking for the group explained that their base pay had not kept up with inflation, and the higher incentive pay restored their real income to its prior level.

On the vacation issue, the group was deadlocked. Several of the workers wanted to take their vacations during the same two-week period and could not agree on who should go. Some workers argued that they should have priority because they had more seniority, while others argued that priority should be based on productivity, as in the past. Because it was quitting time, the group concluded that Kathy would have to resolve the dispute herself. After all, wasn't that what she was being paid for?

Copyright © 1987 by Gary Yukl

Questions

1. Were the two decisions appropriate for a group decision procedure according to the Vroom-Yetton model?
2. What mistakes were made in using participation, and what could have been done to avoid the difficulties the manager encountered?
3. Where these two decisions appropriate ones for introducing participation into the department?

CASE 3

Participative Decision-Making

Shaji Kurian[1] is concerned and somewhat worried about the forthcoming yearly leadership appraisal committee's report in which the company is going to announce the *Leader of the Year* award. Among other criteria, participative decision-making has been assigned the highest weight in the evaluation. Previously, all recipients of this award have been promoted.

Kurian is a branch manager (BM)[2] at MRT Tires Limited, based in Delhi. He is among the seven BMs who report to the Regional Sales Head. He has four area sales managers (ASMs) and 12 sales managers reporting to him. MRT Tires is a leading tire manufacturer and a highly reputed tire brand in India. Kurian has been working with MRT for the last 14 years and has been consistently performing and being rewarded with bonuses and regular promotions. In all previous appraisals, the sales revenue targets have been the key criteria

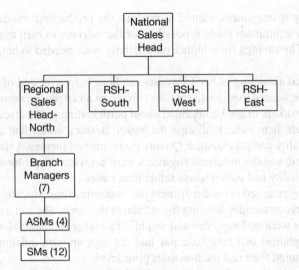

FIGURE 4 Organizational Hierarchy

for promotion. Kurian has been known in the firm as the "Sales Tiger" and has always been over-achieving his targets. But this time, it is different.

As BM, in addition to achieving the sales revenue target, Kurian is responsible for developing a team for the next level of leadership. The organization is very consciously promoting participative decision-making across the hierarchy. It wants to develop a leadership team from within the organization, which the employees perceive as a welcome move. In fact, all the BMs were sent for a leadership training with a special focus on participative decision-making at IIM Lucknow. The organization has also introduced a 360-degree feedback mechanism. This employee appraisal system required ratings on performance from channel partners, distributors, support staff, and subordinates as well. Kurian was less worried about the others than about his immediate subordinates, who were supposed to rate him on his participative decision-making style.

Kurian's concern stemmed from the diverse nature of his team members.[3] He had four subordinates – Gurinder, Rajendra, Sita, and Nishant – who have been allocated specific areas in Delhi to generate sales revenue. Although he often consults with all his team members about almost all the strategic decisions related to his branch, more recently, he has developed a tendency to seek suggestions selectively. For example, whenever he is needed to organize a local customer event to promote sales, he makes Nishant in charge. For local media planning, he often seeks advice from Gurinder. Rajendra regularly contributes to the development of promotion and marketing schemes. Sita participates in almost all the exercises. This seems to have been working in Kurian's favor—it reflects in the sales numbers of his branch, which is among the top three branches in the country.

Although he is confident that his team members will rate him adequately on participative decision-making, he senses dissatisfaction in the team. At one time, during a party at the branch, Gurinder complained about Sita's participation in all decisions, despite her poor performance. Rajendra also expressed that his participation is limited in all local events, which are a regular feature of the branch. Sita, though, seemed satisfied with her level of

---

[1]Kurian is 52 years old and has been in the sales department of various tire manufacturing organizations for 28 years. He is a graduate and holds a diploma in sales from a local college.

[2]Refer to Figure 5 for the organizational hierarchy.

[3]Refer to Table 11 for a profile of the ASMs.

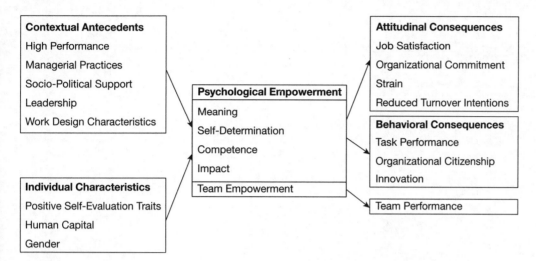

FIGURE 5 Integrated Individual and Team Empowerment Framework (Seibert, Wang, and Courtright, 2011)

participation, yet complained about the time consumed in meetings. In some of the meetings, he had invited SMs too, and all the ASMs had reservations about this.

TABLE 11	Profile of ASMs			
	Rajendra	Gurinder	Nishant	Sita
Age	24	39	41	36
Gender	M	M	M	F
Marital Status	Unmarried	Married	Married	Divorced
Education	MBA	BA	B.Com	BA
Native	Chennai	Ludhiana	Delhi	Jaipur
Sales Experience (months)	24	216	240	72
Tilre Industry Experience	24	140	190	60
Sales Experience in Tilre Industry	24	140	132	72
Languages Known	Telugu, English	Punjabi, Hindi, English	Punjabi, Hindi	Hindi, English
Sales Target Achievement (avg 2 years)	89%	112%	102%	66%

Kurian is clear that he cannot seek an equal level of participation from all his team members, despite their enthusiasm. However, he is worried about how he can manage to get good ratings from them. He is also wondering if it is practically possible to have 100 percent participative decision-making.

Questions

1. What process is Shaji Kurian following to have participative decision-making?
2. Why does Kurian involve Sita in all decisions and what value does he expect this would generate?

Leading Change and Innovation

From Chapter 4 of Leadership in Organizations, Eighth Edition. Gary Yukl. Copyright © 2013 by Pearson Education, Inc. Publishing as Prentice Hall. All rights reserved.

Leading Change and Innovation

Learning Objectives

After studying this chapter, you should be able to:

- Understand reasons for resisting change.
- Understand the psychological processes involved in making major changes.
- Understand how to develop an appealing vision for the organization.
- Understand how to implement a major change in an organization.
- Understand the characteristics of a learning organization.
- Understand how leaders can increase learning and innovation.

Leading change is one of the most important and difficult responsibilities for managers and administrators. It involves guiding, encouraging, and facilitating the collective efforts of members to adapt and survive in an uncertain and sometimes hostile environment. For some theorists, this is the essence of leadership. The subject became especially relevant in the 1980s when many private and public sector organizations were confronted with the need for major changes to cope with globalization, deregulation, sweeping social and political changes, and the technological revolution in products and services.

Major change in an organization is usually guided by the top management team, but other members of the organization can initiate change or contribute to its success. This chapter describes different types of change, common change processes, and reasons for member *resistance to change*. The chapter also explains the importance of collective learning in teams and organizations. Finally, the chapter provides guidelines for leaders on behaviors for encouraging and facilitating change and collective learning.

Types of Change in Teams and Organizations

Many types of changes can be made by leaders, and some types are more difficult than others. The focus of a change effort may involve roles, attitudes, technology, strategy, economics, or people.

Roles or Attitudes

One useful distinction is between efforts to change attitudes versus efforts to change roles, structures, and procedures (Beer, Eisenstat, & Spector, 1990). The attitude-centered approach involves changing attitudes and values with persuasive appeals, training programs, team-building activities, or a culture change program. In addition, technical or interpersonal skills may be increased with a training program. The underlying assumption is that new attitudes and skills will cause behavior to change in a beneficial way. The leader seeks to convert resisters into *change agents* who will transmit the *vision* to other people in the organization.

The role-centered approach involves changing work roles by reorganizing the workflow, redesigning jobs to include different activities and responsibilities, modifying authority relationships, changing the criteria and procedures for evaluation of work, and changing the reward system. The assumption is that when work roles require people to act in a different way, they will change their attitudes to be consistent with the new behavior. Effective behavior is induced by the new role requirements and reinforced by the evaluation and reward system. An example will clarify the difference between the two approaches to organizational change.

A company is having difficulty getting people in different functionally specialized departments to cooperate in developing new products rapidly and getting them into the marketplace. One approach is to talk about the importance of cooperation and use a process analysis intervention or team-building activity to increase understanding and mutual respect among people from different functions. This approach assumes that increased trust and understanding will increase cooperation back in the workplace. Another approach is to create cross-functional teams that are responsible for the development of a new product, and then reward people for contributions to the success of the team. This approach assumes that people who cooperate to achieve a common goal will come to understand and trust each other.

Over the years, there has been controversy about which approach is the most effective. Either approach can succeed or fail depending on how well it is implemented. Beer et al. (1990) argue that a role-centered program is more likely to be successful than an attitude-centered program. However, the two approaches are not incompatible, and the best strategy is to use them together in a mutually supportive way. Efforts to change attitudes and skills to support new roles reduce the chance that the role change will be subverted by opponents before it has a chance to succeed.

Technology

Another type of change is in the technology used to do the work. Many organizations have attempted to improve performance by implementing new information and decision support systems. Examples include networked workstations, human resource information systems, inventory and order processing systems, sales tracking systems, or an intranet with groupware for communication and idea sharing among employees. Such changes often fail to yield the desired benefits, because without consistent changes in work roles, attitudes, and skills, the new technology will not be accepted and used in an effective way.

Strategy

Still another major type of change is in the competitive strategy for achieving the major objectives of the team or organization. Examples of strategy changes for a company include introduction of new products or services, entering new markets, use of new forms of marketing, initiation of Internet sales in addition to direct selling, forming alliances or joint ventures with other organizations, and modifying relationships with suppliers (e.g., partnering with a few reliable suppliers). To be successful, changes in the competitive strategy may require consistent changes in people, work roles, organization structure, and technology. For example, the decision to begin providing a more intensive type of customer service may require service personnel with additional skills and better technology for communicating with customers.

Economics or People

Internal changes in an organization may emphasize economics or people (Beer & Nohria, 2000). The first approach seeks to improve financial performance with changes such as downsizing, restructuring, and adjustments in compensation and incentives. The second approach seeks to improve human capability, commitment, and creativity by increasing individual and organizational learning, strengthening cultural values that support flexibility and *innovation*, and empowering people to initiate improvements. Attempts to make large-scale change in an organization often involve some aspects of both approaches, but incompatible elements can undermine the change effort if not carefully managed. For example, making drastic layoffs of employees to reduce costs can undermine the trust and loyalty needed to improve collective learning and innovation. It is difficult to improve organizational performance unless a leader can find ways to deal with the trade-offs and competing values involved in making major change.

Change Processes

Change process theories describe a typical pattern of events that occur from the beginning of a change to the end, and in some cases they describe how earlier changes affect subsequent changes. The theories may identify distinct phases in the process, stages in the reaction of individuals, or effects of repeated changes on people.

Stages in the Change Process

One of the earliest process theories was Lewin's (1951) force-field model. He proposed that the change process can be divided into three phases: unfreezing, changing, and refreezing. In the unfreezing phase, people come to realize that the old ways of doing things are no longer adequate. This recognition may occur as a result of an obvious crisis, or it may result from an effort to describe threats or opportunities that were not evident to most people in the organization. In the changing phase, people look for new ways of doing things and select a promising approach. In the refreezing phase, the new approach is implemented and it becomes established. All three phases are important for successful change. An attempt to move directly to the changing phase without first unfreezing attitudes is likely to meet with apathy or strong resistance. Lack of systematic diagnosis and problem solving in the changing phase will result in a weak change plan. Lack of attention to consensus building and maintenance of enthusiasm in the third stage may result in the change being reversed soon after it is implemented.

According to Lewin, change may be achieved by two types of actions. One approach is to increase the driving forces toward change (e.g., increase incentives and use position power to force change). The other approach is to reduce restraining forces that create resistance to change (e.g., reduce fear of failure or economic loss, co-opt, or remove opponents). If the restraining forces are weak, it may be sufficient merely to increase driving forces. However, when restraining forces are strong, a dual approach is advisable. Unless restraining forces can be reduced, an increase in driving forces will create an intense conflict over the change, and continuing resistance will make it more difficult to complete the refreezing phase.

Stages in Reaction to a Change

Another process theory describes a typical pattern of reactions to changes imposed upon people (Gebert et al., 2003; Jick, 1993; Krause, 2004; Woodward & Bucholz, 1987). The theory builds on observations about the typical sequence of reactions to sudden, traumatic events such as the death of a loved one, the breakup of a marriage, or a natural disaster that destroys one's home (Lazarus, 1991). The reaction pattern has four stages: denial, anger, mourning, and adaptation. The initial reaction is to deny that change will be necessary ("This isn't happening" or "It's just a temporary setback"). The next stage is to get angry and look for someone to blame. At the same time, people stubbornly resist giving up accustomed ways of doing things. In the third stage, people stop denying that change is inevitable, acknowledge what has been lost, and mourn it. The final stage is to accept the need to change and go on with one's life. The duration and severity of each type of reaction can vary greatly, and some people get stuck in an intermediate stage. Understanding these stages is important for change leaders, who must learn to be patient and helpful. Many people need help to overcome denial, channel their anger constructively, mourn without becoming severely depressed, and have optimism about adjusting successfully.

Prior Experience and Reactions to Change

Despite the extensive literature providing guidance on how to initiate and manage change, many efforts fail to meet expectations (Burke, 2002). Large-scale change in organizations is difficult to study, and much of the research involves anecdotal accounts or case studies in a single organization. However, recent years have seen an increase in research on conditions affecting the success of change efforts in organizations. The research has examined how contextual factors and individual factors jointly determine the amount of resistance or commitment to change.

How a person reacts to change depends in part on the person's general confidence about coping with change successfully. This confidence is affected by prior experience with change as well as by traits, such as self-confidence, risk tolerance, openness to new experiences, and internal locus of control orientation (Erwin & Garman, 2010).

Competing hypotheses can be made about the effects of experiencing repeated, difficult change (Jick, 1993). One hypothesis is that experiencing traumatic change will "inoculate" people and leave them better prepared to change again without such an intense or prolonged period of adjustment. For example, having experienced and survived the loss of two jobs in five years, Sally is confident about taking more risky, less secure jobs in the future. The rival hypothesis is that repeated change leaves people less resilient and more vulnerable to adverse effects from subsequent change. The explanation involves prolonged stress and the inability to resolve the emotional trauma of an earlier change. For example, after losing two jobs in five years as a result of downsizing, Linda cannot deal with the threat of losing another job and seeks early retirement. A third possibility is that repeated change makes some people more resilient and others less resilient, depending on their personality traits and social support system.

Research on the cumulative effects of experiencing repeated, intense changes is still limited, but it suggests that the more common effect is to increase stress and frustration (Rafferty & Griffin, 2006). The stress caused by earlier changes and a person's self-efficacy for change jointly determine how the person will react to more changes (Herold et al., 2007).

Even for people with strong confidence in their ability to handle change, frequent changes in a short period of time can undermine commitment. People are likely to feel frustration and a sense of injustice if the burden of implementing change is placed on them without adequate support from the organization. Feelings of being unjustly treated are intensified when most of the benefits of the changes will accrue to others, such as owners and top management.

Reasons for Accepting or Rejecting Change

Many efforts to implement major change in an organization are unsuccessful, and resistance to change is a major reason for failure. One explanation for the outcome of a proposed change is in terms of leader power and the types of influence processes that leaders use. Compliance with the change is likely if people believe that it is a legitimate exercise of leader authority (legitimate power), or if they fear punishment for resisting the change (coercive power). Commitment to support a change initiative is likely when people trust their leaders and believe that the change is necessary and effective (strong referent and expert power). However, resistance to change is common in organizations, and it can occur for several reasons that are not mutually exclusive (Connor, 1995; Fedor, Caldwell, & Herold, 2006).

Proposed Change Is Not Necessary

A change is likely to be resisted if there is no clear evidence of a serious problem or opportunity that would justify major change. The signs of a developing problem are usually ambiguous at the early stage, and it is easy for people to ignore or discount them. Even when a problem is finally recognized, the usual response is to make incremental adjustments in the present strategy, or to do more of the same, rather than to do something different.

Proposed Change Is Not Feasible

Another reason for resistance is the belief that a proposed change cannot be implemented successfully. Making a change that is radically different from anything done previously will appear difficult if not impossible to most people. If earlier change programs initiated by the same leaders were unsuccessful, it creates cynicism and makes people doubtful the next one will be any better. The self-confidence of people who must implement change also influence how they view it. Change makes some expertise obsolete and requires learning new ways of doing the work. Individuals who lack self-confidence will be reluctant to give up established procedures for new ones that may be too difficult to master.

Change Is Not Cost Effective

A change may be resisted because the benefits would not justify the costs necessary to implement the change. Major change always entails some costs, and they may be higher than any likely benefits. Resources are necessary to implement change, and resources already invested in doing things the traditional way will be lost. Performance invariably suffers during the transition period as the new ways are learned and new procedures are debugged. More resistance is likely when it is not possible to accurately estimate costs in relation to benefits and people are pessimistic about the benefits.

Change Would Cause Personal Losses

Even if a change would benefit the organization, it may be resisted by people who would suffer personal loss of income, benefits, or job security. Major changes in organizations invariably result in some shift in power and status for individuals and subunits. Some jobs may be eliminated or modified, resulting in layoffs or transfers to new locations. People responsible for activities that will be cut back or eliminated may lose the basis for their current status and power. A change will be perceived as unfair by people if it has adverse consequences for them and they have little or no influence over decisions about the change.

Proposed Change Is Inconsistent With Values

Another reason for resistance is that the proposed change appears inconsistent with an individual's values and ideals. If a proposed change is viewed as unethical, illegal, or inconsistent with strong beliefs about proper behavior, it is more likely to be resisted, even if it would provide tangible benefits to the person. When the values violated by a proposed change are embedded in a strong organization culture, resistance will be widespread.

Leaders Not Trusted

In some organizations, change is resisted because the leaders who propose it are distrusted, and this distrust can magnify the effect of other sources of resistance. Even without an obvious threat, a change may be resisted if people imagine hidden, ominous implications that will not be discovered until it is too late to do anything about them. Mutual mistrust may encourage a leader to be secretive about the real reasons for change or some of the risks, thereby further increasing suspicion and resistance. Resistance may also reflect resentment that changes were proposed by leaders who are not viewed as having legitimate authority to make them, or who are seen as using the changes to further personal ambitions and desire for more power.

Summary

Resistance to change is not merely the result of ignorance or inflexibility. It can occur for several reasons and is a natural reaction by people who want to protect their self-interests and sense of self-determination. Rather than viewing resistance only as an obstacle to batter down or circumvent, it can be viewed as energy that can be redirected to improve change (Ford, Ford, & D'Amelio, 2008; Jick, 1993; Maurer, 1996). Active resistance indicates the presence of strong values and emotions that could serve as a source of commitment if opponents are converted to supporters. It is essential to discuss a proposed change with the people who will be affected to learn about their concerns and their ideas about the best course of action.

Implementing Change

Organization scholars have been interested in determining how the approach used to implement change affects the success of the effort. It is likely that the outcome will depend in part on what is changed, how and when the change is implemented, who participates in the process, and how much influence each participant has. The outcomes for a change can be judged in different ways, including commitment of people to the change, successful implementation of the change, and the extent to which the change results in the desired benefits and avoids negative consequences.

Determining What to Change

Before initiating major changes, leaders need to be clear about the nature of the problem and the objectives to be achieved. Just as in the treatment of a physical illness, the first step is a careful diagnosis to determine what is wrong with the patient. The *organizational diagnosis* can be conducted by the top management team, by outside consultants, or by a task force composed of representatives of the various key *stakeholders* in the organization.

An incorrect diagnosis or an inappropriate change program will not provide the desired benefits. A common mistake is to implement a generic change program that is currently popular without a careful diagnosis of the problems confronting the organization. Some examples of popular change programs in past years include downsizing, delayering, total quality management, reengineering, self-managed teams, outsourcing, and partnering with suppliers. Change programs often fail to solve organizational problems and sometimes make them worse (Beer et al., 1990). The benefits obtained from changes made in one part of the organization often fail to improve the overall performance of the organization and may cause new problems for other subunits (Goodman & Rousseau, 2004).

Understanding Systems Dynamics

To understand the reasons for a problem and how to deal with it requires a good understanding of the complex relationships and *systems dynamics* that occur in organizations (Gharajedaghi, 1999; Goodman & Rousseau, 2004; Senge, 1990). Knowledge of systems dynamics is helpful both for identifying the nature of a problem and for anticipating the likely effects of changes made to resolve it.

Systems dynamics involve complex relationships, multiple causes and outcomes, delayed effects, and cyclical causality. Problems have multiple causes, which may include actions taken earlier to solve other problems. If the diagnosis only identifies one of several problems, the changes may fail to achieve the desired outcome. In large systems such as organizations, actions have multiple outcomes, including unintended side effects. A change in one part of a system will eventually affect other parts, and reactions to the change may cancel out the effects. Changes that have delayed effects tend to obscure the real nature of the relationship. Sometimes actions that appear to offer quick relief may actually make things worse in the long run, whereas the best solution may offer no immediate benefits, but the delayed benefits are substantial. A leader who is impatient for quick results may keep repeating inappropriate remedies, rather than pursuing better remedies that require patience and short-term sacrifice.

Understanding the complex interdependencies among organizational processes and the implications of efforts to make changes requires cognitive skills and "systems thinking" (Senge, 1990). When making decisions or diagnosing the cause of problems, it is essential to understand how the different parts of the organization are interrelated. Even when the immediate objective is to deal with one type of challenge, such as improving efficiency, leaders need to consider the likely consequences for other performance determinants and the possibility that any immediate benefits will be nullified by delayed effects. An example is when a manager downsizes the workforce to reduce costs, but pressure to maintain the same output requires expensive overtime and use of consultants (including some of the same people who were downsized), thereby negating most of the cost savings.

Another common phenomenon is a reinforcing cycle wherein small changes grow into much bigger changes that may or may not be desirable. A positive example is when a change made to improve processes in one subunit is successful, and other subunits are encouraged to imitate it, resulting in more benefits for the organization than initially expected. A negative example is when rationing is introduced to conserve a scarce resource and people stockpile more of it than they currently need, thereby causing more shortages and problems.

Responsibility for Implementing Major Change

Large-scale change in an organization is unlikely to be successful without the support of top management. However, contrary to common assumptions, major changes are not always initiated by top management, and they may not become involved until the process is well under way (Beer, 1988; Belgard, Fisher, & Rayner, 1988). Major changes suggested by lower levels may be resisted by top managers who are strongly committed to traditional approaches and do not understand that the old ways of doing things are no longer appropriate. The major transformation of an organization often requires the replacement of top management by new leaders with a mandate for radical change.

The essential role of top management in implementing change is to formulate an integrating vision and general strategy, build a coalition of supporters who endorse the strategy, then guide and coordinate the process by which the strategy will be implemented. Complex changes usually involve a process of experimentation and learning, because it is impossible to anticipate all the problems or to prepare detailed plans for how to carry out all aspects of the change. Instead of specifying detailed guidelines for change at all levels of the organization, it is much better to encourage middle and lower-level managers to transform their own units in a way that is consistent with the vision and strategy. Top management should provide encouragement, support, and necessary resources to facilitate change, but should not try to dictate the details of how to do it.

The Pace and Sequencing of Changes

A debate continues among change scholars about the optimal pace and sequencing of desired changes. Some scholars have advocated rapid introduction of changes throughout the organization to prevent the buildup of resistance, whereas other scholars favor a more gradual introduction of change to different parts of the organization at different times. The limited amount of longitudinal research does not yet provide clear answers to these questions, but some evidence favors the latter approach (e.g., Beer, 1988; Hinings & Greenwood, 1988; Pettigrew, Ferlie, & McKee, 1992). In a 12-year study of 36 national sports organizations in Canada, Amis, Slack, and Hinings (2004) found evidence that major change was more successful when it was implemented slowly, beginning in highly visible, important ways that convey the message that the change is a serious, long-lasting effort. Controversial changes occurred in a nonlinear way, with delays and reversals as aspects of the change were modified to deal with opponent concerns or postponed until a time when opponents would be more receptive to them. This process provided opportunities for the change agents to establish trust and use a process of collaborative problem solving for contentious issues.

Whenever feasible it seems beneficial to change interdependent subunits of the organization simultaneously so that the effects will be mutually supporting. However, in a large organization with semiautonomous subunits (e.g., separate product divisions) simultaneous change is not essential, and it may not be feasible to implement change in all subunits at the same time. One way to demonstrate the success of a new strategy is to implement it on a small scale in one subunit or facility on an experimental basis. A successful change that is carried out in one part of an organization can help to stimulate similar changes throughout the organization. However, it is unwise merely to assume that the same changes will be appropriate in all subunits, especially when they are very diverse. This type of mistake is more likely to be avoided when middle managers are allowed to have a major voice in determining how to implement a strategy in their own organizational subunits (Beer, Eisenstat, & Spector, 1990).

Successful implementation of a major new strategy usually requires changes in the organizational structure to make it consistent with the strategy. However, when structural change is likely to be resisted, it may be easier to create an informal structure to support the new strategy and postpone changes in the formal structure until people realize that they are needed. Informal teams can be created to facilitate the transition, without any expectation that these temporary structures will become permanent. For example, after temporary task forces were created to plan and coordinate changes in one company, they eventually evolved into permanent cross-functional committees with formal authority to plan and monitor continuing improvements in product quality and operational procedures.

Guidelines for Implementing Change

Successful implementation of change in organizations requires a wide range of leadership behaviors. Some of the behaviors involve political and administrative aspects, and others involve motivating, supporting, and guiding people. Even the people who initially endorse a change will need support and assistance to sustain their enthusiasm and optimism as the inevitable difficulties and setbacks occur. Major change is always stressful and painful for people, especially when it involves a prolonged transition period of adjustment, disruption, and dislocation. The following guidelines describe current thinking about the best way to implement a major change in an organization (see summary in Table 1). The guidelines are based on theory, research findings, and practitioner insights (Beer, 1988; Connor, 1995; Jick, 1993; Kotter, 1996; Nadler et al., 1995; Pettigrew & Whipp, 1991; Rubin, Dierdorff, Bommer, & Baldwin, 2009; Self & Schraeder, 2009; Tichy & Devanna, 1986). Although the guidelines describe actions a chief executive can take, many of them also apply to other leaders who want to make major changes in their team or department.

- **Create a sense of urgency about the need for change.**

When changes in the environment are gradual and no obvious crisis has occurred, many people fail to recognize emerging threats (or opportunities). An important role of the leader is to persuade other key people in the organization of the need for major changes rather than incremental adjustments. To mobilize support for proposed changes, it is essential to explain why they are necessary and to create a sense of urgency about them. Explain

TABLE 1	Guidelines for Implementing a Major Change

- Create a sense of urgency about the need for change.
- Communicate a clear vision of the benefits to be gained.
- Identify likely supporters, opponents, and reasons for resistance.
- Build a broad coalition to support the change.
- Fill key positions with competent change agents.
- Use task forces to guide the implementation of changes.
- Empower competent people to help plan and implement change.
- Make dramatic, symbolic changes that affect the work.
- Prepare people for change by explaining how it will affect them.
- Help people deal with the stress and difficulties of major change.
- Provide opportunities for early successes to build confidence.
- Monitor the progress of change and make any necessary adjustments.
- Keep people informed about the progress of change.
- Demonstrate continued optimism and commitment to the change.

why not changing will eventually be more costly than making the proposed changes now. If people have little sense of the problems, it is important for the leader to provide relevant information and help people understand what it means. For example, distribute a summary of customer complaints each week with selective quotes from irate customers. Arrange for people to meet with dissatisfied customers. Prepare analyses of costs involved in correcting quality problems. Compare the performance of the organizational unit to the performance of key competitors as well as to unit performance in prior years.

- **Communicate a clear vision of the benefits to be gained from change.**

When it is necessary to make major changes in an organization, a vision of what the changes will do to achieve shared objectives and values is very helpful in gaining commitment for the change. The desirable characteristics of a vision and guidelines for developing an appealing vision are described later in this chapter.

- **Identify likely supporters, opponents, and reasons for resistance.**

To evaluate the feasibility of various strategies for accomplishing major change in the organization, a leader must understand the political processes, the distribution of power, and the identity of people whose support is necessary to make the change happen. Before beginning a major change effort, it is useful to identify likely supporters and opponents. Time should be set aside to explore each of the following questions. Which key people will determine whether a proposal will be successfully implemented? Who is likely to support the proposal? How much resistance is likely and from whom? What would be necessary to overcome the resistance? How could skeptics be converted into supporters? How long will it take to get approval from all of the key parties?

- **Build a broad coalition to support the change.**

The task of persuading people to support major change is not easy, and it is a too big job for a single leader to do alone. Successful change in an organization requires cooperative effort by people who have the power to facilitate or block change. It is essential to build a coalition of supporters, both inside and outside the organization. A supportive coalition may be even more important in pluralistic organizations that have collective leadership (e.g., hospitals, universities, professional associations) than in hierarchical business organizations where the top management team may have sufficient power to authorize major change (Denis, Lamothe, & Langley, 2001). The first step is to ensure that the executive team is prepared to undertake the difficult task of implementing major change in the organization, and some changes in the team may be necessary. Supporters are needed not only within the top executive team, but also among middle and lower levels of management. In a study by Beer (1988) of six companies undergoing a major change effort, the companies with a successful transformation had more middle managers who supported the changes and possessed relevant skills to facilitate it. The external members of the coalition may be consultants, labor union leaders, important clients, executives in financial institutions, or officials in government agencies.

- **Use task forces to guide implementation of changes.**

Temporary task forces are often useful to guide the implementation of major change in an organization, especially when it involves modification of the formal structure and the relationships among subunits. Examples of typical responsibilities for a task force include exploring how key values in the vision can be expressed more fully; developing action plans for implementing a new strategy that cuts across subunits; designing procedures for performing new types of activities; and studying how the appraisal and reward structure can be modified to make it more consistent with the new vision and strategy. The composition of each task force should be appropriate for its responsibilities. For example, a task force to improve customer service should include people from all the functions that affect the quality of this service, and the task force should actually meet with some important customers. The leader of each task force should be someone who understands and supports the new vision and has skills in how to conduct meetings, manage conflict, and involve people in constructive problem solving.

- **Fill key positions with competent change agents.**

It is especially important to get the commitment of people directly responsible for implementing the change—the people in key positions who will make it happen. These "change agents" must support the change with their actions as well as their words. They should be people who are committed to the vision and have the ability to communicate it clearly. Whenever possible, people in key positions who cannot be won over to the new vision and strategy should be replaced. If left in place, opponents may go beyond passive resistance and use political tactics in an effort to block additional change. Pockets of resistance can develop and grow strong enough to prevent the new strategy from being implemented successfully. Acting quickly to remove opponents who symbolize the old order not only removes people who will resist change, but also signals that you are serious about the change.

- **Empower competent people to help plan and implement the change.**

A major change is less likely to be successful if top management tries to dictate in detail how it will be implemented in each part of the organization. Whenever feasible, the authority to make decisions and deal with problems should be delegated to the individuals or teams responsible for implementing change. Competent supporters in key positions should be empowered to determine the best way to implement a new strategy or support a new program, rather than telling them in detail what to do. Empowering people also means reducing bureaucratic constraints that will impede their efforts and providing the resources they need to implement change successfully.

- **Make dramatic, symbolic changes that affect the work.**

If feasible, make dramatic, *symbolic changes* that affect the everyday lives of organization members in significant ways. When members are immediately affected, it becomes more obvious that the change is really going to happen and they need to adjust to it. One type of symbolic change involves how the work is done and the authority of various parties over the work. For example, in a manufacturing company that adopted a new strategy of total product quality, the position of quality inspector was eliminated, production employees were given the responsibility for checking quality and correcting any quality problems, quality circles were established to identify ways to improve quality, and employees were empowered to stop the production line to correct quality problems. Another type of symbolic change involves where the work is done. In a large insurance company that reorganized from a functionally specialized hierarchy into 14 small, semiautonomous divisions, the chief executive officer (CEO) sold the old high-rise office building and relocated each division into its own, separate, low-rise facility. The move emphasized to employees the new strategy of empowering each division to find its own ways to improve customer service. Symbolic changes may also involve cultural forms such as symbols, ceremonies, and rituals.

- **Prepare people for change by explaining how it will affect them.**

Even when a change is necessary and beneficial, it will require difficult adjustments by the people who are most affected. If people are unable to handle the stress and trauma of change, they will become depressed or rebellious. Even enthusiastic change agents are not immune from the difficulties experienced in a long-term change effort. Alternating successes and setbacks may leave change agents feeling as if they are on an emotional rollercoaster ride. Ambiguity about progress and the recurring discovery of new obstacles will increase fatigue and frustration. These negative aspects of change are easier to deal with if people expect them and know how to cope with them. Rather than presenting change as a panacea without any costs or problems, it is better to help people understand what adjustments will be necessary. However, it is essential to be enthusiastic and optimistic about the likely success of the change, despite serious obstacles. Change agents should be careful to avoid any cynicism, because it will undermine confidence and commitment. One approach to prepare people for change is to provide a realistic preview of some typical types of problems and difficulties, then discuss what can be done to avoid or resolve these problems. It may be useful to ask people who have experienced a similar change to speak about their experiences and what they did to get through the change successfully. Social networks can be used to enable people to get advice and support from each other more easily.

- **Help people deal with the stress and difficulties of major change.**

When radical changes are made, many people experience personal pain at the loss of familiar things to which they had become attached. The trauma of change may be experienced regardless of whether the change involves new strategies and programs, new equipment and procedures for doing the work, new facilities, new management practices, or new leaders. It is difficult for people to accept the failure of past decisions and policies, and it may be necessary to help them accept the need for change without feeling personally responsible for the failure. Leaders can encourage people to take advantage of available training on how to manage stress, anxiety, and depression. It may be useful to form support groups to help people cope with the disruptions caused by a major change. Sometimes ceremonies or rituals are useful to help people express their grief and anger over the loss of sentimental elements of the old organization. An example is provided by the following description of a special management conference held in a large electronics company that had recently undergone many changes (Deal, 1985, p. 321).

> The conference opened with a general discussion of culture and then continued with three successive small-group sessions of thirty participants each. When asked for metaphors to capture the essence of the company, the group overwhelmingly came up with transitive images: afloat in a stormy sea without an anchor, a two-headed animal, and so on. Each group specifically addressed the issue of loss. In the last session, the CEO was present; the word had spread that the discussions were yielding some significant perceptions. The tension in the room was obvious. At one point, the participants were asked to name what they had lost, and these were written on a flip chart. The list included values, symbols, rituals, ceremonies, priests, and heroes. As people contributed specific losses, someone got up and dimmed the lights. The emotion was obviously high. The group then launched into a discussion of the positive features of the company in its new incarnation. The CEO incorporated much of the preceding discussion into an excellent closing speech, and the company moved ahead.

- **Provide opportunities for early successes to build confidence.**

The confidence of an individual or team can be increased by making sure people experience successful progress in the early phases of a new project or major change. Some skeptics will only become supporters after they see evidence of progress in initial efforts to do things a new way. Kouzes and Posner (1987) recommend breaking up a challenging task into initial small steps or short-term goals that do not appear too difficult. People are more willing to undertake an activity if they perceive that their efforts are likely to be successful and that the costs of failure would not be great. As the initial steps or goals are accomplished, people experience success and gain more self-confidence. Then, they are willing to try for larger wins and to invest more resources in the effort.

- **Monitor the progress of change and make any necessary adjustments.**

Innovative changes are by nature ventures into uncharted waters, and it is impossible to predict all of the obstacles and difficulties that will be encountered. Many things must be learned by doing, and monitoring is essential for this learning. Feedback about the effects of change should be collected and analyzed to evaluate progress and refine *mental models* about the relationship among key variables that affect the organization's performance. Monitoring is also important to coordinate different aspects of the change. Accurate, timely information is needed about the effect of the changes on people, processes, and performance. This information can be gathered in a variety of ways, one of which is to hold frequent progress review meetings with people in key positions.

- **Keep people informed about the progress of change.**

A major change, like any other crisis, creates anxiety and stress in people who are affected by it. When a new strategy does not require many visible changes in the early stages of implementation, people will begin to wonder whether the effort has died and things are going back to the way they were. People will be more enthusiastic and optimistic if they know that the change program is progressing successfully.

One way to convey a sense of progress is to communicate what steps have been initiated, what changes have been completed, and what improvements have occurred in performance indicators. Hold ceremonies to announce the inauguration of major activities, to celebrate significant progress or success, and to give people recognition for their contributions and achievements. These celebrations provide an opportunity to increase optimism, build commitment, and strengthen identification with the organizational unit. Recognizing the contributions and accomplishments of individuals makes the importance of each person's role in the collective effort more evident.

When obstacles are encountered, explain what they are and what is being done about them. If the implementation plan must be revised, explain why it was necessary. Otherwise, people may interpret any revisions in the plan or schedule as a sign of faltering commitment.

- **Demonstrate optimism and continued commitment to the change.**

Responsibility for guiding various aspects of the change can be delegated to other change agents, but the leader who is identified as the primary proponent and sponsor of the change must continue to provide the attention and endorsement that signal commitment to see it through to the end. Initial enthusiasm and support for a major change may decline as problems are encountered, setbacks occur, and people come to understand the necessary costs and sacrifices. People look to their leaders for signs of continued commitment to the change objectives and vision. Any indication that the change is no longer viewed as important or feasible may have ripple effects that undermine the change effort. Supporters will be lost and opponents encouraged to increase overt resistance. Continued attention and endorsement signal a leader's commitment to see the change program through to a successful conclusion.

The leader should persistently promote the vision guiding the change process and display optimism that the inevitable setbacks and difficulties will be overcome. The leader must reject easy solutions for dealing with immediate problems when these solutions are inconsistent with the underlying objectives of the change effort. Demonstrating commitment is more than just talking about the importance of the change. The leader must invest time, effort, and resources in resolving problems and overcoming obstacles. When appropriate, the leader should participate in activities related to the change. For example, attendance at a special meeting or ceremony relevant to the change effort has a clear symbolic meaning for other people in the organization that the change must be important.

How Visions Influence Change

The success of a major change will depend to a great extent on how well leaders communicate the reasons why proposed change is necessary and beneficial. Success is more likely if leaders articulate a vision of a better future that is attractive enough to justify the sacrifices and hardships the change will require. The vision can provide a sense of continuity for followers by linking past events and present strategies to a vivid image of a better future for the organization. The vision provides hope for a better future and the faith that it will be attained someday. In the hectic and confusing process of implementing change, a clear vision helps to guide and coordinate the decisions and actions of many people in widely dispersed locations.

Desirable Characteristics for a Vision

A number of writers have attempted to describe the essential qualities of a successful vision (Bennis & Nanus, 1985; Kantabutra, 2009; Kotter, 1996; Kouzes & Posner, 1995; Nanus, 1992; Tichy & Devanna, 1986). A vision should be simple and idealistic, a picture of a desirable future, not a complex plan with quantitative objectives and detailed action steps. The vision should appeal to the values, hopes, and ideals of organization members and other stakeholders whose support is needed. The vision should emphasize distant ideological objectives rather than immediate tangible benefits. The vision should be challenging but realistic. To be meaningful and credible, it should not be a wishful fantasy, but rather an attainable future grounded in the present reality. The vision should address basic assumptions about what is important for the organization, how it should relate to the environment, and how people should be treated. The vision should be focused enough to guide decisions and actions, but general enough to allow initiative and creativity in the strategies for attaining it. Finally, a successful vision should be simple enough to be communicated clearly in five minutes or less.

Elements of a Vision

The term *vision* has many different meanings, which creates widespread confusion. It is unclear whether a mission statement, strategic objective, *value statement*, or slogan constitutes an effective vision. In the absence of direct research on this question, one way to answer it is to examine each construct in relation to the desirable characteristics for a vision.

The *mission statement* usually describes the purpose of the organization in terms of the type of activities to be performed for constituents or customers. In contrast, an effective vision tells us what these activities mean to people. The core of the vision is the organization's mission, but different aspects of it may be emphasized. A successful vision tells you not only what the organization does, but also why it is worthwhile and exciting to do it.

A successful vision makes the typical dull mission statement come alive, infusing it with excitement, arousing emotions, and stimulating creativity to achieve it. Consider this vision for a car company:

> We will create an empowered organization to unleash our creativity and focus our energies in cooperative effort that will enable us to develop and build the best personal vehicles in the world, vehicles that people will treasure owning because they are fun to use, they are reliable, they keep people comfortable and safe, and they enable people to have freedom of movement in their environment without harming it.

This vision conveys an image of what can be achieved, why it is worthwhile, and how it can be done. Note that the vision is flexible enough to encourage the possibility of finding alternative power sources in the future and developing other types of vehicles besides conventional ground cars (e.g., fusion-powered air cars, as in the movie *Back to the Future*).

Value statement is a list of the key values or ideological themes considered important for an organization. The values usually pertain to treatment of customers, treatment of organization members, *core competencies*, and standards of excellence. Common themes include satisfying customers, achieving excellence in products or services, providing an innovative product or service, developing and empowering employees, and making important contributions to society. A value statement provides a good beginning for developing a more complete vision. However, just listing values does not clearly explain their relative priority, how they are interrelated, or how they will be expressed and achieved. An effective vision statement provides a glimpse of a possible future in which all the key values are realized at the same time.

Slogans are statements used to summarize and communicate values in simple terms. However, a slogan is limited in how many values can be expressed. Consider the following examples: technology is our business, quality is job one, we feel good when you feel good, all the news people want to read, and partners in making dreams come true. Only the last slogan has more than one value; it describes the ideal service provided to customers and the ideal relationship among the providers. Slogans can be useful as part of a larger vision, but overemphasis on a simplistic slogan can trivialize the vision and diminish important values not included in the slogan (Richards & Engle, 1986).

Strategic objectives are tangible outcomes or results to be achieved, sometimes by a specific deadline. A performance objective may be stated in terms of the absolute level of performance (e.g., profits, sales, return on investment), or the relative level of performance (e.g., becoming number one in the industry or region, outperforming a traditional rival). Neither type of objective is likely to involve enduring, ideological themes. Performance objectives are useful to guide planning and facilitate evaluation of progress, but the focus of a vision should be on values and ideological themes, not on improvement of economic outcomes or outperforming rivals. If performance objectives are included in a vision, they should be regarded as milestones along the way toward achieving ideological objectives.

Project objectives are defined in terms of the successful completion of a complex activity (e.g., developing a new type of product, implementing a new MBA program, establishing a subsidiary in China). These objectives can emphasize economic outcomes, ideological outcomes, or both. For example, a pharmaceutical company has a project to develop a new vaccine that will prevent a disease; successful completion of the project will improve profits, provide health benefits to society, and enhance scientific knowledge. A limitation of most project objectives is their relatively short-time perspective. When the project is completed, the vision is ended. Project objectives can be included in the long-term vision for an organization, or a supplementary vision can be built around an especially important project. However, no single project should be allowed to eclipse the fuller, more enduring vision for the organization.

To understand what an effective project vision looks like, it is helpful to examine a specific example. When Walt Disney conceived the idea of Disneyland, it was an entirely new type of activity for his company, and it was unlike any earlier amusement park. It would be expensive to build, and it was uncertain whether enough visitors would be attracted to yield a profit. At the time it was not obvious that Disneyland would become such a phenomenal success, and people were skeptical about the risky project. An inspiring vision was needed to gain support from other key members of top management and outside investors. Disney's vision for the park was described in the following way (Thomas, 1976, p. 246):

> The idea of Disneyland is a simple one. It will be a place for people to find happiness and knowledge. It will be a place for parents and children to spend pleasant times in one another's company: a place for teachers and pupils to discover greater ways of understanding and education. Here the older generation can recapture the nostalgia of days gone by, and the younger generation can savor the challenge of the future. Here will be the wonders of Nature and Man for all to see and understand. Disneyland will be based upon and dedicated to the ideals, the dreams and hard facts that have created America. And it will be uniquely equipped to dramatize these dreams and facts and send them forth as a source of courage and inspiration to all the world. Disneyland will be something of a fair, an exhibition, a playground, a community center, a museum of living facts, and a showplace of beauty and magic. It will be filled with the accomplishments, the joys and hopes of the world we live in. And it will remind us and show us how to make those wonders part of our own lives.

Most of the evidence about the importance of a vision for successful change in organizations comes from leadership research that is focused more on the process of envisioning than on the content of the vision. The visions articulated by effective leaders are sometimes elaborate and sometimes simple. Descriptive studies on the content of organizational visions found that most of them were expressed in the form of a performance objective or value statement that was very brief, strategic, and future oriented (Larwood, Falbe, Kriger, & Miesing, 1995; Ruvio, Rosenblatt, & Rachel Hertz-Lazarowitz, 2010). A study by Berson, Shamir, Avolio, and Popper (2001) found that leaders who were rated as highly transformational were more likely to develop visions that were future oriented and reflected a high level of optimism and confidence. A study of small entrepreneurial firms by Baum, Locke, and Kirkpatrick (1998) found that CEOs for the fastest growing firms were more likely to communicate a vision that emphasized future growth. The results from these studies seem to suggest that few organizations actually have a well-developed vision with significant ideological content. In recent years, some scholars have begun to question whether the importance of a vision for organization change has been overstated. More research is needed to determine what type of vision is sufficient to guide and inspire change in organizations and the conditions where an ideological vision is most important.

Guidelines for Developing a Vision

It is extremely difficult to develop a vision that will elicit commitment from the many diverse stakeholders whose support is needed for major change. Such a vision cannot be generated by a mechanical formula. Judgment and analytical ability are needed to synthesize the vision, but intuition and creativity are important as well. To develop an appealing vision, it is essential to have a good understanding of the organization (its

TABLE 2	Guidelines for Formulating a Vision

- Involve key stakeholders.
- Identify shared values and ideals.
- Identify strategic objectives with wide appeal.
- Identify relevant elements in the old ideology.
- Link the vision to core competencies and prior achievements.
- Continually assess and refine the vision..

operations, products, services, markets, competitors, and social-political environment), its culture (shared beliefs and assumptions about the world and the organization's place in it), and the underlying needs and values of employees and other stakeholders. In most cases, a successful vision is not the creation of a single, heroic leader working alone, but instead it reflects the contributions of many, diverse people in the organization (Tichy & Devanna, 1986). The vision is seldom created in a single moment of revelation, but instead it takes shape during a lengthy process of exploration, discussion, and refinement of ideas. The following guidelines for developing visions (see summary in Table 2) are based on leadership theories, empirical research, and practitioner insights (e.g., Conger, 1989; Kotter, 1996; Kouzes & Posner, 1987; Nadler, Shaw, Walton, & Associates, 1995; Nanus, 1992; Peters, 1987; Peters & Austin, 1985; Strange & Mumford, 2005; Tichy & Devanna, 1986; Trice & Beyer, 1993).

- **Involve key stakeholders.**

A single leader is unlikely to have the knowledge needed to develop a vision that will appeal to all the stakeholders whose support is necessary to accomplish major organizational change. Even when the initial ideas for a vision originate with the leader, it is desirable to involve key stakeholders in refining these ideas into a vision with widespread appeal. Key stakeholders may include owners, executives, other members of the organization, customers, investors, joint venture partners, and labor unions.

Often, the best place to begin is with senior executives, the group most likely to have the broad perspective and knowledge necessary to understand the need for change. An important source of ideas for a vision is to discuss beliefs and assumptions about the determinants of performance for the organization and changes that will affect future performance. It is easier to develop an ambitious but realistic vision for the organization if the key executives have accurate shared beliefs about the determinants of company performance and opportunities for the future. A shared "mental model" is useful both for developing a credible vision and for strategic planning.

Executives are not the only stakeholders to consult when formulating a vision. It is also essential to understand the values, hopes, and aspirations of other people in the organization. Gaining this insight can be difficult if people are unable or reluctant to explain what is really important to them. Kouzes and Posner (1987, p. 115) described how leaders may learn about the needs and values of followers:

> Leaders find the common thread that weaves together the fabric of human needs into a colorful tapestry. They seek out the brewing consensus among those they would lead. In order to do this, they develop a deep understanding of the collective yearnings. They listen carefully for quiet whisperings in dark corners. They attend to the subtle cues. They sniff the air to get the scent. They watch the faces. They get a sense of what people want, what they value, what they dream about.

- **Identify shared values and ideals.**

The appeal of a vision depends on its ideological content as well as on its relevance for the challenges facing the organization. If the vision embodies shared values and ideals for most members of the organization, it is more likely to elicit their commitment. Thus, another useful procedure is to identify and understand what values and ideals can be incorporated in the vision. Discovery of shared values often requires considerable time and effort, and there is no guarantee of success. If serious disagreement exists about the essential qualities for an ideal organization, then it will be difficult to find a vision that transcends these differences.

One approach is to ask executives to develop a personal vision statement describing what they see as their ideal future role in the organization. The personal vision statements can be examined to identify shared values and appealing images of how the organization should be transformed. Another approach for identifying shared values and ideals is to ask people to describe what the best possible future would look like for the organization. One technique suggested by Tichy and Devanna (1986) is to ask executives to write a magazine article in journalistic style describing the organization as they would like it to be at a specified time in the future. A variation of this technique is a role play in which half of the executives (the "reporters") interview the remaining executives and ask them to describe how they would like the organization to be in 10 years. Still another technique is to have people describe a fictitious organization that would be able to compete effectively with the leading companies in a specified market. The group then determines how the current organization differs from the fictitious one and looks for ways to close the gaps.

- **Identify strategic objectives with wide appeal.**

It is sometimes easier to get agreement on strategic objectives than on a more elaborate vision, and a group discussion of objectives can provide insight about values and ideals to include in a vision. The first step is to ask people to identify specific performance objectives that are challenging and relevant to the mission of the organization. Then ask people to discuss the relative importance of the various objectives and the reasons why an objective is important. Look for shared values and ideals that can become the basis for a vision with wide appeal.

- **Identify relevant elements in the old ideology.**

Even when radical change is necessary in an organization, some elements in the current ideology may be worthy of preservation. Look for values and ideals that will continue to be relevant for the organization in the foreseeable future. Sometimes traditional values that were subverted or ignored can serve as the basis for a new vision, as in the following example:

> A manufacturing company that once had a reputation for making the best products in the industry decided to pursue a strategy of cost reduction to compete with the inexpensive products of foreign competitors. The strategy was not successful. After several years of declining sales the company lost its dominant position in the market and its products were perceived to be of inferior quality. Major changes were made to implement a new strategy that emphasized quality and innovation rather than low price. The strategy was justified as a return to key values from the glorious early years of the firm.

- **Link the vision to core competencies and prior achievements.**

A successful vision must be credible. People will be skeptical about a vision that promises too much and seems impossible to attain. Leaders face a difficult task in crafting a vision that is both challenging and believable. Lofty visions often require innovative strategies, and untested strategies are risky and difficult to assess. In the absence of a tested strategy, people need a basis for believing the vision is attainable. One way to build follower optimism about the vision is to link it to their ability to collectively solve problems and overcome difficult obstacles. If people have been successful in past efforts to accomplish difficult objectives, the leader can use these successes to build confidence in their ability to do it again.

> When President Kennedy first articulated his visionary objective to land a man on the moon by the end of the decade, only about 15 percent of the necessary technology and procedures had been developed, and it was not evident that so many difficult things could be done successfully in such a short time. However, the availability of scientists and engineers with the necessary expertise and confidence to tackle these formidable problems made the vision more credible. The objective was successfully achieved in less time than initially expected.

- **Continually assess and refine the vision.**

A successful vision is likely to evolve over time. As strategies to achieve the vision are implemented, people can learn more about what is feasible and what is not. As progress is made toward achieving the vision, new possibilities may be discovered, and objectives that seemed unrealistic may suddenly become attainable. Although some continuity in the vision is desirable, it is helpful to keep looking for ways to make the vision more appealing and credible (e.g., new metaphors, slogans, and symbols that capture the essence of the vision). The development of a vision is an interactive, circular process, not a simple, linear progression from vision to strategy to action. A review of strategy may provide the ideas for a new vision, and information about changing conditions may require major revisions rather than just minor adjustments.

In his seminal piece, John Kotter (1995) illustrated why transformation efforts fail. He provided the following steps as guidelines for a successful change process:

1. **Establish a great-enough sense of urgency.**

   Kotter suggests that for change to be successful, 75 percent of a company's management needs to "buy into" the change. For change to happen, the entire company must really want it. This might spark the initial motivation to get things moving.

2. **Form a powerful coalition.**

   The change process often requires strong leadership and visible support from key people within the organization.

3. **Create a vision for change.**

   A change initiative naturally comes along with many great ideas and solutions. A leader needs to link these concepts to an overall vision that people can grasp easily and remember.

4. **Communicate the vision.**

   The call for change will probably have strong competition from other day-to-day communications within the company. As a result, a leader needs to communicate the vision frequently and powerfully, and embed it within everything.

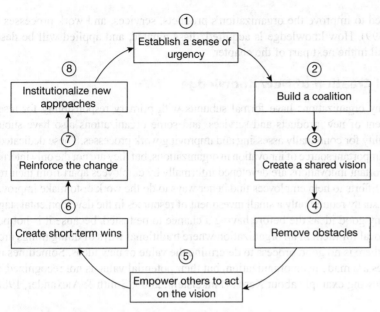

FIGURE 1 Leading the Change

Source: John P. Kotter, *Leading Change*, HBS Press, 1996

5. **Remove obstacles.**

Let go! Removing obstacles that often come in the form of peoples' desire for status quo becomes necessary to execute the vision and can help the change move forward.

6. **Create short-term wins.**

Leaders must create short-term targets, not just one long-term goal. On accomplishing these short-term targets, the leaders must celebrate them, to keep the change process rolling.

7. **Build on the change.**

Kotter argues that many change projects fail because victory is declared too early. Real change runs deep. Quick wins are only the beginning of what needs to be done to achieve long-term change.

8. **Anchor the change in the culture.**

The leader must prepare the team for the next change. This is specifically mandated in the VUCA (volatility, uncertainty, complexity, and ambiguity) business environment.

Collective Learning and Innovation

The environment of most organizations is becoming increasingly dynamic and competitive. Competition is becoming more intense, customer expectations are rising, less time is available to develop and market new products and services, and they become obsolete sooner. To succeed in this turbulent environment, organizations need to have people at every level who are oriented toward learning and continuous improvement.

Organizational learning involves acquiring and using new knowledge. The new knowledge can be created internally or acquired from outside the organization (Nevis et al., 1995). After new knowledge is acquired, it must be conveyed to the people who need it and applied to improve the organization's products, services, and work processes (Crossan et al., 1999). How knowledge is acquired, disseminated, and applied will be described in more detail in the next part of the chapter.

Internal Creation of New Knowledge

Many organizations have formal subunits with primary responsibility for research and development of new products and services, and some organizations also have subunits with responsibility for continually assessing and improving work processes. These dedicated subunits can be an important source of innovation in organizations, but they are not the only internal source; many important innovations are developed informally by employees apart from their regular job activities. Efforts to help employees find better ways to do the work or to make improvements in products usually require only a small investment of resources in the developmental stage.

Many good ideas die before having a chance to be tested, because it is not possible to gain approval for them in an organization where traditional ways of doing things are favored, or where there is no good process to determine the value of new ideas. Sometimes important discoveries are made in an organization, but their potential value is not recognized, as shown in the following example about Xerox (Finkelstein, 2003; Smith & Alexander, 1988).

> Several major discoveries were made at the Palo Alto Research Center, including the graphic user interface, the mouse, the Ethernet, and the laser printer. Except for the laser printer, executives at Xerox failed to recognize the potential value of these discoveries. Microsoft and Apple would eventually earn billions of dollars from the sale of products that incorporated the unused discoveries. According to Steve Jobs, the CEO of Apple, Xerox missed the opportunity to become the dominant company in the computer industry.

To facilitate the development and approval of innovations, it is helpful to have sponsors or champions who will shepherd new ideas through the long and tedious review and approval process in organizations. Also important is an impartial but systematic process for reviewing and assessing new ideas suggested by individual employees or teams. Examples include "venture boards" or "innovation teams" to identify high potential ideas and determine which ideas will receive additional funding and development (Pryor & Shays, 1993).

External Acquisition of New Knowledge

An important leadership function is to encourage and facilitate external acquisition of relevant knowledge. New ideas and knowledge also be acquired from a variety of outside sources, including: publications on results of applied research, books or articles describing practitioner experiences, and observation of best practices used elsewhere. Other sources include purchasing the right to use specific knowledge from another organization, getting advice from consultants who have relevant expertise, hiring outsiders with special expertise, entering joint ventures with another organization to increase learning opportunities, and acquiring another organization that has relevant expertise and patents.

The process of examining best practices used in successful organizations is sometimes called "*benchmarking*" (Camp, 1989), and an example is provided by Main (1992).

> The benchmarking manager for Xerox read an article about the success of L.L.Bean, the catalog retailer, in filling customer orders quickly and accurately. He organized a fact-finding visit to the headquarters office of L.L.Bean in Freeport, Maine. The team found that good planning and software support helped to make Bean three times faster than Xerox in filling small orders. The team used this knowledge to help redesign the procedures used at Xerox warehouses, resulting in significant improvements.

Another example is provided by Peters and Austin (1985).

> The owner of a chain of successful dairy stores conducts regular visits to competing stores accompanied by several of his employees. They look for things the competitor does better, and everyone is challenged to find at least one good idea that can be used. Nobody is allowed to discuss things done better by their store, which would bias the visitors to look for negative rather than positive things. During the return trip in the van, the discussion of ideas and how to implement them provides a unique opportunity for each employee to become an empowered member of a team of retailing experts.

Imitating the best practices of others can be beneficial, but it is essential to evaluate their relevance before adopting them. It is also important to remember that imitation alone seldom provides much of a competitive advantage. Rather than simply copying what others are doing, it is usually better to improve their best practices, and to invent new approaches not yet discovered by competitors.

Exploration and Exploitation

When describing the objectives of collective learning in organizations, a distinction is often made between *exploration* and *exploitation* (Benner & Tushman, 2003; March, 1991). Exploration involves finding innovative new products, services, processes, or technology, whereas exploitation involves learning how to make incremental improvements in existing products, services, or processes. Both learning processes are necessary to some extent in organizations, and their relative importance will depend on the competitive strategy and the pace of change in the external environment (e.g., He & Wong, 2003; O'Reilly & Tushman, 2004; Tushman & O'Reilly, 1996). There is growing evidence that successful firms are able to develop new products and services (involving exploration) simultaneously with delivery of existing ones in an efficient way (which involves exploitation).

A difficult challenge for leaders is how to gain the benefits of both learning processes and avoid adverse side effects (Miller, 1990; Yukl & Lepsinger, 2004). Too much emphasis on exploration may result in excessive costs for acquiring new knowledge (e.g., for R&D), but too much emphasis on exploitation can reduce flexibility and discourage development of new products and services. Introducing new products too quickly can reduce the profitability of established products that are still selling well and paying off their developmental costs, but waiting too long can result in the loss of competitive advantage. Effective leaders balance the trade-offs and integrate the processes in a way that is appropriate for the situation.

Effective leaders also recognize opportunities for combining the two types of learning. For example, methods usually associated with exploitation can be used to reduce costs for expensive forms of exploration, such as research in the pharmaceutical industry. Methods usually associated with exploration can be used to improve the efficiency of established processes and to reduce the cost of traditional products and services.

Knowledge Diffusion and Application

New knowledge is of little value unless it is made available to people who need it and is used by them. Some organizations are successful at discovering knowledge, but fail to apply it effectively. One example is provided by a multinational company that established a "center of marketing excellence" in its Australian operations (Ulrich, Jick, & Von Glinow, 1993). Successful pilot programs increased market share by 25 percent, but the lessons learned never reached the European and U.S. divisions, where the benefits would have been even greater. Similar examples can be found in many organizations.

Secrecy is the enemy of learning, and easy access to information about the organization's operations, including problems and failures, facilitates learning. There are several different approaches to encourage and facilitate knowledge sharing in organizations (Earl, 2001). An increasing number of companies have sophisticated information systems to facilitate easy access by employees to relevant information. An employee with a difficult task can discover how other people in the organization handled a similar task in the past, and employees can interact with each other to get advice and support about common problems.

A more formalized mechanism for translating learning into practice is to describe best practices and effective procedures in written or electronic manuals. For example, when the U.S. Army discovers an effective way to conduct some type of operation, it is translated into doctrine to guide others who will be performing the same operation. Formal doctrine can be useful, but it is not as flexible or easily updated as posting best practices and lessons learned on an interactive network. Moreover, formal doctrine often ends up being used in a way that discourages subsequent learning and innovation.

Another approach for diffusing new knowledge in an organization is a special purpose conference to facilitate sharing of new knowledge and ideas among the subunits of an organization. General Electric conducts "best practice" workshops to encourage sharing of ideas among managers. A large government agency holds a conference each year to enable participants from different facilities to present new ideas and informally discuss how to improve service quality.

Seminars and workshops can be used to teach people how to perform new activities or use new technology. When it is not feasible for people to attend a conference or workshop, a team of experts can be dispatched to different work sites to show people how to use new procedures. An alternative approach is to transfer individuals with new knowledge to other units, or assign them on a temporary basis to teach others. A person who has participated in a successful change can serve as a catalyst and consultant for change in another unit.

Learning Organizations

All organizations learn things, but some do it much better than others. The term *learning organization* has been used to describe organizations that learn rapidly and use the knowledge to become more effective (e.g., Crossan et al., 1999; Fiol & Lyles, 1985; Huber, 1991; Levitt & March, 1988). In these organizations, the values of learning, innovation, experimentation, flexibility, and initiative are firmly embedded in the culture of the organization (Baer & Frese, 2003; James, 2002; Kotter & Heskett, 1992; Miron, Erez, & Naveh, 2004; Popper & Lipshitz, 1998). Resources are invested in promoting learning, knowledge is made easily available to anyone who needs it, and people are encouraged to apply it to their work. The advantage of a learning culture is shown by the way a hospital responded to a physicians strike (Meyer, 1982).

The hospital that adapted most successfully had a culture in which innovation, professional autonomy, and entrepreneurial activity were strong values. The administrator anticipated the strike and asked a task force to develop scenarios describing how it would affect the hospital. Supervisors were asked to read the scenarios and develop contingency plans. When the strike actually occurred, the hospital was able to adapt quickly and continue making profits, despite a drastic drop in the number of patients. When the strike ended, the hospital was able to re-adapt quickly. In the process the hospital even discovered some new ways to cut operating costs.

Most organizations fall short of this ideal. A major obstacle is the common belief that top management should have most of the responsibility for leading change and innovation. This belief encourages a top-down approach to innovation, rather than a collaborative approach that includes emergent processes. Many CEOs are too insulated to recognize opportunities and threats immediately, and bottom-up initiatives help an organization to be more flexible and adaptive. Top management can help to avoid or overcome this obstacle by implementing systems and programs that support local initiatives and emergent processes of learning and innovation. People at all levels should be empowered to deal with problems and find better ways of doing the work. Innovation programs should nurture ideas and support changes initiated by people at lower levels in the organization. The process of discovery and *diffusion of knowledge* can be accelerated by encouraging accurate communication, implementing appropriate information systems, allowing greater access to information, and encouraging people to use social networks to increase their access to relevant information and ideas. All leaders in the organization need to communicate and model values relevant for a learning culture. Finally, the appraisal and compensation system should provide equitable rewards for knowledge creation, sharing, and application (Bartol & Srivastava, 2002; Yukl, 2009).

Guidelines for Enhancing Learning and Innovation

Leaders at all levels can help to create conditions favorable to learning and innovation. The following guidelines (see Table 3) are based on theory, research findings, and practitioner insights (e.g., Berson, Nemanich, Waldman, Galvin, & Keller, 2006; Cavaleri & Fearon, 1996; Chaston, Badger, Mangles, & Sadler-Smith, 2001; Garvin, 1993; James, 2002; McGill, Slocum, & Lei, 1993; Madsen & Desai, 2010; Nadler et al., 1995; Sabherwal & Becerra-Fernandez, 2003; Schein, 1993; Senge, 1990; Ulrich, Jick, & Von Glinow, 1993; Vera & Crossan, 2004; Yeung, Ulrich, Nason, & Von Glinow, 1999; Yukl, 2009; Zhang & Bartol, 2010).

- **Recruit talented, creative people and empower them to be innovative.**

New and better ways to accomplish work unit objectives are more likely to be found by people who are talented and creative. One way for a leader to facilitate innovation is to recruit people who have the skills and enthusiasm to develop new ideas, and then empower them to pursue these ideas by providing necessary time and resources. An example of this type of leadership is provided by Anne Sweeney (Bisoux, 2006).

TABLE 3	Guidelines for Increasing Learning and Innovation

- Recruit talented, creative people and empower them to be innovative.
- Encourage appreciation for flexibility and innovation.
- Encourage and facilitate learning by individuals and teams.
- Help people improve their mental models.
- Evaluate new ideas with small scale experiments.
- Leverage learning from surprises and failures.
- Encourage and facilitate sharing of knowledge and ideas.
- Preserve past learning and ensure continued use of relevant knowledge.
- Set innovation goals.
- Reward entrepreneurial behavior.

Sweeney is the president of Disney-ABC Television Group and one of the most powerful and successful women in business. Her achievements include the successful creation of new ventures such as Nickelodeon. Sweeney has a passion for innovation and uses her leadership skills to encourage and facilitate change. She hires people who are talented, enthusiastic about their work, and unafraid of change. She expects them to serve as internal entrepreneurs to keep the company relevant, and she gives them the autonomy they need to be creative.

• Encourage appreciation for flexibility and innovation.

Major change will be more acceptable and less disruptive if people develop pride and confidence in their capacity to adapt and learn. Confident people are more likely to view change as an exciting challenge rather than an unpleasant burden. To develop an appreciation for flexibility and adaptation, encourage people to view all practices as temporary. Each activity should be examined periodically to determine whether it is still needed and how it can be improved or eliminated. Encourage subordinates and peers to question traditional assumptions about the work and to "think outside the box" when solving problems. Encourage people to apply creative ideas for improving work processes. Encourage and support relevant learning practices and quality improvement programs (e.g., benchmarking, Six Sigma, TQM, quality circles).

• Encourage and facilitate learning by individuals and teams.

Organizations can learn only when individual members of the organization are learning (Senge, 1990). More individual learning will occur if the organization has strong cultural values for personal development and lifelong education, and it provides training and development programs to help individuals learn new skills. Opportunities for learning are also increased by empowering individuals or teams to try new and innovative approaches for doing the work. However, providing learning opportunities is not enough to guarantee actual learning will occur. Leaders should keep subordinates informed about relevant learning opportunities (e.g., workshops, training programs, college courses) and make it easier for them to pursue these opportunities (e.g., allowing time and providing education subsidies). Leaders can also encourage and facilitate collective learning in teams by using procedures such as after activity reviews. Finally, leaders can provide tangible rewards to encourage individuals to acquire new knowledge and apply it to improve their job performance.

• Help people improve their mental models.

People have conscious beliefs and implicit assumptions about the causes of performance and the source of problems. These "mental models" influence how they interpret events and information about the effects of decisions and actions (Cannon-Bowers, Salas, & Converse, 1993; Senge, 1990). Leaders can help people improve their mental models about the way things work in organizations and the reasons for success or failure. One form of collective learning is to analyze feedback about prior performance. How such feedback is interpreted depends on what assumptions are made about the causal relationships among variables and how much time is necessary for decisions and actions to have visible effects. A poor mental model about causal relationships is likely to result in inaccurate interpretation of performance feedback. For collective learning to be successful, team members must be able to develop a shared mental model that is accurate and use it to interpret performance feedback. As noted earlier in this chapter, to develop a better understanding of complex problems often requires systems thinking. By helping people to understand complex systems, a leader can increase their ability to learn and solve problems. In this way, the leader also helps people understand that they are not powerless and can collectively influence events in the organization.

- **Evaluate new ideas with small scale experiments.**

One way to assess the feasibility of new ideas is to test them on a small scale. In recent years, the trend has been for more organizations to use small experiments and controlled tests to facilitate learning. A well-known example of an organization with an experimental orientation is Wal-Mart, which regularly conducts hundreds of tests in its stores on sales promotions, displays, and improving customer service. Small-scale experiments provide an opportunity to try out new ideas without the risks entailed by major change programs. People who are skeptical about a controversial new approach may be willing to experiment on a small scale to evaluate it. The amount of learning that results from an experiment depends on how well it is designed and executed. Even a simple experiment can provide useful information. However, experiments do not always produce useful knowledge, and the results may even be misleading. Careful planning is needed to ensure that a controlled test yields clear, meaningful results.

- **Leverage learning from surprises and failures.**

Surprises usually provide a good opportunity for learning. Things that turn out just as expected confirm existing theories or assumptions but do not provide new insights. Unfortunately, many people tend to discount or ignore unexpected information that does not fit their theories or assumptions about how things work. Some of the most important scientific discoveries resulted from investigating unexpected "accidents" or "anomalies" that would be overlooked by people only interested in confirming prior beliefs or favorite theories. It is helpful to specify in advance what results are expected from an activity or change and the underlying assumptions on which the prediction is based. Otherwise, instead of using unexpected results to reevaluate the model, people are more likely to overlook them or assume that they could have been predicted in advance. Make specific predictions and the reasons for them a regular part of the planning process, and make evaluation of outcomes in relation to predictions a regular part of the review process for activities. Use unexpected failures as an opportunity to learn more about a strategy or process, rather than looking for someone to blame for them.

- **Encourage and facilitate sharing of knowledge and ideas.**

Leaders at all levels should facilitate the timely dissemination of new ideas and knowledge in the organization. Attend meetings with people from different subunits of the organization (or send a representative) to discuss ideas for solving common problems. Encourage subordinates to share relevant ideas and knowledge with other people in the organization who can use it to improve their own performance. Encourage subordinates to support and make use of knowledge management programs (e.g., a resource directory, databases, and groupware). Invite experts or outside consultants to inform members of the unit or team about relevant discoveries, new technology, and improved practices.

- **Preserve past learning and ensure continued use of relevant knowledge.**

A common mistake is to assume that once something has been learned in an organization it remains in the "organizational memory." However, knowledge that is not being used may not be retained in an accessible form, and knowledge that resides only in the heads of individuals may be lost when they leave the organization. Sometimes an organization implements best practices for avoiding serious problems, but the practices are later abandoned and the organization eventually has a disaster that could have been prevented (Kletz, 1993). It is important for leaders to ensure that useful knowledge is preserved and relevant practices continue to be used. Advances in the technology for information processing have made it easier to find relevant knowledge quickly, while still preserving the security of proprietary knowledge.

- **Set innovation goals.**

The pressure of meeting normal task deadlines tends to leave little time for reflective thinking about ways to make things better. A leader should encourage entrepreneurial activity and help employees find the time to pursue their ideas for new or improved products and processes. One way to increase the number of creative ideas is to set innovation goals for individuals or teams. A special meeting is scheduled on a monthly or quarterly basis to discuss these ideas and review progress. Goals can also be set for the application of ideas to improve products and work processes. For example, some companies set a goal to have new products or services (e.g., those introduced within the last three years) account for a substantial percentage of sales each year.

- **Reward entrepreneurial behavior.**

Employees who invent new products or suggest ways to improve existing products and processes should receive appropriate recognition and equitable rewards. The support and cooperation of many people are needed to get new ideas accepted and implemented effectively in an organization. It is essential to provide recognition and equitable rewards not only to the individuals or teams who contribute creative ideas, but also to individuals who serve as sponsors, advocates, and champions for innovations.

Summary

One of the most important and difficult leadership responsibilities is to guide and facilitate the process of making a major change in an organization. A major change may involve a variety of different objectives, including attitudes, roles, technology, competitive strategy, economics, and people. The change process can be described as having different stages, such as unfreezing, changing, and refreezing. Moving too quickly through the stages can endanger the success of a change effort. People typically transit through a series of emotional stages as they adjust to the need for a drastic change in their lives. Understanding each of these change processes helps leaders guide and facilitate change.

A major change is unlikely to be successful unless it is based on an adequate diagnosis of the problem or opportunity that was the reason for making it. This diagnosis should include systems thinking about complex relationships, multiple causes and outcomes, delayed effects, cyclical causality, and the potential for unintended consequences. When planning a major change, it is also desirable to anticipate likely resistance and plan how to avoid or resolve it. There are many reasons for resisting, and resistance should be viewed as a normal defensive response, not as a character weakness or a sign of ignorance.

Before people will support radical change, they need to have a vision of a better future that is attractive enough to justify the sacrifices and hardships the change will require. To be inspiring, the vision must include strong ideological content that appeals to organization members' shared values and ideals concerning customers, employees, and the mission of the organization. The vision is usually created in an interactive process involving key stakeholders.

A leader can do many things to facilitate the successful implementation of change. Political actions include identifying likely supporters and opponents, creating a coalition to approve changes, forming teams to guide the implementation of changes, filling key positions with competent change agents, making symbolic changes that affect the work, and monitoring the progress of change to detect problems that require attention. People-oriented actions include creating a sense of urgency, articulating a clear vision of the likely benefits, preparing people for change, helping them cope with change, providing opportunities for early successes, keeping people informed, demonstrating continued commitment to the change program, and empowering people to help plan and implement change.

It is important for leaders to influence the acquisition, retention, and application of relevant knowledge that can provide a competitive advantage. Leaders can help to create the conditions favorable to organizational learning and an appropriate balance of exploration and exploitation. New knowledge and innovative ideas can be discovered through reflection, research, and systematic learning activities, or acquired externally by imitation, purchase of expertise, or participation in joint ventures. The discovery of new knowledge is of little use unless it is disseminated to people who need it and used to improve products, services, and processes. Individual leaders can do many things to encourage and facilitate learning and innovation in the organization.

Review and Discussion Questions

1. What are the major reasons for resistance to change?
2. What are the process theories of change and how are they useful?
3. What are the desirable characteristics for a vision?
4. What are some guidelines for developing a compelling vision?
5. What are some reasons why efforts to change organizations often fail?
6. What are some guidelines to help leaders implement change?
7. What is a learning organization and what kind of learning occurs in it?
8. How can leaders increase collective learning and innovation?

Key Terms

benchmarking	innovation	stakeholders
change agents	learning organization	symbolic changes
core competencies	mental models	systems dynamics
diffusion of knowledge	mission statement	value statement
exploitation	organizational diagnosis	vision
exploration	resistance to change	

CASE 1

Ultimate Office Products

Ultimate Office Products was an old, established manufacturing company in the turbulent office products industry. Discount merchandisers and office product superstores were spreading rapidly and altering the traditional distribution channels once dominated by wholesalers and smaller retail stores. The growing power of the superstores was forcing manufacturers to improve customer service. The traditional manufacturers were being challenged by new companies more willing to cut prices and use technologies favored by the superstores, such as electronic orders and billing. Ultimate Office Products was losing market share and profits were declining.

Richard Kelly was the director of information systems, a newly created position in the company. When the CEO met with Richard to discuss his new responsibilities and objectives, she explained that it was essential to speed up order processing and improve customer service. Richard knew that the order processing system used by the company was obsolete. He prepared a plan to automate the system and got approval from the CEO for it. Then, he purchased new computer workstations and a software package to support them. The software would enable customers to make electronic orders, and it would improve order processing, billing, and inventory control. However, months after the equipment and software arrived, it was still waiting to be used. The managers from sales, production, accounting, shipping, and customer service could not agree about the requirements of the new system, which was necessary to get it operating. These managers were Richard's peers, and he had no direct authority over them. Even though he encouraged cooperation, meetings among the managers usually ended with heated accusations about who was responsible for the company's problems. Most of the managers disagreed about the reason for the delays in filling orders, and some questioned the need for an expensive new system. Meanwhile, the CEO was becoming impatient about the lack of progress. She made it clear that, after spending a small fortune on new technology, she expected Richard to find a way to resolve the problem. Richard decided it was time to take a different approach.

His first step was to gather more information about the reasons for delays in processing and filling orders. He began by having his staff map the workflow from the time orders were received until the filled orders were shipped. As he suspected, many unnecessary activities created bottlenecks that could be eliminated to speed up the process. The problems extended across functional boundaries and required changes in all departments. The preliminary results were presented to the CEO, who agreed on the need for dramatic improvements and authorized Richard to begin reengineering the process. Despite having the support of the CEO, Richard knew that widespread commitment would be needed for major changes to be successful. Richard met with the department managers to get their assistance in forming some cross-functional task forces. Although he knew that one task force would probably be enough to determine what changes were needed, he wanted to involve more people in the change process so that they would understand and support it. An outside consultant was secured to advise the task forces in their work.

Each task force examined a different aspect of the problem. They analyzed processes, met with key customers to learn what they wanted, and visited other companies to learn how they processed orders more efficiently. As people began working together to understand the system, they began to realize how serious the problems were. The participants were able to put aside their functional biases and cooperate in finding ways to improve efficiency and customer service. Each team made recommendations to the steering committee, composed of

Richard and the department managers. The CEO also attended these meetings to emphasize their importance. When one of the department managers opposed a change, everyone in the meeting looked at the CEO, who made it clear that she supported the task force recommendation. Within a year, the company eliminated many of the steps formerly required to process an order, and the average number of days to fill an order was reduced by nearly half. Many more orders were being made electronically, and most mistakes in the billing process were eliminated. As people discovered that they could actually change things for the better, many of them volunteered to serve on teams that would continue to look for ways to improve quality and customer service.

Copyright © 1996 by Gary Yukl

Questions

1. Why did Richard fail in his first attempt to implement change? *Mariah*
2. Identify subsequent actions by Richard that were more effective for implementing change in the organization. *Rebecca*
3. Evaluate the change leadership provided by the CEO. *Austin*

CASE 2

The Fruit Company

The Fruit Company grows and markets watermelons and pineapples in Kochi, Kerala. The company has been in the produce business for the last 50 years and has some of the finest land for growing these fruits. It has also been quite successful in marketing its products.

Until now, the company has been a family business run by senior Mishra, whose father and uncle started the business. His son, junior Mishra, has been working as an assistant since he returned from IIM Lucknow after completing his two-year Management course.

There are three major sets of activities that must be accomplished to grow and market the two fruits. One group of workers and managers works in the fields, handling the growth and harvest of the watermelons and pineapples. Another group of workers and managers works in development research. This group is made up largely of agriculture scientists who attempt to improve the varieties grown and to increase crop yield. Marketing is handled by

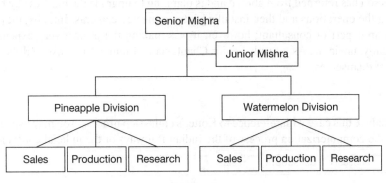

Option 1

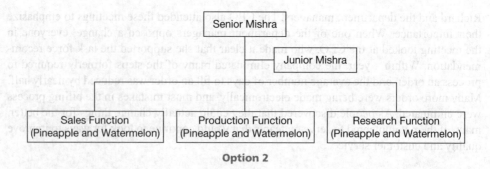

Option 2

several sales personnel who call on wholesalers and fruit distributors in the region. The sales force is very large and has been, like all other employees, very effective.

Senior and junior Mishra have been managing the firm without many formal policies and procedures. The company has a few set rules, procedures, and job descriptions. Senior Mishra believes that after people know their job, they should and would do it well. However, the firm has grown fairly large, and senior and junior Mishra believe that it is necessary to develop a more-formal organizational structure. They have two options, as shown in Figure 2.

Questions

1. Identify which of the two options provided in the figure is more suited for the firm.
2. Identify the challenges the Mishras are likely to face in implementing these changes.

CASE 3
Chaurasia and Sons

Manubhai Chaurasia owns electronics stores by the name of Chaurasia and Sons in Uttar Pradesh. There are 30 branches across the state. He is a direct dealer of low-cost items (below ₹25000); for higher-cost items, he depends on local distributors. With customers who deal in both cash and credit, he has an understanding with local personal financing firms. However, only well-known customers can avail personal financing. He has a total of 300 employees, of which 100 are on commissions, 40 on commissions and salary, and the remaining on salary only. The firm has not suffered any attrition due to its friendly policies.

His son has returned from abroad and is planning to upgrade the business by first computerizing the operations and then installing interconnected cameras. Initially, they thought of hiring an expert or consultant; however, it was making the project very expensive and, consequently, unviable. As a result, senior Chaurasia and junior Chaurasia will have to run the project themselves.

Question

1. Analyze this case with reference to Kotter's eight-step process. You may use references to the computerization process of the Indian Railways or the judicial courts in India.

Leadership Traits and Skills

Learning Objectives

After studying this chapter, you should be able to:

- Understand how leader traits and skills are related to effective leadership.
- Understand the types of research methods used to study leadership traits and skills.
- Understand what traits and skills are most relevant for effective leadership.
- Understand what traits and skills best predict success in a managerial career.
- Understand how the relevance of a trait or skill depends on the situation.
- Understand the limitations of the trait approach.

One of the earliest approaches to studying leadership was the trait approach, which involved a search for traits and skills that predict whether a person will attain positions of leadership and be effective in these positions. This chapter reviews research on the individual attributes of successful leaders. The emphasis is on traits and skills that contribute to managerial effectiveness and advancement, rather than on traits that predict who will emerge as a leader in an informal group. The chapter begins with an explanation of basic concepts and research methods in the trait approach. Then major findings about traits and skills related to effective leadership are reviewed, and some situations that affect the relevance of the skills are described. The chapter ends with several guidelines for managers based on the findings.

Introduction to the Trait Approach

The constructs used most often in the trait approach include traits, skills, and values of individual leaders. Each type of construct and the major types of research in the trait approach are explained briefly in this section of the chapter.

From Chapter 6 of *Leadership in Organizations,* Eighth Edition. Gary Yukl. Copyright © 2013 by Pearson Education, Inc. Publishing as Prentice Hall. All rights reserved.

Individual Attributes Relevant for Leadership

The term *trait* refers to a variety of individual attributes, including aspects of personality, temperament, needs, motives, and values. Personality traits are relatively stable dispositions to behave in a particular way. Examples include *self-confidence,* extroversion, *emotional maturity,* and energy level. Needs (or motives) are another type of trait that involves a desire for particular types of stimuli or experiences. Psychologists usually differentiate between physiological needs (e.g., hunger, thirst) and social motives such as achievement, esteem, affiliation, power, and independence. Needs and motives are important because they influence attention to information and events, and they guide, energize, and sustain behavior. Considerable evidence shows that most traits are jointly determined by learning and by an inherited capacity to gain satisfaction from particular types of stimuli or experiences (Bouchard, Lykken, McGue, Segal, & Tellegen, 1990; Zhang, Ilies, & Arvey, 2009). Some traits (e.g., social needs) are probably more influenced by learning than others (temperament, physiological needs).

Values are internalized attitudes about what is right and wrong, ethical and unethical, moral and immoral. Examples include fairness and justice, honesty, freedom, equality, altruism, loyalty, civility (courtesy and politeness), pragmatism, and performance orientation (excellence). Values are important because they influence a person's preferences, perception of problems, and choice of behavior.

Self-concepts, self-identities, and *social identities* involve values and beliefs about a person's occupation, relationships to others, and worthwhile roles and activities. It is usually assumed that people are intrinsically motivated to defend their self-esteem and to maintain consistency among their core values, social identities, and behavior.

The term *skill* refers to the ability to do something in an effective manner. Like traits, skills are determined jointly by learning and heredity (Arvey, Zhang, Avolio, & Krueger, 2007). Skills may be defined at different levels of abstraction, ranging from general, broadly-defined abilities (e.g., intelligence, interpersonal skill) to narrower, more specific abilities (verbal reasoning, persuasive ability).

The term *competency* may involve traits or skills, and *competencies* often include a combination of related skills and traits. Competencies are often used to describe qualities considered relevant for managers in a particular organization or profession, in which case they are more useful for consultants than for researchers.

Types of Research on Leader Traits and Skills

Several types of research have been used in the trait approach. In the first type of study, researchers seek to discover traits and skills that predict whether a person will pursue a leadership career or emerge as an informal leader in a group (Lord, DeVader, & Alliger, 1986; Stogdill, 1974). Some studies compare leaders to non-leaders in the same profession in terms of their scores on measures of traits and skills. Other studies examine the traits and skills of individuals who emerge as leaders in a group problem-solving exercise.

The second type of research seeks to discover how the traits and skills of managers are related to measures of leadership effectiveness in their current management positions (Bass, 1990; Boyatzis, 1982). Measures of traits and skills are obtained using tests, coded critical incidents, leader self-ratings, or ratings by other people; then these measures are correlated with measures of leadership effectiveness (e.g., subordinate satisfaction or performance, unit performance, ratings of leader effectiveness by bosses). Meta-analyses of a large number of these studies can provide an estimate of the relationship between each type of trait or skill and leadership effectiveness (e.g., Judge, Piccolo, & Kosalka, 2009).

The third type of research uses longitudinal studies conducted over a period of several years to discover traits and skills that predict advancement to higher levels of management. Relevant traits and skills are measured with tests, interviews, and biographical information collected during the selection process or in assessment centers used to identify promising candidates for promotion. These measures are correlated with the rate of advancement to higher level management positions and other indicators of eventual career success (e.g., Bray, Campbell, & Grant, 1974; Howard & Bray, 1988; McClelland & Boyatzis, 1982; Miner, 1978).

A fourth type of research compares managers who advanced successfully to top management to managers who initially advanced but then *"derailed"* in their careers because they were dismissed, opted for early retirement, or simply reached a "plateau" without any chance of further advancement (McCall & Lombardo, 1983a; McCartney & Campbell, 2006). Information about the traits, skills, and career experiences of each manager are collected and analyzed to identify similarities and differences for derailed and successful managers. In another version of this research, executives and middle managers rated the extent to which various flaws are likely to derail a management career in the United States and Europe (Lombardo & McCauley, 1988; Van Velsor & Leslie, 1995).

Overview of Findings in the Trait Research

Hundreds of studies were conducted over a period of several decades to examine how traits and skills are related to leadership emergence, effectiveness, and career advancement. The initial conclusions reached in Stogdill's (1974) literature review were confirmed by subsequent reviews and meta-analyses (Bass, 1990, 2008; Judge et al., 2009; Zaccaro, 2007). Some traits and skills increase the likelihood that a leader will be effective, but they do not guarantee effectiveness. A leader with certain traits can be effective in one situation but ineffective in a different situation. Furthermore, two leaders with a different pattern of traits can be successful in the same situation. With regard to different criteria, such as advancement, unit performance, subordinate satisfaction, management of crises, the pattern of traits and skills that best predicts the criterion varies somewhat from one criterion to another.

Findings in Research on Derailed Managers

Research at the Center for Creative Leadership on managers who succeed or derail in their careers provides some interesting insights about traits and skills that determine advancement to top management. Most of the managers had strong *technical skills;* they had a string of prior successes; and they were initially viewed by others as "fast risers" in their company. Every manager had both strengths and weaknesses; none of the successful executives had all of the strengths, and none of the derailed managers had all of the weaknesses. Sometimes the reason for derailing was obvious, but other times it appeared to be just a matter of bad luck involving events beyond a manager's control (e.g., unfavorable economic conditions or losing political battles). Sometimes the importance of a success factor seemed to depend in part on the organization culture. For example, derailment often involved weak *interpersonal skills,* but this factor was more important in some organizations than in others.

The researchers used a mix of traits, skills, and other competencies (e.g., ability to build and lead a team, ability to adapt to change) to describe their interpretation of the descriptive data they collected. Managers who derailed were less able to handle pressure. They were more prone to moodiness, angry outbursts, and inconsistent behavior, which undermined their interpersonal relationships with subordinates, peers, and superiors. In contrast, the successful managers were calm, confident, and predictable during crises.

Managers who derailed were more likely to be defensive about weaknesses and failures. They reacted by attempting to cover up mistakes or blame other people. The successful managers admitted mistakes, accepted responsibility, and then took action to fix the problem. Moreover, having dealt with the problem, they did not continue to dwell on it, but turned their attention to other things. In the more recent studies, the ability to learn and adapt to change was an especially important success factor.

The successful managers were more focused on the immediate task and the needs of subordinates than on competing with rivals or impressing superiors. In contrast, many of the derailed managers were too ambitious about advancing their career at the expense of others, and they were more likely to betray a trust or break a promise. McCall and Lombardo (1983b, p. 28) gave the following example: "One executive didn't implement a decision as promised, causing conflicts between marketing and production that reverberated down through four levels of frustrated subordinates."

Managers who derailed were usually weaker in interpersonal skills. The most common reason for derailment was insensitivity, which was reflected in abrasive or intimidating behavior toward others. This flaw had been tolerated when the person was a lower-level manager, especially when the manager had outstanding technical skills, but at higher levels technical skills could not compensate for being insensitive. Some of the derailed managers could be charming when they wanted to, but over time it became evident that beneath the facade of charm and concern for others was a selfish, inconsiderate, and manipulative person. In contrast, the successful managers were more sensitive, tactful, and considerate. They were able to understand and get along with all types of people, and they developed a larger network of cooperative relationships. When they disagreed with someone they were direct but diplomatic, whereas the derailed managers were more likely to be outspoken and offensive. These interpersonal skills are especially relevant for building and leading a cooperative team, which was a key success factor in the recent studies.

For most managers who derailed, their technical brilliance was a source of successful problem solving and technical achievement at lower levels of management where their expertise was usually greater than that of subordinates. However, at higher levels this strength could become a weakness if it led to overconfidence and arrogance, causing the manager to reject sound advice, to offend others by acting superior, and to micromanage subordinates who had more expertise. Some managers were unable to shift from a focus on technical problems to the more strategic perspective needed at a higher level of management. Some derailed managers had technical expertise only in a narrow functional area, and they advanced too quickly to learn skills needed to perform higher-level jobs effectively. Successful managers usually had experience in a variety of different types of situations where they acquired a broader perspective and expertise in dealing with different types of problems.

Personality Traits and Effective Leadership

Over a period of several decades, the four methods described earlier were used to examine a variety of different personality traits related to managerial effectiveness and advancement. The choice of traits and the labels used for them have varied from study to study, but the results have been fairly consistent across different research methods. This section summarizes and integrates the findings regarding the most relevant aspects of personality for effective leadership by managers and administrators in large organizations (see also Table 1). The relevance of traits and skills is explained by linking them back to behaviors.

TABLE 1	Specific Traits Related to Leadership Effectiveness

- High energy level and stress tolerance
- Internal locus of control orientation
- Emotional maturity
- Personal integrity
- Socialized power motivation
- Moderately high achievement orientation
- Moderately high self-confidence
- Moderately low need for affiliation

Energy Level and Stress Tolerance

The trait research finds that energy level, physical stamina, and stress tolerance are associated with managerial effectiveness (Bass, 1990; Howard & Bray, 1988). High energy level and stress tolerance help managers cope with the hectic pace, long hours, and unrelenting demands of most managerial jobs. Physical vitality and emotional resilience make it easier to cope with stressful interpersonal situations, such as a punitive boss, a troubled subordinate, an uncooperative peer, or a hostile client. Effective problem solving requires an ability to remain calm and stay focused on a problem rather than panicking, denying the problem exists, or attempting to shift responsibility to someone else. In addition to making better decisions, a leader with high stress tolerance and composure is more likely to stay calm and provide confident, decisive direction to subordinates in a crisis.

Managerial jobs often have a high level of stress due to the pressure to make important decisions without adequate information and the need to resolve role conflicts and satisfy incompatible demands made by different parties. Tolerance of stress is especially important for executives who must deal with adverse situations where the leader's reputation and career, or the lives and jobs of subordinates, may hang in the balance. Bill George describes the pressures he felt as CEO of Medtronics (George, 2003, p. 16):

> I felt it every day as problems mounted or sales lagged. I knew that the livelihood of tens of thousands of employees, the health of millions of patients, and the financial fortunes of millions of investors rested on my shoulders and those of our executive team. At the same time I was well aware of the penalties for not performing, even for a single quarter. No CEO wants to appear on CNBC to explain why his company missed the earnings projections, even by a penny.

Self-Confidence

The term *self-confidence* is defined in a general way to include several related concepts such as self-esteem and self-efficacy. Most studies on leader self-confidence or self-efficacy found that it is related positively to effectiveness and advancement (see Bass, 1990). Self-confidence differentiated between effective and ineffective managers in a study of critical incidents by Boyatzis (1982), and self-confidence predicted subsequent advancement to higher levels of management in the assessment center research at AT&T (Howard & Bray, 1988). Other research finds that self-confidence is essential for charismatic leadership.

The relationship of self-confidence to leadership effectiveness can be understood by examining how this trait affects a leader's behavior. Without strong self-confidence, a leader is less likely to make influence attempts, and if an influence attempt is made, it is less likely to be successful. Leaders with high self-confidence are more likely to attempt difficult tasks and to set challenging objectives for themselves. Confident leaders take more initiative to solve problems and introduce desirable changes (Paglis & Green, 2002). Leaders who have high expectations for themselves are likely to have high expectations for subordinates as well (Kouzes & Posner, 1987). These leaders are more persistent in pursuit of difficult objectives, despite initial problems and setbacks. Their optimism and persistence in efforts to accomplish a task or mission are likely to increase commitment by subordinates, peers, and superiors to support the effort. Leaders with self-confidence are likely to be more decisive in a crisis, where success often depends on the perception by subordinates that the leader has the knowledge and courage necessary to deal with the crisis effectively. Finally, self-confidence is related to an action- oriented approach for dealing with problems. Leaders with low self-confidence are more likely to put off dealing with difficult problems or to shift responsibility to someone else (Kipnis & Lane, 1962).

There are some clear advantages of having self-confidence, but if it becomes excessive some dysfunctional behaviors may occur. Excessive self-confidence may make a leader overly optimistic about the likely success of a risky venture, and it may result in rash decisions and denial of evidence that a plan is flawed. A manager with extremely high self-confidence is inclined to be arrogant, autocratic, and intolerant of dissenting viewpoints, especially if the manager is not emotionally mature. Because the manager is unresponsive to ideas and concerns expressed by others, the benefits of participative leadership are unlikely to be realized. Thus, in situations where the leader does not have vastly superior expertise than subordinates, a moderately high amount of self-confidence may be better than either extremely high self-confidence or low self-confidence.

The arrogance and know-it-all attitude associated with excessive self-confidence has another negative side effect. An arrogant manager will have difficulty in developing cooperative relationships with people who are not dependent on the manager's specialized expertise. Acting arrogant toward people who have more expertise than the manager may create enemies who are able to derail the manager's career.

Internal Locus of Control

Another trait that appears to be relevant to managerial effectiveness is called the *locus of control orientation,* which is measured with a personality scale developed by Rotter (1966). People with a strong internal locus of control orientation (called "internals") believe that events in their lives are determined more by their own actions than by chance or uncontrollable forces. In contrast, people with a strong external control orientation (called "externals") believe that events are determined mostly by chance or fate and they can do little to improve their lives.

Because internals believe that they can influence their own destiny, they take more responsibility for their own actions and for the performance of their organization. Internals have a more future-oriented perspective, and they are more likely to proactively plan how to accomplish objectives. They take more initiative than externals in discovering and solving problems. They are confident in their ability to influence people and are more likely to use persuasion rather than coercive or manipulative influence tactics (Goodstadt & Hjelle, 1973). They are more flexible, adaptive, and innovative in their response to a problem and in their management strategies (Miller, Kets de Vries, & Toulouse, 1982). When setbacks or failures occur, they are more likely to learn from them rather than just dismissing them as bad luck.

Research on the relationship of this trait to managerial effectiveness is still limited, but the results suggest that a strong internal locus of control orientation is positively associated with managerial effectiveness. For example, Miller and Toulouse (1986) conducted a study of chief executive officers in 97 firms and found that internals were more effective than externals in terms of objective criteria such as profitability and sales growth. The relationship was stronger for firms in dynamic environments where it is more important to have major product innovations. Howell and Avolio (1993) conducted a study of 76 executives in a large financial institution and found that internals had better business-unit performance than externals for the year following the measurement of personality.

Emotional Stability and Maturity

The term *emotional maturity* may be defined broadly to encompass several interrelated motives, traits, and values. A person who is emotionally mature is well adjusted and does not suffer from severe psychological disorders. Emotionally mature people have a more *self-awareness* of strengths and weaknesses, and they are oriented toward self-improvement instead of denying weaknesses and fantasizing success. People with high emotional maturity are less self-centered (they care about other people), they have more self-control (are less impulsive, more able to resist hedonistic temptations), they have more stable emotions (are not prone to extreme mood swings or outbursts of anger), and they are less defensive (are more receptive to criticism, more willing to learn from mistakes). They are more likely to be at a high level of cognitive moral development. As a result, leaders with high emotional maturity maintain more cooperative relationships with subordinates, peers, and superiors. The following description (George, 2003, p. 15) includes many of these attributes:

> I too have struggled in getting comfortable with my weaknesses—my tendency to intimidate others with an overly challenging style, my impatience, and my occasional lack of tact. Only recently have I realized that my strengths and weaknesses are two sides of the same coin. By challenging others in business meetings, I am able to get quickly to the heart of the issues, but my approach unnerves and intimidates less confident people. My desire to get things done fast leads to superior results, but it exposes my impatience with people who move more slowly. Being direct with others gets the message across clearly but often lacks tact. Over time I have moderated my style and adapted my approach to make sure that people are engaged and empowered and that their voices are fully heard.

Most of the empirical research on traits shows that key components of emotional maturity are associated with managerial effectiveness and advancement (Bass, 1990). A study by McCauley and Lombardo (1990) with a measure called Benchmarks found that managers with good self-awareness and a desire to improve had higher advancement. Self-objectivity and general adjustment predicted advancement in the AT&T research by Howard and Bray (1988). Other research has found that effective executives have a good understanding of their own strengths and weaknesses, and they are oriented toward self-improvement rather than being defensive (e.g., Bennis & Nanus, 1985; Tichy & Devanna, 1986). The research on socialized and *personalized power orientation* also provides evidence about the importance of emotional maturity for effective leadership.

Power Motivation

Someone with a high *need for power* enjoys influencing people and events and is more likely to seek positions of authority. Most studies find a strong relationship between need for power and advancement to higher levels of management in large organizations (e.g., Howard & Bray, 1988; McClelland & Boyatzis, 1982; Stahl, 1983). People with a strong need for power seek positions of authority and power, and they are likely to be more attuned to the power politics of organizations.

A strong need for power is relevant to managerial role requirements involving the use of power and influence. Managers in large organizations must exercise power to influence subordinates, peers, and superiors. People who are low in need for power usually lack the desire and assertiveness necessary to organize and direct group activities, to negotiate favorable agreements, to lobby for necessary resources, to advocate and promote desirable changes, and to impose necessary discipline. A person who finds such behavior difficult and emotionally disturbing or who believes it is wrong to exercise power over others is unlikely to satisfy the role requirements of a managerial job (Miner, 1985).

A strong need for power is desirable, but a manager's effectiveness also depends on how this need finds expression. The empirical research indicates that a *socialized power orientation* is more likely to result in effective leadership than a *personalized power orientation* (Boyatzis, 1982; House, Spangler, & Woycke, 1991; McClelland & Boyatzis, 1982; McClelland & Burnham, 1976). Only a few studies have examined the behaviors associated with each power orientation, but the results indicate significant differences (McClelland, 1975, 1985).

Managers with a personalized power orientation use power to aggrandize themselves and satisfy their strong need for esteem and status. They have little inhibition or self-control, and they exercise power impulsively. According to McClelland and Burnham (1976, p. 103), "They are more rude to other people, they drink too much, they try to exploit others sexually, and they collect symbols of personal prestige such as fancy cars or big offices" Personalized power leaders seek to dominate subordinates by keeping them weak and dependent. Authority for making important decisions is centralized in the leader, information is restricted, and rewards and punishments are used to manipulate and control subordinates. The leader tries to play off different individuals or factions against each other to keep them weak. Assistance and advice to a subordinate is done in a way that demonstrates personal superiority and the inferiority and dependence of the subordinate. Sometimes personalized power leaders are able to inspire subordinate loyalty and team spirit, but adverse consequences are more likely to occur. When problems are encountered in the work, subordinates are reluctant to take any initiative in solving them. Instead of acting quickly to deal with a problem, they ignore it or wait for explicit directions from the leader. Any subordinate loyalty that may occur is to the leader rather than to the organization, and when the leader departs, there is likely to be disorder and a breakdown in team spirit.

Managers with a socialized power orientation are more emotionally mature. They exercise power more for the benefit of others, are hesitant about using power in a manipulative manner, are less egoistic and defensive, accumulate fewer material possessions, have a longer-range view, and are more willing to take advice from people with relevant expertise. Their strong need for power is expressed by using influence to build up the organization and make it successful. Because of their orientation toward building organizational commitment, this kind of leader is more likely to use a participative, coaching style of managerial behavior and is less likely to be coercive and autocratic. Such leaders "help make their subordinates feel strong and responsible, bind them less with petty rules, help produce a clear organizational structure, and create pride in belonging to the unit" (McClelland, 1975, p. 302).

Personal Integrity

Integrity means that a person's behavior is consistent with espoused values, and the person is honest, ethical, and trustworthy. Integrity is a primary determinant of interpersonal trust. Unless one is perceived to be trustworthy, it is difficult to retain the loyalty of followers or to obtain cooperation and support from peers and superiors. Moreover, a major determinant of expert and referent power is the perception by others that a person is trustworthy. Values related to integrity include honesty, loyalty, fairness, justice, and altruism.

Several types of behaviors are related to integrity. One important indicator of integrity is the extent to which one is honest and truthful rather than deceptive. Leaders lose credibility when people discover that they have lied or made claims that are grossly distorted. Another indicator of integrity is keeping promises. People are reluctant to negotiate agreements with a leader who cannot be trusted to keep promises. A third indicator of integrity is the extent to which a leader fulfills the responsibility of service and loyalty to followers. The trust of followers will be lost if they discover the leader exploited or manipulated them in pursuit of self-interest. A fourth indicator of integrity is the extent to which a leader can be trusted not to indiscriminately repeat something said in the utmost confidence. People will not pass on important but sensitive information to a leader who cannot be trusted to keep a secret. A key determinant of perceived integrity is the extent to which a leader's behavior is consistent with values articulated repeatedly to followers. A leader who hopes to inspire others to support an ideology or vision must set an example in his or her own behavior. Finally, integrity also means taking responsibility for one's actions and decisions. Leaders appear weak and undependable when they make a decision or take a position on an issue, then try to deny responsibility later if the decision is unsuccessful or the position becomes controversial.

Integrity was mentioned as an important value by most of the 45 British chief executives in a study by Cox and Cooper (1989). The CCL research described earlier found that lack of integrity was common among the managers whose career derailed, whereas managers who succeeded were regarded as having strong integrity. The successful managers were honest and dependable, as reflected in the following precept (McCall & Lombardo, 1983b, p. 30): "I will do exactly what I say I will do when I say I will do it. If I change my mind, I will tell you well in advance so you will not be harmed by my actions" Integrity is an important aspect of ethical, authentic, and spiritual leadership.

Narcissism

Narcissism is a personality syndrome that includes several traits relevant to effective leadership, such as a strong need for esteem (e.g., prestige, status, attention, admiration, adulation), a strong personalized need for power, low emotional maturity, and low integrity. This personality syndrome can be measured with a self-report scale called the Narcissistic Personality Inventory (Raskin & Hall, 1981).

Researchers with a background in clinical psychology and psychoanalysis have described the origins of narcissism and the behaviors associated with it (Kets de Vries & Miller, 1984, 1985; Raskin, Novacek, & Hogan, 1991). People whose parents have been emotionally unresponsive and rejecting may come to believe that they cannot depend on anyone's love or loyalty. In an effort to cope with their inner loneliness and fear, these extreme narcissists become preoccupied with establishing their power, status, and control. They have fantasies of success and power. They have a grandiose, exaggerated sense of their own self-importance and unique talents. To support this self-deception, they seek continuous attention and admiration from others.

Because they are so preoccupied with their own ego needs, narcissists have little empathy or concern for the feelings and needs of others. They exploit and manipulate others to indulge their desire for self-aggrandizement without feeling any remorse. They expect special favors from others without feeling any need for reciprocity. Narcissists tend to oversimplify human relationships and motives and see everything in extreme good and bad terms. People are viewed either as loyal supporters or as enemies. Narcissists are very defensive and view criticism by others as a sign of rejection and disloyalty. Narcissists can be charming and helpful when they want to impress someone who is important, but they are likely to be aggressive and cruel with people who have little power, especially someone who opposes them or stands in their way. The following example describes a narcissistic manager:

> He was very talented in handling technical problems, but his remarkable results were achieved at a horrible cost to others. He was moody, volatile, and completely devoid of sensitivity, kindness, or patience. Any subordinate who made a serious mistake was loudly criticized in front of others with scathing remarks or questions such as "How could you be so stupid?" He did not tolerate any disagreement, and subordinates were afraid to suggest changes that would make the unit more effective. Ironically, he could be charming and pleasant when it suited his purpose, which was usually when interacting with top management.

The research on narcissism provides additional insights into the difficulties encountered by leaders with low emotional maturity and a personalized power orientation (House & Howell, 1992; Rosenthal & Pittinsky, 2006). Narcissists in leadership positions have a number of characteristic flaws (Glad, 2002; Kets de Vries & Miller, 1984, 1985). They surround themselves with subordinates who are loyal and uncritical. They make decisions without gathering adequate information about the environment. In the belief that they alone are sufficiently informed and talented to decide what is best, objective advice is not sought or accepted from subordinates and peers. They tend to undertake ambitious, grandiose projects to glorify themselves, but in the absence of an adequate analysis of the situation, the projects are likely to be risky and unrealistic. When a project is not going well, they tend to ignore or reject negative information, thereby missing the opportunity to correct problems in time to avert a disaster. When failure is finally evident, the narcissistic leader refuses to admit any responsibility, but instead finds scapegoats to blame. Finally, because they exploit the organization to compensate for their own sense of inadequacy, extreme narcissists are unable to plan for an orderly succession of leadership. They see themselves as indispensable and cling to power, in contrast to emotionally mature executives who are able to retire gracefully when their job is done and it is time for new leadership.

Despite the many negative aspects of narcissism, this personality syndrome may also have some positive aspects, at least in limited situations (Rosenthal & Pittinsky, 2006). Research on U.S. presidents (Deluga, 1998) and CEOs of computer and software companies (Chatterjee & Hambrick, 2007) found that some of the most and least successful leaders were narcissistic. The strong self-confidence and optimism of narcissistic leaders facilitates their efforts to influence others to pursue bold, innovative objectives, which may or may not prove to be feasible and worthwhile. Despite questionable motives for proposing risky new initiatives, a narcissistic person is sometimes successful in leading an organization's response to serious threats or unusual opportunities. Of course, this potential benefit does not mean that a narcissistic leader is more effective than a leader who has strong selfconfidence and optimism combined with a socialized power orientation and high emotional maturity.

Achievement Orientation

Achievement orientation includes a set of related needs and values, including *need for achievement*, willingness to assume responsibility, performance orientation, and concern for task objectives. Many studies have been conducted on the relationship of achievement orientation to managerial advancement and effectiveness (see Bass, 1990). However, the results have not been consistent for different criteria (e.g., advancement, effectiveness) and for different types of managerial positions (e.g., entrepreneurial managers, corporate general managers, technical managers).

The relationship of achievement motivation to managerial effectiveness is complex. Some studies find a positive relationship between achievement motivation and effectiveness (e.g., Stahl, 1983; Wainer & Rubin, 1969), but other studies find a negative relationship (House, Spangler, & Woycke, 1991) or no evidence of a strong, significant relationship (Miller & Toulouse, 1986). One possible explanation for these inconsistent findings is that the relationship of achievement motivation to managerial effectiveness is curvilinear rather than linear. In other words, managers with a moderately high amount of achievement motivation are more effective than managers with low achievement motivation, or managers with very high achievement motivation.

Research on the behavioral correlates of achievement orientation is still limited, but some relationships appear likely. Compared to managers with a weak achievement orientation, managers with a strong achievement orientation are likely to have a strong concern for task objectives; they are more willing to assume responsibility for solving task-related problems; they are more likely to take the initiative in discovering these problems and acting decisively to solve them; and they prefer solutions that involve moderate levels of risk rather than solutions that are either very risky or very conservative. These managers are likely to engage in task behaviors such as setting challenging but realistic goals and deadlines, developing specific action plans, determining ways to overcome obstacles, organizing the work efficiently, and emphasizing performance when talking to others (Boyatzis, 1982). In contrast, a manager with a weak achievement orientation is not motivated to seek opportunities involving challenging objectives and moderate risks and is less willing to take the initiative to identify problems and to assume responsibility for solving them.

A strong achievement orientation may also result in behavior that undermines managerial effectiveness. If need for achievement is the dominant motive for a manager, it is likely that the manager's efforts will be directed toward his or her own individual achievement and advancement rather than toward the achievements of the team or work unit headed by the manager. The manager tries to accomplish everything alone, is reluctant to delegate, and fails to develop a strong sense of responsibility and task commitment among subordinates (McClelland & Burnham, 1976; Miller & Toulouse, 1986). It is especially difficult for this type of person to function effectively in a management team in which leadership responsibility is shared.

The way in which achievement orientation finds expression in a manager's behavior depends on the overall motive pattern of the manager. Achievement motivation enhances leadership effectiveness only if it is subordinated to a stronger need for socialized power, so that the manager's efforts are directed toward building a successful team. When combined with a personalized need for power, strong achievement motivation may be focused on career advancement at any cost. This type of manager will neglect task objectives and the development of subordinates in an effort to build a personal reputation as a fast-rising star. Task decisions will be guided by a desire for short-term achievements, even though unit performance may suffer in the longer run. The manager is likely to take personal control over promising, highly visible projects and will take most of the credit for success. A manager who is very competitive may refuse to cooperate with peers who are viewed as potential rivals. As found in the CCL study, the result is likely to be initial advancement but eventual derailment when a manager with overriding personal ambition and excessive competitiveness makes too many powerful enemies.

Additional insights are provided by research on the Type A personality, which appears to combine a strong achievement orientation with a strong need for control over events (Baron, 1989; Nahavandi, Mizzi, & Malekzadeh, 1992; Strube, Turner, Cerro, Stevens, & Hinchey, 1984). Managers with this personality syndrome have high expectations for themselves and are very competitive. They set high performance objectives, compare themselves with others, and want to win any contest. Type A managers are also highly concerned about time; they feel rushed much of the time, try to do more than one thing at a time, and are impatient with delays. They prefer to maintain control over all aspects of their work, which makes them poor delegators and reluctant to work in a team (Miller, Lack, & Asroff, 1985). Finally, Type A managers tend to be more angry and inclined to express their hostility when unable to control events. They are demanding, intolerant of mistakes, and critical of people who are not as intensely dedicated. This behavior pattern makes it more difficult for them to maintain cooperative relationships.

Need for Affiliation

As noted earlier in this chapter, people with a strong *need for affiliation* receive great satisfaction from being liked and accepted by others, and they enjoy working with people who are friendly and cooperative. Most studies find a negative correlation between need for affiliation and managerial effectiveness. The ineffectiveness of managers with a high need for affiliation can be understood by examining the typical pattern of behavior for such managers. These managers are concerned primarily about interpersonal relationships rather than the task, and they are unwilling to allow the work to interfere with harmonious relationships (Litwin & Stringer, 1966; McClelland, 1975). They seek to avoid conflicts or smooth them over rather than confront genuine differences. They avoid making necessary but unpopular decisions. They dispense rewards in a way designed to gain approval, rather than rewarding effective performance. They show favoritism to personal friends in making assignments and allowing exceptions to rules. This pattern of behavior often leaves subordinates feeling "weak, irresponsible, and without a sense of what might happen next, of where they stand in relation to their manager, or even of what they ought to be doing" (McClelland & Burnham, 1976, p. 104).

It is clearly undesirable for a manager to have a strong need for affiliation, but a very low need for affiliation may also have undesirable consequences. A person with low need for affiliation tends to be a "loner" who does not like to socialize with others, except perhaps the immediate family or a few close friends. This type of person may lack the motivation to engage in the many social and public relations activities that are essential for a manager, including those involved in establishing effective interpersonal relationships with subordinates, superiors, and peers. As a result, this type of person may fail to develop effective interpersonal skills and may lack confidence in being able to influence others. Thus, it is likely that the optimal level of affiliation motivation is moderately low rather than either high or extremely low.

The Big Five Personality Traits

Describing leaders in terms of their individual profiles would be easier if there was an integrative conceptual framework with a small number of meta-categories that encompass all of the relevant traits. The proliferation of personality traits identified over the past century has resulted in efforts to find a smaller number of broadly defined categories that would simplify the development of trait theories. One such effort that appears promising is referred to as the five-factor model of personality or the "Big Five" model (e.g., Digman, 1990; Hough, 1992). The five broadly defined personality traits in the taxonomy have somewhat different labels from one version to another. The traits include surgency (or extroversion), dependability (or conscientiousness), adjustment (or neuroticism), intellectance (or openness to experience), and agreeableness.

TABLE 2	Correspondence of the Big Five Traits with Specific Traits
Big Five Personality Traits	**Specific Traits**
Surgency	Extroversion (outgoing) Energy/Activity Level Need for Power (assertive)
Conscientiousness	Dependability Personal Integrity Need for Achievement
Agreeableness	Cheerful and Optimistic Nurturance (sympathetic, helpful) Need for Affiliation
Adjustment	Emotional Stability Self-Esteem Self-Control
Intellectance	Curious and Inquisitive Open Minded Learning Oriented

Based on Hogan et al. (1994).

In recent years, leadership scholars have shown increasing interest in using this taxonomy to facilitate interpretation of results in the massive and confusing literature on leadership traits (e.g., Goodstein & Lanyon, 1999; Hogan, Curphy, & Hogan, 1994). Table 2 shows how the five broad trait categories correspond to many of the specific traits found relevant for leadership emergence, advancement, or effectiveness in the trait studies reviewed earlier in this chapter.

Reviews and meta-analyses of studies on the five factors find that most of them are related to leader emergence, behavior, or effectiveness (e.g., Bono & Judge, 2004; Judge, Bono, Ilies, & Gerhardt, 2002). Effective leaders had higher scores on extroversion, conscientiousness, and openness to learning from experience, and lower scores on neuroticism. However, the results were not consistent across studies or for different types of organizations. One likely reason for inconsistent results is the use of different measures to represent the five factors, including surrogate measures that do not adequately represent a factor. Another reason for inconsistent results may be the use of different criterion variables (e.g., leadership emergence, advancement, or effectiveness; subjective or objective measures).

Not all scholars agree that the Big Five model of personality is better than taxonomies with more specific traits (cf., Block, 1995; Hough, 1992). If both relevant and irrelevant traits are included in a broadly defined factor, the accuracy of prediction will be lower. Even when the component traits are all relevant, they may not have the same relationship with different criteria of leadership effectiveness. More research is needed to determine whether the *big five traits* predict and explain leadership effectiveness better than the specific component traits. Such research should be based on a theory that clearly describes how specific leader traits are related to specific types of behavior that mediate the effects of the traits on leadership effectiveness.

Skills and Effective Leadership

The early research on leader characteristics identified several skills that are related to the advancement and effectiveness of leaders. Many different taxonomies have been proposed for classifying managerial skills, but the most useful and parsimonious taxonomy uses the three broadly defined skill categories shown in Table 3. Similar versions of this taxonomy were proposed by Katz (1955) and Mann (1965). The technical skills are primarily concerned with things, the interpersonal skills (or "social skills") are primarily concerned with people, and the *conceptual skills* (or *"cognitive skills")* are primarily concerned with ideas and concepts.

Some writers differentiate a fourth category of skills (called *administrative skills* or *strategic management skills)* that includes selected aspects of the other three categories and are defined in terms of the ability to perform a particular type of managerial function or behavior such as planning, negotiating, and coaching (e.g., Hooijberg, Hunt, & Dodge, 1997; Hunt, 1991; Mumford, Campion, & Morgeson, 2007).

Technical Skills

Technical skills include knowledge about methods, processes, and equipment for conducting the specialized activities of the manager's organizational unit. Technical skills also include factual knowledge about the organization (rules, structure, management systems, employee characteristics), and knowledge about the organization's products and services (technical specifications, strengths, and limitations). This type of knowledge is acquired by a combination of formal education, training, and job experience. Acquisition of technical knowledge is facilitated by a good memory for details and the ability to learn technical material quickly. Effective managers are able to obtain information and ideas from many sources and store it away in their memory for use when they need it.

Managers who supervise the work of others need extensive knowledge of the techniques and equipment used by subordinates to perform the work. Technical knowledge of products and processes is necessary to plan and organize work operations, to direct and train subordinates with specialized activities, and to monitor and evaluate their performance. Technical expertise is needed to deal with disruptions in the work due to equipment breakdowns, quality defects, accidents, insufficient materials, and coordination problems. Ample evidence indicates that technical skills are related to the effectiveness of civilian and military leaders, especially at lower levels of management (see Bass, 1990). The CCL study (McCall

TABLE 3	Three-factor Taxonomy of Broadly Defined Skills

Technical Skills: Knowledge about methods, processes, procedures, and techniques for conducting a specialized activity, and the ability to use tools and equipment relevant to that activity.

Interpersonal Skills: Knowledge about human behavior and interpersonal processes, ability to understand the feelings, attitudes, and motives of others from what they say and do (empathy, social sensitivity), ability to communicate clearly and effectively (speech fluency, persuasiveness), and ability to establish effective and cooperative relationships (tact, diplomacy, listening skill, knowledge about acceptable social behavior).

Conceptual Skills: General analytical ability, logical thinking, proficiency in concept formation and conceptualization of complex and ambiguous relationships, creativity in idea generation and problem solving, ability to analyze events and perceive trends, anticipate changes, and recognize opportunities and potential problems (inductive and deductive reasoning).

& Lombardo, 1983a) on derailed managers found that technical knowledge about products and work processes is related to effectiveness and advancement at lower levels of management, but it becomes relatively less important at higher levels of management.

Technical knowledge is also relevant for entrepreneurial managers. The inspirational vision of a new product or service may seem to spring from out of nowhere, but it is actually the result of many years of learning and experience. Research on entrepreneurs who started successful companies or introduced important new products in established companies suggests that their technical knowledge is the fertile ground in which the seeds of inspiration take root to yield innovative products (Westley & Mintzberg, 1989). Some examples include Edwin Land, the inventor of the instant camera and founder of Polaroid Corporation; Steve Jobs, the cofounder of Apple Computer; and Mark Zukerberg, the cofounder of Facebook. It is not enough to have an intimate knowledge of the products and processes for which a manager is responsible. Managers also need to have extensive knowledge of the products and services provided by competitors. Strategic planning is unlikely to be effective unless a manager can make an accurate evaluation of the organization's products (or services) in comparison to those of competitors (Peters & Austin, 1985).

Conceptual Skills

In general terms, conceptual (or cognitive) skills involve good judgment, foresight, intuition, creativity, and the ability to find meaning and order in ambiguous, uncertain events. Specific conceptual skills that can be measured with aptitude tests include analytical ability, logical thinking, concept formation, inductive reasoning, and deductive reasoning. Cognitive complexity involves a combination of these specific skills and is defined as the ability to develop concepts and categories for describing things, the ability to identify patterns and understand complex relationships, and the ability to develop creative solutions to problems. A person with low cognitive complexity sees things in simplistic black and white terms and has difficulty in seeing how many diverse elements fit together to make a meaningful whole. A person with high cognitive complexity is able to see many shades of gray and is able to identify complex patterns of relationships and predict future events from current trends.

Conceptual skills are essential for effective planning, organizing, and problem solving. A major administrative responsibility is coordination of the separate, specialized parts of the organization. To accomplish effective coordination, a manager needs to understand how the various parts of the organization relate to each other and how changes in one part of the system affect the other parts. Managers must also be able to comprehend how changes in the external environment will affect the organization. Strategic planning requires considerable ability to analyze events and perceive trends, anticipate changes, and recognize opportunities and potential problems.

A manager with high cognitive complexity is able to develop a better mental model of the organization to help understand the most critical factors and the relationships among them. A model is like a road map that depicts the terrain for a region, shows where things are located in relation to each other, and helps you decide how to get from one place to another. Managers with weak conceptual skills tend to develop a simplistic mental model that is not especially useful because it is unable to describe the complex processes, causal relationships, and flow of events in the organization and external environment. In the CCL study described earlier, weak conceptual skills were one reason for managers who derailed (McCall & Lombardo, 1983b, p. 26): "The charming but not brilliant find that the job gets too big and the problems too complex to get by on interpersonal skills."

Conceptual skills have been measured with a variety of different methods, including traditional aptitude tests, situational tests, interviews, critical incidents, and constructed response tasks. Research with traditional pencil-and-paper measures of conceptual skills finds strong evidence that they are related to managerial effectiveness, especially in high-level managerial positions (Bass, 1990). Cognitive skills measured with incident interviews differentiated between effective and ineffective managers in a study by Boyatzis (1982). Cognitive skills measured in an assessment center predicted advancement to higher levels of management in a study at AT&T (Howard & Bray, 1988). In a longitudinal study of managers in four companies, cognitive complexity measured with an individual assessment interview predicted managerial advancement remarkably well 4-8 years later (Stamp, 1988). With constructed response tasks, leaders say how they would solve representative types of problems described in a set of scenarios, and then raters determine the level of skill demonstrated by the answers. In a large sample of army officers at different ranks, complex problem-solving skills that were measured in this way were related to career achievement (Connelly et al., 2000).

Interpersonal Skills

Interpersonal (or social) skills include knowledge about human behavior and group processes, ability to understand the feelings, attitudes, and motives of others, and ability to communicate clearly and persuasively. Specific types of interpersonal skills such as empathy, social insight, charm, tact and diplomacy, persuasiveness, and oral communication ability are essential to develop and maintain cooperative relationships with subordinates, superiors, peers, and outsiders. Someone who is charming, tactful, and diplomatic will have more cooperative relationships than a person who is insensitive and offensive.

Interpersonal skills are essential for influencing people. Empathy is the ability to understand another person's motives, values, and emotions, and social insight is the ability to understand what types of behavior are socially acceptable in a particular situation. Understanding what people want and how they perceive things makes it easier to select an appropriate influence strategy, and persuasiveness and oral communication influence attempts more successfully. Another interpersonal skill is the ability to use cues from others to understand one's own behavior and how it affects other people. This skill is sometimes called "self-monitoring," and it helps people adjust their behavior to fit the requirements of the situation (Snyder, 1974; Zaccaro, Foti, & Kenny, 1991). Influence tactics and impression management tactics are used more effectively by people who have strong interpersonal skills.

Interpersonal skills also enhance the effectiveness of relationship-oriented behaviors. Strong interpersonal skills help a manager listen in an attentive, sympathetic, and non-judgmental way to somebody with a personal problem, complaint, or criticism. Empathy is important for understanding the needs and feelings of others and determining how to provide support and sympathy. Empathy is also useful for determining effective ways to resolve conflicts. Even managerial behaviors that are primarily task-oriented (e.g., making assignments and giving instructions) require considerable interpersonal skill to be enacted in a way that reflects a concern for people as well as task objectives. Some people have a misconception that interpersonal skill is nothing more than considerate behavior to be "turned on" in special situations. Katz (1955, p. 34) takes a different viewpoint:

> Real skill in working with others must become a natural, continuous activity, since it involves sensitivity not only at times of decision making but also in the day-by-day behavior of the individual... . Because everything a leader says and does (or leaves unsaid or undone) has an effect on his associates, his true self will, in time, show through. Thus, to be effective, this skill must be naturally developed and unconsciously, as well as consistently, demonstrated in the individual's every action.

The trait research described earlier in this chapter shows consistently that interpersonal skills are important for managerial effectiveness and advancement (Bass, 1990). In the AT&T study, interpersonal skills predicted managerial advancement. In research on leadership competencies by Boyatzis (1982), interpersonal skills differentiated between effective and ineffective managers, regardless of the situation. In the CCL research, deficiencies in interpersonal skills were a major reason for managers who eventually derailed in their management careers. McCall and Lombardo (1983b, p. 28) describe an incident involving an abrasive manager who derailed:

> The manager walked into the subordinate's office, interrupting a meeting, and said, "I need to see you." When the subordinate tried to explain that he was occupied, his boss snarled, "I don't give a goddamn. I said I wanted to see you now."

Managerial Competencies

Although competencies are commonly regarded as skills, they usually involve a combination of specific skills and complementary traits. Competencies are frequently used to describe desirable attributes for managers in a particular company or profession, but some scholars have proposed generally relevant competencies for managers. Examples include *emotional intelligence, social intelligence,* and learning ability. These competencies include some of the same skills and traits described earlier in the chapter, but they are defined and measured in unique ways.

Emotional Intelligence

Emotions are strong feelings that demand attention and are likely to affect cognitive processes and behavior. Some examples of emotions include anger, fear, sadness, joy, shame, and surprise. Even after the intensity of an emotion fades, it is likely to linger as a positive or negative mood, which can also affect leadership behavior (George, 1995). Emotional intelligence includes several interrelated component skills. Empathy is the ability to recognize moods and emotions in others, to differentiate between genuine and false expression of emotions, and to understand how someone is reacting to your emotions and behavior. Self-regulation is the ability to channel emotions into behavior that is appropriate for the situation, rather than responding with impulsive behavior (e.g., lashing out at someone who made you angry, or withdrawing into a state of depression after experiencing disappointment). Emotional self-awareness is an understanding of one's own moods and emotions, how they evolve and change over time, and the implications for task performance and interpersonal relationships. Another aspect of emotional intelligence that requires both self-awareness and communication skills is the ability to accurately express one's feelings to others with language and nonverbal communication (e.g., facial expressions, gestures). Emotional intelligence can be learned, but a significant improvement probably requires intensive individual coaching, relevant feedback, and a strong desire for significant personal development (Goleman, 1995).

Emotional intelligence is relevant for leadership effectiveness in several ways (Goleman, 1995; Goleman, Boyatzis, & McKee, 2002; Mayer & Salovey, 1995). Leaders with a high level of emotional intelligence are more capable of solving complex problems, planning how to use their time effectively, adapting their behavior to the situation, and managing crises. Self-awareness makes it easier to understand one's own needs and likely reactions if certain events occurred, thereby facilitating evaluation of alternative solutions. Self-regulation facilitates *emotional stability* and information processing in stressful situations, and it helps leaders maintain their own optimism and enthusiasm about a project or mission in the face of obstacles and setbacks. Empathy is associated with strong social skills that are needed to develop cooperative interpersonal relationships. Examples include the ability to listen attentively, communicate effectively, and express appreciation and positive regard. The ability to understand and influence emotions in others will help a leader who is attempting to arouse enthusiasm and optimism for a proposed activity or change. A leader with high emotional intelligence will have more insight about the type of rational or emotional appeal that is most likely to be effective in a particular situation.

In research on the consequences of emotional intelligence, some studies use a self-report measure (e.g., Wong & Law, 2002), but other studies use a performance-based measure (e.g., Mayer, Salovey, Caruso, & Sitarenios, 2003). As yet there is only a limited amount of research to support the proposition that emotional intelligence enhances leadership effectiveness (see Joseph & Newman, 2010). The extent to which emotional intelligence can improve the prediction of leadership effectiveness beyond measures of cognitive intelligence and other traits has not been clearly determined. There is a continuing controversy about the usefulness of emotional intelligence. Some critics claim that it uses well-known traits and skills and adds no important new insights about effective leadership (e.g., Landy, 2005; Locke, 2005).

Social Intelligence

Social intelligence is defined as the ability to determine the requirements for leadership in a particular situation and select an appropriate response (Cantor & Kihlstrom, 1987; Ford, 1986; Zaccaro, Gilbert, Thor, & Mumford, 1991). The two primary components of social intelligence are *social perceptiveness* and *behavioral flexibility*.

Social perceptiveness is the ability to understand the functional needs, problems, and opportunities that are relevant for a group or organization, and the member characteristics, social relationships, and collective processes that will enhance or limit attempts to influence the group or organization. A leader with high social perceptiveness understands what needs to be done to make a group or organization more effective and how to do it. Social perceptiveness involves the conceptual skills and specific knowledge needed for strategic leadership, including the ability to identify threats and opportunities that are jointly determined by environmental events and the core competencies of the organization, and the ability to formulate an appropriate response. Social perceptiveness also involves interpersonal skills (e.g., empathy, social sensitivity, understanding of group processes) and knowledge of the organization (structure, culture, power relationships), which jointly determine whether it is feasible to initiate change and the best way to do it.

Behavioral flexibility is the ability and willingness to vary one's behavior to accommodate situational requirements. A leader with high behavioral flexibility knows how to use a variety of different behaviors and is able to evaluate his or her behavior and modify it as needed. High behavioral flexibility implies a mental model with fine distinctions among different types of leadership behavior rather than a simplistic taxonomy. The person must have a large repertoire of skilled behaviors from which to select, as well as knowledge about the effects and limiting conditions for each type of behavior. Behavioral flexibility is facilitated by self-monitoring, because leaders who are high on self-monitoring are more aware of their own behavior and how it affects others. Whether social intelligence is used primarily to achieve collective rather than personal objectives probably depends on the leader's emotional maturity and socialized power motivation.

Considerable overlap is apparent between social intelligence and emotional intelligence, although the latter construct seems to be more narrowly defined (Kobe, Reiter-Palmon, & Rickers, 2001; Salovey & Mayer, 1990). Social intelligence also appears to include political skill, which is the ability to understand how decisions are made in organizations and how to use political tactics to influence decisions and events. More research is needed to clarify how social intelligence is related to emotional intelligence and political skill. More research is also needed to assess how each component skill in social intelligence is related to leadership effectiveness.

Learning Ability

In a turbulent environment in which organizations must continually adapt, innovate, and reinvent themselves, leaders must be flexible enough to learn from mistakes, change their assumptions and beliefs, and refine their mental models. One of the most important competencies for successful leadership in changing situations is the ability to learn from experience and adapt to change (Argyris, 1991; Dechant, 1990; Marshall-Mies et al., 2000; Mumford & Connelly, 1991). This competency is distinct from other conceptual skills (e.g., verbal reasoning, creative thinking) and from social skills. It involves "learning how to learn," which is the ability to irrespectively analyze your own cognitive processes (e.g., the way you define and solve problems) and to find ways to improve them. It also involves self-awareness, which is an understanding of your own strengths and limitations (including both skills and emotions).

In a study of 1,800 high-level military officers, this competency predicted self-reported career achievements (Zaccaro et al., 1997). A study of military officers by Marshall-Mies et al. (2000) provides additional evidence that the ability to learn and adapt is important for leadership effectiveness. In research on derailment by civilian managers, this ability was considered an important success factor by American and European executives (Van Velsor & Leslie, 1995).

The ability to learn from experience and adapt to change probably involves traits as well as skills (Spreitzer, McCall, & Mahoney, 1997). Traits that appear relevant include achievement orientation, emotional stability, self-monitoring, and an internal locus of control orientation. Managers with these traits are motivated to achieve excellence; they are inquisitive and open-minded; they have the confidence and curiosity to experiment with new approaches; and they actively seek feedback about their strengths and weaknesses.

Entrepreneurial Ability and Leadership

It remains debatable whether individuals who are motivated by the spirit of entrepreneurship and leadership are more similar in their personality than they are different, and what is the crucial personality difference between them (Chan et al., 2015, pp. 163). Researchers (e.g., Renko et al., 2015) propose that entrepreneurial abilities and leadership traits together influence team and organizational performance, and they term this phenomenon "entrepreneurial leadership." They argue that entrepreneurial leadership involves influencing and directing the performance of group members toward achieving those organizational goals that involve recognizing and exploiting entrepreneurial opportunities.

Entrepreneurial leadership encompasses the establishment of clear goals, creation of opportunities, empowerment of people, preservation of organizational intimacy, and development of a human resource system. Entrepreneurial leadership entails the ability to influence others to manage resources strategically to emphasize both opportunity-seeking and advantage-seeking behaviors. It is a type of leadership that is capable of sustaining innovation and adaptation in high-velocity and uncertain environments.

Situational Relevance of Skills

Managers need many types of skills to fulfill their role requirements, but the relative importance of the various skills depends on the leadership situation. Relevant situational moderator variables include managerial level, type of organization, and the nature of the external environment.

Level of Management

One aspect of the situation influencing skill importance is a manager's position in the authority hierarchy of the organization (Boyatzis, 1982; Gentry, Harris, Baker, & Leslie, 2008; Jacobs & Jaques, 1987; Katz, 1955; Mann, 1965; Mumford & Connelly, 1991; Mumford, Marks, Connelly, Zaccaro, & Reiter-Palmon, 2000). Skill priorities at different levels of management are related to the differing role requirements at each level. Figure 1 shows the relative importance of the three broad skill categories to leadership effectiveness for low-level managers, middle-level managers, and top executives. Managerial level affects not only the relevance of the three broad categories of skills described earlier (i.e., conceptual, interpersonal, technical), but also the relative importance of specific types of skills within each category.

In general, higher levels of management have a greater number and variety of activities to be coordinated; the complexity of relationships that need to be understood and managed is greater; and the problems that need to be solved are more unique and ill-defined (Jacobs & Jaques, 1987, 1990; Jaques, 1989; Mumford & Connelly, 1991). Whereas a department supervisor may have to coordinate the work of employees with mostly similar jobs, a CEO must coordinate the diverse activities of several organizational units, each with large numbers of people. Increasing complexity as one ascends to higher levels in an organization is reflected in increased requirements for conceptual skills. Top executives need to analyze vast amounts of ambiguous and contradictory information about the environment in order to make strategic decisions and to interpret events for other members of the organization. Executives need to have a long-term perspective and the ability to comprehend complex relationships among variables relevant to the performance of the organization. A top executive must be able to anticipate future events and know how to plan for them. The quality of strategic decisions ultimately depends on conceptual skills, even though some technical knowledge is necessary to make these decisions, and interpersonal skills are necessary for

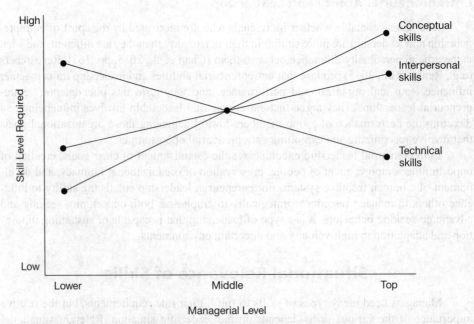

FIGURE 1 Relative Importance of Skills for Different Levels of Management

developing relationships, obtaining information, and influencing subordinates to implement decisions (Katz & Kahn, 1978).

The role of middle-level managers is primarily one of supplementing existing structure and developing ways to implement policies and goals established at higher levels (Katz & Kahn, 1978). This role requires a roughly equal mix of technical, interpersonal, and conceptual skills. Low-level managers are mainly responsible for implementing policy and maintaining the work flow within the existing organizational structure; for these managers, technical skills are relatively more important than conceptual skills or interpersonal skills.

The skill requirements for managers at each level vary somewhat depending on the type of organization, its size, the organization structure, and the degree of centralization of authority (McLennan, 1967). For example, technical skills are more important for top executives in organizations where operating decisions are highly centralized. Likewise, more technical skill is needed by top executives who have functionally specialized roles (e.g., selling to key customers, product design) in addition to general administrative responsibilities. More conceptual skills are needed by middle- and lower-level managers who are expected to participate in strategic planning, product innovation, and leading change.

Type of Organization

An interesting question about managerial skills is the extent to which they are transferable from one type of organization to another. Writers generally agree that lower-level managers cannot easily transfer to a different functional specialty (e.g., from sales manager to engineering manager), because the technical skills needed at this level of management are so different across functions. However, less agreement is evident about the transferability of skills across organizations at the executive level.

Katz (1955) proposed that top-level managers with ample human relations and conceptual skills can be shifted from one industry to another with great ease and no loss of effectiveness. Some other writers contend that the transferability of skills for top executives is limited due to variations in ownership, traditions, organizational climate, and culture (Dale, 1960; Kotter, 1982; McLennan, 1967; Shetty & Peery, 1976). Different industries have unique economic, market, and technological characteristics. Familiarity with technical matters, products, personalities, and tradition is a type of knowledge that is acquired only through long experience in the organization. Only the general components of conceptual and technical skills can be used in a different situation; the unique knowledge component of these skills must be relearned. Moreover, an executive who moves to a different industry must develop a new network of external contacts, whereas the old network would still be relevant for a move to another organization in the same industry. In general, it seems to be more difficult for an executive to make a successful transition to a different industry or type of organization, especially if the new position requires extensive technical expertise and an extensive network of external contacts (Kotter, 1982; Shetty & Peery, 1976).

External Environment

Recent research and theory on how organizations evolve and adapt to a changing environment suggests that the mix of skills needed for effective leadership may change as the situation changes. The skills needed by an entrepreneurial manager to build a new organization are not identical to the skills needed by the chief executive of a large, established organization. The skills needed to lead an organization with a stable, supportive environment are not identical to the skills needed to lead an organization facing a turbulent, competitive environment (Hunt, 1991; Lord & Maher, 1991; Quinn, 1992).

Unprecedented changes affecting organizations are changing the nature of managerial work. To cope with these changes, most managers may need more of the new competencies as well as the skills identified in earlier research. As the pace of globalization, technological development, and social change continues to increase, so will the premium on competencies such as cognitive complexity, empathy, self-awareness, cultural sensitivity, behavioral flexibility, systems thinking, and the ability to learn from experience and adapt to change (Conger, 1993; Gentry, Harris, Baker, & Leslie, 2008; Hunt, 1991; Nadkarni & Herrmann, 2010; Van Velsor & Leslie, 1995).

Evaluation of the Trait Approach

Considerable progress has been made in identifying traits and skills relevant for managerial effectiveness and advancement. Nevertheless, this line of research has been hindered by some methodological and conceptual limitations. Most trait studies are not guided by a theory that explains how traits are related to managerial effectiveness and advancement. It is difficult to interpret the relevance of abstract traits except by examining how they are expressed in the actual behavior of leaders and the types of influence processes related to leader decisions and actions. Few trait studies include mediating processes to explain why leadership traits and skills are relevant for predicting effectiveness in the current position or career success.

Another limitation of the trait approach is the lack of attention in many studies to the leadership context. As in the behavior research, the relevance of different traits and skills will depend in part on the nature of the leadership position, the types of challenges facing the leader, and the criteria used to assess effectiveness.

TABLE 4	Negative Aspects of Very Low or Very High Trait Scores

Self-confidence

- too little: indecisive, avoids risks, and does not seek to influence others
- too much: arrogant, acts too quickly, and takes too many risks

Need for Esteem

- too little: does not seek recognition or build a reputation for high expertise and reliability
- too much: preoccupied with reputation and status, exaggerates achievements, covers up mistakes and failures or blames others

Need for Affiliation

- too little: does not try to form strong relationships or build a social support network
- too much: overly concerned about being liked and accepted by others, over-uses ingratiation, and will not risk popularity by asking for sacrifices or insisting on better performance

Need for Independence

- too little: dependent on others for direction, rule oriented, avoids taking initiative
- too much: resents authority, too quick to ignore rules and standard procedures

Altruism (value)

- too little: selfish, indifferent about the needs of others, may exploit them for personal gain
- too much: overly generous and forgiving, unable to ask for sacrifices or maintain discipline

Performance Orientation (value)

- too little: the person accepts weak performance and does not push for improvement
- too much: the person is a perfectionist and is overly demanding and never satisfied

Most trait studies on the relationship of traits and skills to effective leadership only test for simple, linear relationships. However, the relationship is often curvilinear, and a moderate amount of the trait is usually optimal rather than the maximum amount (e.g., Le et al., 2010). Examples of traits for which either a very low or very high level is undesirable are shown in Table 4. When the relationship is curvilinear, a study that only tests for a linear relationship will yield incorrect results, and the practical implications for leaders may be incorrect.

Most trait studies examined how single traits or skills are related to leadership effectiveness or advancement. This approach fails to consider how the traits are interrelated and how they interact to influence leader behavior and effectiveness. A more holistic approach is needed to examine patterns of leader traits and skills in relation to leader effectiveness (Kaplan & Kaiser, 2006; McCall, Lombardo, & Morrison, 1988; Quinn, 1988). Sometimes the optimal pattern involves a balance among related traits. For example, effective leaders balance a high need for power with the emotional maturity required to ensure that subordinates are empowered rather than dominated.

The concept of balance has been described for individuals, but it applies to shared leadership as well. For example, balance may involve several different leaders in a management team who have complementary attributes that compensate for each other's weaknesses and enhance each other's strengths (Bradford & Cohen, 1984). A better understanding of leadership in an organization may be gained by examining the pattern of traits for the executive team rather than focusing on the traits of a single leader such as the chief executive officer.

Guidelines for Managers

The finding that particular skills and traits are positively related to managerial effectiveness and advancement has some practical implications for people in planning their own managerial careers. The following guidelines (summarized in Table 5) are based on research, theory, and practitioner findings about traits and skills.

- **Learn about your strengths and weaknesses.**

It is essential for leaders to understand what is required for success in their current position and how well their traits and skills will enable them to do what is required. Understanding of strengths makes it easier to build on them and become more effective. Understanding of weaknesses makes it easier to correct them or compensate for them. Take advantage of opportunities to gain systematic feedback about strengths and weaknesses from multisource feedback programs and assessment centers.

- **Maintain a high level of self-awareness.**

Self-awareness includes a good understanding of one's own needs, emotions, abilities, and behavior. Awareness of your emotional reactions to events facilitates information

TABLE 5	Guidelines for Understanding and Improving Relevant Competencies

- Learn about your strengths and weaknesses
- Maintain self-awareness
- Identify and develop skills relevant for a future leadership position
- Remember that a strength can become a weakness
- Compensate for weaknesses

processing and decision making in stressful situations, and it helps you maintain optimism and enthusiasm about a project or mission in the face of obstacles and setbacks. Awareness of your behavior and its influence on others makes it easier to learn from experience and to assess your strengths and weaknesses. Insights can be gained by monitoring your own behavior and its consequences. It is also important to be receptive to feedback from others about positive and negative aspects of behavior as they perceive it.

- **Identify and develop skills relevant for a future leadership position.**

Effective managers are more oriented toward continuous learning and selfdevelopment. Learn what traits and skills are useful for the type of leadership role or position you want to have in the future. Determine which skills need to be strengthened and seek opportunities to develop them. Some training may be obtained in specialized management development workshops run by one's employer or by consulting companies. Other approaches for developing new skills include challenging assignments, personal coaching, and self-development activities.

- **Remember that a strength can become a weakness.**

A trait or skill that is a strength in one situation can later become a weakness when the situation changes. People tend to emphasize a skill that brings repeated success early in their careers, and later when it is no longer as relevant, the strength becomes a weakness. For example, a study conducted by CCL researchers found that staff managers who performed brilliant analytical work could not develop the action orientation necessary to implement ideas when they moved into a line position. Successful line managers had the opposite problem; they seemed incapable of the reflective analysis and cooperative teamwork that was necessary in a staff position. Any trait taken to an extreme can also become a weakness, even when the situation has not changed. Confidence can become arrogance, innovation can become recklessness, decisiveness can become rashness, integrity can become fanaticism, and global vision can become lack of focus.

- **Compensate for weaknesses.**

One way to compensate for weaknesses is to select subordinates who have complementary strengths and allow them to assume responsibility for aspects of the work they are more qualified to perform. Sometimes it is appropriate to delegate responsibilities to qualified individuals, and other times it is better to have a management team (in which you are a member) share the responsibility for a particular problem or challenge.

Summary

The early trait studies attempted to identify physical characteristics, personality traits, and abilities of people who were believed to be "natural leaders" Hundreds of trait studies were conducted, but individual traits failed to correlate in a strong and consistent manner with leadership effectiveness. More progress was made after researchers included additional traits and skills and used better measures of traits and outcomes. Nevertheless, much of the trait research continues to have weaknesses such as lack of adequate attention to situational variables, mediating processes, curvilinear relationships, and trait interactions. As in the case of leadership behavior, some scholars have emphasized broadly defined categories of traits and skills that can make it more difficult to identify and understand important relationships.

Some personality traits found to be relevant for leadership advancement or effectiveness include energy level and stress tolerance, self-confidence, internal control orientation, emotional stability, extroversion, conscientiousness, and integrity. The motive pattern characteristic of many effective managers includes a socialized power orientation and a moderately strong need for achievement with an emphasis on collective performance rather than individual performance.

To be successful, a leader also needs interpersonal, cognitive, and technical skills. The relative priority of the three types of skills and the optimal mix of specific skills probably depends on the type of organization, the level of management, and the nature of the challenges confronting a leader. Some skills such as persuasiveness, analytical ability, speaking ability, and memory for details will help a leader be successful in any situation, whereas some other skills are not easily transferred to a different type of position. Competencies involve a combination of traits and skills, and some competencies examined in recent leadership research include emotional intelligence, social intelligence, and the ability to learn and adapt to change. The uniqueness and relevance of these competencies continues to be a controversial subject in the leadership literature.

The trait approach has important implications for improving managerial effectiveness. Information about traits and skills relevant for different types of managerial positions is useful for people who are planning a managerial career. The information is also useful for selecting people to fill managerial positions, for identifying training needs in the current job, and for planning management development activities to prepare the person for promotion to higher- level jobs.

Review and Discussion Questions

1. What traits are the best predictors of managerial performance and advancement?
2. Is it possible to have too much of a good thing with some traits?
3. Why is it important to consider the joint effects of different traits and skills?
4. What are the major reasons for managers to derail in their careers?
5. How are technical, conceptual, and interpersonal skills related to managerial effectiveness?
6. To what extent are the effects of traits and skills dependent on the situation?
7. Which skills are most important at lower, middle, and higher levels of management?
8. What are emotional and social intelligence, and how are they relevant for leadership?

Key Terms

big five personality traits
cognitive skills
competencies
conceptual skills
derailed careers
emotional intelligence
emotional maturity

emotional stability
interpersonal skills
locus of control orientation
need for achievement
need for affiliation
need for power
personalized power

orientation
self-awareness
self-confidence
social intelligence
socialized power orientation
technical skills

CASE 1

National Products

Susan Thomas is the vice president for human resources at National Products, a manufacturing company with 500 employees. The company has an opening for a general manager in one of its product divisions, and the president asked Susan to review the backgrounds of three department managers who are interested in being promoted to this position. She is expected either to recommend one of the three internal candidates or to begin recruitment of external candidates. The internal candidates are Charley Adams, Bill Stuart, and Ray Johnson. The following information about each candidate was obtained from performance records, interviews with the candidates, and discussions with the boss of each candidate.

Charley Adams

Charley Adams has been a production manager for the past eight years. He is an easy-going person who loves to swap jokes and tell stories. Charley stresses the importance of cooperation and teamwork. He is uncomfortable with conflict, and he tries to smooth it over quickly or find an acceptable compromise.

Before becoming a manager, Charley was always willing to take on extra assignments for his boss and to provide helpful advice to less experienced coworkers in his department. Charley is proud of his reputation as a "good team player" and a loyal "company man." It is important to Charley to be liked and appreciated by people in the organization.

Charley comes from a cultural background emphasizing the importance of close family ties. He holds frequent Sunday dinners at which the entire Adams clan gathers for an afternoon of swimming, baseball, eating, and singing. On Saturdays, Charley likes to play golf with friends, including some of the other managers in the company.

Charley wants his department to have a good performance record, but he is reluctant to jeopardize relations with subordinates by pushing them to improve their performance beyond current levels, which he believes are adequate. When Charley gives out performance bonuses to subordinates, he usually tries to give something to everyone.

Bill Stuart

Bill Stuart has been the manager of an engineering department for three years. He was promoted to that position because he was the best design engineer in the company and was ambitious to further his career by going into management. At the time, Bill had little understanding of what the job would be like, but he saw it as both an opportunity and a challenge.

Bill grew up as somewhat of a loner. He still feels awkward around people he doesn't know well, and he dislikes social functions such as cocktail parties and company picnics. As a design engineer, Bill preferred assignments where he could work alone rather than team projects. He is impatient with bureaucratic authority figures and he is critical of corporate policies that he regards as too restrictive. Bill gets along well with his present boss, because he is left alone to run his engineering group in his own way.

Bill likes challenging assignments, and he tries to save the most difficult and interesting design projects for himself. Although Bill usually performs these tasks effectively, his preoccupation with them sometimes takes time away from some of his managerial responsibilities, such as developing and mentoring subordinates.

Ray Johnson

Ray Johnson has been a corporate marketing manager for five years. He grew up in a poor ethnic neighborhood where he learned to be tough in order to survive. He has worked hard to get where he is, but for Ray, good performance has been a way to get ahead rather than something he enjoys for its own sake.

Ray lives in a large house with a big swimming pool in the best part of town, and he likes to throw big parties at his home. He wears expensive clothes, drives a luxury car, and he belongs to the best country club. Ray is married, but fancies himself as quite a playboy and has had many affairs, including some with female employees.

Ray views the organization as a political jungle, and he is quick to defend himself against any threats to his reputation, authority, or position. He tries to undermine or discredit anybody who criticizes or opposes him. He keeps a tight control over the operations of his department, and he insists that subordinates check with him before taking any action that is not routine.

Copyright © 1978 by Gary Yukl

Questions

1. What are the dominate motives for each candidate?
2. What are the implications of these traits for the success of each candidate if selected for the general manager position?
3. Should Susan recommend one of these candidates for the position, or look for external candidates?

CASE 2

Excerpts from the Autobiographies of M. K. Gandhi, Nelson Mandela, and Martin L. King

About Parents

King

He [King's father] has always been a very strong and self-confident person. I have rarely ever met a person more fearless and courageous than my father, notwithstanding the fact that he feared for me. He never feared the autocratic and brutal person in the white community. (Carson, 1998, pp. 4–5).

Gandhi

My father was a lover of his clan, truthful, brave, and generous, but short-tempered… But he was incorruptible and had earned a name for strict impartiality in his family as well as outside. (Gandhi, 1929, pp. 15).

Mandela

My father had a stern manner and did not spare the rod when disciplining his children. He could be exceedingly stubborn, another trait that may unfortunately have been passed down from father to son… my father possessed a proud rebelliousness, a stubborn sense of fairness that I recognize in myself. (Mandela, 1994, pp. 15)

About Childhood

King

The second incident happened when I was about six years of age… The climax came when he [King's friend] told me one day that his father had demanded that he would play with me no more. I never will forget what a great shock this was to me… The question arose in my mind: How could I love a race of people who hated me and who had been responsible for breaking me up with one of my best childhood friends? This was a great question in my mind for a number of years. (pp. 7)

Gandhi

I do not remember having ever told a lie, during this short period, either to my teachers or to my schoolmates… Two other incidents belonging to the same period have always clung to my memory… To follow truth and to go through all the ordeals Harishchandra went through was the one ideal it inspired in me. (pp. 16)

Mandela

As a leader, I have always followed the principles I first saw demonstrated by the regent at the Great Palace. I have always endeavored to listen to what each and every person in a discussion had to say before venturing my own opinion. Oftentimes, my own opinion will simply represent a consensus of what I heard in the discussion. (pp. 18)

About Adolescence

King

My days in college were very exciting ones. There was a free atmosphere at Morehouse, and it was there I had my first frank discussion on race… They encouraged us in a positive quest for a solution to racial ills. I realized that nobody there was afraid. Important people came in to discuss the race problem rationally with us… As stated above, my college training, especially the first two years, brought many doubts into my mind. It was then that the shackles of fundamentalism were removed from my body. More and more, I could see a gap between what I learned in Sunday school and what I was learning in college. My studies had me skeptical, and I could not see how many of the facts of science could be squared with religion. (pp. 13–15).

Gandhi

All this had its due effect on me. I was beaten. It began to grow on me that meat-eating was good, that it would make me strong and daring, and that, if the whole country took to meat-eating, the English could be overcome. A day was thereupon fixed for beginning the experiment. It had to be conducted in secret… I cannot say that I did not know then that I should have to deceive my parents if I began eating meat. But my mind was bent on the "reform." It was not a question of pleasing the palate. I did not know that it had a particularly good relish. I wished to be strong and daring and wanted my countrymen also to be such, so that we might defeat the English and make India free. The word *Swaraj* I had not yet heard. But I knew what freedom meant. The frenzy of the "reform" blinded me. And having ensured secrecy, I persuaded myself that mere hiding the deed from parents was no departure from truth. (pp. 12).

Mandela

I could hardly believe my ears. His boldness in speaking of such delicate matters in the presence of Dr. Wellington and other whites seemed utterly astonishing to us. Yet at the same time, it aroused and motivates us, and began to alter my perception of men like Mr. Wellington, whom I had automatically considered my benefactor... I was galvanized, but also confused by Mqhayi's performance (pp. 36–37).

SOURCES:

- Carson, C., 1998, *The Autobiography of Martin Luther King, Jr.* (New York: Warner Books).
- Gandhi, M. K., 1929, *An Autobiography. The Story of My Experiments with Truth* (Ahmedabad, India: Navajivan).
- Mandela, N. R., 1994, *Long Walk to Freedom* (Boston: Little, Brown).
- Morselli, D. and Passini, S. (2010). Avoiding Crimes of Obedience: A Comparative Study of the Autobiographies of MK Gandhi, Nelson Mandela, and Martin Luther King, Jr. *Peace and Conflict,* 16(3): 295–319.

Questions

1. Analyze the commonalities and differences in the above text with reference to the leadership development of three great leaders of the world.
2. How does Gandhi differ from Mandela in his approach toward internalizing life instances?

Contingency Theories and Adaptive Leadership

Contingency Theories and Adaptive Leadership

Learning Objectives

After studying this chapter you should be able to:

- Understand how aspects of the situation can enhance or diminish effects of leader behavior.
- Understand key features of the early contingency theories of effective leadership.
- Understand the benefits and limitations of contingency theories.
- Understand the findings from empirical research on contingency theories.
- Understand how to adapt leader behavior to the situation.
- Understand how to manage disruptions and other crises.

Much of the early research on effective leadership reflects an implicit assumption that some leader traits (e.g., intelligence, self-confidence) or broadly-defined behaviors (e.g., task-oriented, relations-oriented, participative) are positively related to subordinate performance or satisfaction in all situations (Stogdill, 1974). However, the research failed to provide strong support for universal conceptions of effective leadership. The lack of consistent results stimulated interest in developing "*contingency theories*" that can explain why the traits or behaviors required for effective leadership vary for different situations. In the 1970s and 1980s, several contingency theories were proposed, including *path-goal theory, situational leadership theory,* the LPC contingency model, leader substitutes theory, cognitive resources theory, the multiplelinkage model, and the *normative decision model.*

The purpose of this chapter is to describe and evaluate early contingency theories and the evidence from research on them. The first section of the chapter provides a general description of contingency theories and how they differ from universal theories of effective leadership. The next section describes three different types of situational influences. Then several early contingency theories are briefly described, conceptual limitations common to most of the theories are identified, the research findings are summarized, and limitations of the research are identified. A general evaluation of the contingency approach is made next, and ways are suggested for developing stronger theories and improving the research. The chapter ends with guidelines for adaptive leadership and guidelines for handling immediate crises.

General Description of Contingency Theories

Contingency theories describe how aspects of the leadership situation can alter a leader's influence and effectiveness. Most of the early contingency theories were focused on dyadic influence on one subordinate, but a few of the theories included leader influence on group processes.

Types of Variables

The contingency theories of effective leadership have at least one predictor variable, at least one dependent variable, and one or more situational variables. The leadership attributes used as independent variables were usually described in terms of broad meta-categories (e.g., task and relations behavior). The dependent variable in most of the theories was subordinate satisfaction or performance, and in a few cases it was group performance. Most of the situational variables were conditions the leader is not able to change in the short term, including characteristics of the work (e.g., task structure, role interdependence), characteristics of subordinates (e.g., needs, values), characteristics of the leader (expertise, interpersonal stress), and characteristics of the leadership position (leader authority, formal policies).

Some contingency theories also include *mediating variables* (sometimes called "intervening variables") to explain the influence of leader behavior and situational variables on performance outcomes. The mediators are usually subordinate characteristics that determine individual performance (e.g., role clarity, task skills, self-efficacy, task goals), but mediators can also include group-level characteristics that determine team performance (e.g., collective efficacy, cooperation, coordination of activities, resources). A theory is more complex and difficult to test if it includes many specific behaviors, mediating variables, and situational variables.

Causal Effects of Situational Variables

The situational variables used in contingency theories can have different types of causal effects, and more than one type of effect can occur for the same situational variable (Howell, Dorfman, & Kerr, 1986; James & Brett, 1984; Yukl, 2009).

Situation Directly Effects Outcomes or Mediators.   A situational variable can directly influence an outcome such as subordinate satisfaction or performance, or a mediating variable that is a determinant of the outcomes. When a situational variable can make a mediating variable or an outcome more favorable, it is sometimes called a *"substitute" for leadership*. An example is when subordinates have extensive prior training and experience. The need for clarifying and coaching by the leader is reduced, because subordinates already know what to do and how to do it. A substitute can indirectly influence leader behavior if it becomes obvious to the leader that some types of behavior are redundant and unnecessary. A situational variable can also affect the relative importance of a mediating variable as a determinant of performance outcomes. For example, employee skill is a more important determinant of performance when the task is very complex and variable than when the task is simple and repetitive. Here again, the situational variable can indirectly influence leader behavior if it is obvious to the leader that some types of behavior are more relevant than others to improve performance for the leader's team or work unit.

Situation Directly Influences Leader Behavior.   A situational variable may directly influence a leader's behavior but only indirectly influence the dependent variables. Aspects of the situation such as formal rules, policies, role expectations, and organizational values can encourage or constrain a leader's behavior, and they are sometimes called *demands* and *constraints*.

In addition to the direct effect of the situation on leader behavior, there may be an indirect effect on dependent variables. For example, a company establishes a new policy requiring sales managers to provide bonuses to any sales representative with sales exceeding a minimum standard; sales managers begin awarding bonuses, and the performance and satisfaction of the sales representatives increases.

Situation Moderates Effects of Leader Behavior.   A situational variable is called an *enhancer* if it increases the effects of leader behavior on the dependent variable but does not directly influence the dependent variable. For example providing coaching will have a stronger impact on subordinate performance when the leader has relevant expertise. This expertise enables the leader to provide better coaching, and subordinates are more likely to follow advice from a leader who is perceived to be an expert. An enhancer can indirectly influence leader behavior if a leader is more likely to use a behavior because it is perceived to be relevant and effective. A situational *moderator variable* is called a *neutralizer* when it decreases the effect of leader behavior on the dependent variable or prevents any effect from occurring. For example, offering a pay increase to an employee for working extra days may fail if the employee is rich and does not need the money. Employee indifference to pay rewards is a neutralizer for this type of influence tactic.

Early Contingency Theories

Six contingency theories are described in this chapter, including *path-goal theory, leadership substitutes theory, situational leadership theory, the LPC contingency model, cognitive resources theory, and the multiple-linkage model.*

Path-Goal Theory

The initial versions of path-goal theory described how a leader's task-oriented behavior ("instrumental leadership") and relations-oriented behavior ("supportive leadership") influence subordinate satisfaction and performance in different situations (Evans, 1970; House, 1971). The theory was later extended to include participative leadership and achievement-oriented leadership (e.g., Evans, 1974; House, 1996; House & Mitchell, 1974).

Consistent with the expectancy theory of motivation, leaders can motivate subordinates by influencing their perceptions about the likely consequences of different levels of effort. Subordinates will perform better when they have clear and accurate role expectations, they perceive that a high level of effort is necessary to attain task objectives, they are optimistic that it is possible to achieve the task objectives, and they perceive that high performance will result in beneficial outcomes. The effect of a leader's behavior is primarily to modify these perceptions and beliefs. According to House (1971, p. 324), "The motivational function of the leader consists of increasing personal payoffs to subordinates for work-goal attainment and making the path to these payoffs easier to travel by clarifying it, reducing roadblocks and pitfalls, and increasing the opportunities for personal satisfaction en route."

Leader behavior can also affect subordinate satisfaction. According to House and Dessler (1974, p. 13), ". . . leader behavior will be viewed as acceptable to subordinates to the extent that the subordinates see such behavior as either an immediate source of satisfaction or as instrumental to future satisfaction" Depending on the situation, leader behavior may affect satisfaction and performance in the same way or in different ways.

According to path-goal theory, the effect of leader behavior on subordinate satisfaction and effort depends on aspects of the situation, including task characteristics and subordinate characteristics. These situational moderator variables determine both the potential for increased subordinate motivation and the manner in which the leader must act to improve motivation. Situational variables also influence subordinate preferences for a particular pattern of leadership behavior, thereby influencing the impact of the leader on subordinate satisfaction.

One key proposition of the theory involves the moderating influence of situational variables on instrumental leadership. Task-oriented behavior has a stronger effect on role clarity, self-efficacy, effort, and performance when subordinates are unsure about how to do their work, which occurs when they have a complex and difficult task and little prior experience with it. Another key proposition is that supportive leadership has a stronger effect when the task is very tedious, dangerous, and stressful. In this situation supportive leadership increases subordinate confidence, effort, and satisfaction.

Leadership Substitutes Theory

Kerr and Jermier (1978) identified aspects of the situation that make task-oriented behavior ("instrumental leadership") or relations-oriented behavior ("supportive leadership") by the designated leader redundant or ineffective. Later versions included additional behaviors such as contingent reward behavior (Howell, Bowen, Dorfman, Kerr, & Podsakoff, 1990; Podsakoff, Niehoff, MacKenzie, & Williams, 1993).

The situational variables include characteristics of the subordinates, task, and the organization that serve as *substitutes* by directly affecting the dependent variable and making the leader behavior redundant. The substitutes for instrumental leadership include a highly structured and repetitive task, extensive rules and standard procedures, and extensive prior training and experience for subordinates. The substitutes for supportive leadership include a cohesive work group in which the members support each other, and an intrinsically satisfying task that is not stressful. In a situation with many substitutes, the potential impact of leader behavior on subordinate motivation and satisfaction may be greatly reduced. For example, little direction is necessary when subordinates have extensive prior experience or training, and they already possess the skills and knowledge to know what to do and how to do it. Likewise, professionals who are internally motivated by their values, needs, and ethics do not need to be encouraged by the leader to do high-quality work.

Some situational variables (called *neutralizers*) prevent a leader from using forms of behavior that would improve subordinate satisfaction or unit performance. For example, a leader with no authority to change ineffective work procedures cannot make changes that would improve efficiency. Howell et al. (1990) contend that some situations have so many neutralizers that it is difficult or impossible for a leader to succeed. In this event, the remedy is to change the situation and make it more favorable for the leader by removing neutralizers, and in some cases by increasing substitutes.

Situational Leadership Theory

Hersey and Blanchard (1977) proposed a contingency theory called Situational Leadership Theory. It specifies the appropriate type of leadership behavior for a subordinate in various situations. Behavior was defined in terms of directive and supportive leadership, and a revised version of the theory also included decision procedures (Graef, 1997). The situational variable is subordinate maturity, which includes the person's ability and confidence to do a task.

According to the theory, for a low-maturity subordinate the leader should use substantial task-oriented behavior such as defining roles, clarifying standards and procedures, directing the work, and monitoring progress. As subordinate maturity increases up to a moderate level, the leader can decrease the amount of task-oriented behavior and increase the amount of relationsoriented behavior (e.g., consult with the subordinate, provide more praise and attention). For high-maturity subordinates, the leader should use extensive delegation and only a limited amount of directive and supportive behavior. A high-maturity subordinate has the ability to do the work without much direction or monitoring by the leader, and the confidence to work without much supportive behavior by the leader.

The primary focus of the theory is on short-term behavior, but over time the leader may be able to increase subordinate maturity with a developmental intervention that builds the person's skills and confidence. How long it takes to increase subordinate maturity depends on the complexity of the task and the subordinate's initial skill and confidence. It may take as little as a few days or as long as a few years to advance a subordinate from low to high maturity on a given task. Hersey and Blanchard recognized that subordinate maturity may also regress, requiring a flexible adjustment of the leader's behavior. For example, after a personal tragedy such as a death of loved ones, a subordinate who was highly motivated may become apathetic. In this situation the leader should increase supervision and use a developmental intervention designed to restore maturity to the former high level.

The LPC Contingency Model

Fiedler's (1967; 1978) LPC Contingency Model describes how the situation moderates the effects on group performance of a leader trait called the least preferred coworker (LPC) score. The interpretation of LPC scores has changed several times over the years, and what the measure actually means is still questionable.

Fiedler's (1978) interpretation is that LPC scores reveal a leader's motive hierarchy. A high LPC leader is strongly motivated to have close, interpersonal relationships and will act in a considerate, supportive manner if relationships need to be improved. Achievement of task objectives is a secondary motive that will become important only if the primary affiliation motive is already satisfied by close, personal relationships with subordinates. A low LPC leader is primarily motivated by achievement of task objectives and will emphasize task-oriented behavior whenever task problems arise. The secondary motive of establishing good relations with subordinates will become important only if the group is performing well and has no serious task-related problems.

An alternative interpretation suggested by Rice (1978) emphasizes leader values rather than motives. According to this interpretation, leaders with a low LPC score value task achievement more than interpersonal relations, whereas leaders with high LPC scores value interpersonal relations more than task achievement (Rice, 1978). These value priorities are assumed to be reflected in the amount of task-oriented and relations-oriented behaviors used by leaders.

The relationship between a leader's LPC score and group performance depends on a complex situational variable called situational favorability, which is jointly determined by task structure, leader position power, and the quality of leader-member relations. The situation is most favorable when the leader has substantial position power, the task is highly structured, and relations with subordinates are good. According to the theory, low LPC leaders are more effective when the situation is either very favorable or very unfavorable, whereas high LPC leaders are more effective when there is a moderate level of situational favorability. The theory does not clearly identify mediating variables to explain how leader LPC and situational favorability jointly determine group performance. Two different approaches can be used by a leader to maximize effectiveness. One approach is to select the appropriate type of behavior for the situation, and the other approach is to try to change the situation to fit the leader's preferred pattern of behavior.

Cognitive Resources Theory

Cognitive resources theory (Fiedler, 1986; Fiedler & Garcia, 1987) describes the conditions under which cognitive resources such as intelligence and experience are related to group performance. According to the theory, the performance of a leader's group is determined by a complex interaction among two leader traits (intelligence and experience), one type of leader behavior (*directive leadership*), and two aspects of the leadership situation (interpersonal stress and the distribution of knowledge about the task).

Interpersonal stress for the leader moderates the relation between leader intelligence and subordinate performance. Stress may be due to a boss who creates role conflict or demands miracles without providing necessary resources and support. Other sources of stress include frequent work crises and serious conflicts with subordinates. Under low stress, leader intelligence facilitates information processing and problem solving, and it is likely to improve the quality of autocratic leader decisions. However, when there is high interpersonal stress, strong emotions are likely to disrupt cognitive information processing and make intelligence difficult to apply. The leader may become distracted and unable to focus on the task. In this stressful situation a leader who has already learned a high quality solution in previous experience with similar problems is usually more effective than an intelligent but inexperienced leader who tries to find new solutions.

A participative decision is more effective when the members of the group have relevant knowledge and information not possessed by the leader, whereas an autocratic decision is more effective when the leader has more expertise about the task than subordinates. This aspect of the theory is similar to a key feature of the Normative Decision Model. However, Cognitive Resources Theory does not include explicit mediating variables to explain how interpersonal stress, leader intelligence, and leader experience affect the use of participative decision procedures, or how decision procedures influence the performance of the leader's group.

Multiple-linkage Model

The *multiple-linkage model* (Yukl, 1981, 1989) was developed after the other early contingency theories, and it includes ideas from some of those theories. However, the broadly defined leadership behaviors in most earlier theories were replaced by more specific types of behaviors. Other unique features include a larger number of mediating and situational variables, and more explicit description of group-level processes. The explanation of how these variables are relevant includes ideas from the literature on motivation, organization theory, and team leadership. The multiple-linkage model describes how managerial behavior and situational variables jointly influence the performance of individual subordinates and the leader's work unit. The four types of variables in the model include managerial behaviors, mediating variables, criterion variables, and situational variables.

Mediating Variables

The mediating variables in the model are based on earlier research and theory on determinants of individual and group performance (e.g., Hackman, Brousseau, & Weiss, 1976; Likert, 1967; McGrath, 1984; Porter & Lawler, 1968). The mediating variables are defined primarily at the group level, like theories of team leadership.

Task commitment: members strive to attain a high level of performance and show a high degree of personal commitment to unit task objectives.

Ability and role clarity: members understand their individual job responsibilities, know what to do, and have the skills to do it.

Organization of the work: effective performance strategies are used and the work is organized to ensure efficient utilization of personnel, equipment, and facilities.

Cooperation and mutual trust: members trust each other, share information and ideas, help each other, and identify with the work unit.

Resources and support: the group has budgetary funds, tools, equipment, supplies, personnel, facilities, information, and assistance needed to do the work.

External coordination: the activities of the group are synchronized with the interdependent activities in other subunits and organizations (e.g., suppliers, clients).

The mediating variables interact with each other to determine the effectiveness of a group or organizational subunit. A serious deficiency in one mediating variable may lower group effectiveness, even though the other mediating variables are not deficient. The greater the relative importance of a particular mediating variable, the more group performance will be reduced by a deficiency in this variable. The relative importance of the mediating variables depends on the type of work unit and other aspects of the situation. Table 1 lists aspects of the situation that affect the level of a mediating variable or make it more important.

Situational Variables

Situational variables directly influence mediating variables and can make them either more or less favorable. Situational variables also determine the relative importance of the mediating variables as a determinant of group performance. Mediating variables that are both important and deficient should get top priority for corrective action by a leader. Conditions that make a mediating variable more favorable are similar to "substitutes" for leadership. In a very favorable situation, some of the mediating variables may already be at their maximum short-term level, making the job of the leader much easier. Situational variables affecting each mediating variable are briefly described in this section.

Situational variables that can influence task *commitment* include the formal reward system and the intrinsically motivating properties of the work itself. Subordinate task commitment is more important for complex tasks that require high effort and initiative and have a high cost for any errors. Member commitment to perform the task effectively will be greater if the organization has a reward system that provides attractive rewards contingent on performance, as in the case of many sales jobs. Intrinsic motivation is likely to be higher for subordinates if the work requires varied skills, is interesting and challenging, and provides automatic feedback about performance.

Situational variables that affect subordinate *ability and role clarity* include the nature of the work, the prior training and experience of the leader's subordinates, and the effectiveness of the organization's recruitment and selection processes. Subordinate skills are more important when task are complex and difficult to perform, they require strong technical skills, the cost of errors is high, and disruptions in the work are likely. An organization with effective recruiting and high salaries is more likely to attract qualified people with relevant job skills and prior experience. Role requirements are easier to understand and the work is easier to perform when the task is simple and repetitive, subordinates have extensive prior experience, and the organization has clear rules and standard procedures for the work. Role ambiguity is more likely to be a problem when the task has multiple performance criteria and priorities are unclear, when the nature of the work or technology is changing, or when the work is affected by frequent changes in plans or priorities determined by clients or higher management.

Situational variables that affect the *organization of the work* and assignment of tasks to individuals include the type of technology, the variety of tasks performed by the leader's

TABLE 1	Conditions Affecting Mediating Variables in the Multiple-linkage Model	
Mediating Variable	**Conditions Where Already High**	**Situations Where Most Important**
Subordinate effort and commitment	• Interesting, challenging, intrinsically motivating task. • Subordinates have strong work ethic values. • Organization reward system has large rewards for performance.	• Complex, labor-intensive work requiring high subordinate initiative and persistence. • Work unit has high exposure tasks and mistakes are very costly.
Subordinate ability and role clarity	• Work is simple and repetitive. • Subordinates have extensive prior training and experience. • Organization provides detailed formal rules and procedures.	• Complex, difficult tasks require a high level of technical skill. • High exposure task for which mistakes are very costly. • Serious disruptions or immediate crises are likely.
Organization of work and task assignments	• Organization specifies optimal way to structure the work. • Subordinates are all highly skilled in doing all the tasks.	• Work unit has complex, unique tasks that require good strategies. • Work unit has several different tasks and a high variation in member skills.
Cooperation and teamwork	• Group has stable, homogeneous, compatible membership. • Members have shared goals consistent with task objectives. • Rewards are based primarily on group performance.	• Task roles in the work unit are highly inter-dependent. • Subordinates must share scarce equipment or limited facilities. • Subordinates work together in close proximity for long time.
Resources needed to do the work	• Organization provides adequate resources as needed. • Organization has good inventory control system for materials.	• The work requires large amounts of scarce resources. • Work unit is highly dependent on unreliable sources of supply.
External coordination	• Organization has structural mechanisms for achieving lateral coordination. • External coordination is done by higher management or designated specialists.	• Work unit has high lateral interdependence with other units in the same organization. • Frequent changes in priorities or schedules due to client demands or unreliable suppliers or vendors.

work unit, the variation in subordinate skills, and the amount of work rules and standard procedures that are determined by staff experts or union contracts. When the work unit performs one basic type of task and subordinates are all highly skilled, it is easy to organize unit activities and make task assignments that will achieve a high level of efficiency. An effective performance strategy for organizing activities and assigning tasks is more important when the work unit has complex, unique, and important projects and members who differ with regard to their skills. For some types of projects, an efficient organization of activities can be achieved by qualified staff experts who use operations management and project management software.

Situational variables that affect *cooperation and teamwork* include the nature of the work, the size of the group, the stability of membership, the similarity among members in values and background, and the reward system. Cooperation and teamwork are more important when the group has specialized, interdependent tasks or when members work alone but must share equipment and scarce resources. More cohesiveness and cooperation are likely in small groups with a stable, homogeneous membership. Cooperation is increased by rewards that are based primarily on contributions to group performance rather than on individual performance.

The adequacy of *resources* that are necessary to do the work is influenced by the nature of the work, the organization's formal budgetary systems, procurement systems, and inventory control systems, as well as by economic conditions at the time. Ensuring an adequate level of resources is more important when work unit performance is highly dependent on getting scarce resources from the organization or outside sources, and when the providers of resources are unreliable. An adequate level of resources is more likely to be provided to a work unit when the organization is prosperous and growing than when the organization is in decline and faces severe resource shortages.

The need for *external coordination* is affected by the formal structure of the organization. High lateral interdependence increases the amount of necessary coordination with other subunits, but this coordination may be facilitated by special integrating mechanisms such as integrator positions and cross-functional committees (Galbraith, 1973; Lawrence & Lorsch, 1967). A high level of dependency on outsiders such as clients or subcontractors for resources or approvals increases the need for external coordination with them, but it may be achieved by designated project managers or liaison specialists rather than by work unit managers.

Short-Term Actions to Correct Deficiencies

A basic proposition of the theory is that leader actions to correct any deficiencies in the mediating variables will improve group performance. A leader who fails to recognize opportunities to correct deficiencies in key mediating variables, who recognizes the opportunities but fails to act, or who acts but is not skilled will be less than optimally effective. An ineffective leader may make things worse by acting in ways that increase rather than decrease the deficiency in one or more mediating variables. For example, a leader who is very manipulative and coercive may reduce subordinate effort rather than increasing it.

Table 2 summarizes possible short-term actions to deal with deficiencies in the mediating variables. Leaders may influence group members to work faster or do better quality work (e.g., by offering special incentives, by giving an inspiring talk about the importance of the work, by setting challenging goals). Leaders may increase member ability to do the work (e.g., by showing them better methods for doing the work, by clearing up confusion about who is responsible for what). Leaders may organize and coordinate activities in a more efficient way (e.g., by finding ways to reduce delays, duplication of effort, and wasted effort; by matching people to tasks better; by finding better ways to use people and resources). Leaders may obtain resources needed immediately to do the work (e.g., information, personnel, equipment, materials, supplies). Leaders may act to improve external coordination by meeting with outsiders to plan activities and resolve conflicting demands on the work unit.

TABLE 2	Leader Actions to Deal with Deficiencies in Mediating Variables

Subordinates are apathetic or discouraged about the work.

- Set challenging goals and express confidence subordinates can attain them.
- Articulate an appealing vision of what the group could accomplish or become.
- Use rational persuasion and inspirational appeals to influence commitment.
- Lead by example.
- Use consultation and delegation.
- Provide recognition.
- Reward effective behavior.

Subordinates are confused about what to do or how to do their work.

- Make clear assignments.
- Set specific goals and provide feedback about performance.
- Provide more direction of on-going activities.
- Provide instruction or coaching as needed.
- Identify skill deficiencies and arrange for necessary skill training.
- Recruit and hire skilled people to work in unit.

The group is disorganized and/or it uses weak performance strategies.

- Develop plans to accomplish objectives.
- Identify and correct coordination problems.
- Reorganize activities to make better use of people, resources, and equipment.
- Identify and eliminate inefficient and unnecessary activities.
- Provide more decisive direction of on-going activities in a crisis.

There is little cooperation and teamwork among members of the group.

- Emphasize common interests and encourage cooperation.
- Encourage constructive resolution of conflict and help mediate conflicts.
- Increase group incentives and reduce competition.
- Use symbols and rituals to build identification with the work unit.
- Use teambuilding activities.

The group has inadequate resources to do the work.

- Requisition or borrow specific resources needed immediately for the work.
- Find more reliable or alternative sources of supplies.
- Ration available resources if necessary.
- Initiate improvement projects to upgrade equipment and facilities.
- Lobby with higher authorities for a larger budget.

External coordination with other subunits or outsiders is weak.

- Network with peers and outsiders to develop more cooperative relationships.
- Consult more with peers and outsiders when making plans.
- Keep peers and outsiders informed about changes.
- Monitor closely to detect coordination problems quickly.
- Meet with peers and outsiders to resolve coordination problems.
- Negotiate favorable agreements with peers and outsiders for group outputs.

Some aspects of the situation limit a leader's discretion in making changes and reacting to problems. These influences are similar to Stewart's (1976) "constraints" and Kerr and Jermier's (1978) "neutralizers." The extent to which a leader is capable of doing something in the short run to improve any of the mediating variables is limited by the position power, organizational policies, technology used to do the work, and legal-contractual restrictions (e.g., labor-management agreements, contracts with suppliers, requirements mandated by government agencies). Constraints may prevent a leader from rewarding or punishing members, changing work assignments or procedures, and procuring supplies and equipment.

The model does not imply that there is only one optimal pattern of managerial behavior in any given situation. Leaders usually have some choice among mediating variables in need of improvement, and different patterns of behavior are usually possible to correct a particular deficiency. The overall pattern of leadership behavior by the designated leader and other group members is more important than any single action. In this respect, the model is similar to Stewart's (1976) "choices". However, a leader whose attention is focused on mediating variables that are not deficient or not important will fail to improve unit performance.

Long-Term Effects on Group Performance

Over a longer period of time, leaders can make larger improvements in group performance by modifying the situation to make it more favorable. Effective leaders act to reduce constraints, increase substitutes, and reduce the importance of mediating variables that are not amenable to improvement. These effects usually involve sequences of related behaviors carried out over a long time period. More research has been conducted on short-term behaviors by leaders than on the long-term behaviors to improve the situation. Useful insights are provided by literature on leading change, making strategic decisions, and representing the team or work unit. Some examples of possible actions a leader may take to improve the situation are as follows:

1. *Gain more access to resources needed for the work by cultivating better relationships with suppliers, finding alternative sources, and reducing dependence on unreliable sources.*
2. *Gain more control over the demand for the unit's products and services by finding new customers, opening new markets, advertising more, and modifying the products or services to be more acceptable to clients and customers.*
3. *Initiate new, more profitable activities for the work unit that will make better use of personnel, equipment, and facilities.*
4. *Initiate long-term improvement programs to upgrade equipment, and facilities in the work unit (e.g., replace old equipment, implement new technology).*
5. *Improve selection procedures to increase the level of employee skills and commitment.*
6. *Modify the formal structure of the work unit to solve chronic problems and reduce demands on the leader for short-term problem solving.*

Conceptual Weaknesses in Contingency Theories

The early contingency theories have many conceptual weaknesses that make them difficult to test and limit their practical utility. Weaknesses typical of the early theories are described in this section, but not every theory has every weakness.

Over-emphasis on Behavior Meta-categories

Broadly defined categories of leader behavior can make a theory more parsimonious and less complex, but they have limited utility for understanding effective leadership in different situations. The diverse component behaviors in a meta-category such as instrumental or supportive leadership are not equally relevant for influencing an outcome variable, and a situational moderator variable may affect the component behaviors in different ways. For example, a stressful task may increase the value of some relations behaviors (e.g., supportive leadership) but not others (delegation). In any given situation some task-oriented behaviors will be more relevant than others, and some may have negative consequences. It is easier to understand how to improve leadership effectiveness when a theory includes specific types of behavior and describes the situations in which each type of behavior is relevant.

Ambiguous Description of Relationships

Most of the contingency theories do not clearly indicate whether the form of the relationship between the independent variable and the dependent variable changes as the situational variable increases (Podsakoff, MacKenzie, Ahearne, & Bommer, 1995). A leader behavior that has a positive effect on the dependent variable in some situations may have no effect or a negative effect in other situations. Thus, a high level of a leader behavior may be optimal in one situation, but a moderate or low level of the behavior may be optimal in a different situation. A contingency theory should identify situations where the form of the relationship changes and too much of the behavior (or any amount of it) has a negative effect rather than a positive effect.

Inadequate Explanation of Causal Effects

Most contingency theories do not provide an adequate explanation of the underlying reasons for the proposed relationships. A clear explanation requires mediating variables that are determinants of the primary dependent variable (e.g., performance or satisfaction) and can be influenced by leader behavior and aspects of the situation. Some of the contingency theories have no mediating variables, and others are too limited in the types of mediating processes used to explain effective leadership. The mediating variables in most of the theories involve dyadic leader influence on an individual subordinate rather than influence on collective processes in teams and work units. The early contingency theories were developed before it became obvious that multi-level issues are important, and even in theories that include group-level processes it is seldom clear whether the leader is influencing only an individual subordinate or the entire group.

Lack of Attention to Behavior Patterns

Most contingency theories explain only the separate, independent effects of each type of leadership behavior included in the theory. Complex interactions among different behaviors (or traits) receive little if any attention. For example, the effects of task-oriented and relationsoriented behaviors are not independent. A high level of relations behavior may not improve performance unless the leader also uses appropriate task-oriented behaviors (Blake & Mouton, 1982; Fleishman & Harris, 1962; Yukl, 1981). The importance of examining joint effects is even greater for specific behaviors than for the meta-categories, because the optimal pattern of specific behaviors will vary more as the situation changes. For example, the need for some task and relations behaviors may remain high for a leader, but the optimal mix of specific behaviors will vary somewhat for different tasks and for different subordinates.

Lack of Attention to Joint Effects of Situational Variables

Most contingency theories do not explicitly consider how multiple situational variables interact in their moderating effects. The enhancing effects of one situational variable may be dependent on another situational variable. An example is provided by Vroom and Yetton (1973). The benefits of allowing participation by subordinates who have relevant information lacked by the leader (one situational variable) are dependent on a high level of goal congruence (another situational variable), because subordinates may be unwilling to share information that would be detrimental to their future welfare (e.g., ways to improve productivity that would also endanger their job security). A contingency theory can provide a more complete explanation of leader effectiveness if the interacting effects of situational variables are described.

Failure to Distinguish Between Mediators and Situational Moderators

As noted earlier, mediators are conceptually distinct from situational variables that directly influence leader behavior (demands and constraints) or situational variables (substitutes) that directly influence the mediators (or the outcomes). Confusion about causal relationships is created and potential for leader influence is underestimated when a mediator is treated as an exogenous situational variable beyond the leader's control. For example, the level of subordinate skills is usually influenced both by the aspects of the situation (e.g., type of tasks performed, selection and training systems for the organization) and by the leader's behavior (e.g., clarifying and coaching). Most contingency theories also fail to explain how leaders may improve work unit performance over a longer time period by reducing constraints and increasing substitutes.

Research on Contingency Theories

A contingency theory is supported by a pattern of results consistent with the propositions of the theory. Most of the research on the early contingency theories of leadership used survey methods, and many studies had the same respondents provide ratings on all variables. Review articles or meta-analyses of relevant research have been published for path-goal theory (Podsakoff, MacKenzie, Ahearne, & Bommer, 1995; Wofford & Liska, 1993), situational leadership theory (Fernandez & Vecchio, 1997; Graef, 1983, 1997; Thompson & Vecchio, 2009), leadership substitutes theory (Dionne, Yammarino, Atwater, & James, 2002; Podsakoff, Niehoff, MacKenzie, & Williams, 1993; Podsakoff et al., 1995), cognitive resources theory (Vecchio, 1990), the LPC contingency model (Peters, Hartke, & Pohlmann, 1985), and the normative decision model (Vroom & Jago, 1988). No research has directly tested all aspects of the multiple-linkage model, but several of the propositions are supported by findings in studies using descriptive research methods such as critical incidents, diaries and observation, case studies, and comparative field studies (e.g., Peterson & Van Fleet, 2008; Yukl & Van Fleet, 1982). Some of the propositions are similar to those in other contingency theories, and studies conducted to test those theories provide evidence relevant for assessing the multiple-linkage propositions.

In general, the evidence supporting contingency theories of effective leadership is inconsistent and difficult to interpret. As noted earlier, the ambiguity and conceptual problems in contingency theories makes them more difficult to test, and most studies used weak research methods (Schriesheim & Kerr, 1977; Yukl, 1989). As yet, none of the contingency theories have been adequately tested, and stronger research methods are needed to provide more conclusive results. Instead of relying so much on survey field studies with convenience samples, it is desirable to make more use of other relevant research methods.

Examples of methods that are likely to be more useful include comparative field studies of effective and ineffective leaders in different situations, longitudinal studies of how well leaders adapt to changes in the situation over time, field experiments with leaders trained to diagnose the situation accurately and select appropriate behaviors, and laboratory experiments with observation of leaders in team simulations conducted over a period of several weeks. Alternative methods for measuring leadership behavior (e.g., observation, diaries, interviews, and critical incidents) should be used more often, and ineffective forms of leadership behavior should be examined in addition to effective forms of behavior (e.g., Amabile, Schatzel, Moneta, & Kramer, 2004; Yukl & Van Fleet, 1982).

Measures of how often a particular type of behavior is used by a leader are not enough; it is also essential to consider whether the behavior is used when and where it is appropriate and in a skillful way. Most studies on the contingency theories only examine one or two aspects of the leadership situation, and behavior is usually defined in terms of a broad meta-category such as task-oriented, relations-oriented, or participative leadership. To understand adaptive leadership, it is also necessary to see how specific aspects of leader behavior change as the situation changes.

Finally, researchers need to pay more attention to the overall pattern of leadership behavior rather than examining each type of behavior separately. Effective leaders combine behaviors that are complementary, and different behaviors are woven together into a complex tapestry such that the whole is greater than the sum of the parts (Kaplan, 1988). More than one pattern of specific behaviors may be equally effective in the same situation, but it is essential to find a good balance between behaviors with competing objectives. Examples of competing values emphasized in this "duality approach" are controlling vs. empowering, strategic vs. operational objectives, and concern for people vs. concern for task objectives (Hooijberg, 1996; Kaiser & Overfield, 2010; Kaplan & Kaiser, 2006; Quinn, Spreitzer & Hart, 1992; Yukl & Mahsud, 2010).

Comparative Evaluation of Contingency Theories

Table 3 lists the major features of the contingency theories described in this chapter and the Vroom and Yetton's (1973) normative decision model. The table makes it easier to compare the theories with respect to their content and empirical support. All seven theories contain situational moderator variables, but the variety of situational variables is greater in some theories than in others. It seems desirable for a contingency theory to include many relevant aspects of the situation, but to do so makes a theory difficult to test. Mediating variables are helpful to explain how leaders influence subordinate performance, but only three of the theories have explicit mediating (or intervening) variables. Simple theories seem to have more appeal than complex theories, but simple theories are less useful for explaining effective leadership.

One basis for evaluating a leadership theory is in terms of practical applications for improving leadership effectiveness. Some behavioral scientists have questioned whether the early contingency theories have any utility for showing managers how to become more effective. For example, McCall (1977) contends that the hectic pace of managerial work makes it impossible to stop and analyze the situation with a complicated model, and he also questions the implicit assumption of most contingency theories that there is a single best way for the manager to act within a given situation. Leaders face an immense variety of rapidly changing situations, and several different patterns of behavior may be equally effective in the same situation.

Most contingency theories do not provide sufficient guidance in the form of general principles to help managers recognize the underlying leadership requirements and choices in the myriad of fragmented activities and problems confronting them. What may be needed is a theory with both universal elements (e.g., general principles) and situational elements (e.g., guidelines to help identify desirable behaviors for a particular type of situation). However, despite the limitations of the situational theories and research,

TABLE 3	Comparison of Seven Contingency Theories of Effective Leadership				
Contingency Theory	Leader Traits	Leader Behaviors	Situational Variables	Mediating Variables	Validation Results
Path-goal Theory	None	Instrumental, supportive, participative, achievement	Many aspects	A few	Many studies, some support
Situational Leadership Theory	None	Directive, supportive, delegation	Subordinate maturity	None	Few studies, some support
Leadership Substitutes Theory	None	Instrumental, supportive	Many aspects	None	Few studies, inconclusive
LPC Contingency Model	LPC	None	Task structure, L-M relations	None	Many studies, some support
Cognitive Resource Theory	Intelligence, experience	Participative	Stress, group ability	None	Few studies, some support
Normative Decision Theory	None	Specific decision procedures	Many aspects	Decision quality and acceptance	Many studies, strong support
Multiplelinkage Model	None	Many specific behaviors	Many aspects	Many	Few studies, some support

they serve to remind leaders that it is essential to monitor changes in the situation and adjust their behavior in appropriate ways.

Guidelines for Adaptive Leadership

In order to be effective, leaders need to adapt their behavior to changing situations. The following guidelines can help leaders be more flexible and adaptive to their situation (see summary in Table 4). The guidelines are based on findings in research on contingency theories and other research using descriptive methods such as critical incidents, observation, case studies, and biographies.

TABLE 4	Guidelines for Adaptive Leadership

- Understand your leadership situation and try to make it more favorable.
- Increase flexibility by learning how to use a wide range of relevant behaviors.
- Use more planning for a long, complex task.
- Consult more with people who have relevant knowledge.
- Provide more direction to people with interdependent roles.
- Monitor a critical task or unreliable person more closely.
- Provide more coaching to an inexperienced subordinate.
- Be more supportive to someone with a highly stressful task.

- **Understand your leadership situation and try to make it more favorable.**

Contingency theories can be used to help understand your leadership situation. The relevant theories include not only the ones described in this chapter, but also theories that consider the leadership context. Identify demands, constraints, and choices in your position. Look for ways to increase substitutes and reduce constraints. Find new sources of resources, advice, and assistance.

- **Increase flexibility by learning how to use a wide range of relevant behaviors.**

One way to increase flexibility and adaptation is to learn how to use a wide range of task, relations, and change behaviors that may be relevant for any situation or challenge you are likely to face in the job. The first step is to identify the types of behaviors and skills that are likely to be useful and assess your current strengths and weaknesses for them.

- **Use more planning for a long, complex task.**

For a long, complex task with many interrelated activities performed by a large group of people over a considerable period of time (e.g., weeks or months), careful planning is necessary to complete the task on time and within budget. Planning is easier when the steps necessary to carry out the task are known in advance, and the environment is relatively predictable. Some examples of such activities include a construction project, installation of new equipment, introduction of new information systems, and the design and execution of a training program. Guidelines for project planning include the following steps: (1) identify the list of necessary activities, (2) determine the optimal sequence for them, (3) estimate when each activity should begin and end, (4) determine who should be responsible for performing each activity, and (5) identify the resources needed for it.

- **Consult more with people who have relevant knowledge.**

A major prescription of the Vroom-Yetton (1973) model was the need for more participative leadership when the task is complex and unstructured, and subordinates (or team members) have relevant knowledge and creative ideas about how to perform the task. An additional condition for effective use of consultation is goal congruence. The quality of decisions is likely to be improved when the leader consults with people who have both relevant expertise and strong commitment to achieve task objectives. Sometimes it is appropriate to hold meetings to jointly solve problems, and other times it is more appropriate to consult with one or two individuals before making a decision.

- **Provide more direction to people with interdependent roles.**

Role interdependence among group members increases role ambiguity, because it requires frequent mutual adjustments in behavior. A team will not achieve high performance unless the actions of its members are closely coordinated. Even when the individual tasks seem relatively structured, members may be confused about how to make mutual adjustments to coordinate their actions. Confusion is greater when team members lack prior experience in performing a particular task together, which is likely in a newly formed team, a team with new members, or a team with a new type of task. Intensive direction by the leader is sometimes needed to coordinate the interdependent actions of different team members, but the amount of required direction may be reduced if the team practices complex activities and members become accustomed to working together closely. Examples include sports teams (e.g., basketball, ice hockey), rescue teams, combat teams, and teams that operate complex equipment (e.g., airplanes, submarines).

- **Monitor a critical task or unreliable person more closely.**

Monitoring provides information needed to detect and correct performance problems. More frequent and intensive monitoring is appropriate for a critical task that involves high exposure, so that problems can be detected before they get so bad that they will be costly and difficult to correct. However, the appropriate amount of monitoring depends also on the reliability of the subordinates who are doing the task. The less dependable and competent a subordinate is, the more monitoring is needed.

- **Provide more coaching to an inexperienced subordinate.**

When the work is complex and a subordinate is inexperienced at doing it, more instruction and coaching by the leader is needed. Lack of experience is likely for subordinates who are new to the job, but it also occurs when there is a major change in how the work is done (e.g., new technology, reconfigured jobs). A leader with strong expertise can help a person discover the reasons for weak performance and provide any necessary coaching or instruction.

- **Be more supportive to someone with a highly stressful task.**

A person who becomes emotionally upset will have more difficulty performing a task successfully, especially if it requires reasoning and problem solving. Stress is increased by unreasonable demands, uncontrollable problems, difficult interpersonal relations (e.g., critical, abusive customers), dangerous conditions (e.g., firefighting, combat, police work), and the risk of costly errors (surgery, financial advisor, aircraft maintenance). People in such situations have more need for emotional support from leaders and coworkers.

Guidelines for Managing Immediate Crises

One type of leadership situation that is especially challenging is an immediate crisis or disruption that endangers the safety of people or the success of an activity. Examples of this type of crisis include serious accidents, explosions, natural disasters, equipment breakdowns, product defects, sabotage of products or facilities, supply shortages, health emergencies, employee strikes, sabotage, a terrorist attack, or a financial crisis. Researchers and some practitioners have identified types of leader actions and decision processes that are effective in immediate crises (e.g., DeChurch et al., 2011; Heifetz, Grashow, & Linsky, 2009; Mitroff, 2004; Muffet-Willett & Kruse, 2008). The amount of research is limited, but the findings suggest some practical guidelines for leaders (see summary in Table 5).

- **Anticipate problems and prepare for them.**

Many types of problems that occur only infrequently can be very disruptive and costly. Examples include accidents, medical emergencies, terrorist attacks, supply shortages,

TABLE 5	Guidelines for Dealing with Disruptions and Immediate Crises

- Anticipate problems and prepare for them.
- Learn to recognize early warning signs for an impending problem.
- Quickly identify the nature and scope of the problem.
- Direct the response by the unit or team in a confident and decisive way.
- Keep people informed about a major problem and what is being done to resolve it.
- Use a crisis as an opportunity to make necessary changes.

strikes, sabotage, and natural disasters. If possible, it is worthwhile to plan in advance how to avoid them. For problems that are unavoidable, contingency plans should be made to cope with them effectively when they eventually occur. Look for best practices found in analysis of past experience with similar problems. Implement training on how to respond to different types of disruptions and emergencies. If appropriate, have the team or work unit practice procedures for handling an emergency, and conduct after-activity reviews to assess prepared-ness and facilitate learning.

- **Learn to recognize early warning signs for an impending problem.**

Some types of problems have early warning signs, and a leader should learn to rec-ognize them. A common response to signs that unpleasant events will soon occur is to deny the signs and do nothing in the hope that the problem will go away. However, for some types of disruptions an early response can reduce the impact and costs. The responsibility for detecting emerging problems should be shared with all employees who have opportunities to observe these signs.

- **Quickly identify the nature and scope of the problem.**

It is essential for the leader to make a quick but systematic analysis of the situation. However, despite the pressure to act quickly, the analysis should not be hasty and superficial. Unless the cause of the problem is identified correctly, time and resources will be wasted in trying to solve the wrong problem. Even when the cause of the problem is obvious, the scope of the problem may not be known initially, and it can be a factor in selecting an appropriate response. Either underestimating or overestimating the scope of a problem can result in an inappropriate response.

- **Direct the response by the unit or team in a confident and decisive way.**

The need for more direction is especially great for a team that must react quickly in a coordinated way to cope with a serious crisis or emergency for which it is unprepared. Knowing how to remain calm and deal with a crisis in a systematic but decisive manner requires a leader with considerable skill and confidence. The leader should provide clear, confident direction to guide the response of the team or unit. However, the leader should also remain receptive to relevant information and suggestions from followers. Followers often have important information and useful suggestions on how to deal with a crisis, especially when it is a novel one.

- **Keep people informed about a major problem and what is being done to resolve it.**

In the absence of timely and accurate information about a crisis, harmful rumors are likely to occur, and people may become discouraged and afraid. A manager can help prevent unnecessary stress for subordinates by interpreting threatening events and emphasizing positive elements rather than leaving people to focus on negatives. When feasible, it is helpful to provide short, periodic briefings about progress in efforts to deal with the crisis.

- **Use a crisis as an opportunity to make necessary changes.**

When a crisis is more than a temporary disruption and is likely to happen again, it should be viewed as a good opportunity to make changes. When the immediate response to a crisis is successful, it can result in a false sense of relief that things can return to normal. However, if the crisis is a warning that traditional strategies or practices are no longer adequate to meet future challenges, then major changes are desirable. The crisis can be an opportunity to gain support for major changes that may otherwise be resisted. Even if major changes are unnecessary, a leader should encourage followers to look for ways to avoid similar crises in the future, or to improve contingency plans for responding to crises that cannot be avoided.

Summary

The managerial job is too complex and unpredictable to rely on the same set of standardized responses for all situations. Effective leaders are continuously reading the situation and determining how to adapt their behavior to it. They seek to understand the task requirements, situational constraints, and interpersonal processes that determine which course of action is most likely to be successful. This chapter examined several contingency theories that prescribe different patterns of leader behavior (or traits) for different situations.

The path-goal theory of leadership examines how aspects of the situation determine the optimal level of each type of leadership behavior for improving subordinate satisfaction and effort. In the situational leadership theory, the appropriate mix of task and relations behavior for the leader depends on the confidence and skill of a subordinate in relation to the task. Leadership substitutes theory identifies aspects of the situation that make leadership behavior redundant or irrelevant. The LPC Contingency theory described how situational favorability moderates the relationship between a leader trait (LPC) and group performance. Cognitive resources theory examines the conditions under which cognitive resources such as intelligence and experience are related to group performance. The *multiple-linkage model* describes how leader behavior and aspects of the situation jointly influence individual or group performance. A leader can improve group performance by taking direct action to correct any deficiencies in the mediating variables, and over time the leader can improve group performance by taking action to make the situation more favorable.

The early contingency theories reviewed in this chapter are complex and difficult to test. Most of the theories have conceptual weaknesses such as over-emphasis on broadly-defined behaviors, exclusion of relevant situational variables, and unclear explanation of causal relationships and mediating processes. Most studies conducted to test the contingency theories used weak research methods, and the results are difficult to interpret. None of the theories has been adequately tested, but the research provides support for some propositions in some of the theories. Additional knowledge about situational variables has been gained in research on more recent theories of effective leadership.

The lack of strong, consistent results in research on contingency theories does not justify the conclusion that situational variables are irrelevant for understanding effective leadership. In an increasingly turbulent and uncertain world, flexible adaptive leadership seems even more relevant today than it was decades ago when the contingency theories were first proposed. Better contingency theories are needed to help managers understand and overcome the challenges confronting them. In future theories it is desirable to include both universal elements (e.g., general principles) and situational elements (e.g., guidelines to help identify desirable behaviors for a particular type of situation).

Review and Discussion Questions

1. What is a situational moderator variable?
2. Briefly explain the path-goal theory.
3. Briefly explain the leadership substitutes theory.
4. Briefly explain the multiple-linkage model.
5. Identify similarities and differences among the contingency theories in this chapter.
6. In what situations are planning, clarifying, and monitoring most likely to be effective?
7. In what situations are supporting, coaching, and mentoring most likely to be effective?
8. What are some guidelines for dealing with a serious disruption or crisis?

Key Terms

cognitive resources theory
contingency theories
directive leadership
mediating variable

moderator variable
multiple-linkage model
normative decision model
neutralizer

path-goal theory
situational leadership theory
substitute for leadership

CASE 1

Foreign Auto Shop

Part 1

Alan has been the owner and manager of a small auto repair shop for seven years. The auto shop has a steady and loyal clientele who appreciate the fact that they receive quick, reliable service at a fair price. Alan employs seven mechanics and two office workers.

Gil and Hans are the two oldest mechanics, and they are the easiest to supervise. When Alan assigns work to them (mostly high-precision, specialist jobs), they do it quickly and hardly ever make a mistake. Bart and Herbie are also skilled mechanics. Bart specializes in repairing motorcycles, and Herbie is a whiz at troubleshooting engine problems. Three younger workers do the jobs that call for lower-level skills, under Alan's more careful guidance. Kirk has a degree in Industrial Arts, but he couldn't get a job in his specialty without moving to another city, and he seems to have resigned himself to auto repair work. LaMont enjoys working on sports cars and is getting to be quite an expert at operating the electronic diagnostic machines. Joanie does general mechanical work and does it well.

Alan takes care of customers when they drop off their cars in the morning, then he plans the work schedule and assigns the mechanics to work on particular cars. Most of the work is done by individual mechanics, but occasionally a job requires two mechanics to work together. The work of repairing cars and conducting routine maintenance on them is well-defined; there are standard procedures and standard times to perform each type of repair task. Mechanics receive feedback about the quality of their work from testing the car and from customers (who will complain if something is not fixed properly). Alan does not spend much time actually directing or supervising the repair work. He leaves the mechanics alone unless they are having a problem and need technical advice. He almost never tells someone to do something in a directive way. Instead, he suggests various ways to deal with a problem, or he shows them how he would have handled it. When not busy with administrative responsibilities, Alan enjoys working alongside his mechanics, where he is available to answer any questions about the work. Alan's style of leadership suits his easy-going personality.

Alan also encourages his employees to participate in making decisions such as what new equipment to purchase or how to improve quality. They know that Alan is sincere in asking for their opinions and is not just doing it as a manipulative strategy to minimize their opposition to decisions that have already been made. Alan's fairness and openness have earned him the continuing respect and trust of his employees.

SOURCE: Adapted from William J. Wasmuth and Leonard Greenhalgh, *Effective Supervision: Developing Your Skills Through Critical Incidents*. Prentice Hall, Copyright © 1979

Questions

1. What is the usual leadership situation in the auto repair shop (consider the nature of the task, subordinates, and environment)?
2. Describe Alan's typical leadership style and evaluate whether it is appropriate for the leadership situation.

Part 2

Alan looked anxiously out of his office window. The sky was very dark over the nearby hills, and the storm seemed to be advancing rapidly toward the valley where his auto repair shop was located. Just to be on the safe side, Alan went out and rolled up the windows of the customer's cars in the parking lot. He noticed the creek was already running high, the result of melting snow during the warm spring days. Before he could get back into the shop, a sudden downpour of huge drops of rain soaked his clothing. Some of the mechanics laughingly teased him for "not having enough sense to come in out of the rain."

After 15 minutes of the pelting rain, Alan realized that this was no ordinary rainstorm. He went out to look at the creek again and found that it had already risen to almost the height of its banks. Alan figured it wouldn't be long before the muddy water would flood the parking lot and come swirling around the shop doors. He ran back into the shop and announced in a loud voice that the creek was going to flood. He told three of his mechanics to drop everything and start moving the cars. The cars that were parked next to the creek needed to be driven, pushed, or towed up to the high ground across the road. Alan told the other mechanics to put the tools away and help move all the boxes of parts and supplies off the floor and into the storage racks in the storeroom and the office. Alan had everybody's attention, but nobody seemed to be moving. If anything the mechanics seemed to be amused.

Kirk strolled over to Alan with a tolerant smile on his face. "Come on, Alan," he said. "There's no sweat. The water's never been more than an inch deep in the parking lot. We've never had any inside . . ." Alan interrupted him, looking him right in the eye, and said in an assertive way, "Listen Kirk, and listen good! You and the rest of the crew are going to do what I say, and you're going to do it now! We can talk later about whether it was a good idea"

This time, the mechanics dropped everything and began preparing for a flash flood. Alan barked instructions as he helped them move everything that could be damaged by water. All of the boxes were off the floor before the first trickle of water came under the door. By the time the water was ankle-deep, all the cars inside the shop had been jacked up and were sitting on cement blocks.

At its peak, the water was 10 inches deep in the shop, but by then the rain had stopped and the sun was already shining. The water level began to recede slowly, but it didn't drop below the shop-floor level until after 9 p.m. At 10 p.m. the mechanics voluntarily returned to the shop to help with the cleanup, which was not completed until 3 a.m. Alan personally thanked each one and gave them all the next morning off.

The next afternoon, Alan gave an informal "speech" during the coffee break. He gave the mechanics all the credit for avoiding thousands of dollars of property damage. He even went to the trouble of pointing out particular contributions each of them had made. For instance, he thanked LaMont for his quick thinking in throwing the master switch before the water reached the electric outlets. He thanked Kirk for the idea of jacking up all the disabled cars inside the shop. And so on until everyone's contribution, no matter how minor, had been recognized.

At 5 o'clock, everyone left but Gil, the oldest mechanic. He decided to stay and chat with Alan. "You really surprised us yesterday!" Gil told Alan. "We could hardly believe it was you"

"Whaddaya mean?" Alan asked, pretending to be offended. "You sounded like my old drill sergeant!" Gil chuckled. "Usually, you're so mild mannered we forget you're the boss!" "May be I'm a little too mild mannered," Alan replied. "When I told you guys to prepare for the flood you all laughed at me."

Questions

1. Describe Alan's leadership style during the flood, and evaluate how appropriate it was for the leadership situation.
2. Identify effective behaviors by Alan after the flood subsided.
3. How should Alan behave toward his employees in the future?

CASE 2

Generating Followership*

It was raining very heavily in Mumbai. During the rains, long and frequent traffic jams are regular phenomena on the busy roads here. There are stories of people being stuck on the roads the entire night during the monsoons in Mumbai. I, too, was once stuck in such a jam, where I experienced a very uncommon incident.

I saw that there was no sign of the jam clearing that day. The traffic snarl was definitely because of the rains, but it had an additional cause too. A roadside tree fell onto the center of the road. The tree was huge and without a crane, it was difficult to move it even an inch. I could see that people had already lost hope of going home that day.

The jam consisted of several types of vehicles in addition to the typical cars. There was a tractor full of building construction material. There were many two-wheelers and some local buses. To add to the chaos, there was a school bus, probably carrying kids back from some picnic, as they were not in school uniform.

There were many roadside shops, which included a small grocery store, some *paan* and cigarette hawkers, and local tea vendors, among others. The road was full of people, desperate to move. I left the car and joined a group of people who were also stuck like me.

We suddenly noticed beacon lights and sirens moving toward the jam. We were filled with a new ray of hope, as we thought that the local governance body had sent some help.

The sirens came closer and, naturally, became louder. To our surprise, it was not help but probably a minister with his caravan of security guards. For some time, the caravan remained stationary, and we continuously heard the siren and endured the dancing beacon lights.

After some time, there was another round of movement of some VIP vehicles, but this time, on the other side of the tree. The sound of the siren now doubled and became immensely irritating. We then noticed the minister exiting his vehicle, covered by security guards—some holding guns and others holding umbrellas for the minister. The minister was then taken to the other side of the tree, where he drove off in the vehicles on the other side. As the minister moved away, the people still stuck on the road heard the diminishing sound of the sirens. This added to their already peaking frustration.

Suddenly, I noticed a kid from the school bus moving toward the tree, alone. The caretaker of the bus ran after him, shouting his name. The kid ran faster toward the tree. This diverted our attention. The kid was nearly eight years old, holding a small backpack, and of medium built. In all, he appeared to be a normal kid, from an ordinary family.

The race between the kid and the caretaker ended when the kid finally reached the tree. He climbed on top of the fallen tree and looked around. He had a very unique and amusing smile. We all thought this was a play-in-the-making for the kids now. However, the kid then did something extremely unusual. He climbed down, put his hands beneath the tree, and tried moving it aside. Of course, this was beyond his physical capacity, but he kept trying. He was shouting as a lifter in a gym would while trying to pick up heavy weights.

At first, there was no movement. Then suddenly, all the kids jumped out of the bus and joined him. They all attempted to lift the heavy tree. Very shortly, they were joined by some more thoroughly drenched people. After that, as if a movement had built up, everyone on the road and shops around joined in. I ran myself, thinking more of passing time and having fun. After nearly 200 people joined in, we started hearing quirky and crackling sounds. We noticed a slight movement in the tree. And then, within no time, miraculously, the tree was lying on the side of the road. I saw the kid who initiated it sitting peacefully in his bus and waving at us, congratulating us and smiling.

Many years have gone by, but the memory of that smile is still fresh in my mind.

(*The case has been developed by Prof. Nishant Uppal based on his classroom experience).

Questions

1. Explain the contingents of evolved and designated leaders in this case.
2. What are the leadership characteristics of the kid who initiated the process?
3. Why could the kid generate followership among strangers?

CASE 3

Is Anyone a Born Leader

Karambir Kang was born as normal as a parent could hope for—with blue eyes, pale skin, and weighing 11 pounds. He was the first child born to the Kang family. He was the darling of his relatives. They described him as a lovely, simple boy. Because, even as a kid, he didn't fight with other children. Sometimes, he teased his sister, but it was the normal brother-sister banter. He always had friends over at the house.

Binny, as Kang was fondly called, made friends easily, owing to his jovial nature. But he was capable of being serious as well. He made his parents proud with his extra-curricular activities like representing his school in quizzes, acting in plays etc. In George Bernard Shaw's *Arms and the Man*, he played Major Petkoff, the character who gave comic relief. The play was a satire on the foolishness of war and violence.

In college, Binny continued to be a simple person who listened to his favorite radio channels–BBC and Voice of America–and would narrate the day's world events to his father. When his friends were drinking, he'd be the one making sure everyone got home. In all, he had all the makings of an ordinary citizen and a family man.

Then, came November 26, 2008.

It was not just the police, the National Security Guard, and the media that'd been up working relentlessly for 60 hours to bring things under control in the wake of the terrorist attacks in Mumbai. One location of the terrorist attack was Taj Mahal Palace Hotel, Mumbai, where Kang worked as General Manager.

When Kang heard about the attacks, he immediately took charge. He supervised the evacuation process and coordinated the efforts of firefighters amid the chaos. His wife and two young children were in a suite on the sixth floor of the hotel, where the general manager traditionally lived. Kang was sure that they would be safe. By midnight, the sixth floor was in flames, and there was no hope of anyone surviving. Kang continued with the rescue efforts until noon the next day. Only then did he call his parents to tell them that the terrorists had killed his wife and children. His father, a retired general, told him, "Son, do your duty. Do not desert your post." Kang replied, "If it [the hotel] goes down, I will be the last man out."

SOURCES:

- Elizabeth Flock, "Karambir Kang: The Stoic," *Forbes India*, December 29, 2009, accessed on December 9, 2016, at http://forbesindia.com/article/person-of-the-year-09/karambir-kang-the-stoic/8102/1.
- Deshpandé, R., and Raina, A. (2011). The Ordinary Heroes of the Taj. *Harvard Business Review*, December 2011.

Questions

1. What are the sources of leadership of Karambir Kang?
2. Is Karambir Kang a born leader? Give reasons for your answer.

Power and Influence Tactics

Learning Objectives

After studying this chapter, you should be able to:

- Understand the process by which power is acquired or lost in organizations.
- Understand the consequences of power for leadership effectiveness.
- Understand ways to use power effectively.
- Understand the different types of influence tactics used in organizations.
- Understand how the tactics are used to influence subordinates, peers, and superiors.
- Understand effective ways to use the tactics.

Influence is the essence of leadership. To be effective as a leader, it is necessary to influence people to carry out requests, support proposals, and implement decisions. In large organizations, the effectiveness of managers depends on influence over superiors and peers as well as influence over subordinates. Influence in one direction tends to enhance influence in other directions.

In the first part of this chapter, several constructs used in the power and influence literature are defined, different sources and types of power are described, how power is gained or lost is discussed, and the implications of power for leadership effectiveness are explained. The second part of the chapter describes different influence tactics that can be used by leaders and how leaders can be more effective in influencing subordinates, peers, and bosses.

Power and Influence Concepts

Terms such as power, authority, and influence have been used in different ways by different writers, and the differences can create confusion. Thus, it is worthwhile to begin by clarifying how key terms will be used in this chapter, including power, authority, influence processes, influence tactics, and influence outcomes.

Power

The concept of *power* is useful for understanding how people are able to influence each other in organizations (Mintzberg, 1983; Pfeffer, 1981, 1992). Power involves the capacity of one party (the "agent") to influence another party (the "target"), but this influence has been described and measured in several different ways. The term may refer to the agent's influence over a single target person, or over multiple target persons. Sometimes the term refers to potential influence over things or events as well as attitudes and behavior. Sometimes the agent is a group or organization rather than an individual. Sometimes power is defined in relative rather than absolute terms, in which case it means the extent to which the agent has more influence over the target than the target has over the agent.

It is difficult to describe the power of an agent without specifying the target person(s), the influence objectives, and the time period. An agent will have more power over some people than over others and more influence for some types of issues than for others. Furthermore, power is a dynamic variable that changes as conditions change. How power is used and the outcomes of influence attempts can increase or reduce an agent's subsequent power. In this text, the term *power* is usually used to describe the absolute capacity of an individual agent to influence the behavior or attitudes of one or more designated target persons at a given point in time.

Authority

Authority involves the rights, prerogatives, obligations, and duties associated with particular positions in an organization or social system. A leader's authority usually includes the right to make particular types of decisions for the organization. A leader with direct authority over a target person has the right to make requests consistent with this authority, and the target person has the duty to obey. For example, a manager usually has the legitimate right to establish work rules and give work assignments to subordinates. Authority also involves the right of the agent to exercise control over things, such as money, resources, equipment, and materials, and this control is another source of power.

The *scope of authority* for the occupant of a managerial position is the range of requests that can properly be made and the range of actions that can properly be taken. Scope of authority is much greater for some managers than for others, and it depends in large part on the influence needed to accomplish role requirements and organizational objectives (Barnard, 1952).

Influence Processes

The psychological explanation for interpersonal influence involves the motives and perceptions of the target person in relation to the actions of the agent and the context in which the interaction occurs. Kelman (1958) proposed three different types of influence processes, called instrumental compliance, *internalization,* and *personal identification.* The influence processes are qualitatively different from each other, but more than one process can occur at the same time. For example, a target person may become committed to implement a new program proposed by the agent because the target person identifies with the agent, believes in the ideals of the program, and expects to gain tangible benefits from supporting it.

Instrumental Compliance. The target person carries out a requested action for the purpose of obtaining a tangible reward or avoiding a punishment controlled by the agent. The motivation for the behavior is purely instrumental; the only reason for compliance is to gain some tangible benefit from the agent. The level of effort is likely to be the minimum amount necessary to gain the rewards or avoid the punishment.

Internalization.   The target person becomes committed to support and implement proposals espoused by the agent because they appear to be intrinsically desirable and correct in relation to the target's values, beliefs, and self-image. In effect, the agent's proposal (e.g., an objective, plan, strategy, policy, procedure) becomes linked to the target person's underlying values and beliefs. Commitment occurs regardless of whether any tangible benefit is expected, and the target's loyalty is to the ideas themselves, not to the agent who communicates them.

Personal Identification.   The target person imitates the agent's behavior or adopts the same attitudes to please the agent and to be like the agent. The motivation for the target probably involves the target person's needs for acceptance and esteem. By doing things to gain approval from the agent, the target is able to maintain a relationship that satisfies a need for acceptance. Maintaining a close relationship with an attractive agent may help to satisfy the target person's need for esteem from other people, and becoming more like an attractive agent helps the target person maintain a more favorable self-image.

General Types of Influence Tactics

The type of behavior used intentionally to influence the attitudes and behavior of another person is usually called an *influence tactic.* Three general types of influence tactics can be differentiated according to their primary purpose. Some specific influence tactics can be used for more than one purpose, but they may not be equally effective for the different purposes.

Impression Management Tactics.   These tactics are intended to influence people to like the agent (e.g., *ingratiation)* or to have a favorable evaluation of the agent (e.g., self-promotion). Impression management tactics can be used by leaders to influence followers, or by followers to influence a leader.

Political Tactics.   These tactics are used to influence organizational decisions or otherwise gain benefits for an individual or group. One type of political tactic involves an attempt to influence how important decisions are made and who makes them. Examples include influencing the agenda for meetings to include your issues, influencing decision makers to use criteria that will bias decisions in your favor, and selecting decision makers who will promote and defend your interests. Political tactics are also used to defend against opponents and silence critics. Some political tactics involve deception, manipulation, and abuse of power.

Proactive Tactics.   These tactics have an immediate task objective, such as getting the target person to carry out a new task, change the procedures used for a current task, provide assistance on a project, or support a proposed change. The tactics can be used also to resist or modify a request made by someone who is attempting to influence you. Different types of proactive tactics are described later in the chapter.

Influence Outcomes

One useful basis for evaluating the success of an influence attempt is to examine the outcome. The agent may achieve the intended effects on the target, or the outcome may be less than was intended. For an influence attempt that involves a single target person, it is useful to differentiate among three distinct outcomes called commitment, *compliance,* and *resistance.*

Commitment.   The outcome is called commitment when the target person makes a great effort to carry out the request or implement the decision effectively. This outcome is usually the most successful one for a complex, difficult task that requires enthusiasm, initiative, and persistence by the target person in overcoming obstacles.

Compliance.   The outcome is called compliance when the target person is willing to carry out a request but is apathetic rather than enthusiastic about it and will make only a minimal effort. With compliance the target person is not convinced that the decision or action is the best thing to do or even that it will be effective for accomplishing its purpose. However, for a simple, routine request, compliance may be all that is necessary to accomplish the agent's task objectives.

Resistance.   The outcome is called resistance when the target person is opposed to the proposal or request, rather than merely indifferent about it. Resistance can take several different forms: (1) refuse to carry out the request, (2) explain why it is impossible to carry out the request, (3) try to persuade the agent to withdraw or change the request, (4) ask higher authorities to overrule the agent's request, (5) delay acting in the hope that the agent will forget about the request, and (6) make a pretense of complying but try to sabotage the task. Resistance is usually regarded as an unsuccessful outcome, but it can be beneficial if it helps the agent avoid a serious mistake. For example, you develop a detailed plan for a new project, but people find some serious flaws that need to be fixed before they will implement the plan.

The target person's reaction to the agent's request is not the only basis for evaluating success. Influence attempts can also affect interpersonal relationships and the way other people perceive the agent (e.g., ethical, supportive, likable, competent, trustworthy, strong). An influence attempt may improve the relationship or make it less friendly and cooperative.

Power Sources

Efforts to classify types of power usually involve differences in the source or basis for potential influence over another person or event. The early taxonomy proposed by French and Raven (1959) continues to influence current theory and research on power. The five types of power in their taxonomy included *expert power, referent power, legitimate power, reward power,* and *coercive power.* That taxonomy was later extended to include some other types of power. The most useful ways for classifying power sources are described in this section.

Legitimate Power

Power stemming from formal authority over work activities is sometimes called legitimate power (French & Raven, 1959). The influence processes associated with legitimate power are complex. Some theorists emphasize the downward flow of authority from owners and top management, but the potential influence derived from authority depends as much on the consent of the governed as on the ownership and control of property (Jacobs, 1970). Members of an organization usually agree to comply with rules and directions from leaders in return for the benefits of membership. However, this agreement is usually an implicit mutual understanding rather than an explicit formal contract.

Compliance with legitimate rules and requests is more likely for members who identify with the organization and are loyal to it. Compliance is also more likely for members who have an internalized value that it is proper to obey authority figures, show respect for the law, and follow tradition. Acceptance of authority also depends on whether the agent is perceived to be a legitimate occupant of his or her leadership position. The specific procedures for selecting a leader are usually based on tradition and the provisions of a legal charter or constitution. Any deviation from the selection process considered legitimate by members will weaken a new leader's authority.

The amount of legitimate power is also related to one's scope of authority. Higher-level managers usually have more authority than lower-level managers, and a manager's authority is usually much stronger in relation to subordinates than in relation to peers, superiors, or outsiders. However, even for a target person outside of the chain of command (e.g., a peer or outsider), the agent may have the legitimate right to make requests necessary to carry out job responsibilities, such as requests for information, supplies, support services, technical advice, and assistance in carrying out interrelated tasks.

A manager's scope of authority is usually delineated by documents such as an organization charter, a written job description, or an employment contract, but considerable ambiguity about it often remains (Davis, 1968; Reitz, 1977). People evaluate not only whether a request or order falls within a leader's scope of authority, but also whether it is consistent with the basic values, principles, and traditions of the organization or social system. The legitimacy of a request may be questioned if it contradicts basic values of the organization or the larger society to which members of the organization belong. For example, soldiers may disobey an order to shoot everyone in a village that has aided insurgents, because the soldiers perceive this use of excessive force to be contrary to basic human rights.

Reward Power

Reward power is the perception by the target person that an agent controls important resources and rewards desired by the target person. Reward power stems in part from formal authority to allocate resources and rewards. This authority varies greatly across organizations and from one type of management position to another within the same organization. More control over scarce resources is usually authorized for high-level executives than for lower-level managers. Executives have authority to make decisions about the allocation of resources to various subunits and activities, and they have the right to review and modify resource allocation decisions made at lower levels.

Reward power depends not only on a manager's actual control over resources and rewards, but also on the target person's perception that the agent has the capacity and willingness to follow through on promises. The target person's perception of agent reward power is more important than the agent's actual control over rewards. In a classic movie theme, a shabbily dressed millionaire offers a stranger a lot of money to do something, and believing that the agent is poor the stranger refuses. In contrast, well-dressed con artists with little money are sometimes able to borrow valuable items or defer paying for them in the (unfulfilled) hope that they will eventually be important customers.

Sometimes reward power can influence people even when the agent makes no overt influence attempt. People are likely to act more deferential toward somebody who has high reward power, because they are aware of the possibility that the person can affect their job performance and career advancement. For example, people may cooperate more with an agent who has substantial reward power in the hopes of getting some rewards in the future.

The authority relationship is an important determinant of reward power. Managers usually have much more reward power over subordinates than over peers or superiors. One form of reward power over subordinates is the authority to give pay increases, bonuses, or other economic incentives to deserving subordinates. Reward power is derived also from control over tangible benefits such as a promotion, a better job, a better work schedule, a larger operating budget, a larger expense account, and status symbols such as a larger office or a reserved parking space. Possible constraints on a manager's reward power include any formal policies or agreements that specify how rewards must be allocated.

A source of reward power in lateral relations is dependence of a peer on the agent for resources, information, assistance, or support needed to carry out the peer's work. Trading of favors needed to accomplish task objectives is a common form of influence among peers in organizations, and research indicates that it is important for the success of middle-level managers (Cohen & Bradford, 1989; Kaplan, 1984; Kotter, 1982; Strauss, 1962).

Upward reward power of subordinates over their boss is limited in most organizations. Few organizations provide a formal mechanism for subordinates to evaluate leaders. Nevertheless, subordinates usually have some indirect influence over the leader's reputation and prospects for a pay increase or promotion. If subordinates perform well, the reputation of their manager will usually be enhanced. Some subordinates may also have upward reward power based on their ability to acquire resources outside of the formal authority system of the organization. For example, a department chairperson in a university was able to obtain discretionary funds from grants and contracts, and these funds were used to influence the decisions made by the college dean, whose own discretionary funds were limited.

Coercive Power

A leader's coercive power over subordinates is based on authority over punishments, which varies greatly across different types of organizations. The coercive power of military and political leaders is usually greater than that of corporate managers. Over the last two centuries, there has been a general decline in use of legitimate coercion by all types of leaders. For example, most managers once had the right to dismiss employees for any reason they thought was justified. The captain of a ship could flog sailors who were disobedient or who failed to perform their duties diligently. Military officers could execute a soldier for desertion or failure to obey an order during combat. Nowadays, these forms of coercive power are prohibited or sharply restricted in many nations.

Lateral relations provide few opportunities for using coercion. If the peer is dependent on the manager for assistance in performing important tasks, the manager may threaten to withhold cooperation if the peer fails to carry out a request. However, because mutual dependencies usually exist between managers of different subunits, coercion is likely to elicit retaliation and escalate into a conflict that benefits neither party.

The coercive power that subordinates have over superiors varies greatly from one kind of organization to another. In many organizations, subordinates have the capacity to indirectly influence the performance evaluation of their boss. Subordinates can damage the reputation of the boss if they restrict production, sabotage operations, initiate grievances, hold demonstrations, or make complaints to higher management. In organizations with elected leaders, subordinates may have sufficient counter-power to remove a leader from office or to prevent the leader's reelection. In the case of political leaders, the ultimate form of coercive power for subordinates is a violent revolution that results in the imprisonment, death, or exile of the leader.

Referent Power

Referent power is derived from the desire of others to please an agent toward whom they have strong feelings of affection, admiration, and loyalty. People are usually willing to do special favors for a friend, and they are more likely to carry out requests made by someone they greatly admire. The strongest form of referent power involves the influence process called *personal identification*. To gain the agent's approval and acceptance, the target person is likely to comply with agent requests, imitate the agent's behavior, and have similar attitudes.

Strong referent power will tend to increase the agent's influence over the target person even without any explicit effort by the agent to invoke this power. People are more likely to carry out requests made by an agent with strong referent power. When the relationship is characterized by a strong bond of love or friendship, the target person may do things the agent is perceived to want, even without being asked.

Referent power is an important source of influence over subordinates, peers, and superiors, but it has limitations. A request based solely on referent power should be commensurate with the extent of the target person's loyalty and friendship toward the leader. Some things are simply too much to ask, given the nature of the relationship. When requests are extreme or made too frequently, the target person may feel exploited. The result of such behavior may be to undermine the relationship and reduce the agent's referent power.

Expert Power

Task-relevant knowledge and skill are a major source of *personal power* in organizations. Unique knowledge about the best way to perform a task or solve an important problem provides potential influence over subordinates, peers, and superiors. However, expertise is a source of power only if others are dependent on the agent for advice. The more important a problem is to the target person, the greater the power derived by the agent from possessing the necessary expertise to solve it. Dependency is increased when the target person cannot easily find another source of advice besides the agent (Hickson et al., 1971; Patchen, 1974).

It is not enough for the agent to possess expertise; the target person must recognize this expertise and perceive the leader to be a reliable source of information and advice. In the short run, perceived expertise is more important than real expertise, and an agent may be able to fake it for a time by acting confident and pretending to be an expert. However, over time, as the agent's knowledge is put to the test, target perceptions of the agent's expertise are likely to become more accurate. Thus, it is essential for leaders to develop and maintain a reputation for technical expertise and strong credibility.

Actual expertise is gained through a continual process of education and practical experience. For example, in many professions it is important to keep informed about new developments by reading technical publications and attending workshops and seminars. Evidence of expertise can be displayed in the forms of diplomas, licenses, and awards. However, the most convincing way to demonstrate expertise is by solving important problems, making good decisions, providing sound advice, and successfully completing challenging but highly visible projects. An extreme tactic is to intentionally but covertly precipitate crises just to demonstrate the ability to deal with them (Goldner, 1970; Pfeffer, 1977a).

Specialized knowledge and technical skill will remain a source of power only as long as dependence on the person who possesses them continues. If a problem is permanently solved or others learn how to solve it by themselves, the agent's expertise is no longer valuable. Thus, people sometimes try to protect their expert power by keeping procedures and techniques shrouded in secrecy, by using technical jargon to make the task seem more complex and mysterious, and by destroying alternate sources of information about task procedures such as written manuals, diagrams, blueprints, and computer programs (Hickson et al., 1971).

When the agent has a lot of expert power and is trusted as a reliable source of information and advice, the target person may carry out a request without receiving any explanation for it. One example is a patient who takes medicine prescribed by a doctor without knowing much about the medicine. Another example is an investor who purchases stocks recommended by a financial consultant without knowing much about the companies that issued the stocks. However, it is rare for leaders to possess this much expert power. A leader's expertise can be used to present logical arguments and evidence that appears credible. Successful influence depends on the leader's credibility and persuasive communication skills in addition to technical knowledge and analytical ability.

Information Power

Another important source of power is control over information (Raven, 1965). This type of power involves both the access to vital information and control over its distribution to others. Managerial positions often provide opportunities to obtain information that is not directly available to subordinates or peers. Boundary role positions (e.g., marketing, purchasing, public relations) provide easier access to important information about events in the external environment of an organization. However, regardless of the type of position, useful information does not appear as if by magic, and one must actively cultivate a network of sources to provide it (Kotter, 1982).

A leader who controls the flow of vital information about outside events has an opportunity to interpret these events for subordinates and influence their perception and attitudes. Some managers distort information to persuade people that a particular course of action is desirable. Examples of information distortion include selective editing of reports and documents, biased interpretation of data, and presentation of false information. Some managers use their control over the distribution of information as a way to enhance their expert power and increase subordinate dependence. If the leader is the only one who "knows what is going on," subordinates will lack evidence to dispute the leader's claim that an unpopular decision is justified by circumstances. Control of information also makes it easier for a leader to cover up failures and mistakes that would otherwise undermine a carefully cultivated image of expertise (Pfeffer, 1977a).

Control over information is a source of upward influence as well as downward and lateral influence. When subordinates have exclusive access to information needed by superiors to make decisions, this advantage can be used to influence the superior's decisions. Some subordinates actively seek this type of influence by gradually assuming more responsibility for collecting, storing, analyzing, and reporting operating information. If a leader is completely dependent on a subordinate to interpret complex analyses of operating information, the subordinate may be invited to participate directly in making decisions based on these analyses (Korda, 1975). Even when not actively participating in the decision process, a subordinate who provides most of the information for a decision has substantial influence over it (Pettigrew, 1972). Control over operating information also enables subordinates to magnify accomplishments, cover up mistakes, and exaggerate the amount of expertise and resources needed to do their work.

Ecological Power

Control over the physical environment, technology, and organization of the work provides an opportunity for indirect influence over other people. Because behavior is determined in part by perception of opportunities and constraints, it can be altered in subtle ways by rearranging the situation. This form of influence is sometimes called *situational engineering* or *ecological control* (Cartwright, 1965).

One form of situational engineering is to modify the design of subordinate jobs to increase subordinate motivation. Research on job enrichment suggests that significant improvements in work quality and job satisfaction are sometimes possible. The organization of work activities anddesign of formal structure is another form of situational engineering. The grouping of activities into subunits, determination of reporting relationships, and design of information systems are all sources of influence over employee behavior.

TABLE 1	Different Types of Power	
Position Power		**Personal Power**
Legitimate Power		Referent Power
Reward Power		Expert Power
Coercive Power		
Information Power		
Ecological Power		

Another form of situational engineering is control over the physical work environment. For example, lights or auditory signals on equipment can be used to inform the operator that it is time for necessary maintenance, or to warn the operator to discontinue doing something that will cause an accident or breakdown. The workflow design and layout of physical facilities determine which employees interact with each other and who initiates action for whom. Machine-paced assembly lines set the speed at which employees work.

Position and Personal Power

The most general way to classify power sources is the distinction between *position power* and *personal power* (Bass, 1960; Etzioni, 1961; Rahim, 1988; Yukl & Falbe, 1991). Specific types of power can be grouped into these two general categories depending on whether they are derived primarily from the opportunities inherent in a person's position in the organization, or from attributes of the agent and the agent-target relationship. The various types of position and personal power are listed in Table 1. Position power includes potential influence derived from legitimate authority, control over resources and rewards, control over punishments, control over information, and control over the physical work environment. Personal power includes potential influence derived from task expertise, and potential influence based on friendship and loyalty. Position and personal determinants of power interact in complex ways, and sometimes it is difficult to distinguish between them.

How Power Is Gained or Lost

Power is not a static condition; it changes over time due to changing conditions and the actions of individuals and coalitions. How power is gained or lost in organizations is described in social exchange theory, strategic contingencies theory, and theories about *institutionalization of power.*

Social Exchange Theory

In a group, the amount of status and power accorded to an elected or emergent leader by other members depends on the person's loyalty, demonstrated competence, and contribution to the attainment of shared objectives (Hollander, 1958, 1980; Jacobs, 1970). The contribution may involve control over scarce resources, access to vital information, or skill in dealing with critical task problems. In addition to increased status and influence, a person who has demonstrated good judgment accumulates "idiosyncrasy credits" and is allowed more latitude to deviate from nonessential group norms. The authority and position power for appointed leaders make them less dependent on subordinate evaluation of their competence, but they will also gain influence from repeated demonstration of expertise and loyalty to subordinates.

Innovation by a leader can be a double-edged sword. Success resulting from innovation leads to greater credit, but failure leads to greater blame. When a member makes an innovative proposal that proves to be successful, the group's trust in the person's expertise is confirmed, and even more status and influence may be accorded to the person. When an innovative proposal results in failure, the person is likely to lose status and influence. More power is lost if failure appears to be due to poor judgment or incompetence rather than to circumstances beyond the leader's control, or if the leader is perceived to have pursued selfish motives rather than loyally serving the group. Selfish motives and irresponsibility are more likely to be attributed to a leader who willingly deviates from group norms and traditions. The extent of a leader's loss of status and influence following failure depends in part on how serious the failure is to the group. A major disaster results in greater loss of esteem than a minor setback. Loss of status also depends on amount of status the leader had prior to the failure. More is expected of a leader with high status, and such a leader will lose more status if perceived to be responsible for failure. Innovation is not only accepted but expected of leaders when necessary to deal with serious problems and obstacles. A leader who fails to show initiative and deal decisively with serious problems will lose esteem and influence, just as a leader who proposes actions that are unsuccessful.

Social exchange theory emphasizes expert power and authority, and other forms of power do not receive much attention. For example, the theory does not explain how reciprocal influence processes affect a leader's reward and referent power. Most of the evidence for the theory is from research with small groups in a laboratory setting, and the results are not consistent across studies (Hollander, 1960, 1961, 1980; Stone & Cooper, 2009). Longitudinal field research in organizations would be useful to test the theory and determine if it applies to other types of power.

Strategic Contingencies Theory

Strategic contingencies theory explains how some organizational subunits gain or lose power to influence important decisions such as determination of the organization's competitive strategy and the allocation of resources to subunits and activities (Hickson et al., 1971). The theory postulates that the power of a subunit depends on three factors: (1) expertise in coping with important problems, (2) centrality of the subunit within the workflow, and (3) the extent to which the subunit's expertise is unique rather than substitutable.

All organizations must cope with critical contingencies, especially problems in the technological processes used to carry out operations and problems in adapting to unpredictable events in the environment. Success in solving important problems is a source of expert power for subunits, just as it is for individuals. The opportunity to demonstrate expertise and gain power from it is much greater for a subunit that has responsibility for dealing with critical problems. A problem is critical if it is clearly essential for the survival and prosperity of the organization. The importance of a particular type of problem is greater as the degree of interdependence among subunits increases; other subunits cannot perform their own functions unless this type of problem is handled effectively. An individual or subunit will gain more power over important decisions if the critical functions cannot be performed by someone else or made easier by development of standard procedures. In other words, the more unique and irreplaceable the expertise required to solve critical problems, the more power is gained from possessing this expertise.

Increased expert power can result in increased legitimate power. People with valuable expertise are more likely to be appointed or elected to positions of authority in the organization. Subunits with critical expertise are likely to have more representation on boards or committees that make important decisions for the organization.

Some support for the theory was found in several studies (Brass, 1984, 1985; Hambrick, 1981a; Hills & Mahoney, 1978; Hinings, Hickson, Pennings, & Schneck, 1974; Pfeffer & Moore, 1980; Pfeffer & Salancik, 1974). However, the theory fails to take into account the possibility that a powerful subunit or coalition can use its power to protect its dominant position in the organization by enhancing its perceived expertise and by denying potential rivals an opportunity to demonstrate their greater expertise.

Institutionalization of Power

The process for using political tactics to increase influence or protect existing power sources is called "*institutionalization*." Having power makes it easier to use political tactics for influencing important decisions in the organization. A powerful subunit can get its members appointed to key leadership positions where they will promote the subunit's objectives. When it is not possible to control key decisions directly, it may be possible to influence them indirectly by determining the procedures and criteria that will be used in making the decisions.

A powerful subunit or coalition is often able to use its power to maintain a dominant position even after their expertise is no longer critical to the organization (Pfeffer, 1981; Salancik & Pfeffer, 1977). Ambiguity about the nature of the environment and how it is changing provides an opportunity for top executives to interpret events in a biased manner, to magnify the importance of their expertise, and to justify their policies. Control over distribution of information about how well the organization is performing allows top executives to exaggerate the success of past decisions and cover up mistakes. The power of top management can also be used to deny others the resources and opportunity needed to demonstrate their superior expertise. Critics and potential rivals can be silenced, co-opted, or expelled from the organization (Pfeffer, 1981).

The evolutionary shift in power described by strategic contingencies theory can be delayed by the use of these political tactics, but if top management lacks the expertise to develop an appropriate strategy for responding to changes in the environment, the performance of the organization will decline. This process will occur much faster when the organization has strong competition for its products and services, and competitors are able to adapt more rapidly to changes in the environment. Unless the organization replaces top management, it will eventually go bankrupt or be taken over by outsiders who desire its assets.

Consequences of Power

The amount of overall power that is necessary for effective leadership and the mix of different types of power are questions that research has only begun to answer. Studies on the consequences of leader power are inconclusive, but findings indicate that effective leaders have more expert and referent power than less effective leaders, and they rely on their personal power more than on their position power (Hinkin & Schriesheim, 1989; Podsakoff & Schriesheim, 1985; Rahim, 1989; Yukl & Falbe, 1991). However, several of the power studies also indicate that it is beneficial for leaders to have at least a moderate amount of position power (e.g., Dunne, Stahl, & Melhart, 1978; Rahim & Afza, 1993; Thambain & Gemmill, 1974; Warren, 1968; Yukl & Falbe, 1991).

The amount of necessary power for a leader will depend on what needs to be accomplished and on the leader's skill in using the available power. Some leadership situations require more power than others for the leader to be effective. More influence is necessary in an organization where major changes are required, but there is strong initial opposition to the leader's proposals for change. It is especially difficult for a leader who recognizes that the organization will face a major crisis in coming years, a crisis that can be overcome only if preparations are begun immediately, but the evidence of the coming crisis is not yet sufficiently strong to persuade members to act now. A similar situation is the case where a leader desires to make changes that will require short-term sacrifices and a long period of implementation before the benefits are realized, but there is opposition by factions with a short-term perspective. In such situations, a leader will need sufficient expert and referent power to persuade people that change is necessary and desirable, or sufficient position and political power to overcome the opposition and buy time to show that the proposed changes are necessary and effective. A combination of personal and position power increases the likelihood of success, but forcing change is always risky. Maurer (1996, p. 177) describes one successful example:

> When Leonard Bernstein became conductor of the Vienna Philharmonic, he reintroduced the symphonies of Gustav Mahler. The orchestra hated Mahler; they felt his music was overblown and pompous . . . Although Bernstein certainly had the power to program whatever he wished, it was a risky move. Orchestras notoriously show their disdain for conductors they disrespect by engaging in malicious compliance. All the notes are correct—so no one can be reprimanded—but they play without spirit . . . Although [they did not agree with Bernstein's] decision . . . he was highly respected by the members of the orchestra . . . He was a world class musician. So, for Leonard Bernstein they played Mahler beautifully. Eventually, it seems, most of the orchestra grew to enjoy playing the music of their hometown boy.

Questions about the optimal mix of power for leaders are complicated by the interdependence among different sources of power. The distinction between position and personal power is sometimes convenient, but it should not be overdrawn. Position power is important, not only as a source of influence but also because it can be used to enhance a leader's personal power. Control over information complements expert power based on technical skill by giving the leader an advantage in solving important problems and by enabling a leader to cover up mistakes and exaggerate accomplishments. Reward power facilitates development of a deeper exchange relationship with subordinates, and when used skillfully, it enhances a leader's referent power. The authority to make decisions and the upward influence to get them approved enables a leader to demonstrate expertise in problem solving, and it also facilitates development of stronger exchange relationships with subordinates. Some coercive power is necessary to buttress legitimate and expert power when a leader needs to influence compliance with rules and procedures that are unpopular but necessary to do the work and avoid serious accidents. Likewise, coercive power is needed by a leader to restrain or banish rebels and criminals who would otherwise disrupt operations, steal resources, harm other members, and cause the leader to appear weak and incompetent.

However, too much position power may be as detrimental as too little. Leaders with a great deal of position power may be tempted to rely on it instead of developing personal power and using other approaches (e.g., *consultation,* persuasion) for influencing people to comply with a request or support a change. The notion that power corrupts is especially relevant for position power (Glad, 2002). Throughout history many political leaders with strong position power have used it to dominate and exploit subordinates.

How easily power can corrupt leaders is demonstrated in an experiment conducted by Kipnis (1972). He found that leaders with greater reward power perceived subordinates as objects of manipulation, devalued the worth of subordinates, attributed subordinate efforts to their own power use, maintained more social distance from subordinates, and used rewards more often to influence subordinates. Although only a laboratory experiment with students, the research clearly points out the dangers of excessive position power. In general, a leader should have only a moderate amount of position power, although the optimal amount will vary somewhat depending on the situation.

What about personal power? Are there also dangers from having a great deal of expert and referent power? Personal power is less susceptible to misuse, because it erodes quickly when a leader acts contrary to the interests of followers. Nevertheless, the potential for corruption remains. A leader with extensive expert power or charismatic appeal will be tempted to act in ways that will eventually lead to failure. McClelland (1975, p. 266) describes this phenomenon:

> How much initiative he should take, how persuasive he should attempt to be, and at what point his clear enthusiasm for certain goals becomes personal authoritarian insistence that those goals are the right ones whatever the members of the group may think, are all questions calculated to frustrate the well-intentioned leader. If he takes no initiative, he is no leader. If he takes too much, he becomes a dictator, particularly if he tries to curtail the process by which members of the group participate in shaping group goals. There is a particular danger for the man who has demonstrated his competence in shaping group goals and in inspiring group members to pursue them. In time both he and they may assume that he knows best, and he may almost imperceptibly change from a democratic to an authoritarian leader.

Studies of the amount of influence exercised by people at different levels in the authority hierarchy of an organization reveal that effective leaders create relationships in which they have strong influence over subordinates but are also receptive to influence from them. Instead of using their power to dictate how things will be done, effective executives empower members of the organization to discover and implement new and better ways of doing things.

One of the best ways to ensure leaders remain responsive to follower needs is to promote reciprocal influence and discourage arbitrary actions by the leader. Rules and policies can be enacted to regulate the exercise of position power, especially reward and coercive power. Grievance and appeals procedures can be enacted, and independent review boards established to protect subordinates against misuse of power by leaders. Bylaws, charter provisions, and official policies can be drafted to require leaders to consult with subordinates and obtain their approval on specified types of decisions. Regular attitude surveys can be conducted to measure subordinate satisfaction with their leaders. When appropriate, periodic elections or votes of confidence can be held to determine whether the leader should continue in office. Recall procedures can be established to remove incompetent leaders in an orderly manner. Finally, leaders themselves can facilitate reciprocal influence by encouraging subordinates to participate in making important decisions, and by fostering and rewarding innovation.

Guidelines for Using Power

The research on power is still too limited to provide clear guidelines on the best ways to exercise it. Nevertheless, by drawing on the findings from research in many different social science disciplines, it is possible to develop some tentative guidelines for leaders. The guidelines are usually worded in terms of influencing subordinates, but many apply as well to influencing other people. Some guidelines involve using influence tactics described later in the chapter.

TABLE 2	Guidelines for Using Legitimate Authority

- Make polite, clear requests.
- Explain the reasons for a request.
- Don't exceed your scope of authority.
- Verify authority if necessary.
- Follow proper channels.
- Follow up to verify compliance.
- Insist on compliance if appropriate.

How to Use Legitimate Power

Authority is usually exercised with a request, order, or instruction that is communicated orally or in writing. The way in which legitimate power is exercised affects the outcome (see Table 2). A polite request is more effective than an arrogant demand, because it does not emphasize a status gap or imply target dependence on the agent. Use of a polite request is especially important for people who are likely to be sensitive about status differentials and authority relationships, such as someone who is older than the agent or who is a peer rather than a subordinate.

Making a polite request does not imply you should plead or appear apologetic about a request. To do so risks the impression that the request is not worthy or legitimate, and it may give the impression that compliance is not really expected. A legitimate request should be made in a firm, confident manner. In an emergency situation, it is more important to be assertive than polite. A direct order by a leader in a command tone of voice is sometimes necessary to shock subordinates into immediate action in an emergency. In this type of situation, subordinates associate confident, firm direction with expertise as well as authority. To express doubts or appear confused risks the loss of influence over subordinates.

The order or request should be stated very clearly using language that the target person can understand. If the request is complex, it is advisable to communicate it in writing as well as orally. Oral requests should be made directly to the target person rather than relying on someone else to relay it to the target person. An intermediary may misinterpret the message, and you also lose the opportunity to assess the target person's reaction. If there is any question about your right to make a request or assignment, then it is important to verify this authority, which is a type of *"legitimating tactic"* described later.

Instances of outright refusal by subordinates to carry out a legitimate order or request undermine the leader's authority and increase the likelihood of future disobedience. Orders that are unlikely to be carried out should not be given. Sometimes a subordinate will delay in complying with an unusual or unpleasant request to test whether the leader is really serious about it. If the leader does not follow up the initial request to check on compliance, the subordinate is likely to conclude that the request may be ignored.

How to Use Reward Power

Reward power can be exercised in several ways (see Table 3). When the agent offers to give the target person a reward for carrying out a request or performing a task, it is called an exchange tactic, and the use of such tactics is described in more detail later in this chapter. Another common way to use reward power is to create a formal incentive system that provides tangible rewards for good behavior or a monetary bonus for performance that exceeds standards.

How reward power is exercised affects the outcome. Compliance is most likely if the reward is something valued by the target person. Thus, it is essential to determine what

TABLE 3	Guidelines for Using Reward Power

- Offer the type of rewards that people desire.
- Offer rewards that are fair and ethical.
- Don't promise more than you can deliver.
- Explain the criteria for giving rewards and keep it simple
- Provide rewards as promised if requirements are met.
- Use rewards symbolically (not in a manipulative way).

rewards are valued, and a leader should not assume that it will be the same for everyone. Another essential condition is that the agent must be perceived as a credible source of the reward. Leader should be careful to avoid making unrealistic promises or failing to provide a promised reward to people who deserve it.

Even when the conditions are favorable for using rewards, they are more likely to result in compliance rather than commitment. Most incentives are unlikely to motivate someone to put forth extra effort beyond what is required to complete the task and get the reward. The target person may be tempted to neglect aspects of the task not included in the specification of performance criteria or aspects not easily monitored by the agent. If rewards are used in a manipulative manner, they may result in resistance rather than compliance. The power to give or withhold rewards may cause resentment among people who dislike being dependent on the whims of a powerful authority figure, or who believe that the agent is manipulating them to his or her own advantage. Even an attractive reward may be ineffective if seen as a bribe to get the target person to do something improper or unethical.

When rewards are used frequently as a source of influence, people may come to perceive their relationship to the leader in purely economic terms. They will expect a reward every time they are asked to do something new or unusual. It is more satisfying for both parties to view their relationship in terms of mutual loyalty and friendship. Rather than using rewards as incentives in an impersonal, mechanical way, they should be used in a more symbolic manner to recognize accomplishments and express personal appreciation for special contributions or exceptional effort. Used in this way, reward power can be a source of increased referent power.

How to Use Coercive Power

Coercive power is invoked by a threat or warning that the target person will suffer undesirable consequences for noncompliance with a request, rule, or policy. The threat may be explicit, or it may be only a vague comment that the person will be sorry for failing to do what the agent wants. The likelihood of compliance is greatest when the threat is perceived to be credible, and the target person strongly desires to avoid the threatened punishment. Credibility will be undermined by rash threats that are not carried out despite noncompliance by the target person. Sometimes it is necessary to establish credibility by demonstrating the will and ability to cause unpleasant consequences for the target person. However, even a credible threat may be unsuccessful if the target person refuses to be intimidated or believes that a way can be found to avoid compliance without being detected by the agent.

It is best to avoid using coercion except when absolutely necessary, because it is difficult to use and likely to result in undesirable side effects. Coercion often arouses anger or resentment, and it may result in retaliation. In work organizations, the most appropriate use of coercion is to deter behavior detrimental to the organization, such as illegal activities, theft, violation of safety rules, reckless acts that endanger others, and direct disobedience of legitimate requests. Coercion is not likely to result in commitment, but when used skillfully

TABLE 4	Guidelines for Using Coercive Power to Maintain Discipline

1. Explain rules and requirements, and ensure that people understand the serious consequences of violations.

2. Respond to infractions promptly and consistently without showing any favoritism to particular individuals.

3. Investigate to get the facts before using reprimands or punishment, and avoid jumping to conclusions or making hasty accusations.

4. Except for the most serious infractions, provide sufficient oral and written warnings before resorting to punishment.

5. Administer warnings and reprimands in private, and avoid making rash threats.

6. Stay calm and avoid the appearance of hostility or personal rejection.

7. Express a sincere desire to help the person comply with role expectations and thereby avoid punishment.

8. Invite the person to suggest ways to correct the problem, and seek agreement on a concrete plan.

9. Maintain credibility by administering punishment if noncompliance continues after threats and warnings have been made.

10. Use punishments that are legitimate, fair, and commensurate with the seriousness of the infraction.

in an appropriate situation, there is a reasonably good chance that it will result in compliance. Table 4 has guidelines for using coercion primarily to maintain discipline with subordinates (Arvey & Ivancevich, 1980; Preston & Zimmerer, 1978; Schoen & Durand, 1979).

How to Use Expert Power

Some guidelines for exercising expert power are shown in Table 5. When an agent clearly has much more relevant expertise than target persons, the effects of the expert power will be automatic. For example, a renowned expert physician recommends a form of treatment, and the patient accepts the recommendation without any doubts. However, in many cases an agent will not have such an obvious advantage in expertise, and it will be necessary to use the expertise to provide information, explanations, and evidence that supports a request or proposal. If there is any question about the agent's expertise, it is helpful to verify it by providing appropriate documents and evidence, or by describing prior success in dealing with similar problems.

Proposals or requests should be made in a clear, confident manner, and the agent should avoid making contradictory statements or vacillating between inconsistent positions. However, it is important to remember that superior expertise can also cause resentment if

TABLE 5	Ways to Use and Maintain Expert Power

- Explain the reasons for a request or proposal and why it is important.
- Provide evidence that a proposal will be successful.
- Don't make rash, careless, or inconsistent statements.
- Don't lie, exaggerate, or misrepresent the facts.
- Listen seriously to the person's concerns and suggestions.
- Act confident and decisive in a crisis.

TABLE 6	Ways to Gain and Use Referent Power

- Show acceptance and positive regard.
- Be supportive and helpful.
- Use sincere forms of ingratiation.
- Keep promises and commitments.
- Make self sacrifices to benefit others.
- Lead by example (use role modeling).
- Explain the personal importance of a request.

used in a way that implies the target person is ignorant or helpless. In the process of presenting rational arguments, some people lecture in an arrogant, condescending manner. In their efforts to sell a proposal, they fire a steady stream of arguments, rudely interrupting any attempted replies and dismissing any objections or concerns without serious consideration. Even when the agent is acknowledged to have more expertise, the target person usually has some relevant information, ideas, and concerns that should be considered.

How to Use Referent Power

Some specific ways to gain and use referent power are summarized in Table 6. Referent power is increased by showing concern for the needs and feelings of others, demonstrating trust and respect, and treating people fairly. However, to achieve and maintain strong referent power usually requires more than just flattery, favors, and charm. Referent power ultimately depends on the agent's character and integrity. Over time, actions speak louder than words, and someone who tries to appear friendly but manipulates and exploits people will lose referent power. Integrity is demonstrated by being truthful, expressing a consistent set of values, acting in a way that is consistent with one's espoused values, and carrying out promises and agreements (French & Raven, 1959).

One way to exercise referent power is through "role modeling." A person who is well liked and admired can have considerable influence over others by setting an example of proper and desirable behavior for them to imitate. When identification is strong, imitation is likely to occur even without any conscious intention by the agent. However, because people also imitate undesirable behavior in someone they admire, it is important to be aware of the examples that one sets. For example, some famous entertainers have a very negative influence on young fans who imitate their reckless and self-destructive behavior.

An agent with limited referent power may find it useful to remind the target person of favors done in the past or events when their friendship was very important. Finally, when relying on referent power as a source of influence, it is important to ensure that the target person understands how important a request is for you. Thus, the agent may say something like: "I would really appreciate it if you can do this, because it is really important to me"

Proactive Influence Tactics

As explained earlier, behavior used intentionally to gain acceptance of a request or support for a proposal is called a *proactive influence tactic*. Two research programs used inductive and deductive approaches to identify distinct types of proactive tactics

Kipnis, Schmidt, and Wilkinson (1980) developed a preliminary taxonomy by analyzing critical incidents that described successful and unsuccessful influence attempts. Then, the tactics identified with this inductive approach were used to develop a self-report agent questionnaire called the *Profiles of Organizational Influence Strategies* (POIS). Schriesheim and Hinkin (1990) later conducted a factor analysis of the POIS using data from samples of agents who rated their own use of the tactics in upward influence attempts with their boss. This study found support for six of the proposed tactics (i.e., rationality, exchange, ingratiation, assertiveness, coalition, and upward appeal), but not for the remaining two tactics (blocking and sanctions). Limited support for the revised version of the questionnaire was also found in a subsequent study of upward influence (Hochwarter et al., 2000). However, there has been no systematic research to validate the questionnaire as a measure of tactics used to influence subordinates and peers. The original and revised versions of the POIS have been used in many studies on proactive tactics (see Ammeter et al., 2002).

Another program of research was carried out by Yukl and his colleagues using several different research methods (i.e., critical incidents, diaries, questionnaires, experiments, and scenarios). A series of studies conducted over a period of more than a decade eventually identified 11 distinct tactics that are used to influence people in organizations (Yukl, Lepsinger, & Lucia, 1992; Yukl, Chavez, & Seifert, 2005; Yukl, Seifert, & Chavez, 2008). These tactics are defined in Table 7. Five of these tactics are similar to ones in the POIS *(rational persuasion,* ingratiation, exchange, pressure, and coalition) and seven other tactics were identified in the critical incidents or suggested by theories about leadership and power. The *Influence Behavior Questionnaire* (IBQ) was developed in the survey research to measure target ratings of agent influence behavior. Target ratings are usually more accu-

TABLE 7	Definition of the 11 Proactive Influence Tactics

Rational Persuasion: The agent uses logical arguments and factual evidence to show a proposal or request is feasible and relevant for attaining important task objectives.

Apprising: The agent explains how carrying out a request or supporting a proposal will benefit the target personally or help advance the target person's career.

Inspirational Appeals: The agent makes an appeal to values and ideals or seeks to arouse the target person's emotions to gain commitment for a request or proposal.

Consultation: The agent encourages the target to suggest improvements in a proposal or to help plan an activity or change for which the target person's support and assistance are desired.

Collaboration: The agent offers to provide relevant resources and assistance if the target will carry out a request or approve a proposed change.

Ingratiation: The agent uses praise and flattery before or during an influence attempt, or expresses confidence in the target's ability to carry out a difficult request.

Personal Appeals: The agent asks the target to carry out a request or support a proposal out of friendship, or asks for a personal favor before saying what it is.

Exchange: The agent offers an incentive, suggests an exchange of favors, or indicates willingness to reciprocate at a later time if the target will do what the agent requests.

Coalition Tactics: The agent seeks the aid of others to persuade the target to do something, or uses the support of others as a reason for the target to agree.

Legitimating Tactics: The agent seeks to establish the legitimacy of a request or to verify authority to make it by referring to rules, policies, contracts, or precedent.

Pressure: The agent uses demands, threats, frequent checking, or persistent reminders to influence the target to carry out a request.

rate than the type of agent's self-ratings used in the POIS. The remainder of this section describes each type of tactic and how it is commonly used in organizations to influence a subordinate, peer, or boss.

Rational Persuasion

Rational persuasion involves the use of explanations, logical arguments, and factual evidence to explain why a request or proposal will benefit the organization or help to achieve an important task objective. This tactic may also involve presentation of factual evidence that a project or change is likely to be successful. Rational persuasion is a flexible tactic that can be used for most influence attempts and target persons. This tactic is very useful when the target person shares the agent's objectives but does not initially recognize that the agent's request or proposal is the best way to attain their shared objectives. The use of a rational appeal that involves evidence and predicted outcomes is more effective if the agent is perceived to have high expertise and credibility. Rational persuasion is unlikely to be effective if the agent and target have incompatible objectives, or the agent lacks expertise and credibility.

Apprising

Apprising involves an explanation of how a request or proposal is likely to benefit the target person as an individual. The benefits may involve the person's career advancement, job satisfaction, or compensation. Apprising may involve the use of facts and logic, but unlike rational persuasion, the benefits described are for the target person, not for the organization or the mission. Unlike *exchange tactics,* the benefits to be obtained by the target person are not something the agent will provide to the target, but rather something that is likely to happen when the agent's request is carried out or the proposal is implemented.

This tactic is more likely to be used with subordinate or peers than with bosses. Successful use of apprising requires unique knowledge about the likely personal benefits associated with an activity or change, and a subordinate is much less likely than a superior to be a credible source of such knowledge. An exception is the situation where the subordinate is experienced but the boss is new to the organization.

Inspirational Appeals

This tactic involves an emotional or value-based appeal, in contrast to the logical arguments used in rational persuasion and apprising. An inspirational appeal is an attempt to develop enthusiasm and commitment by arousing strong emotions and linking a request or proposal to a person's needs, values, hopes, and ideals. Some bases for appealing to most people include their desire to be important, to feel useful, to support their values, to accomplish something worthwhile, to perform an exceptional feat, to be a member of the best team, or to participate in an exciting effort to make things better.

This tactic can be used in any direction, but it is especially appropriate for gaining commitment to work on a new project, and this type of request is most likely to be made with subordinates or peers. An inspirational appeal is also an appropriate tactic to gain support for a proposed change that involves values and ideals.

Consultation

This tactic involves inviting the target person to participate in planning how to carry out a request, revise a strategy, or implement a proposed change. Consultation can take a variety of forms, but unlike the leadership behavior with the same name, the target person is only invited to help determine how the objective should be attained, not to help decide what the objective should be. As with rational persuasion, consultation is more likely to be effective if the agent and target have shared objectives. Consultation is useful for discovering if the target person has concerns about the feasibility of a proposal or likely adverse consequences. The agent can explore ways to avoid or resolve any issues that are revealed (which involves the tactic called *collaboration).*

Consultation can be used in any direction, but it is likely to be used more often with subordinates and peers than with bosses. This tactic is especially appropriate when you have the authority to plan a task or make a change, but you need the target person to help carry out the work or implement the change. The authority to assign work and make changes is greatest in a downward direction and least in an upward direction. Consultation can be used in an attempt to gain support or approval from superiors for a proposed change or new project, but superiors already have authority to review such decisions and do not need an invitation from the subordinate to modify the proposal. In a lateral direction, consultation is very useful to elicit concerns and suggestions from peers who may be committed to support an activity or change unless their needs and opinions are taken into account.

Exchange

This influence tactic involves the explicit or implicit offer to reward a person for doing what you request. The tactic is especially appropriate for a request that offers no important benefits for the target person and would involve considerable effort and inconvenience. With exchange tactics, you offer something valued enough by the target person to motivate compliance with a request. The promised benefit may involve tangible rewards, scarce resources, information, advice or assistance on another task, career support, or political support. An exchange tactic is unlikely to be effective unless the target person believes the agent is able to provide the promised benefit and can be trusted to actually deliver it.

Exchange tactics are more likely to be used in influence attempts with subordinates and peers than with bosses. Control over rewards is greatest in a downward direction and least in an upward direction. One type of reward that can be offered only to subordinates is a pay increase, bonus, promotion, better assignments, or a better work schedule. It is also more socially acceptable to offer incentives to subordinates than to bosses. Managers have little to offer bosses who are not already expected as part of their job responsibilities, and any incentive offered to a boss may be viewed as a bribe. Managers usually have some control over rewards desired by peers, but the rewards are more likely to be task related (e.g., provide resources, assistance, information, political support) rather than personal benefits.

Collaboration

This influence tactic involves an offer to provide necessary resources and/or assistance if the target person agrees to carry out a request or approve a proposal. Collaboration may seem similar to exchange in that both tactics involve an offer to do something for the target person. However, there are important differences in the underlying motivational processes and facilitating conditions. Exchange involves increasing the benefits to be obtained by carrying out a request, and it is especially appropriate when the benefits of compliance would otherwise be low for the target person. Collaboration involves reducing the difficulty or costs of carrying out a request, and it is especially appropriate when compliance would be difficult for the target person. Exchange usually involves an impersonal trade of unrelated benefits, whereas collaboration usually involves a joint effort to accomplish the same task.

Collaboration is used least often in an upward direction. A boss usually has more control over discretionary resources than subordinates and can usually require subordinate assistance on an essential activity. With subordinates and peers, there is more opportunity to propose ways to facilitate the target person's ability to carry out a request.

Ingratiation

Ingratiation is behavior that makes someone feel better about you. Examples include giving compliments, doing unsolicited favors, acting deferential and respectful, and acting especially friendly and helpful before making a request. When ingratiation is perceived to be sincere, it tends to strengthen positive regard and make a target person more willing to consider a request.

This tactic is more likely to be used in influence attempts with subordinates or peers than with bosses. Praise and compliments can be used with anyone, but they are more credible and meaningful when the agent has higher status and expertise than the target person. Thus, ingratiation is likely to be viewed as less sincere when used in an influence attempt with a boss. Ingratiation may be viewed as manipulative if it is used just before asking for something; so in general, it is more useful as part of a long-term strategy for building cooperative relations than as proactive influence tactic.

Personal Appeals

A *personal appeal* involves asking someone to do a favor based on friendship or loyalty to you, or it may also involve an appeal to the person's kindness and generosity. This influence tactic is not feasible when the target person dislikes the agent or is indifferent about what happens to the agent. A personal appeal is most useful for getting assistance or information or for requesting a personal favor unrelated to the work. The tactic is more socially acceptable with a peer or outsider than with a subordinate or boss. It is awkward to request a personal favor from a subordinate and should not be necessary except in very unusual circumstances. A personal appeal to a boss involves issues of equity and may be perceived as favoritism by other subordinates.

Legitimating Tactics

Legitimating tactics involve attempts to establish one's legitimate authority or right to make a particular type of request. Legitimacy is unlikely to be questioned for a routine request that has been made and complied with many times before. However, legitimacy is more likely to be questioned when you make a request that is unusual, when the request clearly exceeds your authority, or when the target person does not know who you are or what authority you have. There are several different types of legitimating tactics, most of which are mutually compatible.

Legitimating tactics are most often relevant for influence attempts with peers or outsiders, where role relationships are often ambiguous and agent authority less well defined. For downward influence attempts with subordinates, legitimating may be used when implementing major changes or for dealing with an unusual crisis. For upward influence attempts, legitimating may be used for requests involving personnel matters, especially if the superior is new and unfamiliar with relevant policies, contract agreements, and standard practices.

Pressure

Pressure tactics include threats, warnings, and assertive behavior such as repeated demands or frequent checking to see if the person has complied with a request. Pressure tactics are sometimes successful in eliciting compliance with a request, particularly if the target person is just lazy or apathetic rather than strongly opposed to it. However, pressure is not likely to result in commitment and may have serious side effects. The harder forms (e.g., threats, warnings, demands) are likely to cause resentment and undermine working relationships. The target person may try to avoid you, discredit you, or restrict your power. The softer forms (e.g., persistent requests, reminders that the person promised to do something) are more likely to gain compliance without undermining your relationship with the person.

Pressure tactics are most likely to be used with subordinates and least likely to be used with bosses. The authority and power needed to make threats or warnings credible is much greater in a downward direction than in a lateral or upward direction, and pressure is often considered more appropriate for influence attempts with subordinates than with peers or bosses.

Coalition Tactics

Coalition tactics involve getting help from other people to influence the target person. The coalition partners may be peers, subordinates, superiors, or outsiders. Coalition partners may actively participate in influence attempts with the target person, or the agent may only use their endorsement of a request or proposal. When a coalition partner actively participates in the effort to influence the target person, the influence attempt usually involves other influence tactics as well. For example, the coalition partner may use rational persuasion, exchange, or pressure to influence the target person. When the agent gets help from the immediate superior of the target person, the process is sometimes called an upward appeal, but it is still an example of a coalition tactic rather than an entirely different type of proactive tactic.

Coalition tactics are more likely to be used to influence peers or bosses than subordinates, and it is especially appropriate to gain their support for a proposed change or new initiative. It is seldom necessary to use coalition tactics to influence subordinates. Managers have many ways to influence subordinates, and in western countries they are expected to do so without getting help from other people.

Effectiveness of Proactive Tactics

Proactive influence tactics are not always needed in an influence attempt. When a request is clearly legitimate, relevant for the work, and something the target person knows how to do, then it is often possible to get target compliance by using a "simple request" based on legitimate power. However, when a person is likely to resist a simple request, the use of proactive influence tactics can help to make the influence attempt more successful. The influence tactics are especially useful for a request or proposal that is unusual, controversial, or difficult to do, or when the agent has little authority over the target person (e.g., a peer, boss, or client).

The effectiveness of each type of proactive tactics depends on several aspects of the situation in which it is used (e.g., Kipnis et al., 1980; Yukl & Falbe, 1990; Yukl, Falbe, & Youn, 1993; Yukl, Guinan, & Sottolano, 1995; Yukl, Kim, & Chavez, 1999; Yukl, Kim, & Falbe, 1996; Yukl & Tracey, 1992). Relevant aspects of the situation include the type of agent-target relationship, the agent's power and authority, the agent's interpersonal skills, the type of influence objective, and the extent to which the request is seen as appropriate and acceptable by the target person. A tactic is more likely to be successful if the target person perceives it to be a socially acceptable form of influence behavior, the agent has sufficient position and personal power, the agent has strong interpersonal skills, and if the tactic is used for a request that is legitimate and consistent with target values and needs.

The outcome of an influence attempt also depends on the extent to which the agent is trusted by the target and perceived to have integrity. Any tactic can be used in a way that is unethical. To preserve a reputation for integrity it is essential to avoid using tactics in a way that is deceptive or manipulative. The proactive tactics should be used in ethical ways to accomplish worthwhile objectives, not to exploit others for personal gain.

Even though the outcome of an influence attempt depends on the situation, research on consequences of influence attempts finds that some tactics tend to be generally more effective than others (e.g., Falbe & Yukl, 1992; Fu & Yukl, 2000; Yukl, Fu, & McDonald, 2003; Yukl & Tracey, 1992). Findings in the research on tactic effectiveness and how the tactics are commonly used in different situations are summarized in Table 8. Research on how the tactics are used with different targets and how tactics are combined and sequenced is still limited, but those findings are also summarized in the table. This section of the chapter describes the findings about the relative effectiveness of the tactics when used individually and when combined and sequenced in different ways.

Effects of Individual Tactics

The four tactics that are generally most effective include rational persuasion, consultation, collaboration, and inspirational appeals. These *"core tactics"* are often successful for influencing target commitment to carry out a request or support a proposal. A strong form

TABLE 8	Summary of Findings for Proactive Influence Tactics			
Influence Tactic	Directional Use of Tactic	Sequencing Results	Used Alone or in Combination	General Effectiveness
Rational Persuasion	Widely used in all directions	Used more for initial request	Used frequently both ways	High
Inspirational Appeal	More down than up or lateral	No difference	Used most with other tactics	High
Consultation	More down and lateral than up	No difference	Used most with other tactics	High
Collaboration	More down and lateral than up	Not studied	Used most with other tactics	High
Apprising	More down than lateral or up	Not studied	Used most with other tactics	Moderate
Ingratiation	More down and lateral than up	Used more for initial request	Used most with other tactics	Moderate
Exchange	More down and lateral than up	Used most for quick follow-up	Used both ways equally often	Moderate
Personal Appeal	More lateral than down or up	Used more for initial request	Used both ways equally often	Moderate
Coalition Tactic	More lateral and up then down	Used most for delayed follow-up	Used both way equally often	Low/Moderate
Legitimating Tactic	More down and lateral than up	Used most for quick follow-up	Used most with other tactics	Low
Pressure	More down than lateral or up	Used most for delayed follow-up	Used both ways equally often	Low

of rational persuasion (e.g., a detailed proposal, elaborate documentation) is much more effective than a weak form of rational persuasion (e.g., a brief explanation, an assertion without supporting evidence).

Ingratiation, exchange, and apprising are moderately effective for influencing subordinates and peers, but these tactics are difficult to use for proactive influence attempts with superiors. Personal appeals can be useful for influencing a target person with whom the agent has a friendly relationship. However, this tactic is only relevant for certain types of requests (e.g., getting assistance, getting a personal favor, changing a scheduled meeting or deadline), and it is likely to result in target compliance rather than commitment.

Pressure and legitimating tactics are not likely to result in target commitment, but these tactics can be useful for eliciting compliance. As noted earlier, compliance is sometimes all that is needed to accomplish the objective of an influence attempt.

A coalition can be effective for influencing a peer or superior to support a change or innovation, especially if the coalition partners use direct tactics such as rational persuasion and inspirational appeals. However, use of a coalition is not likely to be effective if it involves the use of pressure tactics by coalition partners and is viewed as an attempt to "gang up" on the target person. The least effective form of coalition is likely to be an upward appeal to an authority person, and this form of coalition is likely to be saved as a last resort for resolving a conflict with a peer who can cause the failure of an important project.

Combining Tactics

It is often feasible for a manager to use more than one direct influence tactic at the same time or in a sequence. An influence attempt is more likely to be successful if two or more different tactics are combined. However, the outcome will depend on the potency of the component tactics and the extent to which they are compatible with each other. Compatible tactics are easy to use together and they enhance each other's effectiveness. The research on tactic combinations is very limited, but it suggests that some tactics are more easily combined than others.

Rational persuasion is a very flexible tactic, and it is usually compatible with any of the other tactics. The effectiveness of a soft tactic such as consultation, inspirational appeals, and apprising can be enhanced by combining it with rational persuasion. For example, rational persuasion can be used to clarify why a proposed change is important, and consultation can be used to involve the target person in finding an acceptable way to implement the change. An inspirational appeal that involves values and ideals can also involve reasons why the request or proposal is important to the organization or mission. The explanation of why a request is beneficial for the organization can also include reasons why it is beneficial to the person. For example, a proposed change to increase profits may also help the target person get a promotion.

Combinations of "soft" tactics, such as consultation, ingratiation, and inspirational appeals and collaboration are usually more effective than use of one soft tactic alone. For example, it is especially useful to combine consultation and collaboration. Consultation will elicit target person concerns, and collaboration can be used to help alleviate them.

Some tactics are clearly incompatible. For example, a hard form of pressure is incompatible with personal appeals or ingratiation because it undermines the feelings of friendship and loyalty that are the basis for these soft tactics. A hard form of pressure also tends to undermine the trust necessary for tactics such as consultation and collaboration. However, rational persuasion, consultation, and collaboration are unlikely to be effective when the target person does not share the agent's task objectives. In this situation, some pressure may be necessary to motivate target willingness to find a mutually acceptable agreement. Threats or the use of upward appeals to authority figures may help convince the target person that cooperation is more beneficial than noncooperation. The use of pressure tactics to gain cooperation requires considerable skill, and it should be used only after other tactics have failed.

Sequencing Tactics

Influence attempts often involve a series of separate influence episodes that occur over a period of days or weeks. Some tactics are used more in initial influence attempts and other tactics are used more in follow-up influence attempts. The reasons for tactic selection described earlier can be used to explain sequencing differences in the use of different influence tactics. In general, it is reasonable to assume that a manager will initially select tactics that are likely to accomplish an objective with the least effort and cost.

Most initial influence attempts involve either a simple request or a relatively weak form of rational persuasion. These tactics are easy to use and entail little in the way of agent costs. Ingratiation is likely to be used early, because it is more credible to use it as part of the rationale for a request (e.g., say that the person is highly qualified to do a task). If some target resistance is anticipated, then the agent is likely to use a stronger form of rational persuasion, and "soft" tactics, such as personal appeals, consultation, collaboration, apprising, and inspirational appeals. In the face of continued resistance by a target, the agent will either escalate to "harder" tactics or abandon the effort if the request does not justify the risks of escalation. Pressure, exchange, and coalitions are likely to be saved for follow-up influence attempts, because they involve the greatest costs and risks. Legitimating may be used either early or late, depending on how the target is likely to perceive the legitimacy of a request. This tactic should be used early if the agent believes that the target person is likely to have any doubts about legitimacy.

Using the Tactics to Resist Influence Attempts

In proactive influence attempts, the agent initiates the interaction, but effective leaders must also be able to handle an undesirable influence attempt initiated by someone else. Most of the tactics used for proactive influence attempts can also be used to resist or modify a request made by someone else such as a boss, peer, subordinate, or client. For example, when used as a resistance tactic, rational persuasion may involve explaining why the agent's proposed plan is unlikely to be successful. Collaboration may involve an offer to help accomplish the agent's objective in different way. Apprising may involve explaining why a proposed activity or change is likely to result in unfavorable personal outcomes for the agent (the "beware what you wish for" tactic). Legitimating may involve explaining how the agent's request is inconsistent with company rules or a formal contract. Pressure may involve a threat to resign or to pursue legal action against the agent if an unethical request or proposal is not withdrawn.

Guidelines for Specific Tactics

This section offers specific guidelines for using the four core tactics (rational persuasion, inspirational appeals, consultation, and collaboration), and they are summarized in Table 9. Guidelines for the other seven tactics are summarized in Table 10. The guidelines for how to use the tactics are suggestions rather than prescriptions, because it is always necessary to evaluate the situation and determine whether a tactic is feasible and relevant. Some of the tactics can take many different forms, and it is important to determine the best way to a tactic.

TABLE 9	Ways To Use the Core Tactics

Rational Persuasion

- Explain in detail why a request or proposal is important.
- Use facts and logic to make a clear case in support of a request or proposal
- Provide evidence that a request or proposal is feasible.
- Explain why a proposal is better than the alternatives.

Inspirational Appeals

- Describe a proposed change as an exciting and worthwhile opportunity.
- Link a proposed activity or change to the person's ideals and values.
- Describe a clear, appealing vision of what can be accomplished by a project or change.
- Use a dramatic, expressive style of speaking and positive, optimistic language.

Consultation

- State your objective, and ask what the person can do to help attain it.
- Ask for suggestions on how to improve a tentative proposal.
- Involve the person in planning action steps to attain an objective.
- Respond in a positive way to any concerns expressed by the person.

Collaboration

- Offer to show the person how to perform a requested task.
- Offer to provide necessary resources.
- Offer to help the person solve problems caused by a request.
- Offer to help the person implement a proposed change.

Rational Persuasion

Rational appeals involve logical arguments and factual evidence that a proposal or request is desirable because it is important for the organization or team and is feasible to do.

- **Explain the reason for a request or proposal.**

People are more likely to comply with a request if they understand the reason why it is necessary and important. When asked to do something unusual, people may wonder whether it is really necessary or just an impulsive whim. Explain how a proposed activity would solve a problem in your work or help you carry out your job responsibilities more effectively. Explain how a proposal would help to achieve an important objective you share in common with the person, such as improved quality, service, or productivity.

- **Provide evidence that your proposal is feasible.**

It is not enough for a request or proposal to be relevant, it must also be seen as practical and realistic to gain the person's enthusiastic support and cooperation. The target person may exaggerate the difficulties or anticipate obstacles that are unlikely to occur. If the person has doubts about the feasibility of a request or proposal, provide supporting evidence for it. Explain the underlying theoretical rationale for assuming that a proposed plan of action will lead to the desired objective. Describe a specific sequence of action steps that could be used to accomplish the objective. Cite supporting evidence from empirical research (e.g., a pilot study, a survey showing a favorable response to a proposed new product, service, or change). Describe how a similar approach was successful when used in the past by yourself or someone else. If appropriate, provide an actual demonstration for the person to observe (seeing is believing).

TABLE 10	Ways to Use the Other Tactics

Apprising

- Explain how the person could benefit from carrying out a requested task.
- Explain how the task you want the person to do would help his/her career.
- Explain why a proposed activity or change would be good for the person.
- Explain how a proposed change would solve some of the person's problems.

Exchange

- Offer something the person wants in exchange for providing help on a task or project.
- Offer to do a specific task or favor in return for compliance with a request.
- Promise to do something for the person in the future in return for his or her help now.
- Offer to provide an appropriate reward if the person carries out a difficult request.

Ingratiation

- Say that the person has the special skills or knowledge needed to carry out a request.
- Praise the person's past achievements when asking him/her to do another task.
- Show respect and appreciation when asking the person to do something for you.
- Say that there is nobody more qualified to do a task.

Legitimating

- Explain that your request or proposal is consistent with official rules and policies.
- Point out that your request or proposal is consistent with a prior agreement or contract.
- Use a document to verify that a request is legitimate (e.g., a work order, policy manual, contract, charter).
- Explain that a request or proposal is consistent with prior precedent and established practice.

Personal Appeal

- Ask the person to do a favor for you as a friend.
- Ask for his/her help as a personal favor.
- Say that you are in a difficult situation and would really appreciate the person's help.
- Say you need to ask for a favor before telling the person what it is.

Pressure

- Keep asking the person in a persistent way to say yes to a request.
- Insist in an assertive way that the person must do what you ask.
- Repeatedly check to see if the person has carried out a request.
- Warn the person about the penalties for not complying with a request.

Coalition

- Mention the names of others who endorse a proposal when asking the person to support it.
- Get others to explain to the person why they support a proposed activity or change.
- Bring someone along for support when meeting with the person to make a request or proposal.
- Ask someone with higher authority to help influence the target person.

- **Explain why your proposal is better than competing ones.**

Sometimes your proposal is competing with other proposals for the person's support. In this case, it is not only necessary to show that your proposal is feasible, but also to show that it is better than any of the alternatives. Point out the advantages of your proposal in comparison to the alternatives (e.g., more likely to accomplish the objective, less costly, more likely to be approved, easier to implement, less risk of undesirable side effects). Point out the weaknesses and problems with each competing proposal. Your comparison will be more credible if you also acknowledge some advantages of competing proposals rather than ignoring them altogether, especially if the person is already aware of these advantages. If feasible, cite evidence from a test of the competing proposals to show that yours is better.

- **Explain how likely problems or concerns would be handled.**

All proposals and plans have weaknesses and limitations. A proposal is more likely to be accepted if you anticipate any obvious limitations and find ways to deal with them. Explain how you propose to avoid potential problems, overcome likely obstacles, and minimize risks. If the person expresses any unanticipated concerns about your proposal, discuss ways to deal with these concerns rather than ignoring them or dismissing them as unworthy of consideration.

Inspirational Appeals

An inspirational appeal is an attempt to develop enthusiasm and commitment by appealing to the target person's emotions and values.

- **Appeal to the person's ideals and values.**

Most people aspire to be important, to feel useful, to accomplish something worthwhile, to make an important contribution, to perform an exceptional feat, to be a member of the best team, or to participate in an exciting effort to make things better. These aspirations are a good basis for emotional appeals. For example, the task of developing a new type of software may be likened to the role of a missionary who is going to revolutionize the way computers are used in society. Some values and ideals that may be the basis for an inspirational appeal include patriotism, loyalty, liberty, freedom, justice, fairness, equality, excellence, altruism, and environmentalism.

- **Link the request to the person's self-image.**

A proposed activity or assignment may be linked to values that are central to the person's self-image as a professional, a member of an organization, an adherent of a particular religion, or a member of a political party. For example, most scientists have strong values about the discovery of new knowledge and its application to improve humanity; most physicians and nurses have strong values about healing people and keeping them healthy. A proposed change or activity may be described as something that will advance new knowledge, improve health care, enrich the lives of all members of the organization, serve one's god, or demonstrate loyalty to one's country.

- **Link the request to a clear and appealing vision.**

Efforts to introduce major changes or innovations are more likely to be successful when they involve an appealing vision of what could be accomplished or how the future could look if the proposed activity or change is implemented successfully. The vision may be an existing one the target person is known to embrace, or one you created to help gain commitment to a new project or activity. The vision should emphasize ideological values rather than tangible economic benefits (used in rational appeals to self-interest). However, it is not necessary to ignore economic benefits; they may be integrated into the overall vision of what can be accomplished as long as it is clear that they are not the primary objective.

- **Use a dramatic, expressive style of speaking.**

A dramatic, expressive style of speaking often increases the effectiveness of an emotional appeal. Conviction and intensity of feeling are communicated by one's voice (e.g., tone, inflection, pause), facial expressions, gestures, and body movement. Use a strong, clear tone of voice, but vary the pace and intensity. Use pauses at appropriate times to emphasize key words, maintain interest, and arouse excitement. Maintain strong eye contact, use strong gestures, and move around to display energy and intensity of feeling.

- **Use positive, optimistic language.**

Confidence and optimism about a project or change can be contagious. It is especially important to foster optimism when the task is very difficult and people lack self-confidence. State your personal belief in the project and your strong commitment to see it through to a successful conclusion. Use positive language to communicate your confidence that a proposed project or change will be successful. For example, talk about the wonderful things that "will" happen when a change is made, rather than what "may" happen.

Consultation

With this tactic, the target person is invited to help plan a task or improve a proposed change in order to gain more commitment for it.

- **State your objective and ask what the person can do to help.**

When you do not expect the target person to be enthusiastic about helping you accomplish an objective, it is helpful to explain why it is important (rational persuasion) then ask the person what he or she can do to help you attain it. If you have a good relationship, the target person is likely to suggest some ways to be of assistance. Show appreciation for any suggestions and explore their feasibility. Once the person has agreed to provide some assistance, it is easier to ask for additional things that build on the initial offer.

- **Ask for suggestions on how to improve a tentative proposal.**

More participation is likely if you present a proposal as tentative and encourage people to improve it, rather than asking people to react to an elaborate plan that appears complete. People will be less inhibited about expressing concerns for a proposal that appears to be in the development stage rather than complete. The agent and target person should jointly explore ways to deal with any serious concerns or incorporate promising suggestions. A stronger version of this tactic is to ask the target person to write the initial draft of a proposal that you want him or her to support. Of course, this procedure is only feasible if the person agrees with you about the objective and has the expertise to develop a credible proposal.

- **Involve the person in planning how to attain an objective.**

Present a general strategy, policy, or objective and ask the target person to suggest specific action steps for implementing it. If the action plan will be detailed, it is best to schedule a meeting at a later time to review the plan and reach a mutual agreement about it. This tactic is especially useful for assigning responsibilities to a subordinate or asking a peer to carry out supporting activities on a project. To be feasible, the target person should have at least moderate agreement with the strategy or objective.

- **Respond to the person's concerns and suggestions.**

Consultation is used mostly as a proactive influence tactic, but opportunities arise to use it also as a reactive tactic. Sometimes when asking the target person to carry out an assignment or provide assistance on a task, the person expresses concerns about it or suggestions for improving it. Whenever feasible, try to deal with the target person's concerns, even if it requires some modification of your initial plans. Ask the person for suggestions about how to deal with concerns. Good suggestions for improving an activity should be utilized whenever feasible.

Collaboration

Collaboration involves an offer to help the target person carry out a request for you, and it can help reduce the difficulty or cost of carrying out a request.

- **Offer to show the person how to perform a requested task.**

If a request involves a task that has not been performed previously by the target person, and the person is worried about not being able to perform the task successfully, then a good way to increase commitment is to offer to show the person how to do the task. Offer to provide instruction to the person or arrange for someone else who is qualified to provide instruction. It is also useful to offer guidance and advice when a request or assignment does not involve a completely new task but there are special requirements and the person is uncertain about what is expected.

- **Offer to provide necessary resources.**

Sometimes the target person is reluctant to do a requested task because it requires supplies, equipment, information, or other resources that are not readily available. If the task requires additional resources that are essential for task performance but difficult to obtain, offer to provide them or help the person get them.

- **Offer to help the person solve problems caused by a request.**

A request is more likely to be resisted if it will cause new problems that will increase the cost of compliance beyond an acceptable level. Try to anticipate such problems and be prepared to offer ways to avoid them or help the person deal with them. In many cases, the agent will not be aware of the problems caused by a request, but target concerns can be elicited with the skillful use of consultation and active listening by the agent.

- **Offer to help the person implement a proposed change.**

A major source of resistance to change is the extra work that would be involved in implementing it in the target person's unit or job. To gain the person's support and approval for a proposed change, offer to help the person implement it. A requirement for the use of this tactic is the capability to actually provide assistance in implementing the proposed change, which is most likely when the target person is a subordinate.

Power and Influence Behavior

Power and influence behavior are distinct constructs, but the relationship among specific forms of power, specific influence behaviors, and influence outcomes is complex

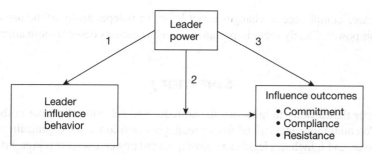

FIGURE 1 Effects of Agent Power and Influence Behavior on Influence Outcomes

and not well understood. Different types of effects are possible, and they are not mutually exclusive (see Figure 1).

Agent power may directly affect the agent's choice of influence tactics (as depicted by arrow #1). Some tactics require a particular type of power to be effective, and a leader with relevant power is more likely to use these tactics. For example, exchange tactics require reward power, which provides an agent with something of value to exchange with the target person. Strong forms of pressure such as warnings and threats are more likely to be used by an agent who has some coercive power over the target person. Rational persuasion is more likely to be used when the agent has the knowledge to explain why a request is important and feasible.

Some influence tactics may have a direct effect on target attitudes and/or behavior, regardless of the agent's power. However, in the majority of influence attempts, it is likely that power acts as a moderator variable to enhance or diminish the effectiveness of the tactics used by the agent. This moderator effect of power (depicted by arrow #2) is most likely to occur for types of the power directly relevant to the tactics used in an influence attempt. For example, expert power probably moderates the effect of rational persuasion. A proposal explaining why it is important to change operating procedures is more likely to be successful if made by someone perceived to have relevant expertise. A similar moderating effect probably occurs for reward power and exchange tactics. An agent with high reward power is likely to have more success offering an exchange than an agent with little reward power.

It is also possible that agent power can enhance the success of an influence tactics for which the power is not directly relevant (also depicted by arrow #2). An agent with strong referent power may be more successful when using rational persuasion to gain support for a proposal. An agent with strong coercive power may be more successful in gaining compliance with a simple request, even though no pressure or exchange tactics are used. Strong expert power may increase the credibility of a request unrelated to the agent's expertise. For example, a famous scientist influences people to participate in a risky financial venture that does not involve the scientist's field of expertise.

Another possibility (depicted by arrow #3) is that agent power can influence the target person regardless of whether the agent makes any overt influence attempt. In organizations, people act more deferential toward somebody who has high position power, because they are aware of the possibility that the person can affect their job performance and career advancement. People are less likely to criticize or contradict a powerful agent, because they do not want to risk the agent's displeasure. People are more likely to cooperate with an agent who has strong referent power, even if the agent does nothing to encourage such cooperation.

Little research has investigated the complex relationships between power and influence. There is only limited evidence for the proposition that power influences the choice of influence tactics, that power moderates the effectiveness of a specific influence tactic, or that power increases compliance or changes target behavior independently of the use of tactics based on this power. Clearly these important research questions deserve more attention.

Summary

Power is the capacity to influence the attitudes and behavior of people in the desired direction. Potential influence derived from a manager's position in the organization is called position power, and it includes legitimate power, reward power, coercive power, information power, and ecological power. Potential influence derived from the characteristics of the person who occupies a leadership position is called personal power, and it includes expert and referent power.

Power for an individual or group can increase or decrease as conditions change. Social exchange theory explains how power is gained and lost as reciprocal influence processes occur over time between leaders and followers in small groups. Strategic contingencies theory explains the acquisition and loss of power by different subunits of an organization (e.g., functional departments or product divisions) and the implications of this power distribution for the effectiveness of the organization in a changing environment. Theories of power institutionalization explain how political tactics are used to increase power and protect existing power.

The amount of power necessary for leader effectiveness depends on the nature of the organization, task, and subordinates. However, a moderate amount of position power is usually optimal. A leader with extensive reward and coercive power is tempted to rely on them excessively, which can cause resentment and rebellion. On the other hand, a leader lacking sufficient position power to reward competent subordinates, make necessary changes, and punish chronic troublemakers will find it difficult to develop a high-performing group or organization. The success of a manager depends greatly on the manner in which power is exercised. Effective leaders rely more on personal power than on position power and they use power in a subtle, careful fashion that minimizes status differentials and avoids threats to the target person's self-esteem. In contrast, leaders who exercise power in an arrogant, manipulative, domineering manner are likely to engender resentment and resistance.

The relationship between power and influence behavior is complex. Power can influence the leader's choice of tactics and it can enhance their effectiveness. Leader power may also influence others even without a direct influence attempt by the leader. Three distinct types of influence tactics found by scholars are impression management tactics, political tactics, and proactive tactics. Eleven distinct proactive tactics have been identified using several types of research methods. Proactive influence tactics are useful when a simple request is not sufficient for eliciting the desired level of compliance or commitment. What tactics are used depends on the situation, and the choice of tactics will vary somewhat depending on whether the target person is a subordinate, peer, or superior.

The outcome of an influence attempt may be target commitment, compliance, or resistance. Some tactics tend to be more effective than others, and the ones most likely to elicit target commitment are rational persuasion, consultation, collaboration, and inspirational appeals. However, these core tactics do not always result in task commitment, because the outcome of any particular influence attempt is affected strongly by other factors in addition to the type of influence tactics used by the agent. It is evident that combining different tactics is beneficial in some cases but not others. Knowing how to successfully combine different forms of influence requires considerable insight and skill on the part of the manager. Any tactic can fail if it is not used in a skillful, ethical way, or it is inappropriate for the influence objective and situation.

Review and Discussion Questions

1. What is the difference between position power and personal power?
2. What types of power are related most strongly to leadership effectiveness?
3. How much position and personal power do leaders need to be effective?
4. What are some guidelines for using position and personal power effectively?
5. Briefly define the four proactive core tactics.
6. Which proactive tactics are most likely to result in target commitment?
7. How can the proactive tactics be used to resist or modify influence attempts by others?
8. How are power and influence behavior related to each other and to influence outcomes?

Key Terms

apprising	information power	personal power
coercive power	ingratiation	position power
collaboration	inspirational appeals	pressure tactics
commitment	institutionalization of power	proactive influence tactic
compliance	internalization	rational persuasion
consultation	legitimate power	referent power
ecological power	legitimating tactic	resistance
exchange tactics	personal appeal	reward power
expert power	personal identification	scope of authority

CASE 1

Restview Hospital

Mary Carter was the accounting manager at Restview Hospital, a large residential health care facility. The facility administrator, Jack Morelli, explained that he wanted to modernize Restview's system of accounts billing. He asked Mary to investigate available software packages that would be compatible with their computer system. Jack explained that he and the Restview board of directors would like to make a decision about this matter at the board meeting next month.

A week later, Jack asked Mary about her progress, and she reported that she had identified two vendors with appropriate software packages. Jack asked why her list of potential vendors did not include Standard Software Systems, the vendor from which they purchased the software currently used to process Restview's payroll. Standard had just recently developed a software package for accounts billing as a new addition to their product line, but few hospitals were using it. The preliminary information gathered by Mary suggested that Standard's software package was less appropriate for Restview than the packages offered by the other vendors. However, Mary knew that the president of Standard Software was a personal friend of Jack, and she agreed to include Standard among the vendors selected for further consideration.

During the next two weeks, sales representatives from each vendor were invited to make a presentation at Restview to demonstrate and explain their product. Mary had planned to invite the board members to these presentations, but Jack said they were too busy to attend.

When the presentations were held, Mary and her office staff asked many questions, but Jack looked bored and said very little. Mary also visited some other hospitals that were already using each type of software package to get firsthand opinions about how well they worked and the difficulties experienced in installing them. During the course of her investigation, she learned that Standard's new software package was less flexible and less user-friendly than the others. All three software packages were about the same price, but the software package from Reliable Computer was clearly the best one for Restview's needs. She prepared a short report to Jack detailing the advantages and disadvantages of each product and making her recommendation.

The next day Mary met with Jack to give him the written report and summarize her findings in person. She explained the reasons for her recommendation to purchase the software package from Reliable Computers, and she reviewed the evidence supporting it. Mary also offered to present her findings to the board of directors at their next meeting, but Jack said he could handle it himself. The board meeting was held the following week, and afterward Jack informed Mary that they decided to go with the software package from Standard. He explained that the board wanted to reward Standard for excellent customer service last year when installing their payroll software at Restview. Two years later, after thousands of dollars of unnecessary expense, the accounts billing software was still not operating smoothly for Restview.

Copyright © 1992 by Gary Yukl

Questions

1. How would you explain the board's decision to purchase the software package from Standard?
2. How much power relative to this decision did Mary, Jack, and the president of Standard Software possess, and what type of power was it?
3. What could Mary have done to gain more influence over the decision?

CASE 2

Sporting Goods Store

Bill Thompson is the new manager of a retail sporting goods store in Vermont that is part of a national chain. Bill, who is 25 years old, has been working for the company for four years. Before his promotion, he was the assistant manager for two years at a company store in Delaware. Last week he was briefly introduced to the employees by his boss, the regional manager.

The profit performance of this store is below average for its location, and Bill is looking forward to the challenge of improving profits. When he was an assistant manager, he was given mostly minor administrative duties and paperwork, so this assignment will be his first opportunity to show he can be an effective manager. The base salaries of the 20 employees who work in Bill's store are set by the company, but appraisal ratings by the store manager influence the size of an employee's annual merit raise. These recommendations must be justified to the regional manager, especially if they are not consistent with individual and department sales. Bill can suspend or fire employees with the approval of his boss, but in practice it is difficult to do so unless the recommendation is supported by a strong case.

The store layout and most prices are set by the headquarters office. However, store performance can be affected to a limited extent by the store manager. One way is to keep the cost of employees low is by making sure they are working efficiently and not taking excessive sick days. Another way is to ensure that employees are providing a high level of customer service so that customers will return to make other purchases rather than going to a different store next time. Customer service depends on knowing the products well, being polite, providing prompt service, and making sure that inventories of popular goods are maintained so that customers can find what they want. Pay is low for this type of retail selling job, turnover is high, and it takes a few months for a new employee to learn the merchandise well enough to be helpful to customers. Thus, it is also desirable to keep competent employees satisfied enough to stay with the company.

Although it is only his first week on the job, Bill believes that he has already discovered some of the problems at this store. Among the various departments in the store, the ski department has the highest potential profits during the winter, because skiing and snowboarding are popular winter sports in Vermont. At the current time the department's sales are about average for company stores in the Northeast region, with potential for considerable improvement. On several occasions Bill noticed a line of customers waited to be served in the ski department, and he overheard some of them grumbling about how long it takes to get served. One customer said he was leaving to go to another store that didn't make him "wait all day to have the privilege of spending hundreds of dollars on ski equipment." Bill observed that Sally Jorgenson, the department manager, spends a lot of time socializing with her salespeople and with customers, including friends who drop in to visit and talk about ski conditions, resorts, fashions, equipment, racing, and so forth. Bill, who doesn't ski, cannot understand what they find so interesting to talk about. He wonders why anybody in their right mind would want to spend a small fortune and risk permanent injury to hurtle down a mountain in blizzard conditions, and then stand in long lines and ride up a freezing chairlift just to do it all over again!

Copyright © 1987 By Gary Yukl

Questions

1. How much of each type of power does Bill have at this time?
2. What influence tactics could be used in this situation to influence Sally? Explain what you would actually say to Sally in the process of using each tactic.
3. What should Bill do to improve store performance?

CASE 3

Promotion Dilemma

Rahul Srivastava is the CEO and MD of Enjoy Fit, a chain of premium fitness centers in India, with its head office at Delhi. Enjoy Fit has 22 branches across India; however, it has a dominant presence in the North, with over 12 branches. Rahul has plans to expand in the East and South, where there are only three branches. Usually, each branch has a manager, three weight-training instructors, two aerobics instructors, two yoga instructors, and three to four helpers and cleaners. Enjoy Fit has a great reputation in India because of the quality, domain knowledge, and customer orientation of its staff. Many of the instructors are national-level champions in their domains.

Rahul has traditionally hired managers from Delhi and sent them to different locations after the initial orientation. However, other branch employees are hired locally. In addition, most of the managers across locations have grown within the organization and been promoted from being instructors. Rahul usually checks the mobility of the employees before he hires them. Enjoy Fit has enjoyed low attrition rate among its employees as well as customers.

Rahul has two instructors who are now due for promotions and there is only one vacancy for a manager's position at a new location. Here are the profiles of these two instructors.

1. Arvind is a weight-training instructor. He is an undergraduate in physical training and is 31 years old. Arvind has been with Enjoy Fit for nearly six years now. He has won the Weight Lifting National Championship twice. In all, he is an expert in his domain.

   Arvind has some very loyal clients; however, they are limited. Being a hard taskmaster, he often offends new clients. He uses slang and colloquial language, which motivates those who are committed; however, it often irritates new clients who are there only for fitness and not body building. This behavior of Arvind has earned him the confidence of clients who are committed to bodybuilding. However, many middle-aged and senior clients do not see him as suitable for their fitness needs. Arvind has won two national and three state-level championships. He also had limited instances of injuries.

2. Dharmendra is a yoga instructor. He has been trained in a local yoga institute. Because of the humble financial condition of his family, he could not go to college. Dharmendra is 36 years old and has been employed by Enjoy Fit for the past 12 years. He teaches the basic and preliminary levels of yoga to new clients. After the clients have learned the basics, they are transferred to teams who teach advanced yoga.

   Dharmendra is more of a friend than an instructor. He has many clients who had begun with him and now are at advanced stages but are still friends with him. In fact, because of his good relationships with clients, he has had many new clients referred to him.

Questions

1. Of the two instructors, whom should Rahul promote?
2. Analyze the situation from the perspective of various sources of power with Arvind and Dharmendra.

CASE 4

Mahatma Gandhi's Address

Before presenting a statement to Lord Selborne, M. K. Gandhi addressed His Excellency, and his speech is as follows:

"Before I deal with the statement I am to baud to your Excellency, I have been asked to mention two matters that have occurred during your recent tour through the Transvaal. Your Excellency is reported to have said at Potchefstroom that, 'no non-refuges British Indians would be allowed to enter the Colony until the Representative Assembly has considered the question next year.'

If the report is correct, it would, as I hope to show this afternoon, be a very grave injustice to the vested rights of the Indian community. At Ermelo, your Excellency is reported to have used the expression 'Coolie Storekeepers.' This expression has given very great offence to the British Indians in the Colony, but the British Indian Association has assured them that the expression has probably not been used by your Excellency or if it has, your Excellency is incapable of giving thereby any intentional offence to British Indian storekeepers. The use of the word "coolie" has caused a great deal of mischief in Natal. At one time, it became so serious that the then Justice, Sir Walter Wagg, had to intervene and put down the use of that expression in connection with any but indentured Indians, it having been imported into the Court of Justice. As your Excellency may be aware, it means 'laborer' or 'porter.' Used, therefore, in connection with traders, it is not only offensive, but a contradiction in terms."

Pt. Jawahar Lal Nehru's First Address as the Prime Minister of India

Tryst with Destiny

"Long years ago, we made a tryst with destiny, and now that time comes when we shall redeem our pledge, not wholly or in full measure, but very substantially. At the stroke of the midnight hour, when the world sleeps, India will awake to life and freedom. A moment comes, which comes but rarely in history, when we step out from the old to new, when an age ends, and when the soul of a nation, long suppressed, finds utterance.

It is fitting that at this solemn moment, we take the pledge of dedication to the service of India and her people and to the still larger cause of humanity with some pride.

At the dawn of history, India started on her unending quest, and trackless centuries, which are filled with her striving and the grandeur of her successes and her failures. Through good and ill fortunes alike, she has never lost sight of that quest or forgotten the ideals which gave her strength. We end today a period of ill fortunes and India discovers herself again.

The achievement we celebrate today is but a step, an opening of opportunity, to the greater triumphs and achievements that await us. Are we brave enough and wise enough to grasp this opportunity and accept the challenge of the future?

Freedom and power bring responsibility. That responsibility rests upon this assembly, a sovereign body representing the sovereign people of India. Before the birth of freedom, we have endured all the pains of labor and our hearts are heavy with the memory of this sorrow. Some of those pains continue even now. Nevertheless, the past is over and it is the future that beckons to us now.

That future is not one of ease or resting but of incessant striving so that we might fulfill the pledges we have so often taken and the one we shall take today. The service of India means the service of the millions who suffer. It means the ending of poverty and ignorance and disease and inequality of opportunity.

The ambition of the greatest man of our generation has been to wipe every tear from every eye. That may be beyond us, but so long as there are tears and suffering, so long our work will not be over.

And so we have to labor and to work, and work hard, to give reality to our dreams. Those dreams are for India, but they are also for the world, for all the nations and people are too closely knit together today for any one of them to imagine that it can live apart.

Peace has been said to be indivisible; so is freedom, so is prosperity now, and so also is disaster in this One World that can no longer be split into isolated fragments.

To the people of India, whose representatives we are, we make an appeal to join us with faith and confidence in this great adventure. This is no time for petty and destructive criticism, no time for ill will or blaming others. We have to build the noble mansion of free India where all her children may dwell.

The appointed day has come—the day appointed by destiny—and India stands forth again, after long slumber and struggle, awake, vital, free, and independent. The past clings on to us still in some measure and we have to do much before we redeem the pledges we have so often taken. Yet the turning point is past, and history begins anew for us, the history which we shall live and act and others will write about.

A new star rises, the star of freedom in the east, a new hope comes into being, a vision long cherished materializes. May the star never set and that hope never be betrayed by!

On this day, our first thoughts go to the architect of this freedom, the father of our nation, who, embodying the old spirit of India, held aloft the torch of freedom and lighted up the darkness that surrounded us. We have often been unworthy followers of his and have strayed from his message. We shall never allow that torch of freedom to be blown out, however high the wind or stormy the tempest.

We have hard work ahead. There is no resting for any one of us till we redeem our pledge in full, till we make all the people of India what destiny intended them to be.

We are citizens of a great country, on the verge of bold advance, and we have to live up to that high standard. All of us, to whatever religion we may belong, are equally the children of India with equal rights, privileges, and obligations.

And to India, our much-loved motherland, the ancient, the eternal and the ever-new, we pay our reverent homage and we bind ourselves afresh to her service. Jai Hind. Jai Hind."

Questions

1. What are the different influencing techniques used in these two speeches?
2. What are the contextual differences in time when these speeches were made?

Dyadic Relations and Followers

Learning Objectives

After studying this chapter, you should be able to:

- Understand why different dyadic relationships develop between a leader and subordinates.
- Understand how leaders are influenced by attributions about subordinates.
- Understand appropriate ways to manage a subordinate with performance deficiencies.
- Understand how leaders and followers attempt to manage impressions.
- Understand how attributions and implicit theories influence follower perception of a leader.
- Understand how followers can have a more effective relationship with their leader.

Sudhir, a freedom fighter and now a social activist, was once engaged in a fierce debate with his 10-year-old grandson, Rajul. This debate was about a pencil that Rajul had picked up from his classroom in school. He was arguing that when he picked up the pencil, all the students had left for the day. And if he had left the pencil, it would have ended up in the dustbin after the sweeping and cleaning that took place every day after school. Sudhir was trying to explain to Rajul that he should have given the pencil to his class teacher, or submitted it in the Lost and Found department of the school. According to Sudhir, this was an act of theft and Rajul should have avoided it.

After listening to this debate for some time, Rajat, Rajul's father, walked up to them and tried to enquire about the debate. At the end, Rajat understood that his father had a point. He tried to explain the situation to Rajul politely and patiently. He said, "Rajul, if you need pencils, you can ask me. Have I ever denied you such petty things? In future, you ask me for as many pencils as you want, I will get them for you from my office."

After listening to this statement, Sudhir took a deep breath of frustration and left the room.

Most of the early research on leadership behavior did not consider how much leaders vary their behavior with different subordinates. However, dyadic relationships are not identical for all of a leader's direct subordinates. This chapter begins with a theory that describes how a unique *exchang e relationship* is developed with each subordinate and the implications of these relationships for effective leadership. Next, attribution theory is examined to discover how leaders interpret subordinate performance and decide how to react to it. Research on upward *impression management* is examined to see how subordinates attempt to influence a leader's perception of their competence and motivation. This part of the chapter also has some guidelines on how leaders can deal with unsatisfactory performance and improve the quality of the exchange relationship.

The chapter then turns to follower-based approaches to leadership. Most leadership literature over the past half-century has focused on leaders. The attitudes and behavior of leaders have been examined in detail, but until recently, follower attitudes and behavior were only examined as an indicator of leader influence and effectiveness. Without followers there would be no leaders, and interest in studying followership has been increasing. This chapter describes research on follower evaluation of leader effectiveness. The chapter includes guidelines on how to be an effective follower while remaining true to one's values. The chapter ends with a brief discussion about integrating leader and follower roles in organizations.

From Chapter 9 of *Leadership in Organizations,* Eighth Edition. Gary Yukl. Copyright © 2013 by Pearson Education, Inc. Publishing as Prentice Hall. All rights reserved.

Leader-Member Exchange Theory

Leader-member exchange (LMX) theory describes the role-making processes between a leader and each individual subordinate and the exchange relationship that develops over time (Dansereau, Graen, & Haga, 1975; Graen & Cashman, 1975). The basic premise of the theory is that leaders develop an exchange relationship with each subordinate as the two parties mutually define the subordinate's role. The exchange relationships are formed on the basis of personal compatibility and subordinate competence and dependability. According to the theory, most leaders develop a high-exchange relationship with a small number of trusted subordinates who function as assistants, lieutenants, or advisors. These relationships are formed gradually over a period of time, through reciprocal reinforcement of behavior as the exchange cycle is repeated over and over again. Unless the cycle is broken, the relationship is likely to evolve to the point where there is a high degree of mutual dependence, loyalty, and support.

The basis for establishing a high-exchange relationship is the leader's control over outcomes that are desirable to a subordinate. These outcomes include such things as assignment to interesting and desirable tasks, delegation of greater responsibility and authority, more sharing of information, involvement in making some of the leader's decisions, tangible rewards such as a pay increase, special benefits (e.g., better work schedule, bigger office), personal support and approval, and facilitation of the subordinate's career (e.g., recommending a promotion, giving developmental assignments with high visibility). In return for receiving these benefits, the subordinate in a high-exchange relationship provides various types of benefits to the leader (Wilson, Sin, & Conlon, 2010). The subordinate is usually expected to work harder, to be more committed to task objectives, to be loyal to the leader, and to carry out additional responsibilities such as helping with some of the leader's administrative duties.

The benefits to the leader from a high-exchange relationship are evident. Subordinate commitment is important when the leader's work unit has tasks that require considerable initiative and effort on the part of some members to be carried out successfully. The assistance of committed subordinates can be invaluable to a manager who lacks the time and energy to carry out all of the administrative duties for which he or she is responsible. However, the high-exchange relationships create certain obligations and constraints for the leader. To maintain these relationships, the leader must provide attention to the subordinates, remain responsive to their needs and feelings, and rely more on time-consuming influence methods such as persuasion and consultation. The leader cannot resort to coercion or heavy-handed use of authority without endangering the special relationship.

A low-exchange relationship is characterized by less mutual influence. These subordinates need only comply with formal role requirements (e.g., duties, rules, standard procedures, and legitimate directions from the leader), and each subordinate receives only the standard benefits for the job (such as a salary). The early version of the theory described an "in-group" of subordinates with high-exchange subordinates and an "outgroup" of subordinates with low-exchange relationships, but later versions did not make such a sharp dichotomy and included the possibility of a high-exchange relationship with all of a leader's subordinates.

Research on LMX

The way in which LMX has been defined has varied substantially from study to study. Quality of exchange relationship is usually assumed to involve such things as mutual trust, respect, affection, support, and loyalty. However, sometimes LMX is defined to include other aspects of the relationship, such as negotiating latitude, incremental influence, shared values, affect, reciprocity, obligation, and mutual trust (see Ferris et al., 2009; Schriesheim, Castro, & Cogliser, 1999). Several different measures of LMX have been used since the theory was first proposed, making it more difficult to compare results from different studies.

Only a small number of studies have measured LMX from the perception of both the leader and the follower (e.g., Deluga & Perry, 1994; Liden, Wayne, & Stilwell, 1993; Markham, Yammarino, Murry, & Palanski, 2010; Phillips & Bedeian, 1994; Scandura & Schriesheim, 1994; Sin, Nahrgang, & Morgeson, 2009; Zhou & Schriesheim, 2009, 2010). It is reasonable to expect agreement about something as important as a leader-subordinate relationship, but the amount of agreement is often low, especially when there has been limited time together and limited interaction frequency. The reason for a lack of stronger agreement is not clear, but it appears to involve a difference in the basis for evaluating it. Subordinate ratings of LMX are strongly influenced by how supportive and fair the leader is with the subordinate, whereas leader ratings of LMX are strongly influenced by judgments about the subordinate's competence and dependability. More research is needed to determine what LMX scores from each source actually mean and to clarify the implications of measuring exchange relationships from different perspectives.

Determinants and Consequences of LMX

Most of the research on LMX theory has examined how LMX is related to other variables. This research includes a large number of survey field studies, a smaller number of laboratory experiments, a few field experiments, and a few studies that used observation and analysis of communication patterns within high versus low LMX relationships (e.g., Fairhurst, 1993; Kramer, 1995).

One set of studies examined factors that predict the quality of the exchange relationship for a dyad. A favorable relationship is more likely when the subordinate is perceived to be competent and has values and attitudes that are similar to those of the leader. Some personality traits for the leader and subordinate may also be related to their exchange relationship. For example, a study by Nahrgang, Morgeson, and Ilies (2009) found that high scores on extraversion and agreeableness for both leader and member predicted development of a more favorable exchange relationship in the early stages of a new team simulation exercise, presumably because these traits are associated with a more supportive and trusting style of interaction. However, after the initial period of interaction, performance was a more important determinant of LMX.

Another set of studies examined how LMX is related to leader and subordinate behavior. When the exchange relationship is favorable, behavior by the leader is more supportive and includes more consultation and delegation, more mentoring, less close monitoring, and less domination of conversations. The behavior of a high LMX subordinate includes more support of the leader, more honest communication with the leader, and less use of pressure tactics (e.g., threats, demands) to influence the leader. It is not clear how much a new subordinate can directly influence the role-making process, for example by using impression management behavior, but it is likely that some subordinates are proactive about developing a favorable relationship rather than passively accepting whatever the leader decides to do.

A substantial body of research has now examined the relationship between LMX and outcomes such as subordinate attitudes and performance, and detailed reviews of research on the correlates of LMX can be found in various articles (e.g., Erdogan & Liden, 2002; Gerstner & Day, 1997; Ilies, Nahrgang, & Morgeson, 2007; Liden, Sparrowe, & Wayne, 1997; Schriesheim et al., 1999). The research found that a favorable downward exchange relationship was usually correlated with more role clarity, higher satisfaction, stronger organizational commitment, more citizenship behaviors, and better subordinate performance. A favorable exchange relationship is also correlated with a high level of subordinate trust, although reciprocal causality is likely (Dirks & Ferrin, 2002). Most of the research on correlates of LMX involved survey field studies, but a rare field experiment found that leaders trained to develop favorable exchange relationships with their subordinates had subsequent gains in the objective performance and satisfaction of their subordinates (Graen, Novak, & Sommerkamp, 1982; Scandura & Graen, 1984). To incorporate the results of the research on outcomes, the revised theory included the prescription that the leader should try to establish a special exchange relationship with all subordinates if possible, not just with a few favorites (Graen & Uhl-Bien, 1995).

A few studies also found that a leader's upward dyadic relationship affects downward dyadic relationships (Cashman, Dansereau, Graen, & Haga, 1976; Graen, Cashman, Ginsburgh, & Schiemann, 1977). A manager who has a favorable exchange relationship with the boss is more likely to establish favorable exchange relationships with subordinates. A favorable upward relationship enables a manager to obtain more benefits for subordinates and to facilitate their performance by obtaining necessary resources, cutting red tape, and gaining approval of changes desired by subordinates. Subordinates feel less motivation to incur the extra obligations of a special exchange relationship if the leader has little to offer in the way of extra benefits, opportunities, and empowerment. The research found that the effects of a manager's upward relationship were felt by subordinates regardless of their own relationship with the manager. Managers with a favorable upward relationship with their own boss were described by subordinates as having more technical skill, providing more outside information, allowing more participation in decision making, allowing more subordinate autonomy, and providing more support and consideration.

Evaluation of LMX Theory

LMX theory still has a number of conceptual weaknesses that limit its utility (Dienesh & Liden, 1986; Schriesheim et al., 1999; Vecchio & Gobdel, 1984). Revisions of the theory have attempted to remedy some of the deficiencies, but additional improvements are needed. The theory needs more elaboration about the way exchange relationships evolve over time. Despite the growing body of research on LMX, we still know little about how the role-making process actually occurs. The theory implies that exchange relationships evolve in a continuous, smooth fashion, starting from initial impressions. The few longitudinal studies suggest that LMX relationships may form quickly and remain stable. However, evidence from other research on dyadic relationships suggest that they typically progress through a series of ups and downs, with shifts in attitudes and behavior as the two parties attempt to reconcile their desire for autonomy with their desire for closer involvement (see Fairhurst, 1993). To resolve these inconsistencies, longitudinal research is needed, with methods that can record the pattern of interactions over time in more detail and probe more deeply into each party's changing perceptions of the relationship.

The theory would be improved by a clear description of the way a leader develops different dyadic relationships, how they affect each other, and how they affect group performance. Research on the antecedents and consequences of LMX differentiation was reviewed in a recent article (Henderson, Liden, Glibkowski, & Chaudhry, 2009). Some differentiation is likely to benefit group performance, especially if it is perceived by members as fair and appropriate to facilitate team performance (Liden, Erdogan, Wayne, & Sparrowe, 2006). However, as differentiation increases, there is more likely to be feelings of resentment among low-exchange members who believe the leader's "favorites" are getting more benefits than they deserve (McClane, 1991; Yukl, 1989). The negative effects of extreme differentiation will be greater in some types of situations than in others. For example, negative effects are more likely for an interacting team, because competition and hostility among members can undermine necessary cooperation. Leader behaviors directed at selected individuals to increase their self-efficacy and identification with the leader may have positive effects for those individuals but negative effects on group performance (Wu, Tsui, & Kinicki, 2010).

The challenge for a leader is to develop differentiated relationships with some subordinates to facilitate achievement of the team's mission, while maintaining a relationship of mutual trust, respect, and loyalty with the other subordinates. It is not necessary to treat all subordinates exactly the same, but each person should perceive that he or she is an important and respected member of the team rather than a "second-class citizen." Not every subordinate may desire more responsibility, but each person should perceive an equal opportunity based on competence rather than arbitrary favoritism.

There has been little research on situational conditions affecting the development of exchange relationships (Green, Anderson, & Shivers, 1996). Some aspects of the situation that are likely to be relevant include demographic attributes of work unit members, job characteristics, work unit characteristics (e.g., size, function, stability of membership), and type of organization. These situational variables may affect the type of dyadic relationships that occur, the underlying exchange processes, and the implications for effective leadership. For example, in a large work unit with diverse activities, it is desirable to have one or more assistant managers if the organization has not created formal positions for them, whereas an assistant manager is less important in small units with simple activities.

Leader Attributions About Subordinates

How a leader acts toward a subordinate varies depending on whether the subordinate is perceived as competent and loyal, or incompetent and untrustworthy. The assessment of competence and dependability is based on interpretation of the subordinate's behavior and performance. Attribution theory describes the cognitive processes used by leaders to determine the reasons for effective or ineffective performance and the appropriate reaction (Green & Mitchell, 1979; Martinko & Gardner, 1987; Mitchell, Green, & Wood, 1981; Wood & Mitchell, 1981).

Two-Stage Attribution Model

Green and Mitchell (1979) described the reaction of a manager to poor performance as a two-stage process. In the first stage, the manager tries to determine the cause of the poor performance; in the second stage, the manager tries to select an appropriate response to correct the problem. Several studies confirm the major propositions of the model (see review by Martinko, Harvey, & Douglas, 2007).

Managers attribute the major cause of poor performance either to something internal to the subordinate (e.g., lack of effort or ability) or to external problems beyond the subordinate's control (e.g., the task had inherent obstacles, resources were inadequate, information was insufficient, other people failed to provide necessary support, or it was just plain bad luck). An external attribution is more likely when (1) the subordinate has no prior history of poor performance on similar tasks; (2) the subordinate performs other tasks effectively; (3) the subordinate is doing as well as other people who are in a similar situation; (4) the effects of failures or mistakes are not serious or harmful; (5) the manager is dependent on the subordinate for his or her own success; (6) the subordinate is perceived to have other redeeming qualities (popularity, leadership skills); (7) the subordinate has offered excuses or an apology; or (8) evidence indicates external causes. Managers with prior experience doing the same kind of work as the subordinate are more likely to make *external attributions,* perhaps because they know more about the external factors that can affect performance (Crant & Bateman, 1993; Mitchell & Kalb, 1982). Manager traits such as internal locus of control orientation can also influence attributions (Ashkanasy & Gallois, 1994).

A perceived reasons for a problem influences the manager's response to it (e.g., Dugan, 1989; Offermann, Schroyer, & Green, 1998; Trahan & Steiner, 1994). When an external attribution is made, the manager is more likely to respond by trying to change the situation, such as providing more resources, providing assistance in removing obstacles, providing better information, changing the task to reduce inherent difficulties, or in the case of bad luck, by showing sympathy or doing nothing. When an *internal attribution* is made and the manager determines that the problem is insufficient ability, the likely response is to provide detailed instruction, monitor the subordinate's work more closely, provide coaching when needed, set easier goals or deadlines, or assign the subordinate to an easier job. If the problem is perceived to be lack of subordinate effort and responsibility, then the likely reaction is to give directive or nondirective counseling, give a warning or reprimand, punish the subordinate, monitor subsequent behavior more closely, or find new incentives.

Other Determinants of Leader Attributions

Attributions about subordinates and the leader's reaction are affected by a leader's position power (Kipnis, Schmidt, Price, & Stitt, 1981; McFillen & New, 1979). The more position power a leader has, the more likely the leader will attribute effective performance and acceptable behavior by a subordinate to extrinsic factors (i.e., done only to gain rewards or avoid punishments) rather than to intrinsic motivation.

Research on attributions also found that the exchange relationship influences the manager's perception of a subordinate's performance (Duarte, Goodson, & Klich, 1994; Heneman, Greenberger, & Anonyuo, 1989; Lord & Maher, 1991). Leaders appear to be less critical in evaluating the performance of subordinates when there is a high-exchange relationship than when there is a low-exchange relationship. Effective performance is more likely to be attributed to internal causes for a high-exchange member and to external causes for a low-exchange member. In contrast, poor performance is likely to be attributed to external causes for a high-exchange member and to internal causes for a low-exchange member.

The leader's behavior toward the subordinate is consistent with the attribution about performance. For example, effective behavior by a high-exchange subordinate is more likely to be praised, and mistakes by a low-exchange subordinate are more likely to be criticized. Thus, the leader's perception of a subordinate tends to become a self-fulfilling prophecy. Low-exchange subordinates get less support, coaching, and resources, yet when they make mistakes or have performance difficulties, the manager blames them rather than recognizing situational causes and his or her own contribution to the problem.

The bias of many managers toward making internal attributions about poor performance by a subordinate is in sharp contrast to the self-serving bias of subordinates to blame their mistakes or failures on external factors (Martinko & Gardner, 1987). These incompatible biases make it more difficult for the manager to deal with performance problems. The manager's bias results in greater use of punitive actions, which are resented all the more by subordinates who do not feel responsible for the problem (Harvey, Martinko, & Douglas, 2006; Tjosvold, 1985). Thus, a major implication of the attribution research is the need to help managers become more careful, fair, and systematic about evaluating subordinate performance. Managers need to become more aware of the many options available for dealing with different causes of performance problems and the importance of selecting an appropriate one.

Leader Influence on Follower Emotions

Understanding the influence of a leader on followers requires an analysis of the emotions and moods of both parties in addition to their cognitions, actions, and decisions. Emotions are brief, intense reactions (e.g., joy, passion, elation, surprise, anger, sadness, despair, grief) to an event or person, whereas moods are longer, less intense, and are not focused on a specific event or person. Moods can affect the performance of individuals or groups, and leaders can influence the mood of followers in various ways. An important research question in recent years is how follower moods or emotions are affected by the leader's mood or emotions, and the implications for effective leadership (Ashkanasy & Jordan, 2008; Bono, Foldes, Vinson, & Muros, 2007; Gooty, Connelly, Griffith, & Gupta, 2010).

Forms of influence that can influence a positive mood among followers include acting cheerful and enthusiastic, making an inspiring visionary speech about a new initiative, and expressing optimism and confidence when followers are discouraged by problems and stress in their work. The process may involve emotional contagion from leader to followers and among the followers themselves. In some situations, influence can be increased by the expression of negative emotions. For example, by expressing anger and disappointment, a leader can emphasize the seriousness of criticism for irresponsible actions or behavior that seriously endangers others. However, the effective use of negative emotions by a leader requires considerable skill.

The influence processes involving emotions and mood can occur at a group or organizational level as well as at a dyadic level (Dasborough, Ashkanasy, Tee, & Tse, 2009). Through a process of emotional contagion, the emotions of individual followers can spread to others. Positive or negative emotions can affect cognitive attributions about a leader and perception of the leader's effectiveness by other members of the organization besides direct subordinates.

Guidelines for Correcting Performance Deficiencies

Correcting performance deficiencies is an important but difficult managerial responsibility. People tend to be defensive about criticism, because it threatens their self-esteem and may imply personal rejection. Many managers avoid confronting subordinates about inappropriate behavior or poor performance, because such confrontations often degenerate into an emotional conflict that fails to deal with the underlying problem, or does so only at the cost of lower respect and trust between the parties. Corrective feedback may be necessary to help a subordinate improve, but it should be done in a way that will preserve a favorable relationship or improve a relationship that is already strained.

Insights about the most effective way to provide corrective feedback are provided by the research on dyadic leadership processes, together with related research on counseling, feedback, and conflict. Effective managers take a supportive, problem-solving approach when dealing with inappropriate behavior or deficient performance by a subordinate. The following guidelines show how to improve communication and problem solving while reducing defensiveness and resentment (see summary in Table 1).

- **Gather information about the performance problem.**

Before confronting a subordinate about a performance deficiency, it is helpful to have the facts straight. It is especially important to do some fact finding when you did not directly observe the subordinate doing something improper. Gather information about the timing (when did problems occur, how many times), magnitude (what were the negative consequences, how serious were they), antecedents (what led up to the problems, what was the subordinate's involvement), and scope (did the problems occur only for the subordinate, or did others experience the same problems). If information about a subordinate's unsatisfactory behavior is second hand (passed on by somebody else), try to obtain a detailed account from the party who initiated the complaint. If the problem occurred previously, identify any prior actions that were taken to deal with it.

- **Try to avoid attribution biases.**

There may be more than one reason for inadequate performance, and the leader should not assume that a performance problem is due to a lack of subordinate motivation or competence. As noted previously, a performance deficiency may be due to situational causes, internal causes, or a combination of both. Situational causes that are usually beyond the control of the subordinate include the following: shortages in supplies, materials, or personnel; unexpected or unusual events (e.g., accidents, bad weather, sabotage, lawsuits, new regulations); resource levels below budgeted levels due to last-minute cuts or shifts in priorities; and failure by people in other parts of the organization or outsiders to carry out their part of a project

TABLE 1	Guidelines for Correcting Performance Deficiencies

- Gather information about the performance problem.
- Try to avoid attribution biases.
- Provide corrective feedback promptly.
- Describe the deficiency briefly in specific terms.
- Explain the adverse impact of ineffective behavior.
- Stay calm and professional.
- Mutually identify the reasons for inadequate performance.
- Ask the person to suggest remedies.
- Express confidence that the person can improve.
- Express a sincere desire to help the person.
- Reach agreement on specific action steps.
- Summarize the discussion and verify agreement.

properly and on time. Internal causes for poor performance usually involve low motivation or deficiencies in subordinate skill. Examples of this type of problem include the following: failure to carry out a major action step on schedule, failure to monitor progress to detect a problem before it becomes serious, showing poor judgment in dealing with a problem, procrastinating in dealing with a problem until it gets worse, failure to notify superiors about a problem that requires their attention, making an avoidable error in the performance of a task, failure to follow standard procedures and rules, and acting in an unprofessional manner.

- **Provide corrective feedback promptly.**

Corrective feedback should be provided soon after the problem is noticed rather than waiting until a later time when the person may not remember the incident. Deal immediately withimproper behavior that you observe, and handle other performance problems (complaints about a subordinate, substandard quality or productivity) as soon as you can conduct a preliminary investigation. Some managers save up criticisms for the annual appraisal meeting or scheduled progress review meetings, but this practice is likely to be ineffective. By delaying feedback, you lose the opportunity to deal with the problem immediately before it becomes worse. Moreover, by not responding to inappropriate or ineffective behavior, the wrong message may be sent, namely that the behavior is acceptable or not of any consequence. Finally, a person is likely to be more defensive after hearing a barrage of criticisms at the same time.

- **Describe the deficiency briefly in specific terms.**

Feedback is more effective if it involves specific behavior or specific examples of performance deficiencies. Vague, general criticism ("Your work is sloppy") may not communicate what the person is doing wrong and is easier for the person to deny. Provide specific examples of what was done, where it occurred, and when it occurred. For example, instead of saying a person is rude, point out that he interrupted you twice this week with trivial questions when you were talking to other people (describe when the incident happened and give examples). When criticizing performance, cite specific examples of unsatisfactory performance. For example, point out that two customers complained about slow service by the person's department. Avoid exaggeration such as "You are always late." Keep the description of ineffective behavior brief. The longer the person has to listen to criticism, even when constructive, the more defensive the person is likely to get.

- **Explain the adverse impact of ineffective behavior.**

Corrective feedback is more useful if it includes an explanation of the reason why a person's behavior is inappropriate or ineffective. For example, describe how the behavior causes problems for others and interferes with their work. Describe the discomfort and distress you or others experienced as a result of the person's inappropriate behavior. Describe how the person's behavior jeopardizes the success of an important project or mission and express your personal concern about it.

- **Stay calm and professional.**

It is appropriate to show concern about a performance problem or mistake, but corrective feedback should be provided without expressing anger or personal rejection. A manager who blows up, yells at the person, and makes insulting remarks (e.g., calling the person stupid and lazy) is unlikely to motivate the person to improve his or her performance. Moreover, this type of behavior impedes problem solving and undermines the relationship between manager and subordinate. Avoid accusations and insults ("Why did you do such a stupid thing?") that will make the person defensive. Criticize behavior instead of the person. Make it clear that you value the person and want to help him or her to deal with the performance problem.

- **Mutually identify the reasons for inadequate performance.**

Even after a preliminary investigation into the causes of a performance problem, you may lack important information that would change your perception of it. It is essential to listen to the subordinate's explanation for the problem, rather than jumping to conclusions about the causes. Give the person an opportunity to explain errors, inadequate performance, or inappropriate behavior. Sometimes the person may not know the reason or may make excuses rather than admitting responsibility. Be careful to differentiate between situational causes and personal causes. Personal causes of inadequate performance are harder to detect, because a subordinate is usually reluctant to admit mistakes and failures. When probing to discover these causes, ask what lessons were learned from the experience and what the subordinate would do differently if given the opportunity to go back and start over again. Keep the discussion of personal causes focused on specific behavior that was ineffective or inappropriate rather than on personal attributes such as poor judgment, irresponsibility, or lack of motivation. Mutually identify all of the important reasons in a careful, systematic manner, rather than moving immediately to a discussion of corrective actions.

- **Ask the person to suggest remedies.**

It is essential to get the person to take responsibility for dealing with a performance deficiency. Improvement is unlikely if the person makes excuses and denies responsibility for the problem. Commitment to improve is more likely if the person suggests ways to deal with the problem. Thus, when discussing how to correct performance deficiencies, begin by asking for suggestions rather than telling the person what to do. Use open-ended questions such as "What ideas do you have for improving performance?" and "What can we do to avoid this problem in the future?" Encourage the person to consider a variety of possible remedies, rather than focusing quickly on one narrow remedy. Try to build on the subordinate's ideas rather than merely pointing out limitations. If the subordinate fails to identify some promising remedies, try to present your own ideas as variations of the subordinate's ideas. State your ideas in a general, tentative way ("What about the possibility of . . . ?") and let the subordinate develop the details so he or she feels some ownership of the improvement plans.

- **Express confidence that the person can improve.**

A subordinate who lacks self-confidence and is discouraged about doing poorly on a task is less likely to improve. One important leadership function is to increase a person's confidence that difficult things can be achieved with a concerted effort, despite past failures. Mention the beneficial qualities that can help the person do better. Describe how others overcame similar failures or setbacks. Express confidence that the person will succeed. Research shows that subordinates perform better when the leader has high expectations for them (Eden, 1990; McNatt, 2000).

- **Express a sincere desire to help the person.**

It is essential to communicate your intention to help the person do better. Be alert for opportunities to provide assistance to the subordinate by using your knowledge, influence, or contacts. Subordinates may be reluctant to ask for help if they believe that it is an admission of weakness. If a person's performance is being affected by personal problems (e.g., family problems, financial problems, substance abuse), be prepared to offer assistance if it is requested or is clearly needed. Examples of things that a leader can do include the following: help the person identify and express concerns and feelings, help the person understand the reasons for a personal problem, provide new perspectives on the problem, help the person identify alternatives, offer advice on how to deal with the problem, and refer the person to professionals who can provide assistance.

- **Reach agreement on specific action steps.**

It is essential to identify concrete action steps to be taken by the subordinate. If you discuss possible remedies but end the discussion without agreement on specific action steps, the person may walk away from the meeting without a clear understanding of what he or she is expected to do. Likewise, it is not enough to tell the subordinate to try to do better. Unless the person makes an explicit promise to carry out specific action steps, he or she may quickly forget about the discussion. As part of the explicit agreement, you should clearly state any action steps you will take to help the subordinate improve performance.

- **Summarize the discussion and verify agreement.**

After agreement has been reached, summarize the essence of the discussion. The purpose of a summary is to check for agreement and mutual understanding. As you end the meeting, repeat your willingness to provide assistance and indicate that you are available to discuss any additional problems or complications that may arise. You may also want to set a tentative date and time for a follow-up meeting to review progress.

Follower Attributions and Implicit Theories

Just as leaders make attributions about follower competence, followers make attributions about leader competence and intentions. Followers use information about leader actions, changes in the performance of the team or organization, and external conditions to reach conclusions about responsibility for success or failure. More attributions are made for someone who occupies a high-level position with substantial prestige and power, especially in cultures where leaders are viewed as heroic figures (Calder, 1977; Konst, Vonk, & Van der Vlist, 1999; Meindl, Ehrlich, & Dukerich, 1985; Pfeffer, 1977b).

Determinants of Follower Attributions about Leaders

Several interrelated factors determine how followers assess leader effectiveness (Awamleh & Gardner, 1999; Choi & Mai-Dalton, 1999; Ferris, Bhawuk, Fedor, & Judge, 1995; Lord & Maher, 1991; Meindl, Ehrlich, & Dukerich, 1985; van Knippenberg, van Knippenberg, De Cremer, & Hogg, 2004). One factor is the extent to which clear, timely indicators of performance are available for the leader's team or organization. A leader is usually judged more competent if his or her unit is successful than if it is unsuccessful. The performance trend will also influence follower assessment of the leader. A leader is more likely to be judged competent if performance is improving than if it is declining. Moreover, if performance suddenly increases (or decreases) soon after the leader's term of office begins, more credit or blame for the change will be attributed to the person than if performance remains stable or changes slowly.

Followers also consider the leader's actions. A leader who has done something that could explain a change in performance will be attributed more responsibility for it. Leaders who take direct actions that appear relevant get more credit for performance improvements than leaders who do not. Direct actions that are highly visible to followers influence attributions more than indirect actions that are not visible. The importance of direct action is increased when followers perceive an immediate crisis. A leader who acts decisively to resolve an obvious crisis is considered highly competent, whereas a leader who fails to take direct action in a crisis, or whose action has no apparent effect is likely to be judged incompetent. The uniqueness of changes made by a leader also influences attributions about the leader's competence. Leaders who make innovative changes in the strategy (what is done or how it is done) get more credit for success and more blame for failure than leaders who stick with a traditional strategy.

Followers also use information about the situation to reach conclusions about responsibility for success or failure. Improving performance is less likely to be credited to the leader when external conditions are favorable (e.g., the economy is improving and sales are up for all firms in the industry). Likewise, declining performance is less likely to be blamed on the leader when external conditions are unfavorable (e.g., a new competitor enters the market). Followers may also consider constraints on the leader's decisions and actions (e.g., new government regulations, pressure from superiors). A leader who appears to have considerable power and discretion in deciding what to do is attributed more responsibility for success or failure than a leader who is viewed as a puppet or figurehead.

Followers judge leader intentions as well as leader competence. A leader who appears to be more concerned about followers and the mission than about personal benefit or career advancement will gain more follower approval. Credibility is increased when the leader expresses strong and consistent convictions about a program or change and explains why it is necessary without exaggerating the benefits or ignoring the costs. Dedication to the organization is indicated when the leader takes personal risks to accomplish important objectives and does not benefit materially from them (Yorges, Weiss, & Strickland, 1999). A leader who makes visible self-sacrifices in the service of the organization will be viewed as more sincere and committed. In contrast, leaders who appear insincere or motivated only by personal gain get less credit for making changes that are successful, and receive more blame for making changes that are unsuccessful.

The mood of the followers can also affect attributions about leader intentions. Leaders are more likely to be seen as manipulative and self-serving if followers are in a negative mood (Dasborough & Ashkanasy, 2002). Followers also consider the extent to which the leader appears to be similar to them in terms of values, beliefs, and other qualities they consider important (e.g., religion, gender, ethnic background). Followers who identify strongly with the group or organization are likely to have more trust in a leader who appears to be "one of them" and will make more favorable attributions about the leader (Hogg, Hains, & Mason, 1998). The effect of perceived similarity (called "leader prototypicality") seems to be stronger for leader assessments made after a group failure than after a group success (Giessner, van Knippenberg, & Sleebos, 2009).

It is more difficult to assess leader competence when reliable indicators of performance are absent, followers have no opportunity to observe the leader's actions, or a long delay occurs before leader actions affect performance. Just as leaders tend to be biased toward making internal attributions about followers, followers seem to have a bias toward making internal attributions about leaders, especially when information is ambiguous. Followers usually attribute success or failure more to the leader's personal qualities (e.g., expertise, initiative, creativity, dedication) than to situational factors beyond the control of the leader. Coaches are praised when the team is winning consistently and blamed for repeated losses. The CEO of a company gets credit for increasing profits and is blamed for declining profits.

Implications of Follower Attributions about Leaders

How followers perceive a leader has important implications for the leader and the organization. Leaders perceived to be competent are likely to retain their position or be advanced to a higher position, whereas leaders perceived to be incompetent are likely to be replaced. Leaders who are judged to be competent gain more power and have more discretion to make changes. The amount of legitimate power and discretion allowed a leader depends on the perception by followers and other stakeholders (e.g., board of directors, banks, government agencies, stockholders) that the leader has the expertise to solve important problems facing the organization. This perception depends in large part on how the leader's earlier decisions and actions are interpreted. Attributions about a leader's competence are especially important for top executives, because their long-term influence on the survival and prosperity of the organization depends on their discretion to make innovative, major changes in key areas of organization strategy (Lord & Maher, 1991).

Implicit Leadership Theories

How leaders are evaluated is affected by implicit leadership theories, which are beliefs and assumptions about the characteristics of effective leaders (Eden & Leviatan, 1975; Epitropaki & Martin, 2004; Gioia & Sims, 1985; Lord, Foti, & DeVader, 1984; Offermann, Kennedy, & Wirtz, 1994; Rush, Thomas, & Lord, 1977; Shondrick, Dinh, & Lord, 2010). The implicit theories involve stereotypes and prototypes about the traits, skills, or behaviors that are relevant for a particular type of position (e.g., executive vs. lower-level leader, manager vs. military officer), context (e.g., crisis vs. noncrisis situation), or individual (e.g., male vs. female leader, experienced vs. new leader). Implicit theories are developed and refined over time as a result of actual experience, exposure to literature about effective leaders, and other social-cultural influences (Lord, Brown, Harvey, & Hall, 2001). The implicit theories are influenced by individual beliefs, values, and personality traits, as well as by shared beliefs and values about leaders in the organizational culture and the national culture (Gerstner & Day, 1997; Keller, 1999). Some differences in implicit theories are likely among countries with diverse cultures.

Beliefs about the ideal qualities for a particular type of leader (prototypes) influence the expectations people have for leaders and their evaluation of the leader's actions. *Implicit theories of leadership* determine the perceived relevance of various types of leader behavior (Lord & Maher, 1991). Leaders who do things that are relevant for the situation but inconsistent with follower expectations may be evaluated less favorably than leaders who conform to role expectations. Follower beliefs about desirable leader qualities are influenced by gender role expectations, ethnic stereotypes, and cultural values. The same type of leader behavior may be evaluated more or less favorably depending on the identity of the leader (e.g., male vs. female) and the cultural values of followers (e.g., individualism vs. collectivism). Implicit theories and prototypes about ideal leaders are more important when followers agree about them and identify strongly with their group or organization (e.g., Hogg et al., 2006).

Implicit leadership theories, prototypes, and attributions can jointly influence ratings on leadership behavior questionnaires. For example, a leader who is liked or perceived to be effective may be rated higher on behaviors in the rater's conception of an ideal leader than on behaviors not included in this "prototype," regardless of the leader's actual use of the behaviors. Effective performance by a leader's group or organization may be attributed to the leader's use of behaviors assumed to be relevant for performance, even though the respondent did not observe the behaviors or did not remember them correctly. If most respondents in a survey study have a similar implicit theory, their biases may influence the factor structure found for a leader behavior questionnaire. The effects of biases from prototypes and attributions can increase the correlations among behaviors considered desirable and make them appear to be part of the same meta-category. The problem complicates the interpretation of results in survey research on broadly-defined conceptions of effective leaders, such as transformational leadership, authentic leadership, and servant leadership.

Impression Management by Leaders and Followers

Impression management is the process of influencing how others perceive you. Tactics such as excuses and apologies are used in a defensive way to avoid blame for weak performance or to seek forgiveness for a mistake. Other tactics are used to elicit a positive effect and respect from others (e.g., Gardner & Martinko, 1988; Godfrey, Jones, & Lord, 1986; Jones & Pitman, 1982; Tedeschi & Melburg, 1984; Wayne & Ferris, 1990; Wortman & Linsenmeier, 1977). Impression management tactics that seem especially relevant for the study of leadership in dyads are exemplification (a tactic that involves behavior intended to demonstrate dedication and loyalty to the organization and its members), ingratiation (a tactic that involves behavior intended to influence the target person to like the agent and perceive the agent as someone who has desirable social qualities), and self-promotion (a tactic that involves behavior intended to influence favorable impressions about your competence and value to the organization).

Impression Management by Followers

Most studies on impression management have examined how followers attempt to influence bosses. Wayne and Ferris (1990) developed a self-report agent questionnaire to measure how subordinates use impression management tactics for upward influence in organizations. Their study found support for a three-factor model that included "supervisor-focused tactics" (similar to ingratiation), "job-focused tactics" (similar to exemplification), and "self-focused tactics" (similar to self-promotion).

Research on the effects of upward impression management on job outcomes has some limitations that complicate interpretation of the results. An outcome such as a pay increase or job promotion may depend more on a subordinate's actual skills and performance than on the use of self-promotion tactics to focus attention on these qualifications. Moreover, the effectiveness of impression management tactics depends to a great extent on the interpersonal skills of the agent (Ammeter et al., 2002; Turnley & Bolino, 2001), and these skills are also a determinant of performance. It is difficult to assess the independent effects of impression management tactics unless these other likely determinants of job outcomes are also measured, which seldom occurs in the research.

Impression Management by Leaders

Many leaders attempt to create the impression that they are important, competent, and in control of events (Pfeffer, 1977b, 1981). Successes are announced and celebrated, and failures are covered up or downplayed. Salancik and Meindl (1984) analyzed annual reports for a sample of corporations over a period of 18 years and found that top management consistently credited themselves for positive outcomes and blamed negative outcomes on aspects of the environment.

Impression management tactics can be manipulative, but some of the same behaviors can also be used in a positive way by leaders. Praise (a form of ingratiation) can be used to build the confidence of subordinates and improve their performance. Announcing achievements that demonstrate progress in implementing a change initiated by the leader (a form of self-promotion) can increase follower optimism and commitment to make the change successful. Forms of exemplification such as showing courage, making personal sacrifices, volunteering to do extra duties, and acting consistent with espoused values are ways to lead by example and inspire follower commitment to a vision or strategy.

Follower Contributions to Effective Leadership

The tendency to credit successful events to leaders obscures the significant contributions of followers (Baker, 2007). Motivated, competent followers are necessary for the successful performance of work carried out by the leader's unit. Consider the following example (Kelley, 1992).

> Today most people regard the role of Thomas Jefferson in writing the Declaration of Independence as an example of effective leadership by someone who would later become one of our most famous presidents. At the time, however, Jefferson was in a follower role. He was a junior member of the committee and was assigned the task by John Adams and Benjamin Franklin. Few people outside the Continental Congress knew that Jefferson was the principal author, and he received no public recognition until eight years later when his role was explained in a newspaper article.

Followers can contribute to the effectiveness of a group by maintaining cooperative working relationships, providing constructive dissent, sharing leadership functions, and supporting leadership development. This section examines alternative conceptions of the follower role and describes how followers can actively contribute to the effectiveness of their leader.

Follower Identities and Behavior

How followers act in a group or organization can be explained in part by their self and social identities (Collinson, 2006; Lord & Brown, 2004). The follower identities are complex and not necessarily consistent. For example, the self-identity of a loyal member who conforms with norms and policies prescribed by the organization may be inconsistent with the self-identity of a courageous follower who challenges bad decisions and unethical practices. Researchers have begun to study how self and social identities help to explain how followers perceive leaders and how they comply with or resist influence attempts by leaders (e.g., Carsten et al., 2010). Deference, passivity, and obedience will reflect the personality traits of followers, their relationship to the leader, the type of organization, and cultural values such as power distance.

Chaleff (1995) noted that many people define the role of follower in terms of conformity, weakness, and passivity. This negative conception is strongly influenced by early childhood experiences at home and in school, where others are responsible for our behavior but we are not responsible for their behavior. As adults, passivity in follower roles is encouraged by the fact that leaders typically are more powerful, have higher status, are older, and have more experience. The reluctance to challenge a leader is even worse for an established leader who is widely seen as brilliant and successful. Chaleff argues that it is essential to replace this negative conception of followers with a positive conception. In short, effective followers are courageous, responsible, and proactive.

The reason why courageous followers are likely to be more effective stems from the fact that all leaders have weaknesses as well as strengths. Followers can influence whether the strengths are fully utilized and the weaknesses overcome. Some of the qualities that contribute to leadership effectiveness (e.g., self-confidence, strong convictions, a passion for change) also make a leader prone to excessive ambition, risk taking, or righteousness. Followers can help the leader avoid these excesses. Rather than complaining about their leader, followers with valid concerns should help the leader to do better.

To be effective as a follower, it is necessary to find a way to integrate two different follower roles, namely to implement decisions made by a leader and to challenge decisions that are misguided or unethical. Followers must be willing to risk the leader's displeasure, but the risk can be reduced by developing a high level of mutual trust and respect. In such a relationship, a leader is likely to view criticism and dissent as an honest effort to facilitate attainment of shared objectives and values, rather than as an expression of personal rejection or disloyalty.

It takes time and effort to help a leader grow and succeed. If the leader is less competent than you or has been elevated to a position you really deserved, it is especially difficult to make this extra effort. Thus, effective followers are more likely to be people with a strong commitment to the organization and its mission. However, mentoring a weak leader is not without its benefits. In the process of helping the leader, the follower will also learn and develop.

Integrating Leader and Follower Roles

Many members of an organization have the dual roles of leader and follower. For example, a middle manager is the leader of an organizational unit but also a follower of a higherlevel manager. How to integrate these two diverse roles is an interesting question with important implications for leadership effectiveness.

To be effective in both roles simultaneously, it is necessary to find a way to integrate them. Inevitable role conflicts and dilemmas make integration of the two roles difficult. Superiors expect the leader to represent their interests and implement their decisions, but subordinates expect the leader to represent their interests and to challenge decisions that are unwarranted or unfair. Leaders are expected to initiate and guide change, but they are also expected to encourage and support "bottom-up" changes suggested by followers. A leader is held responsible for everything that happens in the team or work unit, but encouraged to empower followers to act on their own in resolving problems. Leaders are also expected to develop followers, which may involve gradually turning over most leadership responsibilities to one or two subordinates designated as likely successors. Issues of how to balance competing interests and resolve role conflicts deserve more attention in the leadership literature.

Self-Management

Self-management is a set of strategies used to influence and improve an individual's own behavior (Manz & Sims, 1980; Sims & Lorenzi, 1992). Self-management is based primarily on control theory. After comparing one's current condition to the desired condition, a person can use behavior in an effort to reduce any discrepancy, monitor progress to assess consequences, and make any necessary corrections in behavior. When a person determines what tasks will be done and how the work will be done, this process is sometimes called *self-leadership* (Manz, 1991). Selfmanagement and self-leadership are appropriately viewed as motivation and self-regulation theories rather than as a leadership theory, but they can serve as a partial substitute for leadership. By taking more responsibility for their own lives, followers do not need to depend so much on leaders to direct and motivate them. Leaders can encourage and facilitate self-management as a way to influence follower satisfaction and development.

Self-management Strategies

Self-management includes both behavioral and cognitive strategies (Sims & Lorenzi, 1992). The behavioral strategies include self-goal setting, self-monitoring, manipulation of cues, self-reward (or criticism), and rehearsal of planned actions. The cognitive strategies include positive *self-talk* and mental imagery.

Behavioral self-management strategies are useful when you are reluctant to do a necessary task or want to change your behavior. For example, set realistic goals to accomplish a task or change a behavior, including subgoals that can be achieved quickly (e.g., a goal to write the first page of a report today; a goal to get through the next hour without saying "you know" to anyone). Then, monitor your own behavior to note what you did and how others reacted (e.g., noticing each time you say something that annoys others; trying different ways of communicating ideas to see which one people respond to most favorably). Compliment yourself for doing something correctly, and reward yourself when you complete a difficult task or accomplish a goal or subgoal (e.g., go to a movie, purchase something you want). Use self-criticism or selfpunishment after acting in an inappropriate way or relapsing into behavior you want to change; for example, after making a careless mistake, work extra hours to correct it. Rehearse a difficult behavior by yourself to improve skill and build confidence you can do it (e.g., practice a presentation in front of the mirror with a tape recorder). Rearrange cues in the immediate physical environment; remove cues that encourage undesirable behavior and replace them with cues that encourage desirable behavior (e.g., go to a quiet place where you will not be disturbed to write a report; purchase only healthy food to avoid being tempted to eat junk food).

Cognitive self-management strategies help you to build self-confidence and optimism about doing a difficult task. One cognitive strategy is positive self-talk, which means emphasizing positive, optimistic thoughts and avoiding negative, pessimistic thoughts (Manz, 1992). An example is to interpret a difficult situation as an opportunity rather than as a problem. The confidence and determination needed to improve are more likely to be found by concentrating on what can be done to make things better than by dwelling on the difficulties or what can go wrong.

To increase positive self-talk, it is necessary to do more than just look for the silver lining in a dark cloud. It is essential to identify and suppress destructive thinking patterns, such as viewing success and failure as extreme conditions with nothing in between, exaggerating the significance of a mistake or setback, stereotyping yourself negatively, dismissing positive feedback as irrelevant ("She's just saying that to be kind"), and assuming blame for something that is not your responsibility. This type of thinking encourages overreaction to mistakes, setbacks, or periods of slow improvement in performance when you are learning a complex new activity or task. A more constructive pattern of thinking is to view performance as a continuum rather than a dichotomy, understand the process involved in learning a complex activity, look for and celebrate signs of progress, accept positive feedback, and be careful about attributing responsibility for failure. Identify destructive thoughts (e.g., "It's hopeless; even after practicing for a week I still made several mistakes") and replace them with constructive thoughts (e.g., "I improved by 20 percent this week, and with additional practice I will do even better").

Another cognitive strategy for self-management is mental imagery, which can be used instead of actually practicing a difficult task. First, you visualize yourself doing the task. Then, you imagine how it would feel to experience the satisfaction of performing it successfully. Before performing an activity, many professional athletes mentally rehearse it, carefully visualizing each movement and how it will feel (Sims & Lorenzi, 1992).

Effects of Self-Management

The consequences of self-management and self-leadership have been assessed in a variety of ways. One research method is to administer a self-report questionnaire such as the one developed by Houghton and Neck (2002), then correlate the scores with measures of each respondent's satisfaction and performance. Another method is a field experiment in which employees are trained to use more self-management, then subsequent job performance of these employees is compared to performance by a control group of employees who did not receive the training. Most studies find that individual self-management can increase satisfaction and performance (see Stewart, Courtright, & Manz, 2010).

How Leaders Encourage Self-Management

A leader can do several things to encourage and facilitate self-management by followers. Encouragement is especially important when followers are dependent on the leader for direction and are not intrinsically motivated by the work. According to some theorists (Manz & Sims, 1991; Sims & Lorenzi, 1992), a primary role of the leader is to help subordinates develop skills in self-management. Leadership activities include explaining the rationale for self-management, explaining how to use behavioral and cognitive self-management strategies, encouraging efforts to use these techniques, and providing enough autonomy to make selfmanagement feasible. The leader should model the use of self-management strategies to set an example for subordinates. The leader should also share information subordinates need to do the work, including sensitive information about strategic plans and the financial performance of the organization. As subordinates develop skills and confidence in self-management, the leader should encourage them to take more responsibility for their own work activities.

Recent Studies in the Field of Leader-Follower Relationships

In a recent study, Mary Uhl-Bien et. al. (2014) demonstrated a complex relationship between leaders and followers. The study suggests that the relationship between the behaviors of leaders and their followers depends upon many complicated variables and the complex relationships among them (see Figure 1). The study also highlights that the final outcome from the exchange of leaders and their followers can be viewed from two perspectives—leaders and followers. As can be seen in figures 2 and 3, the behavioral outcome from leader-follower exchanges mutually depend on each other, and the behaviors of leaders and followers both may be analyzed as a starting point.

Guidelines for Followers

The research on followers has some practical applications (Chaleff, 1995; Kelley, 1992; Whetton & Cameron, 1991). The following guidelines deal with issues such as how to improve one's relationship with a leader, how to resist improper influence from the leader, how to provide advice and coaching to the leader, and how to challenge flawed plans and

	Follower Traits	Follower Motivation	Follower Perceptions and Constructions	
Followership Characteristics	• Political Skill • Goal Orientation • Machiavellianism	• Mission Consciousness • Motivation to Lead • Power Orientation	• FIFTs • Role Orientations • Romance of Leadership • Followership Identity	
	Leader Power	Leader Perceptions and Constructions	Leader Affect	
Leader Characteristics	• Dependence on Leader • Empowerment	• Leader Identity • LIFTs • Perceived Follower Support • Satisfaction with Follower	• Positive and Negative State and Trait Affect	
	Followership Behaviors	Leadership Behaviors		
Followership (and Leadership) Behaviors	• Proactive Behavior • Initiative Taking • Obedience • Resistance • Upward Influence • Voice • Dissent • Feedback Seeking • Advising	• Consultation with Followers • Feedback Seeking • Democratic/Autocratic Decision Making • Development of Followers		
	Individual Follower Outcomes	Individual Leader Outcomes	Relationship Outcomes	Leadership Process Outcomes
Followership Outcomes	• Informal Leadership • High Potential • Follower Effectiveness • Organizational Advancement	• Energy/Burnout/Motivation • Leader Derailment	• LMX • Trust	• Higher Ethical Thinking/ Unethical Conduct • Advancing Change/ Maintaining the Status Quo • Mission Fulfillment • Goal Accomplishment

FIGURE 1 Theoretical Constructs and Variables for the Study of Followership

Source: Uhl-Bien, M., Riggio, R. E., Lowe, K. B., & Carsten, M. K. (2014). Followership theory: A review and research agenda. *The Leadership Quarterly*, 25(1), 83-104.

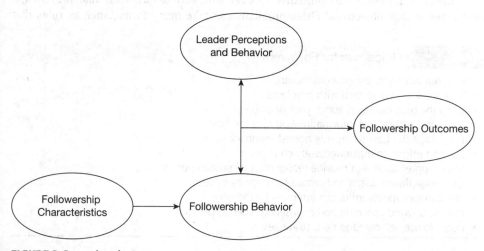

FIGURE 2 Reversing the Lens

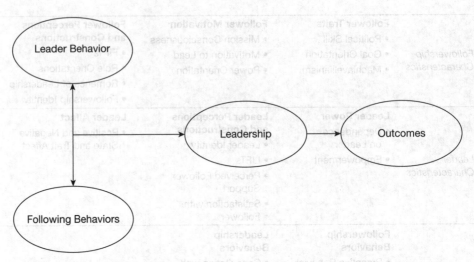

FIGURE 3 The Leadership Process

policies (see Table 2). Underlying themes in the guidelines include maintaining credibility and trust, taking responsibility for your own life, and remaining true to your own values and convictions.

- **Find out what you are expected to do.**

It is difficult to be viewed as competent and reliable if you have role ambiguity and are unsure what you are expected to do. You may be working very hard, but doing the wrong things or doing things the wrong way. It is an important leader responsibility to clearly communicate the role expectations for subordinates. Nevertheless, many leaders fail to explain job responsibilities, scope of authority, performance standards, and the relative priority of different aspects of performance. Sometimes the message is inconsistent, such as when the leader says something is important but acts as if it is not. Sometimes the leader asks for something that is inconsistent with the needs of a client or customer. Followers should be assertive but diplomatic about resolving role ambiguity and conflict.

- **Take the initiative to deal with problems.**

Effective followers take initiative to deal with serious problems that prevent the attainment of task objectives. These problems can take many forms, such as rules that

TABLE 2	Guidelines for Followers

- Find out what you are expected to do.
- Take the initiative to deal with problems.
- Keep the boss informed about your decisions.
- Verify the accuracy of information you give the boss.
- Encourage the boss to provide honest feedback to you.
- Support efforts to make necessary changes.
- Show appreciation and provide recognition when appropriate.
- Challenge flawed plans and proposals made by bosses.
- Resist inappropriate influence attempts by the boss.
- Provide upward coaching and counseling when appropriate.
- Learn to use self-management strategies.

prevent attainment of task objectives, a process that does not achieve the desired results, traditions that are obsolete, conflicts between individuals with interrelated jobs, and unsatisfactory performance by someone over whom you have no authority. Taking initiative may mean pointing out the problem to the boss, suggesting ways to deal with the problem, or if necessary, handling the problem yourself. One way to gain support for changing a flawed process is to conduct a pilot demonstration to show the superiority of a different approach. Taking initiative often involves risks, but if done carefully it can make you a more valuable follower.

- **Keep the boss informed about your decisions.**

Followers who take more initiative to deal with problems also have a responsibility to keep the leader informed about their actions and decisions. It is embarrassing for a leader to hear from someone else that changes have been made. An uninformed leader may appear incompetent to others, and lack of knowledge about ongoing changes may also adversely affect the leader's own actions and decisions. How much and how often you inform the boss about your decisions and actions is a complex issue that may be a subject of continuing discussion and revision as conditions change. Finding the right balance is much easier within a relationship of mutual trust and respect.

- **Verify the accuracy of information you give to the boss.**

An important role of followers is to relay information to their leader. Control over what information is passed on gives a follower power over the leader's perception of events and choices. It is an important responsibility for followers to provide accurate, timely information needed by the leader to make good decisions. The responsibility includes relaying bad news as well as good news. It is important to verify the accuracy of information you are trusted to obtain for the leader. Rumors, complaints, and reports of problems can have a disproportionate effect on the leader's decisions if not verified. It is also important to acknowledge when your information is limited or questionable. Rather than pretending to have expertise about a matter, say that you will look into it immediately and get back to the leader as soon as possible.

- **Encourage the boss to provide honest feedback to you.**

One way to improve mutual trust with the leader is to encourage honest feedback about your performance. If the leader is uncomfortable about expressing concerns about a subordinate's performance, it may be necessary to probe for more information. For example, ask the leader to identify the strongest and weakest aspects of your work. Ask what you can do to be more effective. After an initial response, ask if the leader has concerns about any other aspects of your performance.

- **Support efforts to make necessary changes.**

Contrary to the myth of heroic leaders, most major changes require a cooperative effort of many people in the organization. Leaders need the encouragement and support of loyal followers to overcome resistance to change in organizations. Look for opportunities to express support and encouragement to a leader who is frustrated by difficulties encountered in trying to implement necessary change. Offer to provide assistance to a leader who is temporarily overwhelmed with new work or too preoccupied with an immediate crisis to handle other work that still must be done.

- **Show appreciation and provide recognition when appropriate.**

Leaders can feel unappreciated and taken for granted. It is appropriate to express appreciation when a leader makes a special effort to help you with a problem, represent your interests, or promote your career in the organization. It is also helpful to provide praise when the leader carries out a difficult activity successfully (e.g., negotiating a favorable contract with a client, lobbying successfully for a larger budget, finding a solution to a difficult problem, persuading superiors to authorize a proposed change). These forms of supporting are one way followers can provide feedback to the leader and reinforce desirable leadership practices. Praising the leader is a form of ingratiation that can be used in a manipulative way, but when praise is sincere it can help promote a more favorable relationship with a leader.

- **Challenge flawed plans and proposals made by bosses.**

One of the most valuable contributions a follower can make is to provide accurate feedback about the leader's plans and proposals. To minimize defensiveness, begin with a comment that shows respect and a desire to be helpful in accomplishing shared objectives. For example:

> You know I respect what you are trying to accomplish, and I hope you won't mind if I express some honest concerns about this proposal.

Describe any obvious faults in a plan or proposal using specific terms rather than vague generalities and avoid making the critique personal. If appropriate, suggest getting reactions from other credible people before going ahead with a plan or proposal that is questionable. Following is an example:

> This change may cause some serious problems for the operations group. Shouldn't we consult with them first before going ahead with it? They are likely to have some good ideas on how to avoid problems that are not obvious to us.

Sometimes a boss may be unwilling to listen to concerns about a decision or policy that is unethical, illegal, or likely to have adverse consequences for the organization. In this situation, it may be necessary to escalate your influence attempt and use pressure tactics such as threats and warnings. Threatening to resign is one way for a follower to express deep concern over a controversial decision. However, such threats should not be used lightly, and they are appropriate only after a serious effort has been made to influence the boss in other ways, such as rational persuasion and use of coalitions. The threat should be expressed with conviction but not personal hostility. Following is a specific example:

> I cannot live with this decision, because it violates our basic principles and poses a serious risk to our people. Unless the decision can be changed, I will have no choice but to resign from my position.

- **Resist inappropriate influence attempts by the boss.**

Despite the obvious power advantage a boss holds over a subordinate, it is not necessary to comply with inappropriate influence attempts or be exploited by an abusive leader. Followers often have more counter-power than they realize, and have some things they can do to deter a leader accustomed to exploiting people who are unassertive. It is essential to challenge abuse early before it becomes habitual, and the challenge must be firm but diplomatic. Point out the use of inappropriate or manipulative influence tactics (e.g., "I don't respond well to threats" or "This offer might be misconstrued by some people as a bribe"). Insist on your rights ("It's not right to ask me to cancel my vacation plans at the last minute to do this job when other people around here have the time and skills to do it."). Remind the leader of a promise about to be violated ("Didn't you promise that assignment to me just last month?"). Point out the negative consequences of complying with an inappropriate request. For example, explain how compliance with a demand to do something immediately will interfere with your other work or jeopardize an important project.

- **Provide upward coaching and counseling when appropriate.**

Coaching is usually viewed as a leader behavior, but subordinates also have opportunities to coach the boss, especially one who is new and inexperienced. Upward coaching is easier to do when a follower has already developed a deep and trusting exchange relationship with the leader. Be alert for opportunities to provide helpful advice on technical matters (the leader may be reluctant to ask for help). Model effective behaviors the leader can learn from and imitate.

Upward counseling is awkward, but at times it is appropriate and even appreciated by a boss. One form of counseling is to help the leader understand actions that are ineffective. For example, describe how inappropriate behavior is having a different effect than the leader intended ("I'm sure you didn't mean to imply Sue is unreliable when you said . . . , but that's how she took it"). Another form of counseling is to be a good listener when the leader needs someone in whom to confide about worries and concerns. Look for opportunities to ask questions about things the leader should consider in handling a difficult problem.

- **Learn to use self-management strategies.**

As noted earlier, cognitive and behavioral strategies for self-management can be useful to increase feelings of empowerment and job satisfaction, reduce dysfunctional behavior, and improve individual performance. Self-development aids are available to guide individuals in using these strategies effectively.

Summary

Leader-member exchange (LMX) theory describes how leaders develop exchange relationships over time with different subordinates. A favorable exchange relationship is more likely when a subordinate is perceived to be competent, reliable, and similar to the leader in values and attitudes. A leader's upward influence is another important determinant of the potential for establishing a favorable exchange relationship with subordinates. The behavior of the leader and subordinate is different in favorable exchange relationships than in unfavorable exchange relationships. Exchange relationships with subordinates have implications for leadership effectiveness. Subordinate satisfaction, commitment, and performance are usually higher when the relationship is favorable. Some differentiation of exchange relationships with subordinates may be necessary, but too much can be detrimental.

A manager's reaction to mistakes or failures by a subordinate depends in part on attributions about the reasons for poor performance. Attribution theory explains how managers interpret performance information and make judgments about the competence and motivation of a subordinate. Managers may unwittingly create a self-fulfilling prophecy if their behavior is based on a biased perception about the ability and motivation of individual subordinates. For their part, subordinates can use impression management tactics to influence the leader to view them more favorably. Followers often do things to appear competent, loyal, and reliable. When a subordinate's performance is unsatisfactory, corrective feedback is more likely to be successful if the leader is supportive rather than hostile and encourages the subordinate to take ownership of the problem.

How followers view leader competence and intentions has implications for leadership effectiveness. Followers are susceptible to the same types of attributions as leaders. A leader who takes visible actions that are followed by improvements in group performance will be viewed as more competent than one who takes no action or acts without apparent success. Leaders use impression management tactics in an effort to appear more decisive, competent, powerful, and trustworthy.

Self-management is a way for followers to become more effective as individual contributors. Self-management strategies can be used to increase confidence, spur greater effort, and manage time more effectively. One way for a leader to empower subordinates is to encourage and facilitate their self-management activities.

Followers are more likely to be effective if they view themselves as active and independent rather than passive and dependent on the leader. Followers can help make their leader more effective by providing accurate information, challenging weak decisions, resisting inappropriate influence attempts, giving support and encouragement, and providing coaching and advice.

All leaders are also followers, and to be effective in both roles, it is essential to find a way to integrate them. Moreover, it is essential to find appropriate ways to share leadership functions within teams, across authority levels, and between interdependent subunits of the organization.

Review and Discussion Questions

1. Briefly explain leader-member exchange theory.
2. What are some possible benefits and costs of developing different exchange relationships?
3. Is it possible to develop different dyadic relationships and still treat everyone fairly?
4. Use attribution theory to explain how leaders interpret the reason for poor performance.
5. How can subordinates influence a leader's perceptions about them?7
6. What are some guidelines for corrective feedback?
7. What factors influence follower attributions about leader competence?
8. What are some guidelines for improving effectiveness as a follower?

Key Terms

empowerment	implicit theories of leadership	leader-member exchange
exchange relationship	impression management	self-management
external attribution	internal attribution	self-talk

CASE 1

Cromwell Electronics

Dan Dalton was the marketing vice president (VP) for Cromwell Electronics. Ten months earlier he had appointed Ed Corelli as the manager of a newly formed marketing unit for the eastern region. The unit was responsible for developing marketing presentations, advertising campaigns, and promotions for the sale of Cromwell products in the eastern region. The unit had six marketing specialists; two were long-time employees, and the other four were newly hired. Ed was promoted to the position based on a good reputation as a marketing specialist. Even though the marketing unit was new, Dan expected its performance to be better by now. The marketing unit for the western region was formed at the same time, and it had higher performance. Dan reflected on the comments made by two of Ed's subordinates when asked how they liked working for him.

Pat Posner had worked for the company for nearly 10 years. He commented that Ed was "a great manager" Pat especially liked the high level of autonomy he was allowed. Pat said, "Ed gives me complete discretion to plan the marketing campaigns for my set of products. If I have a problem, he encourages me to look at it from different perspectives, but he doesn't say what he wants me to do about it. He trusts me to solve my own problems. When I make a mistake, which seldom happens, he doesn't get upset. Instead, he expects me to learn from it" Pat also noted that Ed showed sincere appreciation for good performance. "My marketing campaign for the new product was very successful, and I really appreciated the recognition Ed gave me in the monthly unit meeting. He also told me that he would try to get me a pay increase."

Katie O'Toole, one of the new employees, was less satisfied with Ed as a manager. "Sometimes I wish Ed would give me more direction. He is always pushing me to make my own decisions. Maybe if I had more experience I would like it, but right now it makes me feel very insecure. I never really know if I am doing what he expects. When I go to him for help with a problem, he turns the question around and asks what I would do. He doesn't seem to understand that I wouldn't ask if I already knew the answer. And when I do something wrong, he doesn't seem to care. Ed likes to pretend that mistakes will go away if you don't talk about them" Katie had another complaint as well. She said, "He seems to favor the two employees who have been with the company longer. He gives them the most interesting assignments, he consults with them more about his plans for the unit, and he recommends them for larger pay increases." Katie noted that Sally and George, both new employees, agreed with her complaints about Ed.

At lunch later that day, Dan asked Ed how things were going in his unit. Ed replied that he was disappointed in some of the new marketing specialists. Only one of the new employees (Linda) was performing well. The others seemed to lack drive and initiative. Ed emphasized that he tried to avoid any favoritism, which had been a serious problem for a former boss. Although he gave the most complex assignments to the marketing specialists with more experience, everyone had challenging assignments and opportunities to excel. Ed had attended the company workshop on empowerment, and he was trying to give employees the autonomy they needed to learn and develop new skills on the job. He was careful not to supervise too closely or criticize mistakes. He provided recognition for outstanding achievements and recommended pay raises for good performance. Ed asked his boss, "What am I doing wrong?"

Questions

1. What theories from this chapter are relevant for analyzing the case?
2. Evaluate Ed's behavior as a manager, and identify effective and ineffective actions.
3. What should Dan say or do now?

CASE 2

American Financial Corporation

Betty Powell is the manager of human resources for American Financial Corporation, a large financial services company. When she arrived back in her office Monday after being away for a week, she discovered that a staffing report due the day before was still not finished. The report was for the vice president of the company's brokerage division, and Betty was supposed to give him the report by Wednesday.

Six weeks earlier Betty had asked Don Adams, one of her subordinates to collect the information and to write the staffing report. At that time she told him what should be included in the report and when it was due. It is not the first time Don has missed a deadline. His work is careful and meticulous, but he appears to be compulsive about checking and rechecking everything several times to avoid any mistakes.

Betty called Don and asked him to meet with her immediately. When Don came into her office, she greeted him and asked him to sit down. The following dialogue occurred.

"Don, I understand the staffing report for the brokerage division is not completed yet. The division vice president needs that report to prepare his annual budget, and he is putting a lot of pressure on me to get it to him immediately. When I gave you this assignment, you assured me that six weeks was ample time to do it."

"I'm sorry that the report wasn't ready on schedule," responded Don, "but it turned out to be much more complex than I initially expected. I had to spend extra time verifying the figures from the branch offices, because they just didn't look right. Just when I thought..."

"Look Don," interrupted Betty, "this is not the first time you have been late on an important project. You're supposed to be a professional, and professionals plan their work and get it done on time."

"It would not be very professional to do a report full of mistakes," replied Don. "It's important to me to do quality work that I can be proud of. It's not my fault that the branch managers don't keep accurate records"

"What types of mistakes did you find when you checked their records?" asked Betty.

"Well . . . , I didn't actually find any mistakes," replied Don, looking embarrassed, "but after I entered the information into the computer and did the preliminary analysis, I discovered that the records were missing for one of the branch offices. I lost a week waiting to get the missing information, but without it the report would not provide an accurate picture of the division's staffing needs. It's a good thing I noticed the . . . "

Betty interrupted impatiently, "Don, we have interns to do things like checking computer records and making sure they are complete. It sounds to me like you are not very efficient about managing your time. If you delegated some of these simple tasks, you wouldn't get so far behind in your work."

"The interns were busy working on the new financial reports," Don protested. "I don't get enough clerical support on any of my projects, and that's why they are sometimes late"

"Why didn't you inform me there were problems that might delay the report?" asked Betty, her voice showing she was becoming very annoyed. "I could have found you some clerical support."

Don was now becoming more defensive. "I tried to let you know last week, but you were on the West Coast for the management training workshop. I left a message for you to call me"

"Don, you have an excuse for everything, and nothing is ever your fault," Betty said sarcastically. "You seem to be incapable of planning the action steps needed to do a project like this one. You should have checked the records before you began the data analysis. As for the missing records, it wouldn't surprise me if they are buried somewhere under the piles of stuff laying around your office. You have the messiest office in the company."

Don looked sullen but did not reply. Betty continued her tirade.

"Don, your career in this company is going to be very short unless you get your act together. I want that report in my hands by noon tomorrow, and no more excuses."

Copyright © 1988 By Gary Yukl

Questions

1. What did Betty do wrong prior to the meeting, and what could have been done to avoid missing the deadline?
2. What did Betty do wrong in the meeting itself, and what could have been done to make the meeting more effective?
3. What should Don have done to be more effective?

Leadership in Teams and Decision Groups

Learning Objectives

After studying this chapter, you should be able to:

- Understand the processes that determine group performance.
- Understand how leaders can influence group processes and improve performance.
- Understand the leadership challenges for different types of teams.
- Understand effective procedures for leading teams.
- Understand the primary leadership functions in decision groups.
- Understand procedures for leading successful meetings.

Most organizations have small subunits (departments, sections) that perform a functional task (e.g., production, operations, sales, accounting, research) under the supervision of an appointed manager. In many of these subunits, the members perform the same type of work, but they work alone, do not depend on each other, and need little coordination (e.g., sales representatives, professors, tax accountants, machine operators). This type of work unit is sometimes called a *coacting group,* because there is little role interdependence among the members.

The word *team* is correctly used to describe an *interacting group* that is small and has members with a common purpose, interdependent roles, and complementary skills.

To clarify the distinction, interacting teams are found in basketball and soccer, whereas in bowling or wrestling the "teams" are actually coacting groups. Dyadic leadership theories are useful for describing leadership in coacting groups, but for interacting teams some additional leadership processes are needed to explain team performance.

A growing trend in organizations is to give more responsibility for important activities to teams, and in some cases they are empowered to make decisions formerly made by individual managers. Several distinct types of teams can be found in organizations, including functional

TABLE 1	Common Characteristics of Four Types of Teams			
Defining Characteristic	Functional Operating Team	Cross-Functional Team	Self-Managed Operating Team	Top Executive Team
Autonomy to determine mission and objectives	Low	Low to moderate	Low to moderate	High
Autonomy to determine work procedures	Low to moderate	High	High	High
Authority of the internal leader	High	Moderate to high	Low	High
Duration of existence for the team	High	Low to moderate	High	High
Stability of the membership	High	Low to moderate	High	High
Diversity of members in functional background	Low	High	Low	High

work teams, *cross-functional teams, self-managed teams,* and top executive teams. Table 1 compares the different types of teams with regard to duration of the team's existence, stability of team membership, functional diversity of members, authority of the internal leader, autonomy to determine the mission, and autonomy to determine work processes. The extent to which members are co-located or geographically dispersed (*"virtual teams"*) is another basis for describing teams, but some degree of virtuality may be found in any type of team. This chapter examines what has been learned about effective leadership in functional work teams, cross-functional teams, and self-managed teams.

A related topic is leadership in the context of group meetings. Meetings are commonly used to make decisions in organizations. Behavioral scientists have been studying leadership processes in such meetings for more than four decades, and practitioners have also contributed to our knowledge about the subject. The last section of the chapter examines effective leadership in meetings held to solve a problem or make a decision. The chapter begins with a description of collective processes that determine team performance.

Determinants of Team Performance

In the past half century, theoretical explanations for team performance have been proposed by many scholars (DeChurch & Mesmer-Magnus, 2010; Gladstein, 1984; Hackman, Brousseau, & Weiss, 1976; Hewett, O'Brien, & Hornik, 1974; Kozlowski & Ilgen, 2006; McGrath, 1984; O'Brien & Kabanoff, 1981; Pearce & Ravlin, 1987; Shiflett, 1979; Wofford, 1982; Zaccaro, Rittman, & Marks, 2001). Several performance determinants have been identified for work groups and teams (see Table 2). Empirical studies on small groups and teams show that leaders can influence these performance determinants, and their relative importance depends on the type of team and situation (Burke et al., 2006; Hulsheger, Anderson, & Salgado, 2009). Each performance determinant and ways for leaders to influence it is briefly explained in this section of the chapter.

TABLE 2	Determinants of Team Performance

- Commitment to task objectives and strategies
- Member skills and role clarity
- Internal organization and coordination
- External coordination
- Resources and political support
- Mutual trust, cohesiveness, and cooperation
- Collective efficacy and potency
- Accurate, shared mental models
- Collective learning
- Member diversity

Commitment to Task Objectives and Strategies

Member commitment to task objectives and *performance strategies* for attaining them facilitates cooperation, innovation, and extra effort to accomplish difficult tasks (Hulsheger et al., 2009; Mathieu & Rapp, 2009; Pearce & Ensley, 2004; Podsakoff, MacKenzie, & Ahearne, 1997). Leadership behaviors that are especially relevant for increasing member commitment to shared objectives include: (1) articulating an appealing vision that links the task objectives to member values and ideals; (2) explaining why a project or new initiative is important; (3) setting task objectives that are clear and challenging; (4) planning relevant performance strategies for attaining the objectives; and (5) empowering members to participate in planning activities and developing creative solutions to problems.

In general, there is a positive correlation between member empowerment and group performance (Burke et al., 2006). However, empowerment is not always successful, and many conditions facilitate or inhibit the effects of empowerment in teams (Cox, Pearce, & Perry, 2003; Seers, Keller, & Wilkerson, 2003). Examples include group size, diversity of members, the interpersonal skills and maturity of members, the nature of the task or mission, and competing loyalties of members to external constituents.

Member Skills and Role Clarity

Group performance will be higher when members have the knowledge and skills necessary to do the work, and they understand what to do, how to do it, and when it must be done (Morgeson, Reider, & Campion, 2005). Member skills and clear role expectations are more important when the task is complex and difficult to learn. A leader can do several things to improve member skills. When the team is being formed, or replacements are needed for departing members, the leader can influence the selection of new members and ensure an appropriate mix of complementary skills (Klimoski & Jones, 1995). In a newly formed team, or when the team has a new type of task to perform, the leader can clearly explain member responsibilities and relevant procedures for performing specific types of activities (Marks, Zaccaro, & Mathieu, 2000). At appropriate times in the performance cycle, leaders can assess the skills of current members to identify any deficiencies, provide constructive feedback and coaching, and arrange for members to receive necessary instruction in other ways (e.g., from more experienced members, or in workshops and courses).

Internal Organization and Coordination

The performance of a team depends not only on the motivation and skills of members, but also on how members are organized to use their skills. The design of work roles and the assignment of people to them determine how efficiently the team carries out its work. Performance will suffer if a team has talented people but they are given tasks for which their skills are irrelevant, or if the team uses a performance strategy that is not consistent with member skills.

Team performance also depends on the extent to which the interdependent activities of different members are mutually consistent and synchronized. A high level of coordination is especially important when the team performs a complex task under rapidly changing conditions. Coordination is determined by decisions made during the planning phase prior to the start of a new task, and a team will usually perform a new task better if members plan an explicit strategy that takes into account potential obstacles and problems that could limit performance (Hackman & Morris, 1975; Tesluk & Mathieu, 1999). Coordination is also facilitated by adjustments in member behavior during the team's performance of the task (Rico, Sanchez-Manzanares, Gil, & Gibson, 2008).

The increased importance of cooperation and coordination among interdependent members of teams makes leadership more difficult than in coacting work groups. A leader can do several things to ensure that necessary activities are well organized and carried out in a timely, efficient way. Relevant leadership behaviors include: (1) planning how to make efficient use of personnel and resources; (2) making contingency plans to deal with possible obstacles and emergencies; (3) involving members with relevant expertise in planning team activities; (4) leading meetings to collectively solve problems and plan activities; (5) planning how to schedule and sequence activities to avoid unnecessary delays or wasted time; (6) and actively monitoring and directing the work.

When the team performs a complex task under rapidly changing conditions, it may be necessary to have members share some of the responsibility for internal coordination. The leader can help members learn to anticipate each other's reactions to changing conditions and quickly adjust their own behavior as needed. Developing member skills about how to work together as a team is facilitated by ensuring that they understand how their roles are inter-related and by frequent rehearsal of complex activities. Training together under realistic conditions is especially important for teams that have difficult, dangerous activities to perform (e.g., combat teams, disaster relief teams, emergency medical teams, SWAT teams, firefighting teams).

External Coordination

The performance of a team also depends upon adjusting their activities to be consistent with the activities in other parts of the organization, and the importance of this *external coordination* increases as interdependence increases (Marrone, 2010; Marks, DeChurch, Mathieu, Panzer, & Alonso, 2005). It is essential for leaders to facilitate communication and coordination not only with other parts of the same organization, but also with outsiders whose decisions and actions affect the group (Ancona, 1990; Galbraith, 1973; Marks, Zaccaro, & Mathieu, 2000; Sundstrom, DeMeuse, & Futrell, 1990).

Many specific types of leadership behaviors are relevant for improving external coordination and adaptation. Examples include: (1) maintaining a network of contacts who can provide relevant information; (2) encouraging members to develop their own networks of useful contacts; (3) consulting with other subunits about plans and decisions that affect them; (4) monitoring progress in operations involving other subunits or organizations; (5) meeting with clients or users to learn more about their needs; and (6) negotiating agreements with clients. As in the case of internal coordination, responsibility for the leadership functions can be shared by members of the team.

Resources and Political Support

Group performance also depends on getting essential resources, and political support from outside sources (Ancona & Caldwell, 1992; Druskat & Wheeler, 2003; Marrone, Tesluk, & Carson, 2007; Peters, O'Connor, & Eulberg, 1985; Tesluk & Mathieu, 1999). Relevant resources may include budgetary funds, tools and equipment, supplies and materials, and facilities. A production team cannot maintain a high level of output without a dependable supply of materials. An air force crew will be rendered ineffective if they have no jet fuel to fly their plane. Maintaining a dependable supply of resources is especially important when the work cannot be done without them and no substitutes can be found. Resource acquisition is less important for a group that needs few resources to do the work or has its own ample supply of resources.

An important leadership responsibility is to obtain essential resources, assistance, and support from outside sources. Examples of relevant leadership behaviors include: (1) planning the resources required for a special project or activity; (2) lobbying with superiors or outsiders to provide additional resources; (3) influencing superiors to authorize use of unusual equipment, supplies, or materials; (4) promoting and defending the reputation of the team with superiors; (5) establishing cooperative relationships with outsiders who are a potential source of necessary resources and assistance; and (6) negotiating favorable agreements with suppliers and vendors.

Cooperation and Mutual Trust

Cooperation and mutual trust are important determinants of performance in groups where member roles are highly interdependent. A high level of cooperation and mutual trust is more likely when members identify with the team or work unit, value their membership, and are very cohesive (Barrick, Stewart, Neubert, & Mount, 1998; Watson, Kumar, & Michaelsen, 1993; Van der Vegt & Bunderson, 2005). It is more difficult to have a high level of *cohesiveness* and group identification in newly formed teams, in teams with frequent changes in membership, in teams with members who represent competing subunits of the organization, in teams with members who are culturally diverse, in teams with emotionally immature members, and in teams with members who must work in close proximity for long periods of time under stressful conditions (e.g., crew of a submarine). Social identity theories of effective leadership describe the processes by which leaders help to define the identity of a group and the meaning of membership (e.g., Reicher, Haslam, & Hopkins, 2005; van Knippenberg, van Knippenberg, De Cremer, & Hogg, 2004). There are many ways a leader can increase mutual trust and *collective identification* with the team. Examples include: (1) articulating an appealing vision of what the team can jointly accomplish; (2) using symbols and rituals to make membership more unique and desirable; (3) conducting *team building* activities; and (4) making recognition and rewards contingent on member contributions to team performance.

High cohesiveness can be a mixed blessing when a group is making decisions. A cohesive group of people with similar values and attitudes is more likely to agree on a decision, but such groups sometimes foster a phenomenon called "groupthink" (Janis, 1972). When members of a cohesive group are unwilling to risk social rejection for questioning a majority viewpoint or presenting a dissenting opinion, the critical evaluation of ideas is inhibited and creativity is reduced. The group strives to maintain the illusion of internal harmony by avoiding open expression of disagreement, and they may agree too quickly without a complete, objective evaluation of the alternatives. Members in these groups may develop an illusion of invulnerability, which will cause them to overestimate the probability of success for a risky course of action. If the group has a shared illusion of moral superiority, it will be easier to justify a course of action that would normally be considered unethical by individual members.

Collective Efficacy and Potency

Member commitment depends in part on the shared belief of members that the team is capable of successfully carrying out its mission and achieving specific task objectives (Bandura, 2000; Guzzo, Yost, Campbell, & Shea, 1993; Pearce, Gallagher, & Ensley, 2002). This shared belief is called *"collective efficacy"* or *"potency."* Several studies provide evidence that it is related to team performance, (e.g., Campion, Papper, & Medsker, 1996; Chen & Bliese, 2002; Gibson, 2001; Gibson, Randel, & Earley, 2000; Gully, Incalcaterra, Joshi, & Beaubien, 2002; Mulvey & Klein, 1998; Pearce, Gallagher, & Ensley, 2002; Wu, Tsui, & Kinicki, 2010). Collective efficacy is likely to be higher for a team with strong member skills, a high level of mutual trust and cooperation, ample resources, and a relevant performance strategy. Prior success can increase collective efficacy, which in turn can enhance a team's subsequent performance. A downward spiral can also occur, with failure resulting in lower collective efficacy, negative affect, and additional declines in performance. High collective efficacy is desirable, but the perception of capabilities should be realistic; as noted earlier, overconfidence can encourage a team to pursue very risky strategies that will fail.

A leader can influence collective efficacy in several ways (Bass, Avolio, Jung, & Berson, 2003; Eden, 1990; Gil, Rico, Alcover, & Barrasa, 2005; Kouzes & Posner, 1987; Lester, Meglino, & Korsgaard, 2002; Sivasubramaniam, Murry, Avolio, & Jung, 2002; Sosik, Kahai, & Avolio, 1998; Srivastava, Bartol, & Locke, 2006; Sutton & Woodman, 1989). Behaviors that influence collective efficacy include: (1) expressing optimism and confidence in the team; (2) setting realistic goals or targets that will provide an opportunity to experience early success; (3) helping the team find ways to overcome obstacles; and (4) celebrating progress and important achievements.

Accurate, Shared Mental Models

The term "mental model" is commonly used to describe conscious beliefs and implicit assumptions about the causes of performance and the best way to improve it (Cannon-Bowers, Salas, & Converse, 1993; Klimoski & Mohammed, 1994; Senge, 1990). Research on teams found that they are likely to have higher performance if members have a shared mental model that is accurate (Edwards, Day, Arthur, & Bel, 2006; Lim & Klein, 2006; Mohammed, Ferzandi, & Hamilton, 2010). Problem solving is more difficult when team members have different assumptions about the cause of the problem. A shared understanding about cause-effect relationships can facilitate the development of effective strategies and plans by a team and increase their commitment to implement them. However, group performance is unlikely to improve unless the mental model is not only shared but also accurate.

Leaders can help members identify their assumptions about cause-effect relationships, determine ways to assess the accuracy of these assumptions, and jointly develop a more accurate mental model. Ways to improve understanding and agreement about causes of problems and good solutions include the following: (1) hold a meeting to discuss member assumptions and beliefs and identify any supporting evidence; (2) examine relevant publications on the subject; (3) implement more accurate measures of team processes and performance determinants; (4) conduct controlled experiments to assess cause-effect relationships; and (5) conduct after-activity reviews to improve learning from experience (see description later in this chapter). Research on teams provides evidence for the importance of this leadership function (Edmondson, 2003; Morgeson, DeRue, & Karam, 2010).

Member Diversity

The extent to which members vary with regard to personality, demographic attributes (e.g., age, gender, ethnic identity, education), and functional specialization has implications for group processes and outcomes (Joshi & Roh, 2009; Kearney, Gebert, & Voelpel, 2009; Triandis, Kurowski, & Gelfand, 1994; Watson, Kumar, & Michaelsen, 1993). Groups with diverse membership are likely to be less cohesive, because people tend to be less accepting of others who have different beliefs, values, and traditions. Diversity can also impede communication when members use different language, jargon, measures, or criteria. On the positive side, having members with different perspectives, experiences, and knowledge can result in more creative solutions to problems. The importance of diversity for group performance varies somewhat for different types of groups and different situations (Horwitz & Horwitz, 2007). It is easier to convert diversity into cooperative problem solving when members are highly interdependent for attainment of important shared objectives, but making it happen is a major leadership challenge. A leader with authority to select members can try to select members who are diverse in terms of their background and relevant knowledge.

Group Process Dichotomies

Some scholars have proposed a broad two-factor classification of group processes that can affect the importance of the performance determinants and the relevance of different leadership functions (Bales, 1950; Katz & Kahn, 1978; Marks, Mathieu, & Zaccaro, 2001). The two dichotomies described in this section can be used together to help understand effective leadership in a group or team.

One distinction is between *transition phase* and *performance phase* of group activities. The transition phase involves determining who will be members of the group and making initial decisions about performance strategies, work assignments, and member roles in the group. If the mission, objectives, and formal leadership roles for the group are not already determined by the parent organization, then these decisions must be made as well. The transition phase is very important in a newly formed group, or when an existing group is given responsibility for a new type of project. The performance phase involves implementing and executing performance strategies, maintaining member commitment and cooperation, monitoring and assessing performance, and resolving any problems in the work. Groups typically alternate between the two phases, and the phases can overlap when unexpected problems require revision of earlier plans and decisions.

Another distinction is between *internal processes* versus *external processes*. The internal processes involve relationships among the group members and decisions about work procedures and member roles. The external processes involve interactions and relationships with the larger organization and outsiders such as clients and suppliers. Both types of processes occur during the transition and performance phases. Leadership may be provided by an elected or appointed leader, by individual members, and by an external leader in the organization with authority over group tasks, procedures, and resources.

Functional Work Teams

In a functional operating team, the members are likely to have jobs that are somewhat specialized but still part of the same basic function (e.g., equipment operating crew, maintenance crew, combat squad, submarine crew, SWAT team). The teams typically continue operating for a long duration of time, and the membership is relatively stable. There is usually an appointed leader who has considerable authority for internal operations and managing

TABLE 3	Leader Behaviors Influencing Performance Determinants for Teams
Leadership Behavior	**Performance Determinant**
Visioning, expressing confidence, celebrating progress	Task commitment, collective efficacy
Recruiting and selecting competent team members	Member skills, collective efficacy
Coaching, training, and clarifying role expectations and priorities	Member skills and role clarity, individual and collective efficacy
Planning and organizing team activities and projects	Efficiency and internal coordination, collective efficacy
Facilitating collective learning by the team	Adaptation to change, performance quality (e.g., strategies, collective efficacy)
Team building and constructive resolution of conflict	Mutual trust and cooperation, member identification with the team
Networking, monitoring/scanning of the external environment	Adaptation to change, external coordination, quality of performance strategies
Representing, promoting, lobbying, negotiating	Resources and political support, external coordination

external relationships with other parts of the organization. Most leadership responsibilities are carried out by this formal leader, but other group members (such as an assistant leader) may perform specific leadership functions.

Effective leadership in functional work teams may require many specific types of leadership behavior. Examples of specific behaviors that can be used to influence each type of performance determinant are listed in Table 3. The optimal pattern of behavior is not the same for each type of functional team. The appropriate pattern of behavior will depend on the situation and the relative importance of the performance determinants at that time.

Many of the required leader behaviors in a functional work team are similar to task-oriented and relations-oriented behaviors. If team members are not highly motivated and performance is less than it should be, then the leader may need to inspire and challenge members to increase their commitment to team objectives. If major changes are being implemented by the organization, then some change-oriented behaviors may be needed. How much external behavior (e.g., representing, lobbying) is needed will vary depending on coordination requirements with other parts of the organization, variation in the demand for the group's products or services, and the adequacy of resources already provided by the organization. To cope with disruptions and immediate crises, some problem-solving and crisis management behaviors may be necessary.

Cross-functional Teams

Cross-functional teams are being used increasingly in organizations to improve co-ordination of interdependent activities among specialized subunits. The team usually includes representatives from each of the functional subunits involved in a project, and it may include representatives from outside organizations such as suppliers, clients, and joint venture partners. The team is given responsibility for planning and conducting a complex activity that requires considerable coordination, cooperation, and joint problem solving among the parties (Ford & Randolph, 1992). Examples of these activities include developing a new product and bringing it into production, implementing a new information system, identifying ways to improve product quality, planning an ad campaign for the client of an advertising agency, carrying out a consulting project, developing a new health care program in a hospital, and developing a new MBA program in a university.

Separate cross-functional teams may be formed in an organization for different activities, projects, or clients. Some cross-functional teams may be permanent additions to the formal structure of the organization, but most of the teams are temporary and only exist until they complete their task or mission. The membership may be stable over the life of the team, or it may change as some functions become more important and others decline in importance (e.g., product development teams). The members may work for the team either on a part-time or fulltime basis. In many cross-functional teams, the members are also in a functional subunit of the organization, and in some cases they are members of more than one cross-functional team.

Benefits and Limitations of Cross-functional Teams

Cross-functional teams offer many potential benefits to an organization (Ford & Randolph, 1992; Manz & Sims, 1993). The teams allow flexible, efficient deployment of personnel and resources to solve problems as they are discovered. Functional expertise is preserved because team members maintain close contact with their respective functional areas. Coordination is improved and many problems are avoided when people from different functions come together to work on a project at the same time, rather than working on it sequentially. The diversity of member backgrounds fosters communication with external sources of ideas and information, and it increases creativity in the generation of ideas and problem solutions (Keller, 2001). Working on a cross-functional team helps members learn to view a problem or challenge from different perspectives, rather than from only a narrow functional viewpoint. Members can learn new skills that will be carried back to their functional jobs and to subsequent teams.

Many organizations have reported great success with cross-functional teams. For example, a cross-functional team at Chrysler developed innovative new subcompact (the Neon) in a record time of only 42 months and at a fraction of the cost of developing new models at other car companies (Woodruff, 1993). At Hallmark Cards, the use of teams drastically reduced the time needed to bring new holiday and greeting cards to market from more than three years to less than one year, while also improving quality and responsiveness to changing customer preferences (George & Jones, 1996). However, cross-functional teams are not always successful, and effective leadership is required to meet the challenges inherent in the use of these teams.

The same conditions that create potential advantages for a cross-functional team also create difficulties (Denison, Hart, & Kahn, 1996; Ford & Randolph, 1992). Members of crossfunctional teams usually have conflicting loyalties to the team and their home department. Members may be more concerned about protecting their functional turf than about accomplishing team objectives. Decisions can become difficult and time consuming if members need to get approval from their functional superiors before agreeing to a major change. The team usually has tight deadlines to meet for completing its work, which puts additional pressure on the leader to resolve disagreements and maintain steady progress.

Meetings are time consuming, and it can be difficult to get sufficient participation from team members who also have responsibilities in a functional department or other cross-functional teams. The functional diversity of the members increases communication barriers, because each function usually has its own jargon and ways of thinking about things (Cronin & Weingart, 2007). The functional subunits represented by team members often have different objectives, different priorities, and a different time orientation. These differences can create conflicts, as shown in the following example from a large petrochemicals company (Stern, 1993).

> A team was formed to develop a better plastic resin. Members from the research department wanted to spend several months developing a new resin. Members from the production and marketing departments wanted to alter the existing product and quickly get it into production. The project was stalled for a long time because the different factions could not agree about a strategy.

Leadership in Cross-functional Teams

Most cross-functional teams have a formal leader who is selected by higher management, because a strong leader is needed to deal with the difficult challenges facing the teams. To gain commitment and resolve disagreements, the designated leader needs substantial position power and good interpersonal skills. Higher management should appoint a qualified leader and provide a clear mission, necessary resources, and political support for the implementation of ideas developed by the team.

Despite the extensive use of cross-functional project teams during the past 20 years, research on the skills required for effective leadership in these teams is still limited. However, the research suggests that team leaders need technical expertise, cognitive skills, interpersonal and political skills, and administrative skills relevant for project management (Ford & Randolph, 1992; Mumford, Hunter, Eubanks, Bedell, & Murphy, 2007; Mumford, Scott, Gaddis, & Strange, 2002). Table 4 explains how each type of skill is relevant for leadership in cross-functional project teams.

Creativity is an important requirement for the success of most cross-functional project teams. In their review of research on leading creative teams, Mumford et al. (2002) found three themes that described essential processes: (1) idea generation, (2) idea structuring, and (3) idea promotion. These themes indicate specific roles or types of leadership behavior that are relevant for each process. With regard to idea generation, it is essential for the leader to stimulate and facilitate creativity by members. With regard to idea structuring, it is important for the leader to provide clear objectives for the project and explain how it is relevant for the

TABLE 4	Skills Required for Leading Cross-functional Project Teams

Technical expertise: The leader must be able to communicate about technical matters with team members from diverse functional backgrounds.

Project management skills: The leader must be able to plan and organize the project activities, select qualified members of the team, and handle budgeting and financial responsibilities.

Interpersonal skills: The leader must be able to understand the needs and values of team members, to influence them, resolve conflicts, and build cohesiveness.

Cognitive skills: The leader must be able to solve complex problems that require creativity and systems thinking, and must understand how the different functions are relevant to the success of the project.

Political skills: The leader must be able to develop coalitions and gain resources, assistance, and approvals from top management and other relevant parties.

organization, but also to allow ample autonomy with regard to how the project objectives will be attained. With regard to idea promotion, necessary resources and support for the project must be obtained from the parent organization.

From interviews and observations of teams, Barry (1991) identified four leadership roles that appear to be essential for teams that solve problems, manage projects, or develop policies for an organization. The roles include (1) envisioning, (2) organizing, (3) social integrating, and (4) external spanning. Envisioning provides a shared objective, organizing helps the team decide how to attain it, social integrating helps to maintain internal cohesiveness, and external spanning helps to keep group decisions compatible with the needs of stakeholders outside the team. The four roles also provide a parsimonious way to describe the specific leadership behaviors used in cross-functional groups to build task commitment, develop effective performance strategies, ensure member trust and cooperation, obtain necessary resources, and maintain external coordination. Table 5 shows a modified version of the four-role taxonomy that incorporates other findings in team leadership.

The relative importance of the different leadership roles varies somewhat depending on the stage of group development. For example, envisioning is especially important when the group is forming, whereas organizing is more important after the group has agreed on an objective. Even when the capacity to provide each type of leadership is present, the team will not be successful unless the leader and members understand that different patterns of leadership are needed at different times. Research on cross-functional teams indicates that the leader must be flexible and adaptive as conditions change (e.g., Lewis, Welsh, Dehler, & Green, 2002).

TABLE 5	Leadership Behaviors Needed in Cross-functional Team

Envisioning

- Articulating strategic objectives or a vision that inspires commitment by team members.
- Helping the team understand and improve their assumptions and mental models regarding the relationships among task variables.
- Suggesting creative ideas and encouraging the team to consider innovative performance strategies.

Organizing

- Planning and scheduling team activities to achieve coordination and meet project deadlines.
- Helping the team establish standards and methods for assessing progress and performance.
- Arranging and conducting meetings to solve problems and make decisions in a systematic way.

Social Integrating

- Encouraging mutual trust, acceptance, and cooperation among team members.
- Facilitating open communication, equal participation, and tolerance of dissenting views.
- Mediating conflicts among members and helping them find integrative solutions.

External Spanning

- Monitoring the external environment of the team to identify client needs, emerging problems, and political processes that will affect the team.
- Promoting a favorable image of the team among outsiders.
- Influencing people outside the team to provide adequate resources, approvals, assistance, and cooperation.

The difficulties and obstacles facing many cross-functional teams are so great that the formal leader may be unable to carry out all of the relevant leadership roles alone. The different lines of research on leadership in cross-functional teams all indicate that success requires the efforts of multiple leaders (Barry, 1991; Cohen & Bailey, 1997; Mumford et al., 2002). Some of the internal leadership responsibilities may be shared at times with individual members of the team who have special expertise about a particular aspect of the project. However, the teams should not be self-managed. Research on the use cross-functional project teams without a strong, designated leader find that they are less likely to be successful, because too much time is consumed by process problems and unresolved conflicts (Cohen & Bailey, 1997).

Self-managed Work Teams

In self-managed work teams (sometimes called *semi-autonomous work groups),* much of the responsibility and authority usually vested in a manager's position is turned over to the team members (Cohen, 1991; Katzenbach & Smith, 1993; Orsburn, Moran, Musselwhite, & Zenger, 1990; Wellins, Byham, & Wilson, 1991). Most self-managed work teams are responsible for producing a distinct product or service. Any type of team can be "self-managed," but this form of team governance is typically used for teams that perform the same type of operational task repeatedly and have a relatively stable membership over time. Unlike cross-functional project teams, the members of self-managed teams typically have similar functional backgrounds (e.g., maintenance technicians, production operators). The members often take turns performing the various tasks for which the team is responsible. When members learn to perform multiple tasks, it increases team flexibility, makes the work more interesting, and provides an opportunity to learn new skills.

Self-managed teams are used most often for manufacturing work or process production, but they are finding increasing application to service work. Examples of companies that have used self-managed teams include AT&T, Colgate-Palmolive Company, Cummins Engine Company, Digital Equipment Corporation, General Electric, General Foods, Goodyear Tire and Rubber, Motorola, Procter and Gamble, TRW, Volvo, Xerox, and the Saturn division of General Motors.

The parent organization usually determines the mission, scope of operations, and the budget for self-managed teams. The amount of authority for other types of decisions varies greatly from one organization to another. Each team is usually given authority and responsibility for operating decisions such as setting performance goals and quality standards, assigning work, determining work schedules, determining work procedures, making purchases of necessary supplies and materials, dealing with customers and suppliers, evaluating team member performance, and handling performance problems of individual members. The teams are usually allowed to make small expenditures for supplies and equipment without prior approval, but in most organizations any recommendations for large purchases must be approved by management. Sometimes self-managed teams are also given the primary responsibility for personnel decisions such as selecting, hiring, and firing team members, and determining pay rates (within specified limits).

Benefits and Limitations of Self-managed Teams

Self-managed work teams offer a number of potential benefits, including stronger commitment of team members to the work, more effective management of work-related problems, improved efficiency, more job satisfaction, less turnover, and less absenteeism. Having team members cross-trained to do different jobs makes the work more interesting for members and increases the flexibility of the team in dealing with personnel shortages resulting from illness or turnover. Their extensive knowledge of work processes helps team members solve problems and suggest improvements. Finally, the changeover to self-managed teams typically reduces the number of managers and staff specialists in an organization, which lowers costs.

How many of these potential benefits are realized depends greatly on how the teams are implemented in an organization. One determinant is the amount of autonomy provided to the team, and member's feelings of collective empowerment (Kirkman & Rosen, 1999; Tesluk & Matthieu, 1999). Giving authority to a self-managed team rather than to an individual leader does not necessarily result in collective feelings of empowerment. The team may use the same type of social pressure on members to conform to strict group norms and established procedures (Barker, 1993; Sinclair, 1992).

Reviews of the literature on self-managed teams (Cohen & Bailey, 1997; Goodman, Devadas, & Hughson, 1988; Kirkman & Rosen, 1999; Pearce & Ravlin, 1987) suggest that this form of employee empowerment can improve job satisfaction and team performance. However, much of the evidence is based on weak research methods or anecdotal reports published in business periodicals. Only a small number of experimental or quasi-experimental field studies have been conducted to evaluate self-managed teams (e.g., Banker, Field, Schroeder, & Sinha, 1996; Cohen & Ledford, 1994; Cordery, Mueller, & Smith, 1991; Pasmore, 1978; Pearson, 1992; Wall, Kemp, Jackson, & Klegg, 1986). These studies found some favorable outcomes for self-managed teams, but the results were not consistent from study to study and did not substantiate the large performance improvements claimed in some anecdotal reports.

Self-managed teams are difficult to implement, and they can be a dismal failure when used in inappropriate situations or without competent leadership and support (Hackman, 1986; Lawler, 1986). If interpersonal conflicts cannot be resolved in a constructive way that will ensure a high level of interpersonal trust and cooperation, then the team may restructure itself with more independent roles, thereby reducing the potential benefits and performance gains (Langfred, 2007). The research on self-managed teams suggests several conditions under which the potential advantages are likely to be realized, and they are listed in Table 6 (Carson, Tesluk, & Marrone, 2007; Cohen & Bailey, 1997; Goodman, Devadas, & Hughson, 1988; Hackman, 1986; Kirkman & Rosen, 1999; Mathieu, Gilson, & Ruddy, 2006; Pearce & Ravlin, 1987; Stewart, Courtright, & Manz, 2009; Sundstrom, DeMeuse, & Futrell, 1990).

Leadership in Self-managed Teams

When describing leadership in self-managed teams, it is helpful to differentiate between internal and external leadership roles. The internal leadership role involves management

TABLE 6	Facilitating Conditions for Self-Managed Teams

- Clearly defined, shared objectives
- Complex and meaningful task
- Small size and stable membership
- Members can determine work processes
- Members have relevant skills
- Member access to relevant information
- Appropriate recognition and rewards
- Strong support by top management
- Competent external leader

responsibilities assigned to the team and shared by group members. It is typical for self-managed teams to have an internal team leader who is elected by the members, and the position may be rotated among different members on a regular basis (e.g., quarterly or annually). Whether elected or appointed, the team leader does not simply replace the former first-line manager. In self-managed teams, most important responsibilities are usually shared by group members, not concentrated in the team leader. The primary responsibility of the internal leader is to coordinate and facilitate the process of making and implementing team decisions (e.g., conduct meetings, prepare work schedules and administrative paperwork).

Internal leadership in self-managed teams can take other forms besides rotation of the team leader position among members, and the amount of shared leadership and what aspects are shared can vary significantly (Carson et al., 2007). One form of shared leadership occurs when members meet to discuss important matters and make a group decision. A member with relevant expertise may assume responsibility for providing coordination and direction on specific team activities. Routine administrative tasks may be assigned to individual members, or someone with a strong interest in a task may take the initiative to do it without being asked. Difficult supervisory functions such as enforcing group norms may be performed collectively, as in the following example described by Barker (1993).

> A small manufacturing company changed from traditionally managed work groups to selfmanaged teams. The team members collectively formulated standards of appropriate behavior. The new standards were more demanding than the earlier work rules, and compared to the supervisors of the traditionally managed work groups, the team was less tolerant of unacceptable behavior. Members first confronted an offender with a reminder of the standards or a warning to improve, then they used their coercive power to dismiss anyone who was not willing to do what was expected.

The role of an external leader involves managerial responsibilities not delegated to the team. The external leaders may be middle managers, special facilitators, or some of the previous first-line supervisors. Each external leader usually works with several teams. One leadership role that is especially important when the team is formed is to serve as a coach, facilitator, and consultant to the team. Considerable coaching and encouragement are usually necessary to get a new team off to a successful start. The type of coaching needed to facilitate shared leadership is different from providing specific advice about better procedures for doing the work. Leadership coaching includes helping members learn how to plan and organize the work, make group decisions, resolve conflicts, and cooperate effectively as a team. Most of these skills are difficult for members to learn, and it may take several months for the team to become proficient in managing its own task and interpersonal processes. During this learning period, an important function of the external leader is to build the self-confidence of team members. As the group evolves, members can gradually assume more responsibility for coaching new members and improving their own working relationships.

Another important role is to obtain necessary information, resources, and political support from the organization. Because external leaders serve as a linking pin between the team and organization, it is essential to build and maintain cooperative relationships and an effective exchange of information. The external leader must be able to influence team members to think and behave in ways that increase team effectiveness, and to influence other people in the organization to do what is necessary to facilitate team effectiveness. Unlike leaders of traditional *functional teams,* external leaders of self-managed teams are less likely to use their legitimate power in directive ways to influence the team; instead, they are more likely to ask questions and use influence based on their expert and referent power (Druskat & Wheeler, 2003).

A competent external leader is important for the success of self-managed teams, not only in the transition phase but also in the performance phase (Cohen, Chang, & Ledford, 1997; Gibson & Vermeulen, 2003; Morgeson, 2005; Morgeson & DeRue, 2006). As the team continues to develop, the external leader should communicate clear expectations about new responsibilities of members for regulating their own behavior. To improve external coordination in a dynamic environment, the external leader should clearly communicate objectives and changing priorities, facilitate collective learning, and continue to help the team obtain necessary resources and political support from the organization. Finally, it is often necessary for the external leader to assist the team in dealing with unusual, disruptive events, and the leader can help the team to understand the problem and coach members in how to respond effectively.

Virtual Teams

In virtual teams, the members are geographically separated and they seldom if ever meet face-to-face (Bell & Kozlowski, 2002). Most of the communication among members relies on computer and telecommunications technology (e.g., e-mail, videoconferencing, groupware, cellular phones). There has been a rapid increase in the use of virtual teams in organizations, and some writers have predicted that they will revolutionize the workplace of the future (Townsend, DeMarie, & Hendrickson, 1998). There are several reasons for increased use of virtual teams, including the rapid pace of globalization, increased use of joint ventures, employee desire for more flexibility in work arrangements (e.g., telecommuting, independent contractors), growing emphasis on service and knowledge management activities, and need for more flexibility and innovation in product development and delivery of customized services.

Any type of team can be virtual, but the most common form is a cross-functional team. A virtual team may be either a temporary arrangement to carry out a specific task, or a more durable arrangement to carry out ongoing responsibilities such as solving technical problems, planning recurring events, coordinating activities among dispersed units of an organization, and maintaining external coordination with suppliers and clients.

Benefits and Limitations of Virtual Teams

Virtual teams can provide several potential benefits compared to a co-located team. With virtual teams it is possible to involve the most qualified persons who are available to work on a project or make a decision, regardless of where they are located. For example, in a two-year project to develop a new type of refrigerator, Whirlpool used a virtual team with experts from the United States, Italy, and Brazil (Geber, 1995). The membership of virtual teams is often fluid, because the technology makes it easy for people to participate in different ways only when they are needed. As compared to teams with members who work together in the same location ("colocated teams"), a virtual team is more likely to have members from different cultures, times zones, and organizations.

Having a diverse, fluid membership creates additional problems and unique leadership challenges that may prevent the team from realizing the potential benefits. The lack of frequent face-to-face contact makes it more difficult to monitor the performance of members, to influence members, and to develop mutual trust and collective identification. It is difficult to gain commitment from diverse members with responsibilities in their local work unit that may be more important to them. Coordination problems may be more difficult to resolve in a virtual team than in a co-located team, especially when members have highly interdependent roles and the environment is dynamic and unpredictable. The leadership challenges are increased when members represent different organizations and are located in different time zones and cultures.

In the past decade there has been an increase in research on the differences between colocated and geographically dispersed teams (see Bell & Kozlowski, 2002; Bordia, 1997; Carte, Chidambaram, & Becker, 2006; Duarte & Snyder, 1999; Martins, Gilson, & Maynard, 2004; Kirkman, Rosen, Tesluk, & Gibson, 2004; Mesmer-Magnus, DeChurch, Jimenez-Rodriguez, Wildman, & Schuffler, In Press; Purvanova & Bono, 2009). It is likely that the same leadership roles are relevant for both types of teams, but the relative importance of these roles and how they are enacted may differ for virtual teams. More research is needed to clarify these issues.

Finally, the rapid pace of development in communication technology will have important implications for virtual teams in the near future. For example, holographic projection technology could be used to make it appear that team members are sitting around the same conference table, even though they are actually in different parts of the world. New developments in artificial intelligence may make it possible for some leadership functions to be shifted from humans to robots. As changes occur in the way virtuality is experienced by a team, earlier research findings will need to be verified and new research methods may be needed.

Guidelines for Leading Teams

A variety of different ways have been identified for leaders to improve member cohesiveness, cooperation, team identification, collective efficacy, and collective learning. The following guidelines based on research, theory, and practitioner insights describe team-building procedures that can be used alone or in various combinations when relevant for the situation (see also Table 7).

- **Emphasize common interests and values.**

Collective identification with a group is stronger when the members agree about objectives, values, priorities, strategies, and the need for cooperation. The leader should emphasize mutual interests, identify shared objectives, and explain why cooperation is necessary to attain them. An example of an appeal to shared values and objectives is provided by the following critical incident from the Korean War (Yukl, 1989, p. 328).

> The commanding officer of a squadron (a lieutenant colonel) learned that interracial trouble had arisen among airmen in his squadron, and he was determined to stop it before it got out of hand. He called together the officers and airmen in his outfit and gave them an inspiring speech about democracy and discrimination. He pointed out that they were

TABLE 7	Guidelines for Leading Teams

- Emphasize common interests and values.
- Use ceremonies, rituals, and symbols to develop collective identification
- Encourage and facilitate social interaction.
- Tell people about group activities and achievements.
- Conduct process analysis sessions.
- Increase incentives for mutual cooperation.
- Hold practice sessions under realistic conditions.
- Use after-activity reviews to facilitate collective learning by the team.

over there to preserve democracy and democratic principles, and discrimination among themselves was no way to attain this purpose. He put the challenge directly to the men and had the two racial groups appoint representatives that could hold meetings to iron out any difficulties that might arise in the future. Not only did this help defuse the conflict, but working conditions and squadron morale were improved also.

- **Use ceremonies, rituals, and symbols to develop collective identification.**

Ceremonies and rituals can be used to increase identification with a group and make membership appear special. Initiation rituals are used to induct new members into a group, and retirement rituals are used to celebrate the departure of old members. Ceremonies are used to celebrate special achievements or mark the anniversary of special events in the history of the group. Rituals and ceremonies are most effective when they emphasize the group's values and traditions. Symbols of group identity such as a team name, slogan, logo, insignia, or emblem may be displayed on flags, banners, clothing, or jewelry. Even a particular type or color of clothing may indicate group membership, as in the case of many urban gangs. Symbols can be effective for helping to create a separate identity for a team. Group identification is strengthened when members agree to wear or display the symbols of membership.

- **Encourage and facilitate social interaction.**

Development of a cohesive group is more likely if the members get to know each other on a personal basis and find it satisfying to interact socially. One way to facilitate pleasant social interaction is to hold periodic social activities such as dinners, lunches, and parties. Various types of outings can be used to facilitate social interaction (e.g., going to a sports event or concert together, or on a camping or rafting trip). When group members work in the same facility, social interaction can be promoted by designating a room for the group to use for meetings and coffee breaks. The room can be decorated with symbols of the group's accomplishments, statements of its values, and charts showing progress in accomplishing group objectives.

- **Tell people about group activities and achievements.**

People tend to feel alienated and unappreciated when they receive little information about the plans, activities, and achievements of their team or department. It is important to keep members informed about these things and to explain how their work contributes to the success of the mission. An example is provided by Admiral Elmo Zumwalt's description of an early command assignment in which he attempted to keep every person on the ship informed about the reason for each tactical exercise and maneuver.

> We made frequent announcements over the loudspeaker about the specific event that was going on. At the beginning and the end of each day, I discussed with the officers who, in turn, discussed with their men what was about to happen and what had just happened, what the competition was doing and what we should do to meet it. We published written notes on the plan of the day that would give the crew some of the color or human interest of what the ship was doing. I had bull sessions in the chief petty officers' quarters, where I often stopped for a cup of coffee. More important than any of the details, of course, was the basic effort to communicate a sense of excitement, fun and zest in all that we were doing. (Zumwalt, 1976, p. 186)

Within 18 months of initiating these practices, his ship moved from last to first place in the squadron with regard to efficiency ratings.

- **Conduct process analysis sessions.**

Process analysis sessions involve frank and open discussion of interpersonal relationships and group processes in an effort to improve them. One approach is to ask each member to suggest ways to make the group more effective. These suggestions should focus on how members communicate, work together, make decisions, and resolve disagreements rather than on the technical aspects of the work. A similar approach is to ask each member to describe how other members could make his or her role in the group easier. The discussion should result in a list of concrete suggestions for improving working relationships. Follow-up meetings can be used to chart progress in implementing the suggestions.

It is usually better to have a trained facilitator conduct the process analysis session instead of the team leader. Discussing interpersonal relationships is more difficult than discussing work procedures, and it takes considerable skill to conduct this type of session. A team leader without training in process consultation may make team relationships worse rather than better. An outside facilitator is likely to be more objective and impartial, which is especially important if the leader is contributing to the difficulties the group has in working together.

- **Increase incentives for mutual cooperation.**

Incentives based on individual performance encourage team members to compete with each other, whereas incentives based on group performance encourage cooperation. One way to increase cohesiveness and team identification is to emphasize formal incentives such as a bonus based on improvements in team performance. Another way is to use spontaneous, informal rewards to emphasize the importance of service to the team. For example, give the members extra days off after the team completes a difficult project, especially one that involved working overtime or on weekends. Hold a special celebration party for team members and their families after the team achieves an important objective.

- **Hold practice sessions under realistic conditions.**

Team performance can be improved by holding frequent practice sessions, and they are very useful for enhancing the confidence of members that they can perform difficult tasks successfully. Unless teams regularly practice how to respond to unusual events such as crises and emergencies, performance is likely to be poor when such events eventually occur. Practice sessions are more beneficial when they are held under conditions that are as realistic as possible. When the task involves a team of people working together, it is best to have them practice complex procedures together. For example, airplane crews practice dealing with emergencies due to equipment failure. Hospital employees conduct simulations to practice dealing with large numbers of casualties from a natural disaster.

- **Use after-activity reviews to facilitate collective learning by the team.**

Collective learning from experience is more likely when a systematic analysis is made after an important activity is finished to discover the reasons for success or failure. The after-activity review (also called an "after-action review," an "after-event review" or a "postmortem") is a procedure for collectively analyzing the processes and resulting outcomes of a team activity (Ellis & Davidi, 2005; Ellis, Mendel, & Nir, 2006; Tannenbaum, Smith-Jentsch, & Behson, 1998). This process is especially useful when teams perform the same type of activity repeatedly. The objective is to identify what was done well and what can be improved the next time a similar activity is conducted. The members should review their initial plans and objectives for the activity, the procedures used to carry out

TABLE 8	Guidelines for Leading an After-activity Review Session

1. Near the beginning make a self-critique that acknowledges shortcomings.
2. Encourage feedback from others and model non-defensive acceptance of it.
3. Ask members to identify effective and ineffective aspects of team performance.
4. Encourage members to examine how group processes affected team performance.
5. Keep the discussion focused on behaviors rather than on individuals.
6. If necessary, provide your own assessment of team performance.
7. Recognize improvements in team performance.
8. Ask members for suggestions on how to improve team performance.
9. Propose improvements not already included in the team's suggestions.

Based on Tannenbaum et al. (1998).

the activity, problems or obstacles encountered in doing the activity, key decisions that were made, and the outcomes. Then the group determines how to use what was learned to improve future performance. For long projects or training simulations, it is also useful to conduct progress review sessions at convenient intermediate points. The use of *after-activity reviews* for evaluating activities and planning improvements is pervasive now in the U.S. Army, and it is slowly gaining acceptance in civilian organizations as well (Baird, Holland, & Deacon, 1999; Ellis & Davidi, 2005). Procedures for leading the reviews are listed in Table 8.

Leading Decision Groups

Groups are used frequently to solve problems and make decisions in organizations. Using a group to make a decision has several potential advantages over decisions made by an individual leader. Groups have more relevant knowledge and ideas that can be pooled to improve decision quality, and active participation will increase member understanding of decisions and member commitment to implement them. On the negative side, group decisions usually take longer, the members may be unable to reach agreement if they have incompatible objectives, and process problems may undermine the quality of decisions.

The process by which a group arrives at a decision is a major determinant of decision quality. Many things can prevent a group from effectively utilizing the information and achieving its full potential. The quality of a group decision depends on the contribution of information and ideas by group members, the clarity of communication, the accuracy of prediction and judgments, the extent to which the discussion is focused on the problem, and the manner in which disagreement is resolved. Common process problems that reduce decision quality include member inhibition, groupthink, false consensus, hasty decisions, polarization, and lack of action planning for implementation.

Appropriate leadership can facilitate effective decision making by a group and help to avoid process problems (Basadur, 2004). The leadership role can be shared to some extent, but members of decision groups often prefer to have one designated discussion leader who has primary responsibility for conducting the meeting (Berkowitz, 1953; Schlesinger, Jackson, & Butman, 1960). An effective leader ensures that the group uses a systematic decision process ("process control"), but does not dominate the discussion ("content control"). The job of conducting a meeting is a difficult one, because the group is likely to be ineffective if the leader is either too passive or too domineering. A considerable amount of skill is needed to achieve a delicate balance between these two extremes. The behaviors and procedures used to achieve this balance are discussed in the remaining sections of this chapter.

TABLE 9	Major Types of Leadership Behavior in Decision Groups
Task Function	**Specific Objective**
1. Process structuring	Guide and sequence discussion
2. Stimulating communication	Increase information exchange
3. Clarifying communication	Increase comprehension
4. Summarizing	Check on understanding and assess progress
5. Consensus testing	Check on agreement
Group Maintenance	**Specific Objective**
1. Gatekeeping	Increase and equalize participation
2. Harmonizing	Reduce tension and hostility
3. Supporting	Prevent withdrawal, reduce tension
4. Standard setting	Regulate behavior
5. Process analyzing	Discover and resolve process problems

Leadership behavior can be classified as task-oriented or relationship-oriented, and a similar distinction can be made for leadership behavior in group meetings. Of course, specific aspects of leadership behavior often involve both task and relationship concerns simultaneously, but the distinction helps to remind group leaders how important it is to balance task and relationship concerns in leading meetings. Several writers have proposed two-factor taxonomies of group leader behavior (Bales, 1950; Benne & Sheats, 1948; Bradford, 1976; Lord, 1977; Schein, 1969). Table 9 shows a simplified, composite taxonomy of task-oriented and group maintenance functions and their primary objectives.

Task-oriented Functions

Task-oriented behavior in a group meeting facilitates the systematic communication, evaluation, and analysis of information and ideas, and it aids problem solving and decision making. Some examples of task-oriented behavior include developing an agenda for the meeting, presenting a problem to the group, asking members for specific information or ideas, asking a member to explain an ambiguous statement, helping the group understand the relevance of ideas, explaining how different ideas are related, keeping the discussion on track, reviewing and summarizing what has been said or done, checking on the amount of agreement among members, suggesting procedures for making a decision, assigning responsibility for follow-up action, and recessing or ending a meeting.

It is not sufficient for a leader simply to carry out the behaviors; a sense of proper timing is also essential (Bradford, 1976). Any task-oriented behavior can be useless or even detrimental if it is premature or overdone. For example, summarizing too soon may discourage contribution of additional ideas on a subject. A discussion may be excessively prolonged if the leader keeps on stimulating communication instead of testing for a *consensus*. It is also important for the leader to have considerable skill in the use of each kind of task-oriented behavior. For example, an unskilled leader who tries to clarify a member's statement may succeed only in creating more confusion. A leader who is unskilled in summarizing may make a summary that leaves out key points and fails to organize contributions in a meaningful way.

Group Maintenance Functions

Group maintenance behavior in a group meeting increases cohesiveness, improves interpersonal relations, aids resolution of conflict, and satisfies the personal needs of members for acceptance, respect, and involvement. Some examples of group maintenance behavior include encouraging participation by quiet members, preventing dominant members from monopolizing the discussion, smoothing over conflict, suggesting compromises, asking members to resolve differences in a constructive way, using humor to reduce tension, expressing appreciation for suggestions and ideas, suggesting norms and standards of behavior, reminding the group of norms agreed upon earlier, asking members for their perception of group processes, and pointing out process problems to the group.

Just as machines need periodic maintenance to keep them running smoothly, so also do human relationships in a group. As with machines, preventive maintenance should be carried out frequently rather than waiting to do corrective maintenance after a serious breakdown. Group maintenance should be an ongoing activity designed to build teamwork and prevent the development of chronic apathy, withdrawal, interpersonal conflict, and status struggles. If allowed to develop, these problems will disrupt the task-oriented activity in a group and reduce the effectiveness of the group.

Group maintenance behavior is needed in most meetings, but it is neglected by many leaders who are unaware of its importance. Standard setting and process analyzing are the aspects of behavior least likely to occur, perhaps because they require an explicit recognition of maintenance needs. As in the case of *task-oriented behaviors,* the *group maintenance behaviors* require skill and a sense of proper timing to be performed effectively.

Who Should Perform the Leadership Functions

Behavioral scientists generally agree that task-oriented behavior and group maintenance behavior are both essential for the effectiveness of decision groups, but they disagree about who should perform these functions and about their relative priority. The traditional view is that the formal leader should direct and control the activities of the group. According to this "leader-centered" view, the group leader should keep discussion focused on the task, discourage expression of feelings, retain control over the final decision (i.e., use consultation rather than group decision), and protect his or her authority in the group. According to Bradford (1976), this kind of group leadership produces some favorable results but at an unacceptable price. Meetings are orderly and decisions get made, but members become apathetic and resentful, which leads to a loss of potential contributions and a reduction in quality of decisions. Acceptance of decisions by group members may also be reduced if members feel manipulated and unable to influence the decisions significantly.

With "group-centered" leadership, the role of the leader is to serve as a consultant, advisor, teacher, and facilitator, rather than as a director or manager of the group. The group maintenance functions are considered to be as important as the task-oriented functions, because feelings and interactions profoundly affect the problem-solving and decision-making processes in a group. Responsibility for both kinds of functions is shared by group members, because no one person can be sensitive to all of the process problems and needs of the group. The leader should encourage expression of feelings as well as ideas, model appropriate leadership behaviors, and encourage members to learn to perform these behaviors themselves. According to Bradford, sharing responsibility for leadership functions will improve the quality of the decisions and make members more satisfied with the group.

Bradford recognized some difficulties in implementing group-centered leadership. He noted that this kind of leadership requires considerable interpersonal skill, maturity, and trust in both the leader and group members. Some leaders are afraid to risk sharing control with group members or dealing openly with emotional behavior. These leaders may also be concerned that the new approach will make them appear weak or incompetent. Some members may be unwilling to deal openly with emotions or may prefer to avoid assuming more responsibility for leadership functions in the group. Many decision groups are only temporary and do not meet over a long enough time to develop the necessary trust, skills, and member commitment. A committee may have unwilling members who prefer to meet as seldom as possible and to assume as little responsibility as possible for committee activities. The traditional approach is often reinforced by ritual and established procedures, which represent additional obstacles to the introduction of group-centered leadership. For example, some decision groups are legally required by their charter or bylaws to follow cumbersome procedural rules (e.g., Robert's rules of order) that are more appropriate for large, formal groups. Despite these many obstacles, Bradford is optimistic about the prospects for successful implementation of group-centered leadership.

Guidelines for Leading Meetings

This section describes specific procedures that leaders can use to improve group effectiveness in solving problems and making decisions. The guidelines for leading meetings (see Table 10) are based on ideas proposed by various scholars over the years (e.g., Basadur, 2004; Janis & Mann, 1977; Jay, 1976; Maier, 1963; Mesmer-Magnus & DeChurch, 2009; Rowland & Parry, 2009; Tropman, 1996; Westaby, Probst, & Lee, 2010).

- **Inform people about necessary preparations for a meeting.**

A problem-solving meeting will be more effective if people know how to prepare for it. To ensure that people plan to attend the meeting, they should be informed in advance about the time, place, and important subjects on the agenda. People who are expected to present briefings, provide technical information, or evaluate a proposal should be given clear guidance and ample time to prepare. Any reports or proposals to be studied in preparation for the meeting should be provided in advance with the agenda.

- **Share essential information with group members.**

When the problem is presented, essential facts known to the leader should be reviewed briefly, including how long the problem has been evident, the nature of the problem symptoms, and what if anything has been done about it up to that time. The amount of information that should be presented depends on the nature of the problem and the group's prior information. The information may be provided prior to the meeting, at the beginning of the meeting, or as the problem diagnosis is made. The leader should be careful to present facts with as

TABLE 10	Guidelines for Leading Decision Group Meetings

- Inform people about necessary preparations for a meeting.
- Share essential information with group members.
- Describe the problem without implying the cause or solution.
- Allow ample time for idea generation and evaluation.
- Separate idea generation from idea evaluation.
- Encourage and facilitate participation.
- Encourage positive restatement and idea building.
- Use systematic procedures for solution evaluation.
- Encourage members to look for an integrative solution.
- Encourage efforts to reach consensus when feasible.
- Clarify responsibilities for implementation.

little interpretation as possible. For example, if the problem is how to increase sales, it is better simply to review sales figures for each district than to make judgments such as "sales are terrible in the central district."

- **Describe the problem without implying the cause or solution.**

The problem should be stated objectively in a way that does not assign blame for it to some or all of the group members. Implying blame will make members defensive and reduce their willingness to help in solving a mutual problem. The problem statement should not suggest the reasons for the problem or possible solutions to it. This kind of statement would limit the consideration of different problem diagnoses by the group. Instead, the problem statement should encourage exploration of a variety of causes and a variety of possible solutions.

- **Allow ample time for idea generation and evaluation.**

The leader should plan meetings so that enough time is available to diagnose the problem, develop alternative solutions, and explore the implications and consequences of each alternative. Even when a group has members who are not inhibited, a strong majority coalition may propose a favored decision and ram it through before the critics have an opportunity to explain their concerns and gather support. The pressure of time is another reason for hasty decisions, and they often occur when a meeting is about to end and members desire to resolve matters quickly to avoid another meeting. When an important decision is being considered but time is not sufficient to evaluate solutions, the leader should try to postpone the decision until another meeting. If an immediate decision is not necessary and it is obvious that more information is needed, the leader may want to adjourn the meeting and arrange for additional information to be obtained.

- **Separate idea generation from idea evaluation.**

Research has found that idea generation is less inhibited when it is separated from idea evaluation (Maier, 1963). Procedures have been developed to reduce inhibition and facilitate idea generation in groups. With *"brainstorming,"* members are encouraged to suggest any idea about the problem that comes to mind, the ideas are written on a blackboard or flip chart, and no positive or negative evaluation of ideas is permitted (including scowls, groans, sighs, or gestures). The rationale is that inhibition would be reduced by deferring evaluation of ideas, domination would be reduced by making contributions brief and spontaneous, and creativity would be increased by mutual facilitation of ideas and a climate of acceptance for strange and novel ideas. Brainstorming improves idea generation in comparison with a regular interacting group, but some inhibition may still occur (White, Dittrich, & Lang, 1980).

The *"nominal group technique"* was developed to correct the deficiencies of brainstorming (Delbecq, Van de Ven, & Gustafson, 1975). During a group meeting (or prior to it) the members are asked to write their ideas on a slip of paper without discussing them. When they are finished, the leader posts the ideas for everyone to see. An alternative that is especially useful for a virtual group is to post ideas on a common web site. Group members are invited to build on ideas already listed or add new ideas stimulated by seeing the list. Then the leader reviews the list with the group to see if there are any questions about the meaning of an idea or its relevance to the objective.

In a recent improvement of this procedure (called "brain writing"), the evaluation of ideas is postponed until a later meeting, and participants are encouraged to continue thinking about the problem and the list of ideas (Paulus & Yang, 2000). The rationale for a follow-up meeting is that members do not have adequate time to reflect upon each other's ideas when they are busy writing ideas of their own, and an "incubation" period is necessary to realize the potential for mutual stimulation of ideas.

- **Encourage and facilitate participation.**

When some members loudly advocate a particular solution and other members remain silent or fail to take a position, the silent ones are usually assumed to be in agreement. In fact, silence may indicate dissent rather than agreement. The leader can use appropriate gatekeeping behavior to facilitate participation and encourage serious discussion of member concerns. Each member should be encouraged to contribute ideas and express concerns, and members should be discouraged from dominating the discussion or using social-pressure tactics (e.g., threats, derogatory comments) to intimidate people who disagree with them. When computer-based groupware is available, it can be used to facilitate anonymous interaction during the posting and evaluation of ideas. After members generate ideas independently, the composite list of ideas can be displayed on each member's computer screen or smart phone. Then any member can add new ideas stimulated by seeing the list, request more information from the (anonymous) source of an idea, or suggest ways to improve an idea. Duplicate ideas can be combined if desired, and a rating procedure can be used to the most acceptable ideas.

- **Encourage positive restatement and idea building.**

Two procedures that are especially useful to create a more supportive climate for idea generation are positive restatement and idea building. One of the most useful techniques for nurturing new ideas is to ask group members to restate another member's idea and find something worthwhile about it before saying anything critical. In a related technique, any member who points out a deficiency or limitation of another's idea is required to suggest a way to correct the deficiency or overcome the limitation. This approach also emphasizes careful listening and constructive, helpful behavior.

- **Use systematic procedures for solution evaluation.**

Procedures have been developed to help decision groups evaluate and compare potential solutions. These procedures are especially useful when members appear to be divided into opposing factions ("polarization"), each with a different solution. With the two-column procedure, members mutually identify and post the advantages and disadvantages of each alternative (Maier, 1963). Members then discuss the advantages and disadvantages and try to agree on an overall ranking of alternatives. A similar but more detailed procedure is cost-benefit analysis. This procedure can be used when the consequences of each solution are fairly certain and it is possible to make reasonably accurate estimates of the benefits and costs in monetary terms. The analysis should be conducted in a systematic manner, and care should be taken to avoid biasing estimates of costs and benefits to support a preferred solution. After all the alternatives have been analyzed, the group selects the best one by using whatever economic criterion seems most appropriate (e.g., maximize net benefit, maximize return on investment).

- **Encourage members to look for an integrative solution.**

When a group is sharply divided in support of competing alternatives, it is sometimes feasible to develop an integrative solution that involves the best features of the rival solutions. One way to begin this procedure is to examine both alternatives closely to identify what features they have in common as well as how they differ. This comparison develops a better understanding and appreciation of the opposing alternative, especially if all group members become actively involved in the discussion. The leader should encourage participation, keep the discussion analytical rather than critical, and post the results of the comparison to provide a visual summary of the similarities and differences. It is also useful to list for each faction the essential qualities of a solution and the relative priorities of different criteria or objectives. Even when it is not possible to develop a hybrid solution, the process may help the group identify an entirely new solution that is superior to the others.

- **Encourage efforts to reach consensus when feasible.**

Voting is a common procedure for making a decision, but whenever feasible, the leader should encourage the group to try to reach a consensus rather than deciding on the basis of a simple majority. A consensus occurs when all members of the group agree that a particular alternative is acceptable, even though it is not necessarily the first choice of every member. A consensus decision usually generates more commitment than a majority decision, but more time is typically needed to make the decision, and a group consensus is not always possible. When the group has a large majority in support of one alternative, but a few dissenters still remain, the leader should carefully weigh the possible benefits of winning them over against the cost of additional discussion time. If adequate time has already been devoted to discussion of alternatives, it is seldom worthwhile to prolong the discussion merely to persuade one or two stubborn members. In this situation, the leader should take the initiative and declare that a group decision has been reached.

- **Clarify responsibilities for implementation.**

Before the meeting ends, the leader should make some provisions for implementing the decision. Necessary action steps should be specified and responsibility for each action step assigned to individuals. Many good decisions made by groups are unsuccessful simply because nobody bothers to ensure that they are implemented. If a follow-up meeting is needed, the preparations required for that meeting should be determined and responsibilities assigned. Also, the date and time should be determined, if possible, when everyone is present. After the meeting, the leader should distribute a summary of what was discussed and decided, and what responsibilities were assigned to whom.

Summary

Organizations increasingly rely on teams to improve quality, efficiency, and adaptive change. Several types of teams are used in organizations, including functional work teams, crossfunctional teams, self-managed teams, virtual teams, and executive teams. The potential advantages of teams include more employee satisfaction and commitment, better quality of products and services, and greater efficiency and productivity. However, the benefits do not occur automatically, and successful implementation depends on the quality of leadership and some facilitating conditions.

Effective leadership in teams usually requires many specific types of leadership behavior. The appropriate pattern of behavior will depend on the type of team and the relative importance of the performance determinants. Some essential leadership processes in teams include building commitment for shared objectives, identifying effective performance strategies and organizing team activities, enhancing member skills and role clarity, building mutual trust and cooperation, identifying and procuring needed resources, maintaining confidence and optimism, and facilitating external coordination.

Leadership is provided in somewhat different ways in the different types of teams. Functional work teams and cross-functional teams usually have an appointed leader with strong position power. In a self-managed team, many of the leadership roles are carried out informally and shared among the members. However, even in teams with a formal leader, it is often beneficial for other members to share responsibility for some of the leadership roles. Virtual teams have members who work in different locations and interact primarily using communications technology. Any type of team can operate with some degree of virtuality.

Team-building activities are used to increase cohesiveness, group identification, and cooperation. Some examples include emphasizing common interests and values, using ceremonies and rituals, using symbols to develop group identification, facilitating social interaction among members, informing members about group activities and achievements, and conducting process analysis sessions.

A group decision is potentially superior to a decision made by a single individual such as the leader, but many things can prevent a group from realizing its potential. Leadership is a major determinant of group effectiveness, and in the context of group meetings it includes both task-oriented and group maintenance functions. The two types of leadership functions require skill and a sense of proper timing to be effective. The leadership role is difficult, because the decision process will be adversely affected if the leader is either too passive or too domineering. To improve problem solving and avoid common process problems, a leader should present the problem in an unbiased manner, encourage the group to consider alternative conceptions of the problem, separate idea generation from idea evaluation, and use systematic procedures for solution evaluation.

Research on leadership in teams has increased in recent years, but it continues to lag behind changes in the use of teams in organizations. The extent to which effective leadership is different in virtual teams has yet to be determined, and rapid advances in technology make it difficult to predict the future relevance of results from past research.

Review and Discussion Questions

1. What factors determine the performance of a team?
2. What leadership processes are important for cross-functional teams?
3. Why is leadership more difficult in cross-functional teams than in functional teams?
4. What leadership roles and processes are important for self-managed teams?
5. Under what conditions are self-managed work teams most likely to be successful?
6. What can be done to improve group cohesiveness and collective identification?
7. What are the major task-oriented and group maintenance functions in decision groups?
8. What can a leader do to improve decision-making processes in a group meeting?
9. Please watch the movie, "Twelve Angry Men" or "Ek Ruka Hua Faisla," and comment on leadership in group decision making.

Key Terms

after-activity reviews	decision support systems	self-managed teams
brainstorming	external coordination	shared mental models
cohesiveness	functional teams	task-oriented behaviors
collective efficacy	group maintenance behaviors	

collective identification   nominal group technique   team building
consensus   performance strategies   virtual teams
cross-functional teams   potency

CASE

The Abilene Paradox*

One July morning in Kota, Rajasthan, it was particularly hot with the temperature hovering at 40ºC. However, the wind was blowing over the cotton farm and through the house, making the afternoon tolerable, even potentially enjoyable. There was a cooler running and adding to the breeze; there was cold lemonade; and finally, there was entertainment—*teen patti* (a popular card game). All in all, it had the makings of an agreeable and enjoyable Sunday. That it was until my father-in-law (who was a retired judge of the Supreme Court) suddenly said, "Let's get in the Austin of England (an expensive vintage car), go to Sawai Madhopur, and have lunch at the 7-Star Hotel there. Their specialty is *kheer mohan*."

I (a newly appointed session judge in Lucknow) thought, "What? Go to Madhopur? 200 kilometers in this dust storm and heat? And in an unairconditioned 1958 Austin?"

But my wife chimed in, "Sounds like a great idea. I'd like to go. How about you, Raghav?" Because my own preferences were obviously out of step with the rest, I replied, "Sounds good to me," and added, "I just hope your mother (who was a retired additional district judge from Jaipur) wants to go."

"Of course I want to go," said my mother-in-law. "I haven't been to Madhopur in a long time."

So, into the car and off to Madhopur we went. My predictions were fulfilled. The heat was brutal. By the time we arrived in Madhopur, we were coated in a fine layer of dust that was cemented with perspiration. The food at the 7-Star Hotel was good, however, it wasn't good enough for the efforts we had put in.

Some four hours and 200 kms later, we returned to Kota, hot and exhausted. We sat in front of the cooler for a long time, in silence. Then, both to be sociable and to break the silence, I said, "It was a great trip, wasn't it?"

No one spoke. Finally, my mother-in-law said, with some irritation, "Well, to tell you the truth, I really didn't enjoy it much and would rather have stayed here. I just went along because the three of you were so enthusiastic about going. I wouldn't have gone if all of you hadn't pressured me into it."

I couldn't believe it. "What do you mean by 'you all'!" I said. "Don't put me in the 'you all' group. I was delighted to be doing what we were doing. I didn't want to go. I only went to satisfy the rest of you. You're the culprits."

My wife looked shocked. "Don't call me a culprit. You, Dad, and Mom were the ones who wanted to go. I just went along to be sociable and to keep you happy. I would have had to be crazy to want to go out in heat like that."

Her father entered the conversation abruptly. "Hell!" he said. He proceeded to expand on what was already absolutely clear. "Listen, I never wanted to go to Madhopur. I just thought you might be bored. You visit so rarely, I wanted to be sure you enjoyed it. I would have preferred to play another game of *teen patti* and eat homemade food."

After the outburst of recrimination, we all sat back in silence. Here we were, four reasonably sensible and intelligent people, who, of our own volition, had just taken a 200-km trip, across a godforsaken desert, in furnace-like temperature, through a cloud-like dust storm, to eat unpalatable food at a hole-in-the-wall restaurant in Madhopur, when none of us had really wanted to go. In fact, to be more accurate, we'd done just the opposite of what we wanted to do. The entire situation simply didn't make sense.

(*Adapted from Harvey, J. B. (1988). "The Abilene Paradox: The Management of Agreement," *Organizational Dynamics, 17*(1), 17-43).

Questions

1. In this situation, who are the culprits and victims?
2. How could the family have avoided going on the trip?
3. Who is the leader in this scenario?

Strategic Leadership in Organizations

From Chapter 11 of *Leadership in Organizations*, Eighth Edition. Gary Yukl. Copyright © 2013 by Pearson Education, Inc. Publishing as Prentice Hall. All rights reserved.

Strategic Leadership
in Organizations

Learning Objectives

After studying this chapter, you should be able to:

- Understand what organizational processes determine a company's performance.
- Understand how top executives can influence organizational processes and performance.
- Understand constraints on strategic leadership and conditions that make it more important.
- Understand the potential advantages of executive teams and how to use them effectively.
- Understand why it is important to monitor the external environment and how to do it.
- Understand the procedures that can be used to formulate a good competitive strategy.

Much of the early leadership literature was concerned with supervisors or middle managers in organizations, but in recent years there has been increased interest in "strategic leadership" by top executives (Cannella & Monroe, 1997). The shift in focus reflects an increased interest in understanding how executives can transform their companies to cope with globalization, increasing international competition, and rapid technological and social change.

This chapter examines what has been learned about effective leadership by top executives in organizations. The chapter begins with a description of the performance determinants that determine the prosperity and survival of an organization. Next is a review of ways leaders can influence these performance determinants. Then the chapter reviews conditions that determine need for strategic change and the amount of influence top executives are likely to have on the organization. Results are reviewed and evaluated for different types of studies that examine the influence of a chief executive officer (CEO) on organizational performance.

The chapter explains why executive teams are relevant for understanding strategic leadership in organizations, and the effective use of executive teams is discussed. Alternative conceptions of organizational leadership are reviewed, including shared and distributed leadership, relational leadership, and complexity theory. Two important responsibilities for top executives are monitoring the external environment to identify threats and opportunities, and formulating strategy for the future survival and prosperity of the organization. These responsibilities are explained and guidelines for them are provided.

Determinants of Organizational Performance

Organizational effectiveness is the long-term prosperity and survival of the organization. To be successful organizations must adapt to their environment, acquire necessary resources, and conduct operations in efficient ways (Katz & Kahn, 1978). Leaders can influence organizational performance in several ways, including decisions about the competitive strategy, human resources, and the management programs, systems, and organization structure. The determinants of organizational performance are closely inter-related, and when deciding how to improve performance leaders should understand the inherent trade-offs and potential synergies (Gupta, Smith, & Shalley, 2006; He & Wong, 2004; Yukl, 2008).

Adaptation to the Environment

The effectiveness of an organization depends on responding in appropriate ways to external threats and opportunities. Adaptation is more important when the external environment is volatile and uncertain, which is likely in situations of rapid technological change, political and economic turmoil, or new threats from competitors or external enemies. A company is more likely to adapt successfully to its environment if it has a relevant competitive strategy specifying the types of products or services to offer and ways to influence potential customers or clients. Successful adaptation sometimes requires major changes in the organization's products and services, or the procedures for marketing and supplying them. A rapid response to changing conditions and the actions of competitors is especially important for an organization with a strategy that emphasizes unique, leading-edge products or services designed to satisfy the changing needs of customers and clients.

Adaptation is enhanced by accurate interpretation of information about the environment; collective learning by members, and accurate mental model about the determinants of performance; effective knowledge management (retention and diffusion of new knowledge within the organization); flexibility of work processes (capacity to change them quickly as needed); innovations in products, services, or processes; and availability of discretionary resources (to support new initiatives and crisis management).

Efficiency and Process Reliability

Efficiency is the use of people and resources to carry out essential operations in a way that minimizes costs and avoids wasted effort and resources. Efficiency is especially important when the competitive strategy of the organization is to offer its products and services at a lower price than competitors, or when a financial crisis occurs and there are insufficient funds to support essential operations. This performance determinant is less important when an organization is able to pass along cost increases to customers, or the organization is highly subsidized by the government or private investors. Efficiency can be increased by redesigning work processes, using new technology, and coordinating unit activities to avoid unnecessary activities and wasted resources. However, efforts to improve efficiency by using new technology may fail if the cost of purchasing and operating the new technology exceeds any savings from a smaller workforce.

Process reliability means avoiding unnecessary delays, errors, quality defects, or accidents. It is an important component of efficiency when defective products or unreliable processes increase costs. Examples include theft or misuse of resources, expenses for correcting or replacing defective products or inadequate services, expenses for repairing or replacing damaged equipment, and lawsuits by customers or employees who are injured by errors, accidents, or exposure to harmful substances. Process reliability is conceptualized primarily as a component of efficiency because it usually increases costs, but sometimes it can also affect adaptation (e.g., if sales are reduced by defective products or poor service) or human resources (e.g., employees are seriously injured or killed by avoidable accidents and hazards).

Process reliability can be improved by using extra resources to ensure that quality and safety standards are maintained, products or services are delivered on time, and accidents are avoided. However, efficiency will not be improved unless the savings from improved process reliability exceeds the cost of the extra resources. Sometimes it is possible to redesign products and simplify work processes in ways that will reduce errors and delays as well as the direct cost of operations (e.g., with re-engineering or Six Sigma programs).

Human Resources and Relations

The term *human capital* is sometimes used to describe the quality of an organization's human resources, which include the relevant skills and experience of members (Hitt & Ireland, 2002). Performance also depends on member motivation and the quality of their social relationships and networks (sometimes called *social capital*). Collective work is performed more effectively by people who have strong skills, strong commitment to task objectives, confidence in their ability to achieve challenging objectives, a high level of mutual trust, and strong identification with the organization and its mission (Crook, Todd, Combs, Woehr, & Ketchen, 2011; Harter, Schmidt, & Hayes, 2002; Pfeffer, 1994, 2005). Talented, dedicated employees are often instrumental for the achievement of both efficiency and innovative adaptation (Huselid, 1995; Mahsud, Yukl, & Prussia, 2011).

At the organizational level, human capital is more important when the organization is heavily dependent on people who have unique talents, require extensive training, and would be difficult to replace if they left (e.g., hospitals, consulting firms, legal firms, advertising agencies, research universities). Human capital is less important for an organization with highly automated processes and few employees, for a "virtual organization" that has outsourced most activities, or for an organization with mostly unskilled jobs and an ample supply of people willing to work for low wages.

Human capital depends in part on organizational policies about human resource acquisition, development, and compensation. Human capital can be improved with the use of relevant human resource programs and systems, such as recruiting, training, compensation, staffing and succession planning (e.g., Becker & Huselid, 1998; Bowen & Ostroff, 2004).

Competitive Strategy

Competitive strategy includes decisions about the types of products or services to offer, the basis for appealing to potential customers (e.g., price, quality, customer service, uniqueness, patriotism), and the methods used to influence potential customers or clients (e.g., advertising, discounts, promotions). The strategy may also involve ways to obtain necessary financial resources (e.g., stocks, bonds, loans, donations), and ways to grow the organization and expand into new markets (e.g., acquisitions, mergers, joint ventures, strategic alliances, franchises). Competitive strategy is an important determinant of the financial performance and survival of organizations (Adner & Helfat, 2003; Carmeli, Gelbard, & Gefen, 2010; Hambrick, 2007; Narayanan et al., 2011; O'Reilly, Caldwell, Chatman, Lapiz, & Self, 2010; Porter, 1980).

Leaders formulate competitive strategy with the use of change-oriented behaviors such as monitoring the external environment, assessing threats and opportunities, identifying core competencies, proposing innovative strategies, and evaluating alternative strategies. Some types of programs and systems for monitoring the external environment can be used to help detect threats and opportunities and identify an appropriate strategy for the organization.

Decisions about competitive strategy have the greatest potential influence on adaptation, but they also affect the relative importance of other performance determinants and their optimal level. For example, the decision to offer lower prices as the primary basis for increasing sales and profits may require a reduction in the cost of operations (e.g., by using improved technology, by using less expensive materials, by reducing the pay and benefits of current or newly hired employees, or by outsourcing high paying jobs to low-wage countries). The decision to provide more unique products or improve customer service may make it necessary to recruit more skilled employees or change the way current employees are trained and rewarded. Implementing a new strategy usually requires some modification of management programs, systems, and structures in the organization, and it may also involve negotiation of new agreements with other organizations (e.g., clients, distributors, suppliers, strategic partners).

Management Programs, Systems, and Structures

Many different types of improvement programs, management systems, and structural forms can be used to influence organizational effectiveness (Yukl & Lepsinger, 2004). Most programs have as the primary objective the improvement of adaptation, efficiency, or human capital (see Table 1).

TABLE 1	Management Programs, Systems, and Structures for Improving Performance

Efficiency and Process Reliability

- Performance management and goal setting programs (e.g., MBO, zero defects)
- Process and quality improvement programs (quality circles, TQM, Six Sigma)
- Cost reduction programs (downsizing, outsourcing, just-in-time inventory)
- Structural forms (functional specialization, formalization, standardization)
- Appraisal, recognition, and reward systems focused on efficiency and process reliability

Human Resources and Relations

- Quality of worklife programs (flextime, job sharing, child care, fitness center)
- Employee benefit programs (health care, vacations, retirement, sabbaticals)
- Socialization and teambuilding (orientation programs; ceremonies and rituals; social events and celebrations)
- Employee development programs (training, mentoring, 360 feedback, education subsidies)
- Human resource planning (succession planning, assessment centers, recruiting programs)
- Empowerment programs (self-managed teams, employee ownership, industrial democracy)
- Recognition and reward programs focused on loyalty, service, or skill acquisition

Innovation and Adaptation

- Competitor and market analysis programs (market surveys, focus groups, consumer panels, comparative product testing, benchmarking of competitor products and processes)
- Innovation programs (entrepreneurship programs, quality circles, innovation goals)
- Knowledge acquisition (consultants, joint ventures, importing best practices from others)
- Organizational learning (knowledge management systems, after-activity reviews, joint ventures)
- Temporary structural forms for implementing change (steering committee, task forces)
- Growth and diversification programs (mergers and acquisitions, franchises, joint ventures)
- Structural forms (research departments, small product divisions, product managers, crossfunctional product development teams)
- Appraisal, recognition, and reward systems focused on innovation and customer satisfaction

Several types of management programs or initiatives have been used to improve efficiency and process reliability (e.g., Benner & Tushman, 2003; Ho, Chan, & Kedwell, 1999; Lawler, Mohrman, & Benson, 2001; Powell, 1995; Waterson et al., 1999). Examples include cost reduction programs (downsizing, outsourcing, just-in-time inventory), process and quality improvement programs (total quality management, Six Sigma, business process re-engineering); performance management and goal setting programs (e.g., management by objectives, zero defects); and appraisal, recognition, and reward systems that emphasize efficiency and reliability. Some programs involve the implementation of standardized procedures that provide a way to ensure that common activities are carried out in an efficient and uniform way across subunits. Another type of improvement program involves the use of new technology to automate work processes and reduce labor costs. Efficiency is also affected by aspects of an organization's formal structure such as formalization, standardization, and the use of functionally specialized subunits (Mintzberg, 1979).

Several types of programs have been used to improve innovation and adaptation (e.g., Damanpour, 1991; Dougherty & Hardy, 1996; Gibson & Birkinshaw, 2004; Teece, 1996; Van de Ven et al., 1999; Vermeulen, Jong, & O'Shaughnessy, 2005). Examples include programs that improve understanding of customer preferences and competitor actions (e.g., market surveys, focus groups, customer panels, comparative product testing, and bench-marking of competitor products and processes). Structural forms that can increase innovation and adaptation include research and development departments, cross-functional product development teams, product managers, and semi-autonomous divisions based on products, market segments or different types of customers (Galbraith, 1973; Mintzberg, 1979).

Many types of management programs and systems are used to improve human capital (e.g., Becker & Gerhardt, 1996; Guzzo, Jette, & Katzell, 1985; Huselid, 1995; Huselid, Jackson, & Schuler, 1997; Ichniowski & Shaw, 1999; Kirkman & Rosen, 1997; Lawler et al., 2001; Molina & Ortega, 2003; Singh, 2003). Employee skills can be improved with recruiting and selection programs, talent management and succession planning programs, and employee development programs (e.g., training, mentoring program, 360 feedback, education subsidies, corporate university). Identification with the organization can be improved with quality of work life programs (flextime, job sharing, child care, fitness center), employee benefit programs (compensation, health care, retirement, sabbaticals), socialization programs (orientation sessions; celebrations, rituals, and ceremonies), employee empowerment programs (employee stock ownership, industrial democracy), and recognition and reward programs based on loyalty, service, and skill acquisition.

Despite some dramatic successes, many improvement programs and management systems fail because they are irrelevant, poorly implemented, or incompatible with the organization's culture and competitive strategy (Abrahamson, 1996; Abrahamson & Fairchild, 1999; Beer, 1988; Benner & Tushman, 2003; Carson, Lanier, Carson, & Guidry, 2000; Powell, 1995; Staw & Epstein, 2000). Management programs and systems intended to improve one performance determinant often have unintended side effects on other performance determinants, and the side effects may be positive or negative. Even if a program is able to achieve its primary objective, adverse side effects may cause it to be abandoned.

How Leaders Influence Organizational Performance

Leaders can do many things to influence the things that determine organizational performance, and two general approaches are described by Flexible Leadership Theory (Yukl, 2008; Yukl & Lepsinger, 2004). One approach is to use leadership behaviors to directly influence individuals and groups. The task-oriented behaviors are used primarily to improve efficiency and process reliability. The relations-oriented behaviors are used primarily to improve human relations and human resources. The change-oriented behaviors are used primarily to improve innovation and adaptation to the external environment.

A second general approach is to make decisions about competitive strategy, organization structure, and management programs. Top executives usually have primary responsibility and authority for decisions about competitive strategy and the creation or modification of formal programs, systems, and structures (Hambrick, Nadler, & Tushman, 1998; Hunt, 1991). However, a coordinated effort by leaders at all levels in the organization is necessary to ensure that a strategy, improvement program, or management system is effectively implemented. Most leadership theories describe the direct influence of leader behavior on subordinate attitudes and motivation, but not the indirect influence on members derived from changing programs and systems. Over a longer period of time, top executives and other leaders in an organization can also influence cultural values with a combination of behaviors, programs, and reward systems.

Direct behaviors and decisions about strategy and programs are complementary forms of leader influence (Yukl, 2008). The direct behaviors can be used to facilitate the implementation of a new strategy or program and their successful use. For example, a new training program is more likely to be successful when leaders encourage subordinates to attend the program and provide them with opportunities to use newly learned skills on the job. A new knowledge management system is more likely to be successful when employees are encouraged to input relevant information and use the system in appropriate ways. A major change in strategy is more likely to be accepted when leaders explain why it is needed and how it will benefit the organization.

Management programs and systems can enhance the effects of direct leadership behaviors (Yukl, 2008). For example, encouraging innovative thinking is much more likely to increase the development of new products and processes when an organization has a well-designed program to facilitate and reward innovation. Without such a program, employees may doubt that their creative ideas will be supported and eventually used by the organization. However, programs and structures can also limit the use of leadership behaviors or nullify the effects of this behavior. For example, it is difficult to empower subordinates when there are elaborate rules and standard procedures for doing the work. It is difficult for a leader to influence subordinates to improve customer service if there is an incentive system with rewards based entirely on the number of customers served, and faster service is achieved by reducing service quality.

Management programs and systems can also serve as substitutes for some types of direct behaviors (Yukl, 2008). For example, company-wide training programs can reduce the amount of training that managers need to provide to their immediate subordinates. Management programs and systems provide a way to ensure that common activities are carried out in an efficient and uniform way across subunits. A company-wide bonus system with clear guidelines is likely to be more equitable than having each subunit manager determine the size and frequency of bonuses and the criteria for awarding them. Training of generic skills that are relevant for all employees is likely to be more efficient and consistent if provided by expert trainers as part of a company training program rather than by many individual managers in the company.

Trade-offs and Synergies

Complex interdependencies and trade-offs among the performance determinants create difficult challenges for leaders (Beer, 2001; Quinn, 1988; Yukl & Lepsinger, 2004). Decisions and actions that are intended to improve one performance determinant can affect the others in a positive or negative way, and unintended consequences are common. A leader who puts too much emphasis on influencing one performance determinant may have an adverse effect on another performance determinant, resulting in lower organizational performance. The following example from Home Depot shows how attempts to improve efficiency can adversely affect both human relations and adaptation (Foust, 2003).

> The company had always encouraged its store managers to view their stores as their own and to manage them as they saw fit. This approach motivated employees to be entrepreneurial and customer-focused, but it increased the cost of operations. When Bob Nardelli became the CEO, he decided to cut costs by centralizing purchasing decisions, reducing inventory, and establishing clear performance standards. Many store managers were upset by the changes and chose to leave Home Depot rather than surrender their autonomy to headquarters. Customers satisfaction was also affected. Inventory reductions meant that customers could no longer be sure of finding what they needed. Using more part-time people (up to half of the workforce) as a cost-cutting measure led to more complaints by customers that they could no longer get advice from knowledgeable, experienced salespeople. Sales declined and there was a sharp drop in the stock price.

When there are difficult trade-offs, it is essential to find an appropriate balance that reflects the relative priorities of the performance determinants and the potential for improving each one (Beer, 2001; Ebben & Johnson, 2005; Gibson & Birkinshaw, 2004; Quinn, 1988; Uotila, Markku, Keil, & Shaker, 2009; Yukl & Lepsinger, 2004). In some cases it is not possible to improve a performance determinant without consistent changes in the others. For example, it is difficult to improve efficiency or innovation if the necessary changes depend on employees who lack the motivation and skills necessary to achieve these objectives. Whenever possible, leaders should look for ways to enhance more than one performance determinant at the same time.

The performance of a team or organization is likely to be better when leaders are able to enhance innovative adaptation and efficiency simultaneously, which is sometimes called "organizational ambidexterity" (Gibson & Birkinshaw, 2004; He & Wong, 2004; O' Reilly & Tushman, 2004; Tushman & O' Reilly, 1996). For example, one study (Gilson, Mathieu, Shalley, & Ruddy, 2005) found that equipment repair teams with highly skilled members (human capital) were able to achieve low costs (efficiency) as well as good customer service (adaptation) with a combination of standardized best practices and creativity in using new approaches. Success in achieving potential synergies requires a good understanding of the complex relationships among performance determinants and the consequences of decisions made to influence them. The following example vividly shows what can go wrong when top executives fail to understand these complexities (Finkelstein, 2003).

> In the 1980s two major problems for General Motors were contentious relations with the auto workers union and increasing competition from low-cost, high quality cars made by Toyota and other Japanese companies. Roger Smith, the CEO of GM, believed that the solution for improving both efficiency and quality was to replace most production workers with robots. He had a vision of GM factories operating at high speed day and night with no worker errors, no strikes, and lower labor costs. The GM executives failed to anticipate the difficulties and high cost of automating production processes, and they did not understand that a much better solution was to use the same lean manufacturing practices that were so effective for Toyota (including supply-chain management, just-in-time inventory, and quality management practices). The cost for capital investment in new equipment and the high costs for skilled technicians to operate and maintain the equipment far exceeded any savings from downsizing the work force. The automated factories

failed to provide the expected improvement in quality, and productivity actually declined during the period from 1984 to 1991. GM invested more than 45 billion dollars in automation, and this amount would have been sufficient to purchase both Toyota and Nissan.

The task of balancing trade-offs among the performance determinants is further complicated by changes in conditions affecting the relative importance of the performance determinants (Yukl, 2008). Examples include changes in economic and political conditions, new competition from other organizations, changes in customer preferences, and changes in technology that affect the processes or products of the company. A leader may achieve a good balance only to find that changing conditions have upset it again. Leaders should frequently assess the situation and determine what types of behavior, programs, management systems, and structural forms are relevant and mutually compatible. Using a particular type of behavior, program, or strategy because it proved successful in the past or for other leaders may not yield the desired results. Considerable skill is required to monitor and diagnose the situation accurately and integrate diverse leadership activities in a way that is relevant for changing conditions (Boal & Hooijberg, 2001; Hooijberg, Hunt, & Dodge, 1997; Yukl & Lepsinger, 2005).

Coordinating Leadership Across Levels and Subunits

Leadership in organizations is a process that involves many formal and informal leaders at all levels and in different subunits of the organization. The fates of different leaders are closely intertwined in complex ways, and the overall performance of the organization is likely to suffer if decisions made by different leaders are not compatible with each other (Yukl, 2008). Even though top executives have primary responsibility for strategic decisions, they are unlikely to be implemented successfully without the support and commitment of middle- and lower-level leaders in the organization (Beer et al., 1990; Huy, 2002; O'Reilly et al., 2010; Wai-Kwong, Priem, & Cycyota, 2001).

Even in organizations with a powerful CEO, the implementation of a new strategy or major change can be delayed by prolonged conflicts among top executives, or by resistance to change from managers at middle and lower levels. Leaders may disagree about the nature of external threats and opportunities, the reasons for past success or failure, the priorities for different objectives, the feasibility of alternative strategies, and the need for major changes. A good understanding of reasons for potential resistance is needed to identify a vision or competitive strategy that will elicit sufficient cooperation and commitment (Connor, 1995; Edmondson, Roberto, & Watkins, 2003; Kotter, 2002; Robbins & Duncan, 1988; Smith & Tushman, 2005).

It is important to understand the complex interdependencies that determine the consequences of strategic decisions for other executives and the overall organization. The primary responsibility for resolving disagreements and achieving integration usually falls on the CEO, and it can be facilitated with the use of appropriate decision processes. However, an alternative approach is to make the entire executive team responsible for integration. The facilitating conditions and essential processes for a "leader centric" or "team centric" approach are described by Smith and Tushman (2005).

It is difficult to achieve cooperation and coordination across levels and subunits in an organization unless the managers have shared ideals and values to guide their decisions. Companies with a "core ideology" that is strong and relevant are more likely to survive and be successful over a long period of time (Collins & Porras, 1997). Top management has primary responsibility for ensuring that the organization has a relevant core ideology, but leaders at all levels must help to build support for it and ensure that it is understood.

Top executives do not have a monopoly on relevant information or new ideas, and innovative changes in organizations often originate from lower levels (Marion & Uhl-Bien, 2001; Yukl & Lepsinger, 2004). There are several ways top management can increase the involvement of middle- and lower-level managers in making strategic decisions (Denis, Lamothe, & Langley, 2001; Sundaramurthy & Lewis, 2003). Managers at different levels can be invited to participate in face-to-face or virtual meetings about strategic decisions. Task forces with representatives from different subunits and levels can be formed to develop a new initiative or determine what types of changes are necessary. Relevant programs and systems can be used to encourage and support proposals from lower-level managers for improving efficiency, adaptation, and human relations.

Effects of the Personality of Top Executives on Organizational Performance

Scholars in organizational theory and industrial psychology widely recognize that a chief executive officer (CEO) serves a unique and central role in the core decision process of organizations by injecting a great deal of their individual attributes, such as experiences, preferences, and dispositions (Hambrick and Mason, 1984). Narcissism is one such personality characteristic that is specifically pertinent to the study of CEO leadership and organizational performance (Chatterjee and Hambrick, 2007).

Literature examining the relationship between a CEO's narcissism and organizational performance conveys two prominent and theoretically divided themes. The first is that the CEO's narcissism provides the requisite force for overcoming inertia and a platform for strategic dynamism and propels actions in highly path-divergent domains (Chatterjee and Hambrick, 2007). The corollary to imparting such grandiosity in a company's current domain is an increase in the number and size of acquisitions and extreme organizational performance (big wins or big losses).

The second theme emerges from leadership literature (Peterson, Galvin, and Lange, 2012; Resick, Whitman, Weingarden, and Hiller, 2009) that provides evidences to the possibilities of a negative relationship between a CEO's narcissism and organizational performance. Because of the grandiose and arrogant disposition of narcissistic leaders, they are more likely to engage in behaviors that create insecurities and dependencies among followers (House and Howell, 1992). As a result, they fail to promote and inculcate a positive organizational culture (Lubit, 2002). Hence, narcissist leadership is found to relate negatively to the development of followers (Peterson et. al., 2012) and equitable credit distributions (Resick et. al. 2009), which are central to servant and contingent reward leadership respectively. In turn, the CEOs' narcissism is shown to affect organizational performance negatively.

The notion that there may be a negative relationship between a CEO's narcissism and organizational performance is more apparent in accounting and finance literature (Chen, Lu, and Sougiannis, 2012; Jenson, 1986) where the narcissist disposition of a CEO seem analogous to their typical "empire-building" tendencies. These tendencies refer to the CEO's motivations for constructing empires (excessive growth and excessive investment) to satisfy their hunger for status, power, compensation, and prestige. The empire-building tendencies germinate conflicts and differences in preferences between the board of directors (representing investors) and the CEO, which consequently decreases operating performance and reduces firm value.

Situations Affecting Strategic Leadership

The opportunity of top executives to exert strong influence on the performance of an organization is greater for some situations than for others. It depends in part on the success of the organization's current strategies in achieving a high level of financial performance, on external conditions that determine if the strategies are effective, on the power of the CEO to make major changes, and on internal and external constraints that limit the decisions of the CEO (Lord & Maher, 1991; Miller & Friesen, 1984; Tushman & Romanelli, 1985; Tushman, Newman, & Romanelli, 1986). Each of these situational influences will be described briefly.

Constraints on Top Executives

Managers face many constraints that limit their discretion. How much influence top executives can have on the performance of their organization is determined in part by internal and external constraints on their decisions and actions (Hambrick & Finkelstein, 1987).

One type of internal constraint involves powerful inside forces or coalitions in the organization. Power and discretion are greater when the CEO is a major owner or shareholder of the firm or when the board of directors is easily influenced to support the CEO. Discretion is also increased when surplus financial reserves are available to fund new ventures, or the firm's prosperity makes it easy to finance innovations by borrowing funds. There is less discretion when the CEO must operate in the shadow of the company founder, satisfy a dominant owner (e.g., the organization is a family-owned firm or the subsidiary of another firm), or answer to a strong board of directors with rigid ideas about the appropriate way to do things. Discretion is also limited when internal factions and coalitions have sufficient power to block changes a leader wants to make (e.g., labor unions, other executives with a strong power base), or there is a strong organization culture that is resistant to change. Large organizations with a strong bureaucracy and standardized ways of doing things have an inertia that is difficult to overcome. People resist change that threatens their status and power, contradicts their values and beliefs, or requires learning new ways of doing things.

External constraints on the discretion of a CEO include the nature of the organization's primary products and services and the type of markets in which the organization operates. Managerial discretion is greater if the organization is in a growth industry that has rapidly increasing demand rather than flat or declining demand, if the organization's products or services can be differentiated from those of competitors (not a standardized "commodity" such as gasoline or cement), and if the organization dominates its markets and faces little or no direct competition (e.g., it is a monopoly or has a dominant share of the market). Discretion is constrained by powerful external stakeholders who can dictate conditions, as when a few major clients account for most of the company's sales, or when the company is dependent on a single source of key materials. The decisions and actions of top executives are limited by environmental regulations, labor laws, safety standards, and legal obligations. Even when the organization is a monopoly, discretion in key areas such as pricing, technology, and product changes may be severely limited by government regulation.

Environmental Uncertainty and Crises

The discretion of an executive to make major changes depends in part on how internal and external stakeholders perceive the current performance of the organization. Major innovative changes are less likely to occur in periods of relative stability and prosperity for the organization. When people do not perceive any crisis, attempts by the leader to make major changes are likely to be viewed as inappropriate, disruptive, and irresponsible. However, in a crisis situation leaders are expected to take more decisive, innovative actions.

The potential influence of a CEO on the organization's performance is much larger when major changes in the environment threaten to undermine the effectiveness of the existing strategy or provide unusual opportunities to pursue a new strategy. A CEO who foresees the need for change and takes bold steps to deal with threats and capitalize on opportunities can have a dramatic effect on the long-term survival and effectiveness of the organization.

However, in the absence of an obvious crisis and declining performance, major changes are risky. In a relatively stable environment, changing a traditional strategy that has been effective can reduce financial performance rather than improving it (McClelland, Liang, & Barker, 2009). It is often costly to implement a new strategy, and a temporary decline in financial performance is likely as added costs are incurred and people learn new ways of doing things (Lord & Maher, 1991). Considerable time is usually required to verify the success of a major change (three to five years), and constituents may become impatient about the lack of faster progress.

When faced with gradual changes in the external environment such as new competition, new technology, or shifts in customer preferences, many executives persist too long in the belief that a previously successful strategy is still relevant (Audia, Locke, & Smith, 2000; Lant, Milliken, & Batra, 1992; Miller & Chen, 1994). When executives identify with the current strategy because they developed it, or their implicit assumptions about it are incorrect, then they are likely to make only incremental changes rather than major changes. Efforts to strengthen the current strategy by cutting costs and tightening controls often results in a temporary improvement in performance, making top management appear to be successful (Johnson, 1992). An entrenched CEO may continue to invest more resources in the current strategy rather than admit that it is failing (Staw & Ross, 1987).

When organizational performance is declining and the survival of the organization is in doubt, it is common to bring in a new CEO from outside the organization with a mandate to make major changes. A new CEO usually makes some initial changes to seek immediate relief, buy time for longer-term solutions, and gain more discretion for future changes. However, if the initial changes are costly to implement and disruptive to operations, the net effect may be a further decline in organizational performance until the benefits of the change finally begin to materialize (Gabarro, 1987; Haveman, 1992). A study of NFL coaches found that major changes were more likely to be successful if the new leader had visible success in a prior position, but the study also found that leaders with a good reputation were usually more cautious about making major changes (Ndofor, Priem, Rathburn, & Dhir, 2009).

Internal and external constraints interact with each other and with the leader's personality and skills to influence the leader's behavior. Over time pressures arise that favor a match between the type of leadership situation and the type of person filling it. The most restrictive situation is one in which internal and external constraints are so severe that the CEO is merely a figurehead who cannot implement any significant strategy changes or innovations. This type of position is unlikely to attract an ambitious, innovative leader, and the organization selection process will favor a conservative, risk-averse, compliant person.

The opposite extreme is the situation with few internal and external constraints and ample discretion. Ambitious, dynamic leaders will be attracted to this type of position. Ample discretion provides opportunities for innovative leadership but does not guarantee it. Even in a situation with few constraints, some leaders lack the cognitive skill to perceive innovative options or the motivation to pursue them.

Organizational Culture

The culture of an organization consists of shared assumptions, beliefs, and values for the members (Schein, 1992, 2004; Trice & Beyer, 1991, 1993). The underlying beliefs and values help members deal with problems of survival in the external environment and problems of internal integration. The culture may be strong or weak, and there may be one dominant culture for the organization or several different cultures within subunits. An organization's culture is a situational influence on leaders, but over time leaders can also influence culture. This section of the chapter explains the functions of culture, the relationship of culture to organizational performance, the influence of leaders on culture, and the difficulty of changing it.

Functions of Culture

A major function of culture is to help people understand the environment and determine how to respond to it, thereby reducing anxiety, uncertainty, and confusion. External issues include the core mission of the organization, concrete objectives based on this mission, strategies for attaining these objectives, ways to measure success in attaining objectives, and the reasons for unexpected events affecting the organization. Objectives and strategies cannot be achieved effectively without cooperative effort, and internal integration involves issues such as the criteria for membership in the organization, the basis for determining status and power, criteria and procedures for allocating rewards and punishments, rules or customs about how to handle aggression and intimacy, and a shared consensus about the meaning of words and symbols. The beliefs that develop about these issues serve as the basis for role expectations to guide behavior, let people know what is proper and improper, and help people maintain comfortable relationships with each other. The internal and external problems are closely interconnected, and organizations must deal with them simultaneously. As solutions are developed through experience, they become shared assumptions that are passed on to new members. Over time, the assumptions may become so familiar that members are no longer consciously aware of them. Shared beliefs and established traditions are an important cultural mechanism for ensuring stability and continuity in an organization or society, and culture can facilitate or limit efforts to make major changes in the organization.

Culture and Organizational Performance

Cultural values can enhance the performance of an organization if they are consistent with the types of processes needed to accomplish the mission and adapt to internal and external challenges (Gordon & DiTomaso, 1992; Kotter & Heskett, 1992). For example, shared values such as flexibility, creativity, and entrepreneurial initiative can facilitate innovation and organizational learning (Baer & Frese, 2003). Shared values about reliability, meeting deadlines, error-free performance, controlling costs, and responsible use of resources, and adherence to best practices and standard procedures can enhance efficiency (Miron et al., 2004). The organization's culture may also include values that are important in the national culture (e.g., performance orientation, uncertainty tolerance), and these values can also have implications for the organization's performance. A strong corporate culture can be a weakness rather than an advantage if shared beliefs and values are not consistent with the strategies necessary for the organization to prosper and survive.

Leader Influence on Culture

The CEO of an organization usually has more influence than other individual managers, but the corporate culture reflects the influence of many different leaders over a considerable period of time (Pfeffer, 1992; Schein, 1992; Trice & Beyer, 1993; Tsui, Zhang, Wang, Xin, & Wu, 2006). The influence of an individual CEO can be substantial for the entrepreneurial founder of a successful company who has led it for many years, or for a turnaround CEO who saves a dying organization by making major changes in strategy and operating practices. The potential influence of leaders on corporate culture increases in a crisis that requires major changes, but the CEO is not the only source of this influence. When one sub-unit is clearly more important than the others for the continued success of the organization, key elements of its subculture may emerge and become central in the corporate culture.

Leaders can influence the culture of an organization in a variety of ways, and the effects are stronger when the different approaches are consistent with each other. One form of leader influence on the organizational culture is the use of ideological appeals and repeated articulation of an inspiring vision for the organization or subunit. Leaders communicate their values when they make statements about values and objectives that are important and formulate long-term strategies and plans for attaining them. Written value statements, charters, and philosophies can be useful, but they have little credibility unless supported by leader actions and decisions. Leaders communicate values and expectations by highly visible symbolic actions relevant for cultural values, such as showing loyalty, self-sacrifice, and service beyond the call of duty. Even when the symbolic actions or decisions of a leader are not directly observed by most members of the organization, they can become the subject of stories and myths and be propagated widely. Leaders also communicate their priorities and concerns in their daily activity by their choice of things to ask about, measure, comment on, praise, and criticize. By not paying attention to something, a leader sends the message that it is not important. The importance of keeping decisions and actions consistent with espoused values is shown in the following example (Newstrom & Davis, 1993).

> The CEO and top executives of a small computer company in the Silicon Valley wanted to create an appropriate culture for the new company. They produced a two-page values statement describing the importance of employee involvement, open communication, high-quality products, and good customer service. The values document was posted in prominent places and distributed to company employees. However, there was a wide discrepancy between the values statement and executive behavior, and most employees knew that secrecy and expediency were the real values. Instead of open communication, meetings were used to announce decisions already made by top management, and employees were not encouraged to suggest ideas or express concerns. Getting the product out the door to customers had top priority, regardless of possible defects. As quality problems increased, many customers became dissatisfied with the company's computers. Sales begin to decline, and two years later the company filed for bankruptcy.

Another approach for influencing culture involves the use of cultural forms such as symbols, slogans, rituals, and ceremonies (Trice & Beyer, 1993). Rituals, ceremonies, and rites of passage can be used to emphasize core values and strengthen identification with the organization. In many organizations new members are required to make a public oath of allegiance, demonstrate knowledge of the ideology, or undergo an ordeal that demonstrates loyalty. Also common are ceremonies to celebrate a member's advancement in rank, to inaugurate a new leader, and to acknowledge the retirement of a member. Rituals and ceremonies may also involve the communication of stories about important events and heroic actions by individuals. However, stories and myths are more a reflection of culture than a determinant of it. To be useful the story must describe a real event and convey a clear message about values.

A third way for leaders to influence culture is creation or modification of formal programs, systems, organization structure, and facilities. Formal budgets, planning sessions, reports, performance review procedures, and management development programs can be used to emphasize some values and beliefs about proper behavior. Orientation programs can be used to socialize new employees and teach them about the culture of an organization. Training programs designed to increase job skills can also be used to teach participants about the ideology of the organization. Values are also communicated by the criteria emphasized in recruiting, selecting, rewarding, promoting, and dismissing people. The effect on culture is stronger if the organization provides realistic information about the criteria and requirements for success, and the personnel decisions are consistent with these criteria.

Difficulty of Culture Change

How difficult it is to change culture depends in part on the developmental stage of the organization (Schein, 1992; Trice & Beyer, 1993). The founder of a new organization has a strong influence on its culture. The founder typically has a vision of a new enterprise and proposes ways of doing things that, if successful in accomplishing objectives and reducing anxiety, will gradually become embedded in the culture. The culture in young, successful organizations is likely to be strong when it is instrumental to the success of the organization, the assumptions are internalized by current members and transmitted to new members, and the founder is still present to symbolize and reinforce the culture. The culture will evolve slowly over the years as experience reveals that some assumptions need to be modified. Eventually, as the organization matures and people other than the founder or family members occupy key leadership positions, the culture will become less uniform, and subcultures may develop in different subunits.

In general, it is much more difficult for leaders to change culture in a mature organization than to create it in a new organization. One reason is that many of the underlying beliefs and assumptions shared by people in an organization are implicit and unconscious. Cultural assumptions are also difficult to change when they justify the past and are a matter of pride. Moreover, cultural values influence the selection of leaders and the role expectations for them. In a mature, relatively prosperous organization, culture influences leaders more than leaders influence culture. Drastic changes are unlikely unless a major crisis threatens the welfare and survival of the organization. Even with a crisis, it takes considerable insight and skill for a leader to understand the current culture in an organization and implement changes successfully.

Research on Effects of Strategic Leadership

The effects of CEO leadership on company performance have been examined in research with different methods. Results will be reviewed for succession studies, intensive case studies, and survey studies of CEO behavior.

Studies of CEO Succession

Research on the consequences of changing the chief executive of an organization is relevant for understanding the importance of strategic leadership. Reviews of succession research provide evidence that changes in the chief executive have important effects on the long-term performance of an organization (Giambatista et al., 2005; Kesner and Sebora, 1994). The research method in most succession studies is an archival field study on CEOs for a sample of business corporations, but a few succession studies have used coaches of professional sports teams. All data is from archival records, and the characteristics of the successors (e.g., internal vs. external) are related to changes in objective measures of organizational performance in the years before and after succession occurs (e.g., Grinyer, Mayes, and McKiernan, 1990). Progress has been made in understanding the reasons for succession, how successors are selected, and the consequences of succession for the organization (Giambatista, Rowe, and Riaz, 2005; Shen and Cannella, 2002; Sobel, Harkins, and Conley, 2007; Zhang and Rajagopalan, 2004).

Descriptive Studies of CEO Decisions and Actions

Several types of descriptive studies have been used to investigate the influence of CEOs on their organizations. Many different sources of information can be used, including interviews, questionnaires, company records, annual reports, and financial databases. Some researchers also use information from secondary sources such as biographies, autobiographies, and magazine articles about organizations and their leaders. Descriptive studies of chief executives usually examine the types of decisions and actions that account for the success or failure of an organization over a period of several years.

A comparative study of several organizations has been used to see if successful CEOs have a similar pattern of strategic decisions and behavior (e.g., Bennis & Nanus, 1985; Nadler et al., 1995), or if CEO actions and communications can explain why some companies have better financial performance than other companies in the same industry (e.g., Makri & Scandura, 2010; McClelland, Liang, & Barker, 2009). An intensive case study of a single organization has been used to examine how a new chief executive leads a dramatic turnaround by a company in decline (e.g., Ghosen & Ries, 2002; Wyden, 1987). A few studies have examined CEOs who were initially successful but later experienced failure in order to determine the reasons for a different outcome (e.g., Finkelstein, 2003; Probst & Raisch, 2005). Descriptive studies of top executives are not limited to corporations, and some are conducted with military leaders, political leaders, or leaders of nonprofit organizations (e.g., Bennis & Nanus, 1985; Burns, 1978; Van Fleet & Yukl, 1986b).

Despite all the difficulties in conducting this type of research, it has provided additional evidence that CEOs can exert significant influence on the performance of their organizations. The descriptive studies also provide insights into the reasons why some chief executives are more effective than others. Successful chief executives identify important threats and opportunities for their organization, take decisive action to resolve serious problems, identify a good competitive strategy, and implement the strategy in a timely way. These CEOs also foster a strong core ideology that is consistent with the mission and strategy.

Survey Studies on CEO Leadership

Several survey studies have examined how leadership by a chief executive is related to a firm's financial performance or rated effectiveness (Angle, Nagarajan, Sonnenfeld, & Srinivasan, 2006; Ensley, Hmieleski, & Pearce, 2006; Jung, Wu, & Chow, 2008; Ling, Simsek, Lubatkin, & Veiga, 2008a, 2008b; Makri & Scandura, 2010; Peterson, Walumbwa, Byron, & Myrowitz, 2009; Tosi, Misangyi, Fanelli, Waldman, & Yammrino, 2004; Waldman, Javidan, & Varella, 2004; Waldman, Ramirez, House, & Puranam, 2001; Wang, Tsui, & Xin, 2011; Zhu, Chew, & Spangler, 2005). Most of these studies were narrowly focused on the effects of charismatic or transformational leadership by a CEO. Leadership behavior was measured with a questionnaire filled out by one or more subordinates, and behavior was correlated with measures of the company's financial performance.

The findings were not consistent across the studies, which may be due in part to large differences in the samples, the measure of leadership behavior, and the measure of organizational effectiveness. Charismatic or transformational leadership was correlated with a measure of organizational effectiveness in some studies but not others. A few studies found that the results were dependent on situational variables such as the size and type of organization and environmental dynamism or uncertainty. None of the studies included adequate measures of performance determinants that explain how a CEO influences financial performance for a large company. Knowledge about firm performance may have biased the ratings of leader behavior. This attribution bias occurs when the CEO of a company known to have strong financial performance is rated more charismatic or transformational than CEOs for companies with weaker performance, despite no actual difference in their behavior. In one study that attempted to control for this bias by including a measure of past performance, a significant effect for CEO charismatic leadership was not found (Angle et al., 2006).

Evaluation of Research on Strategic Leadership

The research on leadership by chief executives of organizations shows that they can influence organizational processes and outcomes, but this influence varies greatly depending on the situation and the traits and skills of the leaders. The succession studies, descriptive studies, and survey studies all have limitations, and more comprehensive research is needed to accurately determine how chief executives can influence the financial performance of their firms. The research should examine a much broader range of actions and decisions by chief executives, including how they influence strategy, structure, programs, systems, and culture. The research should include measures of other relevant mediating processes and performance determinants in addition to member motivation, commitment, and cooperation. Finally, it is essential to gather information about the influence of other top executives and leaders at middle and lower levels in the organization.

Executive Teams

All organizations have a top management group that includes the CEO and other top executives, but organizations differ greatly in the way this group operates. The traditional approach is to have a clear hierarchy of authority with a CEO (usually the chairman of the board, but sometimes the president of the organization), a chief operating officer (usually the president of the organization), and several subordinate executives (e.g., vice presidents) who head various subunits of the organization. This structure is still prominent, but an increasingly popular alternative is to share power within the top management team (Ancona & Nadler, 1989). Executives in the team collectively assume the responsibilities of the chief operating officer in managing the internal operations of the organization, and they assist the CEO in formulating strategy. Another, less common variation is the "office of the chairperson" structure in which the responsibilities of the CEO are shared, even though one executive (the chairperson) usually has more power than the others (the vice chairpersons).

Regardless of the formal structure of an organization, differences will occur in the extent to which strategic leadership is actually shared among the top executives. An organization with an executive team may have an autocratic CEO who allows other executives little influence over strategic decisions, whereas an organization with a traditional hierarchy may have a CEO who empowers other top executives to share responsibility for making strategic decisions.

Executive teams are becoming more acceptable due to their effective use in other countries (such as Japan) and a growing awareness that shared leadership can be beneficial for complex organizations in a turbulent environment. An example of an executive team with an unusual amount of shared leadership comes from Nordstrom Inc., a department store chain (Yang, 1992).

During the 1980s the executive team consisted of three of the founder's grandsons, Bruce, John, and James. The title of President rotated among the three executives. Later in the 1990s, when the company encountered sluggish sales and lower profits, the executive team was modified. The three co-presidents and one other relative were elevated to co-chairmen. They focus on strategy issues, such as expansion plans and selection of store sites. Four non-family members were promoted to the positions of co-president.

They are jointly responsible for making operating decisions on how to conduct the day-to-day affairs of the company. Each co-president is responsible for a different type of merchandise. Although they have considerable autonomy in their own domain of responsibility, they operate as a unified team. They hold weekly meetings and communicate frequently with each other. Despite lively debates, they cooperate in finding solutions that will be best for the customer, their common goal.

Potential Advantages

Executive teams offer a number of potential advantages for an organization (Ancona & Nadler, 1989; Bradford & Cohen, 1984; Eisenstat & Cohen, 1990; Hambrick, 1987; Nadler, 1998). The members often have relevant skills and knowledge that the CEO lacks and can compensate for weaknesses in the skills of the CEO. Important tasks are less likely to be neglected if several people are available to share the burden of leadership. When executives from different subunits meet regularly as a team, communication and cooperation are likely to be improved. The decisions made by a team are more likely to represent the diverse interests of organization members, and involvement in making these decisions will improve member commitment to implement them effectively.

A recent study found that when the CEO allowed other members of a top executive team to influence a strategic decision, the decision quality was better, the decision was perceived as more fair, team members were more committed to implement the decision, their trust in the leader increased, and they identified more with the team (Korsgaard, Schweiger, & Sapienze, 1995). A study of top management teams from 116 Israeli firms found that a high level of mutual understanding and collaboration among members (called "behavioral integration") was related to better quality of strategic decisions and more favorable ratings of organizational performance (Carmeli & Schaubroeck, 2006).

The team approach is also a way to facilitate leadership succession in large, diverse organizations. Experience in dealing with the major issues and decisions facing the organization provides opportunities for executives to develop more relevant leadership skills. Moreover, when several executives share responsibility for strategic leadership of the organization, it is easier for the current CEO and the board of directors to determine which executive in the team is most qualified to become the next CEO.

Facilitating Conditions

The potential advantages of having an executive team depend in part on the situation, and they are especially important in a complex, rapidly changing environment that places many external demands on the CEO (Ancona & Nadler, 1989; Edmondson et al., 2003). Growing turbulence in the environment due to rapid technological changes and increased global competition has made the responsibility for developing successful strategy more difficult for many organizations. Teams are also more important when the organization has diverse but highly interdependent business units that require close coordination across units. In an organization with several diverse business units, a single leader is unlikely to have the broad expertise necessary to direct and coordinate the activities of these units.

The quality of the strategic decisions made by a team is likely to be better if members have a diverse backgrounds and perspectives and their knowledge and skills are relevant for understanding how the organization can adapt in a dynamic, uncertain environment (Bantel & Jackson, 1989; Cannella, Park, & Lee, 2008; Murray, 1989). However, as found in the research on decision groups, the potential benefits of diversity will not be achieved unless the team can process information and make decisions in a way that utilizes the knowledge and ideas of members. Highly divergent interests and differences in preferences and priorities regarding company objectives also make it more difficult to achieve mutual understanding (Colbert, Kristof-Brown, Bradley, & Barrick, 2008; Simsek, Veiga, Lubatkin, & Dino, 2005). It is more difficult to develop mutual trust and cooperation when team members represent subunits with different objectives or members are competing to become the successor to the current CEO.

Making strategic decisions jointly is more likely to yield high quality decisions if the executives have an accurate, shared "mental model" about the determinants of organizational performance, their relative importance, and how they can be influenced to improve performance (Cannon-Bowers et al., 1993; Klimoski & Mohammed, 1994; Senge, 1990). More accurate models can be developed by explicit discussion of differences in how the executives view the world, by improving measures and information systems (to ensure accurate, timely information about key variables), and by conducting experiments on the effects of different types of changes and improvement programs. Relevant training in development of accurate mental models about the causes of important outcomes in complex systems is another way to improve strategic decisions by individual executives and teams (Marcy & Mumford, 2010).

Leadership of Executive Teams

Whether the potential advantages of executive teams are realized depends on the leadership provided by the CEO (Eisenstat & Cohen, 1990). Effective leadership is more likely if the CEO has relevant values, traits, and skills. For example, a comparative case study of 17 CEOs (e.g., Peterson, Smith, Martorana, & Owens, 2003) found that CEO personality was related to the top management team characteristics (optimism, cohesiveness, flexibility, and moderate risk taking), which were related in turn to a measure of financial performance.

Executive teams are more likely to be successful when the CEO selects team members with relevant skills and experience, clearly defines objectives consistent with shared values, gives the team considerable discretion but clearly specifies the limits of team authority in relation to CEO authority, helps the team establish norms that will facilitate group processes, facilitates learning of skills in working together effectively, and encourages openness and mutual trust among team members. The CEO should avoid actions that encourage competition or distrust, such as overtly making comparative evaluations among team members and meeting with individual executives to deal with issues that should be addressed by the entire team.

It is also essential for the CEO to help the team avoid process problems that can prevent them from making good decisions. If the CEO dominates decisions, the potential benefits of diverse members with relevant knowledge may not be realized. The quality of a strategic decision is likely to be better if individuals with the most expertise for that type of decision have ample influence over it. It is also important to make decisions in a timely way. The CEO should seek consensus among the executives who would be the most affected by a decision, rather than prolonging discussion in an effort to achieve consensus among everyone. Here is an example of how a new CEO implemented an effective executive team (George, 2003, pp. 96-97):

> To mold top executives into a well-oiled team and build agreement on major goals and objectives, we formed an executive committee that included the leaders of major company businesses and corporate staff units. Each meeting began with an executive session to discuss issues any member considered important. Then we reviewed and approved all strategies, investments, and financial plans for each business and the company as a whole. I encouraged committee members to make their positions known even on areas of the business for which they were not responsible. This open approach brought us closer together and built a strong sense of commitment to our mutual agenda. The executive

committee actually voted on all major decisions of the corporation, including the release of new products before they went to market, which increased commitment to our decisions and emphasized the vital importance of product quality.

Example of a Study on Executive Teams

Eisenhardt (1989) conducted a study of eight minicomputer firms to investigate how the speed and quality of strategic decisions were affected by the decision processes in these firms. Interviews were conducted with members of the executive team in each company to learn about the process used for important decisions, including when and how they were made. Questionnaires, company documents, and industry reports were used to obtain additional information about decision processes and company performance.

The study found that strategic decisions were both faster and better when the executive team conducted a simultaneous evaluation of several alternatives rather than using the common "satisficing" procedure of examining alternatives sequentially until a satisfactory one is found. An intensive decision process helped the team evaluate the strengths and weaknesses of each alternative, avoid premature commitment to a particular alternative, and identify a fallback position to use if attempts to implement the chosen alternative encountered unexpected obstacles. The executive team was more effective when it considered how a decision was related to other strategic decisions, and when it considered tactical plans (e.g., action steps, budgets, schedules) for implementing a strategic decision as part of the process for evaluating feasibility. This integrative approach appears to provide a better understanding of the alternatives and their implications, and it tends to reduce anxiety about possible adverse consequences, thereby increasing confidence in the team's evaluation and willingness to move forward with a decision.

Emerging Conceptions of Organizational Leadership

Some different ways of conceptualizing leadership have emerged in recent years, and they are eliciting interest among scholars who believe that the currently popular theories are too limited. Examples include shared and distributed leadership, relational leadership and social networks, and emergent processes in complexity theory. These approaches are still evolving, and as yet there is little conclusive research on them. Each approach will be described briefly.

Shared and Distributed Leadership

The theory and research on leadership has long recognized that effective leaders empower others to participate in the process of interpreting events, solving problems, and making decisions (Argyris, 1964; Likert, 1967). In most of these approaches, the focus is on the process by which focal leaders encourage and enable others to share responsibility for leadership functions. The emphasis in the traditional approaches is on using empowerment to make an individual leader more effective. An alternative view of organizations is that distributed leadership, power sharing, and political activities are inevitable in organizations, and they cannot be understood by focusing on the decisions and actions of individual leaders.

Proponents of this perspective recognize that the actions of any individual leader are less important than the collective leadership provided by many members of the organization, including both formal and informal leaders (Day, Gronn, & Salas, 2004). Viewing leadership in terms of reciprocal, recursive influence processes among multiple leaders is different from studying unidirectional effects of a single leader on subordinates. Distributed leadership involves multiple leaders with distinct but inter-related responsibilities. If the various leaders are unable to agree about what to do and how to do it, performance of the team or organization is likely to suffer (e.g., Mehra, Smith, Dixon, & Robertson, 2006).

There are many different ways to share and distribute power and authority in organizations, and some are more successful than others (e.g., Cox, Pearce, & Perry, 2003; Ensley et al., 2006; Gronn, 2002; Locke, 2003; O' Toole, Galbraith, & Lawler, 2003; Pearce & Conger, 2003). A few initial attempts to develop theories of shared leadership are promising (e.g., Ilgen, Hollenbeck, Johnson, & Jundt, 2005; Pearce & Sims, 2000; Mayo, Meindl, & Pastor, 2003; Seers et al., 2003). In addition to the leadership literature, insights about shared and distributed leadership in organizations are provided by several other literatures (e.g., organization theory, public administration, strategic management, and social networks theory).

Several scholars have considered how shared, collective, or distributive leadership is related to team or organizational effectiveness (e.g., Brown & Gioia, 2002; Brown & Hosking, 1986; Carson et al., 2007; Denis, Lamothe, & Langley, 2001; Friedrich, Vessey, Schuelke, Ruark, & Mumford, 2009; Hunt & Ropo, 1995; Lawler, 1986; Pearce & Sims, 2002; Semler, 1989). Despite these efforts, much more research is needed on the distribution of leadership responsibilities among the members of a team or organization. The extent to which different types of leadership roles and decisions can be shared or distributed effectively, the conditions facilitating the emergence and success of shared leadership, and the implications for organizational design are all important questions that require more attention. More intensive, descriptive, and longitudinal research is needed to understand the complex processes involved in shared and distributed leadership.

Relational Leadership

Most theory and research on leadership views it as an influence process and focuses on the actions of people designated as leaders. Relationships are acknowledged to be important in much of the leadership literature, but in "traditional" approaches the focus is on how an individual leader can develop and maintain cooperative relationships. An alternative view of leadership is to describe it as part of the evolving social order that results from interactions, exchanges, and influence processes among many people in an organization.

According to this perspective, leadership cannot be understood apart from the dynamics of the social system in which it occurs (Dachler, 1984, 1992; DeRue & Ashford, 2010; Drath, 2001; Uhl-Bien, 2006). Instead of the traditional focus on a single leader, scholars examine the social processes and patterned relationships that explain how collective activity can accomplish shared objectives. Organizations and other social entities (e.g., teams, coalitions, common interest groups) are defined more by the web of interpersonal relationships than by formal charters, structures, policies, and rules. The relationships are continually being modified as changes occur in the people who are involved in the collective activity, and as changing conditions elicit adaptive responses.

Leaders are defined as the people who consistently influence relationships and collective activities and are expected by others to have this influence (Hogg, 2001; Hosking, 1988; Uhl-Bien, 2006). Their influence is accomplished by interpreting events and explaining cause-effect relationships in a meaningful way, and by influencing people to modify their attitudes, behavior, and goals. Many different people participate in this leadership process, and their diverse and sometimes conflicting interests make it a political process involving the use of social power as well as rational and emotional appeals. Individuals develop and use social networks to gather information and build coalitions to increase their influence over decisions (e.g., Balkundi & Kilduff, 2005).

The methods most appropriate for studying relational leadership are seldom used in leadership research (Uhl-Bien, 2006). It is impossible to understand evolving relationships and reciprocal influence processes among multiple parties by analyzing data from survey studies in which most information is obtained with fixed-response questionnaires at one point in time. Instead, it is necessary to use intensive longitudinal studies and qualitative methods that allow researchers to explore different explanations of unfolding events. An example is the study conducted by Reicher et al. (2005) of leadership in the BBC prison simulation.

Complexity Theory of Leadership

To accurately describe effective leadership in organizations requires theories that are more complex than most of the earlier ones. Distributed leadership, relational dynamics, and emergent processes are not adequately described in the hierarchical leadership theories that focus on the influence of a chief executive or the top management team. Complexity theory involves interacting units that are dynamic (changing) and adaptive, and the complex pattern of behaviors and structures that emerge are usually unique and difficult to predict from a description of the involved units (Marion & Uhl-Bien, 2001). Complex adaptive systems are used to explain how emergent processes can facilitate adaptation by organizations to turbulent environments. The emergent processes provide an alternative explanation for organizational learning, innovation, and adaptation. However, rather than replacing hierarchical theories, it is likely that the two perspectives can be integrated to provide a more complete explanation of effective leadership in large organizations (Hunt, Osborn, & Boal, 2009; Lichtenstein & Plowman, 2009; Uhl-Bien & Marion, 2009; Uhl-Bien, Marion, & McKelvey, 2007; Osborn & Hunt, 2007).

One recent version of the theory identifies three types of leadership processes (Uhl-Bien & Marion, 2009; Uhl-Bien et al., 2007). *Administrative leadership* involves actions and decisions by formal leaders who are responsible for planning and coordinating activities for the organization. *Adaptive leadership* is an emergent process that occurs when people with different knowledge, beliefs, and preferences interact in an attempt to solve problems and resolve conflicts. The result of this process is the production of creative ideas and new conceptions that can facilitate the resolution of conflict and an adaptive response to a threat or opportunity. *Enabling leadership* facilitates the process of emergent solutions by fostering interaction among people who need to be involved, increasing the interdependence among these people, supporting the value of dissent and debate, increasing access to necessary information and resources, and helping to get innovative ideas implemented in the organization. Enabling leadership also involves efforts to keep the administrative and adaptive processes consistent and mutually compatible. For example, it is essential to prevent administrative leaders from dominating or suppressing the interaction and exploration needed to produce creative solutions, but it is also important to prevent adaptive processes from creating destructive conflicts or undermining the essential mission of the organization.

Complexity theory involves emergent processes and adaptive outcomes that are often unpredictable in advance. Research is needed to learn how interactions and relationships change over time, how the historical and contextual factors affect these processes, and how the three forms of leadership interact to create adaptive outcomes for an organization. Instead of relying on survey studies conducted at one point in time, it will be necessary to conduct intensive, studies that include qualitative descriptions of the relevant processes and relationships (e.g., Lichtenstein & Plowman, 2009; Plowman et al., 2007; Schneider & Somers, 2006). Computer simulation is useful tool for testing models based on the descriptive studies (Hazy, 2007). Examples of methods relevant for studying complexity theories of leadership are described in recent publications (e.g., Hazy, 2008; Schreiber & Carley, 2008).

Two Key Responsibilities for Top Executives

Two key functions for top executives in business organizations are to monitor the external environment and formulate a competitive strategy. External monitoring is needed to detect threats and opportunities for the organization, and competitive strategy guides the organization's response to threats and opportunities.

External Monitoring

Top executives need to be sensitive to a wide range of events and trends that are likely to affect their organization (Ginter & Duncan, 1990). Some representative questions likely to be important for a business organization are shown in Table 2. It is essential to learn about the concerns of customers and clients, the availability of suppliers and vendors, the actions of competitors, market trends, economic conditions, government policies, and technological developments. The information may be gathered in a variety of ways (e.g., reading government reports and industry publications, attending professional and trade meetings, talking to customers and suppliers, examining the products and reports of competitors, conducting market research).

External monitoring (also called "environmental scanning") provides the information needed for strategic planning and crisis management. Grinyer et al. (1990) studied 28 British companies that experienced a sharp improvement in performance and a matched sample of firms with only average performance; the top management of the high-performing companies did more external monitoring (e.g., environmental scanning, consultation with key customers) and were quicker to recognize and exploit opportunities. The amount of change and turbulence in the environment will determine how much external monitoring is necessary. More external monitoring is needed when the organization is highly dependent on outsiders (e.g., clients, customers, suppliers, subcontractors, joint venture partners), when the environment is rapidly changing, and when the organization faces severe competition or serious threats from outside enemies (Ginter & Duncan, 1990; Narayanan et al., 2011).

TABLE 2	Questions for External Monitoring

1. What do clients and customers need and want?
2. What is the reaction of clients and customers to the organization's current products and services?
3. Who are the primary competitors?
4. What strategies are they pursuing (e.g., pricing, advertising and promotions, new products, customer service, etc.)?
5. How do competitors' products and services compare to those of the manager's organization?
6. What events affect the acquisition of materials, energy, information, and other inputs used by the organization to conduct its operations?
7. How will the organization be affected by new legislation and by government agencies that regulate its activities (e.g., labor laws, environmental regulations, safety standards, tax policies, etc.)?
8. How will new technologies affect the organization's products, services, and operations?
9. How will the organization be affected by changes in the economy (employment level, interest rates, growth rates)?
10. How will the organization be affected by changing population demographics (e.g., aging, diversity)?
11. How will the organization be affected by international events (e.g., trade agreements, import restrictions, currency changes, wars and revolutions)?

TABLE 3	Guidelines for External Monitoring

- Identify relevant information to gather.
- Use multiple sources of relevant information.
- Learn what clients and customers need and want.
- Learn about the products and activities of competitors.
- Relate environmental information to strategic plans.

Monitoring of the external environment is usually considered more important for upper-level managers than for lower-level managers (Kraut, Pedigo, McKenna, & Dunnette, 1989; Pavett & Lau, 1983). However, the difficulties involved in scanning and interpreting information about environmental changes make this responsibility one that should be shared by managers in an organization. Guidelines for external monitoring are listed in Table 3.

Developing Competitive Strategy

For business organizations, a major part of the strategy is how to compete effectively in the marketplace and remain profitable (Porter, 1980). Some examples of possible competitive strategies include the following: selling a product or service at the lowest price; having superior quality, customer service, or the most innovative products and services; providing a unique product or service in a segment of the market ignored by competing organizations ("niche" strategies); and being the most flexible about customizing products or services to meet each client's needs. Sometimes it is feasible to pursue a mix of strategies at the same time (e.g., have the least expensive "standard" product or service as well as the best customized versions of the product or service). Strategy may also involve the way the product or service is produced, delivered, marketed, financed, and guaranteed.

Reviews of research on strategy formulation and strategic planning by top executives show that it can improve an organization's performance, and that it is more important in a complex and dynamic environment with many threats and opportunities (Miller & Cardinal, 1994; Narayanan et al., 2011). However, a limitation of many studies on effects of strategic planning is the lack of attention to strategy content and implementation. Strategy formulation will not improve organizational performance unless the strategies are relevant and feasible, they are communicated to middle- and lower-level managers, and these managers become committed to implement the strategies.

A relevant strategy takes into account changes in the external environment, and it is realistic in terms of the organization's strengths and weaknesses. The strategy should reflect the core mission and high-priority objectives of the organization. Although strategy may include changing structure or management processes, such changes should be clearly relevant to strategic objectives. For example, it is not enough to propose downsizing, elimination of management layers, or reorganization into separate product divisions without providing a clear purpose for such changes. Unfortunately, many executives who need to improve weak short-term performance will succumb to the appeal of faddish remedies.

Guidelines for Strategic Leadership

One of the most difficult responsibilities for executives is to develop a competitive strategy for the organization, and there are no simple answers on how to do it effectively. The following guidelines (see Table 4) are based on relevant theory, research, and practitioner insights (Bennis & Nanus, 1985; Kotter, 1996; Nanus, 1992; Narayanan et al., 2011;

TABLE 4	Guidelines for Formulating Strategy

- Determine long-term objectives and priorities.
- Learn what clients and customers need and want.
- Learn about the products and activities of competitors.
- Assess current strengths and weaknesses.
- Identify core competencies.
- Evaluate the need for a major change in strategy.
- Identify promising strategies.
- Evaluate the likely outcomes of a strategy.
- Involve other executives in selecting a strategy.

Nohria, Joyce, & Roberson, 2004; Wall & Wall, 1995; Worley, Hitchin, & Ross, 1996). The guidelines do not depict a rigid sequence of steps, but rather a set of overlapping, cyclical activities that must be interwoven in a meaningful way.

- **Determine long-term objectives and priorities.**

It is difficult to make strategic plans without knowing the objectives to be attained and their relative priority. Long-term objectives and priorities should be based on the stated mission and vision for the organization. Strategic objectives for a business organization may involve such things as maintaining a specified profit margin or return on investment, improving market share, and providing the best products or service in the industry. Strategic objectives for an organization with a humanitarian mission may include such things as finding a way to cure or prevent a disease, eliminating illiteracy in a specified population, and ending deaths from drunk driving. Strategic objectives for an educational institution may include improving the learning of essential skills, preparing students for specific careers, and increasing the number of students who graduate.

- **Learn what clients and customers need and want.**

It is essential to learn as much as possible about the specific needs and requirements of customers and what they think about the organization's products and services. It is useful to discover what they like, what they dislike, and how the products or services could be improved. Market surveys are one common source of information about clients and customers, but more personal contacts are also desirable. Some manufacturing organizations have teams of production, engineering, and sales employees from different levels of the organization visit with major clients to learn more about their needs and get ideas for product improvements (Peters & Austin, 1985). Clients and suppliers are also invited to visit the organization's facilities, meet with production and engineering personnel, and attend meetings on how to improve quality, product design, or customer service.

- **Learn about the products and activities of competitors.**

Knowledge about the products and services of competitors provides a basis for evaluating your own products and processes (a process called *benchmarking),* and it provides a source of good ideas on how to improve them. Detailed information about the products and services of competitors is sometimes difficult to obtain but worth the effort. Learning about competitors' products can be accomplished in a variety of ways: use them yourself, conduct comparative product testing, read evaluations conducted by product testing companies or governmental agencies, have customers directly compare the organization's products and services to those of competitors, visit the facilities of competitors, read competitors' advertising literature, and attend trade shows where competitors display and demonstrate their wares.

- **Assess current strengths and weaknesses.**

Strategic planning is facilitated by a comprehensive, objective evaluation of current performance in relation to strategic objectives and compared to the performance of competitors. Much of the information needed for this evaluation is provided by internal and external monitoring. Several types of analysis are useful. Review indicators of organizational performance for the past several years and progress toward achieving strategic objectives. Examine performance (e.g., sales, market share, costs, profits) for each product, service, and market. Identify products or services that are successful and those that are not meeting expectations. Compare the organization's products or services to those of competitors to identify strengths and weaknesses. Compare the efficiency of the organization's processes to that for similar organizations. Identify tangible resources that currently provide an advantage over competitors, such as financial assets, unique equipment and facilities, and patents on products or technology used to do the work. Identify conditions that provide an advantage, such as low operating costs, employees with relevant skills, a special relationship with suppliers, and an outstanding reputation for quality or customer service. Identify weaknesses as well as strengths, and estimate how long current strengths and weaknesses are likely to continue.

The competitive advantage to be gained from current strengths depends on how long they will last and how difficult they are for competitors to overcome or duplicate. For example, a pharmaceutical company with a patented new drug that is better and cheaper than any alternatives has a strong competitive advantage that will likely continue for several years. In contrast, a service company that devises a new and attractive promotion (e.g., special discounts) may enjoy its competitive advantage only for a few weeks or months (as long as it takes competitors to imitate it). An organization that is first into a new market has an advantage, but only if it is difficult for competitors to follow quickly. A product or service that is costly to develop but easy and cheap to duplicate offers little advantage. Capabilities should be evaluated together, not in isolation. A unique resource (e.g., an improved product or process) may offer no competitive advantage if organizational weaknesses or external constraints prevent it from being used effectively. A weakness may not be so serious if it can be corrected quickly or offset by other strengths.

- **Identify core competencies.**

A core competency is the knowledge and capability to carry out a particular type of activity (Barney, 1991). Unlike tangible resources, which are depleted when used, core competencies increase as they are used (Prahalad & Hamel, 1990). A core competency usually involves a combination of technical expertise and application skills. For example, a core competency for W. L. Gore is their expertise about a special type of material (GORE-TEX) and their capability to discover and exploit new uses for this material.

Core competencies provide a potential source of continuing competitive advantage if they are used to provide innovative, high-quality products and services that cannot easily be copied or duplicated by competitors. Core competencies can help an organization remain competitive in its current businesses and diversify into new businesses. Canon's core competencies in optics, acquired as a producer of quality cameras, enabled the company to become a successful producer of copiers, fax machines, semiconductor lithographic equipment, and specialized video systems, while continuing to be a successful producer of cameras and the first to develop a microprocessor- controlled camera. Competence in display systems, which involves knowledge of microprocessor design, ultra-thin precision casing, material science, and miniaturization enabled Casio to be successful in such diverse businesses as calculators, miniature television sets, digital watches, monitors for laptop computers, and automotive dashboards (Prahalad & Hamel, 1990).

- **Evaluate the need for a major change in strategy.**

One of the most important responsibilities of executives is to help interpret events and determine whether the organization needs a different strategy or just incremental improvements in the existing strategy. A new strategy may be needed when there is a performance crisis for the organization and established practices are not sufficient to deal with it. When a serious crisis is imminent, it is appropriate to be pragmatic and flexible rather than defensive and tradition bound in deciding how to respond. In this situation, a leader who attempts to defend the old, obsolete strategy rather than proposing necessary changes is likely to be replaced. However, proposing a different strategy when the current strategy can be easily fixed is also risky, both for the organization and the leader. A new strategy may not be needed if weak performance is caused by temporary conditions or problems in implementing the current strategy.

- **Identify promising strategies.**

If a major change in strategy is necessary, it is better to begin by exploring a range of possible strategies. Focusing attention too quickly on one strategy will preclude finding better ones that are less obvious. Success in finding a new strategy will be greater if the quest is guided by a clear, meaningful conception of the organization's mission, long-term strategic objectives, core competencies, and current performance. Sometimes it is necessary to redefine the mission of the organization to include new activities that are relevant for the environment and the organization's core competencies.

For example, Williams Company was making pipelines for transporting oil and gas, but it was losing business to larger competitors with lower costs. Recognizing that it was unlikely to find a way to compete successfully in the pipeline business, top management looked around for other opportunities to use the company's core competencies. They discovered that their piping was perfect for housing fiber optic cable, a newly emerging market, and they could market it to cable television and telecommunications companies at a lower price than other suppliers in that industry (Worley et al., 1996).

- **Evaluate the likely outcomes of a strategy.**

A strategy should be evaluated in terms of the likely consequences for the attainment of key objectives. Relevant consequences include benefits and costs for the various stakeholders in the organization. The costs include the extra resources and lost productivity associated with any organizational changes necessary to support the strategy. It is difficult to forecast the consequences of a strategic change, especially when competitors can adjust their own strategies to cope with your changes. A number of procedures have been developed to assess likely customer response to a new product or service (market surveys, focus groups, product trials in selected locations or markets).

Scenarios provide another way to improve the evaluation of likely consequences for a proposed change (Van der Heijden, 1996). A scenario is a detailed description of what the future will be like if a proposed change or strategy is pursued. Scenarios can be developed to describe what would happen under the most and least favorable conditions, as well as under the most likely conditions. The process of developing the scenarios often provides insights about unexpected consequences of a strategy and implicit assumptions that were not realistic (Sosik, Jung, Berson, Dionne, & Jaussi, 2005).

- **Involve other executives in selecting a strategy.**

A key responsibility of executives is to make strategic decisions that will improve the organization. However, few leaders are so brilliant that they can make such decisions alone, and a competitive strategy developed with participation by the top management team is more likely to be successful than strategy developed alone by an autocratic CEO (Finkelstein, 2003; Probst & Raisch, 2005). In the event of considerable uncertainty and disagreement about the best strategy, it is wise to select one that is flexible enough to permit later modification after more knowledge about its effectiveness can be obtained. Moderate risk taking is usually beneficial, but it is not wise to take extreme risks with irreversible decisions. Systematic procedures have been developed by scholars and consultants to facilitate the process of strategy formulation by a group of executives. One example is the scenario development procedure called "Quest" (Bennis & Nanus, 1985), which is a two-day exercise held with executives and relevant outsiders to discuss long-range opportunities and risks, and possible reactions by the organization.

Summary

The prosperity and survival of the organization depend on timely adaptation to threats and opportunities, maintaining a high level of efficiency and process reliability, ensuring favorable human relations and resources, and an organizational culture with shared values that are consistent with the mission and competitive strategy. The relative importance of these performance determinants for organizations, and the potential trade-offs among them, are determined by aspects of the situation such as the type of organization and the amount of change in the external environment. When changes in the external environment affect the capacity of the organization to carry out its mission, successful adaptation requires recognition of threats and opportunities, and the willingness to make changes in the processes, products, services, or the competitive strategy of the organization. Flexible, adaptive leadership is essential to deal successfully with the trade-offs, competing objectives, and changing situations. The organizational culture can facilitate or hinder efforts to make major change.

A chief executive has more potential influence on the performance of an organization when there is a crisis and the competitive strategy is no longer aligned with its environment. A major change is more likely to be successful if it is initiated before a crisis becomes serious and the organization no longer has any slack resources, but it is more difficult to initiate a major change when there is no obvious need for it. Major strategic change is most likely to be initiated by a CEO who is an external successor than by a CEO who has been in office for a long time. The different types of research described in this chapter show that despite all the constraints on top executives, they can still have a moderately strong influence on the effectiveness of an organization. The outcome of a major change depends on what type of leadership is provided by mid-level and lower-level managers as well as by top executives, and the leadership decisions at different levels and in different subunits of the organization must be consistent and coordinated.

An executive team is more important in a complex, rapidly changing environment that places many external demands on the CEO. Teams are also more important in an organization with diverse but highly interdependent business units, because a single leader is unlikely to have the broad expertise necessary to direct and integrate the activities of these units. The member characteristics necessary for team effectiveness depend on the organizational context, the external environment, and the leadership provided by the CEO.

External monitoring provides information needed for strategic planning and crisis management. To detect threats and discover opportunities in a timely way, top management must actively monitor relevant sectors of the environment, sources of dependency for the organization, and current performance. Developing a strategy for adapting to the environment is an important responsibility for top executives, and the strategy is more likely to be effective if it builds on core competencies, is relevant to long-term objectives, and is feasible in terms of current capabilities.

Review and Discussion Questions

1. What are the major performance determinants for organizations?
2. How can leaders influence each type of performance determinant?
3. What is organizational culture and how can leaders influence it?
4. What conditions limit the discretion of a CEO?
5. What determines the effectiveness of executive teams?
6. How do shared leadership, relational leadership, and complexity theories increase our understanding of leadership in organizations?
7. Why is external monitoring important for strategic leadership?
8. What are some guidelines for strategy formulation?

Key Terms

adaptation	core competencies	organizational culture
chief executive officer (CEO)	distributed leadership	performance determinants
CEO succession	internal and external	relational leadership
competitive strategy	constraints	strategic leadership
complexity theory	external monitoring	strategic planning
convergence	flexible leadership theory	top management team

CASE 1

Costco

Costco is one of the largest retail sales companies in the United States, and it has more than 500 stores in 37 states and eight countries. Despite low profit margins in the retailing industry, the company is more profitable than most competitors, and it is growing rapidly. In the University of Michigan's annual survey of customer satisfaction with U.S. retailers, Costco has had the highest ratings in recent years.

The company's basic strategy is to provide quality products at the lowest available prices, and the products include clothing, electronics, and food. Costco's leading competitor—Wal-Mart's Sam's Club—offers more variety and some lower priced items, but Costco's products are generally of a higher quality. Around 20% of the products consist of limited-time supplies of deeply discounted luxury goods and other special bargains. Examples include Rolex and Movado watches, gourmet imported chocolates, Waterford crystal, plasma televisions, and Burberry and Coach handbags. This strategy of temporary special bargains creates customer excitement and increases purchases of items that shoppers had not intended to buy when they visited the store.

Charging customers for the privilege of shopping at Costco provides a steady source of revenue for the company and increases customer loyalty. Costco has two types of members: businesses and individuals. Even though the cost of membership is a little higher than for competitors, Costco's card renewal rate was over 86% in 2006, and membership increased by 14%. To increase the value of the memberships and attract additional customers, Costco also offers services such as travel plans, health and home insurance, banking, and financial planning. Individual shoppers average two Costco visits per month, and many travel great distances to stock up on supplies. Unlike most discount stores, Costco has many affluent customers who are "treasure hunting" for the special bargains on luxury goods rather than merely looking for low prices on basic commodities.

Costco's merchandise buyers have to experiment and take big risks with luxury items, because a lot of money is tied up in inventory if the items do not sell quickly. The buyers need to rely on their intuition and creativity to find items that will be popular and profitable. Innovation in design and packaging is also important for making some types of products such as food items more appealing to customers. Recent initiatives, for instance, include the elimination of Styrofoam trays from meat packages and the use of individually sealed packets. The design is more environmentally sound and enables consumers to freeze unused portions without repackaging or rewrapping products.

Costco has generous pay, excellent health benefits, and a good 401(k) plan for its more than 120,000 hourly employees in the Unites States. The average wage for a full-time worker at Costco is around 40% higher than at Sam's Club. Around 82% of Costco employees have health-insurance coverage, as compared with less than half of the employees at Wal-Mart, and Costco employees pay much less of their health premiums. Around 91% of Costco's employees are covered by retirement plans, as compared to 64% of employees at Sam's Club, and company contributions to the plan are nearly twice as high per employee at Costco. The company policy is to promote from within the ranks, and workers at all levels have good opportunities for advancement.

The company has one of the most loyal and productive workforces in the retailing industry. The high level of organizational commitment is reflected in the turnover rate (around 6% for workers on the job for more than one year) which is well below the average rate of 44% for the industry. The cost from turnover (lost productivity, recruiting and training new employees) is 40% lower at Costco than at Sam's Club. Employee theft at Costco is the lowest in the industry. The savings from lower turnover costs, lower employee theft, and higher employee productivity more than offsets the higher cost of compensation at Costco. The operating profit per hourly employee in the United States is nearly twice as high at Costco as at Sam's Club.

The high level of employee motivation and commitment is not only because they are well compensated, but there is also a high level of intrinsic motivation among Costco employees. They are encouraged to suggest ways to improve the stores and product mix, and creativity is valued. Each morning before the store opens there is a conversation about ways to be more efficient and to provide better customer service. All employees are trained to be friendly and helpful when customers need assistance. When shoppers need assistance in locating an item, employees are expected to show them where it is rather than merely pointing to a distant spot or providing vague directions.

The methods Costco uses to minimize costs include a no-frills approach to their stores, which also function as their warehouses. The buildings have metal exteriors and steel racks. Instead of individual products on shelves, there are pallets on steel frames that soar to the ceilings. Above every pallet is a card with a simple product description, and they keep everything as simple as possible for the product displays. Marketing costs are low because Costco does not do any advertising; there is no public relations manager or expensive advertising agency. Instead, Costco depends entirely on happy customers who tell their friends about the fantastic bargains available at Costco stores.

The company keeps layouts standard in its stores to reduce costs and give shoppers a feeling of familiarity at every location. The products sold in each store are similar, except for foods, which vary according to local tastes. Inventory costs are reduced by having only a limited variety of product sizes, and by packaging many products for bulk sales. Products move right from the delivery truck to the sales floor, and the signage looks like it was made with a cheap laser printer. There are not even any shopping bags for customers. A computer system that tracks sales in the stores makes it possible to determine when more fresh foods are needed in the display cases and reduces costs from waste and overproduction.

Jim Sinegal, the CEO of Costco, is very modest about his contribution to the success of the company and quick to share credit with others. He understands how important it is to have talented people working for a company, and he does many things to attract and retain them. At the company headquarters in a Seattle suburb, his office is an open space with no door. His desk is pushed up against the wall so that, at first glance, he appears to be someone else's secretary. Sinegal usually answers his own phone, uses a nametag like other employees, and usually wears one of the low-priced dress shirts sold in his stores. As the cofounder of Costco, Sinegal is a major shareholder, but his annual compensation is only 10% of the average amount for CEOs. He tries to limit his salary and bonus to no more than twice what a Costco store manager earns, and he declined his bonus for the last three years in order to achieve that objective.

At the annual Managers' Conference, Sinegal meets with more than 1,000 Costco managers and product buyers to review the past, discuss the present, and plan the future. He also has monthly budget meetings with groups of around 70 store managers to talk about the importance of exercising tight cost controls, getting the details right, and adhering to the Costco credo. Important values at Costco include hard work, respect for customers, and high ethical standards. Sinegal communicates a strong concern for high performance, but he is not coercive or overly critical. He is careful not to discourage his product buyers when they take risks on new products. Employees are empowered and encouraged to "think outside the box" Sinegal still attends every new store opening, and he tries to visit every Costco store twice a year. He spends nearly half of his time on the road checking out his stores as well as the competition to make sure they are not undercutting Costco's prices.

Sinegal has a strong concern for his employees, and he is perceived as dedicated, caring, and hard-working. He is able to remember the names of most of his managers, and they know him by sight. At a recent annual meeting when he answered a question by stating that he had no plans to retire soon, the audience gave him a spontaneous standing ovation. In 2003, the rising cost of health care made it necessary to increase the employee contribution to their health insurance. Sinegal sent a letter to employees explaining why the increase was necessary, and the letter generated more than 100 responses, nearly all of which were supportive.

Sinegal tries to do what is right for employees, customers, vendors, and stockholders. Recently a major decision was made to put a 90-day limit on customer returns of electronics products. The old policy was unique in American retailing, but it was becoming too costly. The new policy could save the company more than $100 million a year, but Sinegal did not want to change it without a viable alternative. Thus, as part of the new policy, he decided to extend the manufacturer warranty by a year.

Questions

1. Explain the success of Costco in terms of the three performance determinants in flexible leadership theory (efficiency, adaptation, and human capital).
2. Explain how Costco can provide higher compensation to its employees and still be successful in the use of a low price competitive strategy.
3. Use relevant leadership theories to analyze the behavior of the CEO and describe his influence on the company.

CASE 2

Turnaround at Nissan

In 1999, Nissan was in a state of serious decline and had lost money in all but one of the previous eight years. Only Renault's willingness to assume part of Nissan's debt saved the Japanese company from going bankrupt. As part of the deal, the French automaker appointed Carlos Ghosn to become Nissan's chief operating officer. However, there was widespread skepticism that the alliance between Renault and Nissan could succeed, or that someone who was not Japanese could provide effective leadership at Nissan.

During the three months prior to assuming the position of COO at Nissan, Ghosn met with hundreds of people, including employees, union officials, suppliers, and customers, to learn more about the company and its strengths and weaknesses. From these meetings and earlier experiences with turnaround assignments, Ghosn understood that major changes would not be successful if they were dictated by him and the experts he brought with him from Renault. Soon after assuming his new position at Nissan in June 1999, Ghosn created nine cross-functional teams and gave them responsibility for determining what needed to be done to revive the company. Such teams had never been used before at Nissan, and it was unusual in a Japanese company to involve a broad cross-section of managers in determining major changes.

The cross-functional teams examined different aspects of company operations to identify problems and recommend solutions to Ghosn and the executive committee. Several interrelated problems were identified, and they were mostly consistent with Ghosn's initial impressions. The poor financial performance at Nissan was a joint result of declining sales and excessive costs, and weak management was the primary reason for the failure to resolve these problems. Management lacked a coherent strategy, a strong profit orientation, and a clear focus on customers. There was little cooperation across functions, and there was no urgency about the need for major change.

One reason for excessive costs at Nissan was that only half of the available capacity in the company's factories was being used; production capacity was sufficient to build almost a million more cars a year than the company could sell. To reduce costs, Ghosn decided to close five factories in Japan and eliminate more than 21,000 jobs, which was 14 percent of Nissan's global workforce. To simplify production operations at the remaining factories and make them more efficient, Ghosn planned to reduce the number of car platforms by half and the number of powertrain combinations by a third. Plant closings can undermine relations with employees, and Ghosn took steps to ensure that employees knew why they were necessary and who would be affected. In general, he understood that most employees prefer to learn what would happen to them and prepare for it, rather than remaining in a state of uncertainty and anxiety. Ghosn attempted to minimize adverse effects on employees by selling subsidiaries and using natural attrition, early retirements, and opportunities for part-time work at other company facilities.

Purchasing costs represent 60 percent of the operating costs for an automaker, and Nissan was paying much more than necessary for the parts and supplies used to build its cars. After comparing expenses at Nissan and Renault, Ghosn discovered that Nissan's purchasing costs were 25 percent higher. One reason was the practice of purchasing small orders from many suppliers instead of larger orders from a smaller number of global sources. It would be necessary to reduce the number of suppliers, even though this action was unprecedented in a country where supplier relationships were considered sacrosanct. Higher purchasing costs were also a result of overly exacting specifications imposed on suppliers by Nissan engineers. The engineers who worked with the cross-functional team on purchasing initially defended their specifications, but when they finally realized that they were wrong, the team was able to achieve greater savings than expected. Excessive purchasing costs are not the type of problem that can be solved quickly, but after three years of persistent effort it was possible to achieve Ghosn's goal of a 20 percent reduction.

Years of declining sales at Nissan were caused by a lack of customer appeal for most of the company's cars. When Ghosn made a detailed analysis of sales data, he discovered that only 4 of the 43 different Nissan models had sufficient sales to be profitable. Final decisions about the design of new models were made by the head of engineering. Designers were taking orders from engineers who focused completely on performance, and there was little effort to determine what types of cars customers really wanted. To increase the customer appeal of Nissan vehicles, Ghosn hired the innovative designer Shiro Nakamura, who became another key leader in the turnaround effort. The designers would now have more authority over design decisions, and Ghosn encouraged them to be innovative rather than merely copying competitors. For the first time in over a decade, Nissan began coming up with cars that excited customers both in Japan and abroad. Ghosn planned to introduce 12 new models over a three-year period, but the time necessary to bring a new model into production meant that few would be available until 2002.

Another reason for declining sales was Nissan's weak distribution network. In Japan strong brand loyalty is reinforced by efforts to maintain close relationships with customers, and it is essential for the dealerships to be managed by people who can build customer loyalty and convert it into repeat sales. In 1999, many Nissan dealerships in Japan were subsidiaries managed by Nissan executives nearing retirement, and they viewed their role more in social terms than as an entrepreneur responsible for helping the company to increase market share and profits. Ghosn reduced the number of company-owned dealerships (10 percent were closed or sold), and he took steps to improve management at the remaining dealerships.

Saving Nissan would also require major changes in human resource practices, such as guaranteed lifetime employment and pay and promotion based on seniority. Transforming these strongly embedded aspects of the company culture without engendering resentment and demoralizing employees was perhaps the most difficult challenge. The changes would primarily affect nonunionized employees at Nissan, including the managers. A merit pay plan was established, and instead of being rewarded for seniority, employees were now expected to earn their promotions and salary increases through effective performance. Areas of accountability were sharply defined so that performance could be measured in relation to specific goals. New bonuses provided employees an opportunity to earn up to a third of their annual salary for effective performance, and hundreds of upper-level managers could also earn stock options. These and other changes in human resource practices would make it possible for Ghosn to gradually replace weak middle- and upper-level managers with more competent successors.

In October 1999, Ghosn announced the plan for revitalizing Nissan. He had been careful to avoid any earlier leaks about individual changes that would be criticized without understanding why they were necessary and how they fit into the overall plan. The announcement included a pledge that Ghosn and the executive committee would resign if Nissan failed to show a profit by the end of 2000. It was an impressive demonstration of his sincerity and commitment, and it made what he was asking of others seem more acceptable. Fortunately, the primary objectives of the change were all achieved on schedule, and by 2001 earnings were at a record high for the company. That year Ghosn was appointed as the chief executive officer at Nissan, and in 2005, he would become the CEO of Renault as well.

Note: This case is based on information in Ghosn and Ries (2005) and Taylor (2002).

Questions

1. What was done to improve efficiency, adaptation, and human relations, and how were the potential trade-offs among these performance determinants handled?
2. What effective change management practices were used at Nissan?
3. What traits and skills can help to explain the successful strategic leadership by Ghosn?

Charismatic and Transformational Leadership

Learning Objectives

After studying this chapter, you should be able to:

- Understand how charismatic and transformational theories differ from earlier theories.
- Understand similarities and differences between charismatic and transformational leadership.
- Understand how leaders, followers, and the situation affect attributions of charisma.
- Understand the traits, behaviors, and influence processes included in each major theory.
- Understand the benefits and costs of charismatic leadership for followers and the organization.
- Understand how to inspire more follower commitment and optimism.

In the 1980s, management researchers became very interested in the emotional and symbolic aspects of leadership. These processes help us to understand how leaders influence followers to make self-sacrifices and put the needs of the mission or organization above their materialistic self-interests. Theories of charismatic and *transformational leadership* describe this important aspect of leadership.

Charisma is a Greek word that means "divinely inspired gift," such as the ability to perform miracles or predict future events. Weber (1947) used the term to describe a form of influence based not on tradition or formal authority but rather on follower perceptions that the leader is endowed with exceptional qualities. According to Weber, charisma occurs during a social crisis when a leader emerges with a radical vision that offers a solution to the crisis and attracts followers who believe in the *vision*. The followers experience some successes that make the vision appear attainable, and they come to perceive the leader as extraordinary.

From Chapter 12 of *Leadership in Organizations*, Eighth Edition. Gary Yukl. Copyright © 2013 by Pearson Education, Inc. Publishing as Prentice Hall. All rights reserved.

In the past two decades, several social scientists formulated newer versions of the theory to describe *charismatic leadership* in organizations (e.g., Conger & Kanungo, 1987, 1998; House, 1977; Shamir, House, & Arthur, 1993). These "neo-charismatic" theories incorporate some of Weber's ideas, but in other respects they depart from his initial conception about charismatic leadership (Beyer, 1999; Conger, 1989). The newer theories describe the motives and behaviors of charismatic leaders and psychological processes that explain how these leaders influence followers (Jacobsen & House, 2001).

Transformational leadership in another type of theory used to describe how effective leaders inspire and transform followers by appealing to their ideals and emotions. The terms *transformational and charismatic* are used interchangeably by many writers, but despite the similarities there are some important distinctions. This chapter describes the major theories of charismatic and transformational leadership, compares and evaluates the theories, reviews the research findings, and provides some practical guidelines for leaders.

Attribution Theory of Charismatic Leadership

Conger and Kanungo (1987) proposed a theory of charismatic leadership based on the assumption that charisma is an attributional phenomenon. Subsequently, a refined version of the theory was presented by Conger (1989) and by Conger and Kanungo (1998). According to the theory, follower attribution of charismatic qualities to a leader is jointly determined by the leader's behavior, expertise, and aspects of the situation.

Leader Behaviors

Follower attributions of charisma depend on several types of leader behavior. These behaviors are not assumed to be present in every charismatic leader to the same extent, and their relative importance depends to some extent on the leadership situation.

Novel and Appealing Vision.   Charisma is more likely to be attributed to leaders who advocate a vision that is highly discrepant from the status quo, but not so radical that followers will view the leader as incompetent or insane. A leader who supports the status quo or advocates only small, incremental changes will not be viewed as charismatic. The ability to see opportunities that others fail to recognize is another reason for a leader to be viewed as extraordinary. Attributions of charisma are likely for leaders who influence people to collectively achieve objectives that initially seemed impossible.

Emotional Appeals to Values.   Followers are more likely to attribute charisma to leaders who inspire them with emotional appeals to their values and ideals. Leaders who use authority to implement an innovative strategy for attaining important objectives may gain more expert power if the strategy is successful, but unless they articulate an ideological vision to justify the strategy, they are unlikely to appear charismatic. Likewise, followers who meet with the leader to develop a consensus strategy may be satisfied and highly motivated by the experience of empowerment, but the leader will not appear to be extraordinary.

Unconventional Behavior.   Charisma is more likely to be attributed to leaders who act in unconventional ways to achieve the vision. The leader's methods for attaining the idealized goal must differ from conventional ways of doing things in order to impress followers that the leader is extraordinary. The use of innovative strategies that appear successful results in attribution of superior expertise to the leader by followers. The risks inherent in the use of novel strategies make it important for the leader to have the skills and expertise to make a realistic assessment of environmental constraints and opportunities for implementing the strategies. Timing is critical; the same strategy may succeed at one time but fail completely if implemented earlier or later.

Self-Sacrifices.   Leaders are more likely to be viewed as charismatic if they make self-sacrifices for the benefit of followers, and they take personal risks or incur high costs to achieve the vision they espouse. Trust appears to be an important component of charisma, and followers have more trust in a leader who seems less motivated by self-interest than by concern for followers. Most impressive is a leader who actually risks substantial personal loss in terms of status, money, leadership position, or membership in the organization.

Confidence and Optimism.   Leaders who appear confident about their proposals are more likely to be viewed as charismatic than leaders who appear doubtful and confused. Unless the leader communicates self-confidence, the success of an innovative strategy may be attributed more to luck than to expertise. A leader's confidence and enthusiasm can be contagious. Followers who believe the leader knows how to attain the shared objective will work harder, thereby increasing the actual probability of success.

Influence Processes

The primary influence process is *personal identification,* which involves a follower's desire to please and imitate the leader. Charismatic leaders appear so extraordinary, due to their strategic insight, strong convictions, self-confidence, unconventional behavior, and dynamic energy that subordinates idolize these leaders and want to become like them. Leader approval becomes a measure of the subordinate's own self-worth. This approval is expressed by praise and recognition of subordinate behavior and accomplishments, which builds self-confidence and a deeper sense of obligation to live up to the leader's expectations in the future. Many subordinates of charismatic leaders reported that desire for leader approval was their primary source of motivation. At the same time, it was evident that followers were also motivated by fear of disappointing the leader and being rejected.

The influence of a charismatic leader may also involve *internalization* of new values and beliefs by followers. Conger (1989) emphasized that it is more important for followers to adopt the leader's attitudes and beliefs about desirable objectives and effective strategies than merely to imitate superficial aspects of the leader's behavior such as mannerisms, gestures, and speech patterns. A charismatic leader who articulates an inspirational vision can influence followers to internalize attitudes and beliefs that will subsequently serve as a source of intrinsic motivation to carry out the mission of the organization. An example is influencing followers to believe they can collectively overcome formidable obstacles to attainment of the vision.

Facilitating Conditions

Contextual variables are especially important for charismatic leadership because the attribution of exceptional ability to a leader is rare and may be highly dependent upon characteristics of the situation. One important situational variable is follower fear and anxiety about the future. Charismatic leaders are more likely to emerge in crisis situations where people are worried about economic loss, physical danger, or threats to core values. Nevertheless, Weber (1947), Conger and Kanungo do not consider an objective crisis to be a necessary condition for charismatic leadership. Even in the absence of a genuine crisis, a leader may be able to create dissatisfaction with current conditions and provide a vision of a more promising future. To set the stage for proposing new ways, the leader may try to discredit the old, accepted ways of doing things. The impact of unconventional strategies is greater when followers perceive that conventional approaches are no longer effective. Finally, the leader may also precipitate a crisis where none existed previously to set the stage for demonstration of superior expertise in dealing with the problem in unconventional ways.

Self-Concept Theory of Charismatic Leadership

House (1977) proposed a theory to explain charismatic leadership in terms of a set of testable propositions involving observable processes rather than folklore and mystique. Shamir et al. (1993) revised and extended the theory by incorporating more aspects of human motivation and a more detailed description of the underlying influence processes.

Evidence of charismatic leadership is provided by the leader-follower relationship, and a charismatic leader has profound and unusual effects on followers. Followers perceive that the leader's beliefs are correct, they willingly obey the leader, they feel affection toward the leader, they are emotionally involved in the mission of the group or organization, they have high performance goals, and they believe that they can contribute to the success of the mission. Attribution of extraordinary ability to the leader is likely, but in contrast to the attribution theory by Conger and Kanungo (1987), it is not considered a necessary condition for charismatic leadership.

Leader Traits and Behaviors

Charismatic leaders are likely to have a strong need for power, high self-confidence, and a strong conviction in their own beliefs and ideals. The leadership behaviors that explain how a charismatic leader influences the attitudes and behavior of followers include the following: (1) articulating an appealing vision, (2) using strong, expressive forms of communication when articulating the vision, (3) taking personal risks and making self-sacrifices to attain the vision, (4) communicating high expectations, (5) expressing optimism and confidence in followers, (6) modeling behaviors consistent with the vision, (7) managing follower impressions of the leader, (8) building identification with the group or organization, and (9) empowering followers.

Charismatic leaders use language that includes symbols, slogans, imagery, and metaphors that are relevant to the experience and values of followers. Several studies of charismatic leaders have identified specific aspects of their communications that help to communicate an appealing and optimistic vision. For example, a study that content analyzed the speeches of U.S. presidents found more frequent use of metaphors by presidents regarded as very charismatic (Mio, Riggio, Levin, & Reese, 2005). Finally, expression of strong positive emotions such as enthusiasm and optimism about a new initiative, project, or strategy is another way for leaders to influence follower motivation (Sy, Cote, & Saavedra, 2005).

Influence Processes

Personal Identification.   Shamir and his colleagues recognize that personal identification is one type of influence process that may occur for some followers of a charismatic leader. When strong personal identification occurs, followers will imitate the leader's behavior, carry out the leader's requests, and make an extra effort to please the leader. Personal identification and follower attributions of charisma to a leader are more likely when the leader communicates an appealing vision in an expressive and dramatic way, demonstrates courage and conviction, and makes self-sacrifices for followers or the mission (e.g., Choi & Mai-Dalton, 1999; DeCremer, 2002; Halverson, Holladay, Kazama, & Quinones, 2004; Yorges et al., 1999).

However, personal identification is considered a less important source of leader influence over followers than *social identification,* internalization, and augmentation of individual and collective *self-efficacy.*

Social Identification. Strong social identification occurs when people take pride in being part of the group or organization and regard membership as one of their most important social identities (Ashforth & Mael, 1989). They see how their efforts and work roles are related to a larger entity, making their work more meaningful and important. They are more willing to place the needs of the group above individual needs and make self-sacrifices for the sake of the group. Moreover, social identification results in strengthening of shared values, beliefs, and behavior norms among members of the group.

Charismatic leaders can increase social identification by articulating a vision that relates a follower's *self-concept* to shared values and role identities associated with the group (see Conger, Kanungo, & Menon, 2000). By emphasizing the ideological importance of the mission and the group's unique qualifications to perform it, the leader can imbue the group with a unique collective identity. Social identification can also be increased by the skillful use of slogans, symbols (e.g., flags, emblems, uniforms), rituals (singing the organization's song or anthem, saluting the flag, reciting the creed), and ceremonies (e.g., initiation of new members). Other relevant leadership behaviors include telling stories about past successes, heroic deeds by members, and *symbolic actions* by the founder or former leaders.

Internalization. With this influence process, followers embrace the leader's mission or objectives as something that is worthy of their commitment. Sometimes charismatic leaders influence followers to embrace new values, but it is more common for charismatic leaders to articulate a vision describing task objectives in ideological terms that reflect existing follower values. By emphasizing the symbolic and ideological aspects of the work, the leader makes it seem more meaningful, noble, heroic, and morally correct. The ultimate form of internalization occurs when followers come to view their work role as inseparably linked to their selfconcepts and self-worth. They carry out the role because it is a part of their essential nature and destiny.

Self and Collective Efficacy. Task motivation also depends on individual self-efficacy and collective efficacy. Individual self-efficacy is the belief that one is competent and capable of attaining difficult task objectives. People with high self-efficacy are willing to expend more effort and persist longer in overcoming obstacles to the attainment of task objectives (Bandura, 1986). Collective efficacy refers to the perception of group members that they can accomplish exceptional feats by working together. When collective efficacy is high, people are more willing to cooperate with members of their group in a joint effort to carry out their mission. A leader can enhance follower self-efficacy and collective efficacy by articulating an inspiring vision, expressing confidence that it can be accomplished, and providing necessary coaching and assistance (see Kark, Shamir, & Chen, 2003).

Emotional Contagion. The effects of a charismatic leader on followers may also involve *emotional contagion,* although this process was not emphasized by Shamir et al. (1993) when the theory was initially proposed. A leader who is very positive and enthusiastic can influence the mood of followers to be more positive, which is likely to increase their enthusiasm for the work and their perception that they can accomplish difficult objectives (e.g., collective efficacy). Moreover, emotional contagion can occur among followers themselves, so that feelings of excitement and optimism can spread quickly in a group or organization. Bono and Ilies (2006) found that leaders who were viewed as charismatic by followers were also rated higher on expression of emotion and overall effectiveness. The positive mood of followers mediated the relationship between leader expression of emotion and ratings of leader effectiveness.

Facilitating Conditions

The motivational effects of charismatic leaders are more likely to occur when the leader's vision is congruent with existing follower values and identities. Thus, charismatic leaders must be able to understand the needs and values of followers. In addition, it must be possible to define task roles in ideological terms that will appeal to followers. High-technology industries can be linked to values such as scientific progress, economic development, and national pride, but it is more difficult to develop an appealing ideology in industries with controversial products such as alcoholic beverages, tobacco, or firearms. Work roles that have low potential for ideological appeals include simple, repetitive work with little inherent meaning or social significance. However, the following story of the two bricklayers shows that even routine work can be made more meaningful.

> When asked what he was doing, one bricklayer replied that he was making a wall. The second bricklayer replied that he was building a cathedral.

According to the theory, a crisis condition is not necessary for the effectiveness of charismatic leadership. Nevertheless, charismatic leadership is more likely to occur when a group or organization is in serious trouble, there is not an obvious way to resolve the problem, and there is considerable anxiety or even panic among the members (e.g., Bligh, Kohles, & Meindl, 2004; Halverson et al., 2004; House et al., 1991; Pastor, Mayo, & Shamir, 2007; Pillai, 1996; Pillai & Meindl, 1998). Such conditions favor the emergence of a charismatic leader who is able to interpret the crisis and offer credible strategies for coping with it successfully. However, the attribution of charisma may be temporary unless the leader's vision continues to be relevant after the immediate crisis is resolved (Boal & Bryson, 1988; Hunt, Boal, & Dodge, 1999). A good example is provided by the career of Winston Churchill.

> As the prime minister of Britain during World War II, he rallied resistance to Nazi aggression and his inspiring speeches sustained hope for an eventual victory. During that time he was widely viewed in Britain and allied countries as a charismatic leader. However, after the war he had a sharp decline in popularity and was unable to retain his leadership position.

Other Conceptions of Charisma

This section reviews some other conceptions of charisma that provide useful insights into the nature of this complex form of leadership. These conceptions of charisma include psychodynamic processes, close versus distant charismatics, and a typology that differentiates charismatics from ideological and pragmatic leaders.

Psychodynamic Processes

A few theorists have attempted to explain charisma in terms of Freudian psychodynamic processes in followers (Kets de Vries, 1988; Lindholm, 1988). These theorists attempt to explain the unusual and seemingly irrational influence of some charismatic leaders who are idolized as a superhuman hero or worshiped as a spiritual figure. The intense personal identification of followers with such leaders is explained in terms of psychodynamic processes such as regression, transference, and projection. Regression involves a return to feelings and behaviors that were typical of a younger age. Transference occurs when feelings toward an important figure from the past (e.g., a parent) are shifted to someone in the present. Projection involves a process of attributing undesirable feelings and motives to someone else, thereby shifting the blame for things about which one feels guilty.

According to one psychoanalytic explanation, followers suffering from fear, guilt, or alienation may experience a feeling of euphoric empowerment and transcendence by submerging their identity in that of a seemingly superhuman leader. For example, a young man has a severe identity crisis because he is unable to develop a clear conception of an ideal self due to weak or abusive parents. He develops a strong emotional attachment and dependence on a charismatic gang leader who serves as the ideal to emulate. In another example, a person who has caused injury to others suffers from overwhelming guilt. By identifying with a charismatic religious leader who is perceived to exemplify moral values, the person vicariously experiences the leader's moral superiority and is able to overcome the guilt. Followers of a charismatic leader may regress to childhood feelings of dependence on a parent who seemed to have magical powers, they may identify with the leader as an idealized self who exemplifies their wishes and fantasies, and they may be encouraged to project their feelings of guilt and hostility to an external figure or group.

Attributions of charisma are especially likely by people who have feelings of inadequacy, guilt, fear, and alienation, and who share beliefs and fantasies that will serve as the basis for emotional and rational appeals by the leader. For example, the combination of a severe economic depression and the collective shame of defeat in World War I left a fertile ground in Germany for the rise of Hitler. Hero worship and personal identification with charismatic entertainers is more likely to occur among adolescents who have low self-esteem and a weak social identity.

Close and Distant Charisma

Shamir (1995) proposed that attributions of charisma for people who have close contact with the leader differ in some important ways from attributions made by people who only view the leader from a distance. An exploratory study was conducted in Israel to see whether the proposed differences could be verified. Students were interviewed and asked to describe a charismatic leader with whom they had a direct relationship and one with whom they did not have a direct relationship. Responses were content analyzed to identify leader traits, skills, behaviors, and effects.

The results from the initial study support Shamir's proposition that the amount of direct interaction between a leader and followers affects attributions of charisma. Distant charismatics were described more often in terms of their substantive achievements and effects on follower political attitudes. Close charismatics were more often described in terms of their effects on follower motivation, task behavior, and identification with the leader. The findings suggest that attributions of greatness for distant leaders are affected more by performance cues and shared stereotypes, whereas attributions of greatness for close leaders are affected more by leader behavior and interpersonal skills. However, the exploratory study had several limitations, and a subsequent study by Yagil (1998) in the Israeli army did not find support for the proposition that interpersonal qualities are more important in determining attributions of charisma for close rather than distant leaders. A survey study of managers at different levels in Korean companies (Chun et al., 2009) examined the influence of charismatic leadership on close and distant subordinates with multilevel analyses, but the results were mixed.

Attribution of charisma to a distant charismatic leader is likely to be affected also by influence processes among the followers themselves (Meindl, 1990). The perception of a distant leader may be influenced by individuals who promote the leader's reputation and defend controversial actions and decisions by the leader (Galvin, Balkundi, & Waldman, 2010). Emotional contagion can increase follower enthusiasm and devotion to the leader. The qualities attributed to a leader may become highly exaggerated as rumors and stories circulate among people who have no direct contact with the leader. For example, stories about a leader's heroic deeds and exceptional feats may spread among members of a political movement; stories about miracles performed by the leader may spread among members of a religious cult.

Attributions about charisma may be made not only by the members of an organization, but also by outsiders who do not have an opportunity to observe the leaders closely (e.g., investors, customers, suppliers, government officials). Chief executive officers (CEOs) have a variety of ways to influence the impressions of external stakeholders whose confidence and support are important to success and survival of the organization (Fanelli & Misangyi, 2006; Treadway, Adams, Ranft, & Ferris, 2009).

More research is needed to clarify how distance affects attributions of charisma, and stronger methods will be needed to avoid the limitations common in this type of research. Antonakis and Atwater (2002) pointed out the need to make a careful distinction between vertical social distance (proximity in the authority hierarchy of an organization) and physical distance. The frequency and nature of interactions with followers, and the amount of leader position power and control, also determine how distance will moderate the influence of a leader on followers. Advances in communication and social networking technology may allow physically distant followers to experience a virtual relationship that is similar in many respects to the relationship experienced by followers who are physically close to the leader.

Charismatic versus Ideological and Pragmatic Leaders

Another theory involving charismatic leadership differentiates between three types of leaders that can emerge in situations involving crises, turbulence, and uncertainty (Hunter et al., 2011; Mumford, 2006; Mumford, Antes, Caughron, & Friedrich, 2008). In turbulent situations, leaders have more potential influence over the identification of threats and opportunities and the selection of appropriate responses. The three different types of leaders that can emerge in these situations are labeled *charismatic, ideological,* and *pragmatic* leaders. Each type of leader can be effective, but they differ in terms of their traits, behavior, and influence processes. The charismatic and ideological leaders are more effective in situations where there is a high level of political and ideological conflict, whereas pragmatic leaders are more effective when there is little political confict and more emphasis on constructive problem solving.

Ideological leaders are more likely to emerge when there is a strong culture of shared values, and they can articulate a vision that embodies these values. Ideological leaders make emotional appeals to shared values and beliefs, and they involve followers in identifying strategies for resolving a crisis or attaining desirable objectives. To retain the trust of followers, ideological leaders must act in ways that are consistent with the values and vision.

The charismatic leaders appeal to emotions and articulate a vision that builds confidence that the leader can show followers how to resolve a crisis and overcome obstacles to desirable objectives. The vision appeals to some members of the organization who trust the leader and are willing to become loyal followers, but other members who do not share the leader's vision may become opponents.

The pragmatic leaders are more likely to emerge when they are perceived by followers to have the expertise and commitment necessary to guide the process of strategy formation and crisis management. Pragmatic leaders make rational appeals to followers who are able to understand and carry out proposed strategies for achieving shared objectives.

Consequences of Charismatic Leadership

Examples of positive and negative charismatics can be found in studies of political leaders. Franklin D. Roosevelt lifted the United States out of the Great Depression, implemented major social programs such as Social Security, and mobilized the nation for World War II. In the same historical period, Adolf Hitler transformed Germany in a manner resulting in paranoid aggression, persecution, destruction, and the death of millions of people. This section discusses the positive and negative consequences of charismatic leadership for followers and the organization.

Positive and Negative Charismatics

How to differentiate between positive and negative charismatic leaders has been a problem for leadership theory. It is not always clear whether a particular leader should be classified as a positive or negative charismatic. One approach is to examine the consequences for followers. However, most charismatic leaders have both positive and negative effects on followers, and it is not always clear whether a particular outcome is beneficial or detrimental.

A better approach for differentiating between positive and negative charismatics is in terms of their values and personality (House & Howell, 1992; Howell, 1988; Musser, 1987). Negative charis- matics have a personalized power orientation. They emphasize personal identification rather than internalization. They intentionally seek to instill devotion to themselves more than to ideals. They may use ideological appeals, but merely as a means to gain power, after which the ideology is ignored or arbitrarily changed to serve the leader's personal objectives. They seek to dominate and subjugate followers by keeping them weak and dependent on the leader. Authority for making important decisions is centralized in the leader, rewards and punishments are used to manipulate and control followers, and information is restricted and used to maintain an image of leader infallibility or to exaggerate external threats to the organization. Decisions of these leaders reflect a greater concern for self-glorification and maintaining power than for the welfare of followers.

In contrast, positive charismatics have a socialized power orientation. They seek to instill devotion to ideology more than devotion to themselves. In terms of influence processes, they emphasize internalization rather than personal identification. Self-sacrifice and leading by example are used to communicate commitment to shared values and the mission of the unit, not to glorify the leader. Authority is delegated to a considerable extent, information is shared openly, participation in decisions is encouraged, and rewards arc used to reinforce behavior consistent with the mission and objectives of the organization. As a result, their leadership is more likely to be beneficial to followers, although it is not inevitable if the strategies encouraged by the leader are inappropriate.

Howell and Shamir (2005) proposed that follower characteristics help explain the type of charismatic relationship that will occur, but unlike some theorists, they do not believe that attributions of charisma are limited to followers who lack self-esteem and a clear *self-identity*. Followers who lack a clear self-identity and are confused and anxious about their lives are more attracted to a strong leader with a personalized power orientation who can provide a clear social identity for them as disciples or loyal supporters. The followers will identify more with the leader than with the organization or mission. In contrast, followers with a clear self-concept and high self-esteem will be responsive to a leader who can explain how the mission of the group or organization is relevant to their core values and strong self-identity. These followers will identify more with the mission and the organization than with the leader.

Effects of Positive Charismatics

The consequences for followers are better with a positive charismatic leader than with a negative charismatic. They are more likely to experience psychological growth and development of their abilities, and the organization is more likely to adapt to an environment that is dynamic, hostile, and competitive. A positive charismatic leader usually creates an "achievement-oriented" culture (Harrison, 1987), a "high-performing system" (Vaill, 1978), or a "hands-on, value-driven" organization (Peters & Waterman, 1982). The organization has a clearly understood mission that embodies social values beyond mere profit or growth, members at all levels are empowered to make important decisions about how to implement strategies and do their work, communication is open and information shared, and organization structures and systems support the mission. Such an organization has obvious advantages, but Harrison (1987, p. 12) contends that proponents also overlook some potential costs:

> In their single-minded pursuit of noble goals and an absorbing task, people lose their sense of balance and perspective; the end can come to justify the means. The group or organization exploits its environment, and its members—to the detriment of their health and quality of life—willingly exploit themselves in the service of the organization's purpose.

The positive charismatic can lead the organization in coping with a temporary crisis, but if prolonged for a long period of time, a single-minded achievement culture creates excessive stress and causes psychological disorders for members who are unable to tolerate this stress. If an achievement culture is created within one subunit of a larger organization, it may result in elitism, isolation, and lack of necessary cooperation with other subunits. Harrison concludes that subordinating member needs to the mission can be justified in a severe crisis, the moral equivalent of war, but under less demanding conditions a better balance between task concerns and people concerns is appropriate.

The Dark Side of Charisma

The major theories of charismatic leadership emphasize the positive consequences, but a number of social scientists have also considered the "dark side" of charisma (Bass & Steidlmeier, 1999; Conger, 1989; Conger & Kanungo, 1998; Hogan, Raskin, & Fazzini, 1990; House & Howell, 1992; Kets de Vries & Miller, 1985; Mumford, Gessner, Connelly, O'Connor, & Clifton, 1993; O'Connor et al., 1995; Sandowsky, 1995). Negative consequences that are likely to occur in organizations led by charismatics are summarized in Table 1. Two interrelated sets of consequences combine to increase the likelihood that the

TABLE 1   Some Negative Consequences of Charismatic Leaders

- Being in awe of the leader reduces good suggestions by followers.
- Desire for leader acceptance inhibits criticism by followers.
- Adoration by followers creates delusions of leader infallibility.
- Excessive confidence and optimism blind the leader to real dangers.
- Denial of problems and failures reduces organizational learning.
- Risky, grandiose projects are more likely to fail.
- Taking complete credit for successes alienates some key followers.
- Impulsive, nontraditional behavior creates enemies as well as believers.
- Dependence on the leader inhibits development of competent successors.
- Failure to develop successors creates an eventual leadership crisis.

leader's career will be cut short. Charismatic leaders tend to make more risky decisions that can result in a serious failure, and they tend to make enemies who will use such a failure as an opportunity to remove the leader from office.

Practical Implications for Organizations

A few writers have proposed the idea that charismatic leadership is a good solution for the problems of large organizations, but critics point out several reasons why it may not be feasible or desirable to have charismatic leaders occupy important positions in private and public sector organizations (Bryman, 1992; Schein, 1992; Trice & Beyer, 1993).

Charismatic leadership is risky. It is impossible to predict the result when people give too much power to an individual leader in the often irrational hope that he or she will actually be able to deliver on a vision of a better future. The power is often misused while the vision remains an empty dream. History is full of charismatic leaders who caused untold death, destruction, and misery in the process of building an empire, leading a revolution, or founding a new religion.

Charismatic leadership implies radical change in the strategy and culture of an organization, which may not be necessary or appropriate for organizations that are currently prosperous and successful. It is difficult to make radical change in an organization if no obvious crisis exists and many members see no need for change. If there is more than one charismatic leader in the organization and they have incompatible visions, the organization may be torn apart by disruptive conflict. Historical accounts suggest that many charismatic leaders find it too difficult to implement their radical vision within an existing organization, and they leave to establish a new one (e.g., a new business, religious order, political party, or social movement).

Charisma is a rare and transitory phenomenon. The beneficial accomplishments of a charismatic leader may not persist after the leader departs. The early dramatic successes that make a leader appear charismatic can sow the seeds of eventual failure if overconfidence encourages risky decisions that will endanger the organization and its members.

The research on effects of charismatic leaders in organizations is limited, but it suggests that charisma is not a beneficial attribute for most chief executives. The descriptive research found that few leaders of successful organizations were viewed as charismatic (e.g., Bennis & Nanus, 1985; Collins, 2001a, 2001b; Kouzes & Posner, 1987; Peters & Austin, 1985; Tichy & Devanna, 1986). In a study of corporations that examined financial performance in the years before and after a survey conducted to measure CEO charisma, financial performance was predicted by past performance but not by CEO charisma (Angle et al., 2006). Another study of corporations found that CEOs who appeared charismatic were able to persuade their board of directors to give them higher compensation, but these CEOs did not improve financial performance for their companies (Tosi et al., 2004).

Transformational Leadership

Much of the thinking about transformational leadership was influenced by James McGregor Burns (1978), who wrote a best-selling book on political leadership. Burns contrasted transforming leadership with *transactional leadership*. Transforming leadership appeals to the moral values of followers in an attempt to raise their consciousness about ethical issues and to mobilize their energy and resources to reform institutions. Transactional leadership motivates followers by appealing to their self-interest and exchanging benefits. For a political leader, these activities include providing jobs, subsidies, lucrative government contracts, and support for desired legislation in return for campaign contributions and votes to reelect the leader. Transactional leadership may involve values, but they are values relevant to the exchange process, such as honesty, fairness, responsibility, and reciprocity. Finally, Burns also identified a third form of leadership influence based on legitimate authority and respect for rules and tradition. Bureaucratic organizations emphasize this form of influence more than influence based on exchange or inspiration.

The process by which leaders appeal to followers' values and emotions is a central feature in current theories of transformational and visionary leadership in organizations (e.g., Bass, 1985, 1996; Bennis & Nanus, 1985; Sashkin & Fulmer, 1988; Tichy & Devanna, 1986). In contrast to Burns, however, the newer theories of transformational leadership are more concerned with attainment of pragmatic task objectives than with the moral elevation of followers or social reform.

Several theories of transformational or inspirational leadership were proposed, but the version of the theory formulated by Bass (1985, 1996) has influenced leadership research more than any of the others. Building on the ideas of Burns, the essence of the theory is the distinction between transformational and transactional leadership. For Bass (1985), transformational and transactional leadership are distinct but not mutually exclusive processes. With transformational leadership, the followers feel trust, admiration, loyalty, and respect toward the leader, and they are motivated to do more than they originally expected to do. The leader transforms and motivates followers by (1) making them more aware of the importance of task outcomes, (2) inducing them to transcend their own self-interest for the sake of the organization or team, and (3) activating their higher-order needs. In contrast, transactional leadership involves an exchange process that may result in follower compliance with leader requests but is not likely to generate enthusiasm and commitment to task objectives. According to Bass, transformational leadership increases follower motivation and performance more than transactional leadership, but effective leaders use a combination of both types of leadership.

Leader Behaviors

Transformational and transactional leadership behaviors are described in terms of two broad meta-categories of behavior, each with specific subcategories (see Table 2). The original formulation of the theory included three types of transformational behavior. *Idealized influence* is behavior that increases follower identification with the leader, such as setting an example of courage and dedication and making self-sacrifices to benefit followers. *Intellectual stimulation* is behavior that influences followers to view problems from a

TABLE 2	Transformational and Transactional Behaviors

Transformational Behaviors:

- Idealized influence
- Individualized consideration
- Inspirational motivation
- Intellectual stimulation

Transactional Behaviors:

- Contingent reward
- Active management by exception
- Passive management by exception

Based on Bass (1996).

new perspective and look for more creative solutions. *Individualized consideration* includes providing support, encouragement, and coaching to followers. A revision of the theory added another transformational behavior called *inspirational motivation,* which includes communicating an appealing vision, and using symbols to focus subordinate effort (Bass & Avolio, 1990a). Yet another revision by Bass and Avolio (1997) distinguished between idealized influence behavior and attributions of charisma, although it is not clear why the latter scale was retained in a questionnaire designed to measure observable behavior. Any ratings of leadership behavior are susceptible to attribution biases, so the distinction between attributed and behavioral charisma is confusing.

The original formulation of the theory included two types of transactional behavior: *contingent reward* and *passive management by exception.* Contingent reward behavior includes clarification of accomplishments necessary to obtain rewards, and the use of incentives to influence subordinate task motivation. Passive management by exception includes use of contingent punishments and other corrective action in response to obvious deviations from acceptable performance standards. Another transactional behavior called *active management by exception* was added in more recent versions of the theory (Bass & Avolio, 1990a). This behavior is defined in terms of looking for mistakes and enforcing rules to avoid mistakes.

Newer versions of the theory also include *laissez-faire leadership,* which is defined as passive indifference about the task and subordinates (e.g., ignoring problems, ignoring subordinate needs). It is best described as the absence of effective leadership rather than as an example of transactional leadership. The revised version of the theory is sometimes called the "Full Range Leadership Model" (Avolio, 1999). This label is inappropriate because the model does not include several important leadership behaviors (Antonakis & House, 2002; Yukl, 1999a).

Influence Processes

The underlying influence processes for transactional and transformational leadership are not clearly explained, but they can be inferred from the description of the behaviors and effects on follower motivation. The primary influence process for transactional leadership is probably instrumental compliance. Transformational leadership probably involves internalization, because inspirational motivation includes efforts to link the task to follower values and ideals with behavior such as articulating an inspirational vision. A leader can increase intrinsic motivation by increasing the perception of followers that task objectives are consistent with their authentic interests and values (see Bono & Judge, 2004; Charbonneau, Barling, & Kelloway, 2001).

Transformational leadership also appears to involve personal identification. Followers may identify with the leader, imitate the leader's behavior, and embrace the values and ideals espoused by the leader. Personal identification may include follower attributions of charisma to the leader. According to Bass (1985, p. 31), "Charisma is a necessary ingredient of transformational leadership, but by itself it is not sufficient to account for the transformational process."

Other processes that may mediate the effects of transformational leadership on follower performance have been identified in research on the theory. Transformational leadership is highly correlated with trust in the leader (Dirks & Ferrin, 2002). Transformational behaviors such as inspirational motivation (e.g., optimistic visioning) and individualized consideration (e.g., coaching) may increase the self-efficacy of individual subordinates (McColl-Kennedy & Anderson, 2002) and the collective efficacy of teams. Intellectual stimulation may increase the creativity of individual followers (Howell & Avolio, 1993; Keller, 1992; Sosik, Kahai, & Avolio, 1998).

The influence process called *cascading* has been offered as a way to explain how a CEO can indirectly influence the motivation of lower-level employees in an organization (Waldman & Yammarino, 1999). The behavior of a CEO is imitated by subordinates, and *role modeling* is repeated by managers at each lower level. As yet, there is only very limited evidence for cascading of leader behaviors (Bass et al., 1987; Chun et al., 2009). There is no evidence that key CEO behaviors will be imitated by low-level managers, or that lower-level members of an organization will embrace the CEO's vision without a credible strategy and major changes in programs, reward systems, and cultural values.

Facilitating Conditions

According to Bass (1996, 1997), transformational leadership is considered effective in any situation or culture. The theory does not specify any conditions under which authentic transformational leadership is irrelevant or ineffective. In support of this position, the positive relationship between transformational leadership and effectiveness has been replicated for many leaders at different levels of authority, in different types of organizations, and in several different countries (Bass, 1997). The criterion of leadership effectiveness has included a variety of different types of measures. The evidence supports the conclusion that in most if not all situations, some aspects of transformational leadership are relevant. However, universal relevance does not mean that transformational leadership is equally effective in all situations or equally likely to occur.

A number of situational variables may increase the likelihood that transformational leadership will occur or may enhance the effect of such leadership on followers (Bass, 1985, 1996; Hinkin & Tracey, 1999; Howell & Avolio, 1993; Pawar & Eastman, 1997; Pettigrew, 1988; Purvanova & Bono, 2009; Waldman et al., 2001). The change-oriented components of transformational leadership are likely to be more important in a dynamic, unstable environment that increases the need for change, and such leadership is more likely when leaders are encouraged and empowered to be flexible and innovative (e.g., a decentralized organization with an entrepreneurial culture). The cross-cultural research on perceived importance of transformational leadership suggests that it may be used more often in some cultures than in others. Finally, there is growing evidence that the traits and values of followers may determine how they respond to a leader's transformational or charismatic behaviors (e.g., de Vries, Roe, & Taillieu, 2002; Ehrhart & Klein, 2001).

Research on Charismatic and Transformational Leadership

Many studies have investigated how charismatic and transformational leadership are related to measures of leadership effectiveness, such as subordinate satisfaction, motivation, and performance. The research methods include survey studies, laboratory and field experiments, comparative studies with analysis of biographical information for several famous leaders, and intensive case studies of an individual leader. In some studies, it is not clear whether the leaders should be regarded as transformational or charismatic, but communication of an inspiring vision is a common feature in most of the studies.

Survey Studies

Field survey studies have been used more often than any other method for research on transformational and charismatic leadership. Different questionnaires have been developed to measure charismatic leadership (Conger & Kanungo, 1994; Shamir, Zakay, & Popper, 1998) and transformational leadership (Bass, 1985; Bass & Avolio, 1990a; Podsakoff, MacKenzie, Moorman, & Fetter, 1990). However, the Multifactor Leadership Questionnaire (MLQ) or a modified version of it (Bass & Avolio, 1990a) has been used in a majority of the studies on transformational leadership and even for some studies on charismatic leadership.

For the MLQ, subordinates rate how often their leader uses each type of behavior described in the items. Several studies that used factor analysis to assess the construct validity of the MLQ found support for the distinction between transformational and trans-actional leadership, but results for the component behaviors were not consistent from study to study (Antonakis, Avolio, & Sivasubramaniam, 2003; Avolio, Bass, & Jung, 1999; Bycio, Hackett, & Allen, 1995; Carless, 1998; Den Hartog, Van Muijen, & Koopman, 1997; Tejeda, Scandura, & Pillai, 2001; Tepper & Percy, 1994; Yammarino, Spangler, & Dubin-sky, 1998). In addition, the component behaviors for transformational leadership are so highly intercorrelated that most studies use only a composite score for transformational leadership.

Successive revisions of the MLQ have added types of transformational behavior not represented in the initial version. Other questionnaires such as the Transformational Leader Index (Podsakoff et al., 1990) have a different mix of component behaviors, thereby creating additional confusion about the definition of transformational leadership. A few studies using questionnaires with a wider range of behaviors found that transformational leadership was confounded with other behaviors not included in the definition, including empowerment and recognition (Hinkin & Tracey, 1999; Rafferty & Griffin, 2004; Yukl, 1999a).

Most of the survey studies correlated transformational or charismatic leadership with measures of outcome variables, such as individual or group motivation or performance. A small number of survey studies examined the relationship of charismatic and transforma-tional leadership to measures of organizational performance. Meta-analyses of the survey studies found a significant relationship between composite ratings of charismatic or trans-formational leadership and measures of leadership effectiveness (DeGroot, Kiker, & Cross, 2000; Judge & Piccolo, 2004; Lowe, Kroeck, & Sivasubramaniam, 1996; Wang, Oh, Court-right, & Colbert, 2011). The relationship was stronger for subordinate satisfaction and self-rated effort than for an independent criterion of leadership effectiveness (e.g., ratings of the leader by superiors, objective performance of the leader's team or work unit). Only a small number of studies have examined effects of transformational leadership by CEOs on com-pany financial performance, and the results were inconsistent.

The number of survey studies on antecedents of charismatic and transformational leadership is much smaller than the number of studies on outcomes, but they generally sup-port the relevance of traits such as leader power motivation, self-confidence, extraversion, and positive emotions (see review by Walter & Bruch, 2009). However, results have not been consistent in the research on several traits and skills proposed to predict charismatic or transformational leadership, which may be due to the large variety of measures and types of samples used in the research.

The interpretation of results in the survey research on transformational and charis-matic leadership is complicated by confounding with unmeasured behaviors and rater biases such as subordinate attributions and affect towards the leader (Brown & Keeping, 2005). The interpretation of results is also complicated by ambiguity about whether the respondent is describing only dyadic leader behavior (with the respondent) or the leader's behavior with everyone in the work unit (Kark & Shamir, 2002; Schriesheim, Wu, & Scandura, 2009; Wang & Howell, 2010). Given the serious limitations of the survey research on transformational and charismatic leadership, future research should include a wider variety of leadership behaviors and alternative ways of measuring them, such as coding of observations, incident diaries, and interviews with leaders and followers (Yukl, 1999a).

Laboratory and Field Experiments

Several laboratory experiments on charismatic leadership were conducted with university students (e.g., Awamleh & Gardner, 1999; Choi & Mai-Dalton, 1999; Halverson et al., 2004; Howell & Frost, 1989; Hunt et al., 1999; Jaussi & Dionne, 2003; Jung & Avolio, 1999; Kirkpatrick & Locke, 1996; Shea & Howell, 1999; van Knippenberg & van Knippenberg, 2005; Yorges et al., 1999). In a few of these experiments, the leader was an actor who displayed charismatic or transformational behaviors. Other experiments used scenarios that described leader behavior and the situation, and participants indicated how they would likely respond as subordinates in that situation. In two field experiments, the behavior of managers was manipulated with a training intervention to assess the effects on the performance of the organizational unit (e.g., Barling, Weber, & Kelloway, 1996; Dvir, Eden, Avolio, & Shamir, 2002). Most of the laboratory and field experiments provide support for the proposition that some types of charismatic or transformational behavior can have positive effects on followers in some situations. However, all of these studies have limitations that make interpretation of results difficult. More experiments are needed to assess the independent and joint effects of the leader behaviors described in the theories. One promising method is the use of laboratory experiments with realistic, multisession simulations that are meaningful for participants.

Comparative Analyses of Leader Descriptions

Another method used to study charismatic leadership involves analyses of leader descriptions. A variety of sources have been used for this type of research, including biographies about the leader, speeches and writings by the leader, critical incidents about the leader. In some studies the researchers look for common attributes for a sample of leaders widely perceived to be charismatic or successful. Other studies compare leaders widely viewed as charismatic to leaders not considered charismatic. A content analysis is usually conducted to identify characteristic behaviors, traits, influence processes that may be relevant for understanding how the leader influenced followers and the organization.

The large variation in predictors, criteria, and situations in the descriptive studies makes it difficult to find consistent results (e.g., Bligh & Robinson, 2010; Bryman, Stephens, & Campo, 1996; Conger, 1989; Deluga, 1998; House et al., 1991; Howell & Higgins, 1990; Jacobsen & House, 2001; Levinson & Rosenthal, 1984; Mio et al., 2005; O'Connor et al., 1995; Seyranian & Bligh, 2008; Strange & Mumford, 2002; Tichy & Devanna, 1986; Van Fleet & Yukl, 1986a; Westley & Mintzberg, 1989; Willner, 1984; Yukl & Van Fleet, 1982). Nevertheless, the results suggest that some of the specific traits and behaviors in the theories are related to effective leadership.

Example of a Comparative Biographical Study

An example of this type of research is provided by House et al. (1991), who conducted a study on charismatic leadership by U.S. presidents. The first step was to ask several historians to classify as charismatic or noncharismatic each of 31 former presidents who were elected to office and served at least two years of their first term. Then the motive pattern of each president was measured by content analysis of his first inaugural address. The biographies of two or more cabinet members were content analyzed to measure a president's use of charismatic behaviors. Leadership effectiveness was measured in several ways including ratings of presidential greatness made by a sample of historians and analysis of biographical information about the outcomes of each president's decisions and actions during the first term of office. The results were mostly consistent with the theory. Presidents with a socialized power orientation exhibited more of the charismatic leadership behaviors and were more likely to be viewed as charismatic by others. Moreover, the charismatic presidents used more direct action to deal with problems and were rated higher in performance.

Intensive Case Studies

Intensive case studies are another type of method used for research on charismatic leadership (e.g., Cha & Edmondson, 2006; Trice & Beyer, 1986; Weed, 1993). Information about leader behaviors, decisions, and consequences are usually gathered by interviews with leaders and members, and the study may involve observation of key processes, analysis of records, reports, and correspondence, and other sources of information. Some studies are focused on a single leader, but other studies compare successful versus unsuccessful leaders, or charismatic leaders versus non-charismatic leaders. A small number of case studies have examined leaders who transitioned from one position to another (e.g., Roberts, 1985; Roberts & Bradley, 1988) or who experienced initial success followed by eventual failure (e.g., Finkelstein, 2003). These studies tend to show that the effects of charismatic leadership depend greatly on the situation and can vary for the same leader as the situation changes.

Example of an Intensive Case Study

A good example is the study by Roberts (1985) of the same leader in two successive positions. The study began when the leader was the superintendent of a public school district. Data were collected by archival searches, analysis of newspaper articles, participant observation of formal and informal meetings, and interviews with the superintendent, other administrators, board members, staff, teachers, parents, and students. The leader was deemed to be effective, because she was able to implement large, mandated budget cuts in a way that satisfied diverse stakeholders and still allowed progress on implementing desirable educational innovations. Her budget was approved unanimously by the school board after only a brief discussion. The teachers gave her a standing ovation for her efforts, even though the plan required program cuts and elimination of jobs. She was described as a "visionary" who had almost a "cultlike following" in the district.

The actions taken by the leader to achieve this successful outcome were the following: (1) a mission statement was formulated and referred to frequently during the change process; (2) a strategic vision was developed during a series of meetings and workshops involving district personnel; (3) several personnel in key positions were replaced with more competent, dynamic people to support the change effort; (4) performance objectives and action plans were developed for immediate subordinates (the school principals), progress was monitored by reports and meetings, and extensive participation by subordinates was encouraged during this process; (5) temporary task forces were created to involve all stakeholders in recommending where to make the budget cuts and how to deal with other budget and educational issues; and (6) staff members were trained in how to run structured public meetings in which task forces made presentations and solicited suggestions about budget cuts.

Roberts characterized the process as more a matter of creating and managing energy than of shaping culture or managing meaning. The leader was energetic, created enthusiasm, channeled emotions aroused by the budget crisis, and galvanized people into action. The leader helped people recognize that they could make a difference by working together toward common objectives. The following episode provides an example (Roberts, 1985, p. 1035):

> After a scheduled 40-minute presentation to district staff, teachers besieged the stage to ask for more of her time to discuss the various initiatives the district was pursuing. Their requests turned into a four-hour dialogue with 800 people, in which the superintendent shared her hopes, her dreams, her past, her disappointments. Many people were moved

to tears, including the superintendent. A critical point in the exchange came in answer to a question of how people could be certain that what she and the School Board promised would indeed occur. The superintendent's response was, "Well I guess you just have to trust us. I trust you." Dead silence followed as people drew in their breaths and held them for a moment or two. Upon being asked what this silence meant, people responded that the superintendent had proven her point. That was what the dialogue and the honesty were all about. She had trusted them with her thoughts, hopes, and feelings, and they in turn would trust her. Mutual trust had created a bond between the superintendent and her audience.

When the superintendent was appointed to her position, she was not initially perceived as a charismatic leader; this attribution occurred only after she had been in the position for two years and the change process was well under way. Roberts concluded that charisma was attributed to the leader because of the way she resolved the budget crisis, and not as an inevitable result of the leader's personal qualities. This conclusion is consistent with the findings of a follow-up study made after the same individual was appointed the commissioner of education for the state in 1983 (Roberts & Bradley, 1988).

Data for the follow-up study were obtained from a variety of sources. Interviews were conducted with the new commissioner during the four years from 1983 to 1987, and interviews were also conducted with state legislators, representatives from the governor's office, the board of education, school boards, and teacher unions. The commissioner was observed during speaking engagements, meetings with her staff, press conferences, formal and informal presentations to teachers and superintendents, and informal meetings with members of the state department of education. Additional information was obtained from analysis of official documents, newspaper articles, and reports made by special interest groups.

The new commissioner's approach for implementing change at the state level was similar to the one she used as superintendent. She formulated a mission statement and vision for change, and she moved quickly to replace several assistant commissioners with people from outside the education department who would support her programs. Enthusiasm and support were generated by conducting visits to nearly all of the school districts in the state. A survey was conducted to assess public opinion on school issues, and meetings were held with community groups throughout the state to identify public concerns and hopes for the schools.

At the end of her four-year term, the commissioner was evaluated as an effective administrator by the governor, and she was reappointed for another term. People usually described her as innovative and committed, but some peers and subordinates were critical rather than supportive. The commissioner's initiatives had some positive benefits, but they did not generate any widespread support for major change in the education system. Overall, there was no evidence that she was perceived as extraordinary or charismatic in her new position.

Roberts and Bradley (1988) suggested several reasons why the same person was seen as charismatic in one position and not in the other. First, at the district level, a serious crisis justified the need for innovative solutions, whereas at the state level there was no crisis to focus attention and provide a rationale for radical change. Second, as a district superintendent she had much more autonomy and authority than as a commissioner. The latter position was more political and involved a larger and more complex web of stakeholder relationships that served to constrain her actions and make change difficult (e.g., the governor, the legislature, members of the education department, interest groups, teachers' unions, school officials). Third, the large size of the state agency and the complexity of the job as commissioner made it essential to delegate more responsibility, but strong political opposition and bureaucratic resistance undermined her efforts to restructure the education department and build a cooperative team of executives to help implement new initiatives effectively. Finally, as superintendent she was able to inspire strong trust and affection in meetings with constituents, whereas as commissioner a close relationship with constituents did not develop. Speaking to large audiences with intrusive television coverage, her speeches lacked the enthusiasm and vivid, emotional language in her earlier speeches as superintendent to smaller, more informal groups of teachers, principals, and parents.

Comparison of Charismatic and Transformational Leadership

One of the most important issues for leadership scholars is the extent to which transformational leadership and charismatic leadership are similar and compatible. Some theorists treat the two types of leadership as essentially equivalent, whereas other theorists view them as distinct but overlapping processes. Even among theorists who view the two types of leadership as distinct processes, there remains disagreement about whether it is possible to be both transformational and charismatic at the same time.

Conceptual ambiguity and inconsistent definitions make it difficult to compare transformational and charismatic leadership, or even to compare theories of the same general type. In recent years, the major charismatic theories have been revised in ways that appear to move them closer to the transformational theories. The major transformational theories have been revised to incorporate additional forms of effective leadership behavior. The term *transformational* has been broadly defined by many writers to include almost any type of effective leadership, regardless of the underlying influence processes. The label may refer to the transformation of individual followers or to the transformation of entire organizations.

One source of apparent differences in the two types of theories is the emphasis on attributed charisma and personal identification. The essence of charisma is being perceived as extraordinary by followers who are dependent on the leader for guidance and inspiration. Attributed charisma and personal identification are more central for the theory by Conger and Kanungo (1998) than for the theory by Shamir et al. (1993). Bass (1985) proposed that charisma is a necessary component of transformational leadership, but he also noted that a leader can be charismatic but not transformational. The essence of transformational leadership appears to be inspiring, developing, and empowering followers (although empowering is not explicit in most versions of the theory). These effects may reduce attribution of charisma to the leader rather than increase it. Thus, the essential influence processes for transformational leadership may not be entirely compatible with the essential influence process for charismatic leadership, which involves personal identification with an extraordinary leader and dependence on the leader. Some support for this distinction is provided in a study by Kark et al. (2003); they found that personal identification mediates the effect of the leader on follower dependence and social identification mediates the effect of the leader on follower self-efficacy and collective efficacy.

Many of the leadership behaviors in the theories of charismatic and transformational leadership appear to be the same, but some important differences are evident as well. Transformational leaders probably do more things that will empower followers and make them less dependent on the leader, such as delegating significant authority to individuals or teams, developing follower skills and self-confidence, providing direct access to sensitive information, eliminating unnecessary controls, and building a strong culture to support empowerment. Charismatic leaders probably do more things that foster an image of extraordinary competence for the leader and increase subordinate dependence, such as impression management, information restriction, unconventional behavior, and personal risk taking.

Another likely difference between transformational and charismatic leadership involves how often each type of leadership occurs and the facilitating conditions for it. According to Bass, transformational leaders can be found in any organization at any level, and this type of leadership is universally relevant for all types of situations (Bass, 1996, 1997). In contrast, charismatic leaders are rare, and their emergence appears to be more dependent on unusual conditions (Bass, 1985; Beyer, 1999; Shamir & Howell, 1999). They are most likely to be visionary entrepreneurs who establish a new organization, or reformers who emerge in an established organization when formal authority has failed to deal with a severe crisis and traditional values and beliefs are questioned.

Another difference involves the way people react to the leaders. The reactions to charismatics are usually more extreme and diverse than reactions to transformational leaders (Bass, 1985). The affective reaction aroused by charismatics often polarizes people into opposing camps of loyal supporters and hostile opponents. The intense negative reaction by some people to charismatic leaders helps explain why these leaders are often targets for assassination or political tactics to remove them from office. Transformational leaders get a less intense reaction from followers and are unlikely to have this polarizing effect. These leaders are viewed as competent and professional but are not usually considered exciting and exceptional.

The empirical research on transformational and charismatic leadership was not designed to examine issues of comparability and compatibility among different theories. Few studies examine underlying influence processes or go beyond the superficial and often ambiguous data provided by behavior description questionnaires. The issue of comparability cannot be resolved merely by comparing responses on questionnaires commonly used in the survey research on each type of leadership (e.g., Rowold & Heinitz, 2007). The primary difference in the theories involves aspects of the relationships and influence processes that are not captured by these questionnaires. Resolution of this interesting and important question requires additional research with more intensive methods.

Evaluation of the Theories

The available evidence supports many of the key propositions of the major theories of charismatic and transformational leadership. Collectively, the theories appear to make an important contribution to our understanding of leadership processes. They provide an explanation for the exceptional influence some leaders have on followers, a level of influence not adequately explained by earlier theories of instrumental leadership or situational leadership. The new theories emphasize the importance of emotional reactions by followers to leaders, whereas the earlier theories emphasized rational-cognitive aspects of leader-follower interactions. The new theories also acknowledge the importance of symbolic behavior and the role of the leader in making events meaningful for followers. Earlier leadership theories did not recognize that symbolic processes and management of meaning are as important as management of things. Finally, the new theories include a more diverse set of variables (e.g., traits, behaviors, mediating processes, situation) and integrate them better in explanations of effective leadership.

Despite their positive features, the new theories also have some conceptual weaknesses (Beyer, 1999; Bryman, 1993; Yukl, 1999b). Examples include ambiguous constructs, insufficient description of explanatory processes, a narrow focus on dyadic processes, omission of some relevant behaviors, insufficient specification of situational variables, and a bias toward heroic conceptions of leadership. Some of these limitations will be explained in more detail.

Relevance of Antecedents

Some theories specify leader traits and skills that predict the types of behavior and influence processes described for a charismatic or transformational leader, while other theories are vague about these antecedents. Research on antecedents of charismatic and transformational leadership (see Walter & Bruch, 2009) supports the relevance of traits such as power motivation, self-confidence, and extraversion. However, the results are not consistent for some other traits and skills (e.g., emotional maturity, narcissism, conscientiousness, conceptual skills). The inconsistent results may be due to the large variety of measures and types of samples used in the research. Another explanation is that the studies and the literature reviews usually disregard the important differences between positive and negative charismatics, and between charismatic and transformational leadership. Some leader traits and skills seem to be more relevant for predicting these differences than for predicting who will be viewed as charismatic.

Explanation of Mediating Processes

Most theories of transformational and charismatic leadership lack sufficient specification of underlying influence processes. The self-concept theory of charismatic leadership provides the most detailed explanation of leader influence on followers, but even this theory needs more clarification of how the various types of influence processes interact, their relative importance, and whether they are mutually compatible. Most of the theories are still leader-centered, and they emphasize the influence of the leader on followers. More attention needs to be focused on reciprocal influence processes, shared leadership, and mutual influence among the followers themselves.

The theories would be strengthened by including a better explanation of how leaders enhance mutual trust and cooperation, empowerment, collective identification, collective efficacy, and collective learning. The theories need to include more explanation of task-oriented functions of leaders that are essential for the effective performance of a team, and strategic functions that are essential for the financial performance of organizations. Most of the theories fail to explain the leader's external roles, such as monitoring the environment to identify threats and opportunities, building networks of contacts who can provide information and assistance, serving as a spokesperson for the team or organization, negotiating agreements with outsiders, and helping to obtain resources, political support, and new members with appropriate skills.

Most of the theories focus too narrowly on dyadic processes. The charismatic and transformational theories describe how a leader can influence the motivation and loyalty of subordinates, which is relevant for understanding effective leadership. However, these theories are primarily extensions of motivation theory, and much more is needed to explain how leaders build exceptional teams or influence the financial performance and survival of an organization (Beyer, 1999; Yukl & Lepsinger, 2004). A leader may influence followers to be more motivated, creative, and cooperative, but what the followers are motivated to do and how appropriate it is for the situation are also important. Having highly motivated and loyal followers will not prevent disaster if the leader pursues unrealistic objectives or misguided strategies (see Finkelstein, 2003).

Implications for Change and Effectiveness

The theories do not clearly specify how leadership processes are related to change, the necessary facilitating conditions for the leader to influence major change, or how initial change will affect future leadership processes. The vision may be one developed primarily by the leader or merely a minor adaptation of a vision already articulated by higher level leaders or a previous leader. The vision may involve a call for innovative changes, or it may involve a return to traditional values that are no longer dominant determinants of strategic decisions for the organization but remain important for many members. For example, a charismatic leader may emerge as a rebel who successfully resists the implementation of major changes that are inconsistent with traditional values (Levay, 2010).

The theories also lack clarity about the longer-term implications for transformational or charismatic leadership. A leader who is attributed charisma following initial success in innovative responses to threats or opportunities, may lose this charisma if success is only temporary or new initiatives result in serious losses for the organization. A transformational leader may lack the cognitive skills needed to successfully deal with increasingly complex and difficult challenges as the situation changes or the person is promoted to a higher level position.

Identification of Situational Variables

A final limitation is the need for more explanation of situational variables that determine whether transformational or charismatic leadership will occur and how effective it will be (Beyer, 1999; Bryman, 1992; Yukl, 1999b). Progress has been made in identifying some relevant situational variables (e.g., Antonakis & Atwater, 2002; Bass, 1996; Conger & Kanungo, 1998; De Hoogh et al., 2005; House et al., 1991; Howell & Avolio, 1993; Klein & House, 1995; Lapidot, Kark, & Shamir, 2007; Pawar & Eastman, 1997; Pillai, 1996; Pillai & Meindl, 1998; Podsakoff, MacKenzie, Ahearne, & Bommer, 1995; Roberts & Bradley, 1988; Shamir & Howell, 1999; Tosi et al., 2004; Trice & Beyer, 1986, Waldman et al., 2001, 2004; Walter & Bruch, 2010). However, the variation among studies in the type of leaders sampled, the measures of leadership behavior, and the situational variables that were included, yielded results that are inconsistent and difficult to interpret.

Guidelines for Inspirational Leadership

Although much remains to be learned about transformational leadership and related theories, the convergence in findings from different types of research suggests some tentative guidelines for leaders who seek to inspire followers and increase their self-confidence and commitment to the mission. The guidelines (see summary in Table 3) are based on the theories and research findings reviewed in this chapter.

• **Articulate a clear and appealing vision.**

Transformational leaders strengthen the existing vision or build commitment to a new vision. A clear vision of what the organization could accomplish or become helps people

TABLE 3	Guidelines for Transformational Leadership

- Articulate a clear and appealing vision.
- Explain how the vision can be attained.
- Act confident and optimistic.
- Express confidence in followers.
- Use dramatic, symbolic actions to emphasize key values.
- Lead by example.

understand the purpose, objectives, and priorities of the organization. It gives the work meaning, serves as a source of self-esteem, and fosters a sense of common purpose. Finally, the vision helps guide the actions and decisions of each member of the organization, which is especially important when individuals or groups are allowed considerable autonomy and discretion in their work decisions (Hackman, 1986; Raelin, 1989).

The success of a vision depends on how well it is communicated to people (Awamleh & Gardner, 1999; Holladay & Coombs, 1993, 1994). The vision should be communicated at every opportunity and in a variety of ways. Meeting with people directly to explain the vision and answer questions about it is probably more effective than less interactive forms of communication (e.g., letters or e-mail messages to followers, newsletter articles, televised news conferences, videotaped speeches). If a non-interactive form of communication is used to present the vision, then it is helpful to provide opportunities for followers to ask questions afterward (e.g., use e-mail, a hotline, open meetings, or visits by the leader to department meetings).

The ideological aspects of a vision can be communicated more clearly and persuasively with colorful, emotional language that includes vivid imagery, metaphors, anecdotes, stories, symbols, and slogans. Metaphors and analogies are especially effective when they excite the imagination and engage the listener in trying to make sense out of them. Anecdotes and stories are more effective if they invoke symbols with deep cultural roots, such as legendary heroes, sacred figures, and historical ordeals and triumphs. A dramatic, expressive style of speaking augments the use of colorful language in making an emotional appeal (see guidelines for inspirational appeals). Conviction and intensity of feeling are communicated by a speaker's voice (tone, inflection, pauses), facial expressions, gestures, and body movement. The appropriate use of rhyme, rhythm, and repetition of key words or phrases can make a vision more colorful and compelling.

- **Explain how the vision can be attained.**

It is not enough to articulate an appealing vision; the leader must also convince followers that the vision is feasible. It is important to make a clear link between the vision and a credible strategy for attaining it. This link is easier to establish if the strategy has a few clear themes that are relevant to shared values of organization members (Nadler, 1988). Themes provide labels to help people understand issues and problems. The number of themes should be large enough to focus attention on key issues, but not so large as to cause confusion and dissipate energy. It is seldom necessary to present an elaborate plan with detailed action steps. The leader should not pretend to know all the answers about how to achieve the vision, but instead should inform followers that they will have a vital role in discovering what specific actions are necessary.

The strategy for attaining the vision is most likely to be persuasive when it is unconventional yet straightforward. If it is simplistic or conventional, the strategy will not elicit confidence in the leader, especially when there is a crisis. Consider the example of a company that was losing market share in the face of intense competition.

> The CEO proposed to make the company's product the best in the world by improving product design and quality (the old strategy was to keep price low by cutting costs). The product would be designed to be reliable (few moving parts, durable materials, extensive product testing, quality control by every worker) as well as "user friendly" (simple operating procedures, easy-to-read displays, clear instructions). This strategy contributed to the successful turnaround of the company.

- **Act confident and optimistic.**

Followers are not going to have faith in a vision unless the leader demonstrates self-confidence and conviction. It is important to remain optimistic about the likely success of the group in attaining its vision, especially in the face of temporary roadblocks and setbacks. A leader's confidence and optimism can be highly contagious. It is best to emphasize what has been accomplished so far rather than how much more is yet to be done. It is best to emphasize the positive aspects of the vision rather than the obstacles and dangers that lie ahead. Confidence is expressed in both words and actions. Lack of self-confidence is reflected in tentative, faltering language (e.g., "I guess," "maybe," "hopefully") and some nonverbal cues (e.g., frowns, lack of eye contact, nervous gestures, weak posture).

- **Express confidence in followers.**

The motivating effect of a vision also depends on the extent to which subordinates are confident about their ability to achieve it. Research on the *Pygmalion effect* found that people perform better when a leader has high expectations for them and shows confidence in them (Eden, 1984, 1990; Eden & Shani, 1982; Field, 1989; McNatt & Judge, 2004; Sutton & Woodman, 1989). It is especially important to foster confidence and optimism when the task is difficult or dangerous, or when team members lack confidence in themselves. If appropriate, the leader should remind followers how they overcame obstacles to achieve an earlier triumph. If they have never been successful before, the leader may be able to make an analogy between the present situation and success by a similar team or organizational unit. Review the specific strengths, assets, and resources that they can draw on to carry out the strategy. List the advantages they have relative to opponents or competitors. Explain why they are as good as or better than an earlier team that was successful in performing the same type of activity.

- **Use dramatic, symbolic actions to emphasize key values.**

A vision is reinforced by leadership behavior that is consistent with it. Concern for a value or objective is demonstrated by the way a manager spends time, by resource allocation decisions made when trade-offs are necessary between objectives, by the questions the manager asks, and by what actions the manager rewards. Dramatic, highly visible actions can be used to emphasize key values, as in the following example:

> The division manager had a vision that included relationships in which people were open, creative, cooperative, and oriented toward learning. Past meetings of the management team had been overly formal, with detailed agendas, elaborate presentations, and excessive criticism. He began a three-day meeting to communicate his vision for the division by inviting people to a beachfront ceremony where they burned a pile of agendas, handouts, and evaluation forms.

Symbolic actions to achieve an important objective or defend an important value are likely to be more influential when the manager risks substantial personal loss, makes self-sacrifices, or does things that are unconventional. The effect of symbolic actions is increased when they become the subject of stories and myths that circulate among members of the organization and are retold time and again over the years to new employees. In one example recounted by Peters and Austin (1985), the CEO personally destroyed some low-quality versions of the company's product that had been sold previously as "seconds." This widely publicized action demonstrated his commitment to the new policy that, henceforth, the company would make and sell only products of the highest quality.

- **Lead by example.**

According to an old saying, actions speak louder than words. One way a leader can influence subordinate commitment is by setting an example of exemplary behavior in day-to-day interactions with subordinates. Leading by example is sometimes called role modeling. It is especially important for actions that are unpleasant, dangerous, unconventional, or controversial. A manager who asks subordinates to observe a particular standard should also observe the same standard. A manager who asks subordinates to make special sacrifices should set an example by doing the same. Some of the most inspirational military leaders have been ones who led their troops into battle and shared the dangers and hardships rather than staying behind in relative safety and comfort (Van Fleet & Yukl, 1986b). A negative example is provided by the executives in a large company that was experiencing financial difficulties. After asking employees to defer their expected pay increases, the executives awarded themselves large bonuses. This action created resentment among employees and undermined employee loyalty to the organization and commitment to its mission. A more effective approach would be to set an example by cutting bonuses for top executives before asking for sacrifices from other employees.

The values espoused by a leader should be demonstrated in daily behavior, and it must be done consistently, not just when convenient. Top-level leaders are always in the spotlight, and their actions are carefully examined by followers in a search for hidden meanings that may not be intended by the leader. Ambiguous remarks may be misinterpreted and innocent actions may be misrepresented. To avoid sending the wrong message, it is important to consider in advance how one's comments and actions are likely to be interpreted by others.

Summary

Attributions of charisma are the result of an interactive process between leader, followers, and the situation. Charismatic leaders arouse enthusiasm and commitment in followers by articulating a compelling vision and increasing follower confidence about achieving it. Attribution of charisma to the leader is more likely if the vision and strategy for attaining it are innovative, the leader takes personal risks to promote it, and the strategy appears to be succeeding. Other relevant behaviors have also been identified, but they vary somewhat across the different theories. Some leader traits and skills such as self-confidence, strong convictions, poise, speaking ability, and a dramatic flair increase the likelihood of attributed charisma, but also important is a context that makes the leader's vision especially relevant to follower needs.

Charismatic leaders can have a tremendous influence on an organization, but the consequences are not always beneficial. Some entrepreneurs who establish a prosperous company are narcissistic charismatics with a personalized power orientation. These leaders are insensitive, manipulative, domineering, impulsive, and defensive. They consider follower devotion more important than commitment to an ideological vision. Their arrogance and excessive self confidence encourage risky decisions that can cause the downfall of their company. Positive charismatics seek to instill devotion to ideological goals and are more likely to have a beneficial influence on the organization. However, the achievement culture fostered by positive charismatics may also produce some undesirable consequences if the needs of individual followers are ignored. More research is needed to discover whether it is possible to achieve the positive outcomes of charismatic leadership without the negative consequences.

Transformational leaders make followers more aware of the importance and value of the work and induce followers to transcend self-interest for the sake of the organization. The leaders develop follower skills and confidence to prepare them to assume more responsibility and have more influence. The leaders provide support and encouragement when necessary to maintain enthusiasm and effort in the face of obstacles, difficulties, and fatigue. As a result, followers trust the leader and are motivated to do more than they originally expected to do.

The empirical research relevant for the theories of transformational leadership has generally been supportive, but few studies have examined the underlying influence processes that account for the positive relationship found between leader behavior and follower performance. More research is needed to determine the conditions in which different types of transformational behavior are most relevant and the underlying influence processes that explain why the behaviors are relevant.

The theories of transformational and charismatic leadership emphasize that emotional processes are as important as rational processes, and symbolic actions are as important as instrumental behavior. These theories provide new insights into the reasons for the success or failure of leaders, but the underlying explanatory processes in these theories do not provide a sufficient basis for understanding how leaders can influence the long-term financial performance and survival of an organization. To understand how leaders influence organizational processes and outcomes, it is necessary to include aspects of strategic management that are not explicitly described in most charismatic and transformational theories.

Review and Discussion Questions

1. Briefly describe the attribution theory of charismatic leadership.
2. Briefly describe the self-concept theory of charismatic leadership.
3. What problems are charismatic leaders likely to create for an organization?
4. In what type of situation is a charismatic leader most likely to be beneficial?
5. Briefly describe the theory of transformational leadership proposed by Bass.
6. What are similarities and differences between charismatic and transformational leadership?
7. What new insights are provided by theories of transformational and charismatic leadership?
8. What can leaders do to become more transformational?

Key Terms

charisma	self-concept	transactional leadership
charismatic leadership	self-efficacy	transformational leadership
emotional contagion	self-identity	vision
personal identification	social identification	
role modeling	symbolic action	

CASE 1

Astro Airlines

Part 1

Arthur Burton established Astro Airlines in 1980, two years after the airlines were deregulated. Burton's vision for the new airline has two key elements. First, the airline would provide low-cost, no-frills service to people who formerly could not afford to travel by air.

Second, the airline would have a novel type of organization that provided a better way for people to work together, thereby unleashing their creativity and improving productivity. Burton was a dynamic, emotionally stirring speaker with a kind of evangelical fervor, and he took advantage of every opportunity to teach and affirm his vision. He was regarded by many employees as an inspirational leader who made you believe that you could do anything. The climate at Astro Airlines in the initial years was one of enthusiasm, excitement, and optimism.

Instead of the typical bureaucratic organization, the new company had only three levels of management and few support staff. The emphasis was on equality, informality, participative leadership, and self-management. Employees were organized into teams with shared responsibility for determining how to do their work. The teams elected members to represent them in advisory and coordinating councils that met with top management, thereby enabling them to participate in making important decisions. Managers were expected to provide direction but not to dictate methods or police efforts. Employees were expected to perform multiple jobs and to learn new skills. Even the managers were expected to spend some time doing regular line jobs to keep informed about problems and customer needs. The "status perks" found in most large organizations were eliminated. For example, executives answered their own telephones and typed their own letters. New employees were carefully screened, because Burton sought to hire young, enthusiastic employees who were willing to learn new jobs and who could function as part of a cooperative team. All permanent employees were required to share in the ownership of the company, and they could purchase shares of stock at a reduced price.

Burton believed that a strategy of discount fares and convenient schedules with frequent flights would attract new passengers who would normally travel by car, train, or bus, or who would otherwise not travel. By keeping operating costs low, Astro Airlines was able to offer fares that were much lower than those of competitors. The salaries of managers and employees were lower than normal for the airline industry, although employees also received generous fringe benefits, profit sharing, and stock dividends. Costs were also reduced by purchasing surplus aircraft at bargain rates, by reconfiguring aircraft to carry more passengers (e.g., converting first class into coach seats), and by innovative scheduling that allowed the planes to fly more hours each day. Customers were charged for some frills such as meals and baggage handling that other airlines included in the price of the ticket. To reduce space normally needed for ticket counters at terminals, the ticketing for flights was done either in advance by travel agents or on the plane itself with innovative ticketing machines.

The new company was an immediate success, and passenger volume expanded rapidly. In less than three years the company grew from a few hundred employees with three planes to more than 3,000 employees with 22 planes servicing 20 cities. This success occurred despite dismal conditions that caused widespread operating losses in the airline industry, including a severe economic recession, a crippling national strike of air traffic controllers, and brutal price wars. The flexibility of the company and the commitment and creativity of its employees aided its early growth and facilitated rapid adaptation to crises such as the strike of air traffic controllers.

Questions

1. Describe Burton's leadership behavior.
2. Was Burton a charismatic leader in the company at this time? Explain your answer.

Part 2

Despite the early successes, the rapid growth of the company was also creating some serious organizational problems. Employees believed that after the initial chaos of starting up the company, things would settle down and the intensely heavy workload would be alleviated. They were wrong; communication problems increased, the workload remained overwhelming, decisions were taking too long to be made, and too many decisions had to be resolved by top management. These problems were due in part to the informality and absence of structure. As the number of routes, facilities, and flights increased, operational problems became more complex, but formal structures were not developed to deal with them effectively. The number of managers did not increase nearly as fast as the number of nonsupervisory employees. Burton refused to recruit experienced managers from outside the company, preferring to promote current employees into positions for which they initially lacked sufficient expertise. Overburdened managers lacked adequate support personnel to which they could delegate routine responsibilities. Managers complained about the pressure and stress. They spent too much time in meetings, they could not get issues resolved and implemented, and they could not provide adequate training for the rapidly increasing number of new service employees. The new employees were not getting the extensive training and socialization necessary to prepare them to provide quality service, rotate among different service jobs, and use team management practices. Operating problems (e.g., canceled flights) and declining customer service (e.g., rude attendants) alienated customers and eroded the company's reputation.

Adding to the confusion was the worsening conflict between Burton, who as CEO was responsible for strategic planning, and the company president who was responsible for operational management. In 1982, the president resigned, and Burton assumed his responsibilities rather than finding an immediate replacement. At this time Burton finally decided to appoint a task force composed of executives to develop ideas for improving the organization. The task force presented some initial proposals for new managerial roles and structures. Employees were subsequently promoted to these roles, and management training activities were initiated for them. Burton was heavily involved in this training; he conducted some of it himself, and he faithfully attended sessions taught by others, thereby indicating the importance he placed on it. However, other necessary changes in management processes were not implemented, and the position of president was still not filled. In short, Burton seemed unwilling to take the steps necessary to transform Astro Airlines from an entrepreneurial start-up to an established organization. Indeed, his remedy for the firm's problems was to set out on a new growth path rather than to concentrate on consolidation. He believed that what the company needed was an even bigger vision to get people excited again. Thus, he began yet another period of rapid expansion. The airline added new routes, purchased new and larger aircraft, and hired more new employees.

By 1984, Burton no longer seemed content to run a successful regional airline. He continued to make changes designed to transform Astro into an international airline that would compete with the major carriers. He decided to acquire some other regional and commuter airlines that were financially weak. His strategy of rapid expansion was overly optimistic, and it ignored some important changes that were occurring in the external environment. Burton failed to anticipate the likely reactions of major airlines that were stronger financially and prepared to conduct a long price-cutting war to protect their market position. New passenger traffic did not increase enough to justify the cost of the added flights, and Astro was unsuccessful in attracting many business travelers accustomed to frills and better service. The company began to experience losses instead of profits.

Internal problems also worsened in 1985. There was an attempt to unionize the pilots, and a substantial number of pilots quit, complaining that they were exploited and mistreated. Other employees began questioning Burton's sincerity and accused him of being a manipulator. The perception among many employees was that he was now acting like a dictator, and no one dared to cross him. When asked about the absence of independent outsiders on the board of directors, Burton replied that he was the founder and largest shareholder, and he could determine what was best for the company. He fired a key managing officer who had been with the company since it was formed, presumably for challenging him and asking questions he no longer wanted to hear. Another founding executive whom Burton had appointed as president resigned and took several other employees with him to establish a new airline.

In 1986, as financial performance continued to deteriorate, Burton abruptly abandoned the distinctive strategy of discount fares and no-frills service and began offering full service with higher fares to lure business travelers. However, operating losses continued to mount, and in a last desperate move, Burton changed back to his original strategy. It was all to no avail. By the summer of 1986, the losses increased and the company entered bankruptcy proceedings.

Question

1. What dysfunctional aspects of charismatic leadership were displayed by Burton?

CASE 2

Chief Employees' Friend

In the two years since becoming the CEO, Satvinder Singh has systematically changed the perception of employees about the top management of HMC, which is one of the largest pharmaceutical manufacturers in India. Satvinder Singh, 35, does not mind wearing a tucked-in T-shirt to office. He smiles easily and is comfortable before the camera and everybody. He goes to the gym, sometimes within office hours, and has been rated as "The Fittest CEO in India" by a fitness magazine. There are other, more mundane reasons why Singh (referred to as Satts by nearly everyone who knows him, right down to the security guard at the gate, who makes the allowance of adding *saheb*) is at ease while facing the world.

Friendly competitions and birthday parties are held regularly in the company, as are fancy dress shows (Singh dressed as a colorful Punjabi ethnic singer at one of these events). His office has a cutout which says: "HMC/fun@work." Singh has introduced the concept of putting a heart-shaped logo on all internal and external communications, such as letter heads, note pads, and key chains.

Here are some of Satvinder Singh's famous quotes as posted on his informal fan club page on Facebook, created by the employees of HMC:

- "Power should be reserved for weightlifting and bikes, and leadership really involves responsibility."
- "One piece of advice that is always stuck in my mind is that people should be known and treated as humans, not because of their position or title or designation."
- "I've found that more of the greatest ideas surface in informal gatherings and social parties than in formal boardroom meetings."

One of Satinder Singh's most unique and innovative ideas, which was applauded by both internal and external customers, was that he now designates himself as Chief Employees' Friend or CEF.

Questions

1. Analyze the leadership style of Satvinder Singh in light of the following observation: "The management team and board of HMC are happy with organizational performance and employee morale. However, they are worried if they are falling into 'the white knight trap'."

2. Please provide evidences of transformational leadership in the behavior of Satvinder Singh.

Ethical, Servant, Spiritual, and Authentic Leadership

Ethical, Servant, Spiritual, and Authentic Leadership

Learning Objectives

After studying this chapter, you should be able to:

- Understand different conceptions of ethical leadership.
- Understand the difficulties in defining and assessing ethical leadership.
- Understand the individual and situational influences on ethical leadership.
- Understand theories of transforming, servant, spiritual, and authentic leadership.
- Understand the consequences of ethical leadership for followers and the organization.
- Understand ways to promote ethical behavior and oppose unethical practices.

Powerful leaders can have a substantial impact on the lives of followers and the fate of an organization. As Gini (1998) reminds us, the primary issue is not whether leaders will use power, but whether they will use it wisely and well. Powerful leaders can advance their own careers and economic gains at the expense of organization members and the public. Moreover, by making unethical practices appear to be legitimate, a leader can influence other members of the organization to engage in "crimes of obedience" (Beu & Buckley, 2004; Hinrichs, 2007). Interest in ethical aspects of leadership has been growing as public confidence in political and corporate leaders continues to decline. Repeated scandals about these leaders have been publicized in the news media, in books, and in movies (Kouzes & Posner, 1993). Companies with top executives involved in unethical activities during recent years include Enron, Global Crossing, HealthSouth, Qwest, Scandia, Tyco International, and WorldCom (Carson, 2003; Flanagan, 2003). This chapter will examine different conceptions of *ethical leadership*, discuss *ethical dilemmas* commonly faced by leaders, describe leadership theories involving ethical leadership, and identify some things leaders can do to promote ethical behavior in organizations.

Conceptions of Ethical Leadership

Despite the growing interest in ethical leadership, there is considerable disagreement about the appropriate way to define and assess it. In a scientific discipline that values objectivity, even to discuss this subject causes some people to feel uneasy. However, as Heifetz (1994) pointed out, there is no ethically neutral ground for theories of leadership, because they always involve values and implicit assumptions about proper forms of influence.

Defining Ethical Leadership

Ethical leadership has been defined in many different ways. When asked to describe ethical leaders in one study, executives identified several behaviors, values, and motives (e.g., honest, trustworthy, altruistic, fair). A key characteristic was leader's efforts to influence the ethical behavior of others (Trevino, Brown, & Hartman, 2003). Examples include leader statements about the importance of ethics, dissemination of ethical guidelines for members of the organization, modeling ethical behavior to set a visible example for others, including ethical behavior in the assessment of performance, and criticizing or punishing unethical behavior. It is also useful to make a distinction between the ethics of an individual leader and the ethics of specific types of leadership behavior, and both types of ethics are difficult to evaluate (Bass & Steidlmeier, 1999).

Several criteria are relevant for judging individual leaders, including the person's values, stage of moral development, conscious intentions, freedom of choice, use of ethical and unethical behavior, and types of influence used. Famous leaders usually have a mix of strengths and weaknesses with regard to these criteria. One difficulty in evaluating the morality of individual leaders is the subjectivity inherent in determining which criteria to use and their relative importance. The final evaluation can be influenced as much by the qualities of the judge as by the qualities of the leader.

Judgments about the ethics of a particular decision or action usually take into account the purpose (ends), the extent to which behavior is consistent with moral standards (means), and the consequences for self and others (outcomes). The three criteria are usually considered in relation to each other, and a common issue is the extent to which the ends justify the means. For example, is deception justified when the purpose is to help another person avoid serious personal harm?

Moral standards used to evaluate behavior include the extent to which it violates basic laws of society, denies others their rights, endangers the health and lives of other people, or involves attempts to deceive and exploit others for personal benefit. Examples of behavior that is usually considered unethical in Western nations include falsifying information, stealing assets for personal use, blaming others for one's own mistakes, provoking unnecessary hostility and distrust among others, selling secrets to competitors, showing favoritism in return for a bribe, and reckless behavior that is likely to injure others. Judgments about ethical leadership vary somewhat across cultures, but researchers find that some types of leader behavior (e.g., exploiting followers) are considered improper regardless of national culture.

Personal Integrity and Ethical Leadership

Discussions of ethical leadership invariably involve the concept of *personal integrity. Integrity* is an attribute that helps to explain leadership effectiveness. In cross-cultural research on the essential traits for effective leadership, integrityis near the top ofthe list in all cultures that have been studied. Most scholars consider integrity to be an important aspect of ethical leadership, but the meaning of integrity is still a subject of debate (Barry & Stephens, 1998; Locke & Becker, 1998; Simons, 2002; Trevino, Weaver, & Reynolds, 2006).

The most basic definition of integrity emphasizes honesty and consistency between a person's espoused values and behavior. What the leader values and how the person acts are not part of this definition, and critics contend that the values must be moral and the behavior must be consistent with a set of justifiable moral principles (e.g., Becker, 1998). A thief who believes it is morally acceptable to steal from corrupt organizations would not be classified as high in integrity. A limitation of this narrower definition is the difficulty of getting agreement about justifiable moral principles, especially when they are not the same for all cultures.

Behaviors commonly regarded as morally justifiable include observing the same rules and standards applied to others, being honest and candid when providing information or answering questions, keeping promises and commitments, and acknowledging responsibility for mistakes while also seeking to correct them. However, behaviors that appear morally justifiable can be used for unethical purposes. An example is to use kindness to gain the trust of people who will later be exploited. For this reason, it is necessary to consider a leader's intentions and values as well as behaviors when evaluating ethical leadership. To be ethical, the leader must intend no harm and respect the rights of all affected parties (Gini, 1998).

Dilemmas in Assessing Ethical Leadership

Influencing follower commitment and optimism for a task are the central aspects of most theories of effective leadership, but this influence is also the source of ethical concerns. The challenge is to determine when such influence is proper. It is easier to evaluate ethical leadership when the interests of the leader, the followers, and the organization are congruent and can be attained by actions that do not involve much risk or cost. However, in many situations the influence process may involve (1) creating enthusiasm for a risky strategy or project, (2) inducing followers to change their underlying beliefs and values, and (3) influencing decisions that will benefit some people at the expense of others. Each type of influence involves ethical dilemmas.

Influencing Expectations

An important leadership responsibility is to interpret confusing events and build consensus around strategies for dealing with threats and opportunities. Sometimes success requires a strategy or project that is bold and innovative. A risky venture may result in great benefits for followers if completed successfully, but the costs can also be high, especially if the project fails or takes much longer than expected. How the leader influences follower perception of the risks and prospects for success is relevant for evaluating ethical leadership.

Most people would agree that it is unethical to deliberately manipulate followers to do something contrary to their self-interest by making false promises or deceiving them about likely outcomes. One proposed standard for ethical leadership is for the leader to fully inform followers about the likely costs and benefits of a risky venture, and ask followers to make a conscious decision about whether the effort is worthwhile. However, it is often difficult to find any objective basis for predicting the likely outcomes of an innovative strategy and project. If an obvious crisis already exists for the group or organization, expressing doubts and sharing complete information can create panic and ensure failure.

As Heifetz (1994) proposed, it is important to help people understand a problem without demoralizing them. Effective leaders do not dwell too much upon the risks or obstacles, but instead emphasize what can be accomplished with a concerted, shared effort. Hope and optimism can eventually become a self-fulfilling prophecy if combined with effective problem solving. Thus, in situations where sharing information and interpreting events involves competing values, there are complex ethical issues to be resolved. For example, should political leaders withhold information about a possible terrorist attack to avoid the risk of harm caused by mass panic?

Influencing Values and Beliefs

Even more controversial is an attempt to change the underlying values and beliefs of individual followers. Some writers contend that this type of leader influence is clearly unethical, even when the intended outcome is to benefit followers as well as the organization (e.g., Stephens, D'Intino, & Victor, 1995; White & Wooten, 1986). These writers question the implicit assumption that the leader knows what is best for followers, and there is concern about the misuse of power and control over information to bias follower perceptions about problems and events. A special concern is the influence of charismatic leaders on followers who are weak and insecure.

A contrary view is that leaders have a responsibility to implement major changes in an organization when necessary to ensure its survival and effectiveness. A large-scale organizational change will not be successful without changes in member beliefs and perceptions. Effective leaders engage members and other stakeholders in a dialogue to determine what types of changes are necessary and morally right for the organization. How much influence the CEO or any other individual should try to exert on this process, and the form of the influence, are ethical questions that are yet to be resolved.

Multiple Stakeholders and Competing Values

The difficulties in evaluating the effectiveness of leaders include multiple criteria with complex trade-offs and stakeholders with partially conflicting interests. The diverse consequences of a leader's decisions and actions complicate the evaluation of ethical leadership. The same actions that benefit followers in some ways may also harm followers in other ways or at a later time. The same actions that serve the interests of some followers may be contrary to the interests of other followers. Doing what is best for one type of stakeholder (e.g., owners) may not be what is best for others (e.g., employees, customers, the community). Efforts to balance competing values and interests involve subjective judgments about rights, accountability, due process, and social responsibilities. It is more difficult to evaluate ethical leadership when stakeholders have incompatible preferences.

The traditional perspective is that managers in business organizations are agents who represent the interest of the owners in achieving economic success for the organization. From this perspective, ethical leadership is satisfied by maximizing economic outcomes that benefit owners while not doing anything strictly prohibited by laws and moral standards. For example, the decision to move a manufacturing plant from Kansas to Mexico would be considered ethical if it would significantly improve profits, regardless of the effects on plant employees or the local economy. The pursuit of short-term profits is often used as the excuse for making strategic decisions that are harmful to many stakeholders such as employees, customers, and towns where the company has facilities.

A very different perspective is that managers should serve *multiple stakeholders* inside and outside the organization (Block, 1993; Gini, 1998; Greenleaf, 1977; Jones, Felps, & Bigley,

2007; Sharp-Paine, 1994). From this perspective, judgments about ethical leadership must take into account the extent to which a leader balances and integrates the interests of different stakeholders within the constraints imposed by legal and contractual obligations. An integrative orientation appears more ethical than supporting the faction that will provide the highest personal gain for the leader, playing stakeholders off against each other (e.g., by encouraging negative stereotyping and mutual distrust), or trying to ignore substantive conflicts of interest. The following incident described by Nielsen (1989) provides an example of the integrative approach.

> The division manager for a paper products company was confronted with a difficult problem. Top management decided to close some paper mills unless operational costs for them could be reduced. The manager was concerned that cutting costs would prevent the mills from meeting government pollution control requirements. However, unless costs were reduced, the mills would close, seriously hurting the economy of the local community. The manager decided to look for an integrative win-win solution. He asked the research and engineering people in his division to look for ways to make the mills more efficient and also reduce pollution. He asked the operations and financial people in his division to estimate how much it would cost to build better mills, and when the operations would achieve a breakeven payback. When a good solution was found, he negotiated an agreement with top management to implement the plan.

Unfortunately, when different stakeholders have incompatible objectives, an integrative solution is not always possible. Leaders of business organizations sometimes have an opportunity to support a worthy cause, even though it does not provide any short-term benefit to the financial performance of the organization. However, making this type of decision requires courage and strong convictions, because powerful stakeholders may expect a leader to protect their interests, regardless of the harm to people who are not viewed as legitimate stakeholders (Jones et al., 2007). A good example of this type of ethical dilemma is provided by Useem (1998).

> In the 1970s river blindness was one of the world's most dreaded diseases, and it had long frustrated scientists trying to stop the spread of river blindness in developing countries. Then a potential cure for the disease was discovered by researchers at Merck. The new drug (called Mectizan) would cost more than $200 million to develop, and it was needed only by people who could not afford to pay for it. When Roy Vagelos, the CEO of Merck, was unsuccessful in his effort to get governments of developing nations to agree to pay for the drug, it became obvious that Mectizan would never make any profit for Merck. Nevertheless, Vagelos decided to distribute Mectizan for free to the people whose lives depended on it. Many people in the company said the decision was a costly mistake that violated the responsibility of the CEO to stockholders. However, Vagelos believed that the decision was consistent with Merck's guiding mission to preserve and improve human life. The development of Mectizan was a medical triumph and it helped to nearly eradicate river blindness. The humanitarian decision enhanced the company's reputation and helped to attract some of the best scientific researchers in the world to work for Merck.

Determinants and Consequences of Ethical Leadership

Two interesting research questions are the reason for differences in ethical behavior among leaders, and the consequences of ethical leadership for followers and the organization.

Both questions are briefly discussed in this section of the chapter, because they are relevant for understanding the theories of ethical leadership described later in the chapter.

Individual Determinants of Ethical Leadership

Ethical leadership is related to a leader's personality traits and needs (Brown & Trevino, 2006b; De Hoogh & Den Hartog, 2008; Kish-Gephart, Harrison, & Trevino, 2010; Mumford et al., 1993; O'Connor et al., 1995). Most of the traits related to effective leadership are also related to ethical leadership. Unethical, abusive leadership is more likely for a person who has low conscientiousness, high neuroticism, high narcissism, and a personalized power orientation. Emotionally mature leaders with a socialized power orientation, a high level of *cognitive moral development,* and a strong moral identity are more likely to resist the temptation to use their power to exploit others.

Kohlberg (1984) proposed a model describing how people progress through six sequential stages of moral development as they grow from a child to an adult. With each successive stage, the person develops a broader understanding of the principles of justice, social responsibility, and human rights. At the lowest level of moral development, the primary motivation is self-interest and the satisfaction of personal needs. At a middle level of moral development, the primary motivation is to satisfy role expectations and social norms determined by groups, organizations, and society. At the highest level of moral development, the primary motivation is to fulfill internalized values and moral principles. A person at this level may deviate from norms and risk social rejection, economic loss, and physical punishment in order to achieve an important ethical objective. The Kohlberg theory of moral development is similar in many ways to Kegan's (1982) theory of psycho-social development.

Unlike physical maturation, moral development is not inevitable, and some people become fixated at a particular developmental stage. A leader who is at a higher level of development is usually regarded as more ethical than one at a lower level of development. Some research indicates that cognitive moral development is related to ethical decisions in business organizations (e.g., Trevino, 1986; Trevino & Youngblood, 1990). However, a review of research on the theory found a lack of clear evidence that leadership behavior or effectiveness is related to stage of development (McCauley, Drath, Palus, O'Connor, & Baker, 2006).

Another explanation for moral behavior involves self-identity theory. A person with a strong moral self-identity is motivated to act in ways that are consistent with ethical values and beliefs (Reynolds, 2006a). A moral self-identity is less important as a determinant of behavior in the situation where there is a strong consensus about ethical behavior. Most people will conform to the social norms, even if they do not have a strong moral self-identity. However, if there is not a consensus about a moral issue, then judgments about ethical consequences of actions are more important as determinants of behavior.

Decisions about moral behavior are also affected by values involving the consequences of behavior and the observance of formal rules, policies, laws, and traditional practices (Reynolds, 2006a). A person's moral identity usually emphasizes one value over the other. If consequences are more important, the person will favor actions likely to result in the greatest benefit to all affected parties. If formalism is more important, the person will be inclined to obey rules and policies. The impact of these values on behavior is most evident when there are rules or traditions about proper behavior but no strong moral consensus about it. In this situation, people with a strong moral identity and a primary concern for consequences will be the most likely to select a behavior that will result in benefits for others, even if it violates formal rules or laws. In contrast, people with a strong moral identity and primary concern for formality will be the most likely to conform with existing rules or laws, even when the behavior is likely to have adverse consequences for some people.

Situational Influences on Ethical Leadership

Ethical behavior occurs in a social context, and it can be strongly influenced by aspects of the situation (Brown & Trevino, 2006b; Mishina, Dykes, Block, & Pollock, 2010; Kish-Gephart et al., 2010; Trevino, 1986; Trevino, Butterfield, & McCabe, 1998). A dynamic, uncertain environment and a lack of strong regulation by government may encourage more risky decisions and illegal activities intended to improve financial performance. The formal reward system can encourage and support ethical or unethical behavior by leaders and members. Unethical behavior is more likely when performance goals are unrealistically difficult, there is high pressure for increased productivity, there is intense competition for rewards and advancement, and the organization does not have strong cultural values and norms about ethical conduct and individual responsibility. The strong success-oriented culture at Enron and the compensation and performance appraisal systems that supported it encouraged employees to exaggerate results and help hide the company's growing debt (Probst & Raisch, 2005; Reynolds, 2006b). Bill George, the former CEO of Medtronics suggested a way to deal with the temptation to use questionable actions to achieve difficult objectives (George, 2003, pp. 16-17):

> All of us who sit in the leader's chair feel the pressure to perform. Little by little, step by step, the pressures to succeed can pull us away from our core values. The irony is that the more successful we are, the more tempted we are to take shortcuts to keep it going. All leaders have to resist these pressures while continuing to perform, especially when things aren't going well. The test I used with our team at Medtronic is whether we would feel comfortable having the entire story appear on the front page of the New York Times. If we didn't, we went back to the drawing boards and re-examined our decision.

Follower traits and beliefs are another aspect of the situation that can influence unethical leadership. Followers are more likely to passively accept a domineering and abusive leader if they lack self-esteem and self-efficacy and do not have much confidence in their own ability to deal with threats and hardship. Unethical leadership is more likely when people believe that formal leaders should have strong position power and obedience to formal authority is necessary. These beliefs are common in societies with strong cultural values for uncertainty avoidance and power distance. Unethical behavior is also more likely in societies where violence is prevalent, fraud and bribery are accepted, and corruption of officials is widespread (Mumford et al., 2007).

Studies of "abusive supervision" and "toxic leaders" provide insights about the conditions that make it easier for a chief executive to act in ways that are destructive for an organization and its members (Lipman-Blumen, 2005; Padilla, Hogan, & Kaiser, 2007). In organizations that lack mechanisms to limit the power of the chief executive, abusive leaders are more difficult to restrain or remove once they have been appointed or elected. Examples of ways to limit executive power include term limits, an independent board of directors, procedures for follower evaluation of leaders, procedures for appealing decisions by leaders (including decisions about punishment or dismissal), and formal procedures for removing a leader who misuses power or is incompetent.

Consequences of Ethical and Unethical Leadership

Most theories of ethical leadership emphasize the importance of leader influence on followers and the ethical climate of an organization. Many different measures have been used to assess the effects of ethical leadership on followers, and they include some criteria seldom used in the earlier leadership research (e.g., follower values and ethical behavior, follower *self-awareness,* follower feelings of spiritual fulfillment). The theories differ somewhat with regard to the criteria used to assess the effects of ethical leadership. Examples of research on the effects of ethical leadership are provided by a number of studies (Reave, 2005), and there is clear evidence of beneficial effects for followers and for leader-member relations. For example, a study of critical incidents found that a lack of leader integrity was the most frequent reason for erosion of trust by subordinates (Lapidot et al., 2007).

Abusive supervision includes using power and authority to humiliate, ridicule, bully, and otherwise mistreat subordinates (Tepper, 2000). Such behavior is usually regarded as a form of unethical leadership, and the research indicates that it results in negative consequences for followers and the organization. Abusive supervision results in less organizational citizenship behaviors by employees (Zellers, Tepper, & Duffy, 2002), and it also results in more retaliation and displaced aggression toward coworkers and the organization (Mitchell & Ambrose, 2007). For example, a study of abusive behavior by restaurant managers found that it resulted in higher food loss from employee theft and waste (Detert, Trevino, Burris, & Andiappan, 2007).

In research on ethical leadership, consequences are more often assessed for employees rather than for measures of organizational performance. Sometimes effects at the individual and organizational level are consistent, such as when higher employee trust and commitment also result in improved financial performance for the organization. However, in many cases leader decisions do not have consistent effects for different criteria or for different stakeholders. Some ethical decisions will benefit employees or customers but increase costs and reduce short-term financial performance. Examples include providing adequate health care benefits to employees, accepting responsibility for defective products (e.g., recalls and refunds), and keeping commitments despite unexpected expenses.

Conversely, some decisions and actions that improve short-term organizational performance will have adverse consequences for employees or customers. Recent examples include reducing employee rights and benefits, and outsourcing employee jobs to low-cost vendors in other countries. Another dubious practice is to reduce spending on activities that are costly but essential for longer-term performance. An example is less maintenance of equipment, despite the increased risk of costly breakdowns or accidents in the future. How unethical practices are used to inflate profits was revealed in prominent scandals over the past decade. Examples include billing the government or other customers for services that were not provided, falsifying the qualification of applicants for loans or mortgages they are not be able to repay, marketing securities with inflated quality ratings, and counting future sales revenues as current income to prop up the value of the company's stock.

Theories of Ethical Leadership

Several prominent theories in the leadership literature have a strong emphasis on ethical leadership. The theories include *transforming leadership, servant leadership, authentic leadership,* and *spiritual leadership.* The types of values emphasized in these theories are listed in Table 1, and each theory is briefly described in this section of the chapter.

Transforming Leadership

Burns (1978) formulated a theory of transforming leadership from descriptive research on political leaders. For Burns, a primary leadership role or function is to increase awareness about ethical issues and help people resolve conflicting values. Burns (1978, p. 20) described transforming leadership as a process in which "leaders and followers raise one another to

TABLE 1	Explanation of Values Emphasized in Theories of Ethical leadership

1. *Integrity:* Communicates in an open and honest way, keeps promises and commitments, acts in ways that are consistent with espoused values, admits and accepts responsibility for mistakes, does not attempt to manipulate or deceive people.
2. *Altruism:* Enjoys helping others, is willing to take risks or make sacrifices to protect or benefit others, puts the needs of others ahead of own needs, volunteers for service activities that require extra time and are not part of the formal job requirements.
3. *Humility:* Treats others with respect, avoids status symbols and special privileges, admits limitations and mistakes, is modest about achievements, emphasizes the contributions by others when a collective effort is successful.
4. *Empathy and healing:* Helps others cope with emotional distress, encourages acceptance of diversity, acts as a mediator or peacemaker, encourages forgiveness and reconciliation after a divisive conflict.
5. *Personal growth:* Encourages and facilitates the development of individual confidence and ability, even when not important for the current job; provides learning opportunities despite a risk of mistakes; provides mentoring and coaching when needed; helps people learn from mistakes.
6. *Fairness and justice:* Encourages and supports fair treatment of people, speaks out against unfair and unjust practices or policies, opposes attempts to manipulate or deceive people or to undermine or violate their civil rights.
7. *Empowerment:* Consults with others about decisions that will affect them, provides an appropriate amount of autonomy and discretion to subordinates, shares sensitive information with them, encourages them to express concerns or dissenting views without becoming defensive.

higher levels of morality and motivation." These leaders seek to raise the consciousness of followers by appealing to ideals and moral values such as liberty, justice, equality, peace, and humanitarianism, not to baser emotions such as fear, greed, jealousy, or hatred. Followers are elevated from their "everyday selves" to their "better selves." For Burns, transforming leadership may be exhibited by anyone in the organization in any type of position. It may involve influencing peers and superiors as well as subordinates. It can occur in the day-to-day acts of ordinary people, but it is not ordinary or common.

Burns described leadership as a process in which leaders and followers influence each other as the relationships evolve over time. Transforming leadership is an influence process between individuals, but it is also a process of mobilizing power to change social systems and reform institutions. The leader seeks to shape, express, and mediate conflict among groups of people, because this conflict can be useful for mobilizing and channeling energy to achieve shared ideological objectives. Thus, transforming leadership involves not only the moral elevation of individual followers, but also collective efforts to accomplish social reforms. In the process, both the leader and followers will be changed. They will begin to consider not only what is good for themselves, but also what will benefit larger collectivities such as their organization, community, and nation.

Servant Leadership

Another early conception of ethical leadership builds on examples found in the New Testament (Greenleaf, 1977; Sendjaya & Sarros, 2002). In 1970, Robert Greenleaf proposed the concept of "servant leadership," and it became the title of a book published in 1977. Greenleaf proposed that service to followers is the primary responsibility of leaders and the essence of ethical leadership. Servant leadership in the workplace is about helping others to accomplish shared objectives by facilitating individual development, empowerment, and collective work that is consistent with the health and long-term welfare of followers. Other theorists have extended the theory to include a more explicit description of key values and the effects of servant leaders on followers and the organization (Farling, Stone, & Wilson, 1999; Graham, 1991; Searle & Barbuto, 2011; Smith, Montagno, & Kuzmenko, 2004). Different questionnaires have been developed to measure servant leadership, but the best way to define and measure the construct has not been resolved (Barbuto & Wheeler, 2006; Dennis & Bocarnea, 2005; Ehrhart, 2004; Liden, Wayne, Zhao, & Henderson, 2008).

A servant leader must attend to the needs of followers and help them become healthier, wiser, and more willing to accept their responsibilities. Service includes nurturing, defending, and empowering followers. It is only by understanding followers that the leader can determine how best to serve their needs. Servant leaders must listen to followers, learn about their needs and aspirations, and be willing to share in their pain and frustration. The servant leader must empower followers instead of using power to dominate them. Trust is established by being completely honest and open, keeping actions consistent with values, and showing trust in followers. Greenleaf believed that followers of such leaders are inspired to become servant leaders themselves. People should prepare themselves to lead and accept the opportunity when offered. The result will be more people who serve as moral agents in society.

The servant leader must stand for what is good and right, even when it is not in the financial interest of the organization. Social injustice and inequality should be opposed whenever possible. Even the weak and marginal members of society must be treated with respect and appreciation. Greenleaf proposed that providing meaningful work for employees is as important as providing a quality product or service for the customer. He advocated that business organizations should consider social responsibility as one of the major objectives, and the board of directors should take primary responsibility for evaluating and facilitating progress on this objective.

The potential benefits of servant leadership are similar to those suggested by theories of supportive and empowering leadership and theories of spiritual and authentic leadership. Leader integrity and concern for subordinates is likely to increase their trust, loyalty, and satisfaction with the leader. A favorable relationship and increased referent power for the leader make it easier to influence subordinates to carry out requests. The potential benefits derived from development and empowerment of subordinates have been demonstrated in research on participative leadership, supportive leadership, and transformational leadership. The attempt to ensure fairness and equity can influence subordinate perceptions of distributive and procedural justice and increase their loyalty and organizational commitment. If a servant leader is able to influence other leaders to become servant leaders as well, the result may be an employee-oriented culture that attracts and retains talented, committed employees.

Research on the consequences of servant leadership is still limited, but several studies have found positive outcomes such as more commitment, self-efficacy, and organizational citizenship behavior (e.g., Liden et al., 2008; Neubert, Kacmar, Carlson, Chonko, & Roberts, 2008; Walumbwa, Hartnell, & Oke, 2010). The following example provides a good description of a servant leader (Sacks, 2009):

> John Mackey is the CEO and co-founder of Whole Foods Market, the largest and most profitable retailer of organic food in the USA. The company has many stores and billions of dollars in sales. Whole Foods was listed by Forbes as one of the "25 Best Companies to Work For" in 2005. The following year Mackey announced he would reduce his salary to $1 a year and set up a $100,000 emergency fund for employees with serious personal problems. He also instituted caps on executive pay, which was limited to no more than

19 times the average employee salary. Most stock options are awarded to employees who are not executives. In addition to his deep concern for employees, Mackey is a strong supporter of environmental, humanitarian, and animal welfare groups, and 5% of the company's after-tax profits are given to charity every year. Whole Foods was the first grocery chain in the USA to set standards for humane animal treatment by suppliers.

Despite the potential benefits from servant leadership, there may also be some negative consequences for an organization when the welfare of followers is considered more important than financial performance (Anderson, 2009; Graham, 1991). When a corporation is facing difficult economic problems and cuts in expenses are necessary to remain profitable, it is very difficult for a servant leader to balance the competing preferences of owners and employees (Schneider & George, 2011). Conflicts between financial objectives and employee welfare are less intense in nonprofit, voluntary, and public sector organizations, but even for these organizations a reduction in employee benefits may be necessary in a weak economy. More research is needed to clarify the implications of servant leadership for different stakeholders in organizations.

Spiritual Leadership

Spiritual leadership describes how leaders can enhance the intrinsic motivation of followers by creating conditions that increase their sense of spiritual meaning in the work. The popularity of books on spirituality in the workplace suggests that many people are seeking deeper meaning in their work (Chappel, 1993; Fairholm, 1997). Several types of research indicate that people value the opportunity to feel interconnected to others in a mutually supporting community of people who are collectively involved in meaningful activities (Duchon & Plowman, 2005; Pfeffer, 2003). The integration of spirituality with work is difficult if not impossible in organizations that encourage or require employees to act in ways that are inconsistent with their values (Mitroff & Denton, 1999). Consistency between personal values and work objectives is important to leaders as well as to followers.

Fry (2003) makes the point that religion usually involves spirituality, but spirituality does not need religion to be meaningful. Theories of spiritual leadership include values found in major religions (Kriger & Seng, 2005), but the theories do not explicitly include any other aspects of these religions. Confusion about the difference between spirituality and religion may be the major reason why most earlier leadership theories did not include spirituality (Fry, 2003). The leadership theorists wanted to avoid any controversy about implied support for one favored religion.

The definition of spirituality provided by Fry (2003, 2005) includes two essential elements in a person's life. Transcendence of self is manifest in a sense of "calling" or destiny, and the belief that one's activities, including work, have meaning and value beyond being instrumental for obtaining economic benefits or self-gratification (need for power, achievement, esteem). Fellowship is manifest in the need for meaningful relationships and being connected to others in a way that provides feelings of joy and wholeness. Both elements involve altruistic love and faith. Altruistic love is associated with values or attributes such as kindness, compassion, gratitude, understanding, forgiveness, patience, humility, honesty, trust, and loyalty. Faith or hope is associated with values or attributes such as optimism, confidence, courage, endurance, persistence, resilience, and serenity.

By doing things to help people satisfy the two essential needs for transcendence and fellowship in the workplace, spiritual leaders increase their intrinsic motivation, confidence, and organizational commitment. As in the case of transformational leadership, spiritual leaders can enhance the meaningfulness of the work by linking it to follower values and self-identities. In addition, spiritual leaders increase mutual appreciation, affection, and trust among members of the organization. As a result, spiritual leadership can increase cooperation, encourage collective learning, and inspire higher performance.

Much of the knowledge about spiritual leadership for leaders is provided by research on related subjects, and Reave (2005) reviewed more than 150 studies that appeared relevant for understanding spiritual leadership. A few of the studies provide evidence that the opportunity to express spiritual values in one's work is related to a person's mental health, life satisfaction, and intrinsic motivation (e.g., Chappel, 1993; Duchon & Plowman, 2005; Fry, Vitucci, & Cedillo, 2005; Milliman, Czaplewski, & Ferguson, 2003). Research in medicine and positive psychology provides evidence that altruistic love can overcome negative feelings such as fear, anxiety, anger, guilt, hatred, pride, envy, and resentment. Other studies show that a high-commitment organizational climate and highly motivated members will improve organizational performance (e.g., Harter et al., 2002).

The limitations of spiritual leadership theory are similar to those for servant leadership. How leader values and skills influence leader behavior is not clearly specified in the theory, and the processes by which leaders influence followers are not clearly explained. The relative importance of calling and fellowship and how they are interrelated is not clear. The theories include many different values, and it is not clear whether some values are more important than others, or how the values are related to leader behavior. It is not clear how a person becomes a spiritual leader, or what types of life experiences can explain why some leaders are more spiritual than others. Even though the theorists emphasize that spirituality is distinct from religious beliefs, some religious beliefs and cultural values may encourage spiritual leadership, especially for individuals in an organization, community, or nation with strong cultural values and religious traditions. More research is needed to identify conditions that favor spiritual leadership and enhance the influence of such leaders on followers and the organization.

Authentic Leadership

The idea of authentic leadership has received a lot of attention in recent years, and several scholars have provided versions of authentic leadership theory (e.g., Avolio, Gardner, Walumbwa, Luthans, & Mayo, 2004; Gardner, Avolio, Luthans, May, & Walumbwa, 2005; George, 2003; Ilies, Morgeson, & Nahrgang, 2005; Shamir & Eilam, 2005). Authentic leadership is based on positive psychology and psychological theories of self-regulation. The theory attempts to integrate earlier ideas about effective leadership with concerns for ethical leadership. The definition of authentic leadership varies for different theorists, but they all emphasize the importance of consistency in a leader's words, actions, and values. Additional aspects of authentic leadership include positive leader values, leader self-awareness, and a trusting relationship with followers.

Authentic leaders have positive core values such as honesty, altruism, kindness, fairness, accountability, and optimism. These core values motivate authentic leaders to do what is right and fair for followers, and to create a special type of relationship that includes high mutual trust, transparency (open and honest communication), guidance toward worthy shared objectives, and emphasis on follower welfare and development. The self-concepts and self-identities of authentic leaders are strong, clear, stable, and consistent. These leaders have a high self-awareness about their values, beliefs, emotions, self-identities, and abilities. In other words, they know who they are and what they believe. They also have a high degree of self-acceptance, which is similar to emotional maturity.

The behavior of authentic leaders, including their espoused values, is consistent with their actual values. They do not seek leadership positions to gratify a need for esteem, status, and power, but rather to express and enact their values and beliefs. Their actions are strongly determined by their values and beliefs, not by a desire to be liked and admired or to retain their position (e.g., be re-elected). Because authentic leaders are motivated by a desire for selfimprovement and self-verification, they are less defensive and more open to learning from feedback and mistakes.

The influence of authentic leaders with some followers is enhanced by their confidence, clarity of values, and integrity. It is easier for followers to be influenced by a leader who is perceived to be credible, focused, and confident. Followers of authentic leaders have more personal identification with the leader and more social identification with the team or organizational unit. There is also an indirect effect through influence on follower self-concepts and self-identities.

A few of the leadership behaviors used to influence followers are the same ones that are included in other leadership theories. The leader can enhance follower commitment and optimism by articulating an appealing vision, modeling appropriate behaviors, and expressing optimism and encouragement when there are setbacks and difficulties. However, with regard to other leadership behaviors, there is less agreement among different versions of authentic leadership theory.

In most versions of the theory, an authentic relationship means that leader behavior is consistent with the leader's values, and both are consistent with follower values. However, the relative importance of the different types of consistency is unclear. If a leader's values and actions are consistent but most followers reject these values, will followers judge the leader more favorably than a leader who conforms to follower values despite not believing in them? In addition, complete transparency in revealing emotions can have unintended negative effects. For example, when it is essential to build confidence that a team can successfully deal with a serious crisis, a leader who has personal fears or doubts must be careful not to communicate these emotions in a way that will undermine follower confidence.

Follower perception of leader authenticity may be jointly influenced by the leader's ability to express emotional values skillfully enough to be credible, on the extent to which the expressed values and emotions are consistent with follower perception of the situation, and on follower ability to accurately perceive when a leader is expressing genuine emotions and values. Trust will be undermined if the leader appears genuine but the values and emotions are inappropriate for the situation, or if the values and emotions are appropriate but they do not appear to be genuine (Gardner, Fischer, & Hunt, 2009).

Like the other theories of ethical leadership, the authentic leadership theories suffer from a lack of clarity in the definition of essential qualities and the explanation of influence processes (Cooper, Scandura, & Schriesheim, 2005; Guthey & Jackson, 2005; Ladkin & Taylor, 2010). It is unclear whether the theory is a description of attributes actually possessed by effective leaders, or only an ideal form of ethical leadership that people can hope to attain (Caza & Jackson, 2011). More research is needed to verify key propositions and to resolve the paradoxes and ethical dilemmas inherent in some aspects of the theory.

Evaluation of Ethical Leadership Theories

The theories of servant, spiritual, and authentic leadership all share some features in common with theories of transformational and charismatic leadership, but important differences are also evident. This section will compare the various theories and identify issues that require more research and clarification.

Comparison to Transformational and Charismatic Leadership

The ethical leadership theories have more emphasis on leader values than on leader behavior, and more emphasis on consequences for stakeholders than on enhancement of subordinate motivation and performance. For charismatic and transformational theories, these priorities are reversed. The ethical theories are primarily focused on leader values and how they affect the leader's relationship with subordinates. The types of values emphasized in the ethical leadership theories indicate that some types of leadership behavior are more revelant than others, and the behaviors should be consistent with the leaders' values. However, the theories do not specify a list of essential behaviors. The theories describe how ethical leaders can improve the lives of followers, and the leader's effects on followers have implications for improving collective performance, but maximizing performance is not a primary concern.

The initial version of transformational leadership was focused on the effects of specified leader behaviors on subordinate motivation and performance. Leader values are not explicitly specified, and there is no requirement that leader behavior (including espoused values and beliefs) must be consistent with the leader's actual values and beliefs. The transformational behaviors can be used in a manipulative way to influence follower task commitment and loyalty to the leader (Stephens, D'Intino, & Victor, 1995; White & Wooten, 1986). For example, individualized consideration can be used in an inauthentic way to build subordinate loyalty. Inspirational motivation can be used to increase subordinate commitment to task objectives, even though the leader cares only about self-enhancement and career advancement. Intellectual stimulation can be used to increase creative ideas that will enhance the leader's reputation (e.g., the leader may claim credit for them). Idealized influence includes leading by example and making sacrifices, but this behavior may be used to manage follower impressions and gain their trust rather than to express a leader's true concern for the mission or subordinates.

When the potential for unethical use of transformational behaviors was pointed out, the theory was modified to distinguish between authentic and inauthentic transformational leadership (Bass & Steidlmeier, 1999). Both types of leaders use transformational behaviors, but the authentic leaders have integrity and do not attempt to manipulate or exploit followers. However, even in the revised version of the theory, improvement of performance remains a stronger priority than improvement of subordinate welfare and happiness. History is full of examples of leaders who caused much suffering and misery in their dedicated pursuit of virtuous objectives (Price, 2003).

The theories of charismatic and transformational leadership emphasized the effects of leader behavior on the motivation of followers and their relationship with the leader. As the charismatic leadership theories evolved, there was more emphasis on leader values and socialized charismatics were differentiated from personalized charismatics (e.g., Brown & Trevino, 2006a; Howell, 1988; House & Howell, 1992). Nevertheless, follower attribution of charisma to the leader remains a central feature of the theory. In theories of servant, spiritual, and authentic leadership, the leader's values for humility, openness, and transparency in decision making and the emphasis on follower development and empowerment make it unlikely that the leader will be viewed as charismatic.

Proponents of the revised versions of transformational and charismatic leadership theories have attempted to clarify the criteria for determining when this type of leadership is ethical (e.g., Bass & Steidlmeier, 1999; Howell & Avolio, 1992), and examples of these criteria are shown in Table 2. The criteria appear plausible, but they may not take into account all of the complexities and dilemmas in evaluating ethical leadership. How the various criteria can be applied remains a question of discussion and debate.

TABLE 2	Suggested Criteria for Evaluating Ethical Leadership	
Criterion	**Ethical Leadership**	**Unethical Leadership**
Use of leader power and influence	• To serve followers and the organization	• To satisfy personal needs and career objectives
Handling diverse interests of multiple stakeholders	• Attempts to balance and integrate them	• Favors the stakeholders who provide the most benefits
Development of a vision for the organization	• Develops a vision based on the followers' input about their needs, values, and ideas	• Attempts to sell a personal vision as the only way for the organization to succeed
Integrity of leader behavior	• Acts in a way that is consistent with espoused values	• Does what is expedient to attain personal objectives
Risk taking in leader decisions and actions	• Is willing to take personal risks and actions to accomplish mission or achieve the vision	• Avoids necessary decisions or actions that involve personal risk to the leader
Communication of relevant information	• Makes a complete and timely disclosure of information about events, problems, and actions	• Uses deception and distortion to bias follower perceptions about problems and progress
Response to criticism and dissent by followers	• Encourages critical evaluation to find better solutions	• Discourages and suppresses any criticism or dissent
Development of follower skills and self-confidence	• Uses coaching, mentoring, and training to develop followers	• De-emphasizes development to keep followers weak and dependent on the leader

Evaluation of the Ethical Leadership Theories

The ethical leadership theories described in this chapter are still in the early stage of development, and like most new theories there is substantial conceptual ambiguity (Cooper et al., 2005). Conceptual confusion is increased and theory testing made more difficult when theories include many different types of constructs (i.e., leader traits, skills, values, and behaviors; follower values, perceptions, and needs; dyadic, group-level, and organizational explanatory processes; and several different outcome criteria). The development of new measures of ethical leadership is still in the early stages, and more validation research is needed for them. Only a few studies have compared different theories or examined their implications for improving leadership in organizations. The research involves mostly anecdotal accounts and testimonials, plus a few case studies and field survey studies. More research, including some intensive, longitudinal studies, will be needed to clarify the relationships proposed by the theories and determine their utility for explaining effective leadership.

Guidelines for Ethical Leadership

Different approaches have been used to increase ethical behavior in organizations. One approach is for individuals to encourage ethical practices and oppose unethical activities or decisions. Another approach is to use laws, professional standards, and organizational programs to increase awareness of ethical issues, encourage ethical behavior, and discourage unethical practices. The different approaches are not mutually exclusive and can be used together. Each approach will be described briefly.

Ways for Individuals to Promote Ethical Practices

Leaders can do many things to promote ethical practices in organizations (Nielsen, 1989), and they are summarized in Table 3. Following are some guidelines for ethical leadership.

- **Set clear standards for ethical conduct.**

Leaders can set clear standards and guidelines for dealing with ethical issues (e.g., help to establish an ethical code of conduct), provide opportunities for people to get advice about dealing with ethical issues (e.g., ethics hotline), and initiate discussions about ethical issues to make them more salient. Leaders can reinforce ethical behavior by including it in the criteria used to evaluate and reward follower performance. Recognize unusual examples of ethical conduct. Use appropriate disciplinary procedures for intentional violations of clear ethical standards.

- **Model ethical behavior in your own actions.**

Providing advice and guidance about correct behavior on the job and avoidance of ethical problems is useful, but to reduce unethical behavior, it is essential for the leader to model proper behavior as well as espousing it (Dineen, Lewicki, & Tomlinson, 2006). Leaders can do many things to promote honesty, fairness, mutual respect, and transparency. A leader's own actions provide an example of ethical behavior to be imitated by people who admire and identify with the leader. The examples include an honest and open examination of problems involving ethical issues, rather than attempts to ignore them or arrange a coverup. If something said or done by the leader has unintentionally encouraged subordinates to use unacceptable practices, the error should be admitted.

- **Help people find fair and ethical ways to resolve problems and conflicts.**

One important leadership function is to influence people to acknowledge an important problem, rather than denying it, discounting the seriousness of the problem, procrastinating about corrective action, or providing fake remedies and stress-reducing diversions (Heifetz, 1994). Another important function is to help frame problems by clarifying key issues, encouraging dissenting views, distinguishing causes from symptoms, and identifying complex interdependencies. Leaders can facilitate problem solving by helping people get information, by identifying points of agreement and disagreement, and by encouraging

TABLE 3	Guidelines for Ethical Leadership

- Set clear standards of ethical conduct.
- Model ethical behavior in your own actions.
- Help people find fair and ethical ways to resolve problems and conflicts.
- Oppose unethical practices in the organization.
- Implement and support programs to promote ethical behavior.

people to find integrative solutions to conflicts. It is important to proceed at a pace that people can tolerate, because if pushed too fast, people may resort to defensive avoidance mechanisms, such as concluding that temporary relief or limited progress is a complete solution. As noted in the guidelines for leading change, it is important to ensure that people understand the difficulties that will be encountered and the self-sacrifices that will be necessary to succeed, but it is also important to build hope and optimism about finding a solution. These ideas seem especially relevant for evaluating political candidates who oversimplify problems, promise unrealistic solutions, and pander to short-term individual interests rather than collective needs.

- **Oppose unethical practices in the organization.**

Opposition to unethical practices can take many different forms, and it should be viewed as a responsibility of all people, not just formal leaders (Hinrichs, 2007; Nielsen, 1989). Examples include refusing to comply with unethical assignments or rules, threatening to complain to higher management, making actual complaints to higher management, threatening to publicize unethical practices to outsiders, and actually revealing unethical practices to outsiders or a regulatory agency. Opposition to unethical practices is usually a difficult and risky course of action. Speaking out against injustices and opposing unethical practices may put one in danger of retaliation by powerful people in the organization. Many "whistleblowers" discover that their actions can result in dismissal or the derailment of their career in the organization.

Programs to Promote Ethical Behavior

An indirect form of leadership influence on the behavior of followers is to establish programs and systems. Many large organizations have ethical programs, and they often involve both an attempt to strengthen relevant internal values, and features to enforce compliance with ethical guidelines and policies (Weaver, Trevino, & Cochran, 1999). Examples of typical features of ethics programs include a formal code of ethics, an ethical committee that is responsible for developing policies and practices, methods of reporting ethical concerns to the ethics committee or top management, ethics education programs, methods to monitor ethical behavior, and disciplinary processes to deal with unethical behavior.

A study conducted in large U.S. corporations (Weaver et al., 1999) found that top executives with a strong concern for ethical behavior are more likely to implement ethical programs, and the scope of the programs is likely to be broader. The types of leadership values associated with the use of ethics programs are similar to the ones discussed earlier in this chapter (e.g., treating people fairly, doing what is right, ensuring justice is done). The research also indicates that responsibility for ethics should be taken seriously by all executives and not simply delegated to staff professionals. Some ways a top executive can influence the ethical climate in an organization include talking about the importance of positive values, setting an example of ethical behavior, making decisions that show integrity is as important as profits, and enforcing discipline for ethics violations.

The use of ethical programs in an organization is also influenced by environmental pressures, such as media attention for ethical failures and corporate scandals. However, it is better to avoid scandals and financial failure by being proactive and creating a strong ethical climate. An example of the type of policy that can be used to avoid problems is provided by Costco. The company ethics policy includes not accepting gifts from vendors. Costco also sends a yearly letter to the president of every vendor stating that gratuities are not accepted.

Cultural Values, Laws, and Professional Standards

Ethical leadership is also influenced by cultural values, social norms, legal requirements, and professional standards in countries where an organization is located (Svensson & Wood, 2007). It is much easier for managers to oppose unethical practices when there is strong and explicit support for such opposition and the standards for unacceptable behavior are clear rather than ambiguous (Reynolds, 2006a). It is more difficult to discourage unethical behavior in countries where bribes and kickbacks, gender and religious/ethnic discrimination, child labor abuse, hazardous working conditions, unsafe products, deceptive advertising, sexual harassment, and falsifying accounting records to evade taxes are widely accepted practices in organizations. Top executives, political leaders, religious leaders, and opinion leaders in universities, the news media, and professional associations (e.g., American Management Association, Academy of Management) all can help to establish clear ethical standards and a strong concern for the social responsibility in companies, nonprofit organizations, and government agencies.

Summary

Interest in ethical leadership has been increased by cynicism about the motives, competence, and integrity of business and political leaders. Conceptions of ethical leadership include nurturing followers, empowering them, and promoting social justice. Ethical leadership includes efforts to encourage ethical behavior as well as efforts to stop unethical practices. Ethical leaders seek to build mutual trust and respect among diverse followers and to find integrative solutions to conflicts among stakeholders with competing interests. Ethical leaders do not foster distrust or play favorites to gain more power or achieve personal objectives.

Determinants of ethical behavior by a leader include situational influences and aspects of leader personality such as level of cognitive moral development. Leader personality and cognitive moral development interact with aspects of the situation in the determination of ethical and unethical behavior. It is easier to understand ethical leadership when both the individual leader and the situation are considered together.

The criteria for evaluating ethical leadership include leader values and intentions, and the extent to which leader behavior is morally justifiable. Evaluation of morality for individual leaders is complicated by multiple stakeholders, diverse consequences of a leader's actions, delays in visibility of outcomes, and disagreements about the extent to which ends justify means. The difficulties in assessing the effects of ethical and unethical leadership are increased by long delays before consequences are evident and the diverse outcomes for different stakeholders. How ethical leadership is defined and measured deserves more attention in the future.

The theories of ethical leadership emphasize the importance of integrity and ethical behavior. Ethical leaders influence followers to recognize the need for adaptive problem solving that will improve their long-term welfare rather than denying the need or settling for superficial remedies. Transforming leaders seek to raise the consciousness of followers by appealing to ideals and moral values rather than to materialistic desires or negative emotions such as fear and jealousy. Servant leadership theory explains why the primary concern of leaders should be to nurture, develop, and protect followers. Spiritual leadership theory explains how leaders can enhance the spiritual meaning in the work experienced by followers. Authentic leadership theory describes an ideal leader whose behavior is guided by strong positive values. The three theories all focus on the interpersonal relationship between leader and followers, and the ideal relationship is one with high mutual respect, trust, cooperation, loyalty, and openness. The theories all emphasize the importance of leader self-awareness (about values and beliefs) and consistency between values and behavior. The positive values or attributes in the theories are very similar, and they include honesty, altruism, kindness, compassion, empathy, fairness, gratitude, humility, courage, optimism, and resilience.

The theories of ethical leadership described in this chapter emphasize leader values more than behavior, and the long-term welfare and development of followers rather than financial performance. The theories provide important insights about effective leadership by making explicit ethical concerns that are only implicit in most other leadership theories. The theories are still evolving, and they have not been adequately tested with strong research methods. Nevertheless, some ways to encourage and support ethical practices have been identified.

Review and Discussion Questions

1. Why is it so difficult to evaluate ethics and morality for individual leaders?
2. What are some examples of ethical and unethical leadership?
3. Can unethical behavior occur for a leader who has proper values and intentions?
4. Why is it important to study ethical leadership?
5. Compare and contrast the following theories: transforming leadership, servant leadership, spiritual leadership, and authentic leadership?
6. What are some individual and situational determinants of ethical leadership?
7. What can be done to increase ethical behavior and decrease unethical practices?
8. Discuss the cases of Enron, Satyam, and Lehman Brothers and the role of the leadership in the failure of these organizations.
9. Discuss the reasons for the subprime mortgage crisis in the USA from December 2007 to June 2009.

Key Terms

authentic leadership	multiple stakeholders	cognitive moral development
ethical dilemmas	servant leadership	transforming leadership
ethical leadership	self-awareness	
decision quality	spiritual leadership	
integrity		

CASE

Fun and Toys

Fun and Toys, a well-known manufacturer of toys, received news that a second child had died of suffocation after inhaling a part from its Fun Time construction kit. Four days later, an autopsy confirmed the cause of death. Madhusudan Lal, who is the chairperson of Fun and Toys and the grandson of its founder, met with his key executives to discuss this latest development and decide upon a course of action. Here is a brief about the company and the events leading to the meeting.

The Company

Fun and Toys was established in 1911, when the company's founder, Shiv Lal, created a business out of his own small shop of wooden toys. The firm experienced substantial growth over the next 30 years, but never departed from its mission of producing entertaining toys and games. In 1978, the company went into plastics and set up its own manufacturing facilities.

Fun Time

The company diversified and launched a new line of toys called Fun Time, marketed as "the toy that makes toys." It came in a number of variations but common to them all were flexible plastic shapes of various sizes and colors (including windows, brackets, and panels), reusable rubber rivets, and a hand tool. Each kit included an instruction manual to help in assembling a variety of parts from the plastic parts and rivets.

Fun Time had sold very well in 1980, the very first year of introduction. Sales were roughly 10,000 sets, which retailed at ₹150/- to ₹175/- per set. Last year, the total distribution crossed 20,000 sets. For the current Diwali and Christmas season, firm bookings for 35,000 sets were in and goods were ready for dispatch.

Applicable Safety Regulations

The industry's trade association, Toy Manufacturers Association of India (TMAI), had developed a voluntary set of safety standards which were published by the Indian Standards Bureau. These product standards were developed with the help of the Indian Academy of Pediatrics, Consumer Associations, the National Safety Council, and some leading retail organizations.

Safety standards were set for flammability, toxicity, electrical, thermal, and acoustical hazards; and for the sharpness of points and edges. Use-and-abuse tests were also part of the guidelines. Where safety may be dependent upon the age of the child playing with a particular toy, the standard required appropriate labeling.

The Consumer Safety Commission (CSC) was empowered to take steps to remove hazardous toys from the marketplace. It was the responsibility of the manufacturers, distributors, and retailers to bring any evidence of a defect or hazard to the attention of the Indian Standards Bureau under the provisions of the Consumer Safety Act. At the time of launch of the product, Madhusudan was convinced that Fun Time was a safe product. He had assured that all safety measures were taken before the product's introduction in the market.

Events Leading to the Meeting

On April 4, 1992, the legal counsel to the TMAI informed Madhusudan Lal that approximately three months earlier, an eight-year-old boy in Indore had suffocated because a Fun Time rivet had lodged in his right lung. At that time, Madhusudan Lal had commented, "According to the story that reached us, the boy was playing in his home and apparently had a Fun Time rivet in his mouth. He was playing softball with his younger brother when he began to choke. First aid efforts by the boy's parents failed, and he was dead on arrival at the hospital. The autopsy revealed a Fun Time rivet impacted in the right main stem bronchus of his lung.

Later, the attorney representing the boy's family had contacted the CSC and a regional office of the commission had conducted a hazard evaluation of Fun Time. No action was recommended by the CSC. At the time, we concluded the incident was an isolated freak accident, which did not warrant action on our part."

However, on Friday, November 4, 1992, a second accidental death was reported from Mumbai, where a nine-year-old boy in Juhu had suffocated on a Fun Time rivet. The autopsy again revealed the presence of the rivet in the boy's lung.

Before the executive meeting, the chairperson summarized the following facts as they pertained to the decision that would soon have to be made:

- Two deaths have resulted from product misuse.
- Fun Time meets all voluntary and industry safety standards.
- The company is under no pressure from any government agency to do anything.
- In its 100 years of being in business, Fun and Toys never heard of a serious accident or fatality resulting from the use or misuse of any of their products despite having thousands of small parts in them.
- Two deaths have occurred only nine months apart and both appear to involve the same part from the same product—Fun Time.

Initially, the chairperson considered the following alternatives:

1. Do nothing, as both accidents clearly resulted from product misuse.
2. Issue a statement to the consumer and put a warning label on the package, pointing out the hazards of misuse.
3. Modify the product.
4. Recall all Fun Time sets in the market.

The decision, of course, had to take the opinion of the company's top team into consideration. He, therefore, called a meeting on November 11 for the following people:

- General Manager – Manufacturing
- General Manager – Marketing
- General Manager – Finance
- Public Relations Manager
- Legal Advisor

Questions

1. What conflicting issues are likely to emerge in the meeting?
2. Who are the stakeholders of a toy-manufacturing firm and how should Madhusudan try to address the concerns of each stakeholder?

Cross-cultural Leadership and Diversity

Cross-cultural Leadership and Diversity

Learning Objectives

After studying this chapter, you should be able to:

- Understand why cross-cultural research on leadership is important.
- Understand the difficulties of studying cross-cultural leadership.
- Understand how cultural values are related to leader behavior.
- Understand how gender issues have been studied and the limitations of this research.
- Understand the findings in research on gender differences in leadership.
- Understand how to manage diversity and provide equal opportunities.

Most of the research on leadership during the past half century was conducted in the United States, Canada, and Western Europe. However, during the past decade interest in studying leadership in non-Western cultures has increased rapidly (Dickson, Den Hartog, & Michelson, 2003; Dorfman, 2003). A major issue is the extent to which leadership theories developed and tested in one culture can be generalized to different cultures. A related question is to identify differences among countries with regard to beliefs about effective leadership and actual management practices.

   Globalization and changing demographic patterns are making it more important for leaders to understand how to influence and manage people with different values, beliefs, and expectations. The diversity of people in leadership positions is also increasing, and there is strong interest in studying whether the ability to provide effective leadership is related to a person's gender, age, race, ethnic background, national origin, religion, sexual preference, or physical appearance (height, weight, attractiveness). There has been more leadership research on cross-cultural aspects and gender differences than on other types of diversity (Ospina & Foldy, 2009). This chapter will examine three distinct but interrelated subjects: (1) cross-cultural research in leadership, (2) gender differences in leadership, and (3) management of diversity.

Introduction to Cross-cultural Leadership

Research on cross-cultural leadership and leadership in global companies has been increasing rapidly during the last 10 years (Bass, 2008; Smith, Peterson, & Thomas, 2008). This section of the chapter explains why the research is important and describes several different types of cross-cultural research on leadership. The different ways culture can influence leaders and followers are explained, and examples of cross-cultural studies on leadership are described, including the multinational *GLOBE* project.

Importance of Cross-cultural Research

Cross-cultural research on leadership is important for several reasons (Ayman & Korabik, 2010; Connerley & Pedersen, 2005; Dorfman, 1996; House, Wright, & Aditya, 1997). Increasing globalization of organizations makes it more important to learn about effective leadership in different cultures. Leaders are increasingly confronted with the need to influence people from other cultures, and successful influence requires a good understanding of these cultures. Leaders must also be able to understand how people from different cultures view them and interpret their actions. To understand these issues, it is essential to determine if a leadership theory is valid in cultures that differ from the one in which it was developed. Some aspects of a leadership theory may be relevant for all cultures, but other aspects may apply only to a particular type of culture.

Cross-cultural research also requires researchers to consider a broader than usual range of variables and processes, which can provide new insights and improve leadership theories. Research to develop or validate taxonomies of leadership behavior in different cultures can reveal new aspects of behavior that are relevant for effective leadership. Examination of crosscultural differences may cause researchers to pay more attention to possible effects of situational variables not usually included in most leadership theories (e.g., religion, language, history, laws, political systems, ethnic subcultures). Finally, cross-cultural research poses some unique methodological challenges that may result in improved procedures for data collection and analysis.

Types of Cross-cultural Studies

As in the case of the leadership research conducted within a single culture, much of the cross-cultural research involves leader behavior, skills, and traits. The growing body of crosscultural research has examined different types of research questions (Brett et al., 1997). The most common approach has been to explain *cross-cultural differences* in leadership in terms of differences in cultural values. The cross-cultural research on leadership was strongly influenced by the early study of cultural values by Hofstede (1980, 1993), but since then several different sets of cultural values have been proposed (e.g., House et al., 1997; Javidan et al., 2006; Schwartz, 1992; Trompenaars, 1993). Some cross-cultural studies examine how beliefs about effective leadership behavior, skills, and traits are similar or different from one country to another. Other studies examine cross-cultural differences in the actual pattern of leadership behavior, or the effects on outcomes such as subordinate satisfaction, motivation, and performance. Only a small number of studies have examined how cultural values and leadership practices are both changing over time.

Cultural Influences on Leadership Behavior

Cultural values and traditions can influence the attitudes and behavior of managers in a number of different ways (Adler, 1997; Fu & Yukl, 2000; House et al., 1997; Lord

& Maher, 1991). The values are likely to be internalized by managers who grow up in a particular culture, and these values will influence their attitudes and behavior in ways that may not be conscious. In addition, cultural values are reflected in social norms about the way people relate to each other. Cultural norms specify acceptable forms of leadership behavior and may be formalized as social laws limiting the use of power. Most managers will conform to social norms about acceptable behavior, even if they have not internalized the norms. One reason is that deviation from social norms may result in diminished respect and increased social pressure from other members of the organization. Another reason for conformity with social norms is that the use of socially unacceptable forms of behavior is likely to undermine a leader's effectiveness.

Leadership behavior is influenced by other situational variables besides national culture (Bass, 1990; House et al., 1997, 2004). Some examples include the type of organization (e.g., profit vs. nonprofit, public corporation vs. private ownership), the type of industry (e.g., retailing, financial services, manufacturing, telecommunications), and characteristics of the managerial position (e.g., level and function of the manager, position power, and authority). Strong values in the organizational culture may or may not be consistent with the dominant cultural values, especially if an organization is a subsidiary of a foreign-owned company. The different determinants of leader behavior are not always congruent with each other. Some situational variables may have parallel effects across national cultures, but other situational variables may interact with national culture in complex ways.

Even when some types of leadership behaviors are not clearly supported by the prevailing cultural values and traditions in a country, it does not necessarily mean that these behaviors are ineffective. Managers who have little experience with a particular type of leadership behavior may not understand how effective it could be (House et al., 1997). When people learn that new practices are highly effective, they are likely to be widely imitated.

The values and traditions in a national culture can change over time, just as they do in an organizational culture. Cultural values are influenced by many types of changes (e.g., economic, political, social, technological). Countries in which socialism is being replaced by capitalism and emphasis on entrepreneurship are likely to see a shift toward stronger individualism and *performance orientation* values. Countries in which an autocratic political system is replaced by a democratic system are likely to become more accepting of participative leadership and empowerment in organizations. Countries in which strong gender differentiation is gradually replaced by gender equality can be expected to become more accepting of leadership practices that reflect traditional feminine attributes (e.g., nurturing, developing, building cooperative relationships). Cultural values and beliefs about the determinants of effective leadership are likely to change in consistent ways.

Cross-cultural Research on Behavior Differences

Much of the cross-cultural research examines differences among countries with regard to typical patterns of leadership behavior. Scores on behavior questionnaires are analyzed to determine whether a type of behavior is used more in one culture or country than another. For example, Dorfman et al. (1997) found that American managers used more participative leadership than managers in Mexico or Korea. However, a quantitative comparison of scale means from behavior description questionnaires is complicated by methodological problems such as confounding and lack of equivalence (Peng, Peterson, & Shyi, 1991). For example, lower scores may be obtained in one country because the behavior items have a different meaning there, or because respondents in that culture avoid giving very high scores on a questionnaire.

A smaller number of cross-cultural studies attempt to identify qualitative differences in the way a specific type of behavior is enacted in each country. For example, one study found that positive reward behavior was important for leadership effectiveness in different cultures, but the types of behavior rewarded and the way rewards were used differed across cultures (Podsakoff, Dorfman, Howell, & Todor, 1986). Another study found differences in the way managers communicated directions and feedback to subordinates (Smith et al., 1989). American managers were more likely to use a face-to-face meeting to provide directions to subordinates and to give negative feedback (criticism), whereas Japanese managers were more likely to use written memos for directions and to channel negative feedback through peers.

Cross-cultural Research on the Effects of Leader Behavior

Cross-cultural studies also examine differences in the relationship of leadership behavior to outcomes such as subordinate satisfaction and performance. For example, one study found that supportive behavior was significantly related to subordinate satisfaction and leadership effectiveness in the United States but not in Jordan or Saudi Arabia (Scandura, Von Glinow, & Lowe, 1999). Another study found that directive leadership was related to organizational commitment in Mexico and Taiwan, but not in the United States, South Korea, or Japan (Dorfman et al., 1997). Leader contingent reward was related to subordinate organizational commitment in the United States, Mexico, and Japan, but not in Korea or Taiwan. Participative leadership was related to subordinate performance in the United States but not in Mexico or South Korea.

A study by Schaubroeck, Lam, and Cha (2007) examined leadership by bank branch managers in the United States and Hong Kong. They found that the transformational leadership of the branch manager (rated by subordinates) was related to branch performance (rated by higher management) in both countries. However, the effect of transformational leadership on branch performance was enhanced by *power distance* and collectivism values, which were higher in Hong Kong than in the United States.

A study by Fu and Yukl (2000) conducted a cross-cultural study on managers of a multinational company with similar manufacturing facilities in the United States and China. The study used scenarios to assess manager beliefs about the effectiveness of different tactics for influencing people in their organizations. The results indicated that confrontational tactics such as rational persuasion and exchange were viewed more favorably by American managers than by Chinese managers, although rational persuasion was still rated one of the most effective tactics in both countries. The Chinese managers had a stronger preference than American managers for indirect tactics such as giving gifts and favors prior to a request, and getting assistance from a third party. Cross-cultural differences were also found in the ways some types of tactic were commonly used. For example, when attempting to influence a peer, the American managers seldom enlisted help from others except after encountering initial resistance to a direct request. Chinese managers were more likely to ask a mutual friend to find out (in a subtle way) how a peer was likely to respond before making a direct request. This informal approach would avoid embarrassment ("losing face") for the managers and for the peer if the request was refused.

Cultural Value Dimensions and Leadership

This section summarizes major findings in the research on how current cultural values are related to leadership beliefs, leadership behavior, and leadership development practices. The six value dimensions to be discussed include: (1) power distance, (2) *uncertainty*

TABLE 1	Cultural Beliefs about Ideal Leader Attributes
Rated Effective in Most Cultures	**Ratings Varied Across Cultures**
Visionary	Ambitious
Decisive	Cautious
Dynamic	Compassionate
Dependable	Domineering
Encouraging and positive	Formal
Excellence-oriented	Humble (self-effacing)
Honest and trustworthy	Independent
Skilled administrator	Risk taker
Team integrator	Self-sacrificing

Based on Dorfman, Hanges, and Brodbeck (2004).

avoidance, (3) individualism versus collectivism, (4) *gender egalitarianism,* (5) performance orientation, and (6) *humane orientation.*

Power Distance

Power distance involves the acceptance of an unequal distribution of power and status in organizations and institutions. In high power distance cultures, people expect the leaders to have greater authority and are more likely to comply with rules and directives without questioning or challenging them (Dickson et al., 2003). Subordinates are less willing to challenge bosses or express disagreement with them (Adsit, London, Crom, & Jones, 1997). More formal policies and rules are used, and managers consult less often with subordinates when making decisions (Smith et al., 2002).

Participative leadership is viewed as a more favorable leadership attribute in low power distance cultures such as Western Europe, New Zealand, and the United States than in high power distance countries such as Russia, China, Taiwan, Mexico, and Venezuela (Dorfman, Hanges, & Brodbeck, 2004). In low power distance countries, transformational (supportive and inspirational) leadership is more likely to be combined with a participative style of decision making (Den Hartog et al., 1999), whereas in high power distance countries, it is likely to be combined with a directive, autocratic style of decision making. In developing countries with a high power distance culture, people often prefer a "paternalistic" style that combines autocratic decisions with supportive behavior (Dickson et al., 2003; Dorfman et al., 1997).

Uncertainty Avoidance

In cultures with high avoidance of uncertainty, there is more fear of the unknown, and people desire more security, stability, and order. Social norms, tradition, detailed agreements, and certified expertise are more valued, because they offer a way to avoid uncertainty and disorder (Den Hartog et al., 1999; Dickson et al., 2003). Examples of countries with high uncertainty avoidance include France, Spain, Germany, Switzerland, Russia, and India. Some countries with a lower concern about avoiding uncertainty include the United States, United Kingdom, Canada, Denmark, and Sweden.

When there is high uncertainty avoidance, valued qualities for managers include being reliable, orderly, and cautious, rather than flexible, innovative, and risk taking. Managers use more detailed planning, formal rules and standard procedures, and monitoring of activities, and there is less delegation (Offermann & Hellmann, 1997). There is more centralized control over decisions involving change or innovation. For example, one study found that managers in the United Kingdom expected more innovation and initiative from subordinates, whereas managers in Germany expected more reliability and punctuality (Stewart et al., 1994). The study also found that management development in Germany emphasized acquisition of specialized knowledge and experience in a functional area, whereas in the United Kingdom, there was more emphasis on general skills attained from a variety of job experiences.

Individualism (vs. Collectivism)

Individualism is the extent to which the needs and autonomy of individuals are more important than the collective needs of groups, organizations, or society. In an individualistic culture, individual rights are more important than social responsibilities, and people are expected to take care of themselves (Dickson et al., 2003; Gelfand, Bhawuk, Nishi, & Bechtold, 2004; Hofstede, 1980). Examples of countries with strong values for individualism include the United States, Australia, England, and the Netherlands.

The implications of collectivistic values depend in part on whether they are more important for in-groups or the larger society, but most of the cross-cultural research has emphasized *in-group collectivism*. The in-groups may be based on family ties, religious or ethnic background, membership in a political party, or a stable, collaborative business relationship. In a collectivistic culture, membership in cohesive in-groups is an important aspect of a person's self-identity, and loyalty to the group is an important value. People are less likely to change jobs, and members are more likely to volunteer their time to do extra work and "organizational citizenship behaviors" (Jackson, Colquitt, Wesson, & Zapata-Phelan, 2006). In turn, the groups are expected to take care of their members. Examples of countries with strong collectivistic values include China, Argentina, Mexico, and Sweden.

Because people are more motivated to satisfy their self-interests and personal goals in an individualistic culture, it is more difficult for leaders to inspire strong commitment to team or organizational objectives (Jung & Avolio, 1999; Triandis et al., 1993). The preference for rewards based on individual achievements and performance also makes it more difficult for leaders to use team-based rewards and recognition (Kirkman & Shapiro, 2000). The emphasis on individual rights and autonomy makes it more difficult to create a strong culture of shared values for social responsibility, cooperation, and ethical behavior. Because of the transitory nature of careers, selection is likely to be more important than training for ensuring that people have adequate skills.

Gender Egalitarianism

Gender egalitarianism is the extent to which men and women receive equal treatment, and both masculine and feminine attributes are considered important and desirable. In cultures with high gender egalitarianism, there is less differentiation of sex roles and most jobs are not segregated by gender. Women have more equal opportunity to be selected for important leadership positions, although access is still greater for public sector positions than in business corporations. In the absence of strongly differentiated gender-role expectations, men and women leaders are less limited in their behavior, and there is less bias in how their behavior is evaluated by subordinates and by bosses. Examples of countries with strong gender egalitarian values include Norway, Sweden, Denmark, and the Netherlands. Countries with a low level of gender egalitarianism include Japan, Italy, Mexico, and Switzerland.

Cultural values for gender egalitarianism have implications for the selection and evaluation of leaders and for the types of leadership behavior considered desirable and socially acceptable (Dickson et al., 2003; Emrich, Denmark, & Den Hartog, 2005). In cultures with strong "masculine" values for toughness and assertiveness, "feminine" attributes such as compassion, empathy, and intuition are not viewed as important for effective leadership (Den Hartog, 2004; Den Hartog et al., 1999). Participative leadership, supportive leadership, and relations-oriented aspects of transformational leadership are viewed less favorably in cultures with low gender egalitarianism. Leaders are more likely to use direct, confrontational forms of interpersonal influence rather than indirect, subtle forms of influence (e.g., Fu & Yukl, 2000; Holtgraves, 1997). Leaders whose actions display humility, compassion, or conciliation are more likely to be viewed as weak and ineffective in a "masculine" culture.

Performance Orientation

The extent to which high performance and individual achievement are valued is called performance orientation (Javidan, 2004). Related values and attributes include hard work, responsibility, competitiveness, persistence, initiative, pragmatism, and acquisition of new skills. In societies with strong performance orientation values, results are emphasized more than people. What you do is more important than who you are (e.g., gender, family or ethnic background), and individual achievements can be an important source of status and self-esteem. Accomplishing a task effectively can take priority over individual needs or family loyalty.

In a high performance orientation culture, there is more emphasis on leader behaviors that are relevant for improving performance and efficiency. Examples include setting challenging goals or standards, developing action plans with schedules and deadlines, expressing confidence that subordinates can improve performance, developing job-relevant skills in subordinates, encouraging initiative, and providing praise and rewards for achievements. In a high performance orientation culture, the selection of members for a team with an important task is likely to be based on talent, not on friendship or family relations.

A strong concern for task performance is widely believed to be a requirement for effective leadership in any country. Economic development is aided by a strong performance orientation, but concern for improving performance may be stronger in rapidly developing countries than in a country where widespread prosperity already exists (Javidan, 2004). Cultural values may have less influence on task-oriented behavior than core organizational values and a leader's individual needs and personality traits (e.g., achievement motivation, internal locus of control). Taken together, these factors help explain the lack of consistent results in cross-cultural studies on the effects of performance orientation values.

Humane Orientation

Humane orientation means a strong concern for the welfare of other people and the willingness to sacrifice one's own self-interest to help others. Key values include altruism, benevolence, kindness, compassion, love, and generosity. These values tend to be associated with stronger needs for affiliation and belongingness than for pleasure, achievement, or power. Altruism and kindness are not limited to a person's family or ethnic/religious in-group, but instead include a humanitarian concern for everyone. Societies with a strong humane orientation encourage and reward individuals for being friendly, caring, generous, and kind to others (Kabasakal & Bodur, 2004). Such societies are likely to invest more resources in educating and training people for careers and in providing health care and social services to people. The humane values for an individual are influenced by family experiences, parenting, and religious teaching as well as by cultural norms.

Humane orientation values encourage supportive leadership behaviors such as being considerate of a subordinate's needs and feelings, showing sympathy when a subordinate is upset, providing mentoring and coaching when appropriate, offering to provide assistance when needed to deal with a personal problem, and acting friendly and accepting. A leader with strong humane orientation values is likely to be more tolerant, patient, and helpful with subordinates who make mistakes or are having difficulty learning a new task. Humane orientation values are also associated with participative leadership, servant leadership, and teambuilding behaviors (encouraging cooperation and mutual trust). The key values are consistent with a diplomatic, conciliatory style of conflict management that seeks to restore harmonious relations and satisfy each party's important needs. The interest in building friendly, cooperative relationships can extend to people outside of the leader's team or unit, such as

TABLE 2	GLOBE Culture Clusters	
Eastern Europe	**Anglo**	**Sub-Saharan Africa**
Albania	Australia	Namibia
Georgia	Canada	Nigeria
Greece	Ireland	South Africa (black)
Hungary	New Zealand	Zambia
Kazakhstan	South Africa (white)	Zimbabwe
Poland	United Kingdom	
Russia	USA	
Slovenia		
Latin America	**Nordic Europe**	**Confucian Asia**
Argentina	Denmark	China
Bolivia	Finland	Hong Kong
Brazil	Sweden	Japan
Colombia		Singapore
Costa Rica		South Korea
Ecuador	**Germanic Europe**	Taiwan
El Salvador	Austria	
Guatemala	Germany	
Mexico	Netherlands	
Venezuela	Switzerland	
Latin Europe	**Middle East**	**Southern Asia**
France	Egypt	India
Israel	Kuwait	Indonesia
Italy	Morocco	Iran
Portugal	Qatar	Malaysia
Spain	Turkey	Philippines
Switzerland (French)		Thailand

Based on Vroom and Yetton (1973, p. 13).

developing a network of external contacts by socializing with people and doing favors for them. In some countries, humane orientation can also take other forms, such as socializing informally with subordinates and acting paternalistic with regard to the career and social welfare of subordinates and their families.

Culture Clusters

The *cultural value dimensions* are moderately intercorrelated, and examining differences for a single value dimension without controlling for the others makes it difficult to determine their independent effects on leadership beliefs and behavior. For example, in a country that has high power distance and low uncertainty tolerance, it is not clear how much each value influences the emphasis on centralized decisions for a company. For this reason, researchers have grouped countries into clusters based on regional proximity and similarity in language, ethnic background, and religion (Dorfman et al., 2004; Gupta, Hanges, & Dorfman, 2002). The GLOBE researchers grouped 60 countries into 10 clusters, and a discriminant analysis confirmed that the classification of countries into clusters accurately reflected differences in the nine cultural values for each country. The nations in each cluster are shown in Table 2.

The clusters were compared with regard to leadership beliefs, and differences were found among clusters for some of the beliefs about effective leadership. For example, participative leadership is considered more important in the Anglo, Germanic Europe, and Nordic Europe clusters than in the Eastern Europe, Southern Asia, Confucian Asia, and Middle East clusters. Showing a strong humane concern for others is considered more important for effective leadership in the Southern Asia and Sub-Saharan Africa clusters than in the Germanic Europe or Latin Europe clusters. Future research will look more closely at differences in actual leadership behavior that correspond to the differences in values and implicit theories about effective leadership.

Evaluation of Cross-cultural Research

The research on cultural values finds important differences that are relevant for beliefs about effective leadership and actual behavior of leaders. However, conceptual and methodological weaknesses are common, and limitations in the research have been pointed out by several scholars (e.g., Jepson, 2009; Kirkman, Lowe, & Gibson, 2006; Smith, 2006). This section of the chapter summarizes the limitations and suggests some promising research questions for the future.

The conceptual frameworks used in cross-cultural research on leadership affect interpretation of results. Different sets of cultural value dimensions have been proposed by scholars, and disagreements about desirable features have not been resolved. All of the current taxonomies have limitations, and researchers continue to seek a more comprehensive and useful way to describe cultural dimensions. The reliance on broadly defined leadership behaviors in many studies makes it more difficult to get a clear picture of cross-cultural differences in behavior. To understand the joint influence of cultural and organizational values on leadership behavior, it is essential to measure specific aspects of this behavior in addition to broad categories such as participative leadership, supportive leadership, and transformational leadership. The selection of variables and interpretation of results can be biased by cultural differences among researchers in their underlying values and assumptions about human nature and organizational processes (Boyacigiller & Adler, 1991). To minimize this type of problem it is advisable to have a research team with qualified representatives from the different cultures included in the study.

Much of the early research used convenience samples from only a few countries, rather than representative samples from many different countries with controls for type of organization and type of respondent. The assumption that cultural values identified for a nation apply to all types of organizations in that country overlooks the importance of organizational culture, regional differences, and individual differences. Levels of analysis problems are caused by using an overall culture score for values to explain the behavior and performance of individuals. When cross-cultural studies have large samples, it is easy to find significant differences, and researchers have not been consistent about reporting whether the differences have much practical significance.

Another limitation in many cross-cultural studies is too much reliance on survey questionnaires. The serious biases in survey measures of leadership were explained earlier, and additional problems are common when fixed-response questionnaires are used in cross-cultural research. It can be difficult to achieve equivalence in meaning when questionnaires are translated into another language, and there are cultural differences in response biases even for scales with equivalent language (Atwater, Wang, Smither, & Fleenor, 2009; Harzing, 2006). An inherent bias in most survey research on cross-cultural leadership is the assumption that leadership is only a consequence of culture, when it is also a determinant of culture and an interpreter of culture. The use of ethnography and a detailed historical perspective are advocated as more useful approaches for research on the relationship between leadership and culture (Guthey & Jackson, 2011).

The utility of many cross-cultural studies is limited by their failure to acknowledge these problems. Even for well-designed studies, the interpretation of results is often difficult. Many studies fail to include information that could help to explain the reason for cross-cultural differences in leadership. It is useful to learn that a particular type of leadership behavior is used more often or has stronger effects in a particular culture, but it is even better to learn why.

Many research questions need to be examined more closely in the future. Examples of relevant questions for future cross-cultural research on leadership include the following:

1. How does actual behavior of leaders differ across cultural value clusters and for different countries?
2. How are leader values and behaviors jointly influenced by personality (and developmental experiences), company culture, and national culture?
3. What types of leadership traits, skills, and developmental experiences are most useful to prepare someone for a leadership assignment in a different culture?
4. How useful is the distinction between actual and ideal cultural values for understanding implicit theories of leadership and patterns of leadership behavior?
5. What are the implications for leaders when a global organization's values are inconsistent with the social values in some countries where the organization has facilities?
6. What is necessary for effective leadership in a multi-national team with members who differ in their cultural values?
7. How fast are cultural values changing in developing countries, and how are the culture changes relevant for leadership?
8. How much agreement is there across cultures with regard to the essential requirements for ethical leadership, and what are the points of disagreement?

Gender and Leadership

A topic of great interest among practitioners as well as scholars is the possible difference between men and women in leadership behavior and effectiveness. A related topic of great importance is the reason for continued discrimination against women in leadership selection. This section of the chapter will briefly discuss both topics and review what has been learned about gender and leadership.

Sex-based Discrimination

Widespread discrimination is clearly evident in the low number of women who hold important, high-level leadership positions in most types of organizations. The strong tendency to favor men over women in filling high-level leadership positions has been referred to as the *"glass ceiling."* Only a small number of nations have a female head of state (e.g., prime minister, president), and the number of women in top executive positions in large business organizations is also very small, although it has been increasing in recent years (Adler, 1996; Catalyst, 2003; Powell & Graves, 2003; Ragins, Townsend, & Mattis, 1998). In the complete absence of sex-based discrimination, the number of women in chief executive positions in business and government should be close to 50 percent.

Theories of Male Advantage

Throughout the twentieth century, gender-based discrimination was supported by age-old beliefs that men are more qualified than women for leadership roles (Ayman & Korabik, 2010). These beliefs involved assumptions about the traits and skills required for effective leadership in organizations (implicit theories), assumptions about inherent differences between men and women (gender stereotypes), and assumptions about appropriate behavior for men and women (role expectations). As noted earlier, the implicit theories and gender stereotypes are also influenced by cultural values for gender egalitarianism.

There is no empirical support for the belief that men are more qualified to be leaders, and laws now exist in the United States to stop sex-based discrimination. The antidiscrimination laws are based on the premise that men and women are equally qualified to hold leadership positions. Gender stereotypes have been slowly changing, but the belief that men are more qualified to be leaders still persists in segments of the population and it remains strong in countries where it is supported by cultural values.

Theory of Feminine Advantage

A more recent controversy is fueled by claims that women are more likely than men to possess the values and skills necessary for effective leadership in modern organizations (Book, 2000; Carr-Ruffino, 1993; Grant, 1988; Hegelsen, 1990; Rosener, 1990). The difference is a result of childhood experiences, parent-child interactions, and socialization practices that reflect cultural *sex-role stereotypes* and beliefs about gender differences and appropriate occupations for men and women (Cockburn, 1991). These experiences encourage "feminine" values such as kindness, compassion, nurturing, and sharing. Proponents of the "feminine advantage" theory contend that women are more concerned with consensus building, inclusiveness, and interpersonal relations; they are more willing to develop and nurture subordinates and share power with them. Women are believed to have more empathy, rely more on intuition, and be more sensitive to feelings and the quality of relationships.

Proponents of the feminine advantage claim that the changing nature of leadership in organizations has increased the relevance of skills and values that are stronger in women than in men. However, as with earlier claims that men are more qualified to be leaders, the claims that women are more qualified appear to be based on weak assumptions and exaggerated gender stereotypes. Evaluation of assertions about gender superiority in leadership requires a careful consideration of the findings in the empirical research.

Explanations for the Glass Ceiling

Biased beliefs about the skills and behaviors necessary for effective leadership are one reason for sex-based discrimination. For a long time, it was assumed that effective leaders must be confident, task-oriented, competitive, objective, decisive, and assertive, all of which were traditionally viewed as masculine attributes (Schein, 1975; Stogdill, 1974). Effective leadership also requires strong interpersonal skills, and leadership behaviors traditionally viewed as feminine (e.g., supporting, developing, empowering). These skills and behaviors were always relevant for effective leadership, but now they are more important than in earlier times because of changing conditions in work organizations. As popular conceptions of effective leadership become more accurate and comprehensive, role expectations for leaders will become less gender biased.

Sex-based discrimination in leadership selection also reflects the influence of popular stereotypes and role expectations for men and women (Heilman, 2001). For a long time, women were assumed to be unable or unwilling to use the masculine behaviors considered essential for effective leadership. Some laboratory studies found that even when women leaders use masculine behaviors, they are evaluated less favorably than men who use them (e.g., Eagly, Makhijani, & Klonsky, 1992; Rojahn & Willemsen, 1994). However, the effects of gender stereotypes on evaluation of female managers may be overstated in laboratory studies with students. The experience of working for men and women leaders over a period of time can reduce the effects of gender stereotypes on evaluation of the leaders (Powell, 1990). As gender stereotypes change over time in the general population, they will probably become less important as a source of biased role expectations for leaders. Unfortunately, the changes in gender role stereotypes and implicit theories have been slow, especially among male managers (Brenner, Tomkiewicz, & Schein, 1989; Epitropaki & Martin, 2004; Powell, Butterfield, & Parent, 2002).

Other possible reasons for the glass ceiling have been suggested (Ragins et al., 1998; Schein, 2001; Tharenou, Latimer, & Conroy, 1994). The explanations include (1) lack of opportunity to gain experience and visibility in types of positions that would facilitate advancement, (2) higher standards of performance for women than for men, (3) exclusion of women from informal networks that aid advancement, (4) lack of encouragement and opportunity for developmental activities, (5) lack of opportunity for effective mentoring, (6) lack of strong efforts to gain access to leadership positions, (7) difficulties created by competing family demands, (8) lack of strong action by top management to ensure equal opportunity, (9) bias to select and promote individuals who are similar to the (male) managers who make the decisions, and (10) intentional efforts by some men to retain control of the most powerful positions for themselves. The explanations are not mutually exclusive, and they may combine to create an inhospitable corporate climate for female managers.

Interest in studying barriers to advancement for women has been increasing. A study by Bell and Nkomo (2001) found that one of the major barriers (especially for black women) was limited access to social and informal networks in their organizations. A study by Babcock and Laschever (2003) found that women were less likely than men to ask for promotion and initiate the types of negotiations likely to favor it. A study by Lyness and Heilman (2006) found that women needed more of the required skills than men to advance to executive positions, and the difference was greater for the types of positions traditionally held by men. These studies and others have increased our knowledge about barriers to advancement for women, but more research is needed to determine the relative importance of different causes and how the different causes interact to limit the number of women in top leadership positions.

A small number of U.S. companies have made concerted effort over the past two decades to eliminate barriers to advancement of women into top management positions. An example is Xerox, where in the 1980s, female employees formed a Women's Alliance to influence top management to promote more women to management positions. The effort was successful, and Xerox is routinely ranked among the best places for women to work. In 2001, Xerox was one of only a small number of Fortune 500 companies with a female CEO, and her successor CEO at Xerox was an African-American women. The events at Xerox suggest that faster progress could be made if more companies made a similar effort to eliminate barriers to the selection of women and minorities for top management positions.

Findings in Research on Gender Differences

Many studies have compared men and women leaders with regard to their leadership behavior. Reviews of this research on gender and leadership disagree about the results (e.g., Bass, 1990; Dobbins & Platz, 1986; Eagly, Darau, & Makhijani, 1995; Eagly & Johnson, 1990; Powell, 1993). Some reviewers concluded that there is no evidence of important gender differences in leadership behaviors or skills. Other reviewers concluded that there are gender-related differences for some behaviors or skills in some situations. A debate published in *Leadership Quarterly* shows the complexity of the issues and the extent to which scholars disagree (Eagly & Carli, 2003a, 2003b; Vecchio, 2002, 2003).

Many of the early studies on gender differences in leadership behavior involved task and relationship behavior. Eagly and Johnson (1990) conducted a meta-analysis of the gender studies with actual managers and found no gender differences in the use of task-oriented behavior or supportive behavior. However, their study did find that participative leadership was used slightly more by women than by men. In a more recent meta-analysis (Eagly, Johannesen-Schmidt, & Van Engen, 2003), women used slightly more transformational leadership behavior than men, and the primary difference was for individualized consideration, which includes supportive behavior and efforts to develop subordinate's skills and confidence. Results for transactional leadership were mixed and difficult to interpret.

Results from studies on gender differences in leadership effectiveness are also inconsistent. A meta-analysis by Eagly et al. (1995) found no overall difference in effectiveness for men and women managers. However, when role requirements for different types of managerial positions were identified, male managers were more effective than women managers in positions that required strong task skills, and women managers were more effective in positions that required strong interpersonal skills. Because most leadership positions require both types of skills, gender is unlikely to be useful as a predictor of leadership effectiveness for these positions.

Limitations of Research on Gender Differences

Serious limitations in much of the research on gender differences complicate interpretation of the results. One major problem is the lack of a clear definition of gender (Ely & Padavic, 2007). In some cases, it refers to anatomical sex (male vs. female), and in others it refers to a set of personal characteristics often associated more with one sex than with another. These conceptions of gender characteristics are not constant across studies, and it is seldom clear how much empirical support exists for strong differences between men and women.

In comparative studies, a major problem is contamination from extraneous variables (see Ely & Padavic, 2007; Lefkowitz, 1994). Gender is often correlated with other variables known to affect leader behavior (e.g., level, function, time in position, type of organization), and most studies of gender differences in leadership do not control for the differential effects of organizational variables on men and women leaders. People may be attracted to a profession (e.g., women to nursing, men to police work) because it involves the use of "natural" skills and behaviors, or because their opportunities are limited and their choices influenced by strong sex-role stereotypes. If a study includes more women than men in types of leadership positions that require a lot of supportive and participative behavior, then (unless type of position is controlled) the results will seem to indicate that women leaders are generally more supportive and participative. If the study has more men in types of leadership positions that require assertive and decisive behavior, then the results will seem to indicate that men generally have more of these attributes. Unfortunately, most comparative studies reporting male-female differences do not control for this type of contamination.

Another type of biased result can occur in a comparative study that fails to take into account how organizational factors may have a differential influence on the skills of men and women who are in the same type of leadership position. For example, if strong interpersonal and political skills facilitate advancement into executive positions but the standards for selection are more difficult for women than for men, then fewer women will advance but they will have more of these skills than the men who advance. Unless this bias in taken into account, the results comparing male to female executives may be incorrectly interpreted as showing that women generally have stronger interpersonal and political skills.

Differential role expectations can also influence the measurement of leader behavior, skills, or performance for men and women in the same type of leadership position (Eagly & Chin, 2010). For example, if most raters share common gender stereotypes, then their ratings will reflect a combination of a leader's real behavior and the rater's biased perception of it. Thus, stereotypes about gender (or race, ethnic background, age, education) can result in inflated differences when in reality there is no difference.

On the other hand, for male and female leaders in similar positions, role expectations that influence leader behavior can make gender differences more difficult to discover. For example, if strong role expectations in an organization influence women to exhibit "masculine" attributes such as toughness and assertiveness, then it will be more difficult to find significant differences between men and women on these attributes. In an organization without strong role expectations, actual gender differences are more likely to emerge and be noted. Even if women in some type of leadership position have more of the relevant skills than men in that position, ratings of overall leadership effectiveness may fail to reflect this difference if the raters have different role expectations for women, or ratings are biased by the belief that women are less able to do the job effectively.

Another difficulty in evaluating results in research on gender differences in leadership is caused by the type of data analysis and reporting of results. Many studies report tests of statistical differences without reporting effect sizes. In studies with large samples, it is possible to find a difference that is statistically significant but has no practical significance. Knowing the sex of a leader is of no practical help for predicting the person's behavior or effectiveness when there are large differences within each gender group. Studies that fail to provide evidence of practical significance perpetuate exaggerated stereotypes about men and women.

The utility of meta-analyses for interpreting research on gender differences is limited when the results in the published literature are not representative. Significant but small gender differences may result from unrepresentative sampling of studies and confounding within some studies. Assessment of gender differences is seldom the primary purpose for conducting a survey field study on leadership, but most studies include gender in the demographic information about the sample. It is easy to check on any gender differences, and the popularity of the topic means that significant relationships involving gender are likely to be reported more often than nonsignificant relationships.

Identifying Causes and Reducing Discrimination

Most studies on gender and leadership are focused on determining if there is a difference between men and women, not on determining the cause of any differences. If the research is able to find differences with both statistical and practical significance, then it is essential to discover the reasons for them. The types of confounding and biases described earlier are one likely cause of the differences. If significant gender differences remain after these biases are removed, then a possible explanation involves biological differences created by evolutionary processes that occurred over thousands of years in primitive times (Browne, 2006; Geary, 1998). Another possible explanation is that differential treatment during childhood causes men and women to have different values, traits, skills, and ways of dealing with situations. Although not mutually exclusive, these explanations lead to different implications for the selection and training of leaders and the elimination of unfair discrimination. Unfortunately, most studies on gender differences in leadership provide little information about the reasons for any differences that are found. In the absence of such evidence, people are more likely to attribute gender differences to inherent biological factors than to things that could be changed.

Equally important to understanding the reasons for any real gender differences is the need to find ways to eliminate unfair discrimination. The essential skills and behaviors for effective leadership differ somewhat across situations, and some types of leadership positions may provide a slight advantage either to men or to women. However, any gender advantage is likely to be a small one, which means that gender should not be an important qualification for the position.

Female candidates are likely to be rated as less qualified than male candidates for many types of leadership positions unless accurate information about each person's skill and experience is collected and used in the selection decision (Heilman, 2001; Heilman & Haynes, 2005). To avoid bias from gender stereotypes and prejudice, a special effort should be made to ensure that the relevant skills are accurately assessed when selecting leaders. If possible, selection and promotion decisions should made by people who understand how to avoid bias resulting from stereotypes and implicit assumptions. Affirmative action guidelines can provide helpful guidance for avoiding unfair discrimination in the selection of leaders. For leadership positions that require skills more likely to be possessed by male (or female) candidates, providing relevant training and developmental experiences to any candidates who need them will help equalize opportunities for advancement.

Summary of Leader Gender Research

More systematic and comprehensive research is needed to determine the extent of any gender differences in leadership and the reasons for them. It is essential to examine how organizational and cultural factors influence the perceptions and behaviors that shape gender identity. Given the inconsistent findings and limitations of research on gender differences in leadership, the conclusion reached by Powell (1990, p. 74) still seems correct:

> There is little reason to believe that either women or men make superior managers, or that women and men are different types of managers. Instead, there are likely to be excellent, average, and poor managerial performers within each sex. Success in today's highly competitive marketplace calls for organizations to make best use of the talent available to them. To do this, they need to identify, develop, encourage, and promote the most effective managers, regardless of sex.

Managing Diversity

Diversity can take many forms, including differences in race, ethnic identity, age, gender, education, physical appearance, socio-economic level, and sexual orientation. Diversity in the workforce is increasing in the United States and Europe (Milliken & Martins, 1996). More women are entering traditionally male jobs, the number of older workers is increasing, and there is more diversity with regard to ethnic, religious, and racial backgrounds. The increasing number of joint ventures, mergers, and strategic alliances is bringing together people from different types of organizations and national cultures.

Diversity offers potential benefits and costs for a group or organization (Cox & Blake, 1991; Kochan et al., 2003; Milliken & Martins, 1996; Triandis et al., 1994; van Knippenberg & Schippers, 2007). A greater variety of perspectives increases creativity, and full utilization of a diverse workforce will increase the amount of available talent for filling important jobs. However, diversity can also result in more distrust and conflict, lower satisfaction, and higher turnover. An organization is less likely to have shared values and strong member commitment when it has many diverse members who identify primarily with their own subgroup. Thus, managing diversity is an important but a difficult responsibility of leaders in the twenty-first century.

Fostering Appreciation and Tolerance

Leaders can do many things to foster appreciation and tolerance for diversity. Some recommended action steps for individual leaders are listed in Table 3. These actions can be divided into two categories that are similar to the distinction made earlier for ethical leadership behavior. Some actions seek to encourage tolerance and appreciation, whereas other actions challenge discrimination and intolerance.

Diversity training programs provide a formal approach to encourage tolerance, understanding, and appreciation (Cox & Blake, 1991). One objective of diversity training is to create a better understanding of diversity problems and the need for self-awareness about stereotyping and intolerance. Many people are not aware of their own stereotypes and implicit assumptions about diverse groups, nor do they understand that even when real differences exist, they are usually small and do not apply to many people in the group being stereotyped.

TABLE 3	Guidelines for Participative Leadership

Encourage Tolerance and Appreciation

- Set an example in your own behavior of appreciation for diversity.
- Encourage respect for individual differences.
- Promote understanding of different values, beliefs, and traditions.
- Explain the benefits of diversity for the team or organization.
- Encourage and support others who promote tolerance of diversity.

Discourage Intolerance and Discrimination

- Discourage use of stereotypes to describe people.
- Identify biased beliefs and role expectations for women or minorities.
- Challenge people who make prejudiced comments.
- Speak out to protest against unfair treatment based on prejudice.
- Take disciplinary action to stop harassment of women or minorities.

Another objective of diversity training is to educate employees about real cultural or demographic differences and how to respond to them in the workplace. The specific aspects of diversity that are included vary depending on the program (e.g., ethnic background, religion, national culture, age differences, employee sex, sexual orientation, physical disabilities). It is important for people to understand how differences can be an advantage rather than a liability. Avon, Hewlett-Packard, Mobil Oil, Procter & Gamble, and Xerox are just a few examples of companies that have used such programs. A problem with some diversity training programs is their emphasis on placing blame for discrimination rather than on increasing self-awareness and mutual understanding (Nemetz & Christensen, 1996). Leaders who implement diversity training should keep the content of the program consistent with an appealing vision of what appreciation of diversity can mean for all members of the organization.

Structural mechanisms to uncover discrimination and reward tolerance are also helpful. Examples include (1) appraisal criteria that include diversity issues, (2) task forces or advisory committees to help identify discrimination or intolerance and develop remedies, (3) measures that allow systematic monitoring of progress, and (4) hotlines or other special mechanisms that make it easier for employees to report discrimination and intolerance. Efforts to change attitudes are more likely to be successful when diversity training is directed at people who have not already formed strong prejudices, and the organization has a culture that supports appreciation for diversity (Nemetz & Christensen, 1996).

Providing Equal Opportunity

To make full use of the talent represented by the diverse members of the organization, it is essential to eliminate constraints that prevent qualified people from selection for important positions. Many things can be done to facilitate equal opportunity and reduce *discrimination in personnel decisions* (Cox, 1991). Surveys of employee attitudes can be used to identify problems and assess progress. The organizational communications media can be used to describe what is being done to promote equal opportunity and report achievements.

Unfair discrimination can be reduced by the use of selection criteria based on relevant skills rather than biased conceptions. The assessments used for selection and promotion decisions will be more accurate if the raters who make them are trained or otherwise helped to reduce biases caused by racial, ethnic, or gender role stereotypes. The stereotypes can include both positive and negative features, and when they lurk below conscious awareness, their influence on the interpretation and evaluation of another person's behavior is more difficult to detect (Eagly & Chin, 2010). One method for reducing this type of bias is a "structured free recall" intervention (Baltes, Bauer, & Frensch, 2007; Bauer & Baltes, 2002). The raters are asked to recall examples of both positive and negative behaviors by a candidate before rating the person's qualifications for a position.

The advancement by women and minorities is facilitated by mentorship programs that provide adequate advice, encouragement, and assistance. Leadership development programs should provide equal opportunities for people who want to learn relevant skills and gain valuable experience. Affirmative action programs can be helpful if they are well designed and implemented (Harrison et al., 2006). The programs are likely to be less controversial and more successful if the need for them is clearly understood by the members of an organization, and ways are found to encourage affirmative action without imposing reverse discrimination.

The human resources management department usually has primary responsibility for many of the processes that affect diversity and equal opportunity, such as recruiting, selection, employee orientation, performance appraisal, training, and mentoring. However, the responsibility for providing equal opportunity should not be relegated solely to human resource staff specialists. A successful effort to improve diversity and equal opportunity requires strong support by top management and managers at all levels of the organization.

Other approaches for achieving equal opportunity are possible at a national level. Corporate boards of directors have only about 13 to 15 percent women members in the United States and Europe, and efforts are being made to help women penetrate this glass ceiling. Corporate boards determine the selection of CEOs, and more balanced boards should help to increase the number of women CEOs. Some Europe countries have been adopting quotas for the number of women directors. For example, Norway adopted a quota in 2002 and has already reached the mandated level of 40 percent women directors. France and Spain recently passed a similar quota. Efforts to eliminate discrimination in the selection of leaders are not limited to legal options. Individuals can initiate voluntary campaigns to increase equal opportunity, and the following example describes what one CEO is doing in Britain (Baker, 2011).

> Helena Morrissey, the CEO of Newton Investment Management, is trying to increase the number of women on the boards of British companies. In November of 2010, Morrissey formed the 30 percent club to put pressure on companies to employ 30% female directors. She has already persuaded more than 20 CEOs of major British companies to accept this challenge. There are some compelling statistics in favor of her campaign. In a survey of 279 companies in Europe, Brazil, Russia, China and India from 2007 to 2009, McKinsey & Co. found that companies with the greatest share of women on their executive committees had a 41 percent higher return on equity than companies with no women members. A study in the USA found that firms with three or more female directors had a 45 percent higher return on equity and sales than firms without female directors. The timing seems good for Morrissey's initiative. The recent financial crisis has resulted in more challenges to company boards for their lack of adequate oversight of top management, and adding more women directors may make boards more independent. Other countries across Europe are adopting quotas, and unless voluntary efforts are successful in Britain, there will be pressure to adopt quotas there as well.

Summary

With the rapid pace of globalization and economic development, cross-cultural leadership has become an important topic for research. Some leader attributes are considered important for effective leadership in all cultures that have been studied, but other attributes vary in importance from one culture to another. Cultural values and beliefs are likely to influence actual leader behavior, especially when they are also consistent with core values for the organization.

The amount of cross-cultural research is increasing, but the methodological difficulties in conducting this type of research are substantial. Equivalence of meaning is not assured in many studies, the sampling procedures are inadequate, controls for contaminating factors are absent, explanatory variables are not included, and interpretation of results is questionable. Faster progress may require greater use of large-scale research projects such as GLOBE.

Sex-based discrimination in the selection and promotion of leaders continues to be a serious problem in large organizations. There are several different reasons for such discrimination, but more research is needed to understand the causes and find ways to deal with them. Many studies have examined gender-based differences in leadership behavior and effectiveness, but the findings are weak and inconsistent. Future studies need to control for effects of likely contaminating variables, report the magnitude of any significant differences that are found, and measure processes that provide insight into the reasons for the differences.

An important responsibility for leaders in this new century is the management of diversity, which can take many forms. Leaders play an essential role in helping to bring about equal opportunity and elimination of unfair discrimination in selection and promotion decisions. Leaders can do many things to encourage tolerance and appreciation of diversity in organizations. All leaders in the organization should share the responsibility for improving diversity and ensuring equal opportunity. Leadership at the national level is also important in the continuing efforts to eliminate unfair discrimination for all minorities and ethnic groups.

Review and Discussion Questions

1. What are the major research questions in studies of cross-cultural leadership?
2. Why is cross-cultural research on leadership important and worthwhile?
3. What are some difficulties in conducting cross-cultural research on leadership?
4. What cultural value dimensions have been identified, and how are they related to leadership?
5. What leadership attributes are universally viewed as effective and desirable?
6. What leadership attributes have the greatest cross-cultural variability?
7. Why is a "glass ceiling" for women, and what can be done about the problem?
8. What can leaders do to manage diversity in organizations?

Key Terms

cross-cultural differences	gender egalitarianism	performance orientation
cultural value dimensions	glass ceiling	power distance
discrimination in personnel	GLOBE	sex-role stereotypes
decisions	humane orientation	uncertainty avoidance
diversity training	in-group collectivism	

CASE 1

Madison, Jones, and Conklin

After graduating from a prestigious business school, Laura Kravitz accepted a job at Madison, Jones, and Conklin, a medium-sized firm that did accounting and consulting projects for corporate clients. After a series of successful assignments working as a member of a project team, Laura was promoted to a team manager position with broader responsibilities. Laura felt confident about her qualifications. The other team managers seemed to respect her, and clients were happy with the projects she managed. With this record of success, Laura hoped to eventually become a partner in the company. However, as the only woman manager in a male- dominated company, she knew that there would be some obstacles to overcome.

Laura felt that some of the senior managers were very conservative and did not accept her as an equal. In the quarterly planning meetings, these managers were often inattentive when she spoke and seemed unreceptive to her suggestions for improvements. Several times she proposed an idea that was ignored, and the same idea was later suggested by someone else who received the credit for it.

Laura did not have a mentor in the company to tell people about her skills and help to advance her career. Moreover, she did not feel accepted into the informal network of relationships that provided opportunities to interact with senior managers. She did not like to play golf and was not a member of the exclusive golf club to which many of the male managers belonged. She was not invited to most of the social activities hosted by senior managers for friends and select members of the company.

Laura also felt that the assignment of projects was biased. The high-profile projects were always given to the male managers. When Laura asked her boss for more challenging projects, she was told that the older clients usually preferred to deal with men. Because she was not given the more profitable accounts, her performance numbers did not look as good as the numbers for some of the male managers. Two male managers who had joined the company around the same time she was hired were promoted ahead of her.

Frustrated by the apparent "glass ceiling" at the company, Laura asked to meet with the president to talk about her career. The president was surprised to hear that Laura was unhappy about her advancement in the company. He assured her that she was a valuable employee and should be patient about a promotion. However, after another year with little improvement in how she was treated, Laura resigned from the company. With two friends from graduate school who also felt unappreciated, she formed a new company and served as the chief executive officer. In a relatively short time, this company became highly successful.

Questions

1. What forms of gender discrimination did Laura experience?
2. What could Laura have done to overcome the obstacles she encountered?
3. What could the president have done to create equal opportunity in this company?

CASE 2

Cybong.com

Cybong.com is an e-commerce marketplace company dealing in Indian fashion and headquartered in Bengaluru, Karnataka, India. In 2009, the graduates of a premier engineering college in the country founded the company with a focus on personalizing gift items. By 2012, Cybong.com shifted its focus to the online retailing of branded apparel.

While the Indian fashion market is booming, with a huge young population and an increase in employment rate, there are many fashion-based e-portals competing for this lucrative space. Fashion-based e-portals have to struggle hard to get a share of the pie; each trying to establish its own niche.

Cybong understands its shoppers' needs and caters to them with a great choice of apparel, accessories, cosmetics, and footwear, from over 500 leading Indian and international brands.

The company's value proposition revolves around giving consumers the power and ease of purchasing fashion and lifestyle products online. Cybong's offerings such as the largest in-season product catalog, 100 percent authentic products, cash on delivery, and a 30-day return policy make it the preferred shopping destination in the country. To make online shopping easier, a dedicated customer care team is on standby to answer queries 24×7. To provide customized services, Cybong tracks the customers' requirement with a complex recommending system.

Recently, a customer survey taken up by the research wing of the firm revealed some extremely unique findings. This survey was undertaken to understand upcoming customer needs and to know emerging segments and niche in the fashion market. The survey indicated that there is an emergence of a few new customer segments, such as transgender customers, diverse ethnic groups, and people in the higher age group. Thus, the organization realized that currently its customer service executives are not formally trained to handle specific queries that may come from these emerging segments in the future.

Although it is not a significant loss to the uncaptured segment yet, the management of Cybong now realizes the potential of this segment and desires to do something about it. The management also plans to refer to the customer care and IT teams of the Global Leadership and Organizational Behavior Effectiveness (GLOBE) project as well.

Questions

1. What business issues is Cybong likely to face because of a rise in diversified customer segments?
2. Cybong is likely to set up some seats in its call center for diversified customer segments. What recruitment policy must it design? What leadership challenges will Cybong face after setting up seats in its call center for diversified segments?
3. What cultural issues is Cybong likely to face because of the development of diversified market segments?
4. How can the findings of GLOBE help the management of Cybong in strategizing its future course of action?

Developing Leadership Skills

Learning Objectives

After studying this chapter, you should be able to:

- Understand the importance of leadership training and development in organizations.
- Understand the benefits and limitations of different methods for leadership development.
- Understand the organizational conditions that facilitate leadership training and development.
- Understand how leaders can encourage and facilitate leadership development.
- Understand some ways for leaders to develop their own skills.
- Understand why leader development should be consistent with strategic planning.

The increasing rate of change in the external environment of organizations and the many new challenges facing leaders suggest that success as a leader in the twenty-first century will require a higher level of skill and some new competencies. To meet this need, new techniques are being invented and old techniques are being refined. *Leadership development* remains a multibillion dollar business in the United States (Fulmer & Vicere, 1996).

Leadership competencies can be developed in a number of ways, including formal training, developmental activities, and self-help activities. Most formal training occurs during a defined time period, and it is usually conducted away from the manager's immediate work site by training professionals (e.g., a short workshop at a training center, a management course at a university). Developmental activities are usually embedded within operational job assignments or conducted in conjunction with those assignments. The developmental activities can take many forms, including coaching by the boss or an outside consultant, *mentoring* by someone at a higher level in the organization, and special assignments that provide new challenges and opportunities to learn relevant skills. Self-help activities are carried out by individuals on their own initiative. Examples include reading books, viewing videos, listening to audiotapes, and using interactive computer programs for skill building.

The effectiveness of training programs, developmental experiences, and *self-help activities* depends in part on organizational conditions that facilitate the learning of leadership skills and the application of this learning. Facilitating conditions include things such as support for skill development from bosses and coworkers, reward systems that encourage skill development, and cultural values that support continuous learning. This chapter examines various approaches for leadership development and the key facilitating conditions.

Leadership Training Programs

Formal training programs are widely used to improve leadership in organizations. Most large organizations have management training programs of one kind or another, and many organizations send their managers to outside seminars and workshops (Saari, Johnson, McLaughlin, & Zimmerle, 1988). Most leadership training programs are designed to increase generic skills and behaviors relevant for managerial effectiveness and advancement. The training is usually designed more for lower- and middle-level managers than for top executives, and there is usually more emphasis on skills needed by managers in their current position than on skills needed to prepare for promotion to a higher position (Rothwell & Kazanas, 1994). However, the old pattern of selecting mostly "fast track" managers for leadership training and providing it only once or twice during a manager's career is gradually being replaced by a series of leadership training opportunities that are available to any manager in the organization at appropriate points in the individual's career (Vicere & Fulmer, 1997).

Types of Leadership Training Programs

Leadership training can take many forms, from short workshops that last only a few hours and focus on a narrow set of skills to programs that last for a year or more and cover a wide range of skills. Many consulting companies conduct short leadership workshops that are open to managers from different organizations. Other consulting companies design leadership training programs tailored to the needs of a particular organization. Most universities offer management development programs (e.g., Executive MBA) that can be attended on a part-time basis. Many organizations compensate employees for the cost of attending outside workshops and courses. Some large organizations (e.g., General Electric, Motorola, Toyota, Unilever) operate a management training center or corporate university for employees (Fulmer, 1997; Meister, 1994).

A number of training programs are based on the application of a particular leadership theory. Examples include training programs based on least preferred coworker (LPC) contingency theory (Fiedler & Chemers, 1982), the normative decision model (Vroom & Jago, 1988), transformational leadership (Bass, 1996; Bass & Avolio, 1990b), and situational leadership theory (Hersey & Blanchard, 1984).

Design of Leadership Training

The effectiveness of formal training programs depends greatly on how well they are designed. The design of training should take into account learning theory, the specific learning objectives, characteristics of the trainees, and practical considerations such as constraints and costs in relation to benefits. Leader training is more likely to be successful if designed and conducted in a way that is consistent with findings in research on learning processes and training techniques (Baldwin & Padgett, 1993; Campbell, 1988; Howell & Cooke, 1989; Lord & Hall, 2005; Noe & Ford, 1992; Salas & Cannon-Bowers, 2000; Tannenbaum & Yukl, 1992). The program design should take into account learning theory, the specific learning

TABLE 1	Desirable Features for Training Programs

- Specific learning objectives
- Clear, meaningful content
- Appropriate sequencing of content
- Appropriate mix of training methods
- Opportunity for active practice
- Relevant, timely feedback
- Build trainee self-confidence

objectives, characteristics of the trainees, and practical considerations such as available time and costs in relation to benefits (see summary in Table 1).

Effects of Leadership Training

Criteria for assessing the effectiveness of formal training programs include skill learning, behavior change, and performance improvement. How much leadership training can affect these outcomes depends on the personality and ability of trainees, the training design and execution, and supporting conditions in the organization. The relative importance of the different determinants depends in part on the type of training and the outcome measure (see reviews by Alliger, Tannenbaum, Bennett, Traver, & Shotland, 1997; Blume, Ford, Baldwin, Huang, 2010; Taylor, Russ-Eft, & Taylor, 2009).

Learning from Experience

Much of the skill needed for effective leadership is learnt from experience rather than from formal training programs (Davies & Easterby-Smith, 1984; Kelleher, Finestone, & Lowy, 1986; Lindsey, Homes, & McCall, 1987; McCall, Lombardo, & Morrison, 1988). Special assignments provide an opportunity to develop and refine leadership skills during the performance of regular job duties. Coaching and mentoring can be used to help managers interpret their experiences and learn new skills. Managers can emulate the effective behaviors modeled by competent bosses (McCall et al., 1988; Manz & Sims, 1981). Managers can also learn what not to do from observing superiors who are ineffective (Lindsey et al., 1987; McCall et al., 1988).

The extent to which leadership skills and values are developed during operational assignments depends on the type of experiences afforded by these assignments. The relevance of different types of experiences for the development of leadership skills was studied by researchers at the Center for Creative Leadership (CCL) (Lindsey et al., 1987; McCall et al., 1988; McCauley, 1986; McCauley, Lombardo, & Usher, 1989) and in subsequent research (e.g., Dragoni, Tesluk, Russell, & Oh, 2009; Mumford et al., 2000). The research found that *learning from experience* is affected by the amount of challenge in assignments, the variety of tasks and assignments, and the quality of feedback.

Amount of Challenge

A challenging situation is one that involves unusual problems to solve, difficult obstacles to overcome, and risky decisions to make. The research at CCL found that challenge was greatest in jobs that required a manager to deal with change, take responsibility for high-visibility problems, influence people without authority, handle external pressure, and work without much guidance or support from superiors. Some examples of challenging situations include dealing with a merger or reorganization, leading a cross-functional team or task force, implementing a major change, coping with unfavorable business conditions, turning around a weak organizational unit, making the transition to a different type of managerial position (e.g., from a functional line position to a general manager or staff position), and managing in a country with a different culture. These situations required managers to seek new information, view problems in new ways, build new relationships, try out new behaviors, learn new skills, and develop a better understanding of themselves. The CCL researchers developed an instrument called the Developmental Challenge Profile to measure the amount and types of challenge in a managerial position or assignment (McCauley, Ruderman, Ohlott, & Morrow, 1994).

Experiencing success in handling difficult challenges is essential for leadership development. In the process, managers learn new skills and gain self-confidence. Learning from experience involves failure as well as success. The research at CCL also found that managers who experienced adversity and failure earlier in their career were more likely to develop and advance to a higher level than managers who experienced only a series of early successes. Types of hardship experiences found to be significant for development included failure in business decisions, mistakes in dealing with important people, career setbacks, and personal trauma (e.g., divorce, serious injury or illness). However, experiencing failure may not result in beneficial learning and change unless a person accepts some responsibility for it, acknowledges personal limitations, and finds ways to overcome them (Kaplan, Kofodimos, & Drath, 1987; Kovach, 1989; McCall & Lombardo, 1983). Moreover, when the amount of stress and challenge is excessive, support and coaching may be needed to prevent people from giving up and withdrawing from the situation before development occurs.

Variety of Tasks or Assignments

Growth and learning are greater when job experiences are diverse as well as challenging. Diverse job experiences require managers to adapt to new situations and deal with new types of problems. Repeated success in handling one type of problem reinforces the tendency of a person to interpret and handle new problems in the same way, even though a different approach may be more effective. Thus, it is beneficial for managers to have early experience with a wide variety of problems that require different leadership behavior and skills. Some ways to provide a variety of job challenges include making special *developmental assignments,* rotating managers among positions in different functional subunits of the organization, providing assignments in both line and staff positions, and making both foreign and domestic assignments. Variety of challenges can also be designed into simulations. The effectiveness of developmental assignments and simulations designed to increase adaptability can be improved by preparing participants in advance to view problems in new ways and become more flexible in their behavior (Nelson, Zaccaro, & Herman, 2010).

Accurate, Relevant Feedback

More learning occurs during operational assignments when people get accurate feedback about their behavior and its consequences and use this feedback to analyze their experiences and learn from them. Unfortunately, useful feedback about a manager's behavior is seldom provided within operational assignments, and even when available it may not result in learning. The hectic pace and unrelenting demands make introspection and self-analysis difficult in a management job. The extent to which a person is willing to accept feedback depends on some of the same traits that are related to managerial effectiveness (Bunker & Webb, 1992; Kaplan, 1990; Kelleher et al., 1986). People who are defensive and insecure tend to avoid or ignore information about their weaknesses. People who believe that most events are predetermined by uncontrollable external forces (i.e., people who do not have a high internal locus of control orientation) are less likely to accept responsibility for failure or to use feedback to improve their skills and future performance.

The obstacles to learning from experience are greatest at higher levels of management (Kaplan et al., 1987). Executives tend to become isolated from all but a small number of people with whom they interact regularly in the organization, and these people are mostly other executives who are also isolated. Success in attaining such a high position of power and prestige tends to give executives self-confidence about their style of management, and it may progress to a feeling of superiority that causes the executive to ignore or discount criticism from others who are not so successful. Moreover, as executives become more powerful, people become more reluctant to risk offending them by providing criticism.

Developmental Activities

A number of activities can be used to facilitate learning of relevant skills from experience on the job (see Table 2). These developmental activities can be used to supplement informal coaching by the boss or coworkers, and most of them can be used in conjunction with formal training programs. Six of the developmental activities will be described in this section of the chapter, including *multisource feedback* programs, developmental assignments, mentoring, *executive coaching,* simulations, and personal growth programs.

Multisource Feedback Programs

Providing behavioral feedback from multiple sources is a widely used method for management development in large organizations (London & Smither, 1995). Other names for this method are "360-degree feedback" and "multi-rater feedback." Multisource feedback programs can be used for a variety of purposes, but the primary one is to assess the strengths and developmental needs of individual managers. A basic assumption of feedback programs is that most managers lack accurate knowledge about their skills and behavior, and the feedback can be used to improve it. The design and use of 360-degree feedback programs is described in several books (e.g., Lepsinger & Lucia, 1997; Tornow & London, 1998).

In a feedback program, managers receive information about their skills or behavior from standardized questionnaires filled out by other people such as subordinates, peers, superiors, and sometimes outsiders such as clients (see Figure 1). The questionnaires used to provide feedback may be customized for a particular organization, but most feedback workshops still utilize standardized questionnaires. Van Velsor, Leslie, and Fleenor (1997)

TABLE 2	Activities for Facilitating Leadership Development

- Multisource feedback workshops
- Developmental assessment centers
- Special assignments
- Job rotation programs
- Action learning
- Mentoring
- Executive coaching
- Simulations
- Personal growth programs
- Outdoor challenge programs

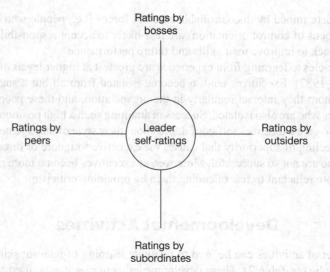

FIGURE 1 Sources of Information for 360-Degree Feedback

described sixteen survey instruments commonly used in feedback workshops and reviewed the empirical evidence about the strengths and limitations of each instrument.

Feedback is likely to be more accurate when the rating questionnaire tracks behaviors that are meaningful and easy to observe. Accurate feedback also depends on gaining the cooperation of a representative set of respondents who interacted frequently with the manager over a period of time and had adequate opportunity to observe the behaviors in the questionnaire. Respondents are more likely to provide accurate ratings if they understand the purpose of the survey, how the results will be used, and the procedures to ensure confidentiality of answers. Ratings are more likely to be accurate if the feedback is used only for developmental purposes and is not part of the formal performance appraisal process (London, Wohlers, & Gallagher, 1990).

Feedback can be presented in a number of different ways, and the format of the feedback report helps to determine how clear and useful the feedback is to the recipients. In most feedback interventions, each participating manager receives a report that compares self-ratings by the manager to ratings made by others and norms for similar managers. The raters by others are usually provided by subordinates who report to the manager (upward feedback) and by the manager's boss. Ratings may also be provided by peers who have had an opportunity to observer the manager's behavior, and when appropriate more than one boss provides feedback. In some feedback reports the ratings are averaged for all raters regardless of direction. Providing feedback separately for each direction (e.g., subordinates, peers, superiors) can make it more informative and easier to interpret, but it requires a larger number of raters. Sometimes the report includes built-in aids for interpreting the results. It is a common practice to highlight large discrepancies between what others say about a manager's behavior and self-ratings by the manager. Self-ratings that are much higher than ratings by others indicate a possible developmental need. Interpretation of feedback is facilitated by norms (e.g., percentile scores) based on a large sample of managers. Ratings of the manager's behavior that are well below "normal" provide another indicator of a possible developmental need.

There has been much discussion but little research on the advantages of different types and forms of feedback. Some writers have questioned the value of providing feedback based on quantitative ratings for abstract traits and vaguely defined behaviors that are difficult to observe and remember. Moses, Hollenback, and Sorcher (1993) suggested providing feedback on what the rater expects the manager would do in a well-defined, representative situation. Kaplan (1993) suggested supplementing numerical feedback with concrete examples of effective and ineffective behavior by the manager. The examples would be obtained by interviewing respondents or including open-ended questions on the survey questionnaire. An example of an open-ended question is to ask respondents what they think the manager should start doing, stop doing, or continue doing (Bracken, 1994). Quantitative feedback about a manager's current behavior can be supplemented with respondent recommendations about desirable changes in the manager's behavior.

The effectiveness of multisource feedback programs depends not only on the type and form of feedback, but also on how it is presented to managers (Kaplan, 1993; Yukl & Lepsinger, 1995). Three common variations are the following: (1) managers just receive a feedback report and are left to interpret it alone; (2) managers receive a feedback report followed by a one-on-one meeting with a facilitator; and (3) managers attend a group workshop with a facilitator to help interpret their feedback reports. A field experiment by Seifert, Yukl, and McDonald (2003) found that a feedback workshop with a facilitator was more effective for changing the behavior of bank managers than merely giving them a feedback report to read. A facilitator can explain the rating categories and their relevance for leadership effectiveness, prepare participants to be receptive to behavioral feedback, encourage participants to interpret the feedback in light of their leadership situation, stress the positive aspects of feedback as well as negatives, help participants work through feelings about adverse feedback, and encourage participants to plan how to use the feedback to improve their leadership effectiveness.

Despite the growing use of multisource feedback programs in recent years, questions remain about the effectiveness of this developmental method (Waldman, Atwater, & Antonioni, 1998). Several studies examined the effects of upward feedback from subordinates (e.g., Atwater, Roush, & Fischtal, 1995; Hegarty, 1974; Heslin & Latham, 2004; Nemeroff & Cosentino, 1979; Reilly, Smither, & Vasilopoulos, 1996; Smither et al., 1995; Wilson et al., 1990), but fewer studies have evaluated the effects of multisource feedback (e.g., Bernardin, Hagan, & Kane, 1995; Hazucha, Hezlett, & Schneider, 1993; Seifert & Yukl, 2010; Seifert, Yukl, & McDonald, 2003). Evidence of positive change in leader behavior was found in some studies but not others. The effects of different types of feedback have been studied in laboratory experiments as well as in experiments and quasi-experimental studies in organizations. A meta-analysis for all types of feedback research found a weak positive effect on performance (Kluger & DeNisi, 1996); the results varied greatly across studies, and a negative effect was found in one-third of the studies.

In summary, the research shows that feedback can be effective in some situations, but it does not support the widespread belief that feedback is always an effective method of leadership development (Waldman et al., 1998). Feedback from other people can help a manager identify strengths and weaknesses, but the manager may not be willing or able to apply the feedback. When multisource feedback is used only for development, managers are usually not required to share the feedback with their boss or to discuss it with the raters. Some participants may dismiss negative feedback or distort its meaning (Conger, 1992). Even when a participant acknowledges a skill deficiency and wants to improve, how to improve may not be evident.

The feedback research on managers has identified several ways to enhance the effects of feedback, including skill training, individual coaching, follow-up activities, and linking the manager's developmental action plan to subsequent appraisal and reward decisions (Hooijberg & Lane, 2009; London & Smither, 1995; Luthans & Peterson, 2003; Nowack, 2009; Seifert & Yukl, 2010). Using more than one feedback cycle can increase the amount of improvement (Seifert & Yukl, 2010; Shipper, 2009). Another way to enhance the effects of feedback is to provide individual coaching to managers for several weeks after the feedback workshop (Kochanowski, Seifert, & Yukl, 2011). Other research found that managers were more likely to improve if they held a meeting with the raters (who were subordinates) to discuss the feedback received from them (Walker & Smither, 1999). Such a meeting provides an opportunity to gain a better understanding of the reason for discrepancies in self and other ratings, and it may increase the manager's sense of accountability to make use of the feedback.

Some progress has been made in determining the potential of feedback as a method of leadership development. However, more research is needed to determine the most useful forms of feedback, the conditions facilitating positive effects, the types of skills or behavior most likely to be improved, and the types of individual most likely to benefit from multi-source feedback.

Developmental Assessment Centers

In assessment centers managerial traits and skills are measured with methods such as interviews, aptitude tests, personality tests, situational tests, a short autobiographical essay, a speaking exercise, and a writing exercise. Information from these diverse sources is integrated and used to develop an overall evaluation of each participant's management potential. The assessment center process typically takes 2 to 3 days, and some data collection may occur beforehand. At first most assessment centers were used only for selection and promotion decisions, but it was subsequently found that they are also useful for developing managers (Boehm, 1985; Goodge, 1991; Munchus & McArthur, 1991; Rayner & Goodge, 1988).

Compared to feedback workshops, developmental assessment centers use more intensive procedures and a more comprehensive set of measures to increase self-understanding, identify strengths and weaknesses, and assess developmental needs. Information about a manager's behavior may be obtained from people who interact with the manager regularly and from observation of the manager in simulations and exercises. The facilitators also collect information about the manager's prior experience, motives, personality traits, skills, interests, and aspirations. Information about behavior and skills is integrated with information about motives, background, experience, and career aspirations to provide a more complete picture of the person's strengths, weaknesses, and potential. The rationale is that behavioral feedback alone is insufficient to change ineffective behavior supported by strong motives, values, and selfconcepts. Helping the person to confront weaknesses and develop a better self-understanding increases the likelihood of behavior change. Participants also receive counseling about developmental needs and career choices. To avoid the inherent dangers in this enhanced feedback, Kaplan and Palus (1994) emphasize the need for careful selection of participants to screen out people who would not benefit from it (or who may not be able to handle the stress).

Studies on participant perceptions of the benefits from developmental assessment centers and similar "feedback intensive programs" suggest that they can enhance self-awareness, help to identify training needs, and facilitate subsequent development of leadership skills (e.g., Fletcher, 1990; Guthrie & Kelly-Radford, 1998; Young & Dixon, 1996). Two studies found evidence that developmental assessment centers can improve the later performance of managers (Engelbracht & Fischer, 1995; Papa & Graham, 1991), but the results are difficult to interpret because other developmental activities were involved (e.g., skill training, special assignments, additional coaching). As with feedback workshops, developmental assessment workshops are likely to be more successful when followed by relevant training or developmental activities. We still do not know much about the underlying psychological processes that occur in developmental assessment centers, and more research on this subject is needed. Finally, the benefits of a developmental assessment center may not be limited to participants;

managers who serve on the staff of these centers may also experience an increase in their managerial skills (Boehm, 1985).

Developmental Assignments

Some developmental assignments can be carried out concurrently with regular job responsibilities, and Lombardo and Eichinger (1989) cataloged types of special assignments that can be used to develop managerial skills in the current job. Some examples include managing a new project or start-up operation, serving as the department representative on a cross-functional team, chairing a special task force to plan a major change or deal with a serious operational problem, developing and conducting a training program for the organizational unit, and assuming responsibility for some administrative activities previously handled by the boss (e.g., preparing a budget, developing a strategic plan, conducting a meeting).

Other developmental assignments may require taking a temporary leave from one's regular job. Examples include working in an assessment center, serving as an understudy or staff member for an exceptional leader in another part of the organization, serving in a temporary liaison position in another organization (e.g., a client or supplier), and serving in a visiting assignment to another organization (e.g., a manager is loaned to a government agency to help implement a major change).

An example of a systematic use of developmental assignments is provided by Citibank in the 1990s (Clark & Lyness, 1991). The development of interpersonal and strategic skills was considered important to prepare managers for advancement to senior executive positions. High-potential managers were given two types of special assignments, each lasting from 3 to 4 years. One assignment involved a major strategic challenge and the other involved difficult people-management challenges.

Research on the effectiveness of developmental assignments is still limited. The longitudinal research on traits and skills provided evidence that diverse, challenging assignments early in one's career facilitated career advancement, and that different skills are learned from different types of challenges and hardship experiences (DeRue & Wellman, 2009; Lindsey et al., 1987; McCall et al., 1988; McCauley et al., 1994; McCauley, Eastman, & Ohlott, 1995; Valerio, 1990). Managers who have a strong learning orientation are more likely to take advantage of developmental opportunities, and they are also more likely to benefit from them (Dragoni, Tesluk, Russell & Oh, 2009).

Most studies on effects of developmental assignments have relied on a managers' retrospective self-reports about developmental experiences and skill acquisition, but the study by DeRue and Wellman (2009) used multiple methods. In addition to a survey measure of developmental challenges, descriptions of developmental experiences were obtained from interviews with managers; then the developmental experiences were related to supervisor ratings of skill improvement by the managers. The researchers found that developmental challenges increased learning up to a point, after which adding more challenge created problems that will reduce learning for some managers unless they are resolved (e.g., by providing more supportive feedback and coaching). As yet nobody has conducted an experiment comparing the effects of different types of developmental assignments in terms of measures of competencies taken before and after the assignment. We still have much to learn about what types of assignments are effective for what type of skills and what type of people.

An important research question is the amount of time required to optimize learning in developmental assignments. Brief assignments may not provide an opportunity to see the consequences of one's actions and decisions or to reflect on one's experiences and comprehend what was learned (Ohlott, 1998). On the other hand, staying in the assignment too long can result in boredom and lost opportunities for more meaningful experiences.

A related question is the optimal sequencing of developmental assignments, which is an important determinant of the amount of challenge in each assignment. Before taking on a big, difficult assignment, it is better to first learn basic knowledge and relevant skills in smaller, less challenging assignments. Otherwise, a person is likely to spend too much time learning the basic things, and may not have sufficient time to learn more complex things that are necessary for later success as a leader. Thus, attempting to move someone too quickly through different developmental assignments can be counterproductive, and the planning of developmental assignments requires careful analysis and a long-term perspective (McCall, 2004).

McCauley, Eastman, and Ohlott (1995) suggested some ways to improve the planning and use of developmental assignments. The challenges and learning opportunities provided by each type of assignment should be matched to the manager's developmental needs, career aspirations, and learning orientation. Managers need to become more aware of the importance of developmental assignments, and they should share in the responsibility for planning them. The challenges and benefits provided by special assignments should be tracked, and this information should be related to career counseling and succession planning. After a developmental assignment is completed, it is important for a manager to reflect on the experience and identify the lessons that were learned. This process of retrospective analysis is likely to increase learning from experience, and it can be facilitated by the boss, a mentor, or a training and development professional (Ohlott, 1998).

Dechant (1994) suggested that learning from special assignments can be facilitated by preparation of a concrete learning plan. The person who has the assignment analyzes the task objectives, context, and job requirements for everyone who will be involved in the task. Skill requirements are compared with available skill resources; any gaps in necessary skills or knowledge are identified; and plans are made to acquire the skills or knowledge needed to carry out the assignment successfully. This process should increase the likelihood that a person will recognize and take advantage of learning opportunities in a special assignment. Learning needs for others are also identified and incorporated into the action plan for the assignment.

The effectiveness of developmental assignments is reduced when bias and discrimination are widespread in the organization. A variety of studies suggest that women are less likely than men to be given challenging, high-visibility assignments (e.g., Ruderman & Ohlott, 1994; Van Velsor & Hughes, 1990). Despite the existence of laws prohibiting it, discrimination based on gender, race, or age still occurs in making assignments and promotions.

Mentoring

Formal mentoring programs are used to facilitate management development in many organizations (Giber, Carter, & Goldsmith, 1999; Noe, 1991). Mentoring is a relationship in which a more experienced manager helps a less experienced protege. The mentor is usually at a higher managerial level and is not the protege's immediate boss (McCauley & Douglas, 1998). Research on mentors (Kram, 1985; Noe, 1988) finds that they provide a psychosocial function (acceptance, encouragement, coaching, counseling) and a career-facilitation function (sponsorship, protection, challenging assignments, exposure and visibility). Mentors can facilitate adjustment, learning, and stress reduction during difficult job transitions, such as promotion to one's first managerial position, a transfer or promotion to a different functional unit in the organization, an assignment in a foreign country, or assignments in an organization that has been merged, reorganized, or downsized (Kram & Hall, 1989; Zey, 1988).

Several studies show that mentoring results in more career advancement and success for the protege (Chao, Walz, & Gardner, 1992; Dreher & Ash, 1990; Fagenson, 1989;

Scandura, 1992; Turban & Dougherty, 1994; Whitely & Coetsier, 1993). A study of NCAA women's basketball coaches and assistant coaches found that the beneficial effects on protege performance are greater when the mentor is successful and the relationship lasts for a long period of time (Tonidandel, Avery, & Phillips, 2007). Mentors may also benefit from the mentoring experience because it is likely to increase their job satisfaction and help them develop their own leadership skills. A study by Wilbur (1987) found that career advancement in a service company was predicted both by mentoring given and mentoring received.

Despite the potential benefits from mentoring, it is not always successful. Research on conditions likely to increase the effectiveness of mentoring suggests that informal mentoring is usually more successful than a formal mentoring program (Noe, Greenberger, & Wang, 2002). The difference may be due primarily to the way a formal program is conducted, including the selection and training of the mentors. The success of a formal mentoring program is probably increased by making participation voluntary, by providing mentors some choice of a protege, by explaining the benefits and pitfalls, and by clarifying the expected roles and processes for both mentor and protege (Chao et al., 1992; Hunt & Michael, 1983). Proteges can be proactive in initiating mentoring relationships rather than waiting for a mentor to select them, especially in an organization that supports this type of developmental activity. Turban and Dougherty (1994) found that proteges were more likely to initiate mentoring relationships and get more mentoring if they had high emotional stability, self-monitoring, and internal locus of control orientation.

Mentoring is also affected by some demographic factors such as age, gender, and race. Women and minorities have more difficulty finding successful mentoring relationships (Ilgen & Youtz, 1986; Ohlott, Ruderman, & McCauley, 1994; Noe, 1988; Ragins & Cotton, 1991, 1993; Ragins & McFarlin, 1990; Thomas, 1990). Common difficulties for women include stereotypes about appropriate behavior, concern about intimacy with men, awkwardness about discussing some subjects, lack of appropriate role models, resentment by peers, and exclusion from male networks. Some of these difficulties remain even when women mentor women. Despite the difficulties, empirical studies found no evidence that gender affects the success of mentoring (e.g., Dreher & Ash, 1990; Turban & Dougherty, 1994).

In general, the research suggests that mentoring can be a useful technique for facilitating career advancement, adjustment to change, and the job satisfaction of a protege. Mentoring also offers advantages such as stronger organizational commitment and lower turnover (Payne & Huffman, 2005). However, the effect of mentoring varies depending on the type of mentoring provided and the type of outcomes examined (Allen, Eby, & Lentz, 2006). As yet few studies have assessed the relationship between the characteristics of mentoring programs and different outcomes. Little is known about the skills, values, and behaviors most likely to be acquired or enhanced in a mentoring relationship, the conditions facilitating development, or the ways a mentor actually facilitates development of leadership competencies in a protege.

Executive Coaching

In recent years individual coaching has become a popular type of developmental intervention for leaders in business organizations (Feldman & Lankau, 2005; Hall, Otazo, & Hollenbeck, 1999; Kilburg, 1996, 2000). The type of leader who receives coaching is usually a high-level executive. The coach is usually a successful former executive or a behavioral scientist with extensive experience as a management consultant.

An executive coach is not a permanent mentor, and the coach is usually employed for a limited period of time ranging from a few months to a few years. Coaching may be provided on a weekly or biweekly basis, and in extreme cases, the coach may be "on call" to provide advice whenever needed. Sometimes the decision to obtain coaching is made by the executive, and other times it is made by higher management to help prepare an executive for advancement, or to prevent derailment. Use of an external coach provides some advantages such as wider experience, greater objectivity, and more confidentiality. An internal coach offers other advantages, such as easy availability, more knowledge of the culture and politics, and a better understanding of the strategic challenges and core competencies.

The primary purpose of executive coaching is to facilitate learning of skills that are relevant for current or future leadership responsibilities. Coaches also provide advice about how to handle specific challenges, such as implementing a major change, dealing with a difficult boss, or working with people from a different culture. Having a coach provides the unusual opportunity to discuss issues and try out ideas with someone who can understand them and provide helpful, objective feedback and suggestions, while maintaining strict confidentiality. Executive coaching is especially useful in conjunction with techniques that provide information about developmental needs but do not directly improve skills (e.g., multisource feedback, developmental assessment center).

Executive coaching offers several advantages over formal training courses, including convenience, confidentiality, flexibility, and more personal attention. One obvious disadvantage is the high expense of one-on-one coaching, even when used for a limited time. The high cost is one reason why personal coaching is used primarily for executives. Another limitation is the shortage of competent coaches. It is important to find a coach who is able to establish a good working relationship with the executive while also remaining objective and professional. The coach should not have a personal agenda such as excessive bias for a particular theory, the desire to sell more consulting time (for an external consultant), or the desire for more power (for an internal consultant). Organizations need clear guidelines regarding the selection and use of executive coaches to avoid the potential problems with this developmental technique (Hall et al., 1999).

The executives who are being coached usually value honest, accurate feedback about strengths and weaknesses, as well as clear, relevant advice about ways to become more effective. Examples of the types of behaviors and skills that can be enhanced by a coach include listening, communicating, influencing people, building relationships, handling conflicts, team building, initiating change, conducting meetings, and developing subordinates. The coach can also provide advice about other things the executive can do to acquire relevant knowledge and skills. Guidelines for effective coaching of executives can be found in books on the subject (e.g., Dotlich & Cairo, 1999). Coaching in leadership skills is not limited to individuals, and coaching the top management team collectively offers some advantages for improving shared leadership processes (Kets de Vries, 2005).

Research on the effects of executive coaching on personal development and leadership effectiveness is limited, but the evidence so far is generally favorable (e.g., Bowles, Cunningham, De La Rosa, & Picano, 2007; Perkins, 2009). The research on assessment of coaching for enhancing leadership skills is complicated by the fact that it usually involves many types of outcomes (attitudes, values, skills, behavior, performance), it is usually combined with other types of interventions and self-help activities, and it is somewhat different for each recipient and coach. A review of leadership coaching studies with recommendations for future research is provided by Ely et al. (2010).

Simulations

Business games and simulations have been used for many years for management training. As with cases, simulations require trainees to analyze complex problems and make decisions. Most business games emphasize quantitative financial information and are used to practice analytical and decision skills taught in a formal training program. The most sophisticated simulations are based on a systems model of the complex causal relationships among important variables for a particular type of company and industry. Participants work individually or in small groups to make managerial decisions about product pricing, advertising, production output, product development, and capital investment. Following is an example of one participant's experience in a computerized simulation of a start-up airline company:

> Sally stared blankly off into space. What had started out so well had turned into a nightmare. She had taken over an airline company that had three planes and gross revenues of $32 million a year, and in just four years she had grown the company to a half-billion-dollar firm with a fleet of 100 aircraft. She had sweated over decisions in the areas of human resources, aircraft acquisition, marketing, pricing, and service scope, and in each case, her airline had triumphed. But then she had reached a turning point. Her market had collapsed. Her service quality had eroded. Losses had piled up so fast that the ability of her company to absorb them was in doubt. It would all turn around though, it had to. All she needed was one more quarter . . . But instead of the next quarter's financial reports she received notification that her creditors were forcing her into bankruptcy. Time had run out . . . What did I do wrong, she thought. All her decisions had seemed to make sense at the time. She reached over and pressed the save button. She would have to analyze her decisions to see what went wrong later. Right now she had another strategy she wanted to try. She hit the restart button to begin the simulation. She was back to having three planes and gross revenues of $32 million. (Kreutzer, 1993, p. 536)

Large-scale simulations emphasize interpersonal skills as much as cognitive skills and decision making. A large-scale simulation typically involves a single hypothetical organization with multiple divisions (e.g., bank, plastics company). Participants are assigned to different positions in the organization and carry out the managerial responsibilities for a period of one or two days. Prior to the simulation, each participant is given extensive background information, such as a description of the organization's products and services, financial reports, industry and market conditions, an organization chart, and the duties and responsibilities of the position. Each participant is also given copies of recent correspondence (e.g., memos, reports) with other members of the organization and outsiders. Participants have separate work spaces, but they are allowed to communicate by various media (e.g., memos, e-mail) and to schedule meetings. Participants make strategic and operational decisions just as they would in a real organization. They react to each other's decisions, but unlike business games, they usually do not receive information about the financial consequences of their decisions during the simulation itself.

After the simulation is completed, participants receive feedback about group processes and their individual skills and behaviors. Feedback is usually provided by observers who track the behavior and decisions of the participants. Additional feedback can be provided by videotaping participant conversations and meetings. The facilitators help the participants understand how well they functioned as executives in collecting and processing information, analyzing and solving problems, communicating with others, influencing others, and planning strategy and operations. The best known large-scale simulation (called Looking Glass) was developed by the Center for Creative Leadership (Kaplan, Lombardo, & Mazique, 1985; Van Velsor, Ruderman, & Phillips, 1989). It is a simulation of a glass manufacturing company. Other large-scale simulations have been developed to depict specific types of organizations such as banks, insurance companies, chemical-plastics companies, and public school systems.

What participants learn from a large-scale simulation depends in part on who participates. If participants are a "family group" of managers from the same organization, their behavior in the simulation will reflect the prevailing culture and relationships in that organization. The feedback to participants in family groups can be used to help them understand and improve their decision-making and conflict resolution processes. For example, most of the managers from one company that participated in the Looking Glass simulation made hasty decisions and looked for information to justify them, rather than carefully gathering information to determine the nature of the problem and available opportunities. During the debrief, participants became aware of their ineffective behavior and realized that it was consistent with the culture of their company.

The research on business games and simulations is still limited, but there is increasing evidence they can be very useful for leadership development (Keys & Wolfe, 1990; Thornton & Cleveland, 1990; Wolfe & Roberts, 1993). Nevertheless, more research is needed to determine what types of learning occur and the conditions that facilitate learning. It was once assumed that interpersonal skills and problem-solving skills would be learned automatically by participants in a simulation. Now it is obvious that the potential benefits are unlikely to be achieved without extensive preparation, planned interventions with specific feedback and coaching during the simulation, and intensive debriefing with discussion of lessons learned after the simulation.

Most large-scale simulations have limitations. The short time period for the simulation makes it difficult for participants to make effective use of behaviors that necessarily involve a series of related actions over time, such as inspirational leadership, networking, team building, developing subordinates, and delegation. A possible remedy is to spread out the simulation sessions over several weeks, which also provides more opportunity for facilitators to provide feedback and coaching after each session. Improved communication technology makes it easier to use virtual meetings among team members who normally work in widely dispersed locations, which can solve some of the logistical problems of holding repeated meetings for team members over a longer period of time. There is a continuing effort to design more flexible and realistic simulations that incorporate more challenging developmental activities and provide more feedback about participant behavior and its consequences for the organization.

Personal Growth Programs

Personal growth programs are designed to improve self-awareness and overcome inner barriers to psychological growth and development of leadership competencies. These programs evolved from the humanistic psychology movement in the 1960s, and many of the founders had prior experience in programs emphasizing development of human potential, such as the Peace Corps and the National Training Laboratories in Bethel, Maine (Conger, 1993).

Personal growth workshops are based on a series of interrelated assumptions about people and leadership. One key assumption is that many people have lost touch with their inner feelings and values. Inner fears and conflicts, which are often unconscious, limit creativity and risk taking. Before one can become a successful leader, it is necessary to reconnect with one's feelings, confront the latent fears, and resolve the underlying conflicts. Another key assumption is that successful leadership requires a high level of emotional and moral development. A person with high emotional maturity and integrity is more likely to put devotion to a worthwhile cause above self-interest and become a supportive, inspiring, and empowering leader. Understanding your own values, needs, and feelings is necessary to determine whether you are able to provide this type of leadership, and indeed, whether it is really what you want to do.

Personal growth programs are usually conducted at a conference center, and the program may last from two days to a week. Participants are usually managers who do not work together, but sometimes a personal growth program is conducted for an intact management group. The programs typically include a series of psychological exercises in which participants attempt to understand their purpose for living and working and share this understanding with each other. Sometimes outdoor challenge activities are incorporated into the program to increase the experience of shared risk taking. An experienced facilitator presents conceptual models and conducts the exercises. The models usually describe how human development occurs, how organizations change over time, and the role of leadership in organizational change.

The process of developing self-understanding begins when participants are asked to explain their reasons for attending the program. In another, more intensive exercise, participants are told to imagine their company has been acquired and only the three best leaders will be retained in the newly merged organization. Each person has five minutes to prepare a two-minute appeal describing his or her positive leadership qualities and reasons to be retained (a variation of this exercise is to imagine that you are at sea in a sinking boat with a small life raft that will only allow three people to be saved). Participants discuss each appeal and vote to determine the three people who have made the most convincing case.

An important exercise near the end of most programs is for each participant to develop a personal vision for the future and present it to the rest of the group. To facilitate development of a vision, participants are encouraged to imagine they are at the end of their lives and have achieved a sense of completion and gratitude; now they must consider what they have done and how they have lived to reach that state. After each presentation, the audience provides feedback on whether they perceive the vision to be sincere and right for the person.

Personal growth programs usually involve strong emotional experiences and are more likely than most training programs to have a lasting effect on participants. The changes may include an increase in interpersonal skills relevant for leadership. However, it is also possible that some participants will change in ways that reduce leadership effectiveness (Conger, 1993). Successful leadership often involves a passionate pursuit of a vision or cause that may require sacrificing aspects of one's personal and family life. The net effect of personal growth programs that encourage people to find a better balance between their work and personal life may be to reduce commitment to the organization. Moreover, increased awareness of unconscious needs and conflicts does not necessarily result in their resolution, and the experience is sometimes more detrimental than helpful to the person. As yet, there are few studies on the consequences of personal growth programs for leaders, followers, or the organization.

Facilitating Conditions for Leadership Development

There is little research comparing the effectiveness of different methods for developing leaders, although meta-analyses of studies on individual methods provide clues about this question (e.g., Collins & Holton, 2004). It is important to remember that the general results for a method do not necessarily indicate how effective it will be for an individual manager. The effectiveness of a method will depend on the types of learning desired, the individuals who will be developed, and facilitating conditions within an organization such as support from bosses, a favorable *learning climate,* and a systematic process for assessing developmental needs and making developmental plans.

Support by the Boss

The immediate boss can facilitate development of leadership skills in subordinates (Hillman, Schwandt, & Bartz, 1990; London & Mone, 1987; Valerio, 1990). However, a

TABLE 3	Ways to Support Leadership Training of Subordinates

Before the Training:

- Inform subordinates about opportunities to get training.
- Explain why the training is important and beneficial.
- Ask others who received the training to explain how it was useful.
- Change the work schedule to make it easier to attend training.
- Give a subordinate time off if necessary to prepare for the training.
- Support preparation activities such as distribution of questionnaires.
- Tell subordinates they will be asked to report on what was learned.

After the Training:

- Meet with the person to discuss what was learned and how it can be applied.
- Jointly set specific objectives and action plans to use what was learned.
- Make assignments that require use of newly learned skills.
- Hold periodic review sessions to monitor progress in applying learning.
- Provide praise for applying the skills.
- Provide encouragement and coaching when difficulties are encountered.
- Include application of new skills in performance appraisals.
- Set an example for trainees by using the skills yourself.

manager who does not understand the importance of coaching and mentoring is unlikely to provide much of it to subordinates. Managers who are preoccupied with immediate crises or their own career advancement are unlikely to spend much time developing subordinates as leaders. Managers who are insecure are unlikely to develop subordinates who could become potential competitors. Development will also be impeded by managers who treat mistakes by subordinates as personal failures rather than learning experiences. Even for managers who want to develop subordinates, it is difficult to find the right balance between providing necessary guidance and encouraging them to solve problems independently. A manager who is overly protective of subordinates and fails to provide enough challenge and honest feedback to them is unlikely to be successful in developing their leadership skills.

How much encouragement and support the boss provides for training and development activities is another determinant of a person's motivation to learn and apply leadership skills (Facteau, Dobbins, Russell, Ladd, & Kudisch, 1995; Ford, Quinones, Sego, & Sorra, 1992; Hand, Richards, & Slocum, 1973; Huczynski & Lewis, 1980; Kozlowski & Hults, 1987; Noe & Schmitt, 1986; Rouiller & Goldstein, 1993; Tracey, Tannenbaum, & Kavanagh, 1995). Some things that can enhance learning and its subsequent application are listed in Table 3.

Learning Climate

The amount of management training and development that occurs in an organization depends in part on prevailing attitudes and values about development, sometimes referred to as the "learning climate" (Ford & Weissbein, 1997). These general conditions augment the influence of the immediate boss. More leadership development is likely when individual learning is regarded as highly important for organizational effectiveness. In such an organization, more resources will be devoted to training, and more effort will be made to explicitly measure and reward learning. Managers will provide more coaching and mentoring when these activities are explicitly measured and rewarded. More members of the organization will be encouraged to seek opportunities for personal growth and skill acquisition. For example, a person is more likely to accept a difficult, high-risk assignment if performance in the assignment will be evaluated in terms of skill development as well as task success. A supportive organizational climate and culture also encourages managers to apply the skills they have learned in training or developmental experiences.

Many things can be done to create and maintain a supportive climate for continuous learning and development. Some examples include the following: (1) make job assignments that allow people to pursue their interests and learn new skills; (2) establish work schedules that allow enough free time to experiment with new methods; (3) provide financial support for continuing education by employees; (4) arrange special speakers and skills workshops for employees; (5) establish a sabbatical program to allow employees to renew themselves; (6) establish a career counseling program to help employees develop self-awareness and find ways to achieve their full potential; (7) establish voluntary skill assessment and feedback programs; (8) make pay increases partly dependent on skill development; (9) provide awards for innovations and improvements; and (10) use symbols and slogans that embody values such as experimentation, flexibility, adaptation, self-development, continuous learning, and innovation.

Criteria for Developmental Assignments

At present, most organizations do not make job assignments that explicitly provide adequate developmental opportunities and a logical progression of learning (Baldwin & Padgett, 1993). The idea of using job assignments for leadership development is somewhat at odds with the traditional approach to selection and placement in an organization, which seeks a good match between manager skills and job requirements (Ruderman, Ohlott, & McCauley, 1990). It is common practice to label someone as a specialist in a particular type of activity or problem and then repeatedly assign the same types of activities or tasks to the person. It is also common for organizations to promote individuals to higher positions within the same functional specialty rather than moving them to management positions in a different functional specialty.

Assigning a challenging job to someone who does not already possess all of the necessary skills can increase development, but there is also a risk of serious mistakes and failure. Even if the person is successful, it will require a longer learning period to master the job. Thus, it is not surprising that most organizations try to select the person with the best skills for a managerial position. More leadership development is likely to occur when executives are aware of the developmental opportunities in operational assignments and value development enough to risk giving important jobs to people who have not already demonstrated experience in performing them (Hall & Foulkes, 1991). Evidence from one study shows that consideration of developmental needs when making succession planning decisions is likely to result in better performance for the organization (Friedman, 1986).

Systems Perspective on Leadership Development

Leadership development is more likely to be successful when top executives have a systems perspective that takes into account related responsibilities and strategic decisions such as selection and appraisal criteria, succession planning, management systems, and competitive strategy. Training programs and developmental activities are more likely to be effective if they are compatible and used in a mutually supportive way, they prepare managers for future positions rather than focusing only on current job requirements, and they consider how to improve the collective leadership for the organization rather than focusing only on developing individuals. Developmental activities also need to be consistent with the competitive strategy, the reward system, the organizational culture, and group-level processes and values. These issues are discussed in this final section of the chapter.

Relationships Among Approaches

The distinction among formal training programs, developmental activities, and self-help activities is useful up to a point, but it implies that the categories are mutually exclusive. In fact, the different categories overlap and are interrelated in complex ways (see Figure 2). Learning acquired from one approach can facilitate or enhance learning from the other approaches. For example, a self-help activity such as using an interactive computer program may be useful to prepare for a developmental assignment. Short courses or work-shops are useful to prepare someone a special operational assignment, or to strengthen skills identified as deficient in a developmental assessment center or feedback intervention.

Sometimes different approaches can used in conjunction with each other. Action learning projects often combine formal training with learning from experience, and participants are encouraged to use self-help activities and peer coaching to acquire additional knowledge as needed for the project. Realistic simulations can be used as a self-contained developmental experience or as part of a formal training course. Some formal leadership development courses now include behavioral feedback for participants from coworkers. Personal growth activities are also included now in some leadership courses. Special mentors can be assigned to people who have developmental assignments, or designated resource people may be available on the Internet to provide advice and coaching as needed.

There has been little research on the relative advantage of training, development, and selfhelp activities for different types of leadership skills. Likewise, little is known about the best way to combine training, development, and self-directed learning activities to maximize their mutual effects. There is clearly need for a more systematic approach to the study of leadership development activities.

Integrating Developmental Activities

In most organizations there is little integration of leadership training and development activities with each other or with related human resources practices such as performance appraisal, career counseling, and succession planning. Decisions about what types of training and development to provide are often influenced by current fads and vendor hype rather than by a systematic analysis of essential competencies that need to be enhanced.

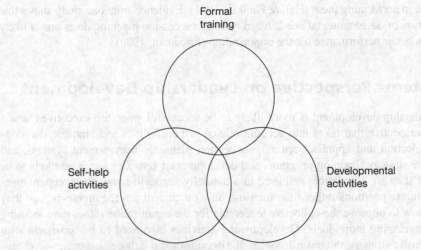

FIGURE 2 Three Ways to Acquire Leadership Competencies

Promotion decisions are often influenced more by a person's prior performance than by rigorous assessment of competencies needed to perform effectively in the next position. As a consequence of poor selection and development, many top executives end up derailing for weaknesses that could have been predicted in advance (McCall, 1998).

Planning of developmental experiences for individual managers is often haphazard and unsystematic when it is determined independently by each manager's current boss and is passed on to the next boss. Few organizations have a specialized position with primary responsibility for planning and coordinating the overall process of leadership development for the organization. McCall (1992) recommended using a developmental facilitator or committee to identify essential competencies for the organization, design tracking systems to assess current skills and developmental needs of individual managers, identify assignments with high developmental potential, sponsor special training programs when needed, find ways to strengthen rewards for managers who develop subordinates, and promote greater use of developmental activities such as mentors, special assignments, and feedback workshops. Another approach is to encourage individuals to take more responsibility for actively seeking developmental experiences. Social networks can be used by an individual to learn about promising developmental assignments and to get assistance in being selected for them (Barthol & Zhang, 2007).

A recent review of best practices in leadership development found that it is facilitated by an integrated approach that includes systematic needs analysis, alignment of development with succession planning, top management support, cultural values for personal development, a program of mutually consistent developmental activities, recognition and rewarding for improvement, and systematic assessment of effectiveness for developmental activities (Leskiw & Singh, 2007).

Leadership Development for the Organization

Most of the literature on leadership development has been focused on improving the skills and behavior of individuals. The emphasis has been on leader development rather than leadership development (Day, 2000). However, as the conceptualization of leadership evolves, so must ideas about leadership development (Day & Harrison, 2007; Van Velsor & McCauley, 2004). If leadership is a shared process that involves the cooperative efforts of many people, then leadership development must also consider how to prepare people to participate in this collective process. Development of individuals is still important, but there is also a need to develop effective leadership processes in teams and in organizations. Progress in understanding what must be done and how to do it will depend in part on progress in theory and research on leadership processes at the group and organizational level. It will also require more intensive, longitudinal research on ways to influence and enhance these leadership processes.

To be optimally effective, leadership development must be consistent with an organization's competitive strategy as well as with other human resource activities (Day, 2000; Fulmer & Vicere, 1996; McCall, 1998; McCauley, 2001). Unfortunately, the developmental activities in most organizations are not based on strategic business objectives, and there is seldom any effort to determine if the activities are relevant to these objectives. The disconnect between developmental activities and strategic objectives probably reflects a lack of understanding about the interdependencies between them. We are only beginning to learn how developmental activities affect the acquisition of leadership competencies, and how the competencies are related to organizational effectiveness. In a time of rapid change, it is not easy to predict the extent to which specific competencies will continue to be relevant in the future. Thus, even when top executives realize leadership development should be guided

TABLE 4	Guidelines for Self-Development of Leadership Skills

- Develop a personal vision of career objectives.
- Seek appropriate mentors.
- Seek challenging developmental assignments.
- Use social networks to learn about developmental opportunities.
- Improve self-monitoring.
- Seek relevant feedback.
- Learn from mistakes.
- Learn to view events from multiple perspectives.
- Be skeptical of easy answers.

by strategic objectives, it is difficult to design developmental systems that will meet the needs of an organization in a turbulent environment. Several scholars have made suggestions on how to improve leadership development and succession planning in organizations (e.g., Fulmer & Vicere, 1996 ; Karaevli & Hall, 2003; London, 2002; McCall, 1998; Moxley & O'Connor-Wilson, 1998).

Guidelines for Self-Development

The focus of this chapter is on what organizations can do to develop the leadership skills of their members, not on what an individual can do to develop his or her own skills. Nevertheless, as noted in the introduction to the chapter, self-help activities provide another approach to enhance leadership skills. Self-development may include diagnosing learning needs and identifying self-help techniques that are relevant and available. Many self-help techniques are available for improving leadership, including practitioner books, instructional videotapes or compact disks, and interactive computer programs. While some of these techniques are intended to be a substitute for formal training programs, some are used to supplement training, and others are intended to facilitate learning from experience. A recent study (Boyce, Zaccaro, & Wisecarver, 2010) examined personality traits associated with propensity for self-development of leadership skills, but more research is needed on the effectiveness of self-learning techniques, the conditions under which they are most effective, and the extent to which they can substitute for formal instruction (Baldwin & Padgett, 1993). Table 4 provides some recommendations for self-development of leadership skills.

Summary

Training of leadership skills is conducted by universities, consulting companies, and organization training centers. Despite the massive volume of formal leadership training that occurs, there is relatively little research to assess its effectiveness. Training methods such as behavior role modeling, cases, simulations, and action learning projects appear promising, but we need to learn more about how to use these techniques for enhancing leadership skills.

The importance of learning from experience on the job is now widely acknowledged, and researchers are now mapping the relationships between specific experiences and specific leadership competencies. In general, more development occurs for managers who experience challenges that require adaptation to new situations and provide opportunity to learn to deal with a variety of different types of problems and hardships. More learning also occurs when people get accurate feedback about their behavior and its consequences and use this feedback to analyze their experiences and learn from them.

Developmental techniques with the potential to increase learning from experience include multisource feedback workshops, developmental assessment centers, special assignments, job rotation, action learning, mentoring, personal growth programs, executive coaching, and outdoor challenge programs. Although most of these developmental techniques are widely used, the amount of research to evaluate their effectiveness is still limited. We are just beginning to learn what types of leadership competencies are enhanced by each technique, the optimal conditions for using a technique, and the type of people most likely to benefit from it.

The extent to which leadership competencies are acquired and used depends on the type of developmental activities that occur (e.g., training, experiential learning, self-learning), facilitating conditions (e.g., boss support, learning environment), and qualities of the individual managers (flexible, pragmatic, learning-oriented). Training and development are more effective when they are mutually consistent, supported by a strong learning culture, and integrated with other human resource activities such as career counseling, staffing decisions, performance appraisal, and succession planning. Leadership development should include shared leadership processes relevant for teams and organizations, and it should be consistent with an organization's strategic objectives. A systems approach to leadership development is as strategically important for long-term organizational effectiveness as product development, marketing, and customer service (Hall & Seibert, 1992; McCall, 1992).

Review and Discussion Questions

1. What features of a training program are likely to make it more effective?
2. What conditions facilitate learning from experience by managers?
3. How are special assignments relevant for development of leadership skills?
4. What are the likely benefits of mentoring for developing leaders?
5. What are the most effective ways to use multisource feedback workshops?
6. What conditions in an organization enhance leadership development?
7. What can be done to integrate the leadership training, development, and self-help activities?
8. Why is it important for the leadership development programs in an organization to be consistent with the human resource management practices and the competitive strategy?

Key Terms

developmental assignments
executive coaching
leadership development

learning climate
learning from experience
mentoring

multisource feedback
self-help activities
simulations

CASE 1

Federated Industries

Patricia Paterson is the new vice president for human resources at Federated Industries, a conglomerate with several diverse subsidiaries. Her primary responsibility is to provide support and advice to each subsidiary and monitor their personnel practices to ensure they are consistent with corporate policy and strategy. She reports directly to the CEO of

Federated. The CEO is concerned that not enough capable leaders are coming up through the ranks. The subsidiaries have complete responsibility for their own internal management development, but the CEO wonders whether it is time for a more uniform approach. The CEO asked Patricia to find out what each subsidiary is doing to develop leadership skills, then report back with recommendations for improving leadership development overall at Federated Industries. Patricia arranged to meet with the personnel directors of the three major subsidiaries and asked each director to prepare a short briefing.

The first director to speak was Peter Proskin, from an engineering company. He explained that his company provides only technical training, because they lack the staff to provide management training. All management training is done outside the company. A manager (or an employee who wants to become a manager) can look at the listing on available training and request any seminar or workshop that appears relevant. If the employee's boss approves the request, the manager is sent to the training at company expense. Some employees are enrolled in the evening MBA degree program at the local university, and they are reimbursed for half of the tuition cost. Peter said they do not pay complete tuition for degree programs, because it is too costly. After some employees finish their MBA, they leave for higher-paying jobs at other companies eager to get people who have managerial as well as technical skills.

The second director to report was Alice Alston, from a company that makes consumer products. She explained that the company provides a program to develop leadership skills in high-potential managers. Managers at each level are encouraged to identify a promising subordinate to mentor. The protege gets lots of personal coaching and is given special, developmental assignments. For example, a couple of junior managers are put on each executive committee to learn about strategic issues and observe how the senior managers work. Other assignments include serving on cross-functional project teams and carrying out improvement projects such as studying work processes and recommending ways to make them more efficient. Alice said that most of the mentors and proteges like the program. However, people not in the program (roughly two-thirds of the employees) sometimes complain about the lack of developmental opportunity in the company.

The last director to speak was Hal Harwick, from an electronics company. Hal explained that they concentrate their training on managers who previously demonstrated their executive capacity. The six most promising managers below the top executive level are selected to participate in a series of seminars held once a month. Each seminar is conducted by one of the top executives, who talks about company activities in his or her area of expertise. Three or four times a year, Hal arranges for an outside consultant to conduct a training workshop on a specific topic such as project management, budgeting, or delegation. The participating managers know they are fast-trackers in line for promotion to top management. They like the program and have told him it is very worthwhile. When one of them is promoted, another promising manager is selected for the program by the top management team. The only drawback is the political infighting that sometimes occurs when executives try to get their proteges selected for the program.

Questions

1. Identify strengths and weaknesses in leadership development at Federated.
2. What types of changes are most likely to improve the leadership development?
3. What additional information is needed to make a good report to the CEO?

CASE 2

Comparing LDP Themes

Here are the basic themes of some leadership development programs (LDPs) from the world's top management development academic institutions.

- "During the leadership program, the participants are introduced to the ideas of leadership, derailment, personality, and emotional intelligence. The program is designed such that it has a mix of training methods: classroom teaching, high-fidelity business simulations, and one-to-one coaching sessions. These methods are used to sensitize and develop essential leadership skills, such as effective listening and communication, presentation, team building, assertiveness, and problem solving."

- "Organizational Leadership Development helps develop organizational mission and vision statements, which serve as foundational guides in the establishment of company objectives. It helps the organization understand the leaders and their expectations, helps individuals at all levels with decision making, raises the professionalism and accountability of everyone by spreading authority, increases transparency and understanding, and facilitates agreement on prioritizing issues, consequently helping the organizations meet their challenges."

- "Today's business leaders influence employees' choices and assist them in reaching goals. Rather than directing and dictating, they inspire and motivate!

  The business world has changed. Instead of pushing people to achieve, successful leaders pull people to succeed, requiring a new skill set to make it to the top.
  Learn how to stop managing and start leading, to play a vital part in your organization's future. A good manager is not always a good leader.
  Learn the differences between managing and leading. Move toward a more direct leadership style and away from a management-based style. Stop pushing and start pulling. 'Leadership Training for Managers' will transform you from yesterday's manager to tomorrow's leader."

- "A Leadership Development program allows you to step back from day-to-day responsibilities, reassess your value to the company, and develop a broader perspective of your leadership capacity. By gaining a deeper understanding of core business functions, you will improve your decision-making skills and learn how to lead cross-functional initiatives in today's shifting global markets. Through a personal case study and professional one-on-one coaching, you will emerge with a personal action plan for addressing the key challenges confronting your organization."

Questions

1. Present a comparative analysis of the training programs described above based on the following aspects:

   - Targeted audience
   - Type and objectives of the program
   - Pedagogy

2. What value does alignment among audience, objectives, and pedagogy add to the LDP?

Overview and Integration

Overview and Integration

Learning Objectives

After studying this chapter, you should be able to:

- Summarize major findings about leadership traits, skills, behavior, and influence processes.
- Understand key points of convergence in findings from the different perspectives.
- Understand similar explanatory processes in dyadic, group, and organizational theories.
- Understand what progress has been made in several decades of research on effective leadership.
- Understand how the methods used to study leadership affect what is learned about it.
- Understand what type of research is most useful for learning about effective leadership.

This chapter examines convergence across different approaches for studying leadership. Similar explanatory constructs in dyadic, group, and organizational theories are described, and some cross-level implications are identified. An *integrating conceptual framework* is presented, and some essential leadership qualities are identified. Limitations in the research on leadership are briefly described and some suggestions made for improving future research. The chapter begins with a summary of what researchers have learned about leadership from the thousands of studies conducted over the past half century.

Major Findings About Effective Leadership

The field of leadership has been in a state of ferment and confusion for decades. Several thousand empirical studies were conducted to understand effective leadership, but the results from most of this research are weak, inconsistent, and difficult to interpret. The confused state of the field can be attributed in large part to the sheer volume of publications, the disparity of approaches, the proliferation of confusing terms, the narrow focus of most research, the preference for simplistic explanations, and over-reliance on weak research methods. As the old adage goes, it is difficult to see the forest for the trees. Nevertheless, despite all these problems, substantial progress has been made in learning about effective leadership. The major findings from different lines of leadership research are summarized briefly.

The Leadership Situation

Most people in leadership positions face relentless and conflicting demands on their time. There is a constant stream of requests, problems, inquiries, and reports from the many different people who interact with a leader. The pattern of necessary interactions with people inside and outside the leader's organization is determined by aspects of the situation such as the nature of the work (e.g., repetitive or variable, uncertain or predictable) and dependencies involving the different parties. The people who interact with a leader communicate role expectations about appropriate behavior, and role conflicts are created by competing demands from different people (insiders vs. outsiders, subordinates vs. bosses). Role expectations and activity patterns are also affected by the nature of the position (e.g., level, function, type of unit or team), the type of organization, the culture of the organization, and the national culture. The decisions and actions of leaders are limited by many internal and external constraints, such as policies, rules, standard procedures, budgetary requirements, and labor laws.

Aspects of the situation also determine the importance of leadership and what type of leadership is needed. Despite all the situational demands and constraints on leaders, they still have choices about what aspects of the job to emphasize, how to allocate their time, and with whom to interact. Effective leaders seek to understand their situation, and they adapt their behavior accordingly. They are able to reconcile the role conflicts, and they take advantage of role ambiguity as an opportunity for discretionary action. They seek to exploit opportunities, expand their range of choices, and shape the impressions formed by others about their competence and expertise.

Leadership Behavior

More research has been conducted on leader activities and behavior than on any other aspect of leadership. The descriptive research found that effective leaders develop a mental agenda of short-term and long-term objectives and strategies. The agenda is used to guide their actions, manage their time, and help them become more proactive. Effective leaders identify problems that are both important and solvable, and they take responsibility for dealing with these problems in a systematic and timely way. By relating problems to each other and to informal objectives, they find opportunities to solve more than one problem at the same time.

Effective leaders find task, relations, and change-oriented behaviors that are appropriate for the current situation. Task-oriented behaviors are used to improve or maintain internal efficiency and coordination in a team or organization. Effective leaders plan and schedule activities in a way that will make better use of people, resources, information, and equipment. They assign tasks, determine resource requirements, and coordinate interrelated activities. They help to clarify objectives, priorities, and standards for evaluating results. They monitor the internal operations of a group or organization to assess performance and detect problems to be resolved. Subunit leaders ensure that internal activities are coordinated with related activities in other parts of the organization, and they obtain necessary information and resources from people outside their work unit.

Relations-oriented behaviors are used to build commitment to work objectives, mutual trust and cooperation, and identification with the team or organization. Effective leaders use a variety of different relations-oriented behaviors. They are supportive (show trust and respect) and provide recognition for accomplishments and contributions. They provide coaching and mentoring to build subordinate skills and self-efficacy. They consult with people who will be affected in important ways by the leader's decisions to discover their concerns and get their suggestions. They empower people to resolve operational problems in their work and provide better service to customers and clients. They use team-building behaviors to increase identification with the group and build member trust and cooperation. Finally, these leaders build and maintain a network of cooperative relationships with outsiders who are a valuable source of information, assistance, and political support.

Change-oriented behaviors are used to modify objectives, strategies, and work processes and facilitate adaptation to the external environment. A major responsibility for top executives is to formulate a competitive strategy that is relevant for the external environment and consistent with the organization's core competencies and ideology. Effective leaders monitor the external environment to obtain information about trends and events that require adaptive changes. The leaders interpret external events, focus attention on threats and opportunities, and relate proposed changes to a clear, appealing vision that is relevant to follower values, ideals, and core competencies. The leaders encourage and facilitate innovative thinking and the creation, acquisition, diffusion, and application of new knowledge to improve products, services, and work processes. To gain approval and support for major change, it is usually necessary to forge a coalition of internal and external supporters. Effective leaders also empower competent change agents to facilitate effective implementation of strategic decisions throughout the organization. Symbolic actions and role modeling are used to show continued personal commitment to a new strategy or major change. Providing opportunities to experience progress and repeated "small wins" gives followers more confidence in themselves, the vision, and the leaders.

Power and Influence

Influence is the *essence of leadership,* and much of the activity of formal leaders involves attempts to influence the attitudes and behavior of people, including subordinates, peers, superiors, and outsiders. How much power and influence a leader needs will depend on the situation. More influence is needed to make major changes in strategy when strong resistance to change is encountered. Influence derived from position power is especially important when it is necessary to control rebels who try to disrupt the activities of the organization or criminals who want to steal its resources. Upward and lateral influence are important for the leader to provide satisfactory benefits, obtain adequate resources, facilitate the work of the team, buffer subordinates from unreasonable demands, and represent their interests effectively.

Position power is derived from aspects of the situation such as the amount of formal authority, control over distribution of rewards and punishments, control over information, and access to important people. Exclusive access to information about internal and external events provides an opportunity to interpret reality for people and influence their decisions. Influence over subordinates is enhanced by having a moderate amount of authority to make necessary changes and dispense tangible rewards and benefits. However, too much position power entails the risk that a leader will be tempted to rely on it and neglect more effective forms of influence for building commitment. Effective leaders develop referent and expert power to supplement their position power and motivate commitment to tasks that require high effort, initiative, and persistence. Referent power is developed by being supportive, caring, fair, and accepting. Expert power is acquired by successfully handling internal problems and external threats.

The manner in which a leader exercises power largely determines whether it results in enthusiastic commitment, passive compliance, or stubborn resistance. Effective leaders exert both position power and personal power in a subtle, easy fashion that minimizes status differentials and avoids threatening the self-esteem of others. Effective leaders attempt to empower followers in ways that are appropriate for the situation. They use power in ethical ways and seek to integrate the competing interests of different stakeholders.

A variety of social influence techniques can be used for developing commitment to task objectives and compliance with requests. Effective leaders use proactive influence tactics that are appropriate for the objectives, context, and relationship. These leaders also use indirect ways of influencing people, such as management systems, reward systems, improvement programs, structural forms, and facilities. Political tactics are used to influence strategic decisions, especially in situations characterized by strong disagreement about organizational objectives and priorities.

The distribution and sharing of power over decisions have important implications for leadership effectiveness in groups and organizations, especially in cultures that value democracy. Extensive participation can result in better decisions when relevant information and ideas are distributed among people, they are willing to cooperate in finding a good solution, and ample time is available to use a participative process. Participants are more likely to understand and accept the decision if the decision process allows sufficient opportunity to present ideas and influence the outcome. The quality of group decisions depends to a considerable extent on whether essential leadership functions are carried out and the group is able to avoid common process problems such as hasty decisions, polarization, and groupthink. Empowerment of individuals or groups is more successful when there is agreement about objectives and priorities, a willingness to assume responsibility for making decisions, and a high degree of mutual trust.

Traits and Skills

Technical, conceptual, and interpersonal skills are needed for most leadership roles and functions. Conceptual skills are necessary to analyze problems, develop creative solutions, identify patterns and trends, differentiate between relevant and irrelevant information, understand complex relationships, and develop effective mental models. Interpersonal skills are needed to influence people, develop cooperative relationships, establish and maintain social networks, understand individuals, facilitate teamwork, and resolve conflicts constructively. Technical skills are needed to understand activities, operational processes, products and services, technology, and legal/contractual requirements. The relative importance of different skills varies greatly from situation to situation, but some specific skills are probably useful in all leadership positions.

Personality traits and core values are also relevant for effective leadership. Traits determine a person's willingness to assume leadership responsibilities and tolerate the stress and relentless pressures of the job. Traits affect a leader's desire to accumulate power, influence people, develop relevant skills, and learn from feedback. Leaders with a high need for power, high self-confidence and an internal locus of control orientation make more influence attempts, and relevant expertise and influence skills make the influence attempts more successful. Leaders with a personalized power orientation seek to accumulate more power, and they exercise it in a manipulative, impulsive, domineering manner intended to aggrandize themselves and gain personal loyalty from subordinates. In contrast, leaders with a socialized power orientation, altruistic values, and a high level of cognitive moral development use power to build commitment to idealized goals, and they seek to empower subordinates by sharing information and using more consultation, delegation, and development of subordinate skills and confidence.

Some traits and skills appear to be especially relevant for effective task-oriented leadership. People with high self-confidence, conscientiousness, internal control orientation, and achievement orientation are more likely to take the initiative to identify and resolve task-related problems. Cognitive and technical skills are needed for planning projects, coordinating complex relationships, directing unit activities, and analyzing operational problems. Cognitive and interpersonal skills are needed to conduct effective problem-solving meetings.

Some traits and skills appear to be especially relevant for effective relations-oriented leadership. Altruistic and humanitarian values encourage supportive leadership and concern for individual subordinates. Emotional maturity, emotional intelligence, and communication skills facilitate development of cooperative relationships and make influence attempts more effective. Personal integrity is essential for maintaining mutual trust and credibility. A socialized power orientation encourages a leader to involve subordinates in determining how to achieve task objectives. An appreciation for individual and cultural differences can help a leader facilitate cooperation and teamwork by diverse followers.

Some traits and skills appear to be especially relevant for effective change-oriented leadership. A strong achievement orientation can be a source of motivation to strive for excellence and pursue innovative improvements. Strong cognitive skills and relevant technical knowledge help a leader to recognize threats and opportunities in the external environment and formulate an appropriate strategy based on the organization's core competencies. Social and emotional intelligence help a leader determine who needs to be influenced to support change and how to do it. Political and communication skills help a leader articulate an appealing vision and persuade people that change is necessary.

The willingness and ability to learn and adapt are important requirements for effective leadership in today's uncertain and turbulent world. Effective leaders are flexible enough to adjust their behavior as conditions change, and they find ways to balance competing values and resolve role conflicts. Relevant skills and knowledge can be acquired through a combination of formal training, developmental activities, and self-learning activities. However, a person's motivation and personality also influence the desire to learn new skills, the willingness to take risks in trying new approaches, and the readiness to accept feedback about deficiencies.

Multilevel Explanatory Processes

A comprehensive description of leadership influence requires a multilevel perspective, and similar explanatory constructs in dyadic, group, and organizational theories can be useful in developing multilevel models (Morgeson & Hofmann, 1999). Explanatory constructs at one level of conceptualization can serve as mediating variables for the effects of leadership at a different level, and higher-level constructs may serve as moderators for the effects of leadership on lower-level processes or outcomes. A mediating process at one level may have beneficial or adverse consequences at other levels. Most leadership theories only describe effects at one level, and the possibility of inconsistent effects across levels is seldom considered. Table 1 lists several sets of constructs that are relevant for explaining effective leadership in dyads, teams, and organizations. Each set of constructs will be briefly described, and some likely multilevel effects are identified.

Motivation and Commitment

Task commitment is an important determinant of individual performance. How leaders can influence a subordinate's task commitment is the primary focus of most dyadic theories of leadership, and in many cases these theories are merely extensions of motivation theories. Influence processes such as internalization and instrumental compliance help to explain how leaders can influence subordinate task commitment. Relevant leader behaviors include inspirational appeals that link the task to the person's values and ideals, setting task goals that

TABLE 1	Similar Explanatory Constructs at Three Levels of Conceptualization	
Dyad	**Group or Team**	**Organization**
Subordinate task commitment	Member commitment to group goals	Mission commitment by all members and subunits
Internalized values and beliefs for subordinates	Group norms and values, shared mental models	Corporate culture and core values for the organization
Subordinate trust and cooperation with leader	Trust and cooperation among members	Integration among subunits, trust of top management
Personal identification with the leader	Collective identification with the team or unit	Collective identification with the organization
Subordinate knowledge and skills	Level and diversity of team member skills	Human capital and employee talent
Role specialization for subordinate	Role specialization in the team or department	Differentiation among subunits of the organization
Subordinate self-efficacy and self-confidence	Collective efficacy or potency for the team	Shared optimism and hope among organization members
Subordinate autonomy and empowerment	Team or unit autonomy and empowerment	Decentralization and power sharing in the organization
Creativity and learning by individual subordinates	Creative problem solving, collective learning by team	Organizational learning, and innovation

are specific and challenging, and explaining how high performance will result in desirable rewards and benefits.

How leaders can influence the task commitment of a team is a key feature of group-level theories of leadership. The mediating processes include leader influence on shared objectives and group norms about acceptable performance. The dyadic behaviors continue to be relevant, but the influence processes are more complex and additional behaviors are required. Leaders must influence member commitment to shared objectives for the team, and it may be necessary to resolve disagreements among members about priorities for different objectives. For example, in temporary committees and project teams, the loyalty of members to their home units may conflict with team objectives. Sometimes it is necessary to influence members to make individual sacrifices such as a reduction in personal benefits to achieve mission objectives. Leaders of teams and work units usually have responsibility for allocating rewards to members, and compensation policies may determine whether it is possible to provide rewards that fairly reflect member contributions to the success of the work unit.

Organizational commitment by members and commitment to mission objectives by subunits are important determinants of organizational performance. Top executives can use the behaviors described in dyadic leadership theories, but research on close and distant leadership suggests that some of the behaviors are only effective for influencing commitment when used during personal interactions with employees. The potential influence from direct behaviors is probably greatest for articulation of an inspiring vision and symbolic actions consistent with the vision. Top executives can also influence member motivation and commitment by their decisions about compensation policies, incentive programs, and criteria for retention and promotion.

Efforts to influence member motivation are complicated by unintended consequences and competing objectives. Policies and programs that encourage competition among individuals or among subunits can have dysfunctional consequences, such as reduced cooperation and failure to share relevant information. When subunits have incompatible objectives or different priorities, conflicts can occur. For example, the marketing manager sets an objective to increase sales and encourages sales representatives to find more customers for a new product, but the production unit cannot provide sufficient amounts of the new product. Conflicts also occur when a powerful subunit has objectives that are incompatible with organizational objectives. When subunits are encouraged to make strategic decisions that maximize their short-term performance, the long-term performance of the organization may suffer.

Social Identification

Personal identification by a subordinate with the leader provides potential influence (referent power) over the subordinate. However, problems will occur if loyalty to the leader is much stronger than loyalty to the mission, and the leader's objectives are not consistent with mission requirements or the objectives of the team or organization.

Collective identification by members with a team or small group has potential benefits such as greater cohesiveness and cooperation and lower turnover. Leaders can increase collective identification by helping to create a unique identity and a favorable reputation for the team. Leaders can interpret events in terms of social identities related to past experiences and shared values of followers. Symbols, rituals, and ceremonies can be used to enhance the visibility of the group and to encourage members to express their loyalty and dedication. Stories, myths, and celebration of current and past achievements can also enhance collective identification.

Despite the potential benefits, strong identification with a team or subunit also has potential risks. For example, members may be unwilling to express concerns or dissent that would improve the group's decisions. Disagreements with other subunits or with top management are more likely to escalate into serious conflicts. In extreme cases, the unit may seek to withdraw from the organization or to use political tactics to undermine opponents in the organization.

Collective identification with the organization can provide benefits in terms of increased organizational commitment, reduced turnover, and higher performance. Member loyalty is especially important for organizations that have difficulty recruiting and retaining qualified members. Top executives can build member loyalty and commitment to the organization with the same behaviors described in team leadership theories. Successful constructions of social identity are likely to be linked to a vision that makes membership worthwhile, and social identification is strengthened by recognizing progress in achieving the shared vision. A compelling vision for the organization can also provide the basis for subunit visions that will make the work of members more meaningful and significant (even if the members provide only routine support services).

Trust and Cooperation

Dyadic theories of effective leadership usually include some aspect of mutual trust and cooperation as a key determinant of reciprocal influence. A leader can improve relations with a subordinate by the use of supportive, considerate behaviors. An important determinant of subordinate trust is the leader's integrity, which includes honesty, fairness, and consistency between actions and espoused values.

The performance of a team usually depends on mutual trust and cooperation among the members, which is more likely when members have shared values and they identify strongly with the group. To enhance and sustain cooperation, leaders can use behaviors such as emphasizing the importance of shared objectives and the need for teamwork, making rewards contingent on contributions to team performance, involving members in decisions that affect the team, facilitating the constructive resolution of disagreements, and using team building activities.

The level of cooperation and coordination among subunits is sometimes called *integration* (Lawrence & Lorsch, 1969). Integration is a determinant of organizational performance, and it is more important when subunits are highly interdependent. The more differentiated the subunits are with regard to their objectives and functional specialization, the more difficult it is to achieve integration. Top executives can facilitate integration by providing structural forms such as cross-functional teams, matrix structures, and integrator positions (e.g., product managers). Management programs can be used to encourage cooperation, such as team building activities for executives (e.g., outdoor challenge program), cross-functional task forces, job rotation for executives from different subunits, and rewards based on contributions to overall firm performance. Sometimes cooperation can be increased by an inspiring vision that will emphasizing shared values for members of the organization, regardless of their subunit function and local objectives.

Knowledge and Skills

Job-relevant skills and knowledge are a major determinant of individual performance. If necessary, leaders can enhance these skills with behaviors such as providing instruction and coaching. A subordinate's level of skill will affect the exchange relationship between the leader and a subordinate, and it determines the possibilities for delegation of more responsibility to a subordinate.

The dyadic behaviors are also relevant for groups, but other behaviors are also necessary for effective leadership. In addition to ensuring that all members have the knowledge and skills needed to perform their individual jobs, a leader is responsible for ensuring that members have the skills needed to operate collectively as a team. This responsibility is more difficult when members have specialized roles that require close coordination, when the team must respond rapidly to crises, and when any errors have serious consequences. Relevant leader behaviors include recruiting talented members with the mix of relevant skills, developing skills that are deficient, simplifying processes to reduce errors, cross-training members on multiple tasks, encouraging peer coaching, conducting team training activities, and conducting after-activity reviews to improve team processes.

The quality of human talent ("human capital") is an important determinant of organizational performance. Talented employees are especially important for highly complex tasks requiring unique skills that are difficult to learn. Most large organizations use human resource programs and systems to improve employee skills and capabilities. Examples include recruiting and selection programs, compensation and benefits programs, training and development programs, appraisal and assessment programs, talent management programs, and succession planning programs. These management programs are seldom included in dyadic or group- level theories of leadership, except as situational variables that enhance or limit the influence of the leader or substitute for direct behaviors by leaders. For example, company-wide training programs can reduce the amount of training that managers need to provide to their immediate subordinates. Top executives in an organization have primary responsibility for decisions to implement or modify human resource programs and systems, but leaders at all levels of the organization will be involved in implementing them.

Acquiring and retaining talented employees can be expensive, and leaders must find an appropriate balance between human resource quality and costs. Leaders must decide the responsibilities for different teams, the skill requirements of team members, and assignment of jobs to members. Decisions made to maximize performance at one level may not maximize performance at other levels. Similar trade-offs occur for decisions about the allocation of scarce resources to different subunits of an organization. Resolving these trade-offs and related conflicts is another challenge for organizational leadership.

Specialization

Most dyadic theories recognize that a primary responsibility of the leader is to assign tasks to individual subordinates who have relevant skills. How leaders plan and organize activities for the work unit is not explicitly described. Therefore, the dyadic theories are most useful for explaining leadership when each subordinate independently performs a similar type of task and there is little need for coordination of activities by different subordinates.

Most group-level theories recognize that a leader's task-oriented behavior includes organizing activities and designing jobs in a way that increases efficiency and makes the best use of member skills. Some degree of role specialization usually improves performance in teams and work units, but too much specialization creates problems that are difficult to overcome. As role specialization and role interdependence increase, it becomes more difficult for leaders to match member skills with job requirements and to coordinate their activities.

Specialization is an important determinant of efficiency for an organization, and it involves not only the design of individual jobs but also the design of subunits and managerial positions with responsibility for planning and coordinating subunit activities (Lawrence & Lorsch, 1969; Mintzberg, 1979). Decisions about organizing and structuring the operations of an organization are an important aspect of strategic leadership. The appropriate type and amount of specialization *(differentiation)* depend in part on the corporate strategy and the nature of the environment. Too much specialization or an inappropriate form of it can adversely impact an organization's performance. Decisions about structural forms involve trade-offs, and it is the responsibility of top management to find an appropriate balance for competing objectives.

Decisions about structural forms and differentiation of activities will affect leadership processes and requirements in an organization. The decision to have functional subunits rather than product divisions affects the responsibilities and skill requirements for leaders at different levels in the organization. The decision to use structural forms such as cross-functional project teams creates a need for team leaders who are able to facilitate cooperation among people with different perspectives, interests, and loyalties.

Perceived Efficacy and Optimism

Confidence and optimism about the possibility of achieving difficult task objectives are motivational concepts that help explain the performance of an individual, team, or organization. When there is little hope that they will be successful, people will not be highly motivated to accomplish a difficult objective. Confidence and optimism depend on skills, task difficulty, resources, and the relative capability of competitors or opponents.

At the dyadic level, a leader can influence the self-efficacy of an individual subordinate in several ways. Examples include providing clear explanations when assigning tasks (to reduce role ambiguity), providing necessary instruction and coaching, providing necessary information and resources, providing encouragement when problems occur, expressing confidence in the ability of a subordinate to do a difficult task, and providing recognition for achievements.

In groups, collective efficacy (or potency) is the perception of members that the group can successfully carry out its task or mission. The same types of leadership behaviors just described can be used to influence collective efficacy in a team, and other relevant behaviors include making assignments that take into account member skills, planning and scheduling activities to avoid delays and meet project deadlines, and solving immediate problems (e.g., accidents, equipment failures, supply shortages, schedule changes initiated by clients or other units). Leaders can also enhance optimism with "pep talks" before difficult activities and by arranging opportunities for the team to experience success in practice sessions.

At the organizational level, collective efficacy includes optimism that a change or new strategy will be successful and confidence that top management is able to guide the organization through difficult times. Leaders can increase confidence and optimism by making inspiring speeches, acting confident and optimistic, explaining what will be done to overcome obstacles or manage crises, taking highly visible actions to deal with problems, keeping members informed about progress, and celebrating significant progress towards achievement of objectives.

Strong optimism usually increases commitment to achieve task objectives, but it may also have negative consequences. When optimism is based on wishful thinking rather than a realistic assessment of actual conditions, it can result in risky decisions or the failure to recognize serious threats that require immediate action by the team or organization in order to avoid a disaster. Negative consequences may also result when some individuals know that they have much more ability than other members of a group or organization, but they do not get more status and rewards. In this situation, self-awareness of superior ability may cause resentment or motivate a person to seek better opportunities elsewhere.

Empowerment

Empowerment involves autonomy, shared responsibility, and influence in making important decisions. Similar concepts of empowerment have been used at all three conceptual levels to explain effective leadership (Seibert, Silver, & Randolph, 2004; Spreitzer, 1995, 2008).

In dyadic theories, empowerment is primarily a result of a leader's use of delegation or consultation with individual subordinates. The potential benefits from this empowerment include improvements in decision quality, employee task commitment, employee initiative in problem solving, and development of employee skills. The extent to which an individual leader can empower subordinates depends in large measure on the leader's own authority, and it is difficult to empower subordinates when there are elaborate rules and standard procedures for doing the work. Other situational variables that make empowerment feasible and beneficial include a subordinate's commitment to task objectives, desire to have more influence, and knowledge that will improve decision quality.

Empowerment is more complex for teams than for dyads, and it usually means allowing the members of a team to make important task decisions collectively. Empowerment may include member influence over selection of an internal leader, the selection of new members, decisions about work procedures, the assignment of tasks to members, and evaluation of each member's performance. In extreme cases, empowerment may include determining the mission and task objectives. The charter, bylaws, or formal policies for the organization often specify how much empowerment is allowed a team or work unit and what decision processes are permitted. The situational variables that determine how much empowerment is feasible also include shared objectives and relevant expertise for members.

One primary form of empowerment for organizational leadership is decentralization of authority for important decisions to subunits and leaders at lower levels. Decentralization can help to improve the quality of decisions, reduce delays in reacting to immediate problems, and enhance development of competent leaders for promotion to higher levels. Empowerment in an organization is encouraged and facilitated by some types of structural forms and empowerment programs (e.g., subsidiaries or product divisions, self-managed teams, quality circles, innovation programs). Many political, voluntary, and professional organizations or associations have charters that empower regular members by allowing them to participate in selecting and evaluating leaders, and by giving them influence over major decisions (e.g., through direct votes or representatives on the board of directors).

Empowerment has both advantages and risks for organizations. Extensive decentralization to interdependent subunits means that many leaders are making interrelated decisions that must be mutually consistent to avoid detrimental effects. Empowerment of subunits that are interdependent but have different priorities increases the need for cooperation and coordination among subunit leaders (Gebert et al., 2003; Locke, 2003; O'Toole et al., 2003). Decentralization can be risky if subunits have objectives that are not consistent with the organization's objectives, and they are allowed to pursue risky strategies that will eventually endanger the organization. Decentralization also means forgoing some potential advantages offered by standardization of work processes and management practices. Thus, it is essential to find an appropriate mix of centralized and decentralized decisions and to ensure that relevant leadership processes occur.

Collective Learning and Innovation

An important form of leadership influence involves improvements in collective learning about effective processes and strategies. Learning is essential for improving adaptation to external change, and it is also a source of incremental improvements in efficiency and human capital. The learning occurs at individual, group, and organizational levels, and learning at each level influences learning at the other levels (Crossan et al., 1999).

The dyadic theories do not explicitly include collective learning as a mediating process, but some of these theories identify ways a leader can encourage and facilitate creativity by an individual subordinate. Examples include encouraging innovative thinking (intellectual stimulation), allowing enough autonomy and time to pursue creative ideas, setting innovation goals, and being receptive to subordinate suggestions about ways to improve products, services, or processes.

Theories of team leadership identify several ways leaders can influence collective learning and creative problem solving (Day et al., 2004; Mumford et al., 2002). The leadership behaviors relevant for influencing creativity by an individual are still relevant, but additional leadership behaviors are needed to explain the synergy and interactive aspects of collective learning and creative problem solving by a group. Leaders can influence the group to use systematic procedures for analyzing problems, encourage the use of helpful procedures for generating creative solutions (e.g., brainstorming), encourage discussion of a broad range of options, and prevent the team from rushing to a decision without carefully considering the potential costs and benefits (e.g., by developing best and worst-case scenarios). Leaders can encourage group members to build on each other's ideas rather than being too critical. Relevant behaviors to facilitate collective learning include encouraging the team to experiment with competing solutions to assess their consequences and using after-activity reviews to improve group performance of repetitive tasks. Some of the leadership behaviors that facilitate creativity, collective learning, and systematic problem solving can be shared among the members of a team.

Top executives can influence collective learning and innovation in an organization (Damanpour, 1991; Jung, Chow, & Wu, 2003; Popper & Lipshitz, 1998). Relevant change-oriented behaviors include encouraging importation of best practices, encouraging internal development of new knowledge, providing appropriate recognition and rewards for entrepreneurial activities, encouraging diffusion of new knowledge in the organization, planning the implementation of innovations, and promoting flexibility and innovation as key values in the corporate culture. In addition to direct behaviors, top management can implement relevant programs to assess, fund, and reward learning and innovation. The success of efforts to increase learning and innovation also requires appropriate leadership by middle and lower-level managers. Many innovative ideas emerge from lower levels, and they should be nurtured and supported by champions and sponsors who appreciate their importance, recognize their relevance, and have sufficient power to ensure they are approved and implemented effectively.

Toward an Integrating Conceptual Framework

Most leadership research has a narrow focus, and there has been little integration of findings from the different approaches. Few of the early studies on leader traits and values included measures of leadership behavior, even though it is evident that traits and values are reflected in a leader's behavior, and the behavior is necessary to explain how leaders influence follower motivation and performance. Most of the early behavior research did not

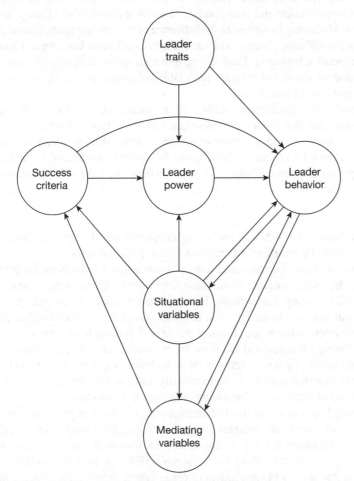

FIGURE 1 An Integrating Conceptual Framework

include leader traits or power, even though they influence a leader's behavior. Few behavior studies included mediating variables that would explain how leader behavior affects outcomes such as subordinate and group performance. The power-influence approach includes some research on influence tactics, but other types of leadership behavior are seldom included. Until recently, little research was conducted on the relationship of leader and follower traits to influence behavior. Finally, most situational theories examine how the situation enhances the effects of selected leader behaviors or traits, rather than taking a broader view of the way traits, power, behavior, and situation jointly interact to determine leadership effectiveness.

Despite the prevailing pattern of segmentation in research on leadership over the past 50 years, the number of studies that straddle more than one approach is increasing, and the different lines of research are gradually converging. Most of the findings from different lines of research are consistent and mutually supportive. When findings from different approaches are viewed as part of a larger network of interacting variables, they appear to be interrelated in a meaningful way. Figure 1 provides an integrating conceptual framework that encompasses each set of variables. The proposed conceptual framework is based on the assumption that a core set of mediating variables determines performance for individuals, groups, or organizations. Mediating variables for the influence of leaders on the performance of individual followers include follower motivation, skills, role clarity, and self-efficacy. Mediating variables for the effects of leader behavior on team performance include cooperation and mutual trust, organization and coordination of activities, collective efficacy, and collective identification. Mediating variables for the influence of leaders on organizational performance includes process efficiency, human and social capital, collective learning and innovation, and adaptive competitive strategies. Leaders can influence these mediating variables in a variety of ways, including the use of relevant leadership behaviors and decisions about strategies, policies, programs, and structures.

The arrow from situational variables to the mediating variables is similar to "substitutes" for leadership that reduce the importance of some types of behavior. Over a longer period of time, the leader may be able to influence some of these situational variables, and this effect is shown by the arrow from leader behavior to situational variables. By taking actions to make the situation more favorable, leaders can indirectly influence the mediating variables and the overall performance of the organization. The arrow from situational variables to the success criteria reflects the direct effect of external conditions that are usually beyond the influence of the leader (e.g., the economy, market conditions, government regulations). These other determinants of organizational effectiveness are sometimes strong enough to overwhelm the efforts of leaders to make improvements.

The model allows for reciprocal influence processes. Leader behavior is both an independent and dependent variable at the same time. Leader behavior is influenced by a variety of factors, including leader traits, leader power, situational demands and constraints, feedback about the success criteria, and feedback about the results of earlier decisions and actions. The reciprocal influence processes occur in the causal links between leader behavior and the mediating variables and are depicted by arrows in both directions. Leader power is determined jointly by leader traits such as technical expertise and persuasiveness, and aspects of the situation such as formal authority and control over rewards. Over time, the feedback effects of success or failure can enhance or diminish leader power.

The model applies to any level of management in a large organization, but the mediating variables and situational variables change somewhat from level to level. Indirect effects are especially important for top management, because over time they can influence the core ideology and cultural values of the organization, the formal structure and management systems, the skills and capabilities of organization members, the competitive strategy, and the network of cooperative relationships and joint ventures with other organizations.

Some mediating variables for executives are situational variables for managers of subunits. For example, top executives determine the overall structure of the organization, whereas a subunit manager organizes subunit activities within the constraints imposed by the larger structure.

Limitations in Leadership Research

The choice of methods and design of studies for much of the leadership research have limited the rate of progress in learning about effective leadership. Beliefs about the most useful research methods and the type of information needed to understand leadership processes are related to biases in the conceptualization of leadership. Until recently, most leadership studies have been guided by theories of dyadic influence processes involving the effects of individual leaders on individual followers. The methods used in most leadership studies are based on questionable assumptions, and available remedies for improving the method are seldom used (Hunter, Bedell-Avers, & Mumford, 2007). This section of the chapter provides a brief description of methodological issues and limitations in many of the leadership studies conducted during the past half century.

Qualitative versus Quantitative Methods

More research is conducted on leader behavior than on any other aspect of leadership, and most of the studies use questionnaires that ask subordinates to retrospectively rate how often or how much a leader has been using a designated type of behavior. The subordinate responses are biased by attributions, stereotypes, and implicit theories about leadership. Several types of evidence raise doubts about the meaning and accuracy of the results. Critics of this survey research contend that it has an inherent bias toward exaggerating the importance of individual leaders, and it is a weak method for studying leadership as a dynamic, shared process embedded in complex social systems.

One alternative approach advocated by some scholars is to make greater use of *qualitative methods* (Bryman, 2004; Bryman, Bresnen, Beardworth, & Keil, 1988; Strong, 1984). One useful method is an intensive, longitudinal case study with data collected from a combination of two or more methods (e.g., interviews, observation, diaries, critical incidents, company records, and open-ended survey questions). The qualitative methods offer some advantages for studying leadership, but these methods also have limitations (House, 1988a; Martinko & Gardner, 1985). Standards for the application and evaluation of qualitative methods are not as explicit as those for traditional quantitative methods, and interpretations based on qualitative methods are sometimes very subjective. Descriptions of past events may be biased by selective memory for aspects of behavior consistent with the respondent's stereotypes and implicit theories about effective leadership. Direct observation is also susceptible to selective attention and biased interpretation of events. Attribution errors may occur if an observer or interviewer has information about unit performance. When observers immerse themselves in an organization for long periods of time in an effort to understand the context and meaning of what they are seeing, they may become involved in the very processes under observation, thereby risking objectivity.

The limitations and advantages of quantitative and qualitative methods make it desirable to use a complementary combination of methods whenever possible (Bryman, 2004). For example, in survey questionnaire studies, researchers could interview some of the respondents to verify that the questionnaire answers are accurately measuring the intended construct and to discover the underlying reasons for some of the quantitative results. A longitudinal case study that uses interviews or observation can include quantitative questionnaires administered periodically to some of the participants.

Survey Versus Experimental Studies

Survey studies are much easier to conduct than experiments and can be completed more quickly, but they do not allow strong inferences about causality. Controlled experiments in laboratory and field settings are appropriate for many types of leadership research, but they constitute only a small proportion (less than five percent) of the thousands of studies conducted on leadership over the past half century (Brown & Lord, 1999; Dipboye, 1990; Wofford, 1999). The most important advantage of an experiment is the opportunity to determine causality. In laboratory experiments, researchers can manipulate leader behavior or situational variables and assess their independent and joint effects. It is relatively easy to measure mediating processes, control for extraneous variables, and examine the effects of conditions seldom found in actual organizations. However, the potential advantages of experiments may not be realized if they are poorly designed and executed. Common limitations of laboratory experiments include the use of weak manipulations, the use of tasks that do not accurately simulate realistic conditions, the use of convenience samples of students who have little work experience, and the use of brief interactions among strangers to study processes that in most organizations would involve people with established relationships.

Field experiments are more difficult to conduct than laboratory experiments but offer some unique advantages. Most field experiments involve realistic working conditions and people who have experience working together. Field experiments can be used to assess the effects of different patterns of leadership behavior, and they provide an excellent way to assess the utility of interventions used to improve leadership (e.g., training, feedback, executive coaching). Common limitations of field experiments on leadership are weak manipulations, nonrandom assignment of participants to experimental treatments, weak assessment of outcome variables, failure to measure mediating processes, and use of an unrepresentative sample that limits external validity. A field experiment on leadership is likely to be more useful if it is based on a relevant and well- specified model, it includes a strong and appropriate manipulation of independent variables, it includes multiple measures of relevant variables, and it is conducted over an appropriate time period. In experiments conducted to evaluate developmental interventions (e.g., feedback or coaching), it is easier to gain approval for a control group if the researcher provides an opportunity for members of the control group to participate in the intervention at a later time.

Level of Analysis

Most survey research on leadership behavior uses an individual, dyadic, or group *level of analysis.* Analysis at the individual level usually involves correlations between variables that are measured within individuals. For example, a subordinate's ratings of leader behavior are correlated with the subordinate's ratings of task commitment across all subordinates in the sample. Dyadic analyses usually involve data obtained from both members of a leader-subordinate dyad, such as correlating subordinate ratings of leader behavior with the leader's ratings of subordinate performance across all dyads in the sample. Group-level analyses often involve individual data that are aggregated to the group level. For example, the leader behavior ratings provided by several subordinates are averaged; then the composite scores for each group are correlated with other composite scores (e.g., cohesiveness, collective efficacy) or group-level measures of outcomes (e.g., group performance, turnover).

The appropriate type of analysis for quantitative data from survey studies depends on the underlying theory of leadership processes and the level of measurement for the variables.

The level of data analysis should correspond to the level of measurement and the proposed relationships in the theory (Klein et al., 1994; Rousseau, 1985). Unless an appropriate level of analysis is used, the results from a study may be misinterpreted. The analysis is more complex for a multilevel theory that includes cross-level effects. Different methods for multilevel analysis are described and compared in a special issue of *Leadership Quarterly* (see Bliese, Halverson, & Schriesheim, 2002).

Many of the early leadership theories were vague about the level of conceptualization for each variable, and many empirical studies used data analyses that are not appropriate for the level of conceptualization (Yammarino, Dionne, & Chun, 2002; Yammarino et al., 2005). When proposed relationships involve variables at different levels of conceptualization or effects that occur at more than one level (e.g., the leader's vision affects both individual self-efficacy and collective efficacy for the team), then it may be necessary to include more than one level of analysis.

Other Methodological Issues

The samples used in many leadership studies are far from ideal. The common approach is to use a convenience sample, one that is easy to get, rather than to plan the type of sample that is appropriate for the research objectives and design. For example, a sample of experienced managers from the same industry is often more useful for a survey study than a convenience sample of undergraduate students with little practical experience in organizations. In comparative studies, the use of convenience samples makes it difficult to identify the effects of unmeasured variables that are confounded with the independent or dependent variables. For example, in a sample of managers from different levels in the organization, level will be confounded with amount of position power, with skills used in promotion decisions, and with types of behaviors required more often at a particular level.

Many leadership studies examine events that occur during a time interval that is too brief for independent variables to have much effect on dependent variables. Longitudinal studies are needed to examine leadership processes that evolve over time, and to assess the delayed effects of leaders on a team or organization. Processes such as developing dyadic relationships, building effective teams, and leading change often require months or years of study. Unfortunately, few researchers are willing to invest that much time in a study. What usually passes for longitudinal research in leadership is a survey study with measures taken a few months apart, rather than an intensive examination of evolving relationships, emerging problems, protracted decisions, sequential changes, and reciprocal influence processes.

The leadership research seems to be biased toward easy methods and faddish topics. Too many studies are merely replications of earlier studies on a popular topic. One researcher publishes a study that is interesting and easy to conduct, and others imitate it with only minor variations (a different sample, a different criterion measure). Too many studies simply correlate one questionnaire with another, even though there is little reason to expect that important relationships exist. The questionnaires are often filled out by the same respondents, and interpretation of results is difficult. Finally, many studies attempt to "prove" a weak theory, and the results are usually inconclusive. It is much better to design research that will "improve" a theory by testing alternative explanations, examining possible confounds, identifying limiting conditions, and assessing practical significance.

Table 2 provides an overview of the methodological biases discussed in this section of the chapter. Common features of leadership studies are contrasted with alternative and less common features. Greater use of the uncommon features would make leadership research more productive. Lowe and Gardner (2001) reached a similar conclusion in their review of leadership studies published in *The Leadership Quarterly*.

TABLE 2	Common and Uncommon Features in Leadership Studies	
Feature	**Common**	**Uncommon**
Research method	Survey study	Experiment
Research objective	Replication	Explore new issues
Level of processes	Individual or dyadic	Group or organizational
Time frame	Short term	Longitudinal
Causality	Unidirectional	Reciprocal
Criterion variables	One or two	Several
Mediating variables	Few or None	Several
Data sources	Single	Multiple
Sample	Convenience	Systematic selection
Level of leader	Supervisor	Executive

Summary of Research Limitations

Even though many different methods of collecting information and analyzing it are available, most of the leadership research during the past half century has relied on weak methods such as survey studies with questionnaires filled out by leaders or their subordinates at one point in time. It is important to select methods that are appropriate for the type of knowledge sought, rather than merely using the most convenient methods. The research question should dictate the methodology and choice of samples, not the other way around. Each type of methodology has limitations, and it is desirable to use *multiple methods* whenever feasible for research on leadership (Jick, 1979; Yukl & Van Fleet, 1982). It is easier to have confidence in the results of leadership research when similar results are found for different research methods, especially if at least one method was an experiment. It is also important to consider the appropriate level of analysis for the theoretical constructs and measures. Multilevel analysis can provide new insights about leadership processes and help to determine whether parallel processes occur at different levels.

Concluding Thoughts

This final section presents my observations about the essence of leadership and some final thoughts about the state of the field.

The Essence of Effective Leadership

This text takes a broad perspective and examines many different aspects of leadership. The different ways of defining leadership, the multitude of different variables examined in the research, and the frequency of weak methods make it difficult to identify the essence of effective leadership. This section presents what I think are the 10 most important leadership functions for enhancing collective work in teams and organizations. In a large organization, the conditions that create a need for these leadership acts are played out at every level of management and in every subunit. The functions can be performed by any member of the organization, but they are especially relevant for people who are elected, appointed, or informally recognized as leaders for a collective activity.

1. ***Help interpret the meaning of events.*** Helping people to find meaning in complex events is important, especially when the pace of change is accelerating and touching every part of our lives. Effective leaders help people interpret events, understand why they are relevant, and identify emerging threats and opportunities.

2. ***Create alignment on objectives and strategies.*** Effective performance of a collective task requires considerable agreement about what to do and how to do it. Helping to build a consensus about these choices is especially important in newly formed groups and in organizations that have lost their way. Effective leaders help to create agreement about objectives, priorities, and strategies.

3. ***Build commitment and optimism.*** The performance of a difficult, stressful task requires commitment and persistence in the face of obstacles and setbacks. Effective leaders increase enthusiasm for the work, commitment to task objectives, and confidence that the effort will be successful.

4. ***Build mutual trust and cooperation.*** Effective performance of a collective task requires cooperation and mutual trust, which are more likely to exist when people understand each other, appreciate diversity, and are able to confront and resolve differences in a constructive way. Effective leaders foster mutual respect, trust, and cooperation.

5. ***Strengthen collective identity.*** The effectiveness of a group or organization requires at least a moderate degree of collective identification. In this era of fluid teams, virtual organizations, and joint ventures, boundaries are often unclear and loyalties are divided. Effective leaders help create a unique identity for a group or an organization, and they resolve issues of membership in a way that is consistent with this identity.

6. ***Organize and coordinate activities.*** Successful performance of a complex task requires the capacity to coordinate many different but interrelated activities in a way that makes efficient use of people and resources. Effective leaders help people get organized to perform collective activities efficiently, and they help coordinate these activities as they occur.

7. ***Encourage and facilitate collective learning.*** In a highly competitive and turbulent environment, continuous learning and innovation are essential for the survival and prosperity of an organization. Members must collectively learn better ways to work together towards common objectives. Effective leaders encourage and facilitate collective learning and innovation.

8. ***Obtain necessary resources and support.*** To effectively carry out its mission, a group must get essential resources, approvals, assistance, and political support from the parent organization and people outside of the unit. Likewise, the survival and prosperity of an organization depend on favorable exchanges with external parties such as clients, customers, and funding agencies. Effective leaders promote and defend the interests and reputation of their unit and help to obtain necessary resources and support for it.

9. ***Develop and empower people.*** The performance of a group or organization is likely to be better if competent members are actively involved in solving problems and making decisions. Relevant skills must be developed to prepare people for leadership roles, new responsibilities, and major change. Effective leaders help develop the skills and confidence of people in their work unit and empower people to become change agents and leaders themselves.

10. ***Promote social justice and morality.*** Member satisfaction and commitment are increased by a climate of fairness, compassion, and social responsibility. To maintain such a climate requires active efforts to protect individual rights, encourage social responsibility, and oppose unethical practices. Effective leaders set an example of moral behavior, and they take necessary actions to promote social justice.

The State of the Field

People have been interested in leadership since the beginning of recorded history, and the study of leadership as a scientific discipline started early in the last century. The massive literature produced by this effort is beset with confusion and ambiguity, but the selective review of theory and research in this text shows that we are making substantial progress in learning about leadership. Nevertheless, much more remains to be learned. Effective leadership at all levels of society and in all of our organizations is essential for coping with the growing social, economic, and environmental problems confronting the world. Learning to cope with these problems is not a luxury but a necessity.

Progress in understanding leadership has been slower than expected from the large volume of publications and the immense amount of effort expended on leadership research. Fortunately, the last decade has witnessed an increase in the richness of research questions and the variety of approaches used to study them, and the field appears to be undergoing an accelerating pace of discovery. With such a vital subject, it is imperative that we continue to upgrade the quality of leadership research and theory. Faster progress will require the efforts of dedicated researchers who value discovery of useful knowledge and are willing to invest the time and effort needed to conduct good research.

Review and Discussion Questions

1. What are some points of convergence in the four major lines of research on effective leadership (traits and skills, behaviors, influence processes, situational variables)?
2. What are some of the most important findings about effective leadership in organizations?
3. What are some explanatory constructs and processes that appear similar in dyadic, group, and organizational level theories?
4. What are some biases and limitations in the way leadership is usually defined and studied?
5. What improvements could be made in the way leadership is studied?
6. If you were asked to identify the 10 most essential functions of leadership, what would be on your list (which may differ from the list suggested by the author)?

Key Terms

essence of leadership	level of analysis	multimethod research
integrating conceptual framework	multilevel explanatory processes	qualitative methods

Index